BRITISH FILM IN[STITU]TE

bfi

FILM AND TELEVISION HANDBOOK 1992

Editor: David Leafe
Deputy Editor: Gill Crawford
Consultant Editor: Wayne Drew
Research: Sue George
Picture research: David Huxley
Additional research/editorial assistance: Karen Alexander, Allen Eyles, Lira Fernandes, Jane Ivey, Jackie Madden, Bernadette Moloney, Susan Oates, Martin Ogden, Pat Perilli, Brian Robinson, Linda Wood
Cover: Calvin McKenzie, Graphic Design, 071 587 5106
Typesetting and Design: Florencetype, Kewstoke, Avon
Advertisement Managers: Marot & Co

With a special thanks for their assistance and advice to BFI staff

Many thanks also to all those who assisted with illustrations: Roy Addison PR, Artificial Eye Film Co, BBC Films, BBC Photograph Library, BBC Picture Publicity, BBC Radio, Blue Dolphin Films, Bray Film Studios, British Screen, British Sky Broadcasting, CNN International, Capital Gold, Castle Premier Releasing, Central Broadcasting Picture Desk, Central Office of Information, Central Television, Channel Four Television, Columbia Tri-Star Films (UK), Consolidated Communications, Contemporary Films, Corbett & Keane, Coutts & Co, Curzon Film Distributors, DDA, Walt Disney Co, Electric Cinema, Electric Pictures, Elstree Studios, Empire Magazine, Entertainment Film Distributors, Film Four International, First Independent Films, Frontline PR, Gala Films, Goldcrest Films & Television, The Grade Co, Granada Television, Guild Film Distribution, HTV International, HandMade Films, Hemdale Film Distribution, Hobo Film Enterprises, ICA Projects, ITN, Independent Television Commission, JAC Publicity, Jazz FM, KM Films, Lynne Kirwin Associates, Kiss FM, LWT, Kim Lewis Marketing (Australia), MCA/Universal, MCEG Virgin Vision, MGM Cinemas, Mainline Pictures, Majestic Films, Manifesto Film & TV Sales, Medusa Communications, Montage Films, National TV Licence Records Office, Oasis, Odeon Cinemas Training Centre, Optimum Communications, Oracle, PSA PR, Palace Pictures, Paramount Pictures, Psychology News, The Radio Authority, Rank Film Distributors, Recorded Cinemas Co, Recorded Picture Co, Richmond Filmhouse, Rogers & Cowan International, The Sales Co, Screen International, Sovereign Pictures, Spectator Entertainment International, Stone Hallinan McDonald, TVS, Terry Farrell & Co, Thames Television, Touchstone Pictures, Twentieth Century Fox Film Co, UCI, UIP (UK), Universal Pictures, Universal Pictorial Press, Warner Bros Distributors, Winsor Beck PR, Working Title Films, Yorkshire Television, Zakiya and Associates, Zenith Productions

21 Stephen Street, London W1P 1PL
Tel: 071 255 1444
Fax: 071 436 7950

Made and printed in Great Britain by Garden House Press, Perivale, Middlesex

British Library
Cataloguing in Publication Data
BFI film and television handbook 1992
1. Great Britain. Cinema Industries. Serials. 2. Great Britain. Television Services. Serials. I. British Film Institute.
348′.8′0941

ISBN 0 85170 317 8

Price £14.95

Cover pictures
(centre) *Cyrano de Bergerac*, French Government-aided and set to be the top earning foreign film in the UK for 1991 (see pp 29, 66 et al) (courtesy of Artificial Eye); (clockwise from top) Margaret Thatcher's hurried decision to fight on in the Tory leadership election provided one of 1990's TV news highlights (see pp 52ff) (courtesy of ITN); Mike Leigh's *Life is Sweet*, one of the diminishing number of British production starts (see p 19) (courtesy of Palace Pictures); the BFI's *Young Soul Rebels*, winner of the Critics' Week prize at Cannes (see pp 12, 21 et al); the Oscar-winning *Creature Comforts*, winner of the BFI Mari Kuttna award in October 1990 and distributed by the BFI on film and on Connoisseur Video (see pp 9, 24, 31, 76 et al); *Prospero's Books*, a British director's re-working of Shakespeare, funded by non-British money (see p 21) (courtesy of Palace Pictures)

CONTENTS

Foreword

By BFI Chairman Sir Richard Attenborough CBE

As we move towards the establishment of the single European market after 1992, the BFI is determined to ensure that Britain's audiovisual industries are fully informed of all the new opportunities that will be on offer. In order to unravel some of the accompanying complexities, this latest edition of the BFI's Handbook contains for the first time a comprehensive overview of European film and television, together with a useful reference section listing the relevant organisations active in Europe.

However, despite the imminent single European market, many in this country who seek funding for their work within the moving image culture face increasingly difficult times and the BFI is committed to helping them in every possible way. The Downing Street seminar in June 1990, described in the Handbook's wide-ranging review of the year, is just one of the high profile initiatives designed to help remedy this situation. On a smaller scale, we hope that the section on funding (another new feature of the Handbook) will clarify some possible routes through this difficult terrain.

Other innovations in this publication include a look back at the year in radio, a medium which, of course, bears directly on the BFI's broadcasting interests. We have also addressed the issue of access to the cinema for people with disabilities, in line with our commitment to equal opportunities for all.

In addition to these invaluable new features, the 1992 BFI Handbook also contains all the usual comprehensive reference sections which those who use it regularly have come to depend upon over the years and which also accurately reflect the scope of the BFI's activities and concerns.

Photo: Terry O'Neill

About the BFI

By BFI Director Wilf Stevenson

Above: The Museum of the Moving Image

THIS Handbook is published by the British Film Institute whose task is to promote the 20th century's major art form, the moving image. In response to questions about how we do this, I sometimes answer that our primary product is influence. Certainly we are responsible for more tangible activities. However, these all contribute to our main purpose, to exert a powerful influence over the development, study and appreciation of the culture of the moving image, be it film or television.

We are in the forefront of discussions about the new broadcasting environment; we are campaigning successfully to establish a national television archive to preserve this long-neglected part of our heritage; our innovative programmes at the National Film Theatre and the Regional Film Theatres continue to discover new aspects of moving image culture; our publications aim to keep enthusiasts abreast of the latest developments in film scholarship, while our education programmes bring to a wider public the delights and challenges of a study of the moving image. Crowning a series of successful initiatives in recent years, we have in the Museum of the Moving Image an institution combining education and entertainment which has already been visited by more than a million people.

So our role is to influence as many people as possible, to encourage the development of the moving image culture and to foster a wider and deeper appreciation and awareness of it. We do this at a national level and with many partners at a regional level. We do it through discussion and debate as well as through the films, books, and other products which we create. Every division participates in achieving this overall goal, as described on the following seven pages.

BFI South Bank

Museum of the Moving Image (MOMI)

THE Museum of the Moving Image explores the unique and magical history of cinema and television, beginning in 2,000 BC with the Javanese Shadow Puppets which were among the earliest experiments with light, shadow and movement. Moving on through a range of early Victorian pre-cinema toys, visitors reach the Temple of the Gods which transports them through the silent era and beyond: the golden age of Hollywood, the birth of television, the development of international cinema and the more recent history of satellite and cable TV. MOMI's award-winning design and exciting interactive exhibits embody its aims to entertain and inform. Amongst others, awards have come from the British Tourist Authority, the Museums Association and BAFTA.

Above: Waiting for the show to begin in NFT1

Below: MOMI's Temple of the Gods

Above: The poster store at the J Paul Getty Jnr Conservation Centre

National Film Theatre

The National Film Theatre aims to bring audiences the widest possible range of film and television from all over the world, screened in the best possible conditions and supported by background notes, lectures and other activities designed to stimulate debate and inform as well as entertain. More than 2,000 films and television programmes are screened annually at the NFT, arranged in seasons centred round a particular director, star, period, genre, idea or issue. A series of live interviews and debates has been sponsored by 'The Guardian' newspaper since 1981. The NFT is also home to the London Film Festival which presents the best of new world cinema and has built up a considerable reputation for introducing directors previously unknown to British audiences.

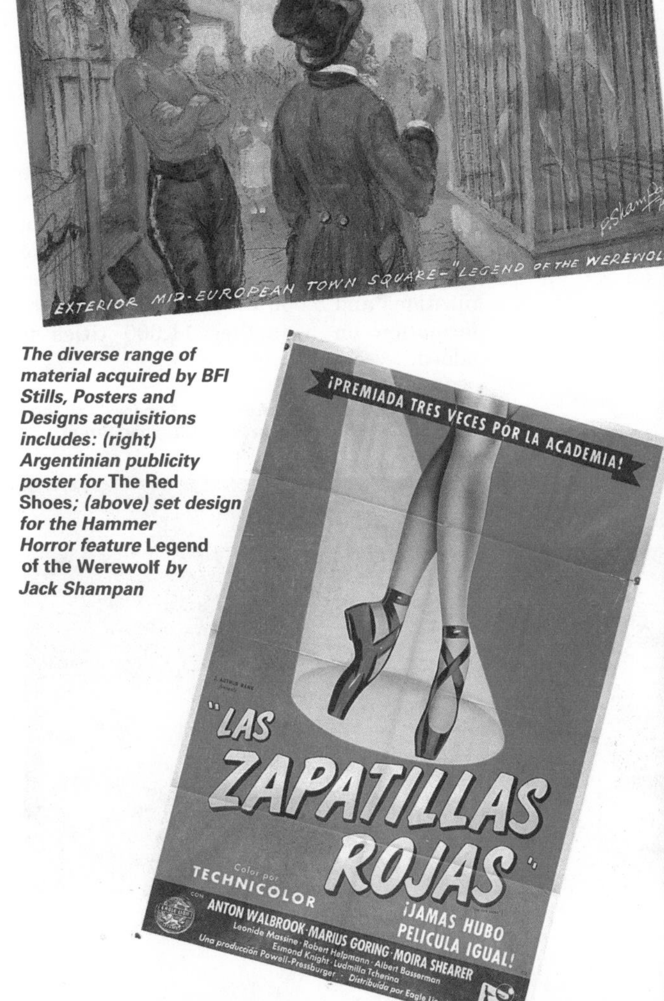

The diverse range of material acquired by BFI Stills, Posters and Designs acquisitions includes: (right) Argentinian publicity poster for **The Red Shoes**; *(above) set design for the Hammer Horror feature* **Legend of the Werewolf** *by Jack Shampan*

BFI STILLS, POSTERS AND DESIGNS

THE BFI's unique collection of illustrations and photographs from cinema and television is developed, preserved and made accessible by BFI Stills, Posters, and Designs. Images from more than 70,000 films and television programmes are held in the collection on some 5 million black and white prints and 700,000 colour transparencies. A fascinating visual account of the development of world cinema and television, these capture the action both on-screen and off. A further 20,000 files contain portraits of film and television personalities and the collection also holds around 15,000 posters and 2,500 set and costume designs including the original work of production designers and art directors.

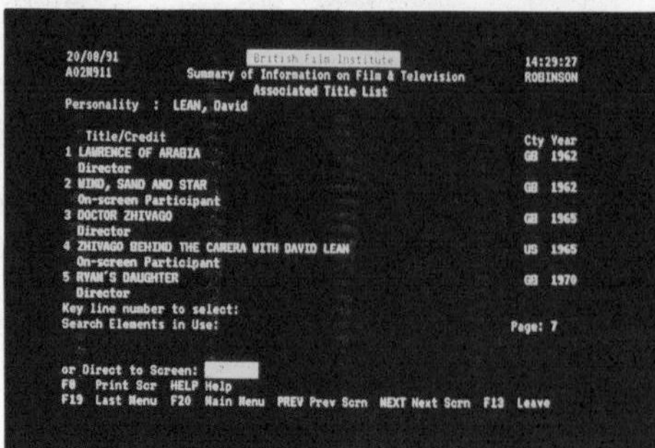

Above: Sample screen from SIFT, the BFI's computerised film and television database

BFI LIBRARY AND INFORMATION SERVICES

THE world's largest collection of information on film and television is held by BFI Library and Information Services which holds both published and unpublished material including books, periodicals, newspaper cuttings, press releases, scripts and theses, as well as special collections of private papers from major figures such as Carol Reed, Michael Balcon, Joseph Losey and Emeric Pressburger. BFI Library and Information Services has moved into the computer age with the arrival of the Summary of Information on Film and Television (SIFT), an on-line database which makes sophisticated information searches possible on more than 400,000 films, television programmes and videos, 280,000 personalities, 115,000 organisations and 5,000 events. Each year, information on a further 11,000 titles is added.

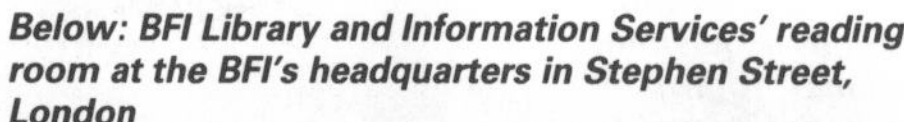

Below: BFI Library and Information Services' reading room at the BFI's headquarters in Stephen Street, London

BFI Exhibition and Distribution

BFI Exhibition and Distribution aims to increase the availability of film, television and video by distributing copies of historic, innovative and newly discovered material for screening and study. The Division also provides programming advice and publicity services to a wide variety of clients, including the BFI-supported network of Regional Film Theatres and is responsible for grant-aiding and monitoring exhibition clients together with some festival and distributor clients. Originally concerned with supplying 16mm prints of 'classics' to mainly education and film

Above: The cavernous film storage vaults at the J Paul Getty Jnr Conservation Centre

society users, and with nurturing the early Regional Film Theatre movement, the Division has expanded to become a major holder of rights and prints on an international scale. The BFI recently moved into video distribution with the launch of its Connoisseur label, releasing landmarks of world cinema. The staff of the Film Society Unit, a part of BFI Exhibition and Distribution, service some three hundred film societies throughout the UK which belong to the British Federation of Film Societies. The FSU gives practical advice on starting, developing and running film societies and offers a range of other services and events.

National Film Archive

THE National Film Archive was founded in 1935 "to maintain a national repository of films of permanent value." Its moving image collection now comprises 175,000 titles dating from 1895 to the present day, covering features and shorts, documentaries, newsreels, television programmes, amateur films and videos, on a comprehensive range of gauges and formats. The NFA began, in the mid-fifties, to acquire television, the recording and preservation of which is now a major part of the Archive's work, aided by substantial annual grants from ITV and Channel Four. Business and private sponsors also contribute to the nitrate film preservation and restoration programmes. There is as yet no law of statutory deposit for film and video production in the UK (as there is for books, for example) and acquisition is mostly by donation.

The J Paul Getty Jnr Conservation Centre, opened in June 1987 at Berkhamsted, Herts, and named after its generous sponsor, is the Archive's storage site for safety film and video, and the location for all preservation and restoration work. Approximately 140 million feet of highly flammable nitrate film is kept at a specially equipped site a further 50 miles away in

Below: Landmarks of world cinema on Connoisseur Video

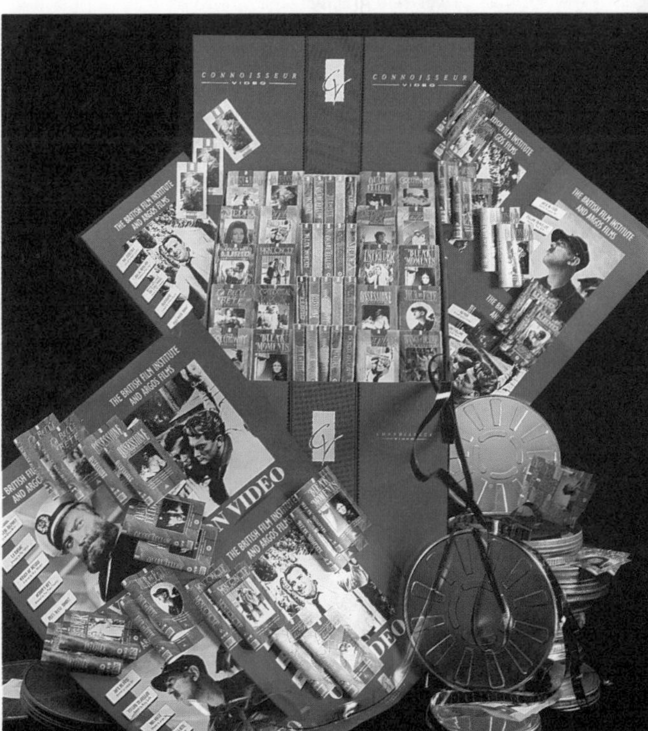

Warwickshire; this material, which shrinks and decomposes with age, is systematically copied on to modern safety film as part of the preservation process.

The Cataloguing section, based in London, provides information, in the form of indexing, descriptive cataloguing and subject analysis on titles held in the collection, and answers personal, telephone and postal enquiries. The Viewing Service organises viewings on the premises for bona fide researchers and arranges loans of material to the National Film Theatre and the BFI-supported network of cinemas and educational venues. It also promotes retrospectives of British cinema at home and abroad. Donor Access handles enquiries specifically from donors and copyright owners, while the Production Library supplies film-makers and TV producers with extracts for use in compilation films and documentary programmes.

Above: The National Film Archive has been archiving television since the 1950s and the BFI recently won statutory backing for the establishment of a National Television Archive

Planning

ALTHOUGH based in London, the BFI is very much a national body and the Planning Unit co-ordinates the regional policies within which other departments carry out their work. The Planning Unit is also responsible for enhancing the BFI's input and influence into development of the regional exhibition and production infrastructure and for helping implement the Institute's Corporate Plan through the co-ordination of pan-Institute activity, for example cultural issues relating to equal opportunities, Europe, etc. The Press Office, contained within the Planning Unit, is responsible for the BFI's corporate image and ensuring that its corporate aspirations receive full public expression.

Research

Communications Group

THE Communications Group co-ordinates various projects which further the BFI's cultural objectives in film and television. It includes the TV and Projects Unit which organised the massive 'One Day in the Life of Television' project which pooled the experiences, via more than

Below: Sabu in* The Thief of Bagdad *which was restored by the National Film Archive

18,000 diaries, of both viewers and those working in the television industry, on 1 November 1988. This culminated in a network ITV documentary and the publication of a book, containing extracts from 800 of the diaries. Research into national viewing patterns continues with 400 'One Day' diarists all over the country writing about their TV viewing three times a year. The Unit's Race and Ethnicity project is another important research initiative, exploring the history of black people in British television since 1936. As well as a comprehensive database, the findings will result in two TV documentaries and a book.

The TV and Projects Unit also organises other conferences and events such as 'Television on BFI South Bank', a regular programme of TV-related screenings and debates at the NFT/MOMI, which brings together audiences and television professionals to highlight TV's achievements and discuss topical broadcasting issues. In many cases, the work of the TV and Projects Unit is supported by books and documentation produced by the publishing arm of the Communications Group.

BFI Education

BFI Education aims to develop knowledge and ideas about the media – film, television and video in particular. By working with people in formal education, from primary to university level, in the community at large, and in many other institutions, the Department tries to ensure that such knowledge and ideas are spread as widely as possible. Its work includes research, teaching, materials production and lobbying, and in all these areas it aims to set agendas and provoke debate. BFI Education strives to enable as many people as possible to discover new ways of thinking about, producing and enjoying these media. A Training Co-ordinator working within BFI Education provides short training courses for Regional Film Theatre staff, produces a guide to short production courses, and represents the BFI on a number of national training initiatives, including the Independent Media Training Federation.

BFI Publishing Services

BFI Publishing Services produces a range of books on film and television on behalf of the various departments within the Research Division, for a readership which ranges from scholars and teachers through

Below: Media education in practice: Julian Bowker of BFI Education in the classroom

Young Soul Rebels, *the latest feature from BFI Production, won the Critics' Week Prize at the Cannes Film Festival*

to the film and broadcasting communities and the general public at large. Its aims are to assist the spread of new ideas and knowledge, to raise the level of public awareness of film and television, and to provide a platform for debate on issues of public concern.

'Sight and Sound'
The cinema, TV and video monthly magazine, 'Sight and Sound' provides sharp feature articles by leading writers and includes an in-depth review, synopsis and full credits for every feature film released and a shorter review of every video.

BFI Production
BFI Production produces a range of projects from short films and videos to feature-length films, acting as producer and co-investor. Focusing on work which is innovative both in theme and style, it aims to encourage challenging and different approaches to cinema in Britain and to foster a film culture which represents the lives and concerns of those people generally under-represented on both sides of the camera. BFI Production also offers grants to a wide range of projects from short films and video to more ambitious pieces on a part-funding package basis through the Production Projects Fund. Channel Four has supported the Production Board since 1985 with an annual subvention (currently £450,000) and the Board is also supported by the Independent Television Association (£50,000). In a given year, BFI Production would also hope to raise extra funding in the form of co-finance and pre-sales tied to individual projects. BFI Production undertakes its own distribution and sales, and its releases over the last few years include *Distant Voices, Still Lives, Venus Peter, Play Me Something, Fellow Traveller, Silent Scream* and *Young Soul Rebels.*

Contacts at the BFI

British Film Institute
21 Stephen Street
London W1P 1PL
Tel: 071 255 1444
Telex: 27624 BFILDNG
Fax: 071 436 7950
Director: Wilf Stevenson
Assistant Director: Michael Prescott

Corporate Press Contacts
Head of Press and Promotions: Wayne Drew

Planning Unit
Head: Irene Whitehead

National Film Archive
(At Stephen Street)
Curator: Clyde Jeavons
Deputy Curator: Anne Fleming
(At the J Paul Getty Jnr Conservation Centre, Kings Hill Way, Berkhamsted, Hertfordshire HP4 3TP. Tel: 04428 76301 Fax: 04428 75607)
Acting Head of Conservation: Tony Cook

BFI Exhibition and Distribution Division
Head of Exhibition and Distribution: Ian Christie
Deputy Head and Head of Exhibition Services: Jayne Pilling
Head of Acquisitions and Rights: Barry Edson
Head of Distribution Services: Heather Stewart
Marketing Officer, Film and Video Distribution: Mark Finch
Head of Film Society Unit: Tom Brownlie
Film Society Unit Information Officer: Peter Cargin

BFI Stills, Posters and Designs
Head: Bridget Kinally

BFI Library and Information Services
Head: Gillian Hartnoll

BFI Research Division
Head of Research: Colin MacCabe
Head of Education: Manuel Alvarado
Head of Publishing Services: Caroline Moore
(Sales enquiries 29 Rathbone Street, London W1P 1AG Tel: 071 636 3289)
Head of Communications Group: Richard Paterson
Head of Trade Publishing: Ed Buscombe
Head of TV and Projects Unit: Tana Wollen
Editor 'Sight and Sound': Philip Dodd

BFI Production
29 Rathbone Street
London W1P 1AG
Tel: 071 636 5587/4736
Fax: 071 580 9456
Head: Ben Gibson
Deputy Head: Angela Topping
Sales: Sue Bruce-Smith
Press and Publicity: Liz Reddish

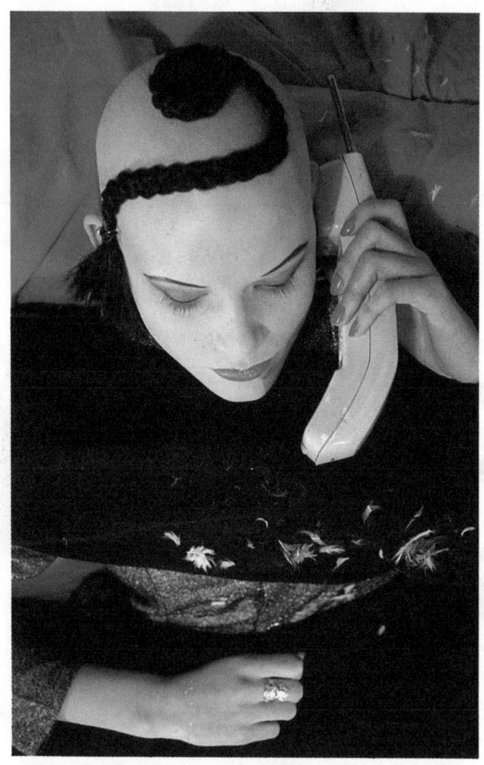

Above:* Floating, *directed by Richard Heslop: one of the 1991 BFI New Directors shorts

BFI South Bank
National Film Theatre and Museum of the Moving Image
South Bank London SE1 8XT Tel: 071 928 3535
Fax: 071 633 9323
Telex: 929229 NATFIL G
Controller: Leslie Hardcastle (from December 1991, Jürgen Berger)
Deputy Controller: Paul Collard
Head of Programming: Deac Rossell
London Film Festival Director: Sheila Whitaker
Head of Marketing: Peter Elliott
Deputy Head of Marketing: Brian Robinson

Facilities for the disabled:
The British Film Institute is working to improve access to its buildings for disabled visitors. Facilities include:

21 Stephen Street: unisex toilet for disabled on ground floor, car parking at rear of building (please contact security staff beforehand to check availability, and on arrival to gain access via

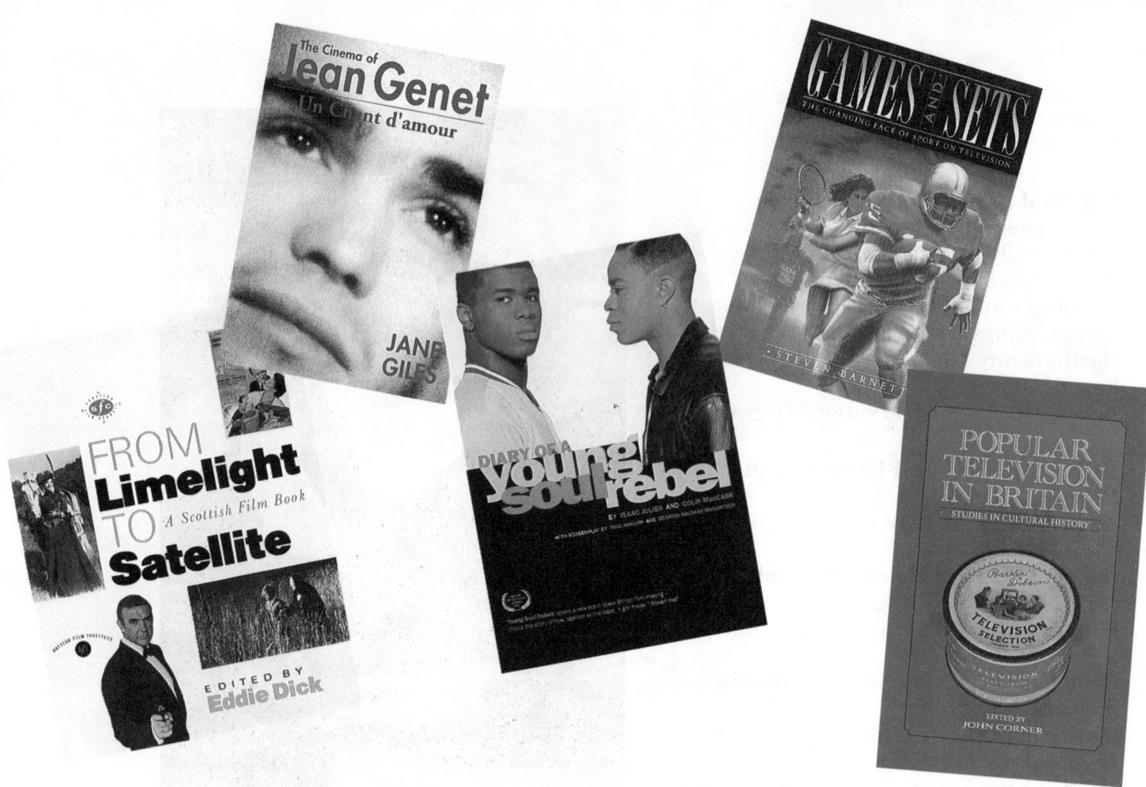

Above: Just some of the varied titles published by the BFI

ramp into rear ground floor corridor). Access to all areas (except nitrate viewing area on roof) via lifts situated in rear ground floor corridor and main reception (no steps into main reception from street). Assistance may be necessary for unaccompanied wheelchair users since there are several heavy fire doors.

Museum of the Moving Image (a leaflet outlining facilities for people with disabilities is available on request from NFT reception): Reduced admission charge, and group rate, for registered disabled people. Unaccompanied wheelchair users are welcome. There are several heavy fire doors in MOMI which may be difficult to use but there is always assistance available.

There are three parking spaces for the disabled on the Royal Festival Hall access road and two on the access road leading to MOMI. Visitors may also use Euro car parks at the Hayward Gallery and National Theatre. There is a ramp from the Hayward Gallery car park to MOMI.

There are no steps into the main foyer of the building where a central telephone call point can be used to gain help with buying tickets and entry to MOMI.

Most areas of the museum are accessible to wheelchair users although in a slightly different order from the usual route. Two scissor lifts and one stair lift operate between the ground and first floor and there is one stair lift between the first and second floor. There are help points placed at each of these lifts to enable disabled visitors to call for assistance.

MOMI's cinema has three wheelchair positions at the front of the auditorium and an induction loop system for those wearing hearing aids incorporating a T switch. There are disabled toilet facilities in the toilets in the first exhibition area.

National Film Theatre: NFT1 has 6 wheelchair positions at the rear of the auditorium which must be booked in advance. A disabled person may occupy seat N1 in NFT2 if accompanied by an able-bodied person who will occupy the adjacent seat. A wheelchair may only be used when the general lighting is on and it must be stored out of the way at the rear of NFT2. There is a unisex disabled toilet situated at the far end of the corridor to the right of the restaurant entrance, near NFT1, and in the black and white passageway off the main NFT/MOMI foyer. NFT1 and NFT2 both have an induction loop system for those with hearing aids incorporating a T switch, and also certain seats with a special earphone facility. Please ask for this service when booking.

29 Rathbone Street: lift access to the first floor offices and ramp access to the technical facilities. Three parking spaces, please contact reception (071 636 5587) before arrival to check availability.

National Film Archive, Berkhamsted: ramps into J Paul Getty Jnr Conservation centre, electronically operated doors, unisex disabled toilet, lift access to all areas.

Cinema 1990-91 – Production

British filmmakers could miss out on the opportunities offered by the single European market argues Ben Keen, executive editor of 'Screen Digest'

WITHIN sight of the symbolic European year of 1992, the year 1990-91 should have seen the British film industry moving steadily towards its, arguably, natural role as the 'Hollywood of Europe'. The argument runs that the UK, with its rich history of creative filmmaking, depth of talent and international language of English, is perfectly placed to take up a leading position in the new European film industry. However, progress towards that goal was not as smooth as it might have been and some would say that few, if any, forward steps were taken.

Many of the relevant issues and problems had been thrashed out at a private seminar organised by the British Screen Advisory Council at the start of 1990. This brought together fifty leading executives from the European continent and the UK to discuss co-operation. A summary of the discussions was published by BSAC in July 1990 as the report 'The European Initiative' which concluded that "the UK is isolated at a time when it should be joining in [with the rest of Europe]."

A Rage in Harlem

A picture emerged of the UK film industry as somehow stranded between the USA and continental Europe, not quite strong enough to be a fully fledged partner to either. It was clear that continental film producers were already working together regularly, while the UK was being left out of the party. With relatively prosperous domestic cinema and television markets plus sizeable government support schemes for film production, French, German and Italian producers make attractive partners for each other while their UK counterparts find it difficult to bring comparable riches to the negotiating table. Consequently, British producers renewed their call for government help to "level the playing field," a plea that was to be echoed throughout the year, particularly when they finally caught the ear of Prime Minister Thatcher in June 1990.

The first quarter of 1990 had given some cause for good cheer, with 16 films going in front of the cameras, the highest number in that period for some years. Optimism continued into the beginning of the period under review. In April 1990 Zenith, the production company responsible for such films as *Wish You Were Here* and *The Dead*, returned to feature film making for the first time since its parent group Carlton Communications sold 49 per cent of the company to the US studio Paramount Communications in November 1989. In the meantime, Zenith, like many British production companies, had turned increasingly to the safer busi-

Above: Scorchers

ness of making television programmes.

While Zenith was making the Hal Hartley-directed comedy *Trust* in New York, two other stalwart British film companies were also active in the USA. In Cincinnati, Palace Pictures started shooting *A Rage In Harlem* while down south in Louisiana, Goldcrest began *Scorchers*. Both Palace and Goldcrest were also busy closer to home; Palace continued its relationship with Irish novelist-turned-director Neil Jordan to make the £2.7 million romantic drama *The Miracle*, while Goldcrest started Don Bluth's $13 million animated feature *Rock-A-Doodle* at the famous Sullivan Bluth Studios in Ireland.

At about the same time, news began to filter through that another well known studio, Bray Film Studios, was to be released from threat of closure by four private investors. Famous for the Hammer House of Horror movies, Bray had looked set to close when its lease ran out in February 1990, but a new management team led by Neville Hendricks and Peter Gray stepped in with a £2 million refurbishment plan based on a belief in a forthcoming cyclical upswing in UK-based production that would keep the studio's four sound stages busy.

Confirmation of planning permission by the Secretary of State for the Environment

Below: The Miracle *continued Palace's link with Neil Jordan*

Top: **Rock-A-Doodle,** *from the renowned Sullivan Bluth studios*
Second: **Jeeves and Wooster** *was shot at Bray Film Studios which were saved from closure by a consortium of private investors*
Third: **Life is Sweet**
Fourth: Artist's impression of Movie Set Street, part of the proposed £2,000 million studio and theme park development for Rainham Marshes

also seemed to clear the way for a major new studio complex to get off the drawing board – MCA/Universal's planned £2,000 million film studio and theme park at Rainham Marshes in Essex. But prospects of this complex being built have faded as the prognosis for the industry has declined.

Those hoping for a revival in the fortunes of UK studios received no solace from a report published in May 1990 by consultants Goodall Alexander O'Hare which pointed to problems of severe overcapacity in studio space – making prospects for their profitability poor. The report found over 960,000 square feet of studio space in the UK, nearly half accounted for by Pinewood, Elstree and Shepperton, but also with over a fifth owned by ITV companies increasingly desperate to supplement their income by hiring out their facilities.

On a further negative note, the sorry saga of the historic Elstree Studios continued in June 1990 when it emerged that Brent Walker, the principal shareholder of Elstree-owner Goldcrest, was intent on selling over half the studio space to Tesco for a 90,000 square feet supermarket.

Elstree had benefited during the 1980s from a stream of big US films, including those made by George Lucas and Steven Spielberg, but in recent years these had faded away to be replaced, rather inadequately, by a mix of television and commercials production. This was exemplified by the August 1990 reopening of stage nine, now promoted as Europe's largest television production stage, under an 18-month deal with television company SelecTV. Of the three big studios, only Pinewood had US productions booked in for the summer of 1990 – Tri-Star's *Robin Hood,* Twentieth Century Fox's *Alien 3,* and Warner's *Shining Through.*

Another name which used to be synonymous with the British film industry – the Rank Organisation – took another step away from the business of production in April 1990 when it sold its industrial training film arm to the Longman Group, part of Pearson, for £11.5 million. Rank Training was a market leader in the field and the

***Above:* *Michael Palin's* American Friends**

sale was probably an indication of the declining fortunes of the industrial film and corporate video market as a whole.

The start of shooting in April 1990 on the low budget feature *Dakota Road* received more than average attention due to it being the first film made under the British Film Partnership Scheme. This scheme was devised by several independent producers and the UK's main film financing organisation British Screen Finance to cut production costs and generate faster returns on investment. In return for a share of revenues above production and distribution costs, the cast, crew and facilities suppliers agreed to lower their fees and work more flexible hours thereby keeping the budget to around £1 million.

Reports back from the set suggested that the scheme engendered a particularly positive spirit on the part of all those involved. Produced by Sarah Radclyffe of Working Title, the tragic drama set in rural England marked the film debut of acclaimed playwright Nick Ward.

May 1990 saw the start of production on Michael Palin's gentle tale *American Friends* and another in Mike Leigh's series of observations on the peculiarities of the British, *Life is Sweet*.

Meanwhile in Cardiff (emerging as a new production centre) the strength of Britain's animation sector was underlined with the first cels being prepared for the animated feature *The Princess And The Goblin*. A $6 million 85-minute adaptation of George MacDonald's 1872 novel, it was put together as a co-production between the Welsh company Siriol Productions and Pannonia Film of Hungary with backing from the Welsh Channel Four (S4C) and Japanese state television. Siriol is notable for reaching out to western as well as eastern Europe through the formation around this time of an alliance with German and French counterparts, under the aegis of the European Commission's MEDIA 92 CARTOON scheme to support the European animation industry.

To prove that the British Commonwealth is still meaningful as an alternative axis to the European Community, a different form of alliance was set up in May to make four films a year over three years under the banner of the Commonwealth Co-production League. This was set up by Channel Four, the Australian Film Commission, and the New Zealand Film Commission and co-ordinated by Zenith and Canadian Sunrise Films. It was followed in June 1990 by the signing of the first official co-production treaty between Australia and the UK, allowing partners to access Australian tax concessions and other support measures.

The big news in June 1990 was of course the British attempt to get support measures for the film industry on to the Govern-

Below:* Dakota Road*: first film made under the British Film Partnership Scheme

The best originating material for cinema and TV.

It is common knowledge that motion picture film is the best originating medium.
However, maintaining the quality of the colour negative in post production for cinema release and television is critical.
AGFA XT has proved that it renders outstanding results when it comes to direct transfer to video and also offers minimal generation loss through intermediate to release print.
Obtaining only the very best on the screen is the essence of filmmaking and that is why cinematographers are relying more and more on AGFA XT.
Agfa-Gevaert Ltd.
Motion Picture Division
27, Great West Road
Brentford
Middlesex TW8 9AX
Tel.: 081-560 2131
AGFA FILM XT 320
AGFA XT 100 & XT 320
COLOUR NEGATIVE FILMS
NEW: XT 100
AGFA NEGATIVE XT 100
AGFA NEGATIVE XT 320
They reflect the best of you.
AGFA
Agfa

Above: **Prospero's Books**

ment's agenda. On 15 June the Prime Minister hosted a Downing Street seminar with a delegation of film producers led by Sir Richard Attenborough and the then Chief Executive of British Screen, Simon Relph.

One immediate outcome was a government nod in the direction of the "uneven European playing field" by pledging £5 million over three years to support UK producers in setting up European co-productions. All other issues were redirected to government-industry working groups, one chaired by the Department of Trade and Industry to examine general structural impediments to attracting more production investment, and another – reporting to Treasury Ministers – to look at fiscal measures for improving the film production environment.

Back at the production front, work was starting on the £1.2 million British Film Institute feature *Young Soul Rebels.* A representation of London black youth experience in the late 1970s, the film was directed by Isaac Julien who emerged out of the low-budget film and video workshop sector. In Holland, the peculiarly English filmmaker Peter Greenaway was beginning his reworking of 'The Tempest' titled *Prospero's Books*, once more funded by non-English money (Dutch, French and Italian), while in New York prolific British producer Eric Fellner (*Pascali's Island, Hidden Agenda*) was overseeing the $9 million drama *Liebestraum* for MGM/UA. Later the same month, Fellner led a management team in buying out his Initial Film and Television company from the collapsed MGMM group.

Another company collapse in July 1990, this time of the large Parkfield Group, sent waves of panic through the UK's video sector and depressed hopes that British video companies would become more proactive investors in film production. Parkfield had been the prime backer of the award-winning gangland drama *The Krays*.

However, there were two very positive developments in July. The BBC conveyed its intention to set up a film production subsidiary with outside financial backing, and Palace Pictures set about doing what most others only talked about – creating an alliance of European film producer-distributors which could function something like a European version of a Hollywood 'major'. The idea was that the partners, from the UK, Spain, Italy, France and Germany, would co-operate in acquiring European rights to US films as well as production and distribution of European films.

August 1990 saw the start, in Budapest, of David Puttnam's collaboration with director Istvan Szabo on the $10.4 million film *Meeting Venus*, the second in his series of projects under the revolving fund put in place by a consortium led by Warner Bros and Japanese group Fujisankei. His backers had been previously responsible for supporting the production of *Memphis Belle* – a film originally intended to portray a British bomber crew but switched to a US crew as its subject for marketing reasons.

Puttnam's track record brings him the level of support and creative autonomy which most other British producers can only dream about. Normal British budget levels are typified by two of the films which went into production in September: the

Above: **The Favour, the Watch & the Very Big Fish**

£1.75 million *The Bridge* and £750,000 production *One Full Moon*. Telling the story behind artist Philip Wilson Steer's painting, *The Bridge* was notable for enticing the US bank Security Pacific to take its first step into British film financing alongside old hands Channel Four and British Screen Finance. Such backing would have been difficult to attract for *One Full Moon*, the first film to be shot under the Ffilm Cymru joint venture between BBC Wales and S4C, and made entirely in the Welsh language.

British banks are not noted for their love of the film industry so the declaration in September 1990 by Coutts & Co, a subsidiary of National Westminster Bank, that it intended to become the main bank for the entertainment industry came as welcome news. Indeed, it was all the more gladly received given the fact that one of the most active UK film financiers, British & Commonwealth, had gone into receivership in June and another, Guinness Mahon, was becoming noticeably more cautious.

Coutts was responsible for helping the most famous modern British film company, Goldcrest, enter a new phase of life through a $50 million management buy-out from the Brent Walker group led by John Quested. After many delays, this finally went through in November.

Prize for most intriguing film title of the year undoubtedly went to *The Favour, The Watch & The Very Big Fish*, which was actually a romantic comedy starring Bob Hoskins, Jeff Goldblum and Natasha Richardson, made as a collaboration between British company Umbrella Films and French company Les Films Ariane. While this was being shot in Paris, Umbrella Films' Simon Perry was announced as the next chief executive of British Screen Finance, succeeding Simon Relph. Guided by Relph, and with vital support from Channel Four, BSF had virtually single-handedly kept the British film industry alive during the 1980s. However, under Relph, only two of the 56 films supported by BSF had been European co-productions, while many more had US participation. Perry declared it his intention to follow his own example and try through BSF to bridge the gap with the European mainland.

At the beginning of 1990 the two film producers' organisations had come together to form The Producers Association. In October 1990 it was the turn of their employees. The two largest film and TV unions, the Association of Cinematograph, Television and Allied Technicians (ACTT) and the Broadcasting and Entertainment Trades Alliance (BETA) voted to merge into the single 60,000 strong Broadcasting Entertainment & Cinematograph Technicians Union (BECTU).

Meanwhile, the dynamic but financially starved low-budget production sector in Britain's regions, which is often forced to work outside union structures, was given a boost by the creation of a new £340,000

***Below: The merger of Sky and BSB was a major blow since BSB had been a major investor in films such as* Hardware**

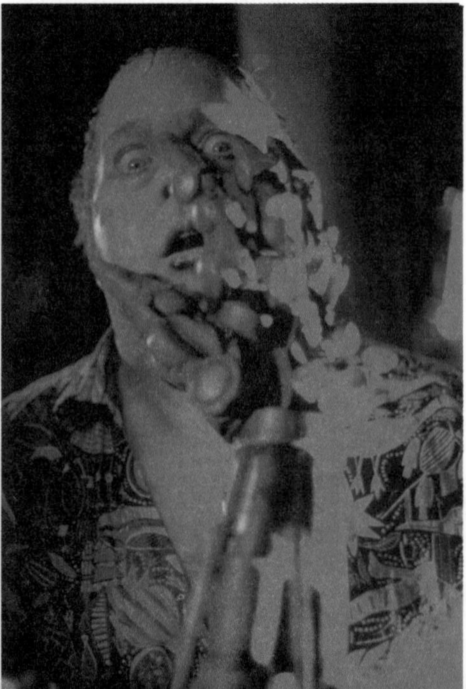

British Film Institute production fund.

Called Production Projects, the new fund was designed to be flexible, offering grants to a wide range of projects from short films and videos to more ambitious pieces on a part-funding package basis, the maximum financial contribution being £30,000.

Overshadowing all else in November 1990 were three corporate acquisition deals which sent repercussions all around the global media industry. In the US, Matsushita became the second Japanese electronics group (after Sony) to buy a Hollywood studio when it confirmed the $6,100 million purchase of MCA/Universal; and Giancarlo Parretti, the colourful Italian entrepreneur, confounded many expectations by pulling off the $1,300 million acquisition of MGM/UA.

Back home, the two horse race for satellite television riches was suddenly reduced to one when British Satellite Broadcasting and Sky Television were merged to form British Sky Broadcasting. For the film industry it seemed a bitter blow since BSB had proven a major ally by investing up front in such films as *The Big Man, Hardware, Chicago Joe And The Showgirl* and *The Rachel Papers*. No one was under any illusions that the cost-conscious Sky-dominated BSkyB would continue in that vein.

The Matsushita takeover of MCA/Universal was an indicator of the accelerating Japanese interest in the film industry which also blossomed into a three-film funding deal for British producer Jeremy Thomas with newly formed Japanese film investment vehicle Nippon Film Development & Finance. Two years previously, Thomas had secured backing from another Japanese company, Shochiku-Fuji, for five films. Shochiku holds 10 per cent of the film financing company, Film Trustees, set up by Thomas and leading distributor Terry Glinwood which also in November acquired a minority stake in Initial Film and Television – the production company which Eric Fellner helped to buy out from MGMM earlier in the year.

The final 1990 tally for feature films made in or from the UK was 53 which, although significantly up on 1989's low of 38, was hardly enough to inspire renewed confidence, particularly as the average budget per film actually fell from £4.1 million in 1989 to £3.6 million in 1990. By contrast, the French industry, heavily supported by government, managed to turn out nearly three times as many features (146) and the Italians were not far behind with 119.

Indicative of French strength, and the country's claim to be the media linchpin of Europe, was the announcement around the turn of the year by the powerful French broadcaster Canal Plus of its intention to set up a major film production arm that would act like a bridge between Europe and Hollywood. The UK sorely misses the kind of $50 million a year commitment to production that such companies are prepared to make. Meanwhile, the rest of Europe is increasingly prepared to usurp Britain's role as Europe's English-language film producer; in continental Europe, at least 19

Below: **London Kills Me*****, written and directed by*** **My Beautiful Laundrette** ***writer Hanif Kureishi***

Above: **The Naked Lunch**

English-language films went into production in 1990 and early 1991, including seven by French companies.

However, the start of 1991 was not all gloom for the UK. Venture capital fund GLE Development Capital, originally set up by the Greater London Council but now entirely independent and already a shareholder in Palace Pictures, agreed to invest £1.2 million in newly formed production company Union Pictures. The latter, co-founded by *Quadrophenia* director Frank Roddam, planned to put the money towards a slate of projects which includes 10 features over two years.

Among films going into production in January, February and March were the £3.1 million Dylan Thomas biography *Dylan* from broadcaster HTV's subsidiary Harlech Films, Working Title's *London Kills Me*, written and directed by *My Beautiful Laundrette* writer Hanif Kureishi, Jeremy Thomas and David Cronenberg's adaptation of William Burroughs' novel *Naked Lunch*, and Derek Jarman's *Edward II*.

Below: Derek Jarman's **Edward II**

Intent on building upon the success of its Oscar-winning *My Left Foot*, in March 1991, Granada Television announced it would formalise its involvement in features with the establishment of a Granada Films subsidiary to make six films in the £5 million-£10 million budget range over five years. In the run-up to the awarding of new ITV franchises in October 1991 it might have been expected that the commercial broadcasters would have withdrawn from the film industry entirely, but several in addition to Granada continued to dabble. HTV, through its Harlech Films arm and its May 1990 acquisition of Vestron Pictures UK, probably had the next strongest commitment, but Anglia, LWT and Yorkshire all showed selected interest.

Bad news came in the March 1991 budget speech when Chancellor Norman Lamont rejected all the fiscal proposals to improve the environment for film investment that had been put forward by the working group formed after the Downing Street seminar. Many felt betrayed by the Government and the gloom was compounded by the realisation that only nine production starts were made in the first quarter of the year, just six of which were shot on British soil and merely four with significant UK funding.

Some consolation came as Britain's brilliant young animator Nick Park walked away with the Oscar for Best Animated Short Film at the March Academy Awards for his poignant and hilarious piece *Creature Comforts*. There was also some satisfaction and perhaps future insights to be gleaned from the fact that *Dances With Wolves*, the winner of seven Oscars and a world hit that would go on to gross over $380 million, was half financed by British company Majestic Films.

Production companies are listed on pp 230-251 of the Directory. Films which went into production during the year are listed on pp 252-263. For feature films released during the period see pp 274-290. Funding sources are listed on pp 176-181.

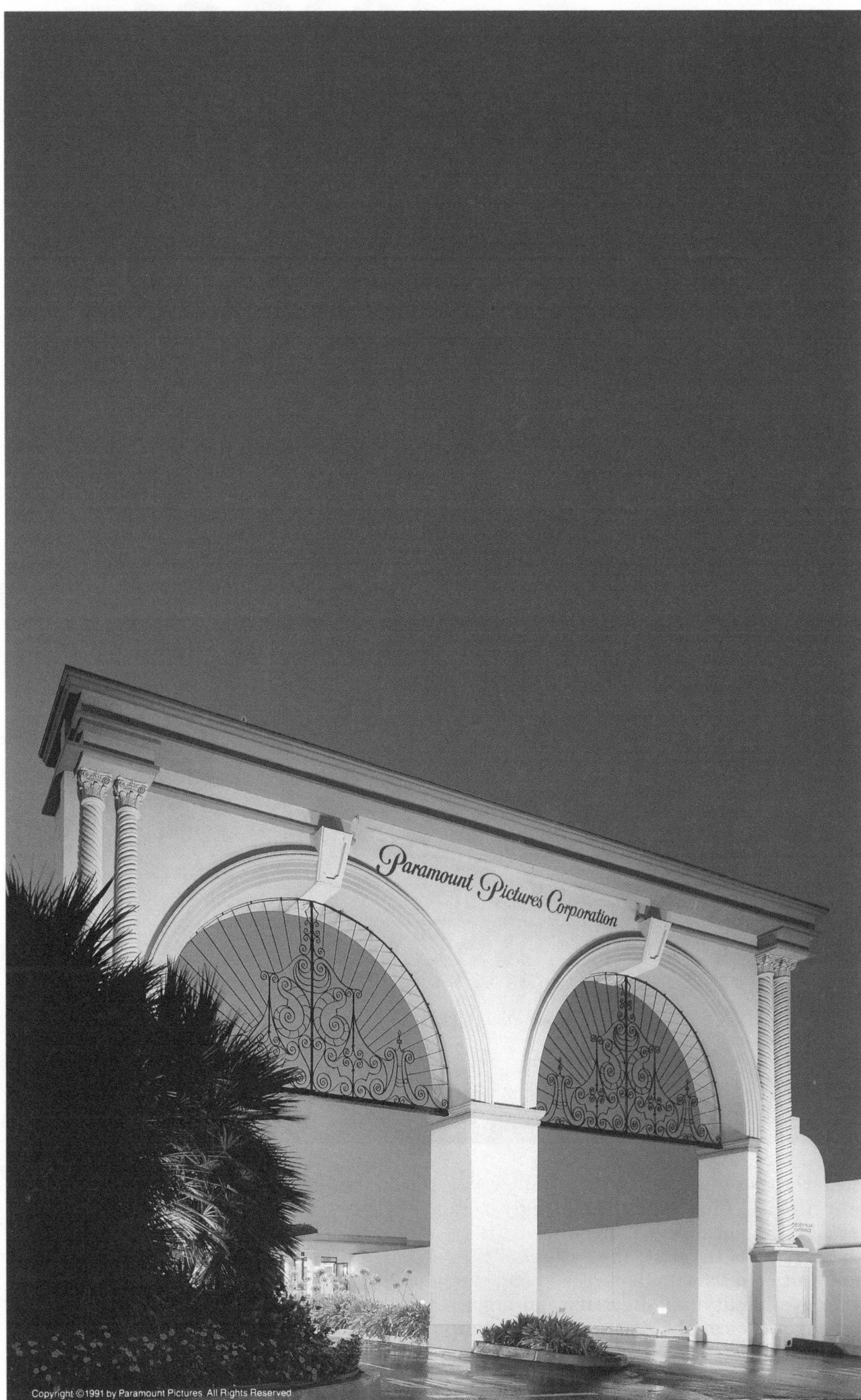
Paramount Pictures Corporation

Cinema 1990-91 – Distribution

Film distribution in Britain continues to offer only limited choice to cinema-goers and video-watchers says Julian Petley in his review of the year

THE main problem with film distribution in Britain is that it delivers a large amount of mainstream Hollywood product fairly effectively to audiences in large metropolitan areas but gives those audiences little opportunity to widen their tastes. Meanwhile, certain audiences (particularly those looking for non-Hollywood, even British, films) and, increasingly, certain geographical areas, remain virtually uncatered for. In short, the system of film distribution does not offer a good recipe for wide availability and diversity and proper consumer choice. The reasons for this state of affairs are structural and deep-seated, as can be seen from the events of the year in review.

Above:* Cinema Paradiso*: top-earning foreign subtitled film in 1990

As outlined in the chapter on exhibition (pp 34-42), both cinema admissions and the number of cinema screens in the UK continued to increase during the year. The increase in admissions was confirmed by the new industry magazine, 'Moving Pictures International', which estimated that, although ticket prices remained stable, gross box office revenues for the Top 100 films showed a 13% increase over the previous year: £234,577,934 compared to £207,536,000.

There are some discrepancies between the box office figures published by 'Moving

***Would-be blockbusters* Back to the Future Part III *(below) and* Dick Tracy *lagged behind surprise successes* Ghost *(above) and* Pretty Woman**

Pictures International' and 'Screen International', its longer established rival. These discrepancies highlight the difficulty, discussed in the 1991 edition of the Handbook, of gathering accurate statistics about film and video distribution.

However, both 'Moving Pictures International''s Top 100 chart and 'Screen International''s Top 70 demonstrate how UK film distribution continued to be dominated by mainstream Hollywood releases. Not only do films from the USA form a significant proportion of the total number of films released (see table 1) but they continue to account for a large percentage of the total box-office revenue earned (see table 2). This dominance of US product can be seen from the fact that the highest placed British film was *Memphis Belle* at 17 with a gross of £4.81 million while *Cinema Paradiso* was the top-earning foreign sub-titled film, grossing £1.02 million and reaching 48 in the chart.

An interesting development within the mainstream dominance of the Top 70/100 charts for 1990 was the way in which big-budget blockbuster sequels such as *Gremlins 2: the New Batch, Die Hard 2: Die Harder*, and prestige pictures such as *Dick Tracy*, lagged behind surprise successes such as *Ghost, Pretty Woman* and *Look Who's Talking*. Also worth noting was the presence of *Total Recall* at number five. This was a remarkable achievement for a film with an '18' certificate which automatically limits its potential audience; the previous year's highest-ranked '18' film was *The Accused*, which didn't even make the Top 10 and took only £3.7 million. *Total Recall* was also the highest-ranking film from an independent distributor, Guild. The film was released on one of the hottest weekends on record, not the best time for cinema-going, and was largely responsible for boosting the London six-day total gross to a record £1,036,633.

The UK advertising campaign for *Total Recall* was rumoured to have cost close to £1 million and the film's success helped push Guild's market share to 4.7% in 1990. Distributors such as Guild and Palace are increasingly operating on the scale of US independents such as New Line, Miramax, Trimax and Samuel Goldwyn. However, although the market shares achieved by Guild and Palace are impressive when compared to those of the other UK independent

Above: **Total Recall***: highest-ranking film from an independent distributor*

distributors, they still account for only a small proportion of the market. As table 3 shows, the lion's share continued to be taken by the five major distributors which release the majority of mainstream Hollywood product shown in the UK: Warner Bros, Rank, Twentieth Century Fox, Columbia Tri-Star and UIP (which distributes films from Paramount, Universal and MGM/UA). Between them, these five companies distributed 18 out of the Top 20 box-office films for 1990, accounting for 89% of the Top 20 box-office revenue.

This left the following independent distributors, specialising in non-mainstream, often foreign, films, with less than 1% shares of the market: Enterprise, Artificial Eye, MCEG Virgin Vision, Gala/Curzon, Medusa, Castle/Premier, Vestron, Pathé Releasing, the BFI, Mainline, and Oasis Releasing. The difficulties facing such independents are illustrated by the fact that, during the year under review, Enterprise went out of business, Medusa closed down its theatrical distribution arm and Oasis scaled down its theatrical releases dramatically to concentrate on exhibition.

Among these difficulties is the shortage of cinema screens in the UK although some independents do also operate cinemas (for example, Artificial Eye, Mainline and Metro). The shortage of screens is a problem also facing the major distributors, particularly in the West End of London which is in serious need of more screens, but where, it seems, cinemas simply do not generate enough revenue to justify the high cost of the prime sites. The majors often have to pencil in releases six or eight months in advance if they want to secure the screen of their choice. However, they are helped considerably by the system of 'alignments' – whereby the two major cinema chains, Metro Goldwyn Mayer Cinemas (operator of the Cannon and MGM cinemas) and Rank (which operates the Odeon chain) each commit themselves to showing the films released by certain of the major distributors. The independent distributors find it far more difficult to find spaces for their films.

Below: **Nuns on the Run***: one of the few British films which made the Top 70*

This problem has not been alleviated by the increase in number of screens outlined in the chapter on exhibition because most of the new screens are contained within multiplexes built by various of the five main multiplex operators, Rank, Warner Bros, UCI, Metro Goldwyn Mayer Cinemas and National Amusements. Rank and Warner Bros are major distributors themselves while UCI and National Amusements, although they have not been absorbed into the system of alignments, are supported by all the major distributors and are, in the main, able to show new product as early as the established duopoly. They have therefore tended to play much the same material as the local Cannon and Odeon cinemas.

The shortage of screens is exacerbated by the tendency of the major exhibitors to hold over successful films for successive weeks and means that the number of films shown in this country, both from Hollywood and elsewhere, is only a tiny fraction of the total numbers potentially on offer. It also seems to be the case that Britain is getting the major new Hollywood releases later than many other European countries.

These problems were highlighted by the business press several times during the year. In March 1991, 'Screen Finance' concluded that: "an increasing slice of the multiplex audience is coming from the 'cannibalisation' of traditional cinema audiences rather than the attraction of new viewers or from any attempt to appeal to audiences not catered for by the duopoly."

Above: **Dances with Wolves*****: repeated Guild's success with*** **Total Recall**

Peter Trowell, then managing director of Hemdale Film Distribution, told 'Screen International' in January 1991 that he believed the multiplexes have little to offer the independent distributor: "With the advent of multiplexes, my company and fellow independents will find it increasingly difficult in 1991 to maintain even the strongest of independent features for more than one or two weeks, because of mounting pressure from the majors."

Below: **Cyrano de Bergerac*****: set to be the top-earning foreign film for 1991***

TABLE ONE: COUNTRY OF ORIGIN OF FEATURE FILMS EXHIBITED IN THE UK BETWEEN 1 APRIL 1990 AND 31 MARCH 1991

Main country of origin	*Number of films*
USA	171
UK	29
Western Europe	41
Eastern Europe	2
Others	19
Total	262

Source: 'Monthly Film Bulletin', published by the British Film Institute

Apart from the shortage of screens, the other major problem facing all distributors is the rising cost of launching a new release, and especially the cost of advertising. Some distributors believe that producers will eventually have to pay a share of advertising and marketing costs. Even the majors are not immune. According to Rank's managing director Fred Turner: "UK theatrical is a loss leader. It can cost anywhere between £500,000 to £1 million to release a film, and around eight out of ten films do not recoup on prints and advertising." The cost of advertising is described by Maj-Britt Kirchner, managing director of Warner Bros UK, as "horrendous, particularly when you are looking at using so many different media outlets." But at least the majors can take advantage of economies of scale, a luxury not available to most of the independents, and certainly not to the smaller ones.

Apart from advertising, there are a number of other costs which have to be met from the third of box revenue left to the distributor after the exhibitor has taken, on average, a two thirds cut. These include poster design and production, the assembling of press packs, the duplication of publicity stills, the hiring of preview theatres, paying for advertising sites on the London

TABLE TWO: TOP TEN BOX OFFICE FILMS FOR 1990

Rank	*Film*	*Total gross (£m)*	*Distributor*
1	Ghost	17.3	UIP
2	Pretty Woman	11.9	Warner Bros
3	Look Who's Talking	10.1	Columbia/ Tri-Star
4	Honey, I Shrunk the Kids	9.4	Warner Bros
5	Total Recall	8.5	Guild
6	Ghostbusters	8.3	Columbia/ Tri-Star
7	Back to the Future: Part III	7.9	UIP
8	Gremlins 2: The New Batch	7.4	Warner Bros
9	Back to the Future: Part II	7.2	UIP
10	When Harry met Sally	7.0	Palace

Source: 'Screen International'

Above:* Nikita *– distributed by Palace which, along with Guild, is increasingly operating on the scale of American independent distributors

Underground, and perhaps hiring the services of a PR company. There are also the fees charged by the British Board of Film Classification – £5.50 per minute for the first hour of a sub-titled/foreign language film and £4.30 per minute for the second hour (£8.00 and £6.00 respectively for English language features).

An interesting insight into this whole process was provided by 'Screen Finance' which examined the cost to Electric Pictures of releasing *La Bête Humaine*, Jean Renoir's 1938 classic, in March 1991. 'Screen Finance' shows how it was easy for Electric Pictures to notch up £5,000 on striking a clean print, importing the film into the country, having sub-titles prepared, exporting the film to Belgium to have the sub-titles put on (this service not being available in English laboratories), and finally bringing it back again. Given these hidden costs, it becomes easier to see how the proper launch of a revival (which at least has the advantage over a totally new film of a good deal of ready made kudos) can cost as much as £20,000.

Of course, it is possible to do it for less: *Rocco and His Brothers* was launched by the BFI in October 1991 for just £4,000, which included the advance to the producer (as part of a six-film 'costs off the top' deal), the striking of a new copy, and publicity for a ten-day run at the National Film Theatre. To date, it has recovered £3,420, of which £1,853 is accounted for by NFT showings. Since 'classics' have, by definition, a long shelf life the film will undoubtedly go into profit: for example, in its four years in distribution Oasis' re-release of *A Bout de Souffle*, which cost £20,000 to launch, grossed over £100,000 at the box office, netting the distributors £38,000 (which has to be split with the BBC, who own the rights).

These various figures demonstrate clearly the huge gulf between what the majors (or the large independents like Guild) and the smaller independents can afford to spend on launching a film, and that launch costs, even comparatively low ones, are a major headache for the independent distributor. It was partly to solve such problems, on a European Community-wide basis, that the EFDO (European Film Distribution Office) programme was established as part of the MEDIA 92 (Measures to Encourage the Development of the Industry of Audiovisual Production) scheme. The programme, which was described in some detail in last year's chapter on distribution, is basically a form of aid which will cover up to 50% of the distribution pre-costs of a low budget film being distributed in at least three different EC countries.

Since 1990 the ceiling for productions has risen from ECU 2.25 million to ECU 4.5 million, taking into account rising production costs but also opening up a new area of the cinema distribution market, and the maximum loan has risen from ECU 70,000 to ECU 100,000. To date EFDO has awarded a total of 241 applications to distributors from the 12 member states, plus Austria and Switzerland. This represents 266 cinema launches of 55 European films. British films which have benefited from the scheme are *Distant Voices, Still Lives, Drowning by Numbers, Resurrected, The Dressmaker* and *Queen of Hearts,* while co-productions aided by EFDO in which Britain has been involved are *Berlin Jerusalem* and *Melancholia*. It should also be noted that the MEDIA programme, now re-christened MEDIA 95, has approved a new project – SOS (Save Our Screens) – which is intended to aid independent exhibition, a sector which clearly enjoys a symbiotic relationship with areas of independent distribution.

One of the more encouraging signs in the field of independent distribution recently has been the resurgence of specialist video labels – for example the BFI's Connoisseur Collection, launched in October 1990, which has now added animation to its impressively varied roster, and the arrival of Palace and Artificial Eye in the 'art-video' sell-through market. It is also possible to buy 'classic' Hollywood films on video for as little as £5 per title. However, a couple of warning notes need to be sounded here.

TABLE THREE: UK MARKET SHARE OF THE MAJOR UK DISTRIBUTORS IN 1990

Company	No of films	Approx gross box-office revenue (£m)
UIP	17	£74,118,061
Warner	19	£70,453,860
Columbia Tri-Star	7	£25,319,000
Palace	5	£13,858,900
20th Century Fox	4	£13,157,108
Guild	4	£10,768,929
Rank	6	£10,202,808

Source: 'Screen International'

Above: Derek Jarman's* The Garden *was distributed by Artificial Eye which is helped in the fight for screens by having its own chain of four cinemas

First, the major distributors, having shied away from video in its early days, are now rapidly consolidating their grip on the business. Concentration in all areas is now on the increase, and the independents' share has begun to shrink.

Second, the rental market has begun to decline in volume and value – down about 5% in the first nine months of 1990 compared to the same period in the previous year, according to statistics collated for the British Videogram Association. If video revenues continue to decline then independent distributors may feel less inclined to distribute 'specialist' or 'minority' titles. It's also worth noting that even the relatively buoyant sell-through market caught rather a fright with the collapse of the Parkfield Group in July 1990.

The reasons for these hiccups in the video industry's hitherto steady year-on-year growth are not immediately obvious, over and above general recessionary factors, but a worrying survey commissioned by 'Satellite TV Finance' suggested that subscribers to Sky Movies reported a significant fall-off in their video renting and buying practices after becoming subscribers. This obviously does not account single-handedly for the industry's current problems, but it may be a worrying pointer to the future.

In more general terms it is certainly possible to discern a process of compression of cinema release, video rental, followed by video sell-through, or the 'third window' as it is sometimes called. Undoubtedly this has a great deal to do with distributors' growing perception of this last as a major profit source. As 'Screen Finance' noted in November 1990, UK film distributors are moving towards a system of much more co-ordinated cinema and video releases: "rental windows are bound not only to be shortened but also to be much more flexible than they have been in the past, with some titles having no rental window at all while others will have four-month, six-month, nine-month or twelve-month windows, depending on the timing of the sell-through release, a process which will undoubtedly have the effect of increasing the share of the video market taken by the High Street retail chains at the expense of the off-High Street rental shops."

On a rather more positive note the MEDIA programme has now begun to take interest in video via the EVE (Espace Vidéo Européen) scheme which, along the lines of EFDO, grants loans to features being distributed on video in at least three European countries. To date 11 films have been supported to the tune of ECU 320,000. These include *Reefer and the Model, The Angelic Conversation, Alice*, and *The Reflecting Skin*, and UK distributors involved include MCEG Virgin Vision and Revision Jettisoundz.

Welcome though they are, however, such initiatives really only tinker with a system whose very structure ensures that certain audiences and geographical areas are considerably less well catered for than others. Perhaps those currently less fortunate will just have to pin their hopes on the future with its promise of HDTV electronic multiplexes, the renaissance of the laser disc and perhaps the wonders of virtual reality.

UK theatrical and non-theatrical distributors are listed on pp 134-143 of the Directory. For feature films released in the UK during 1990-91, see pp 274-290.

Below: Akira Kurosawa's* Dreams*: an unusual combination of an 'art-house' film released by a major distributor

Cinema 1990-91 Exhibition

Cinema operators enjoyed yet another rise in admissions in 1990-91 but the year was not without its problems, as described by Tina McFarling, Deputy Editor of 'Moving Pictures International'

***Below:** The Empire, Leicester Square, London*

Photo: Chris Taylor

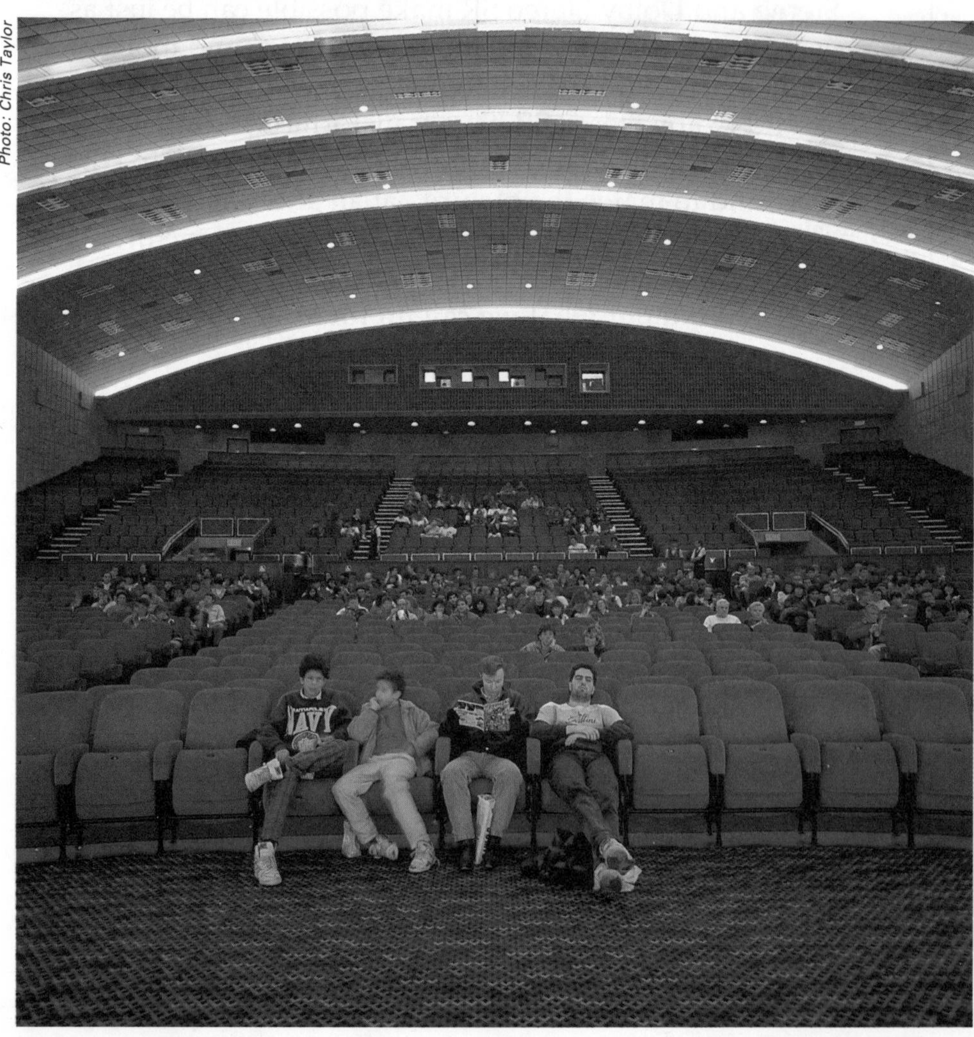

THE cinema exhibition business in the UK continued on a growth path during 1990-91. Admissions increased during 1990, albeit by a marginal 1%, to 96 million and business shifted into an even higher gear in the first three months of 1991, a quarter which recorded the highest number of cinema admissions for the past decade, a total of 24,987,302 admissions. The number of cinema screens up and running increased by 8% (128 screens) to a total of 1,552.

However, without wanting to sound alarmist about a business which has had to battle against negative press for long enough, the events of 1990-91 bear close scrutiny as a number of factors have begun to emerge which could eat into profits and inhibit growth.

These factors essentially separate themselves into those emanating from the business itself, and outside influences such as national and global economics, national and European legislative measures and shifting demographics.

Taking the latter group first, it has been impossible for exhibitors to ignore the effects of global recession. Those adhering to the traditional industry facts of life, or myths (depending on how you look at it), have held firmly to the theory that box-office usually benefits from, or at least holds up, in recession. But both the majors and independent operators have noted the decrease in disposable income of their potential customers with concern.

"These are very difficult times," says Robin Price, managing director of Facealpha, which operates six cinemas. "People have got less money to spend and profit margins are minimal in some areas." Price believes the cinema-going public is watching carefully what it spends, unless films are 'must sees'.

The immediate remedy would seem to be to raise ticket prices, but both majors and independents agree that cinema customers are sensitive to price. National Amusements, which operates the Showcase chain (both in the USA and UK), decided for the first time in 1990 not to raise prices in the USA, because of the economic recession which is affecting cinema along with other leisure industries, and is to keep prices pinned down in the UK. Ira Korff, president of National Amusements, said in early 1991 that he would like to raise the Showcase ticket price from £3.50 to £4.50 but felt the market conditions would make such a move unwise.

A 2.5% increase in the VAT rate announced in the March 1991 Budget posed an added dilemma for exhibitors, whether to pass on the rise to the customer by raising ticket prices or bite the bullet and absorb the rise themselves.

In tackling the general issue of ticket prices, exhibitors have apparently opted for the introduction of a flexible pricing policy. Although the idea of a tiered policy is not new – in the 1980s exhibitors introduced early evening reduced rates on weekdays to combat falling admissions – the ticket sliding scale is likely to be taken further. Cinema-goers in the supposedly affluent South-East have found themselves paying more than their northern counterparts.

In looking to make its pricing policy more flexible, the UK's second largest chain, the Odeon circuit run by Rank, is computing

FROM SEPTEMBER 21ST
ANOTHER 48 HOURS
GRAND OPENING
FRIDAY SEPTEMBER 21ST
OPEN DAY SEPTEMBER 19
SEE THE 10 CINEMAS

Warner's new 10-screen Basingstoke multiplex opened in September 1990

PANAVISION
®
EUROPE

Above: UCI claim annual admissions of 1.4 million for their Gateshead multiplex

local factors, such as the incidence of unemployment in a town and the age structure of the local population, into setting its ticket prices. The exhibitor has not only staggered the lower prices with an 'early bird' rate, but has also addressed the higher range and introduced a premium rate of £0.50 on top of its higher-priced tickets for which the cinema-goer gets a more luxurious seat and more leg space.

Prime multiplex operator UCI staggers its prices according to locality, charging up to £8.00 in the West End of London and £2.75 to £3.75 in the provinces.

Exhibitors have also been hit by the rising cost of development and changes in the business rating system. The major exhibitors believe the effects of the new system have been largely 'swings and roundabouts'. They have had to pay higher rates on some buildings but have been compensated by paying less on others.

Below: The lion roars at Swindon where the first multiplex under the Metro Goldwyn Mayer Cinemas banner opened in March 1991.

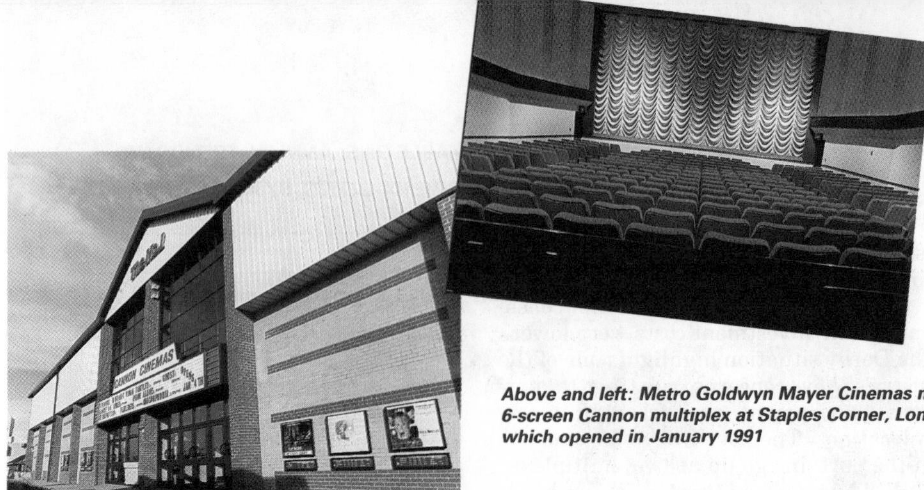

Above and left: Metro Goldwyn Mayer Cinemas new 6-screen Cannon multiplex at Staples Corner, London which opened in January 1991

For the independent operator who does not have the geographical spread or the sheer number of cinemas enjoyed by the major chains the effect has been more sharply felt. Business rates have doubled for some cinemas, placing extra pressure on the sale of concessions, such as sweets and popcorn, to make up the difference.

In the summer of 1990, exhibitors were also faced with the prospect of having to pay more for their cinematograph licences. A Parliamentary bill would have wrestled control for setting the licence rate away from central government and placed it with local authorities which would then have had the right to set their own rates for exhibitors – a move swiftly quashed by the industry trade body, the Cinematograph Exhibitors Association. The setting of the licence rate by local authorities would have been bound to bring about inconsistencies – in much the same way as the former pre-Poll Tax ratings system on homes – depending on the regional and political vagaries of individual councils.

Since cinema embarked upon its programme of revitalisation in the mid-1980s, some £280-£300 million has been invested in buildings. Over 30% of all screens in the UK now have five screens or more (either purpose-built multiplexes or existing but redeveloped cinemas) compared to 1% two years ago. The UK's 49 purpose built multiplexes now take around 35% of the total box office generated by the mainstream releases.

On average, the multiplex operators have been investing around £5 million into each new cinema which has opened although some such as Warner Brothers have been, and are, spending more. But all are now watching costs carefully.

The demise of the construction industry which has witnessed many companies going under, should have provided for more competitive development costings, but as the number of potential sites for new cinemas decreases – owing to market saturation – so the price of land has risen.

Competition between operators perpetuates the industry's reluctance to release investment figures publicly, but it is generally accepted that Warner Bros is still spending more than anyone else – £8 million in the case of its Basingstoke cinema which opened in September 1990 – and at a level which, although not considered impossible by rivals, is conceived of as infeasible on their particular payback terms.

The number of admissions which cinemas need to generate to be viable depends on both the type of operation and the amount invested. The bones of Rank's cinema investment business plan call for each £1 million invested to pull in 300,000 admissions per year. At initial investment levels of £3.5 million per cinema (the cost quoted by other exhibitors who embarked on the multiplex development trail four years ago), 1.05 million admissions would have to be generated on this model. But at the increased cost levels (it is believed that Rank's Romford cinema cost £4.5 million) 1.35 million admissions would have to be generated to meet the company's payback criteria. At this rate, the Warner Basingstoke would have to generate 2.4 million admissions – a level regarded as impossible within most quarters of the film industry.

All the multiplex exhibitors claim that those complexes which have been running for a full 12 months are achieving 1 million admissions a year with UCI's Metro Centre at Gateshead held to be the most successful in the country with around 1.4 million admissions per annum. But UCI and National Amusements admit that their rival multiplexes in Derby are not meeting this generally quoted figure. Even so, they claim that these cinemas are performing according to their business plans since they were among the first multiplexes to open and consequently their investment costs were lower.

The Derby situation highlights one of the industry's key concerns relating to new cinema development: overscreening in certain locations. The past twelve months has seen the curtains go up at two multiplexes in Hull, Thurrock and Preston. A number of other cities such as Manchester, Leeds, Dublin and Glasgow already have, in the case of Manchester, or will have three multiplex cinemas.

Where the population catchment area is substantial and where the cinemas are widely spaced, as they are in Manchester, exhibitors are generally confident that there is sufficient business for all. But in Preston, where the UCI and Rank Odeon cinemas are within popcorn throwing distance of each other, Rank's box office dropped by 15% just a few weeks after UCI opened.

The UK's changing demographics are also now beginning to produce a few shivers down the spines of exhibitors.

A CAVIAR (Cinema and Video Industry Audience Research) report pointed out in April 1990 that cinema's traditionally key audience, the 15-24 year olds (18% of the population and 56% of the cinema's audience), is decreasing as a result of changes in the birth rate. The Henley Centre for Forecasting says the 16-24 year old age group will decline by 3% during the 1990s but will still account for 14% of the population or 6.4 million people by the end of the century and it should continue to enjoy a higher disposable income than other age groups.

The CAVIAR findings also point to some welcome trends. Firstly the level of people who "ever go to the cinema" increased to 64% in November 1990 compared to 60% at the same point in 1989. The number of people "ever watching" rented video cassettes, on the other hand, has remained the same.

The percentage of 7-14 year olds "ever going" remained steady at 85%. The proportion of those "ever going" in cinema's prime age group, the 15-24 year olds, increased from 86% to 87% while the proportion of those in this age bracket who truly have the cinema habit – going once a month or more – increased from 30% to 34%.

TABLE ONE: ANNUAL TRENDS IN CINEMA-GOING, BY AGE GROUP (%)

	1988	1989	1990
All ever go to cinema (age 7+)	56	60	64
Ever go (7–14)	84	85	85
Ever go (15–24)	81	86	87
Ever go (25–34)	64	72	79
Go once a month or more (15–24)	27	30	34
Go once a month or more (25–34)	10	11	11

Source: Cinema and Video Industry Research Association

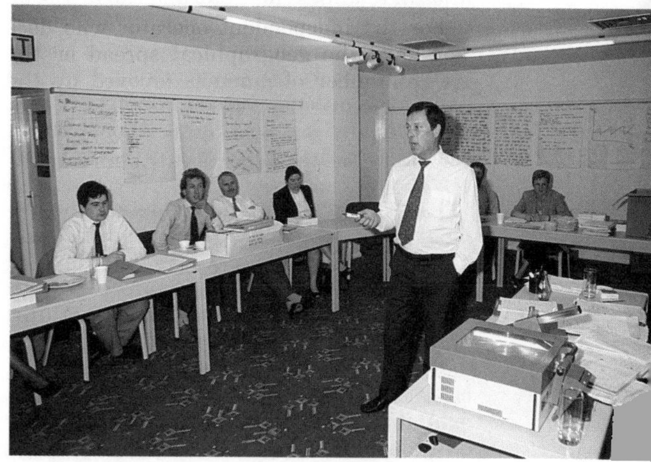

Above: 'Don't build up barriers' exhorts the message on the whiteboard at the Rank training academy which was set up to 'meet the demands of the new market-place'

It is however, the older age group, the 25-34 year olds, which shows the biggest swing towards cinema with 79% now going compared to 72% in November 1989.

Interestingly, the purpose-built multiplexes, expected to appeal most to the mobile 15-24 year olds wanting to imbibe some of America's popular culture, are also winning over older age groups and possibly therefore eating into the audiences of other cinemas.

CAVIAR's survey shows that the multiplex audience tends to be female, with women making up 56% of the audience compared to 38% of the audience in traditional cinemas. Of the multiplex audience, 27% are aged 35 years or over compared to 19% in older cinemas.

Legislative moves were mooted during the year which have raised alarm signals within the industry. These concern changes in working practice, access for the disabled and the possible introduction of a levy on admissions.

Taking these issues in order, the changes in working practices, details of which were leaked in August 1990, would affect all businesses since they are part of draft directives drawn up by the European Commission based on the Social Charter.

Essentially, the measures contained within the directives are aimed at providing uniform European employment guidelines in readiness for 1992 and the lifting of trade barriers within Europe. They would impose strict guidelines on working hours, National Insurance payments and redundancy obligations for the employment of part-time and night workers, who of course comprise a major part of the cinema workforce.

The bottom line would be higher employment costs – and consequently cinemas are back at the key issue; would they have to raise seat prices? The CEA represented the exhibitor point of view but as yet nothing has been heard back from Brussels.

Access to all public buildings including cinemas for the disabled is a matter which exhibitors wholeheartedly support: existing cinemas are being redeveloped and new cinemas are now designed with special thought given to the disabled. But the possibility of various regulations from the Home Office which would impose legal requirements has caused serious qualms among exhibitors who find it financially difficult to have to modify all their cinemas immediately to fall in line with new regulations.

The third concern, that of a possible levy, has raised and is likely to continue to raise the hackles of all exhibitors who only saw the Eady Levy laid to rest by the 1985 Films Act.

The notion of this new levy, or as it has now become dubbed, 'son of Eady', arose from the meetings held by the Department of Trade and Industry's film industry working party which was set up as one of the Downing Street summit recommendations to find new avenues to fund film production.

Exhibitors were not invited to any of the DTI discussions until just before Christmas, some six months after the working party was set up: they have remained politely tight-lipped over what on the surface appears to be a case of crass non-consultation or oversight.

The exhibitors are extremely unlikely to accept the idea of a levy on cinema which doesn't tax related businesses such as television and video. They argue that any pro-

TABLE TWO: UK MULTIPLEXES OPENED BETWEEN APRIL 1990 AND MARCH 1991

Town/City	Screens	Operator
Basingstoke	10	Warner
Bedford	6	MGM Cinemas
Bracknell	10	UCI
Chester	6	MGM Cinemas
Dublin/Tallaght	12	UCI
Edinburgh	12	UCI
Gloucester	6	MGM Cinemas
Harlow	6	MGM Cinemas
Hull	8	Rank
Hull	8	UCI
Ipswich	5	Rank
London Mezzanine	5	Rank
London/Staples Corner	6	MGM Cinemas
Preston	10	UCI
Romford	8	Rank
Thurrock	7	Warner
York	12	Warner

***Source:** 'Moving Pictures International'*

Right: Giancarlo Parretti: quashed management buyout of Metro Goldwyn Mayer Cinemas

fits they make, in the face of considerable financial pressures, are ploughed back into their business. In addition it is certain that although exhibitors are back on the upward path to profits they, and especially the operators of new cinemas, do not have money to burn.

Where the issue of levy now lies is difficult to determine, since some believe that the Treasury is still interested in the idea while others say it has been put on the shelf.

Another measure which has leaked out from the DTI working party meetings, is the possibility of imposing a British film quota on exhibitors, ie cinemas would have to play a certain number of indigenous productions during a year.

This move is likely to be repudiated by exhibitors who, having been told "to stop moaning and get commercial" back in 1985 feel they have now done so. They have always stood by the line of playing the films that people want to see regardless of where they are produced. British films such as *Shirley Valentine, A Fish Called Wanda* and *Buster* have been played widely and successfully, but it is hard to imagine an exhibitor happily taking off *Dances With Wolves* or *Green Card* to play *Buddy's Song* or *The Fool* to fulfil quotas.

Even if the ground on which exhibitors are operating is shifting, the faces of those operating in the business are, for the most part, stable.

MGM Pathé, via Metro Goldwyn Mayer Cinemas, continues to be the UK's largest operator with its 406 screens (134 cinemas) accounting for around 30% of 1990's admissions total. Apart from being the largest operator, it continues to be the most controversial in terms of its ownership.

Intrigue started in August 1990 when the original Pathé based in France was bought by Chargeurs after Italian entrepreneur Giancarlo Parretti was forced to relinquish control of the company. Chargeurs then said it was interested in buying the then 406-screen British circuit as well.

The Menahem Golan-Yoram Globus duo who owned the circuit through the early eighties over-extended themselves and at that time it looked like Parretti, who bought the circuit from Golan and Globus, had fallen into the same abyss through his acquisition of the great American Lion, MGM/UA.

Soon afterwards, a management buyout led by UK managing director Barry

Above: London's Electric Cinema, one of the oldest in Britain

TABLE THREE: NUMBER OF CINEMA SCREENS IN THE UK

	1988	***1990***
Number of cinema sites/ complexes	642	676
Number of screens in sites/ complexes with:		
one screen	336	356
two screens	260	236
three screens	450	387
four screens	88	116
five screens	45	75
six screens	6	48
seven screens	–	7
eight screens	8	56
nine screens	–	18
ten screens	80	150
eleven screens	11	22
twelve screens	–	60
thirteeen screens	–	13
fourteen screens	–	14
Total screens	1,284	1,558

Source: Cinema Advertising Association, 'Screen Digest'

Above: Producer Jeremy Thomas sold his interest in Recorded Cinemas, which includes the Cameo Edinburgh, to partner Chris Blackwell

Jenkins hit the headlines but Parretti's public commitment in October 1990 to retain the circuit quashed the buyout and Jenkins resigned. In December 1990 it was announced that the cinema circuit would be renamed MGM/UA Cinemas (subsequently Metro Goldwyn Mayer Cinemas).

Regardless of board room and financial machinations, the circuit had continued to expand opening multiplexes: on the outskirts of London at Staples Corner, Eastbourne, Brighton, Gloucester, Chester, Bedford and Harlow.

Rank has also remained committed to its national programme of refurbishment and extension as well as opening new purpose-built cinemas in Romford, Hull and Ipswich. With 277 screens within 75 cinemas Rank is estimated to hold a market share of 20.4% or just over 20 million of last year's admissions. It has also installed a training academy at its Brighton cinema to "meet the demands of the new market-place."

TABLE FOUR: NEW CINEMAS BUILT/SCREENS ADDED

	1989	*1990*
MGM Cinemas	12	24
National Amusements	50	–
Rank	23	21
UCI	55	52
Warner	21	22
Total	161	119

Source: 'Moving Pictures International'

Left: Warner's five-screen West End theatre: showcase cinema for the chain which expanded by a further three multiplexes during the year

UCI has been the most prolific multiplex operator opening a further four multiplexes between April 1990 and March 1991 and operating 193 screens within 20 cinemas. The company's ultimate target number of screens for the UK is 300 screens, with 29 screens due to come onstream in the summer months of 1991.

With the maturation of the UK market, UCI is increasingly turning its eyes towards Europe with the acquisition of the Zoo Palast in Berlin and the opening of purpose-built multiplexes in Germany and development deals in the USSR.

Likewise, Warner Bros which has opened cinemas in York, Basingstoke and Thurrock, establishing a UK chain of six cinemas, also focused farther afield with development deals running in the USSR, Spain, Portugal, Japan and Italy.

National Amusements appears to have taken a back seat adding no new sites to its seven-cinema, 85-screen string but the company has started work on a new cinema in Coventry and plans to announce more.

Within the independent sector, a consortium of film people including Sir Richard Attenborough, David Puttnam and Philip Knatchbull got together to open the luxurious single screen Filmhouse in Richmond, while producer Jeremy Thomas sold his interest in Recorded Cinemas, which operates the Gate at Notting Hill and the Cameo Edinburgh (scheduled for expansion), to partner Chris Blackwell. Sadly, at London's oldest cinema, the Electric, business has been more of a struggle.

For an updated list of cinemas, see the Cinemas section on pp 98-113.

Television 1990-91 – Background

Maggie Brown, Media Editor of 'The Independent', examines a momentous year for British broadcasters

YOU do not need the gift of hindsight to recognise that the year 1990-1991 was a watershed in the history of British television. The entire period was dominated by the debate, passage and aftermath of the Broadcasting Act, one of the most controversial pieces of legislation ever to affect the media.

The heart of the Act deals with the technical method of allocating ITV franchises for the ten years from January 1993. But it unleashes, for the first time, a competitive tendering system into television which had been treated, up to now, as primarily a cultural and entertainment medium. Broadcasters, and those from outside ITV wishing to run television franchises, have been asked to price, in cash, the value of the frequencies they desire.

This is an entirely new and market-driven approach to television and has led to fears that the public service programme traditions built into ITV since its start 36 years ago, and largely developed in tandem with the BBC, will be undermined during the 1990s.

Further, the competitive tender process is being extended to new national radio channels, and Channel 5, a quasi-national TV service starting a year or so after the new franchises.

The year breaks neatly into two parts: throughout the summer and autumn of 1990 there was intense lobbying over key aspects of the then Broadcasting Bill. First over the 'exceptional circumstances' clause, allowing the Independent Television Commission, the new licensing body, to choose a bid which offered less money but a higher standard of programming. Second, over a last ditch attempt in the House of Lords to force a much tougher definition of impartiality on broadcasters: right-wingers mounted a lobby against (alleged) television bias.

As a vivid sub-plot there was the drama of satellite television, as British Satellite Broadcasting was launched in April 1990, meeting the same distressing lack of equipment in the shops which rival Sky had experienced a year before. After a hot, tough, summer of unequal competition with the more established and aggressive Sky, the two sides staged an unequal 'merger' engineered by Rupert Murdoch on 2 November 1990, just as the Broadcasting Bill received Royal Assent.

All of this was played out against deepening recession which showed no signs of lifting as 1990 advanced. ITV was jolted to its roots by the realisation that August 1990 advertising revenue was down 17.8% on the previous year. Throughout the 1980s advertising had grown by an annual average of eight per cent. The golden age came to an end, just as the broadcasting duopoly was broken and ITV was producing the rich range of audience-grabbing drama which the advertisers had been pressing for.

The advertising recession played its part in ITN's considerable and as yet unresolved difficulties. The crisis at Independent Television's news organisation is another of the year's themes.

By May 1990 the Broadcasting Bill (as it then was) had been the subject of 800 amendments in House of Commons Committee stage. Its grand design, to shake up commercial television, had been blended with an infusion of pragmatism after inspired efforts by the ITV-funded Campaign for Quality Television. Some of the

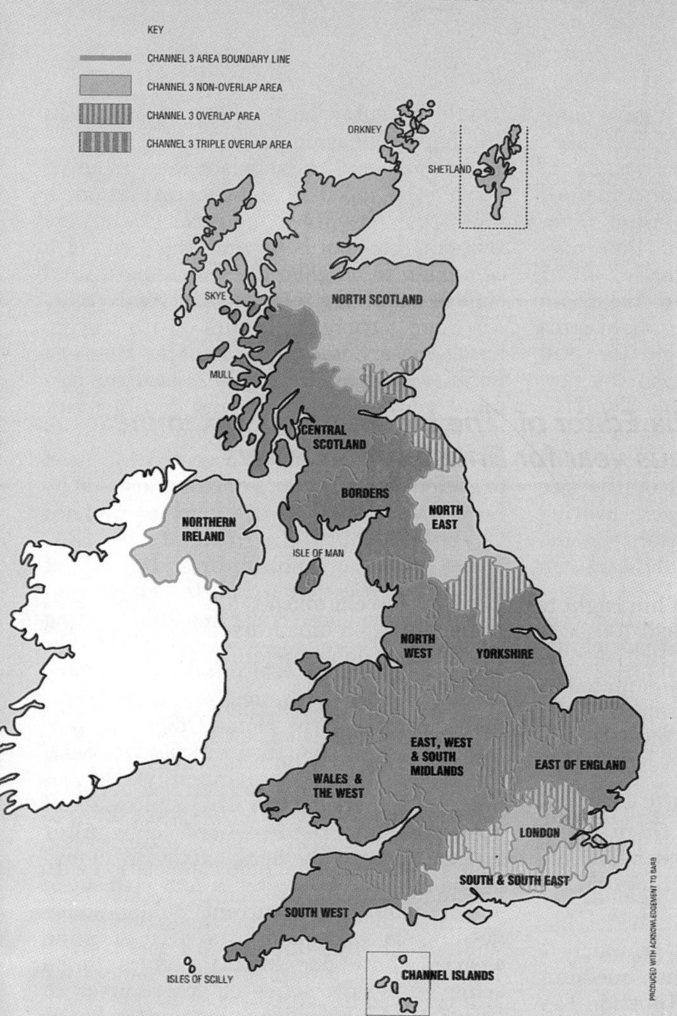

Above: David Mellor MP: accepted key changes

Left: The Channel 3 areas

hardest free market edges were knocked off it as the then Home Office Broadcasting Minister David Mellor accepted key changes.

The Bill had caught the tide of ebbing Thatcherism. Its second reading in the House of Commons on 9 May was surprisingly good-tempered. The map of 15 ITV regional companies had been left untouched, as was the national breakfast franchise.

While ITV franchises were to be auctioned off to the highest bidder, the principle that the market will decide the winner, in all cases, was subverted. An exceptionally high quality bid could act as trumps so that viewers were not deprived of interesting programmes. This concession was enshrined in a June amendment published by the then Home Secretary Douglas Hurd. It is worth recording.

Clause 17(4) says: The Commission may regard the following as exceptional circumstances, which make it appropriate to award the licence to an applicant who has not submitted the highest bid; (a) that the quality of the service is exceptionally high, and (b) that the quality of the proposed service is substantially higher than the quality proposed by the highest bidder.

Cynics say that this clause was designed to save established ITV companies, such as Thames and Granada, operating as producer/broadcasters – making a wide range of programmes. They were under threat from the lightly staffed bidders such as Carlton Communications, aiming to model themselves as Channel Four style publisher/broadcasters.

But the principle has a respectable provenance. It flowed from the 1986 Peacock Committee report on financing the BBC, which was the first to recommend a tendering system, with the proviso that the regulator should pick a lower bid if it gave more value for money in terms of public services.

Nonetheless, the essential design of shaking up commercial television remained intact. The Independent Television Commission (ITC) which replaced the Independent Broadcasting Authority on 1 January 1991, switched from being an interventionist publisher into a more arms length licensing body, though the full change does not take place until the new contracts start in January 1993. The ITC, once the new contracts start, will no longer preview programmes or dictate key details such as programme schedules or the size of game show prizes. New codes covering programme content, impartiality, and advertising rules were published in January/February 1991.

The legislation also made other concessions to public service broadcasting. Operators of new licences for Channel 3, as ITV was re-christened, would have to increase regional programmes and safeguard two vulnerable areas, children's and religious programming.

By June 1990, when the Bill went forward to the House of Lords, there was a successful move, against government advice, to ensure that half of all programmes should be subtitled by 1998, to help deaf and hard of hearing people.

But, just as the lobbyists were winding down in a mood of self-congratulation, a new row of great political bitterness erupted. The Lords became the focus of a campaign to toughen the 'due impartiality' clause, requiring television to treat political and current affairs with even-handedness. Some members of the House of Lords were particularly incensed by personal view programmes and documentary dramas, a bitterness built up over thirty years. The Government accepted the need to stiffen the law after a fierce attack, led by Lord Wyatt of Weeford, supported by Lord Chalfont, deputy chairman of the IBA. There was also confusion over the role of the IBA: critics felt it had too easily conceded the need for change in a July briefing document. There was a strong belief that Margaret Thatcher had intervened to force through an amended, toughened, clause.

By September the Home Office had produced a rewritten clause which provoked a chastened IBA into saying it would not work: at this point the BBC and Channel Four joined in a House of Lords lobby. After further changes the final, expanded, clause introduced the following: a new concept of 'major matters' of current public policy needing special balance; the need to define clearly where due impartiality is to be achieved over a series of programmes to ensure that a balancing viewpoint is heard

Below: An Oracle subtitler prepares an episode of* Coronation Street *for the deaf and hard of hearing. The Broadcasting Act decrees that half of all programmes should be subtitled by 1998

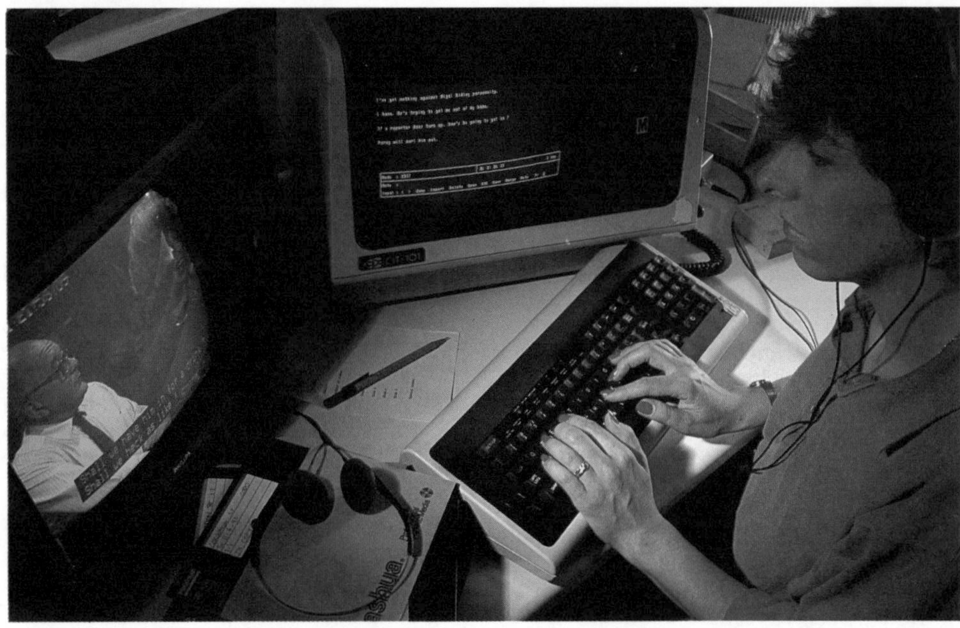

and a legal requirement for broadcasters to publish the dates and times of programmes in an opinionated series. However, the Government did bow to those who warned that too strict a legal definition would force broadcasters to give airtime to undesirable causes: "Due impartiality does not require absolute neutrality on every issue, or detachment from fundamental democratic principles."

Also in September, the BBC returned to the spotlight. While the Government had been directing its attention to ITV, the Corporation had been quietly attempting to reform itself, seeking cuts of £75 million to redirect into salaries and programmes to wrest the top ratings back from ITV.

But, in what was to be one of the last Thatcherite actions against broadcasters, the Home Office decided to call in accountants Price Waterhouse to advise on the BBC's efficiency before settling a new formula for the licence fee. This had been automatically linked to the retail price index for three years.

Price Waterhouse's short, politically inspired report found a top heavy yet under-managed organisation in the throes of painful change. But the wind had changed. The Government, now under John Major's control, took the least vindictive

Above: John Major: his Government took the least vindictive licence fee option

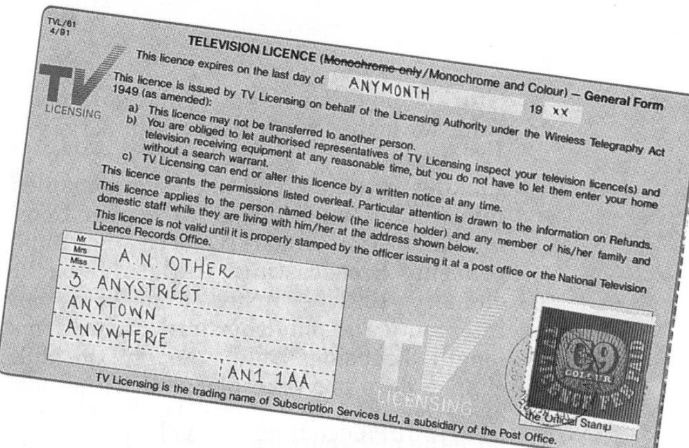

TVL/61
4/91

TV LICENSING

TELEVISION LICENCE (~~Monochrome only~~/Monochrome and Colour) – **General Form**

This licence expires on the last day of ANYMONTH 19 XX

This licence is issued by TV Licensing on behalf of the Licensing Authority under the Wireless Telegraphy Act 1949 (as amended):

a) This licence may not be transferred to another person.
b) You are obliged to let authorised representatives of TV Licensing inspect your television licence(s) and television receiving equipment at any reasonable time, but you do not have to let them enter your home without a search warrant.
c) TV Licensing can end or alter this licence by a written notice at any time.

This licence grants the permissions listed overleaf. Particular attention is drawn to the information on Refunds.

This licence applies to the person named below (the licence holder) and any member of his/her family and domestic staff while they are living with him/her at the address shown below.

This licence is not valid until it is properly stamped by the officer issuing it at a post office or the National Television Licence Records Office.

Mr / Mrs / Miss A.N. OTHER
3 ANYSTREET
ANYTOWN
ANYWHERE
AN1 1AA

the Official Stamp

TV Licensing is the trading name of Subscription Services Ltd, a subsidiary of the Post Office.

option in January 1991, holding the April 1991 licence rise to three per cent below RPI, then returning to the full link for the next four, until the Charter and licence agreement with Government is renewed in 1996. This change of emphasis towards the BBC was further cemented by pamphlets from two Conservative think tanks, the Centre for Policy Studies and the Tory Reform Group, who both stressed its role as a national asset. This mild renaissance in fortunes was underlined during the Gulf War, when Mr Major went out of his way to praise the BBC's best efforts in news and current affairs. BBC Radio, which had expanded with a new Radio 5 service in August, also used the Gulf War to launch an experimental rolling news service, News FM. This was mooted as the prototype for a permanent service.

Towards the end of the year in review, the BBC was preparing for 1 April 1991 when it switched to collecting the licence fee itself, another change flowing from the Broadcasting Act.

Once the Broadcasting Act became law in November 1990 the ITV companies plunged into six months of anxiety and cutbacks. Since multi-bidding was allowed, attempts at unity completely broke down. The ITC issued draft contracts in December 1990 then the final version in February 1991. This proved that the commission wanted a high quality service built on the present range of output and planned to devise extremely detailed contracts, leaving nothing to chance. There was a fixed price to be paid, based on income from advertising and sponsorship, before the cash bid was calculated. Applicants had to deliver a high quality service, but also had to bid if they thought they faced competition.

The quality threshold which applicants had to pass (before the cash bids decided who had won) also included credible business plans which showed bona fide financial backing for the programme plans.

Above: The listings duopoly ended and the battle of the TV and film guides began

It was estimated that ITV companies cut more than 15 per cent of jobs in three months (January to March 1991), bringing ITV's workforce down to 10,000 as incumbents turned their businesses inside out, looking for waste. The key problem during the dark months leading to the year end lay in working out what to bid. This depended on an assessment of advertising revenue growth during the 1990s. And when the ITC revealed final contracts in February 1991, with a deadline for applications of 15 May, they contained a sting. The ITC was backing a central scheduler, a new figure at the centre of ITV, to draw up schedules and order the important peak-time evening programmes, which attract 75 per cent of advertising, and absorb around £440 million annually.

Further, it reserved the right to impose someone if the ITV companies could not agree by early 1992. This need for a central scheduler, separate from the broadcasters, arose because the old system of giving the largest companies a guaranteed right to make peak time programmes was too cosy.

The Office of Fair Trading had been given the right to vet arrangements by the Broadcasting Act, in part to safeguard the interests of independent producers, who had won a 25% quota for their programmes on ITV and the BBC: hungry for work they wanted equal rights of access with ITV companies. But, at a stroke, central scheduling removed sovereignty from the largest ITV companies, who had sorted out the programme schedules between themselves. An ITV franchise increasingly boiled down to making programmes and selling advertising.

There were two other key changes. The system of listings duopoly (the exclusive rights to programme details for BBC and ITV and Channel Four), enjoyed respectively by Radio Times and TV Times, ended on 1 March 1991. From that day any publication could publish listings, provided they took out a licence and paid a fee. The levels set by the copyright owners, BBC Enterprises and Independent Television Publications, provoked outcry and prevented newspapers from expanding into this territory.

Test cases were drawn up to test the fees at the Copyright Tribunal. But readers were subjected to a frenzied courtship, as the rivals published full all-channel details,

Below: The ITC is backing a central scheduler to order peak-time evening programmes such as Granada's **Coronation Street** ***(left) and LWT's*** **Blind Date** ***(right)***

and a listings magazine battle began. Newcomer 'TV Plus' sank after three weeks, but the German company Bauer was poised to strike with 'TV Quick' at a starter price of 10 pence. As the year ended the battle was intensifying and settling into a long hard slog.

The second key development was that ITN found itself in serious difficulties. The organisation, for 35 years a cost centre and service for ITV, had at an early stage of the Broadcasting Bill lobbied to be freed from its (ITV) shareholders. But during the year, as it moved into new headquarters in Gray's Inn Road, it became clear that ITN desperately needed their financial support: an extra £20 million had to be guaranteed in late 1990.

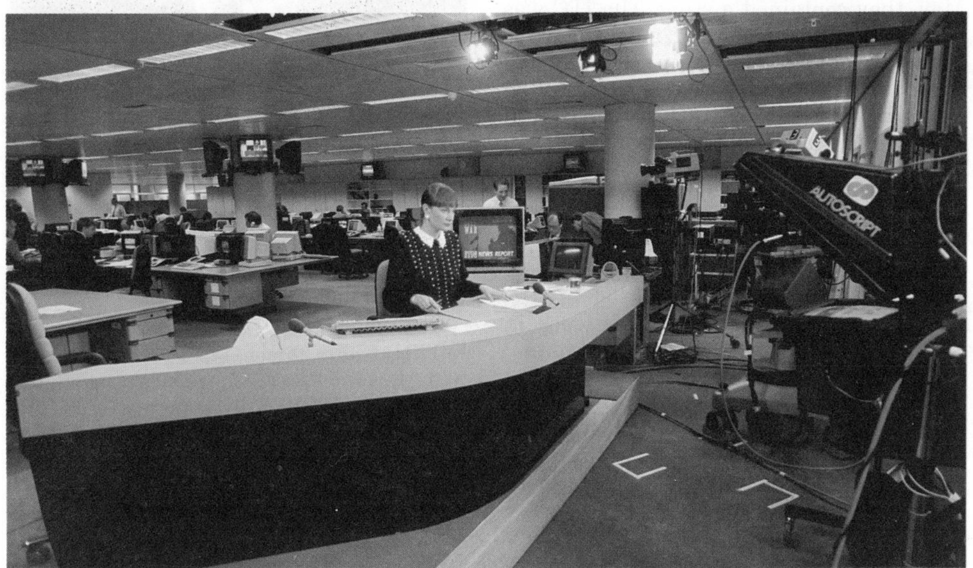

Above: Sue Carpenter reads the news from troubled ITN's new headquarters in Gray's Inn Road

The Act set out to encourage rival news suppliers; it also said that the supplier must be controlled by outside shareholders. Once the ITC designated ITN for this role, it meant that a controlling 51 per cent of shares had to be sold by the end of 1994, to comply with the law.

The companies found a new external chief executive, Bob Phillis, to reform it and try to turn the news machine into a profit maker. Unless it made money, outside shareholders would not buy shares. But he found, on arrival in January 1991, that there had been a serious amount of overspending in the previous year of 1989/90: some £9.8 million had been unaccounted for. Even as this was investigated, and blamed on items such as extravagant satellite links, there was a further £1 million overspend on Gulf War coverage.

The final drama of the year belonged to satellite television. On 29 April 1990 British Satellite Broadcasting began its direct-to-home service with a five channel line-up: Movie Channel, Galaxy (entertainment), Now (lifestyle and arts), Sports and the Power Channel (music). Run from glamorous offices, just south of the River Thames in the Marco Polo building, it was the UK's bona fide satellite operator, holding an IBA licence for the five satellite channels. It was the pioneer of high-powered frequencies and the new TV D-Mac signal. It spent money rather too freely. And its launch was six months later than planned.

But Murdoch's Sky, using the rival, unregulated, Astra satellite, and broadcasting with the existing PAL signal, had already been in operation for 14 months (launched in February 1989) and had a devastating headstart of 400,000 installed dishes, after a tough marketing campaign which had courted subscribers, even if they did not have the ability to pay.

During the long hot summer of 1990 the gap widened as the recession began to grip. In July there were the first tentative meetings between Mr Murdoch and one of BSB's worried investors, Reed International. The

Right: Rupert Murdoch: tentative meetings during the summer of 1990

courtship began in earnest in September when the mounting debts at Sky's parent, News International, forced economies.

At the point of 'merger' on 2 November 1990, a deal which put Sky in the managerial driving seat, BSB had sold only 117,000 dishes, while Sky claimed one million homes. BSB had spent £900 million to get this far; Sky's bill was £400 million.

The merger, which put Mr Murdoch in effective control of a monopoly subscription satellite service, had not been cleared with the IBA, and provoked outrage in Parliament. The Government said that it would not interfere with market forces. A ruthless merger of operations then took place, in which 1,200 people lost their jobs, mostly from BSB. Its offices were put up for rent. The headquarters moved to Sky's Osterley studios and all but the sports and movie channel were eventually closed down, though the BSB satellites continued to broadcast, keeping the prospect of the D-Mac standard alive.

At BSkyB, as the merged service was called, there was then further anguish, as it became clear that the extra £200 million of funds needed for the £6 million a week losses could not be raised through a conventional project loan. There was also a debate about whether the cost of Sky News was justified: it became a more valued service with the Gulf War.

The nail-biting negotiations for the extra financing, designed to see the satellite company beyond 1992, were finally concluded in March 1991. These distractions prevented BSkyB from promoting itself properly, and dish sales declined to a low of 27,000 in January. By the end of March they had returned to a healthier 71,000 with the majority of customers signing up for both subscription film channels. How-

Below: The Movie Channel, inherited from BSB by BSkyB, caters for the family audience while Sky Movies is aimed at the youth audience interested in comedy, horror and adventure

ever, Sky's managers were now trying to cut costs further, by ending their association with Eurosport and by renegotiating costly film contracts with the Hollywood studios.

The ratings show that by March 1991 Sky was received in 7.6 per cent of homes, some 1.66 million out of 21.8 million. In homes equipped to receive satellite, Sky was taking a 26 per cent of weekly viewing, while Astra (which comprises some ten channels) accounted for 38.7 per cent. This compares with the 27.9 per cent share accounted for by BBC1 and BBC2 and 33.2 per cent for ITV and Channel Four. The message is that Sky Television is liked by those who have it, although conventional broadcast television still has the main grip on affections, even if Channel Four and BBC2 are slipping.

So, an extraordinary year ended, with the ITV companies, and their rival bidders, making final adjustments to their licence applications, while continually trawling for advice about when the advertising recession would bottom out.

For further information on UK television companies see pp 296-311.

Cable and Satellite Update

By David Fisher, Editor, 'Screen Digest'

THE impending absorption of the Cable Authority into the new Independent Television Commission (ITC) and the anticipated resultant hiatus in franchising activity caused a flood of applications to be processed during the first eight months of 1990, since when no new franchises have been granted. By the end of that phase 135 franchises had been granted. In the remainder of the country that has not yet been allocated, there are only 13 towns with more than 20,000 homes.

The current phase is one of consolidation as the winners of franchises start to put their money where their bids required it to be put: under the streets. The majority have still to begin this process. Consolidation is also occurring in ownership as franchises change hands and some of the pioneers drop out in favour of mainly North American companies with investment power –notably telecommunications operators prevented from moving into cable in their home territory but now able to offer telephony and data services in the UK in competition with British Telecom and Mercury.

As of 1 January 1991 a total of 422,705 UK homes were connected to cable, including the old 'upgrade' systems that still pass about a million homes. Of these 148,948 were on the new-build broadband networks: 18 per cent of the 828,227 homes passed. Saatchi & Saatchi has forecast that seven per cent of television households will be connected to cable networks by 1994 – compared with about one per cent in early 1991 – and that another seven per cent will be added in each of the two following two-year periods, leading to 5.8 million homes connected by the end of the decade/century.

Television 1990-91 – the Programmes

Peter Fiddick reviews the year's TV programmes

IT was a year more memorable for its politics than its programmes as the Thatcher Government's Broadcasting Bill, unveiled at the end of 1989, became the focus of anxious lobbying, by ITV companies in particular. Nevertheless, the role of television as a window on live events came to the fore, bringing with it both controversy and screen moments to treasure.

There is a certain irony in the way Margaret Thatcher herself provided one of them. In November 1990, what would normally have been a routine re-election of the leader of the Conservative Party erupted into high drama, as it became clear that the Prime Minister had lost the confidence of a crucial number of her Cabinet. One year earlier, her Chancellor of the Exchequer, Nigel Lawson, had suddenly resigned after a long rumbling disagreement over the direction and control of economic policy. Now, it was Sir Geoffrey Howe, Foreign Secretary, who suddenly handed in his resignation, after a similarly long-running difference of approach to Britain's role within the European Community.

Government ministers have come and gone throughout British political history. The tally of leading Conservatives who, across a decade, voluntarily or otherwise, had left Mrs Thatcher's Cabinet, had become a fact of contemporary political life. What made the Howe case different was not his seniority but his resignation statement to the House of Commons. The man noted for his low-key style used the occasion to deliver one of the most stinging attacks on a member of his own party in living memory.

And he did it on television. The televising of the House of Commons, long debated, long delayed, with Mrs Thatcher herself one of the leading resisters, had very quickly become a routine part of media coverage. It made news items about Parliament more easily illustratable than before, but broadcasters found relatively few occasions merited disrupting the normal schedules for live relay. The Howe speech was one of them. Even under the constraints on use of the cameras, imposed by members of Parliament themselves, viewers could see not only the speaker but also his victim, stony-faced, a few feet in front of him.

This was the first moment of high drama caught by the cameras in the history of Parliament. Margaret Thatcher was soon at the centre of the action again. On 20 November 1990, as the first ballot of Conservative MPs for the now hotly contested leadership of their party was held, Mrs Thatcher was conducting "business as usual" at a summit meeting in Paris. Television's early-evening news programmes were extended to catch the result, due around 7pm. Reporters and cameras were injecting live pictures from outside the British embassy in Paris, where Mrs Thatcher was changing between engagements, but even when it became clear that her support was insufficient to prevent a second ballot, the word was that she would not comment.

Peter Sissons, the anchorman of *The Six O'Clock News* on BBC1, was talking on air with political correspondent John Sergeant when the embattled Tory leader was seen emerging from the building. "Look behind you!" Sissons cried – just as Mrs Thatcher strode up, took over the microphone, her media manager Bernard Ingham shouldering the reporter out of the way, and

Above: Prime Minister Margaret Thatcher takes the media by surprise in Paris

announced her intention of fighting on. In fact, it was virtually at the end of her premiership – and the moment caught by television encapsulated its spirit.

It is worth recording the detail, because television's role in these microcosmic moments, surely never to be forgotten by any British elector who saw them (and on 20 November 1990, some 10 million were watching BBC1) may prove in the long run to be more significant than its coverage of the more far-reaching confrontation already in place: the international bid to push Saddam Hussein's Iraqi forces out of annexed Kuwait.

The Iraqis invaded their neighbour in August 1990. It was mid-January 1991 before diplomacy ended and shooting started. The real dangers to world peace were tinged, for the media, with anticipation that this might be their biggest moment. For the British, in particular, the memory of the Falklands campaign, reported under the tightest Government control and long debated afterwards, instilled a determination that this time, with satellite technology improved and access to the arena of war likely to be physically simpler, things would be different.

It did not work out like that. Certainly, when the shooting started, the event was dramatic enough and indicative of television's own changing world. It was approaching midnight, British time, on Wednesday, 16 January 1991, when the first missiles from the American-led alliance forces fell on Baghdad. It was from the target city that the reporting team of CNN, the American 24-hour television news service geared to accessing their network at any time, described it to the world from their hotel bedroom.

But if this was an undoubted coup for CNN, leaving conventional networks hastily clearing space in their schedules, the problems of live coverage of this war in particular and such events in general quickly became clear. The issue was crystallised before the week was out, also by CNN, when Iraqi Scud missiles hit Israel; its correspondent there, reacting instantly, gave credence to the rumour that they were armed with gas-releasing warheads. They were not. Broadcasters were then confronted with the implications of "shooting from the hip" with unchecked information, when, in the new era of global media, their reports were beamed straight back to the target.

In the event they were to remain frustrated in their endeavours to reach the heart of the matter. Iraqi President Saddam Hussein soon decided that his initial policy of allowing foreign reporters to stay and report virtually uncensored was not to his advantage. In Saudi Arabia, meanwhile, the screen geniality of military leaders like US General 'Stormin'' Norman Schwarzkopf – who achieved star status – could not overcome the facts that not only were media activists kept within evident

Above: Media star 'Stormin'' Norman Schwarzkopf, live on CNN, the American news channel which itself became news during the Gulf crisis

Below: Barry Foster returned as Van der Valk in a new series, more than 20 years after the original was screened

boundaries but the main tool of this war – night-time air-raids – might have been designed to cramp television's style. The outcome was screens occupied for long hours with talking pundits, enlivened by videos of 'precision bombing' released by the military. When the war was over, broadcasters were left pondering what seemed a worryingly bloodless television campaign.

As to television's more staple fare, it would not be too outrageous a caricature to suggest that the year's drama was symbolised by the revival, in January 1991, of a popular detective series of two decades earlier, *Van Der Valk*. If the Dutch locations were inevitably somewhat changed, little else was, from the star to the title-music. The public quite liked it.

There were interesting, well-made single dramas to be found, in umbrella series like the BBC's 'Screen One' and 'Screen Two', though few that made ripples. With the BBC, in particular, still hunting for new popular series as long-running series like *Bergerac* and *Howard's Way* approached the end of their natural lives, the dominance of Central's *Inspector Morse*, in a two-hour single-story format, was the more

Right:* Inspector Morse*: conventional and extremely popular

marked. Nothing could be more conventional, but its well-crafted production, attractive locations and increasingly well-honed lead partnership of John Thaw and Kevin Whateley achieved new heights of popularity (including a ratings-boosting repeat on Channel Four).

The most significant impact of drama was perhaps achieved in the drama-documentary branch of the genre. The week of 1 April 1990 brought a major piece from the Granada journalistic stable that has done much to develop it: *Who Bombed Birmingham?* This added a new twist to the technique in that it dramatised the *World In Action* team's own investigative and campaigning efforts to see justice done in the Birmingham case, with actors like John Hurt in the lead. But it was its convincing making of its argument that earned it a place as one of the landmark uses of dramatic form to force public attention on a subject.

Above: **Who Bombed Birmingham?** ***added a new twist to drama-documentary***

Above: **The Trials of Life**

Below: Sky News' popularity was boosted by the Gulf War

The Birmingham film was followed in June by Yorkshire Television's account of the Stalker inquiry into the Royal Ulster Constabulary, *Shoot To Kill*, screened over successive nights. All drama-documentary continues to arouse high passions, and this one proved so highly contentious that the Independent Broadcasting Authority felt moved to organise a day-long professional seminar at the National Film Theatre to discuss the ethics and practice of the technique. Its inherent risks are evident. But its place in the programme-maker's armoury seems to be now well-earned, with the objectors often seeming to respond mainly to what they perceive as its greater power to create a public fuss.

The range of more conventional factual programming was as wide as ever, with the popular favourite being *The Trials of Life*,

Left: Who the hell's Bart Simpson? Sky viewers found out when The Simpsons, *the American animation cult reached their screens*

the last of the BBC Natural History Unit's three mega-series, fronted by David Attenborough and deploying the work of the world's top nature photographers with characteristic skill. Far smaller audiences, and curiously little fuss, greeted the latest of Channel Four's somewhat sporadic efforts at innovation: *Sex Talk* brought together, suitably late at night, a group of people prepared to engage in conversation about their particular proclivities.

In a year strong on sport, the soccer World Cup dominated the schedules and won high ratings in June, aided by the England team's performance. The pulling power of success was to be seen again in the New Year period, as the battle for the League championship and the FA Cup seemed to re-establish the sport in television terms after some years in limbo.

It remains to be seen, however, how television sport develops as a specialist service. In the wake of the sudden merger of the satellite companies Sky and BSB, which put all the new direct-to-home services into the melting-pot, with the new pattern not emerging until the spring of 1991, one casualty was the Eurosport channel. It had been on the receiving end of an anti-cartel complaint to the European Commission from rival Screensport, and Rupert Murdoch decided to cut his losses.

In the same area, the Gulf War brought higher audiences to the Sky News channel, but only for two or three weeks, and it remains to be seen how much the British appetite for rolling news will grow, especially since the new channel has to take its share of cuts in staff and resources.

One of the more unexpected weapons with which the Sky stable, both pre- and post-merger, hoped to attract attention and

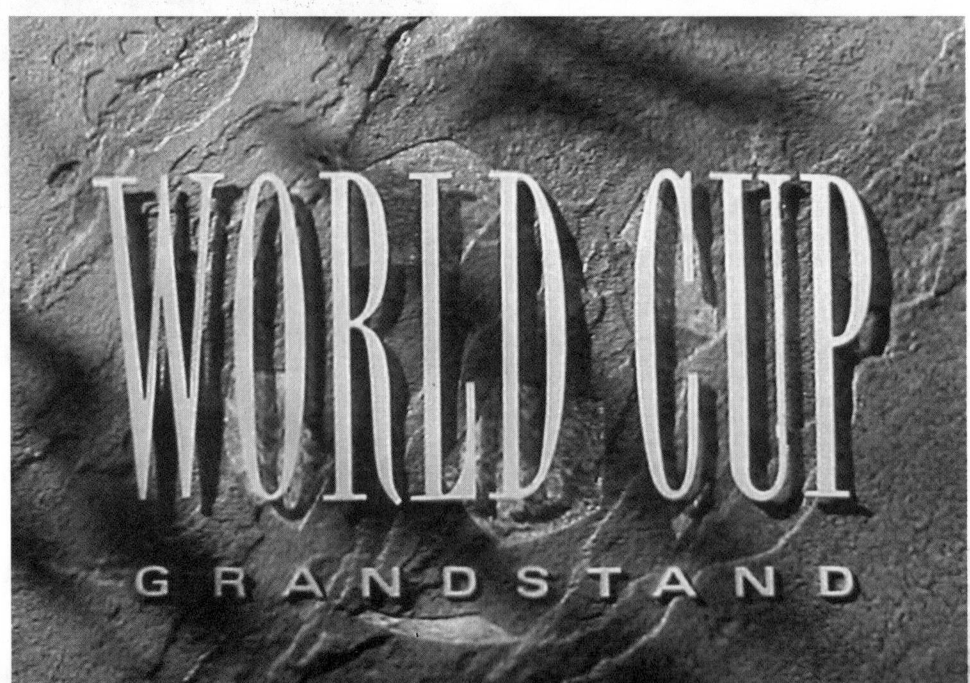

viewers was the arrival of *The Simpsons*, an animated (in the cartoon sense) comedy series originated by the Murdoch empire's Fox channel in the USA, where it quickly attracted a cultish young audience. Whether it could do so in Britain will be a test of the growth of the satellite audience: certainly, in the early days, the following seems to have been too small to let crucial characters and catch-phrases slip into the language.

On the conventional channels, however, imports were the more noticeable as home-made entertainment successes proved elusive (though ITV proved stronger than the others). BBC1 was to be found running *Doogie Howser MD* – the exploits of a child genius surgeon – in peak time, while Channel Four's ratings continued to feature a string of imports – *Cheers, Roseanne, The Cosby Show, The Wonder Years* and more – in its upper reaches.

For further information on UK television companies and programmes see pp 296-311.

***Below: American imports:* Cheers *and (bottom)* Roseanne**

1990's TOP 20 NETWORKED PROGRAMMES (EXCLUDING MULTIPLE SCREENINGS)

No	*Programme*	*Transmitted*	*Channel*	*Audience (millions)*
1	Coronation Street	Mon 1 Jan	ITV	19.21
2	Coronation Street	Wed 10 Jan	ITV	18.90
3	Only Fools and Horses	Tue 25 Dec	BBC1	17.97
4	It'll Be Alright on the Night	Sun 2 Dec	ITV	17.91
5	A View to a Kill	Wed 31 Jan	ITV	17.72
6	ET	Tue 25 Dec	BBC1	17.49
7	The Queen's Speech	Tue 25 Dec	BBC1	16.74
8	Christmas Generation Game	Tue 25 Dec	BBC1	16.73
9	BBC World Cup '90	Wed 4 Jul	BBC1	16.69
10	Coronation Street	Fri 28 Dec	ITV	16.68
11	News and Weather	Tue 25 Dec	BBC1	16.61
12	Inspector Morse	Wed 24 Jan	ITV	16.16
13	ITV World Cup '90	Mon 11 Jun	ITV	15.95
14	Octopussy	Sat 20 Jan	ITV	15.86
15	Blind Date	Sat 3 Feb	ITV	15.79
16	This is Your Life	Wed 1 Jan	ITV	15.65
17	For Your Eyes Only	Sat 13 Jan	ITV	15.22
18	Keeping up Appearances	Mon 3 Dec	BBC1	14.98
19	Eastenders	Thu 27 Dec	BBC1	14.86
20	Watching	Fri 19 Jan	ITV	14.82

***Source:* AGB Television/BARB**

Radio 1990-91

Bevan Jones considers whether the TV industry has anything to learn from the experiences of its radio counterparts during 1990-91

THE hullabaloo surrounding the new framework for commercial television created by the 1990 Broadcasting Act predictably distracted public attention away from the far more radical deregulation of independent radio incorporated in the same Act. Many broadcasting commentators had argued that radio is increasingly used by legislators as a stalking-horse for moves to circumscribe an over-mighty television establishment. Radio, after all, was generally agreed to be in need of change: the BBC's monopoly of national services overlaid a messy mixture of local and regional stations run both by the BBC and commercial operators which few found satisfactory.

All British radio stations have hitherto had to include an element of public service broadcasting, an injunction which had worked well in the world of television but had failed to stimulate an equivalent broad range of programme genres on commercial radio. The survival of high quality prescripted programmes on the BBC networks, which had provided most of the subject matter for most serious newspaper coverage of the medium, also tended to mask the blandness of much music radio. The Act attempted to allow existing and new commercial stations to compete for audiences with little restraint, especially over sources of income. Thus the new Radio Authority's Programme Code, published in January 1991, states baldly: "all programmes may be sponsored, with the exception of news bulletins" and, as with commercial television after 1993, central prescription of programme content and schedules is abolished or drastically reduced.

The reform of the radio system which the Act was supposed to deliver had been mooted as long ago as the early 1980s in response to an unusual alliance of deregulatory free-marketeers, pirate operators with a wide range of motives, and those inspired by overseas examples of non-profit access-oriented community stations run on democratic principles.

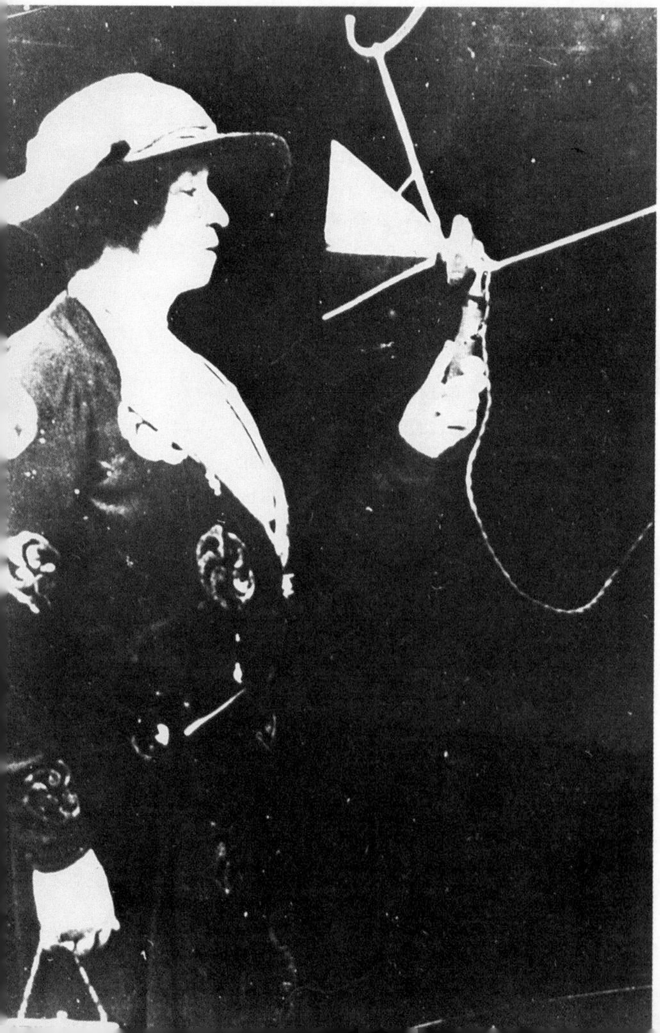

Radio past and present: (left) Dame Nellie Melba makes the first broadcast transmission of entertainment in Great Britain in 1920, two years before the BBC was formed; (right) advertising poster for Kiss 100 FM, London's first ever legal 24-hour 7-day dance music station, launched in September 1990

Their representations were compounded by the persistent failure of most commercial stations to increase their modest two per cent share of advertising expenditure to the sort of levels found in foreign broadcasting markets, where radio routinely achieves between 6% and 12% of net advertising revenue a year.

Six years after the abruptly-cancelled experiment in community radio, some limited diversification of the system had finally appeared through the IBA Radio Division's valedictory 'incrementals' scheme which allowed the licensing of small stations catering for specific cultural and ethnic groups for the first time. Yet during the passing of the Act the notion that radio is a central part of British culture never really broke through the potent mix of hazy nostalgia and commercial opportunism that has characterised political responses to the medium since the arrival of television.

One of the guiding principles of the Act, curiously disinterred when the Bill was in its committee stage, was the encouragement of full-on competition for the BBC's national services through the introduction of national commercial radio. Proposals for the privatisation of Radio 1 and Radio 2 had already foundered because it was never clear what could actually be sold off and had been truly scuttled by a timely BBC threat to replace Dvořák with Duran Duran on the definitively up-market Radio 3.

In the event, the BBC has merely had to surrender the increasingly anomalous luxury of broadcasting the same programmes on different wavebands. Not only has it retained its Rolls-Royce FM frequencies, it even managed to conjure up a fifth national channel on medium wave, Radio 5. This new channel, an eclectic mix of sport, education and youth programmes, reportedly cost a million and a half pounds to set up although it has now emerged that the true running costs are around £17 million a year. With Radio 4 costing around seventy million pounds a year, Radio 5 can certainly claim to be extremely cheap even if its audience share sticks at one per cent. Critics have wondered whether the real motive behind it is a wish by the BBC to retain control of one of its medium-wave frequencies as much as a rational way of tidying up a sprawl of programme genres in which Test Match commentaries and parliamentary debates displace quite different scheduled programmes.

Probably of greater significance was the introduction during the Gulf War of a full-time national news channel on Radio 4's FM frequency. Despite the immense news-gathering capacity of the BBC, intense public interest through British participation in the conflict and the palpable and occasionally excessive enthusiasm of presenters given their heads, longueurs

abounded. The case for a radio equivalent of BSkyB's continuous news service must surely have been dispatched, even before the costs are taken into account.

Which brings us to the saga of the proposals for up to three national commercial radio (Independent National Radio) stations. If there is a case to be made for them, and it should be remembered that each national channel occupies the same frequency space as sixty new local stations, it is that INR should find the biggest conceivable audience and so raise the profile of the medium in the minds of advertisers. One imaginative suggestion was for a Channel Four style service with a remit to fill the gaps in the existing system and perhaps stimulate an independent audio production sector. The commercial radio sector has always had to endure the handicap of being introduced after half a century of BBC monopoly and twenty years after the introduction of commercial television. Despite a quadrupling in the number of stations, the sector's share of total advertising expenditure remained static during the fat years of the 1980s in the face of competition from daytime television and a more aggressive newspaper and magazine market to below 2%, a fifth of what has been achieved by radio in business-driven broadcasting markets.

Independent Local Radio (ILR) was, by common consent, due for a shake-up, if not a shake-out and that was where the notion of INR began. The first problem was that it would inevitably breach the long-standing principle that different parts of the broadcasting system should be funded from different sources.

Overall, national advertising accounts for well over 40% of ILR income. Almost any national service will eat into that and so the ILR lobby swung into action. Government proposals simply to auction off up to three franchises without any prescription as to their character were kicked energetically into touch when it dawned on policy-makers that the result would be three versions of Radio Luxembourg and a decidedly gloomy future for ILR.

The crucial decisions on the character of INR were taken during the Committee stage of the Broadcasting Bill's passage through the House of Lords. The outcome was that the one franchise with real commercial potential, that of FM stereo, was restricted to the less popular musical forms and, like the new commercial television franchises, was to be sold to the highest bidder. A later interpretation by the new Radio Authority (a re-badged IBA Radio Division) determined that this required most of the music it plays – and there has at least never been any doubt that it would play mostly music – should be pre-1960 and therefore pre-stereo. There is an even more absurd aspect to the proscription of pop: it is that a substantial slice (25-30%) of the music played on the most profitable stations around the world is British, and yet Britain is the one country where an

adult-oriented Rock format is largely unavailable.

The only real justification for all this nonsense was to protect ILR's erratic profitability and it therefore sits all the more oddly with the far-reaching de-regulation of the established commercial sector. The fundamental problem of ILR really lies in its original conception, which attempted to transfer the highly successful ITV regional public service model to radio. The injunction on ILR to provide a general entertainment service with moderate public service obligations in return for an effective local monopoly of radio advertising led to a system that was sub-regional but supra-local and a style of programming that had become a weak mono-culture of 'pop and prattle' which delivered few surprises and a lightweight local identity. ILR's protagonists point out that they have tackled the 'best radio in the world' and achieved very respectable ratings. The sector's total income of around £140 million in 1990 earned it an audience share of between a third and 45%, allowing it to claim to be the brand leader in its local market. BBC local radio, by comparison, cost about £60 million for a 10% share, a respectable enough performance given its public duty to provide a higher and more demanding speech-to-music ratio across its output.

The real excitement of the year was the appearance of twenty four 'incremental' stations, licensed under the old Broadcasting Act. As harbingers of a genuinely diversified system, they held great promise: four Afro-Caribbean, three Asian, one multicultural, several small scale community-oriented, a larger number of shoestring commercials and two specialist music stations for London. Sadly, over half of them experienced traumatic changes in staff and ownership almost before they got on air. A combination of high start-up costs and over-hasty launches confirmed the pessimistic predictions of the ILR establishment, who nonetheless went on to take a substantial stake in the financing and management of the new stations. Some consolation can be taken from the belated willingness of the new Radio Authority to learn from the many mistakes and allow new stations much more time to find their own feet in the future.

One major development that gathered during the year attracted virtually no public attention. It was the dispensation given to ILR stations to split their frequencies, so doubling their sales potential. The usual way of doing this was to introduce a 'Gold' format on the less popular, low-definition medium-wave frequency instead of providing the same programmes on AM and FM. Gold, in this usage, normally means Sixties pop, although it has been pointed out that the format bears much the same relationship to historical reality as Disneyland. That such an expansion of the commercial sector took place, by stealth, without any attempt to bring in new operators or any public discussion, set an unfortunate precedent.

Lobbyists were further disappointed by the failure of legislators to confirm in writing the virtues of community radio they were happy to praise in the course of parliamentary debate. It was ironic that a barely tenable definition of pop music found its way into the statute book but that the concept of community radio – owned, managed and made by its audience – should have defeated the politicians. In vain did enthusiasts point out that community radio flourished around the world and that it could sensibly be treated as a third tier of public broadcasting with a distinct operational framework. It would be doubly ironic if Britain's first encounter with access broadcasting comes not through radio but via cable television, with its enormous infrastructural costs and much more problematic production values.

Towards the end of the year, it became apparent what the likely nature of INR 1 might be. At one point it looked as though there might be no applicants for the licence at all though eventually three groups did come forward. It now seems likely that the least interesting option of all will win the day, a 'beautiful music' format dismissively but fairly described in the USA as 'elevator music' and exemplified by London's Melody Radio. It cannot be pretended that the new station will add to the cultural value of the system, even if it does achieve its modest target audience share of around 5% and meet its annual costs of between £7 and £10 million. We face a station not just without speakers, but with minimal human input – the operation may be largely programmed by computer.

British radio is approaching its seventieth birthday in a state of uncertainty. Efforts to re-configure it have had limited success around the margins and it is welcome that ethnic minority communities have at last been given a look-in. But, by and large, the same faces dominate and are likely to do so until the mid-1990s when a new tranche of FM frequencies are promised. What is so disappointing is that new talent and new ways of doing radio have still to compromise with the Corporation and the companies of old or take to piracy, as many metropolitan stations still do, despite the increased powers the 1990 Act had given to the authorities. The free play of market forces has been diverted into a cultural cul-de-sac, at least temporarily, in a medium distinguished by cheapness, flexibility and infinite scope for the imagination.

The one proposal to arise during the course of the year which held out some hope received as much support in principle as it failed to receive in practice. It was for a radio fund, much smaller than the multimillion pound Gaelic Broadcasting Fund which suddenly became politically expedient during the year. The fund would be used to pay for programmes – drama, music, education and so on – which the market is unlikely to deliver. Perhaps a more thoughtful approach to radio policy will emerge and the fund idea will become more than a proposal. Until then, radio is in danger of remaining stuck in its old groove, a medium on which new tunes have yet to be played.

Below: 'Hello, good morning and welcome to Radio 5': Andrew Kelly, 5, of Blackpool, launches the BBC's new national channel with DJ Bruno Brooks

And will radio as so often in the past turn out to be the template for television? Certainly, the 1990 Act goes much further in taking the reins off radio than it does for television. De-regulation of ILR means that all that stations will have to do in order to retain their licence is observe a brief promise of performance and not take too many liberties with such facts as they broadcast. It will only take one station to try to employ 'shock-jock' tactics, Radio Bigot, only one to exploit the almost limitless scope for dubious sponsorship deals, only one to sell slabs of airtime to a televangelist, for the delicate fabric of consumer protection to effectively disappear in the competitive rush. The only real test of success will be the balance sheet and if radio profits at the expense of any notion of the wider public interest, then why should television be treated differently? Perhaps the real campaign for quality broadcasting has just begun.

Right: Lord Chalfont, chairman of the newly-formed Radio Authority

European Overview

BFI Director Wilf Stevenson asks how our film industry compares with the rest of Europe as the single European market approaches

THE well documented collapse of production and investment in the British cinema raises the question of whether this is a Europe-wide industry recession or simply a British phenomenon. With the opportunities of the single European market now fast approaching, how does the United Kingdom stand in comparison to its European Community rivals? The evidence suggests that, although the downturn in investment and production is widespread, the UK has fared worse than its EC partners and is less well-placed to recover during the present decade. The critical factor here may be the virtual absence in this country of fiscal support for investment in the industry, or of direct state subsidies. Without it, the UK may not be in the best position to keep pace with the major film producing countries of Europe.

The likely consequence is that, when the single market comes into operation in 1993, British cinema will be unable to play any sort of dominant economic – or indeed cultural – role.

Table 1 shows the overall decline in production across Europe. Production figures are notoriously unreliable and seldom do two sets of figures agree with each other, so one must approach the actual figures in the table with caution. Nevertheless, it is probably safe to rely on the general trend evidenced in table 1. The UK's static level of production at each end of the decade is, in a sense, less serious than the severe decline in output evident in France, Italy and particularly Spain. It is, however, difficult to be impressed by the British ability to bump along at the bottom of the table while the leading nations have been producing up to four times as many films as we manage. The UK contributed fewer than 10% of the total EC output throughout the period. The point is simple but important: the British film industry is in no sense a major concern when viewed in the European context. It cannot hope, therefore, to occupy a central position in the inevitable economic regrouping which will occur after 1992.

TABLE ONE: FILMS PRODUCED (INCLUDING CO-PRODUCTIONS)

	1980	1985	1986	1987	1988	1989
Belgium	6	7	5	12	15	10
Denmark	13	12	11	12	17	18
France	189	151	134	133	137	136
German Fed Rep	49	64	60	65	57	68
Greece	27	27	20	15	19	–
Ireland	5	2	4	4	5	6
Italy	163	89	114	116	124	117
Luxembourg	0	1	1	1	1	3
Netherlands	7	11	13	18	10	13
Portugal	9	8	6	11	16	–
Spain	118	77	60	69	63	48
UK	38	54	41	57	56	38

Source: 'Screen Digest'

The investment figures in table 2 appear to suggest levels of activity in the UK which would compare favourably with any EC nation. In fact, the figures are distorted by the high level of US investment in producing feature films here, rather than overall investment in the domestic industry.

The common feature about sustaining a film industry in countries with a small domestic market – and that means every European country – is Government support.

Whether one believes in high levels of direct Government spending or simply in schemes to stimulate private investment, the difference between a relatively buoyant

TABLE TWO: TOTAL FEATURE FILM PRODUCTION INVESTMENT

	1987 $m	1988 $m	1989 $m	Share of EC total 1987 %	1988 %	1989 %
Belgium	16.6	21.1	14.0e	1.4	1.6	1.2
Denmark	17.5	14.2	18.8e	1.4	1.1	1.6
France	351.9	423.1	446.5	28.8	32.4	39.0
German Fed Rep	123.9	97.4	114.4e	10.1	7.5	10.0
Greece	4.3	7.6	–	0.3	0.6	–
Italy	222.6	270.6	231.0	18.2	20.8	20.2
Netherlands	13.0	7.1	9.2e	1.1	0.5	0.8
Portugal	2.2	3.6	–	0.2	0.3	–
Spain	77.1	51.4	47.2e	6.3	3.9	4.1
UK	392.1	407.8	263.8	32.1	31.3	23.0

(e = estimated figure)
Source: 'Screen Digest'

industry and a vanishing one lies in some form of state intervention in the market. The extent to which the UK lags behind its EC competitors in this respect is shown in table 3 and the difference is staggering. It is also fatal to our prospects for competing with France, Italy, Spain and Germany. In these countries, a variety of schemes are in operation which aim to smooth the path for investors in film production. France operates a levy on exhibitors, providing returns to producers which must be re-invested in film production. The SOFICA schemes provide tax incentives to stimulate private investment. Germany runs a levy system as well as a number of local and national grant and loan schemes. The Italian national bank is a major source of funding for feature films, while there is again an exhibitors levy. Spanish exhibitors provide 15% of their box-office to producers. This means that in the UK, where a tiny amount of Government money (around £2 million per annum is provided for production), the market conditions here are so unfavourable (relative to our major EC rivals) that in competition with them, the British industry is hopelessly disadvantaged.

This will be the vital factor determining UK participation in the opportunities of 1992 and it is with this in mind that the industry has been arguing with the Government for investment schemes, tax incentives and subsidy arrangements.

The creation of a single European market has the potential to rival the internal market of the United States. Currently, the dominance of American product is a Europe-wide phenomenon although the UK is the worst affected, making up for the absence of domestic production by import-

Below: UCI's 14-screen multiplex in Cologne, Germany

TABLE THREE: GOVERNMENT SUBSIDY TO FILM INDUSTRY (in ECU million)

	1981	1982	1983	1984	1985	1986	1987	1988	1989
Belgium	2.4	2.9	–	4.4	2.6	4.6	5.9	3.0	–
Denmark	–	4.8	–	–	6.9	7.14	7.18	7.7	–
France	–	–	–	–	–	107.5	110.7	111.1	113.1
Germany	–	–	–	–	–	–	51.3	62.4	33.3
Greece	–	–	–	–	–	1.6	–	–	–
Italy	–	–	–	–	114.8[1]	131.2[1]	139.0[1]	146.2[1]	–
		31.8[2]	40.7[2]	51.4[2]	63.4[2]	96.1[2]	129.5[2]	162.2[2]	202.9[2]
Netherlands	–	–	–	–	4.9	4.9	6.4	5.9	–
Portugal	0.63	0.79	0.630	0.628	0.950	1.31	1.05	–	–
Spain	–	–	–	–	30.3	29.5	29.0	35.0	–
UK:									
BFI Grant from OAL	–	9.32	16.68[3]		16.80[4]	11.66	13.9	14.3	16.2
National Film Development Fund		–	–	–	0.71	0.71	0.71	0.71	0.71
British Screen Finance		–	–	–	2.14	2.14	2.14	2.14	2.14

[1] Film investments by the film credit section of the Banca National Del Lavoro (BNL-SACC)
[2] Financial aid by the Fondo Unico Per Lo Spettacolo (FUS)
[3] For the 18 month period ending 30 September 1983
[4] For the 18 month period ending 31 March 1985

Source: BFI Library and Information Services

Below: The highly successful* Cyrano de Bergerac *is one of approximately 50 films a year funded by the French Government. It received £450,000. Bottom: Director Isaac Julien and producer Lynda Myles leaving the Downing Street seminar where the British film industry put its case for investment schemes, tax incentives and subsidy arrangements in June 1990

Photo courtesy of Empire magazine

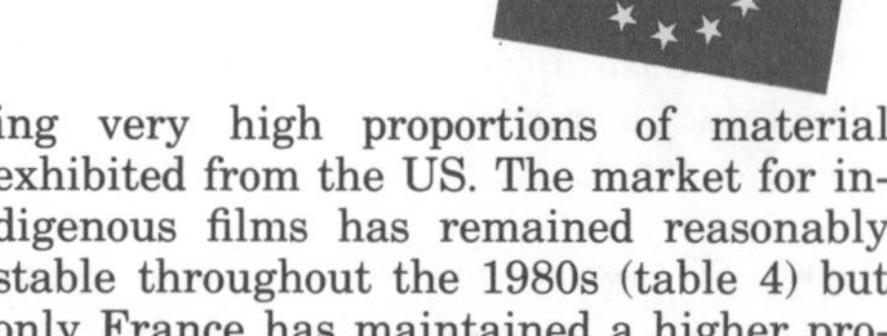
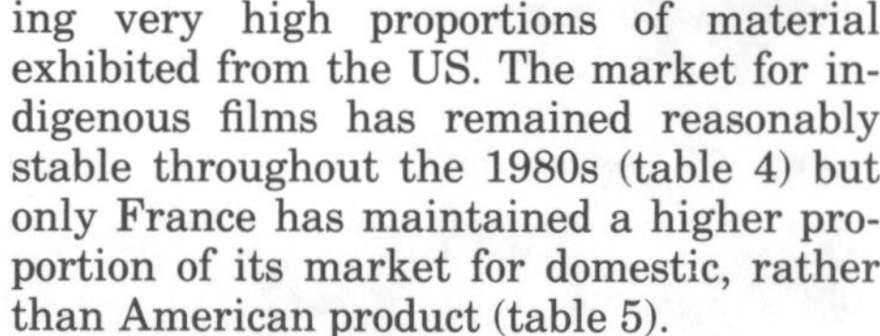
ing very high proportions of material exhibited from the US. The market for indigenous films has remained reasonably stable throughout the 1980s (table 4) but only France has maintained a higher proportion of its market for domestic, rather than American product (table 5).

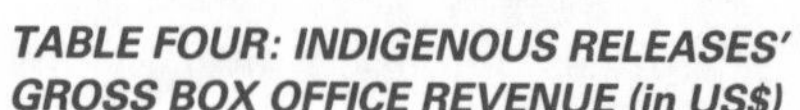
TABLE FOUR: INDIGENOUS RELEASES' GROSS BOX OFFICE REVENUE (in US$)

	1985 $m	1988 $m	1989 $m
Belgium	0.3	0.6	–
Denmark	1.2	2.7	3.0
France	213.9	231.1	191.7
German Fed Rep	59.7	109.5	70.4
Ireland	0.3	0.7	1.0
Italy	83.3	93.2	90.5
Netherlands	1.7	8.6	3.7
Portugal	0.2	0.3	–
Spain	24.0	26.5	18.7
UK	17.0	64.4	78.1

Source: 'Screen Digest'

TABLE FIVE: INDIGENOUS AND US FILMS' SHARES OF NATIONAL MARKETS

	Indigenous films' share				US films' share			
	1980 %	1985 %	1988 %	1989 %	1980 %	1985 %	1988 %	1989 %
Belgium	2.0	0.8	1.0	–	–	61.0	–	–
Denmark	21.0	4.4	6.6	7.5	44.5	61.2	71.0	62.2
France	46.9	44.7	38.6	33.8	35.2	39.1	45.9	–
German Fed Rep	9.3	22.7	23.4	16.7	54.9	59.0	64.4	–
Greece	28.0	13.0	–	–	–	76.0	–	–
Ireland		2.0	3.0	4.0		96.0	94.0	95.0
Italy	43.5	31.8	23.1	21.7	33.7	48.6	56.0	63.1
Netherlands	12.5	3.6	11.9	4.5	46.2	74.3	75.0	–
Portugal	–	1.0	1.0	–	–	48.0	–	–
Spain	18.5	16.2	11.1	7.3	35.0	58.4	64.2	71.4
UK	21.0	10.7	18.7	21.0	78.0	88.0	80.0	78.0

Source: 'Screen Digest'

The attraction of Hollywood films has increased in direct response to the dwindling of domestic production in all EC countries, but the UK (and Ireland) remain at absurdly high levels of dependence on US product. Increasingly, the British are becoming a nation of film consumers but not filmmakers. Nevertheless, Europe's absorption of American culture is a widespread phenomenon as table 6 shows. EC nations pay money to the US for American films, videos and television programmes and receive revenue for export sales and for the use of European facilities by US film companies. The resulting trade balance tells its own story. It remains to be seen whether the single market will begin to shift EC nations' attention towards their own cultural products.

TABLE SIX: BALANCE OF TRADE BETWEEN EUROPE AND THE USA IN FILM, TELEVISION AND VIDEO FOR 1988 (in millions of US$)

	US Revenues in Europe	EC Revenues in America	Trade deficit
Theatrical	693	43	650
Television/ Cable	575	100	475
Video	700	60	640
Total	1,198	203	1,765

Total US revenues from the EC for 1988 amounted to $2.0 billion, total EC revenues from the US for 1988 were $0.2 billion. Source: Idate/'Screen Finance'

The market for films is clearly an important factor in assessing the potential for a European cinema revival. The overall decline – and recent revival – in cinema audiences in the UK fits in with the European pattern more generally. The drop in audiences led in the 1980s to a corresponding decline in the number of cinemas throughout the EC, (table 7). Signs of an increase were evident in the UK and in

TABLE SEVEN: NUMBER OF CINEMAS

	1980	1985	1986	1987	1988	1989
Belgium	500	440	433	407	422	–
Denmark	329	241	221	207	195	–
France	4500	5153	5117	5026	4819	4658
Germany	3354	3418	3262	3252	3246	–
Greece	1100	900	600	500	500	455
Ireland	163	–	–	–	100	–
Italy	8453	4885	4431	4143	3871	–
Luxembourg	12	17	17	17	16	14
Netherlands	523	473	457	438	438	–
Portugal	423	379	373	358	–	–
Spain	4096	3109	2640	2234	1882	–
UK	942	663	660	648	657	676

Note: Figures for Greece, Ireland and the UK since 1986 are estimates.
Source: BFI Library and Information Services/'Cultural Trends'/ 'Screen Digest'

Above: Cable TV operators have made little inroad in the UK. The programmes they offer include those of satellite service BSkyB which transmits to the UK from its uplink near Southampton, pictured above (photo courtesy of NTL)

Germany from 1988. The growth of multiplexes has meant that the decline in the number of screens, which in general parallels the decline in cinemas, has been arrested in this country (table 8), although the trend is still downwards elsewhere in Europe. Admissions, which fell significantly in most countries during the decade, are now beginning to recover in nearly all the member states (table 9). Taking into account the differences in population, France emerges as the leading EC nation of cinema-goers, although the UK has improved its ranking over the decade, catching up with Italy and Germany as admissions per head there slumped (table 10).

Looking at video, the UK leads Europe (indeed, is behind only the USA and Japan) in VCR penetration (table 11). Cable, on the other hand, has made virtually no inroad here. Other evidence suggests that the

TABLE EIGHT: NUMBER OF CINEMA SCREENS

	1980	1985	1987	1988	1989
Belgium	508	440	399	467	395
Denmark	475	429	397	381	366
France	4540	5190	5026	4819	4658
German Fed Rep	3422	3418	3252	3246	3216
Greece	1103	600	700	700	625
Ireland	163	135	140	145	146
Italy	8453	4885	4143	4000	3500
Luxembourg	20	18	18	14	14
Netherlands	523	473	438	445	436
Portugal	423	379	300	290	280
Spain	4096	3109	2234	1882	1802
UK	1574	1251	1215	1250	1424

Source: 'Screen Digest'

TABLE NINE: TOTAL CINEMA ADMISSIONS (millions)

	1980	1981	1982	1983	1984	1985	1986	1987	1988	1989
Belgium	21.6	20.1	20.5	21.4	19.0	17.9	17.7	15.7	15.2	15.0e
Denmark	15.9	16.2	14.3	13.8	11.8	11.3	11.4	11.5	10.0	10.3
France	174.8	189.2	201.9	198.8	190.8	175.0	167.8	136.7	124.7	118.8
German Fed Rep	143.8	141.3	124.5	125.3	112.1	104.2	105.2	108.1	108.9	101.6
Greece	42.9	—	35.0	—	—	23.0	22.0	22.5	17.0	17.5
Ireland	9.5	—	—	—	—	4.5	5.0	5.2	6.0	7.0
Italy	241.9	215.0	195.0	162.0	130.1	123.1	124.8	110.0	93.0	95.2
Luxembourg	0.8	—	—	—	—	0.7	0.7	0.6	0.5	0.5
Netherlands	27.9	26.7	22.0	21.6	17.4	15.3	14.9	15.5	14.8	15.6
Portugal	30.8	30.3	27.3	24.3	18.8	19.0	18.4	16.9	13.0	13.8e
Spain	176.0	173.0	155.9	141.0	118.6	101.1	87.3	85.7	69.6	78.1
UK	101.0	86.0	64.0	65.7	53.8	72.0	75.7	78.4	84.0	94.6

e = estimated figure Source: 'Screen Digest'

TABLE TEN: EUROPEAN CINEMA ADMISSIONS PER HEAD OF TOTAL POPULATION

	Population 1981	average admissions per head and ranking 1980	rank	1985	rank	1988	rank	1989	rank
Belgium	9.93m	2.19	9	1.82	7	1.53	8	1.51	9
Denmark	5.14m	3.10	6	2.21	4	1.95	2	2.00	2
France	56.15m	3.24	4	3.17	1	2.23	1	2.12	1
German Fed Rep	61.23m	2.34	8	1.71	8	1.78	3=	1.66	6
Greece	10.07m	4.45	2	2.32	3	1.70	5	1.74	5
Ireland	3.56m	2.79	7	1.27	9=	1.69	6	1.97	4
Italy	57.55m	4.29	3	2.15	5	1.62	7	1.65	7=
Luxembourg	0.37m	–	–	–	–	1.35	10	1.35	10
Netherlands	14.85m	1.97	10	1.06	11	1.00	12	1.05	12
Portugal	10.46m	3.14	5	1.86	6	1.25	11	1.32	11
Spain	39.28m	4.71	1	2.63	2	1.78	3=	1.99	3
UK	57.19m	1.79	11	1.27	9=	1.47	9	1.65	7=

Source: 'Screen Digest'

video boom has passed its peak in the UK, with signs of a small but significant decline in video rentals in the first quarter of 1990 compared to the same period in 1989.

The 1990s will be a period of change in Europe, economically with the single market, politically following the opening of Eastern Europe and culturally, as European integration makes its inexorable progress. The UK, traditionally aloof from mainland Europe, perhaps stands to lose most. The opportunity to develop our cultural ties with other European nations may not be realised.

The prospects too for Britain to lead the field in exports to the USA – through co-productions in the English language, for example – cannot be guaranteed.

It is in the British nature to be cautious but recent caution has degenerated into complacency, into inertia at a time of rapid economic and cultural change. No one can be certain about the impact of 1992; but we can all be certain that, as matters presently stand, the UK may well be the nation that misses the boat – or, possibly more apt, gets stuck in the tunnel.

TABLE ELEVEN: PERCENTAGE OF HOMES WITH VIDEO RECORDERS/CABLE TV

	Population m	TV homes m	Penetration of TV households: video recorders 1988 %	1989 %	1990 %	cable TV 1989 %
Belgium	9.93	3.43	32.9	39.5	45.6	91.4
Denmark	5.14	2.15	35.5	39.3	42.6	28.2
France	56.15	19.65	35.8	41.6	46.6	1.1
Germany	61.23	30.83	40.0	46.0	51.4	23.8
Greece	10.07	3.06	19.0	23.2	27.1	–
Ireland	3.56	0.94	45.2	49.2	52.5	38.2
Italy	57.55	19.49	15.2	20.0	25.7	–
Netherlands	14.85	5.69	41.2	45.2	49.3	79.0
Portugal	10.46	2.60	27.0	28.9	30.8	–
Spain	39.28	10.69	34.3	40.0	44.9	4.0
UK	57.19	21.13	58.8	63.3	67.0	1.1

Source: 'Screen Digest'

For information on European film and television organisations see pp 206-214 of the Directory.

Below: Ghost, top box-office earner in 1990: one of the many Hollywood films which have benefited from the increase in UK cinema-going

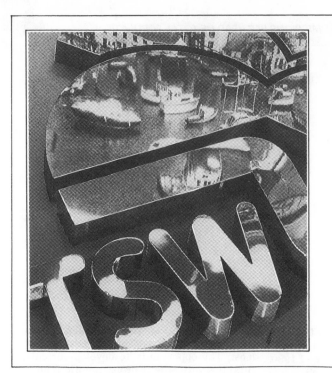

DIRECTORY

ARCHIVES AND LIBRARIES

International Federation of Film Archives (FIAF)
rue Franz Merjay 190
1180 Brussels
Belgium
Tel: (32) 2 343 06 91
Though not itself an archive, FIAF, which has over 50 member archives and many observers from 58 countries, exists to develop and maintain the highest standards of film preservation and access. It also publishes handbooks on film archiving practice which can be obtained from the above address

International Federation of Television Archives (FIAT)
Calle Saturno 10
E-28023 Madrid, Spain
Tel: (34) 1 715 44 32
Fax: (34) 1 715 51 00

NATIONAL ARCHIVES
There are two national archives in the UK that are recognised by FIAF:

Imperial War Museum
Department of Film
Lambeth Road
London SE1 6HZ
Tel: 071 416 5000
Fax: 071 416 5379

National Film Archive
21 Stephen Street
London W1P 1PL
Tel: 071 255 1444
Fax: 071 436 7950
See also p9

REGIONAL COLLECTIONS

East Anglian Film Archive
Centre of East Anglian Studies
University of East Anglia
Norwich
Norfolk NR4 7TJ
Tel: 0603 56161 x2664
David Cleveland
Cathryn Terry
Jane Alvey

North West Film Archive
Manchester Polytechnic
Minshull House
47-49 Chorlton Street
Manchester M1 3EU
Tel: 061 247 3097/8
Maryann Gomes
Marion Hewitt

Northern Film and Television Archive
36 Bottle Bank
Gateshead
Tyne and Wear NE8 2AR
Tel: 091 477 3601
Fax: 091 478 3681
Bob Davis

Scottish Film Archive
Dowanhill
74 Victoria Crescent Rd
Glasgow G12 9JN
Tel: 041 334 4445
Fax: 041 334 8132
Janet McBain, Archivist
Almost exclusively non-fiction film, the collection dates from 1897 to the present day and concerns aspects of Scottish social, cultural and industrial history. Access charges and conditions available on request

Wessex Film and Sound Archive
Hampshire Archives Trust
20 Southgate Street
Winchester SO23 9EF
Tel: 0962 847742
David Lee

NEWSREEL, PRODUCTION AND STOCK SHOT LIBRARIES
These are film and television libraries which specialise in locating material on a particular subject. For other, sometimes more specialised, film libraries consult the 'Researcher's Guide to British Film and Television Collections' and the 'Researcher's Guide to British Newsreels', published by the BUFVC

Archive Film Agency
21 Lidgett Park Avenue
Roundhay
Leeds LS8 1EU
Tel: 0532 662454
Agnese Geoghegan
Film and stills archive. 16mm and 35mm newsreel, documentary and feature material from 1900

Archive Films/Film Images
4th Floor
184 Drummond Street
London NW1 3HP
Tel: 071 383 0033
Fax: 071 383 2333
Footage from silent films, documentaries, newsreels, features, industrial films; 1896-1960s; b/w and colour

Boulton-Hawker Films
Hadleigh, Ipswich
Suffolk IP7 5BG
Tel: 0473 822235
Fax: 0473 824519
Peter Boulton
Educational films produced over 44 years. Subjects include: health, biology, botany, geography, history, archaeology, and the arts

British Movietone News Film Library
North Orbital Road
Denham, Uxbridge
Middx UB9 5HQ
Tel: 0895 833071
Fax: 0895 834893
London Office:
72 Dean Street
London W1V 6DE
Tel: 071 437 7766 x206
Newsreel (1929-1979), b/w, some colour, 35mm

British Pathé News Library
Pinewood Studios
Iver Heath
Bucks SL0 0NH
Tel: 0753 630361
Fax: 0753 655365
George Marshall
35mm newsreel from 1896 to 1970, b/w and colour. Index on text search computer

Chameleon Film and Stockshot Library
The Magistretti Building
Harcourt Place
Leeds LS1 4RB
Tel: 0532 434017
Helen Osman
16mm material from 1970s onwards includes climbing and caving films for use as stockshots. Also output from Trident Television, including *Whicker's World* and Channel 4 programme trims

Educational and Television Films (ETV)
247a Upper Street
London N1 1RU
Tel: 071 226 2298
Documentaries on Eastern Europe, USSR, China, British Labour movement, b/w and colour, 16mm and 35mm, 1896 to present day

Film Archive Management and Entertainment (FAME)
18-20 St Dunstan's Road
London SE25 6EU
Tel: 081 771 6522
Fax: 081 653 9773

Film Research and Production Services
25-27 Heddon Street
London W1R 7LG
Tel: 071 734 1525
Fax: 071 734 8017
Amanda Dunne
Gerard Wilkinson
James Clarkson-Webb
Film holdings, with comprehensive film research and copyright clearance facilities

GB Associates
80 Montalt Road
Woodford Green
Essex IG8 9SS
Tel: 081 505 1850
Malcolm Billingsley
An extensive collection of fact and fiction film from 1896 onwards, 35mm and 16mm

Fred Goodland Collection
81 Farmilo Road
Leyton
London E17 8JN
Tel: 081 539 4412
16mm colour and b/w actuality and entertainment film from the 1890s through to the 1960s. Specialist collections include the early sound period and a wide range of musical material. Extensive research facilities available on tape

Huntley Film Archives
22 Islington Green
The Angel
London N1 8DU
Tel: 071 226 9260
Fax: 071 704 0847
John Huntley
Amanda Huntley
Documentary and newsreel film, 16mm/35mm specialist collections in transport, street scenes, industrial history, music etc from 1895

ITN Film Library Sales
200 Gray's Inn Road
London WC1X 8XZ
Tel: 071 833 3000
Fax: 071 430 4453
Malcolm Smith
Newsreel and TV news coverage worldwide. Colour and b/w, 1956 to present day. Variety of formats including 16mm, 3/4" video, and Beta SP. Copy facility to any format available. Library also offers stills collection and information service

Index Stock Shots
12 Charlotte Mews
London W1P 1LN
Tel: 071 631 0134
Fax: 071 436 8737
Stock footage on film and video, including international locations, aircraft, and wildlife

Kobal Archive Films
4th Floor
184 Drummond Street
London NW1 3HP
Tel: 071 383 0011
Fax: 071 383 0044
Footage and stills from silent films, features, newsreels, industrial films, documentaries; b/w and colour

London Video Access (LVA)
23 Frith Street
London W1A 4XD
Tel: 071 437 2786
Fax: 071 734 2003
LVA is Britain's national centre for video and new media art and houses the most extensive collection of video art in the country. Artists work dating from the 1970s to the present day

LWT Library Clip Services
London Weekend Television
Upper Ground
London SE1 9LT
Tel: 071 261 3771/3690
Fax: 071 261 3224
Judith Steele
Lynne Giddens
Extracts and stockshots from all LWT programmes covering arts, drama, wildlife, London news, popular music, entertainment, current affairs and international GVs

Medi Scene
32–38 Osnaburgh Street
London NW1 3ND
Tel: 071 387 3606
Fax: 071 387 9693
Carol Naylor
Wide range of accurately catalogued medical and scientific shots available on film and video. Part of the Medi Cine Group

Oxford Scientific Films
Long Hanborough
Oxford OX7 2LD
Tel: 0993 881881
Fax: 0993 882808
Stock footage and stills libraries; 16mm, 35mm film and transparencies covering wide range of wildlife and special effects subjects

Post Office Film and Video Library
PO Box 145
Sittingbourne
Kent ME10 1NH
Tel: 0795 426465
Holds a representative selection of documentary programmes made under the GPO Film Unit, including the classic *Night Mail* etc. Catalogue available

RSPB Film and Video Unit
The Lodge
Sandy
Beds SG19 2DL
Tel: 0767 680551
Fax: 0767 692365
Pauline Miller
Over one million feet of 16mm film covering a wide variety of wildlife subjects and their habitats, particularly European birds. Viewing facilities and tape duplication are available on request. See also under Distributors (Non-Theatrical) and Production Companies

Timescape Image Library/Film Images
4th Floor
184 Drummond Street
London NW1 3HP
Tel: 071 383 2777
Fax: 071 383 2333
Original, specially shot 35mm contemporary colour film of America – cities, landscapes, landmarks, people, time-lapse and special effects

Visnews Library
Cumberland Avenue
London NW10 7EH
Tel: 081 965 7733
Fax: 081 965 0620
Pam Turner
Newsreel, TV news, special collections. Colour and b/w, 16mm, 35mm, 1896 to present day and all material pre 1951 and post July 1981 on 1" video

WTN (Worldwide Television News)
The Interchange
Oval Road, Camden Lock
London NW1
Tel: 071 410 5200
Fax: 071 413 8302
David Simmons
David Muddyman
Jane Dickenson
Collection of videotape, film and stills covering world events from the turn of the century. Computerised retrieval system (for all stories from 1980). Libraries in London and New York

Weintraub Feature Film Library
Pinewood Studios
Pinewood Road
Iver, Bucks SL0 0NH
Tel: 0753 631111
Fax: 0753 655813
John Herron
Feature films and stock shot, b/w and colour, 35mm, 1925 to present day

World Backgrounds Film Production Library
Imperial Studios
Maxwell Road
Borehamwood, Herts
Tel: 081 207 4747
Fax: 081 207 4276
Ralph Rogers
Worldwide establishing shots, colour, 35mm and back projection plates, 1964 to present day, supplied to TV series, commercials, features, documentaries and sports programmes

AWARDS

The following awards were presented during 1990 and the first quarter of 1991

BAFTA AWARDS – BRITISH ACADEMY OF FILM AND TELEVISION ARTS

Awarded March 1991 for 1990 films/programmes

BAFTA special award 1991: Deborah Kerr
Academy fellowship: Louis Malle
Michael Balcon award for outstanding British contribution to cinema: Jeremy Thomas
Desmond Davis award for outstanding creative contribution to television: Ray Fitzwalter (Granada TV)
Writer's award: Simon Gray for *Old Flames* (BBC Screen Two)
Richard Dimbleby award: John Pilger (Central TV)
Originality award: *Troubleshooter* (BBC) Sir John Harvey Jones (former Chairman of ICI) and Richard Reisz (series producer)

Film

Best film: *GoodFellas* (USA) Dir Martin Scorsese
Best achievement in direction: Martin Scorsese for *GoodFellas*
Best actress: Jessica Tandy for *Driving Miss Daisy* (USA) Dir Bruce Beresford
Best actor: Philippe Noiret for *Nuovo Cinema Paradiso* (Italy) Dir Giuseppe Tornatore
Best supporting actress: Whoopi Goldberg for *Ghost* (USA) Dir Jerry Zucker
Best supporting actor: Salvatore Cascio for *Nuovo Cinema Paradiso*
Best original screenplay: Giuseppe Tornatore for *Nuovo Cinema Paradiso*
Best adapted screenplay: Nicholas Pileggi for *GoodFellas*
Best film score: Ennio Morricone and Andrea Morricone for *Nuovo Cinema Paradiso*
Best foreign language film: *Nuovo Cinema Paradiso*
Best short film: *Say Goodbye* (UK) (National Film and Television School) Dir Michele Camarda and John Roberts
Best short animated film: *Toxic* (UK) (Royal College of Art) Dir Andrew McEwan

Television

Best single drama: *News Hounds* (BBC Screen One) Prod Sarah Curtis Dir Les Blair
Best drama series/serial: *Oranges Are Not the Only Fruit* (BBC) Prod Philippa Giles Dir Beeban Kidron Script Jeanette Winterson
Best factual series: *The Trials of Life* (BBC) Exec prod Peter Jones
Best light entertainment programme: *Whose Line Is It Anyway?* (Channel 4) Prod Dan Patterson Dir Chris Bould
Best comedy series: *The New Statesman* (YTV) Script Laurence Marks and Maurice Gran Prod David Reynolds Dir Geoffrey Sax
Best news/OB coverage: Channel 4 News Team
Best actress: Geraldine McEwan for *Oranges Are Not the Only Fruit*
Best actor: Ian Richardson for *House of Cards* (BBC) Prod Ken Riddington Dir Paul Seed
Best light entertainment performance: David Jason for *Only Fools and Horses* (BBC) Prod Gareth Gwenlan Dir Tony Dow
Best original music: Tim Souster for *The Green Man* (BBC) Prod David

◀ Old Flames

Snodin Dir Elijah Moshinsky
Best children's programme (entertainment/drama): *Press Gang* (Channel 4) Prod Steven Moffat Script Sandra C Hastie
Best children's programme (documentary/educational): *Ipso Facto* (BBC) Prod Madeline Wiltshire
Flaherty documentary award: *The Last African Flying Boat* (BBC) Dir David Wallace
Huw Wheldon award (best arts programme): *Partnership between Robert Bolt and Sir David Lean* (LWT South Bank Show) Prod David Thomas
Best foreign television programme: *Dekalog (The Ten Commandments)* Dir Krzysztof Kieslowski

BAFTA CRAFT AWARDS 1990

Awarded March 1991

Film

Cinematography: Vittorio Storaro for *The Sheltering Sky* (UK/Europe) Dir Bernardo Bertolucci
Production design: Richard Sylbert for *Dick Tracy* (USA) Dir Warren Beatty
Editing: Thelma Schoonmaker for *GoodFellas*
Sound: J Paul Huntsman, Stephen von Hase, Chris Jenkins, Gary Alexander and D M Hemphill for *The Fabulous Baker Boys* (USA) Dir Steve Kloves
Achievement in special visual effects: The production team for *Honey I Shrunk the Kids* (USA) Dir Joe Johnston
Make-up: John Caglione Jr and Doug Drexler for *Dick Tracy*
Costume design: Richard Bruno for *GoodFellas*

Television

Video lighting: Derek Constable and Keith Reed for *Boon* (Central TV)
Design: Stuart Walker for *Portrait of a Marriage* (BBC)
Film cameraman: The team of *The Trials of Life*
Sound supervisor: Graham Haines for *Boris Godunov: Live from Leningrad* (BBC)
Film sound: Aad Wirtz, Kathy Rodwell and Malcolm Webberley for *Oranges Are Not the Only Fruit*
Film editor: Dick Allen for *Portrait of a Marriage*
Graphics: Lucy Blakstad and Susan Worthy for *Summer on BBC1* promotion
VTR editor: Malcolm Banthorpe for *Casualty (Episodes 1 and 6)* (BBC)
Make-up: Joan Stribling for *Van Gogh* (BBC Omnibus)
Costume design: Dinah Collin for *Portrait of a Marriage*
Video cameraman: Roy Easton, Rolle Luker and Adrian J Fearnley for *The Bill* (Thames TV)

▲ Portrait of a Marriage

▼ Ghost

▲ *BFI Fellows: Krzysztof Kieslowski, Jeanne Moreau, Fred Zinnemann and Derek Jarman with Sir Richard Attenborough*

BFI AWARDS 1990

Awarded October 1990 in association with Ernst & Young

BFI fellowship: Derek Jarman, Krzysztof Kieslowski, Jeanne Moreau and Fred Zinneman
Grierson award (for best documentary): *Four Hours in Mai Lai* (YTV)
Film award: Stephan Evans producer of *Henry V* (UK) Dir Kenneth Branagh
Independent achievement award: Birmingham Film and Television Festival
Archival achievement: *The Making of a Legend: Gone with the Wind* (USA) Dir David Hinton
Technical achievement: *Henry V*
Career in the industry: Monty Berman, costumier
Television award: *The Late Show* (BBC)
Book award: François Truffaut for *Letters* (Faber & Faber)
British book award: Roger Bolton for *Death on the Rock and Other Stories* (W H Allen)
Anthony Asquith film music award: Michael Kamen for *The Krays* (UK)
Anthony Asquith young composer award: Susan George for *That Summer of White Roses* (UK/Yugoslavia) Dir Rajko Grlic
Mari Kuttna award (for animation): *Creature Comforts* Dir Nick Park
Sutherland trophy (for best first/second feature): *The Fabulous Baker Boys* (USA) Dir Steve Kloves

◀ **The Silence of the Lambs**

BERLIN FESTIVAL

Awarded February 1991

GOLDEN BEARS
Grand prix: *La Casa del Sorriso (The House of Smiles)* (Italy) Dir Marco Ferreri
Short film: *Six Point Nine* (USA) Dir Dan Bootzin
SILVER BEARS
Special jury prize: *La Condanna (The Conviction)* (Italy) Dir Marco Bellocchio and *Satana (Satan)* (USSR) Dir Viktor Aristov
Best director: Ricky Tognazzi for *Ultra* (Italy) and Jonathan Demme for *The Silence of the Lambs* (USA)
Best actor: Maynard Eziashi for *Mister Johnson* (USA) Dir Bruce Beresford
Best actress: Victoria Abril for *Amantes (Lovers)* (Spain) Dir Vicente Aranda
Short film: *Posledních 100 let Marx-Leninismu V Čechách (The Last 100 Years of Marx-Leninism in Bohemia)* (Czechoslovakia) Dir Pavel Koutský
FIPRESCI Best film in competition: *Le Petit criminel (The Little Gangster)* (France) Dir Jacques Doillon

Please return undelivered copies to:
BFI Membership, BFI, South Bank, London SE1 8TL

Best film out of competition: *Die Mauer* (Germany) Dir Jurgen Böttcher
OCIC (Catholic Ecumenical) prize: *Le Petit criminel*
International Protestant film prize: *Il Viaggio di Capitan Fracassa (Captain Fracassa's Journey)* (Italy/France) Dir Ettore Scola
GDF (German Art Film Theatre Association) prize: Neil Jordan for *The Miracle* (UK/Eire)
Berliner Morgenpost (audience) prize: *Dances with Wolves* (USA) Dir Kevin Costner
CIAE (International Confederation of Arts Cinemas) prize: *Berdel* (Turkey) Dir Atif Yilmaz
UNICEF prize: *Langitku Rumahku (My Sky, My Home)* (Indonesia) Dir Slamet Rahardjo Djarot
Best short film: *Creature Comforts* (UK) Dir Nick Park
CIFEJ (International Centre of Films for Children and Young People) prize: *Oh! Xiang Xue (Oh! Sweet Snow)* (People's Republic of China) Dir Wang Haowei and *O Psylos (The Flea)* (Greece) Dir Dimitris Spyrou
Special mention: *Lad Isbjørnene Danse (Dance of the Polar Bears* (Denmark) Dir Birger Larsen
Children's jury prize: *Vincent et Moi* (Canada) Dir Michael Rubbo

BROADCASTING PRESS GUILD AWARDS 1990

Presented March 1991

Best single drama: *Shoot to Kill* (YTV)
Best drama series: *House of Cards* (BBC)
Best single documentary: *The Maze – Enemies Within* (BBC Inside Story)
Best documentary series: *The Trials of Life* (BBC)
Best entertainment programme: *Drop the Dead Donkey* (Hat Trick Productions for Channel 4)

▲ Zamri Umi Voskresni (Don't Move, Die and Rise Again)

Best imported programme: *Twin Peaks* (USA – Lynch-Frost Productions for ABC TV)
Best acting performance: Ian Richardson for *House of Cards*
Best on-screen performance (non-acting): John Cole (BBC)
Most memorable outside broadcast: *Mrs Thatcher in Paris* (BBC)

CANNES FESTIVAL 1990

Awarded May 1990

Golden Palm: *Wild At Heart* (USA) Dir David Lynch
Special jury prize: *Hidden Agenda* (UK) Dir Ken Loach
Grand jury prize: *Tilaï* (Burkina Faso) Dir Idrissa Ouedraogo and *Shi No Toge (The Sting of Death)* (Japan) Dir Kohei Oguri
Best director: Pavel Loungine for *Taxi Blues* (USSR/France)
Best actor: Gérard Depardieu for *Cyrano de Bergerac* (France) Dir Jean-Paul Rappeneau
Best actress: Krystina Janda for *Przesluchanie (Interrogation)* (Poland) Dir Ryszard Bugajski
Best artistic contribution: *Matj (Mother)* (USSR) Dir Gleb Panfilov
Golden camera (best first film): *Zamri Umi Voskresni (Don't Move, Die and Rise Again)* (USSR) Dir Vitali Kanievski
Grand prize for superior technical achievement: Pierre Lhomme, director of photography for *Cyrano de Bergerac*
Short film Golden Palm: *The Lunch Date* (USA) Dir Adam Davidson
Short film prize (animation): *De Slaapkamer (The Bedroom)* (Netherlands) Dir Maarten Koopman
Short film prize (fiction): *Revestriction* (France) Dir Barthelemy Bompard
FIPRESCI (international critics' award): *Shi No Toge* (in competition) and *Lebedyne Ozero – Zona (Swan Lake – The Zone)* (USSR) Dir Yuri Illienko (out of competition)
Prix jeunesse (France): *Printemps perdu (Lost Spring)* Dir Alain Mazars
Prix jeunesse (foreign): *Lebedyne Ozero – Zona*
OCIC (Catholic Ecumenical) prize: *Stanno Tutti Bene (Everybody's Fine)* (Italy/France) Dir Giuseppe Tornatore

Stanno Tutti Bene (Everybody's Fine) ▼

FIPRESCI special prize: Manoel de Oliveira
Grand prize (audience): *Abraham's Gold* (Germany) Dir Jorg Graser: Grand prize (young audience): *300 Mil do Nieba (300 Miles to Heaven)* (Poland) Dir Maciej Dejczer
Luis Buñuel prize (Latin American): *Ju Dou* (China/Japan) Dir Zhang Yimou
Prix Perspectives (French cinema): *L'Amour* (France) Dir Philippe Faucon
Prix PROCIREP (producers'): *Passport* (France) Dir Georgi Daneliya
Prix de la Fondation Gan pour le cinéma: *L'Amour*
Prix du Club Espace Cinéma Philip Morris: *Mado, Poste Restante* (France) Dir Alexandre Adabachian
Prix Perspectives (short film): *Dis Moi Oui, Dis Moi Non* (France) Dir Noémie Lvovsky
Prix Canal Plus (short film): *Dis Moi Oui, Dis Moi Non*
Cointreau prize (short film): *Animathon* (Canada) Dir collective
SACD prize: *Outremer* (France) Dir Brigitte Rouan
'Afrique en création' cinema prize: *Tilaï* and *Diplomate à la tomate* (Senegal) Dir Samba Felix N'diaye

▲ The Wonder Years

CESARS

Awarded March 1991 for 1990 films

Best actor: Gérard Depardieu for *Cyrano de Bergerac* Dir Jean-Paul Rappeneau
Best actress: Anne Parillaud for *Nikita* Dir Luc Besson
Best supporting actor: Jacques Weber for *Cyrano de Bergerac* ▶
Best supporting actress: Dominique Blanc for *Milou en mai* Dir Louis Malle
Most promising young actor: Gérald Thomassin for *Le petit criminel* Dir Jacques Doillon
Most promising young actress: Judith Henry for *La Discrète* Dir Christian Vincent
Best director: Jean-Paul Rappeneau for *Cyrano de Bergerac*
Best French film: *Cyrano de Bergerac*
Best foreign film: *Dead Poets Society* (USA) Dir Peter Weir
Best first feature: *La Discrète*
Best screenplay: Christian Vincent and Jean-Pierre Ronssin for *La Discrète*
Best music: Jean-Claude Petit for *Cyrano de Bergerac*
Best short feature: *Foutaises* Dir Jean-Pierre Jeunet
Best documentary short: *La Valise* Dir François Amado
Best cinematography: Pierre Lhomme for *Cyrano de Bergerac*
Best set design: Ezio Frigerio for *Cyrano de Bergerac*
Best sound: Pierre Gamet and Dominique Hennequin for *Cyrano de Bergerac*
Best editing: Noëlle Boisson for *Cyrano de Bergerac*
Best costumes: Franca Squarciapino for *Cyrano de Bergerac*
Career award: Jean-Pierre Aumont and Sophia Loren

42ND PRIMETIME EMMY AWARDS FOR TELEVISION – NATIONAL ACADEMY FOR TELEVISION ARTS AND SCIENCES

Awarded September 1990

DRAMA
Outstanding series: *L.A. Law* (NBC)

Director: Thomas Carter for *Equal Justice (Promises to Keep)* (ABC)
Lead actor: Peter Falk for *Columbo* (ABC)
Lead actress: Patricia Wettig for *thirtysomething* (ABC)
Supporting actor: Jimmy Smits for *L.A. Law*
Supporting actress: Marg Helgenberger for *China Beach* (ABC)
Writing: David E Kelley for *L.A. Law (Blood, Sweat and Fears)*
Guest actor: Patrick McGoohan for *Columbo (Agenda for Murder)*
Guest actress: Viveca Lindfors for *Life Goes On (Save the Last Dance for Me)* (ABC)
COMEDY
Outstanding series: *Murphy Brown* (CBS)
Director: Michael Dinner for *The Wonder Years (Goodbye)* (NBC)
Lead actor: Ted Danson for *Cheers* (ABC)
Lead actress: Candice Bergen for *Murphy Brown* (CBS)
Supporting actor: Alex Rocco for *The Famous Teddy Z* (ABC)
Supporting actress: Bebe Neuwirth for *Cheers*
Writing: Bob Brush for *The Wonder Years (Goodbye)*
Guest actor: Darren McGavin for *Murphy Brown (Brown Like Me)*
Guest actress: Swoosie Kurtz for *Carol & Company (Reunion)* (NBC)
Outstanding special (drama/comedy): *Caroline? (Hallmark Hall of Fame)* (CBS) and *The Incident (A & T Presents)* (CBS)
MINI-SERIES/ SPECIALS
Outstanding mini-series: *Drug Wars: The Camarena Story* (NBC)
Director: Joseph Sargent for *Caroline?*
Lead actor: Hume Cronyn for *Age-old Friends* (HBO)
Lead actress: Barbara Hershey for *A Killing in a Small Town* (CBS)
Supporting actor: Vincent Gardenia for *Age-old Friends*
Supporting actress: Eva-Marie Saint for *People Like Us* (NBC)
Writing: Terrence McNally for *Andre's Mother (American Playhouse)* (PBS)
VARIETY/MUSIC
Outstanding variety/music/comedy series: *In Living Color* (Fox)
Outstanding variety/music/comedy special: *Sammy Davis Jr 60th Anniversary Celebration* (ABC)
Directing: Dwight Hemion for *The Kennedy Center Honors: A Celebration of the Performing Arts* (CBS)
Writing: Billy Crystal for *The Midnight Train to Moscow* (HBO) and James L Brooks, Heide Periman, Sam Simon, Jerry Belson, Marc Flanagan, Dinah Kirgo, Jay Kogen, Wallace Wolodarsky, Ian Praiser, Marilyn Suzanne Miller and Tracey Ullman for *The Tracey Ullman Show* (Fox)
Individual performance: Tracey Ullman for *The Tracey Ullman Show*
Informational series: *Smithsonian World* (PBS)
Informational special: *Dance in America: Bob Fosse Steam Heat (Great Performances)* (PBS) and *Broadway's Dreamers: The Legacy of the Group Theatre (American Masters)* (PBS)
Animated programme: *The Simpsons* (Fox)
Children's programme: *A Mother's Courage: The Mary Thomas Story (The Magical World of Disney)* (NBC)
Individual Achievement (informational programming): George Burns for *A Conversation with...* (Disney) and Gene Lasko for *W Eugene Smith – Photography Made Difficult (American Masters)* (PBS)
Individual achievement (classical music/dance program): Katarina Witt, Brian Orser and Brian Boitano for *Carmen on Ice* (HBO) and Peter Rosen and Alan Skog for *The Eighth Van Cliburn International Piano Competition: How to Make Music* (PBS)
Classical program in the performing arts: *Aida (The Metropolitan Opera Presents)* (PBS)
Music composition for series: Don Davis for *Beauty and the Beast (A Time to Heal)* (CBS)
Music direction: Ian Fraser (director), Chris Boardman, Bill Byers, Bob Florence, J Hill and Angela Morley (arrangers) for *Julie Andrews In Concert (Great Performances)* (PBS)

INTERNATIONAL EMMYS 1990

Awarded November 1990

Best drama: *First and Last* (UK-BBC Pebble Mill) Dir/Prod Alan Dossor Prod Michael Wearing
Best documentary: *J'ai douze ans et je fais la guerre* (France-Canal Plus/FR3)
Best arts documentary: *Bookmark: From Moscow to Pietushki* (UK-BBC) Dir/Prod Paul Pawlikowski
Best performing arts programme: *The Mahabharata* (France/UK) Dir Peter Brook Prod Michael Propper
Best popular arts programme: *Norbert Smith: A Life* (UK-Hat Trick for Channel 4) Dir Geoff Posner Prod Geoffrey Perkins ▲
Children's and young people award: *Living with Dinosaurs* (UK-TVS) Dir Paul Wieland Prod Duncan Kenworthy
International Council Founder's award: Joan Ganz Cooney (co-founder/chairman/CEO of the Children's Television Workshop)

EUROPEAN FILM AWARDS 1990

Awarded December 1990

European film of the year: *Porte Aperte (Open Doors)* (Italy) Dir Gianni Amelio

Living with Dinosaurs ▼

◀ **Twin Peaks**

Young European film of the year: *Henry V* (UK) Dir Kenneth Branagh
European actor of the year: Kenneth Branagh for *Henry V*
European actress of the year: Carmen Maura for *¡Ay, Carmela!* (Spain) Dir Carlos Saura
European supporting actor of the year: Dimitrij Persov for *Matj (Mother)* (USSR) Dir Gleb Panfilov
European supporting actress of the year: Malin Ek for *Skyddsanglen (The Guardian Angel* (Sweden) Dir Suzanne Osten
European discovery of the year: Ennio Fantastichini for *Porte Aperte*
European screenwriter of the year: Vitali Kanievski for *Zamri Umi Voskresni (Don't Move, Die and Rise Again)* (USSR) Dir Vitali Kanievski
European documentary of the year: *Poperechnaya Street* (USSR) Dir Ivars Selecktis
European film composer of the year: No prize awarded
European production designer of the year: Ezio Frigerio (sets) and Franca Squarciapino (costumes) for *Cyrano de Bergerac* (France) Dir Jean-Paul Rappeneau
European cinematographer of the year: Tonino Nardi for *Porte Aperte*
Special jury award: Gian Maria Volonté for his 'genius and generosity' and *December Bride* (Eire) Dir Thaddeus O'Sullivan
European Cinema Society special award: The Association of Soviet Filmmakers
Special mention: *Step Across the Border* (Switzerland) Dir Nicolas Humbert and Werner Penzel
European Cinema Society Lifetime Achievement award: Andrzej Wajda

48TH GOLDEN GLOBE AWARDS

Awarded January 1991

Film

Best drama: *Dances with Wolves* (USA) Dir Kevin Costner
Best comedy/musical: *Green Card* (USA) Dir Peter Weir
Best foreign language film: *Cyrano de Bergerac* (France) Dir Jean-Paul Rappeneau
Best actor (drama): Jeremy Irons for *Reversal of Fortune* (USA) Dir Barbet Schroeder
Best actor (comedy/musical): Gérard Depardieu for *Green Card*
Best supporting actor: Bruce Davison for *Longtime Companion* (USA) Dir Norman Rene
Best actress (drama): Kathy Bates for *Misery* (USA) Dir Rob Reiner
Best actress (comedy/musical): Julia Roberts for *Pretty Woman* (USA) Dir Garry Marshall
Best supporting actress: Whoopi Goldberg for *Ghost* (USA) Dir Jerry Zucker
Best director: Kevin Costner for *Dances with Wolves*
Best screenplay: Michael Blake for *Dances with Wolves*
Best original score: Ryuichi Sakamoto and Richard Horowitz for *The Sheltering Sky* (UK/Europe) Dir Bernardo Bertolucci
Best original song: Jon Bon Jovi for 'Blaze of Glory' from *Young Guns II* (USA) Dir Geoff Murphy

Television

DRAMA
Best series: *Twin Peaks* (ABC)
Best actress: Sharon Gless for *The Trials of Rosie O'Neill* (CBS) and Patricia Wettig for *thirtysomething* (ABC)
Best actor: Kyle MacLachlan for *Twin Peaks*

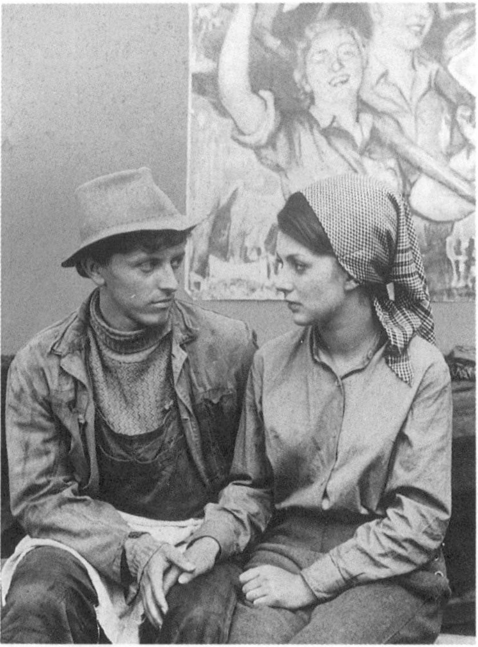

COMEDY/MUSICAL
Best series: *Cheers* (ABC)
Best actress: Kirstie Alley for *Cheers*
Best actor: Ted Danson for *Cheers*
MINI-SERIES OR FILMS MADE FOR TV
Best series: *Decoration Day (Hallmark Hall of Fame)* (NBC)
Best actress: Barbara Hershey for *A Killing in a Small Town* (CBS)
Best actor: James Garner for *Decoration Day*
Best supporting actress: Piper Laurie for *Twin Peaks*
Best supporting actor: Charles Durning for *The Kennedys of Massachusetts* (ABC)
Cecil B DeMille award: Jack Lemmon

KARLOVY VARY FILM FESTIVAL

Awarded July 1990 (biennial event alternating with Moscow)

Grand prize (Crystal Globe): jury declined to award its main accolade this year
Rose of Lidice prize: to the Czech and Slovak filmmakers who were persecuted, banned or sent into exile
Special jury prize: *Byli Jsme To My? (Were we really like this?)* (Czechoslovakia) Dir Antonín Máša
Best director: Janusz Kijowski for *Stan Strachu (State of Fear)* (Poland)
Best actor: Andrej Smirnov for *Černov* (USSR) Dir Sergei Yurski
Best actress: Clotilde de Bayser and Laure Marsac for *Tumultes* (France) Dir Bertrand Van Effenterre
FIPRESCI critics prize: *Ptáčkove, Siroty a Blázni (Birds, Orphans and Fools)* (Czechoslovakia) Dir Juraj Jakubisko
Special mention:

▲ Gravy Train

Smuteční Slavnost (Funeral Ceremony) (Czechoslovakia) Dir Zdenek Sirovy as representative of the banned and blacklisted section
Czech critics prize: *Skriváncí na Nitích (Larks on a String)* (Czechoslovakia) Dir Jirí Menzel

LOCARNO FILM FESTIVAL 1990

Awarded August 1990

Gold Leopard: *Slouchainj Vals (Accidental Waltz)* (USSR) Dir Svetlana Proskurina
Silver Leopard and special jury prize: *The Reflecting Skin* (UK) Dir Philip Ridley and *Metropolitan* (USA) Dir Whit Stillman
Bronze Leopard (technical achievement): Miklos Gurban for his camerawork on *Szurkulet (Dawn)* (Hungary) Dir György Feher
Bronze Leopard (acting): Emer McCourt for *Hush A Bye Baby* (UK/Northern Ireland) Dir Margo Harkin
OCIC (Catholic Ecumenical) prize: *Hush A Bye Baby*

MONTE CARLO TV FESTIVAL 1990

Awarded February 1991

FICTION (SERIES)
Gold nymph (best series): *Marie Curie* (France-FR3)
Silver nymph (best series): *The Gravy Train* (UK-Channel 4)
Silver nymph (best actress): Marie Christine Barrault for *Marie Curie*
Special jury mention: Ian Richardson for *The Gravy Train*
TELEFILM
Gold nymph for best film: *Princes in Exile* (Canada) Dir Giles Walker
Silver nymph (best direction): *The Children of Sin* (USSR-Gostelradio)
Silver nymph (best actor): James Garner for *Decoration Day* (USA-NBC)
Silver nymph (best actress): Annabelle Apsion for *The Widowmaker* (UK-Central/LWT)
Silver nymph (best screenplay): *Felipe ha gli occhi azzuri (Felipe has blue eyes)* (Italy-RAI 1)
Special jury mention: *The Story of Edes Anna* (Hungary-MTV)
NEWS
Gold nymph (best news feature): *The White Tribe of Africa: Drowning in Blood* (UK-BBC Panorama)
Gold nymph (best news report): *Baghdad* (Finland-YLE)
Silver nymph (best news report in terms of quality and authenticity): *The Last Parade of the Red Army* (Netherlands-NOS)
Silver nymph (best news report in terms of journalistic merit): *Chernobyl – They shall harvest no more* (Japan-NHK)
Special jury mention: *La Bête sous la manche* (France-Antenne 2)
SPECIAL PRIZES
Prix du public: *Felipe ha gli occhi azzuri*
International critics prize for news magazine: *First Tuesday: Angel is Missing* (UK-YTV)
Best TV film: *Le Piège* (France-Antenne 2/SFP)
Best news documentary: *Toby's Journey* (USA-ABC)
PRIX UNDA
Documentary: *First Tuesday: Angel is Missing*
Fiction: *The Children of Sin*
Unesco prize: *Princes in Exile*
PRIX URTI
International Grand Prix for documentary: *L'Histoire du soldat Igor Stravinsky* (France-INA)
Youth television prize: *Les pygmées de l'Est Camerounais* (Camerouns-RTV)
Prix de Croix Rouge Monegasque: *Firing Squad* (Canada)
Prince Rainier III Special de S.A.S. prize: *Chernobyl – They shall harvest no more*

MONTREUX FESTIVAL OF LIGHT ENTERTAINMENT 1990

Awarded May 1990

Golden Rose: *Mr. Bean* (UK-ITV)
Silver Rose: *Norbert Smith - A Life* (UK-Channel 4)
Bronze Rose: *Neutral Policy* (Finland-MTV)
Golden Rose for independent producers: Picture Music International for *Nigel Kennedy – Four Seasons* (UK-BBC)
City of Montreux prize for funniest programme: *Mr. Bean*
City of Montreux prize for independent producers: Celador Productions for *Carrott's Commercial Breakdown* (UK-BBC)
Special mention: *The Wonder Years (St Valentine's Day Massacre)* (USA-ABC)
International Press prize: *Mr. Bean*

▼ First Tuesday: Angel is Missing

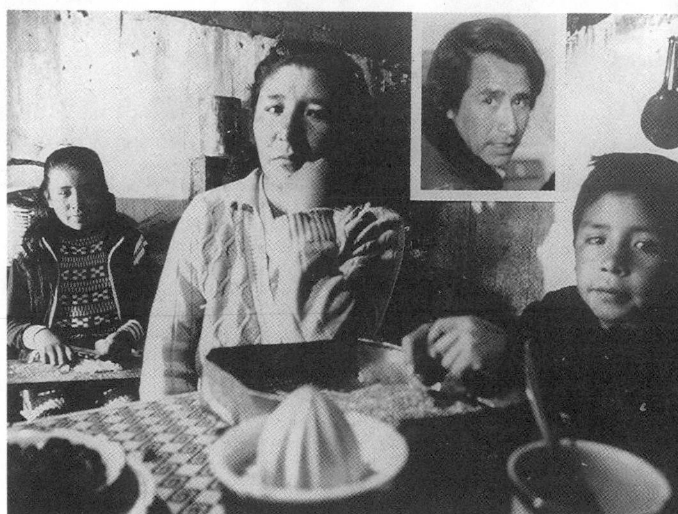

OSCARS – ACADEMY OF MOTION PICTURE ARTS AND SCIENCES

Awarded March 1991 for 1990 Films

Best film: *Dances with Wolves* (USA) Dir Kevin Costner
Best foreign language film: *Reise der Hoffnung (Journey of Hope)* (Switzerland) Dir Xavier Holler
Best director: Kevin Costner for *Dances with Wolves*
Best actor: Jeremy Irons for *Reversal of Fortune* (USA) Dir Barbet Schroeder
Best actress: Kathy Bates for *Misery* (USA) Dir Rob Reiner
Best supporting actor: Joe Pesci for *GoodFellas* (USA) Dir Martin Scorsese
Best supporting actress: Whoopi Goldberg for *Ghost* (USA) Dir Jerry Zucker
Best original screenplay: Bruce Joel Rubin for *Ghost*
Best screenplay adaptation: Michael Blake for *Dances with Wolves*
Best cinematography: Dean Semler for *Dances with Wolves*
Best editing: Neil Travis for *Dances with Wolves*
Best original song: 'Sooner or later (I always get my man)' Music and lyrics by Stephen Sondheim from *Dick Tracy* (USA) Dir Warren Beatty
Best original music score: John Barry for *Dances with Wolves*
Best art direction: Richard Sylbert (art director) and Rick Simpson (set decorator) for *Dick Tracy*
Best costume design: Franca Squarciapino for *Cyrano de Bergerac* (France) Dir Jean-Paul Rappeneau
Best make-up: John Caglione Jr and Doug Drexler for *Dick Tracy*
Best visual effects: *Total Recall* (USA) Dir Paul Verhoeven
Best sound: Russell Williams II, Jeffrey Perkins, Bill W Benton and Greg Watkins for *Dances with Wolves*
Best sound effects editing: Cecilia Hall and George Watters II for *The Hunt for Red October* (USA) Dir John McTiernan
Best short film (animated): *Creature Comforts* (UK) Dir Nick Park
Best short film (live action): *The Lunch Date* (USA) Dir Adam Davidson
Best documentary feature: *American Dream* (USA) Dir/Prod Barbara Kopple Prod Arthur Cohn
Best documentary short: *Days of Waiting* (USA) Dir/Prod Stevan Okazaki
Academy honorary award: Myrna Loy and Sophia Loren for a lifetime's contribution to cinema
Irving G Thalberg Memorial Award: Richard Zanuck and David Brown
Gordon E Sayer award for technical achievement: Stefan Kudelski for the development of the Nagra self-contained movie sound recorder
Academy award of merit: Eastman Kodak Company for the development of T.grain technology
Medal of commendation: Roderick T Ryan, Don Trumbull and Geoffrey H Williamson

Reise der Hoffnung (Journey of Hope) ▶

ROYAL TELEVISION SOCIETY AWARDS 1990

Programme and Performance Awards May 1990

PROGRAMME AWARDS
Light entertainment: *Whose Line Is It Anyway?* (Hat Trick Productions for Channel 4)
Situation comedy: *Blackadder Goes Forth* (BBC)
Single drama: *Nobody Here But Us Chickens* (Greenpoint Films for Channel 4)
Drama series: *A Bit of a Do* (Yorkshire TV)
Drama serial: *Nice Work* (BBC)
Single documentary: *Four Hours in Mai Lai* (Yorkshire TV)
Documentary series: *Around the World in 80 Days* (BBC)
Arts: *Arena – Tales from Barcelona* (BBC)
Outside broadcasts: *Lord Olivier Memorial Service* (BBC)
Regional award: *Charlie Wing* (TVS)
Technique award: Brendan Shore for sound on *Metamorphosis/ Theatre Night* (BBC)
Children's award (factual): *The Lowdown – Brave Heart* (BBC)
Children's award (drama & light entertainment): *Maid Marian and her Merry Men* (BBC)
Special commendation (drama): *A Wanted Man* (BBC)
PERFORMANCE AWARDS
Gold medal: Melvyn Bragg

Cyril Bennett award: Roger Bolton
Judges' award: George Jesse Turner, cameraman for *World in Action*
TECHNOLOGY AWARDS (in memory of Geoffrey Parr)
Research and development: Rank Cintel for the development of URSA Telecine
Communications innovations: BBC, One Man Camera
Operational systems: Quantel, Harry Suite

Television Journalism Awards February 1991

Regional daily news magazine: *Inside Ulster* (BBC Northern Ireland)
Regional current affairs: *For Those in Peril* (BBC South West)
News, home: *Strangeways Siege* (BBC Six O'Clock News)
News, topical feature: *The Iraqi Weapons Link* (Channel 4 News)
News, international: *Nine O'Clock News – Romanian Report* (BBC West)
Current affairs, home: *The Maze – Enemies Within* (BBC Inside Story)
Current affairs, international: *Cutting Edge – Island of Outcasts* (Twenty Twenty Television for Channel 4)
Television news cameraman of the year: Eugene Campbell (ITN)
Television journalist of the year: John Simpson (BBC) and John Cole (BBC)
Judges' award: Sir David Nicholas CBE, Chairman of ITN

VENICE FESTIVAL 1990

Awarded September 1990

Golden Lion: *Rosencrantz and Guildenstern are dead* (UK) Dir Tom Stoppard
Grand jury prize: *An Angel at My Table* (New Zealand) Dir Jane Campion
Silver Lion (best story and screenplay): Helle Ryslinge and Peter Boesen for *Sirup (Syrup)* (Denmark) Dir Helle Ryslinge
Silver Lion (best direction): Martin Scorsese for *GoodFellas*
Volpi Cup for best actor: Oleg Borisov for *Edinstvenijat Svidetell (The Final Testimony)* (Bulgaria) Dir Mikhail Pandourski
Volpi Cup for best actress: Gloria Munchmeyer for *La Luna en el Espejo (The Moon in the Mirror)* (Chile) Dir Silvio Caiozzi
Osella for cinematography: Mauro Nichetti for *Ragazzi fuori (Street Boys)* (Italy) Dir Marco Risi
Osella for editing: Dominique Auvray for *S'en fou la mort (To Hell with Death)* (France) Dir Claire Denis
Italian senate prize: *Raspad* (USSR) Dir Mikhail Belikov
FIPRESCI (Italian critics') prize – Official Selection: *Mathilukal (The Wall)* (India) Dir Adoor Gopalkrishnan
FIPRESCI (International critics') prize – International Critics' week: *La Stazione (The Station)* (Italy) Dir Sergio Rubini and *La Discrète (The Discreet)* (France) Dir Christian Vincent
OCIC (Catholic Ecumenical) prize: *An Angel at My Table*
UNICEF prize: *Mathilukal*
Career awards: Miklos Jancso and Marcello Mastroianni

▲ Cutting Edge – Island of Outcasts

◀ Rosencrantz and Guildenstern are Dead

BOOKSHOPS

Most bookshops stock film and cinema books and, if they don't have the book you want, they are usually happy to order it for you direct from the publisher. However, if the book you are looking for proves elusive or if you are looking for magazines, posters or memorabilia, you might try the specialist mail order services offered by the following bookshops

Arnolfini Bookshop
First Floor
16 Narrow Quay
Bristol BS1 4QA
Tel: 0272 299191
Fax: 0272 253876
Stock: A, B, C, E, F
Opening hours: 10.00-19.00 Monday-Saturday, 12.30-18.30 Sunday
Based in the Arnolfini Gallery, concentrating on the visual arts. No catalogues are issued. Send requests for specific material with SAE

B H Blackwell
48-51 Broad Street
Oxford OX1 3BQ
Tel: 0865 792792
Fax: 0865 794143
Stock: A
Opening hours: 09.00-18.00 Monday, Wednesday-Saturday 09.30-18.00 Tuesday
Literature department has sections on cinema, media studies and performing arts. An international charge and send service is available

Blackwell's Art & Poster Shop
27 Broad Street
Oxford OX1 2AS
Tel: 0865 792792
Stock: A, B, C, F
Opening hours: 09.00-18.00 Monday, Wednesday-Saturday 09.30-18.00 Tuesday
A wide selection of art books, posters, cards, calendars and gift items, all available by mail order

The Cinema Bookshop
13-14 Great Russell Street
London WC1B 3NH
Tel: 071 637 0206
Stock: A, B, C, D
Opening hours: 10.30-17.30 Monday-Saturday
Comprehensive stock of new, out-of-print and rare books. No catalogues are issued. Send requests for specific material with SAE

The Cinema Shop
45 Summer Row
Birmingham B3 1JJ
Tel: 021 236 9879
Stock: A, B, C, D, E, F
Opening hours: 11.30-17.30 Tuesday-Saturday, closed Sunday, Monday
Shop rather than mail order service, but will accept telephone queries

Geoffrey Clifton
Performing Arts Bookshop
44 Brazennose Street
Manchester M2 5EA
Tel: 061 831 7118
Stock: A, B, C, D, E, F
Opening hours: 10.00-17.30 Monday-Saturday
Stock mainly new books but a search service is available for out-of-print titles. Send SAE for details

Cornerhouse Books
70 Oxford Street
Manchester M1 5NH
Tel: 061 228 7621
Stock: A, B, C, E, F
Opening hours: 10.30-20.30 daily
No catalogues are issued. Send requests for specific material with SAE

A E Cox
21 Cecil Road
Itchen
Southampton SO2 7HX
Tel: 0703 447989
Stock: A, B, C, D
Telephone enquiries and orders are accepted at any time. Mail order only. A catalogue, including scarce items, is published at least six times yearly. Send two first-class stamps or three international reply vouchers overseas to receive the current issue

Richard Dalby
4 Westbourne Park
Scarborough
North Yorks YO12 4AT
Tel: 0723 377049
Stock: A, B
Mail order only. Lists issued of rare, out-of-print and second hand cinema books. Free search service for titles not in stock

Dress Circle
57-59 Monmouth Street
Upper St Martin's Lane
London WC2H 9DG
Tel: 071 240 2227
Stock: A, B, C, D, E, F
Opening hours: 10.00-19.00 Monday-Saturday
Specialists in music and soundtracks. A catalogue of the entire stock is issued annually. Send SAE for details

58 Dean Street Records
58 Dean Street
London W1V 5HH
Tel: 071 437 4500/734 8777
Stock: E
Opening hours: 10.00-18.30 Monday-Saturday
Retail shop with recorded mail order service. Over 7,000 titles including soundtracks, original cast shows, musicals and nostalgia. Telephone for information

Film Magic
18 Garsmouth Way
Watford
Herts

Stock: A, B, C, D, E, F
Mail order only.
Comprehensive catalogue costing £1.00 available on request

Anne FitzSimons
62 Scotby Road
Scotby
Carlisle
Cumbria CA4 8BD
Tel: 0228 513815
Stock: A, B, C, D, F
Mail order only.
Antiquarian and out-of-print titles on cinema, broadcasting and performing arts. A catalogue is issued three times a year. Send three first-class postage stamps for current issue

Flashbacks
6 Silver Place
Beak Street
London W1R 3LJ
Tel: 071 437 8562
Stock: C, D
Opening hours: 10.30-19.00 Monday-Saturday
Shop and mail order service. Send SAE and 'wanted' list for stock details

Forbidden Planet
71 New Oxford Street
London WC1A 1DG
Tel: 071 836 4179/379 6042
Stock: A, B, C, D, E, F
Opening hours: 10.00-18.00 Monday-Wednesday, Saturday
10.00-20.00 Thursday, Friday
Science fiction, horror, fantasy and comics specialists. Mail order service available on 071 497 2150

Heffers Booksellers
20 Trinity Street
Cambridge CB2 3NG
Tel: 0223 358351
Stock: A, E
Opening hours: 09.00-17.30 Monday-Saturday
Catalogues of videocassettes and spoken word recordings are issued. Copies are available free on request

David Henry
36 Meon Road
London W3 8AN
Tel: 081 993 2859
Stock: A, B
Mail order only.
A catalogue of out-of-print and secondhand books is issued two or three times a year and there is a search service for titles not in stock. New books can also be obtained to order, including those published in the USA

MOMI Bookshop
South Bank
London SE1 8XT
Tel: 071 928 3535
Stock: A, B, C, D, F
Opening hours: 10.30-19.30 daily
Based in the Museum of the Moving Image. Mail order available with special orders on request

The Media Bookshop
Book Base
PO Box 1057
Quinton
Birmingham B17 8EZ
Tel: 021 429 2606
Stock: A
Mail order only. A complete catalogue of books is produced once a year. Catalogue sent on request

Movie Finds
Mail order only: 2 Laurel Walk
Juniper Close
St Leonards on Sea
East Sussex TN38 9RH
Stock: C, D
Comprehensive catalogue pack available at £1.00

National Museum of Photography, Film and Television
Princes View
Bradford BD5 0TR
Tel: 0274 727488
Fax: 0274 723155
Stock: A, B, C, F
Opening hours: 10.30-18.00 Tuesday-Sunday
Mail order available. Send SAE with requests for information

Offstage Theatre & Cinema Bookshop
37 Chalk Farm Road
London NW1 8AJ
Tel: 071 485 4996
Stock: A, B, D, F
Opening hours: 10.00-18.30 Monday, 10.00-17.30 Tuesday-Saturday, 11.00-18.00 Sunday
Cinema catalogue available. Send SAE for details

Tyneside Cinema Bookshop
10 Pilgrim Street
Newcastle upon Tyne
NE1 6QG
Tel: 091 232 5592
Fax: 091 221 0535
Stock: A, B, C, D, F
Opening hours: 11.30-19.00 Monday-Saturday
Based in Tyneside Cinema. Send requests for specific material with SAE

Vintage Magazine Co
39-41 Brewer Street
London W1R 3FD
Tel: 071 439 8525
Stock: B, C, D, F
Opening hours: 10.00-20.00 Monday-Saturday, 12.00-19.00 Sunday
247 Camden High Street
London NW1
Tel: 071 482 0587
Stock: B, C, D, F
Opening hours: 10.00-18.00 Monday-Friday, 10.00-19.00 Saturday, Sunday
510 Brixton Road
London SW9
Tel: 071 274 7336
Stock: A, B, C, D, F
Opening hours: 10.00-18.00 Monday-Saturday
For details of catalogues, picture library and research services available, call 081 533 7588. Mail order service available. Send requests for specific material with SAE to:
203/213 Mare Street
London E8 3QE

Peter Wood
20 Stonehill Road
Great Shelford
Cambridge CB2 5JL
Tel: 0223 842419
Stock: A, D, F
Mail order, monthly PBFA Hotel Russell London book fair and others in provinces. Visitors are welcome by appointment. A free catalogue is available of all books in stock

A Zwemmer
80 Charing Cross Road
London WC2H 9NJ
Tel: 071 379 7886
Stock: A, B
Opening hours: 09.30-18.00 Monday-Friday, 10.00-18.00 Saturday
A catalogue of new and in-print titles on every aspect of cinema is available on request. Mail order service for all books available through Mail Order Dept.
A Zwemmer Ltd
24 Litchfield Street
London WC2H 9NJ

A – Books
B – Magazines
C – Posters
D – Memorabilia (eg stills)
E – Records, cassettes and compact discs
F – Postcards and greetings cards

CABLE AND SATELLITE

Cable networks in the UK are divided into two categories: the new full-franchise operations (listed by franchise area), and the dwindling number of older systems which have been upgraded to carry satellite programme channels (listed according to ownership)

UK FULL CABLE FRANCHISE AREAS

Franchises which have been granted or offered by the Cable Authority (including 11 previously granted by the Department of Trade and Industry) are arranged in alphabetical order of area. Where appropriate the principal towns in the area are identified under the area name. Unless otherwise stated, services have not yet begun on full franchise networks. Addresses are given where the operator has only one franchise or where a local address is used for the area. Where no address is given see the appropriate reference in the Group ownership section which follows

Aberdeen
Franchise holder: Aberdeen Cable Services
Ownership: Broadcast Satellite Television (see Group ownership) (59.5%), Legal & General Assurance (9%), Time Life International (8%), Standard Life Assurance (8%), Investors in Industry (6%), AT&C
Homes in area: 96,000
Homes passed: 92,381 (1 Jan 1991)
Subscribers: 12,875 – 13.9% (1 Jan 1991)
Date awarded: 1 Nov 1983
Service start date: 1 May 1985

Andover
Franchise holder: Andover Cablevision
Ownership: IVS Cable Holdings (see Group ownership)
Homes in area: 11,500
Homes passed: 1,000 (Jan 1990)
Date awarded: Apr 1988
Service start date: 28 Jun 1989

Avon
Bristol, Bath, Weston-super-Mare, Frome, Melksham etc
Franchise holder: United Artists Communications (Avon)
700 Waterside Drive
Aztec West
Almondsbury
Bristol BS12 4ST
Tel: 0454 612290
Fax: 0454 612416
Ownership: United Artists, US West (see Group ownership)
Homes in area: 300,000
Date awarded: 16 Nov 1988
Service start date: 14 Sep 1990

Aylesbury/ Amersham/ Chesham
Franchise holder: Jones Cable Group (see Group ownership)
Homes in area: 62,000
Date awarded: 31 May 1990

Barnsley
Franchise holder: Cable Communications (Barnsley) – Oyston Communications Group (see Group ownership)
Homes in area: 82,000
Date awarded: 14 Jun 1990

Bearsden/ Milngavie
Franchise holder: Clyde Cablevision (see Group ownership)
Homes in area: 16,000
Date awarded: 7 Jun 1990

Bedford
Franchise holder: Cablevision North Bedfordshire
20 Cosgrove Way
Luton
Beds LU1 1XL
Tel: 0582 401044
Fax: 0582 401055
Ownership: English Cable Partners (see Group ownership), Columbia Management, individuals
Homes in area: 55,000
Date awarded: 14 Jun 1990

Belfast
Franchise holder: Ulster Cablevision
40 Victoria Square
Belfast BT1 4QB
Tel: 0232 249141
Fax: 0232 236130
Homes in area: 136,000
Date awarded: 29 Nov 1983
Build start date: 1 Jun 1990

Birmingham/ Solihull
Franchise holder: Birmingham Cable
Ownership: US West, Comcast, Compagnie Générale des Eaux (see Group ownership), Standard Life Assurance
Homes in area: 465,000
Homes passed: 29,000
Date awarded: 19 Oct 1988
Service start date: Oct 1990

Black Country
Dudley, Sandwell, Walsall, Wolverhampton,

Data for this section has been kindly provided by Screen Digest from its data base, and compiled and presented for the Handbook by David Fisher, Editor of Screen Digest. We gratefully acknowledge the continuing support of Screen Digest in providing this information

urban parts of Bromsgrove, Cannock, Kidderminster
Franchise holder: West Midlands Cable Communications – Lightstream (see Group ownership)
Homes in area: 470,000
Date awarded: 14 Jul 1989
Build start date: Nov 1990

Bolton
Franchise holder: Bolton Cablevision – Pactel Cable UK (see Group ownership)
Homes in area: 135,000
Date awarded: Aug 1985

Bournemouth/Poole/Christchurch
Franchise holder: Bay Cable
1-9 Cotlands Road
Bournemouth
Dorset BH1 3RP
Tel: 0202 294346
Fax: 0202 299569
Ownership: Cross Country, Nynex (see Group ownership)
Homes in area: 130,000
Date awarded: 6 Apr 1990

Bradford
Franchise holder: General Cable
14 Headfort Place
London SW1X 7DH
Tel: 071 259 5244
Fax: 071 235 7206
Ownership: General Cable subsidiary of Compagnie Générale des Eaux (see Group ownership), Yorkshire Water
Homes in area: 175,000
Date awarded: 14 Jun 1990

Brighton/Hove/Worthing
Franchise holder: Southdown Cablevision
Ownership: Cross Country, Nynex (see Group ownership)
Homes in area: 135,000
Date awarded: 20 Oct 1989

Bromley, London Borough of
Franchise holder: Telecommunications Network
Ownership: Cross Country, Nynex (see Group ownership)
Homes in area: 117,000
Date awarded: 16 Mar 1990

Burton-on-Trent/Swadlincote/Ashby
Franchise holder: N-Com Cablevision of Burton
Ownership: N-Com Holding Corporation (see Group ownership)
Homes in area: 40,000
Date awarded: 21 Jun 1990

Bury/Rochdale
Franchise holder: Comment Cablevision Bury and Rochdale (see Group ownership)
Ownership: US Cable (51%), Nynex (49%)
Homes in area: 143,000
Date awarded: May 1990

Calderdale
Halifax, Brighouse
Franchise holder: Telecable of Calderdale – GB Cable (see Group ownership)
Homes in area: 75,000
Date awarded: 14 Jun 1990

Cambridge and district
Cambridge, Newmarket, Ely, Saffron Walden, Huntingdon, St Ives, St Neots, Royston etc
Franchise holder: Cambridge Cable
PO Box 182
Abbey Walk
Cambridge CB1 2QN
Tel: 0223 464201
Fax: 0223 467347
Ownership: Comcast Corporation, Kingston Communications (see Group ownership)
Homes in area: 134,000
Date awarded: 4 Jun 1989
Service start date: 1 Jan 1990

Camden, London Borough of
Franchise holder: Cable Camden – Cable London (see Group ownership)
Homes in area: 70,000
Homes passed: 4,500
Date awarded: 1 Feb 1986
Service start date: Dec 1989

Cardiff/Penarth
Franchise holder: Cardiff Cablevision
Ownership: Insight Communications (see Group ownership)
Homes in area: 103,000
Date awarded: 5 Feb 1986

Carlisle
Franchise holder: Carlisle Cablevision
Ownership: Broadcast Satellite Television (see Group ownership), Vento Cable
Homes in area: 30,000
Date awarded: 21 Jun 1990

Cheltenham/Gloucester
Franchise holder: United Artists Communications (Cotswolds) (see Group ownership)
Homes in area: 90,000
Date awarded: 13 Aug 1985

Cheshire, North
Chester, Ellesmere Port, Warrington, Widnes, Runcorn
Franchise holder: Cheshire Cable
Ownership: Maclean Hunter, Kingston Communications (see Group ownership)
Homes in area: 175,000
Date awarded: Jan 1990

Cheshire, North West
Warrington, Widnes, Runcorn
Franchise holder: Cheshire Cable – Maclean Hunter Cablevision (see Group ownership)
Homes in area: 175,000
Date awarded: 12 Jan 1990

Colchester/Ipswich/Felixstowe/Harwich/Woodbridge
Franchise holder: East Coast Cable
Britannia House
Factory Lane
Brantham
Manningtree
Essex CO11 1NH
Tel: 0206 396066
Fax: 0206 391448
Ownership: Maclean Hunter (see Group ownership), Kingston Communications
Homes in area: 126,000
Date awarded: 21 Jul 1989

Corby/Kettering/Market Harborough/Wellingborough
Franchise holder: Northampton Cable Television
Crest House
Crestwood Road
Northampton NN3 4JJ
Tel: 0604 494949
Fax: 0604 790289
Ownership: CUC UK (80%), Ron Dean (20%)
Homes in area: 90,000
Homes passed (upgrade within Franchise area): 20,000
Date awarded: 21 Jun 1990

Coventry
Franchise holder: Coventry Cable Television
Blackburn House
Whitley Village
London Road
Coventry CV3 4HL
Tel: 0203 505345
Fax: 0203 505445
Ownership: CUC Broadcasting (89.5%) (see Group ownership), Equity and Life Assurance Society (10.5%) (British Telecom sold 75.5% stake to CUC)
Homes in area: 119,000
Homes passed: 113,022 (1 Jan 1991 – build complete)
Subscribers: 14,197 – 12.6% (1 Jan 1991)
Date awarded: 1 Nov 1983
Service start date: 1 Sep 1985

Crawley/Horley/Gatwick
Franchise holder: Mid Downs Cable – Lightstream (see Group ownership)
Block C
Lloyds Court
Manor Royal
Crawley
West Sussex RH10 2PT
Tel: 0293 518070
Fax: 0293 517400
Ownership: Goldcrest Communications, Swedtel, HTV
Homes in area: 40,000
Date awarded: 27 Apr 1989

Croydon/Merton and Sutton/ Kingston and Richmond, London Boroughs of
Franchise holder: United Artists Communications (London South)
Communications House
5 Factory Lane
Croydon
Surrey CR9 3RA
Tel: 081 760 0222
Fax: 081 681 2340
Ownership: United Artists Entertainment (76.25%), US West (23.75%) (see Group ownership)
Homes in area: 373,000
Homes passed (1 Jan 1991):
Croydon 100,000
Merton & Sutton 22,537
Subscribers (1 Jan 1991):
Croydon 23,439 22.6%
Merton & Sutton 5,699 25.3%
Date awarded: Croydon 1 Nov 1983, others 6 May 1989
Service start date: Croydon 1 Sep 1984, Kingston & Richmond Oct 1990, Merton & Sutton May 1990

Cumbernauld/ Kilsyth/Airdrie/ Coatbridge
Franchise holder: Scotcable (see Group ownership)
Homes in area: 55,000
Date awarded: 27 Apr 1989

Darlington
Franchise holder: Britannia Cablevision Darlington (see Group ownership)
Homes in area: 34,000
Date awarded: 21 Jun 1990

Dartford/Swanley
Franchise holder: East London Telecommunications (see Group ownership)
Homes in area: 35,000
Date awarded: 16 Mar 1990

Derby/Spondon
Franchise holder: Derbyshire Cablevision – Pactel Cable UK (see Group ownership)
Homes in area: 85,000
Date awarded: 16 Feb 1990

Devon, South
Exeter, Plymouth, Torbay
Franchise holder: Devon Cablevision – Maclean Hunter (see Group ownership)
Suite 103
City Business Park
Somerset Place
Plymouth PL3 4BB
Tel: 0752 605884
Fax: 0752 605154
Homes in area: 236,000
Date awarded: 15 Dec 1989

Doncaster/ Rotherham
Franchise holder: South Yorkshire Cablevision – Pactel Cable UK (see Group ownership)
Homes in area: 192,000
Date awarded: 10 May 1990

Dorset, West
Dorchester, Weymouth, Portland
Franchise holder: Coastal Cablevision – Leonard Communication (see Group ownership)
Homes in area: 35,000
Date awarded: 10 Feb 1990
Build start date: Jan 1991

Dumbarton/Vale of Leven
Franchise holder: Scotcable (see Group ownership)
Homes in area: 18,000
Date awarded: 17 Apr 1989

Dundee/Monifieth/ Carnoustie
Franchise holder: Tayside Cable Systems (see Group ownership)
Homes in area: 81,000
Date awarded: 19 Jan 1990

Ealing, London Borough of
Franchise holder: Videotron Cable Communications (see Group ownership)
Homes in area: 105,000
Homes passed (Jan 1990): 20,000
Date awarded: 8 Nov 1983
Service start date: 1 Nov 1986

Edinburgh
Franchise holder: Cablevision (Scotland)
Homes in area: 183,000
Homes passed: 4,500
Date awarded: 5 Feb 1986

Enfield
Franchise holder: Cable Camden – Cable London (see Group ownership)
Homes in area: 105,000
Date awarded: 31 May 1990
Build start date: 1 Mar 1991

Epping Forest/ Chigwell/ Waltham Forest/ Loughton/Ongar
Franchise holder: East London Telecommunications (see Group ownership)
Homes in area: 45,000
Date awarded: 3 May 1990

Falkirk/West Lothian
Franchise holder: Scotcable (see Group ownership)
Homes in area: 30,000
Date awarded: 21 Jun 1990

Glamorgan, West
Swansea, Neath, Port Talbot
Franchise holder: Starvision Network – Cable & Satellite Television Holdings
Ownership: Starside Network (Glamorgan) – Starstream Europe (see Group ownership), Cast Services
Homes in area: 110,000
Homes passed: 2,000
Date awarded: 16 Nov 1989

Glasgow, Greater
Franchise holder: Clyde Cablevision (see Group ownership)
Homes in area: 274,000
Date awarded: 7 Jun 1990

Glasgow, Northwest/ Clydebank
Franchise holder: Clyde Cablevision (see Group ownership)
Homes in area: 112,000
Homes passed: 54,736 (1 Jan 1991)
Subscribers: 5,742 – 10.5% (1 Jan 1991)
Date awarded: 1 Nov 1983
Service start date: 1 Oct 1985

Glenrothes/ Kirkcaldy/Leven
Franchise holder: Kingdom Cablevision – Tayside Cable Systems (see Group ownership)
Homes in area: 60,000
Date awarded: 21 Jun 1990

Grantham
Franchise holder: Diamond Cable (see Group ownership)
Homes in area: 14,000
Date awarded: 26 Apr 1990

Great Yarmouth/ Lowestoft/Caister
Franchise holder: Broadland Cablevision – Pactel Cable UK (see Group ownership)
Homes in area: 64,000
Date awarded: 5 Jul 1990

Greater London East
Boroughs of Barking/Dagenham, Bexley, Redbridge
Franchise holder: East London Telecommunications (see Group ownership)
Homes in area: 229,000
Homes passed: 6,000
Date awarded: 15 Dec 1988
Build start date: 25 Jun 1990

Greenock/Port Glasgow/Gourock
Franchise holder: Clyde Cablevision (see Group ownership)
Homes in area: 32,000
Date awarded: 5 Jul 1990

Greenwich/ Lewisham, London Boroughs of
Franchise holder: Videotron Cable Communications (see Group ownership)
Homes in area: 175,000
Date awarded: 7 Apr 1989
Build start date: Nov 1990

Grimsby/Cleethorpes
Franchise holder: Alphavision Communications (see Group ownership)
Homes in area: 63,000
Date awarded: 5 Jul 1990
Build start date: Mar 1991

Guildford/West Surrey
Guildford, Aldershot, Farnborough, Camberley, Woking, Godalming
Franchise holder: Guildford and West Surrey Cablevision
170 Walnut Tree Close
Guildford
Surrey GU1 4RX
Tel: 0483 505200
Fax: 0483 579544
Ownership: Insight Communications (see Group ownership)
Homes in area: 22,000 + 115,000
Date awarded: 29 Nov 1983 + Aug 1985
Service start date: 1 Jul 1987

Hackney/Islington, London Boroughs of
Franchise holder: Cable Hackney and Islington – Cable London (see Group ownership)
Homes in area: 150,000
Date awarded: 13 Apr 1990
Build start date: 1 Mar 1991

Haringey, London Borough of
Franchise holder: Cable Haringey – Cable London (see Group ownership)
Homes in area: 80,000
Date awarded: Sep 1989
Build start date: Sep 1990

Harlow/Bishops Stortford/Stansted Airport
Franchise holder: Stort Valley Cable – IVS Cable Services (see Group ownership)
Homes in area: 43,000
Date awarded: 23 Mar 1990

Harrogate/Knaresborough
Franchise holder: Yorcan Communications
Homes in area: 27,000
Homes passed: 3,925 (jointly with York franchise)
Date awarded: Mar 1990

Harrow
Franchise holder: Telecable of Harrow
Ownership: GB Cable (see Group ownership), Telecable
Homes in area: 79,000
Date awarded: 24 May 1990

Havering, London Borough of
Franchise holder: East London Telecommunications (see Group ownership)
Homes in area: 90,000
Date awarded: Apr 1990

Haywards Heath/Burgess Hill
Franchise holder: N-Com Cablevision (see Group ownership)
Homes in area: 25,000
Date awarded: 5 Jul 1990

Hertford/Cheshunt/Ware/Lea Valley/Hoddesdon
Franchise holder: Cablevision Communications Company – English Cable Partners (see Group ownership)
Homes in area: 60,000
Date awarded: 31 May 1990

Hertfordshire, Central
Stevenage, Welwyn, Hatfield, Hitchin, Baldock, Letchworth
Franchise holder: Cablevision Communications Company – English Cable Partners (see Group ownership)
Homes in area: 100,000
Homes passed: 2,000
Date awarded: 3 Nov 1989

Hertfordshire, South
Watford, Chorleywood, Rickmansworth, Bushey, Radlett, Elstree, Borehamwood, Potters Bar
Franchise holder: Jones Cable Group (see Group ownership)
Homes in area: 95,000
Date awarded: 3 Nov 1989
Service start date: 1 Jan 1991

Hertfordshire, West
Harpenden, Hemel Hempstead, St Albans, Berkhamsted, Tring, Redbourne
Franchise holder: Herts Cable
Knoll House
Maylands Avenue
Hemel Hempstead
Hertfordshire HP2 7DE
Tel: 0442 231311
Fax: 0442 234892
Ownership: CUC Cablevision (see Group ownership), Ron Dean
Homes in area: 100,000
Homes passed: 6,000
Date awarded: 3 Nov 1989
Service start date: 1 Nov 1990

Hillingdon
Franchise holder: Middlesex Cable – Cable Corporation (see Group ownership)
Homes in area: 92,000
Date awarded: 24 May 1990
Build start date: 1 Mar 1990

Hinckley
Franchise holder: N-Com Cablevision of Hinckley (see Group ownership)
Homes in area: 20,000
Date awarded: 6 Apr 1990

Hounslow
Franchise holder: Middlesex Cable – Cable Corporation (see Group ownership)
Homes in area: 79,000
Date awarded: 24 May 1990

Huddersfield/Dewsbury
Franchise holder: Kirklees Communications – Insight Communications (see Group ownership)
Homes in area: 148,000
Date awarded: 14 Jun 1990

Isle of Thanet
see **Thanet, Isle of**

Jersey
Franchise holder: Jersey Cable – IVS Cable Services (see Group ownership)
PO Box 233
St Helier
Jersey JE4 8SZ
Channel Islands
Homes in area: 23,000
Homes passed: 12,000
Subscribers: 7,230 (end 1990)
Service start date: 1987

Kenilworth/Leamington Spa/Stratford-upon-Avon/Warwick
Franchise holder: Heartland Cablevision – CUC Cablevision (see Group ownership)
Homes in area: 50,000
Date awarded: 30 Mar 1990

Kensington/Chelsea, London Boroughs of
Franchise holder: Videotron Cable Comlmunications (see Group ownership)
Homes in area: 68,000
Homes passed: 7,000
Date awarded: 4 Feb 1988
Service start date: 1 Jun 1989

Kent, South East
Dover, Deal, Folkestone, Ashford
Franchise holder: North Downs Cable – Starside Network
The Old Pumping Station
Pluckley Road
Charing
near Ashford
Kent TN27 0AH
Tel: 023371 3939
Fax: 023371 3933
Ownership: Starstream Europe (see Group ownership)
Homes in area; 77,000
Date awarded: 3 May 1990
Build start date: Nov 1990

Lambeth/Southwark, London Boroughs of
Franchise holder: Videotron Cable Communications (see Group ownership)
Homes in area: 191,000
Date awarded: 6 Jul 1989

Lancashire, Central
Preston, Chorley, Leyland
Franchise holder: Cable Communications (Central Lancashire) – Oyston Cable Communications (see Group ownership)
Homes in area: 114,000
Date awarded: 5 Feb 1986
Build start date: Jan 1990

Lancashire, East
Blackburn, Accrington, Nelson, Colne, Rossendale Valley
Franchise holder: East Lancashire Cablevision
Ownership: Maclean Hunter Cablevision (see Group ownership), Kingston Communications, local shareholders
Homes in area: 168,000
Homes passed: 33,500
Date awarded: May 1988
Service start date: 30 Nov 1989
Service: 27 channels + 3 premium channels

Lancaster/ Morecambe
Franchise to be awarded
Homes in area: 40,000

Leeds
Franchise holder: Jones Cable Group (see Group ownership)
Homes in area: 289,000
Date awarded: Mar 1990

Leicester
Franchise holder: Leicester Communications (see Group ownership)
Homes in area: 147,000
Date awarded: 22 Sep 1989
Service start date: 1 Jan 1991

Lincoln
Franchise holder: Alphavision Communications (see Group ownership)
Homes in area: 30,000
Date awarded: 5 Jul 1990

Liverpool, North/Bootle/ Crosby
Franchise holder: Cable Communications (Liverpool) – Oyston Cable Communications (see Group ownership)
Homes in area: 100,000
Date awarded: 5 Jul 1990

Liverpool, South
Franchise holder: Cable Communications (Liverpool) – Oyston Cable Communications (see Group ownership)
Homes in area: 125,000
Date awarded: 29 Nov 1983
Build start date: 1 Jun 1990

London, North West
Boroughs of Barnet, Brent, Hammersmith and Fulham
Franchise holder: Videotron Cable Communications (see Group ownership)
Homes in area: 280,000
Date awarded: 19 Jan 1989

London
see also **Greater London East** and individual boroughs

Loughborough/ Shepshed
Franchise holder: Leicester Communications (see Group ownership)
Homes in area: 30,000
Date awarded: 9 Mar 1990
Service start date: 1 Jan 1991

Luton/Dunstable/ Leighton Buzzard
Franchise holder: Cablevision Bedfordshire – English Cable Partners (see Group ownership)
Homes in area: 104,000
Homes passed: 10,000
Date awarded: Jul 1986
Service start date: Mar 1990

Macclesfield/ Wilmslow
Franchise holder: Telecable of Macclesfield
Ownership: GB Cable, Telecable (see Group ownership)
Homes in area: 45,000
Date awarded: 11 Jul 1990

Manchester/ Salford
Franchise holder: Greater Manchester Cablevision – Pactel Cable UK (see Group ownership)
Homes in area: 363,000
Date awarded: 17 May 1990

Mansfield/Sutton/ Kirkby-in-Ashfield
Franchise holder: Diamond Cable (Mansfield) (see Group ownership)
Homes in area: 58,000
Date awarded: 3 Mar 1990

Melton Mowbray
Franchise holder: Diamond Cable (Melton Mowbray) (see Group ownership)
Homes in area: 30,000
Date awarded: 26 Apr 1990

Motherwell/East Kilbride/Hamilton/ Wishaw/Lanark
Franchise holder: Scotcable (see Group ownership)
Homes in area: 125,000
Date awarded: 27 Apr 1989

Newark on Trent
Franchise holder: Diamond Cable (Newark) (see Group ownership)
Homes in area: 18,000
Date awarded: 26 Apr 1990

Newham/Tower Hamlets, London Boroughs of
Franchise holder: East London Telecommunications (see Group ownership)
Homes in area: 127,000
Homes passed: 48,694 (1 Jan 1991)
Subscribers: 9,386 – 19.3% (1 Jan 1991)
Date awarded: 13 Aug 1985
Service start date: 1 Jan 1987

Newport/ Cwmbran/ Pontypool
Franchise holder: Newport Cablevision
Penhow Film Studio
Newport
Gwent NP6 3AD
Tel: 0633 400900
Fax: 0633 400990
Ownership: Insight Communications (see Group ownership), Dowden Communications (US)
Homes in area: 85,000
Date awarded: 11 Jul 1990

Northampton
Franchise holder: Northampton Cable Television – CUC Cablevision (see Group ownership)
Homes in area: 72,000
Homes passed: 20,000 (narrowband network within franchise area)
Subscribers: 16,000 on narrowband network
Date awarded: 19 Jan 1989
Service start date: 1988 on narrowband network
Build start date: 1 Nov 1990

Norwich
Franchise holder: Norwich Cablevision – Pactel Cable UK (see Group ownership)
Homes in area: 83,000
Date awarded: 21 Jul 1989
Service start date: 2 Apr 1990

Nottingham
Franchise holder: Diamond Cable (Nottingham) (see Group ownership)
Homes in area: 160,000
Homes passed: 25,000
Date awarded: 22 Sep 1989
Service start date: 10 Sep 1990

Nuneaton/ Bedworth/Rugby
Franchise holder: Heartland Cablevision – CUC Cablevision (see Group ownership)
Homes in area: 43,000
Date awarded: 6 Apr 1990

Oldham/Tameside
Franchise holder: Comment Cablevision Oldham and Tameside (see Group ownership)
Homes in area: 170,000
Date awarded: 17 May 1990

Oxford/Abingdon
Franchise holder: Oxford Cable
Ownership: IVS Cable Services (see Group ownership), Flextech
Homes in area: 55,000
Date awarded: 14 Jun 1990

Paisley/Renfrew
Franchise holder: Clyde Cablevision (see Group ownership)
Homes in area: 67,000
Date awarded: 7 Jun 1990

Perth/Scone
Franchise holder: Perth Cable Television
Arran Road
North Muirton
Perth PH1 3DZ
Tel: 0738 38794
Fax: 0738 36867
Ownership: Tayside Cable (see Group ownership)
Date awarded: 19 Jan 1990

Peterborough
Franchise holder: Peterborough Cablevision – Pactel Cable UK (see Group ownership)
Homes in area: 58,000
Date awarded: 21 Jul 1989
Service start date: May 1990

Portsmouth/Fareham/Gosport/Havant
Franchise holder: Britannia Cablesystems Solent (see Group ownership)
Homes in area: 150,000
Date awarded: 2 Feb 1990
Build start date: Dec 1990

Rugby
Franchise holder: Heartland Cablevision – CUC Cablevision (see Group ownership)
Homes in area: 24,000
Date awarded: 6 Apr 1990

St Helens/Knowsley
Franchise holder: Cable Communications (St Helens & Knowsley) – Oyston Cable Communications (see Group ownership)
Homes in area: 100,000
Date awarded: 5 Jul 1990

Salisbury
Franchise holder: Wessex Cable – IVS Cable Services (see Group ownership)
Homes in area: 15,000
Date awarded: 6 Apr 1990

Sheffield
Franchise holder: Sheffield Cable Media
Provincial House
Solly Street
Sheffield S1 4AB
Tel: 0742 701700
Fax: 0742 701274
Ownership: Flextech, Swedtel, Standard Life, Marconi
Homes in area: 210,000
Date awarded: 31 May 1990

Southampton/Eastleigh
Franchise holder: Videotron Cable Communications (see Group ownership)
Homes in area: 97,000
Homes passed: 37, 482 (1 Jan 1991)
Subscribers: 7,967 – 21.3% (1 Jan 1991)
Date awarded: 12 Sep 1986
Service start date: 1 Dec 1990

Stafford/Stone
Franchise holder: Stafford Communications – IVS Cable Services (see Group ownership)
Homes in area: 24,000
Date awarded: Dec 1989

Stockport
Franchise holder: TeleCable of Stockport
Ownership: GB Cable (see Group ownership), AT&C, Telecable
Homes in area: 113,000
Date awarded: 17 May 1990

Stoke-on-Trent/Newcastle-under-Lyne
Franchise holder: Staffordshire Cable
Ownership: Maclean Hunter (see Group ownership), Cable Systems Development, locals
Homes in area: 140,000
Date awarded: 1 Dec 1989

Surrey, North
Elmbridge, Runnymede
Franchise holder: Britannia Cablesystems (see Group ownership)
Homes in area: 71,000
Date awarded: 21 Jun 1990

Surrey, North East
Epsom, Mole Valley, Reigate, Redhill
Franchise holder: Britannia Cablesystems (see Group ownership)
Homes in area: 98,000
Date awarded: 21 Jun 1990

Swindon
Franchise holder: Swindon Cable – British Telecom Visual Communications
Homes in area: 75,000
Homes passed: 57,767 (1 Jan 1991)
Subscribers: 15,552 – 26.9% (1 Jan 1991)
Date awarded: 1 Nov 1983
Service start date: 1 Sep 1984

Tamworth
Franchise holder: N-Com Cablevision of Tamworth (see Group ownership)
Homes in area: 25,000
Date awarded: 6 Apr 1990

Teesside
Middlesbrough, Stockton, Hartlepool
Franchise holder: Britannia Cablesystems Teesside (see Group ownership)
Homes in area: 170,000
Date awarded: 5 Jul 1990

Telford
Franchise holder: Telford Telecommunications – Lightstream (see Group ownership)
Homes in area: 50,000
Date awarded: 26 Apr 1990
Build start date: Dec 1990

Thames Estuary North
Southend, Basildon, Brentwood, Chelmsford
Franchise holder: North Estuary Cable – United Artists International (see Group ownership)
Homes in area: 300,000
Date awarded: 16 Nov 1988

Thames Estuary South
Gravesend, Chatham, Rochester, Gillingham, Maidstone, Sittingbourne
Franchise holder: South Estuary Cable – United Artists International (see Group ownership)
Homes in area: 145,000
Date awarded: 16 Nov 1988

Thames Valley
Reading, Twyford, Henley-on-Thames, Wokingham, High Wycombe, Marlow, Bracknell, Basingstoke, Newbury, Thatcham
Franchise holder: Cable Thames Valley – CUC Cablevision (see Group ownership)
Homes in area: 215,000
Date awarded: 2 Dec 1988

Thamesmead
Franchise holder: Videotron Cable Communications (see Group ownership)
Homes in area: 11,000
Date awarded: 31 May 1990

Thanet, Isle of
Margate, Ramsgate, Broadstairs
Franchise holder: Coastal Cablevision – Leonard Communications (see Group ownership)
Homes in area: 51,000
Date awarded: 16 Feb 1990

Tyneside
Newcastle upon Tyne, Gateshead, North and South Tyneside
Franchise holder: Comment Cablevision (see Group ownership)
Homes in area: 325,000
Date awarded: 14 Dec 1989
Build start date: Sep 1990

Wakefield/Pontefract/Castleford
Franchise holder: Wakefield Cable – Maclean Hunter

Cablevision (see Group ownership)
Homes in area: 94,000
Date awarded: 2 Mar 1990

Waltham Forest, London Borough of
Franchise holder: East London Telecommunications (see Group ownership)
Homes in area: 83,000
Date awarded: 28 Sep 1989

Wandsworth, London Borough of
Franchise holder: Videotron Cable Communications
Homes in area: 100,000
Date awarded: 13 Aug 1985

Wearside
Sunderland/Durham/Washington
Franchise holder: Comment Cablevision Wearside (see Group ownership)
Homes in area: 200,000
Date awarded: 14 Jun 1990

Westminster, London Borough of
Franchise holder: Westminster Cable Television
87-89 Baker Street
London W1M 1AG
Tel: 071 935 6699
Fax: 071 486 9447
Ownership: Strogino (45%), Sanoma (Finland)
Homes in area: 107,000
Homes passed: 51,625 (1 Jan 1991)
Subscribers: 11,525 – 22.3% (1 Jan 1991)
Date awarded: 1 Nov 1983
Service start date: 29 Nov 1985

Wigan
Franchise holder: Cable Communications (Wigan) – Oyston Cable Communications (see Group ownership)
Homes in area: 110,000
Date awarded: 17 May 1990

Winchester
Franchise holder: Videotron Cable Communications
Homes in area: 33,000
Date awarded: 6 Apr 1990
Build start date: 1 Sep 1991

Windsor/Slough/Maidenhead/Ashford/Staines/Stanwell/Heathrow
Franchise holder: Windsor Television
Ownership: Cable Corporation (see Group ownership), CIN Industrial Investments, McNicholas Construction
Homes in area: 110,000
Homes passed: 85,094 (1 Jan 1991)
Subscribers: 13,991 – 16.4% (1 Jan 1991)
Date awarded: 1 Nov 1983
Service start date: 1 Dec 1985

Wirral, The
Franchise holder: Britannia Cablesystems Wirral (see Group ownership)
Homes in area: 120,000
Date awarded: 11 Jul 1990

Wisbech/March/Whittlesey
Franchise holder: Fenland Cablevision – Pactel Cable UK (see Group ownership)
Homes in area: 21,000
Date awarded: 5 Jul 1990

Worcester/Redditch/Droitwich
Franchise holder: Comment Cablevision Worcester (see Group ownership)
Homes in area: 70,000
Date awarded: 14 Jun 1990

York
Franchise holder: Yorcan Communications (see Group ownership)
Homes in area: 47,500
Homes passed: 3,925 (jointly with Harrogate franchise)
Date awarded: 30 Mar 1990
Service start date: 1 Jan 1991

UPGRADE CABLE SYSTEMS

Cable networks which pre-existed the franchise era and usually operate on a limited basis on old installations. These services are gradually being phased out as full franchise network construction proceeds. Because a number are in groups, systems are listed in alphabetical order of ownership
HP – homes passed

A Thomson (Relay)
27 Auld Lea Road
Beith
Ayrshire
Tel: 0505 52118
Areas:
Beith HP 1,700
Dalry HP 900
Kilbirnie HP 1,700
Lochwinnoch HP 400

Bracknell Cable Television
John Scott House
Market Street
Bracknell
Berkshire RG12 1JB
Tel: 0344 424018
Fax: 0344 487564
Ownership: CUC Broadcasting (see Group ownership)
Area:
Bracknell

British Telecom Visual and Broadcast Services
Areas: (total HP 71,360):
Bracknell
Irvine
London (Barbican)
Milton Keynes
Washington

Broadcast Satellite Television
Areas (as Multichannel Television, Northern Region):
Barrow in Furness HP 18,360
Billingham/Teesside/Hartlepool HP 27,752
Birkenhead and Wirral HP 24,025
Burnley HP 18,360
Hull HP 73,040
Lancaster HP 6,936
Tyneside 23,427
(as Multichannel Television, Southern Region):
Brighton HP 21,705
Exeter HP 16,087
Mansfield HP 19,603
Norwich HP 7,120
Nottingham HP 71,976
Plymouth HP 21,000
Rotherham HP 18,102
Southampton HP 21,000
Stoke-on-Trent/Newcastle-u-Lyne HP 46,400
(as Gwent Cablevision):
Tredegar HP 5,200
(As Salford Cable Television):
Salford
(as Medway Cablevision/Sittingbourne Cablevision):
Sittingbourne

Cablecom Investments
c/o Granada Television Rentals
Ampthill
Bedford
Beds MK42 9QQ
Tel: 0234 55233
Areas:
Chicksands HP 800
Lakenheath HP 2,170
Mildenhall HP 950

Davis Cable TV
34a Church Street
Eastbourne
East Sussex BN21 1HS
Area:
East Dean (HP 1,000)

Harris of Saltcoats
104-106 Dockhead Street
Saltcoats
Strathclyde
Tel: 0294 63541
Areas:
Saltcoats HP 6,975
Largs HP 3,300

Maxwell Cable Television
3 Plough Place
London EC4A 1PD
Tel: 071 822 3115
Fax: 071 822 3836
Areas:
Ashford HP 11,000
Basildon HP 26,100
Bristol HP 47,000
Canterbury HP 11,000
Deal/Dover/Folkestone HP 23,000
Eastbourne HP 20,250
Guildford HP 2,236
Hastings HP 30,000
Heads of Valley HP 3,500
Leicester HP 7,654
Maidstone HP 15,000
Merthyr Tydfil HP 13,000
Newbridge/Bargoed HP 42,900
Oxford HP 8,100
Reading HP 14,600
Rhondda HP 35,000
Swansea HP 16,140

Thanet	HP 30,000
Welwyn Garden City/Hatfield	HP 13,100
West Wales	HP 9,200
Worcester	HP 9,964

Sky Cablevision
446 Stratford Road
Sparkhill
Birmingham
Tel: 021 773 6989
Area:
Sparkhill (HP 1,000)

Starvision Network
Ownership: Starstream Europe (see Group ownership)
Area:
Neath/Port Talbot (HP 28,000)

Teleline
3-5 High Street
Princes Risborough
Bucks HP1Y 0AE
Tel: 08444 3196
Area:
Princes Risborough/Wendover
Homes passed: 1,300
Subscribers: 530
Service start date: 1961

West Wales Aerials
97 Rhosman Street
Llandeilo
Dyfed SA19 6HA
Tel: 0558 823278
Area:
Llandeilo and district (HP 1,400)

GROUP OWNERSHIP

Almost all franchises are held as part of groups of holdings. This list identifies the companies and consortia with more than one franchise. In some cases precise composition of share ownership may vary slightly between franchises in a group, especially where local and/or founding directors and managers have retained equity stakes after major groups have taken over the franchise

Alphavision Communications
Franklyn Suite
The Priory
Syresham Gardens
Haywards Heath
West Sussex RH16 3LB
Tel: 0444 415735
Fax: 0444 458322
Ownership: Metro Mobile CTS (US cellular telephone operator), USA Cable Connections (US cable construction company)
Areas:
- Grimsby/Cleethorpes
- Lincoln

Bell Canada Enterprises
30% stake in partnership with Videotron in Videotron Corporation (qv)

Booth Management
see ***English Cable Partners***

Britannia Cablesystems
Capitol House
2-4 Church Street
Epsom
Surrey KT17 4NY
Tel: 0372 744050
Fax: 0372 744059
Ownership:
Mearing-Lynch Cable, Falcon Cable, First Carolina Communications; Camelot Cable (qv) minority in partnership with Nynex (qv)
Areas:
- Darlington
- Middlesbrough/etc
- Portsmouth/etc
- Surrey, North
- Surrey, North East
- The Wirral

British Telecom Visual and Broadcast Services
Room 26/20
Euston Tower
286 Euston Road
London NW1 3DG
Tel: 071 728 3405
Fax: 071 380 2635
Upgrades:
London (Barbican), Irvine, Martlesham Heath, Milton Keynes, Walderslade and Washington

Broadcast Satellite Television (BST)
303 King Street
Aberdeen AB2 3AP
Tel: 0224 646644
Ownership: Graham Duncan
Franchise areas:
Aberdeen Cable 59.5%; (in partnership with Vento Cable Management subsidiary of Vento & Co (US)):
Carlisle; see also Tayside Cable Systems;
Upgrades (see listing for areas)
(as Multichannel Television):
Northern region:
Reservoir Road
Slough Road
Hull
Humberside HU6 7QD
Tel: 0482 470805
Fax: 0482 470806
Southern region:
Unit G
Freeth Street
off Meadow Lane
Nottingham NG2 3GP
Tel: 0602 868989
Fax: 0602 868778
(as Gwent Cablevision):
88 Commercial Street
Tredegar
Gwent NP2 3DN
Tel: 0495 525600
Fax: 0495 717892
(as Salford Cable Television):
102 Mather Way
Salford M6 5JA
Tel: 061 737 9313
(as Medway Cablevision/ Sittingbourne Cablevision):
2-4 William Street
Sittingbourne
Kent ME10 1HR
Tel: 0795 429711
Fax: 0795 422807

Bruncor
(Canadian telecom operator of New Brunswick)
Minority stake in partnership with US Cable

CUC Cablevision (UK)
Link 2
Beaconsfield Plaza
Gillette Way
Reading RG2 0BS
Tel: 0734 756475
Ownership: wholly owned subsidiary of CUC, a Canadian multiple systems cable operator
Areas:
- Corby/Kettering/etc (80%)
- Coventry (89.5%)
- Northampton
- Swindon
- Thames Valley

(as Heartland Cablevision):
- Nuneaton/Bedworth
- Rugby
- Stratford on Avon/etc

(as Herts Cable):
- Hertfordshire, West (80%)

Upgrades: Bracknell

Cable Corporation
Cable House
Waterside Drive
Langley
Berkshire SL3 6EZ
Tel: 0753 44144
Fax: 0753 49310
Ownership: Compagnie Générale des Eaux (30.9%); Standard Life (22.6%); US West (16.9%); Investors in Industry, Drayton Consolidated Trust, McNicholas Construction
Areas:
- Hillingdon
- Hounslow
- Windsor/Slough/ Maidenhead
- Birmingham (small minority stake)

Cable London
Centro House
20-23 Mandela Street
London NW1 0DU
Tel: 071 911 0911
Fax: 071 911 0111
Ownership: Comcast (qv) (37.4%), US West (qv) (37.4%), Rosehaugh, Mercury Communications, McNicholas Construction, Logica UK, 3i
Areas:
- Camden LB
- Enfield
- Hackney/Islington LBs
- Haringey LB

Camelot Cable
Shackleton House
4 Battle Bridge Lane
London SE1 2HR
Tel: 071 403 8786
Ownership: Paul Kagan
Small shareholding in Britannia Cablesystems (qv)

Clyde Cablevision
40 Anderston Quay
Glasgow G3 8DA
Tel: 041 221 7040
Fax: 041 248 2921
Ownership: Insight Communications (qv) (95%), GEC, Cable and Wireless, 3i
Areas:
- Bearsden/Milngavie
- Glasgow Greater

Glasgow North West/Clydebank
Greenock/Port Glasgow/Gourock

Comcast Corporation
Centro House
Mandela Street
London NW1 0DU
Tel: 071 528 0555
Ownership: Comcast Corporation (US)
Areas:
Cambridge/Ely/ Newmarket
with US West:
Birmingham/Solihull
Enfield
Also 37.4% stake in Cable London (qv)

Comment Cablevision
Gibson House
Holly Hill
Felling
Gateshead
Tyne & Wear
WE10 9NQ
Tel: 091 469 8800
Fax: 091 469 1491
Ownership: US Cable (qv)
Areas:
(51%, with Nynex (qv) 49%):
Bury/Rochdale
Oldham/Tameside
Tyneside
(with Bruncor):
Wearside
Worcester

Compagnie Générale des Eaux (CGE)
(French utilities company)
Parent of General Cable; stake in Cable Corporation (qv) 30.9%

Cross Country Cable
4 Cavendish Street
Brighton
East Sussex BN2 1RN
Tel: 0273 606702
Fax: 0273 679962
Ownership: Cross Country Cable (US)
Areas:
51% in partnership with Nynex:
Bournemouth/ Poole/etc
Brighton/Hove/ Worthing
Bromley LB

Diamond Cable
Regency House
2a Sherwood Rise
Nottingham NG7 6JN
Tel: 0602 503021
Fax: 0602 605111
Areas:
Grantham
Mansfield/etc
Melton Mowbray
Newark-on-Trent
Nottingham

East London Telecommunications (ELT)
2 Millharbour
London E14 9TE
Tel: 071 895 9910
Fax: 071 895 9755
Ownership: Jones Cable Group (qv) (45%), Pacific Telesis (qv) (45%), Mercury Communications, 3i, GEC, Prudential Assurance, Robert Fleming Mercantile Investment Trust, Electricity Council Pension Fund, Ferranti International
Areas:
Dartford/Swanley
Epping Forest LB/etc
Havering LB
Greater London East
Newham/Tower Hamlets LBs
Waltham Forest LB

English Cable Partners
Ownership: English Cable Partners (US) (55%); Booth Management (US) (25%); managed by Columbia Management
Areas:
Bedford
Hertford/etc
Hertfordshire, Central
Lea Valley
Luton/South Bedfordshire

GB Cable
Bullin Court Business Centre
Sunderland Street
Macclesfield
Cheshire SK11 6JE
Tel: 0625 428185
Fax: 0625 614202
Areas:
Calderdale
Harrow
Macclesfield/ Wilmslow
Stockport

Insight Communications
Areas:
(as Cardiff Cablevision):
Cardiff/Penarth
(as Clyde Cablevision, qv):
Bearsden/Milngavie
Glasgow Greater
Glasgow North West/Clydebank
Inverclyde
Paisley/Renfrew
(as Guildford and West Surrey Cablevision):
Guildford/West Surrey
(as Kirklees Cable):
Huddersfield/ Dewsbury
(as Newport Cablevision):
Newport/Cwmbran/ Pontypool

IVS Cable Holdings
284 Weyhill Road
Andover
Hampshire SP10 3LS
Tel: 0264 334607
Fax: 0264 332071
Areas:
Andover
Harlow/etc
Jersey
Oxford
Salisbury
Sheffield
Stafford/Stone

Jones Cable Group
PO Box 448
Watford WD1 8QT
Tel: 0923 211440
Fax: 0923 211335
Ownership: Jones Intercable (US)
Areas:
Aylesbury/etc
Hertfordshire, South
Leeds
Also 45% partner in East London Telecommunications (qv)

Kingston Communications (Hull)
Small stake in Cambridge, Maclean Hunter and Diamond Cable franchises

Leicester Communications
12 Elstree Way
Borehamwood
Hertfordshire WD6 1NF
Tel: 081 207 5232
Ownership: Community Communications (46%), Kingston Communications (18%), Leicester CC (7%), Radio Trent (8%), Q Studios (8%), Morgan Grenfell (8%), Alliance & Leicester Building Society (5%)
Areas:
Leicester
Loughborough/ Shepshed

Leonard Communications
4-5 King Street
Weymouth
Dorset DT4 7BH
Tel: 0305 776543
Fax: 0305 760985
Ownership: Leonard Communications International Management
Areas (as Coastal Cablevision):
Dorset, West
Isle of Thanet

Lightstream
44 Church Street
Oldbury
Warley
West Midlands B69 3AE
Tel: 021 544 8244
Fax: 021 544 4057
Ownership: Goldcrest Group, Centreway Trust, RM Douglas Construction
Areas:
Black Country
Crawley/Horley/ Gatwick
Telford

Maclean Hunter Cablevision
Glenfield Park Site 2
Northrop Avenue
Blackburn
Lancashire BB1 5QG
Tel: 0254 680094
Fax: 0254 679236
Ownership: Maclean Hunter Cable TV (Canada)
Areas:
Cheshire, North
Cheshire, North West
Colchester/ Ipswich/etc
Devon, South
Lancashire, East
Stoke-on-Trent/ Newcastle
Wakefield/etc

MTA Cable
Ownership: Malarkey Taylor Associates
Minority stake in partnership with IVS Cable Holdings (qv)

N-Com Cablevision
c/o Swedtel
71 Church Road
Hove
East Sussex BN3 2BB
Tel: 0273 746622

Fax: 0273 746969
Ownership: N-Com Limited Partnership (US)
Areas:
Burton on Trent/Swadlincote/Ashby
Haywards Heath/Burgess Hill/Hinckley
Tamworth

Nynex Corporation
Seaco House
20 Upper Ground
London SE1
Tel: 071 620 0663
Ownership: Nynex Corporation (US)
Areas: majority holding in Britannia Cablesystems (qv); also 49% in partnership with Cross Country Cable and 49% in partnership with US Cable (qqv)

Oyston Cable Communications
Operating as Cable Communications
Ribble View
Frenchwood Avenue
Preston
Lancashire PR1 4QF
Tel: 0772 202888
Ownership: Southwestern Bell (80%), Owen Oyston (17%)
Areas:
Barnsley
Lancashire Central
Wigan
Century Building
Atlantic Way
Brunswick Business Park
Liverpool L3 4BL
Tel: 051 708 0280
Fax: 051 708 0263
Areas:
Liverpool North/Bootle/Crosby
Liverpool South
St Helens/Knowsley

Pactel Cable UK
41-46 Piccadilly
London W1V 9AJ
Tel: 071 287 3760
Ownership: Pacific Telesis Group (California telecom operator)
28 Queensbrook
Bolton Technology Centre
Spa Road
Bolton BL1 4AY
Tel: 0204 365440
Fax: 0204 365417
Areas:
Bolton
Derby/Spondon
Manchester/Salford/etc
29 Metro Centre
Shrewsbury Avenue
Peterborough PE4 0BX
Tel: 0733 230303
Fax: 0733 238405
Areas:
Doncaster/Rotherham (96%)
Peterborough
32a Whiffler Road
Norwich NR3 2AZ
Tel: 0603 787892
Fax: 0603 787851
Areas:
Fenland
Great Yarmouth/etc (Broadland)
Norwich
Also 45% partner with Jones Cable Group in East London Telecommunications (qv)

Scotcable
24a Lenziemill Road
Cumbernauld
Strathclyde G67 2RL
Tel: 0236 447007
Fax: 0236 736832
Areas:
Cumbernauld/etc
Dumbarton/Vale of Leven
Falkirk/West Lothian
Motherwell/etc

Southwestern Bell
(US telecom operator)
Majority shareholder in Oyston Cable Communications (qv)

Starstream Europe
6 Prince Albert Road
London NW1 7SR
Tel: 071 284 0432
Ownership: Starstream Communications
Area:
Kent South East;
(as Starvision Network):
Network House
Baglan Industrial Park
Baglan
Port Talbot SA12 7DJ
Tel: 0639 891111
Fax: 0639 891110
Area:
Glamorgan West;
Upgrades: Neath/Port Talbot

TA Associates
Financial backer for N-Com Cablevision (qv)

Tayside Cable Systems
26 East Dock Street
Dundee
Tel: 0382 25875
Fax: 0382 25882
Ownership: Graham Duncan of Broadcast Satellite Television (qv), Vento Cable Management, Washington Post
Areas:
Dundee/Monifieth/Carnoustie
Glenrothes/etc
Perth/Scone

TeleCable
Sun Alliance House
9 Bond Court
Leeds LS1 2SN
Tel: 0800 777421
Ownership: wholly owned subsidiary of Telecable Corporation (US)
Areas:
Calderdale
Harrow
Macclesfield/Wilmslow
Stockport

United Artists Cable TV International
Unit 1, Genesis Business Park
Albert Drive
Woking
Surrey GU21 5RW
Tel: 0483 750900
Fax: 0483 750901
Areas:
Cheltenham/Gloucester
Thames Estuary North
Thames Estuary South
(as 76.25% partner with US West):
Avon
Croydon LB
Edinburgh
Kingston/Richmond LBs
Merton/Sutton LBs

US Cable Corporation
Areas:
(as 51% partner with Nynex):
Bury/Rochdale
Oldham/Tameside;
(as partner with Bruncor):
Wearside (51%)
Worcester/etc (74%);
(as 74% partner with US West):
Tyneside

US West
16.9% share in Cable Corporation; 37.4% in partnership with Comcast Corporation and others in Cable London; 23.75% in partnership with United Artists; 25% in partnership with US Cable (qqv)

Videotron Cable Communications
Ownership: Videotron of Canada (61%), Bell Canada Enterprises (30%)
West London division:
Parkways
179-181 The Vale
London W3 7QS
Tel: 081 740 4848
Fax: 081 740 4583
Areas:
Ealing LB
Kensington/Chelsea LB
London, North West
South London division:
Belmont House
11-29 Belmont Hill
London SE13 5AU
Tel: 081 852 0123
Fax: 081 852 2232
Areas:
Greenwich/Lewisham LBs
Lambeth/Southwark LBs
Thamesmead
Wandsworth LB
Southern division:
Ocean House
West Quay Road
Southampton SO1 0XL
Tel: 0703 333020
Fax: 0703 335237
Areas:
Southampton/Eastleigh
Winchester

Washington Post Company
Partner in Vento Cable Management (see Broadcast Satellite Television and Tayside Cable Systems)

Yorcan Communications
Viking House
Lysander Close
York YO3 8XB
Tel: 0904 691415
Fax: 0904 690554
Areas:
Harrogate/Knaresborough (91%)
York (91%)

ENGLISH-LANGUAGE SATELLITE-DELIVERED TELEVISION CHANNELS IN EUROPE

All channels transmitting via

satellite in Europe, wholly or partly in the English language. The television standard and encrypting system used are indicated after the name of the satellite. Not all channels are intended for reception in the UK

AFRTS Germany HQ USAFE/PAI
6720 Flugplatz Ramstein
Germany
Ownership: US Government
Satellites: Intelsat VB F15/V F2/V F7 (all B-MAC/MAC, digital audio)
Programming: entertainment

BBC World Service Television
Woodlands
80 Wood Lane
London W12 0TT
Tel: 081 576 2248
Ownership: BBC Enterprises
Satellite: Intelsat VI F4 (PAL/Save)
Programming: entertainment

Bravo
Twyman House
16 Bonny Street
London NW1 9PG
Tel: 071 482 4824
Ownership: United Artists International
Satellite: Intelsat VI F4 (PAL/clear)
Programming: films and classic tv

British Sky Broadcasting (BSkyB)
6 Centaurs Business Park
Grant Way
Syon Lane
Isleworth
Middlesex TW7 5QD
Tel: 081 782 3000
Ownership: News International (48%), Pearson (15%), Chargeurs (15%), Granada Group (11%), Reed International (4%)
See The Movie Channel, Sky Movies Plus, Sky News, Sky One, Sky Sports

CNN International
19-22 Rathbone Place
London W1P 1DF
Tel: 071 637 6700
Ownership: Turner Broadcasting System
Satellite: Intelsat VI F4 (PAL/clear)
Programming: news

Channel E
European Institute for the Media
The University
Manchester M13 9PL
Tel: 061 273 2754
Ownership: VNU, EIM, SES, European Commission, IFCBEBF
Satellite: Astra 1A (PAL/clear)
Programming: education

Children's Channel
9-13 Grape Street
London WC2H 8DR
Tel: 071 240 3422
Ownership: Starstream – Flextech (66.7%), D C Thomson (24.9%), Thames TV (8.2%)
Satellites: Astra 1A, Intelsat, VI F4 (PAL/clear)
Programming: children's

Discovery Channel
Twyman House
16 Bonny Street
London NW1 9PG
Tel: 071 482 4824
Ownership: United Artists International
Satellite: Intelsat VI F4 (PAL/clear)
Programming: documentaries

Eurosport
6 Centaurs Business Park
Grant Way
Isleworth
Middlesex TW7 5QD
Tel: 081 782 3000
Ownership: 14 EBU members and TF1
Satellites: Astra 1A, Eutelsat II F1, DFS-1 Kopernikus (PAL/clear)
Programming: sport

Eurostep
Rapenburg 63
2311 GJ Leiden
Netherlands
Ownership: educational institutions in several countries
Satellite: Olympus 1 (D2-MAC/clear)
Programming: education

Lifestyle
180 Wardour Street
London W1V 8AA
Tel: 071 439 1177
Ownership: W H Smith (74.8%), D C Thomson (20.8%), TVS (2.5%), Yorkshire TV (1.9%)
Satellite: Astra 1A (PAL/clear)
Programming: women's

MTV Europe
20-23 Mandela Street
London NW1 0DU
Tel: 071 383 4250
Ownership: Mirror Group Newspapers (50%), Viacom (50%)
Satellite: Astra 1A (PAL/clear)
Programming: music

The Movie Channel
Ownership: British Sky Broadcasting (qv)
Satellites: Astra 1A (PAL/Videocrypt), Marcopolo-1 (D-MAC/Eurocypher)
Programming: films

One World Channel
93 Wardour Street
London W1V 3TE
Tel: 071 494 2083
Ownership: Development Aid from People to People, Humana
Satellite: Eutelsat I F4 (PAL/clear)
Programming: religion

SIS
17 Corsham Street
London N1 6DR
Tel: 071 253 2232
Ownership: Racal (20%), Ladbroke (18%), Brent Walker (15%), Sears (13%), Bass (12%), RAL (10%), MAI (7%), Tote (5%)
Satellite: Intelsat VI F4 (B-MAC/B-MAC)
Programming: horse racing

Screensport
180 Wardour Street
London W1V 8AA
Tel: 071 439 1177
Ownership: W H Smith (75%), ESPN (25%)
Satellite: Astra 1A (PAL/clear)
Programming: sport

Sky Movies Plus
Ownership: British Sky Broadcasting (qv)
Satellites: Astra 1A (PAL/Videocrypt), Marcopolo-1 (D-MAC/Eurocypher)
Programming: films

Sky News
Ownership: British Sky Broadcasting (qv)
Satellites: Astra 1A (PAL/clear), Marcopolo-1 (D-MAC/Eurocypher)
Programming: news

Sky One
Ownership: British Sky Broadcasting (qv)
Satellites: Astra 1A (PAL/clear), Marcopolo-1 (D-MAC/Eurocypher)
Programming: entertainment

Sky Sports
Ownership: British Sky Broadcasting (qv)
Satellites: Astra 1B (PAL/Videocrypt), Marcopolo-1 (D-MAC/Eurocypher)
Programming: sports

Super Channel
Melrose House
14 Lanark Square
Limeharbour
London E14 9QD
Tel: 071 418 9418
Ownership: Beta Television (58%), Virgin (42%)
Satellite: Eutelsat II F1 (PAL/clear)
Programming: entertainment

Worldnet
US Information Agency
American Embassy
24 Grosvenor Square
London W1A 1AE
Tel: 071 499 9000
Ownership: US Government
Satellite: Eutelsat II F1 (PAL/clear)
Programming: news

CINEMAS

Listed below are the companies who control the major chains of cinemas and multiplexes in the UK, followed by the cinemas themselves listed by area, with seating capacities. The listing includes disabled access information for the London area and BFI-supported cinemas, together with limited information on cinemas nationwide. We hope to extend this in the next edition of the Handbook. The assistance of the organisations who helped compile this information is gratefully acknowledged (see the key at the end of the section for details)

CINEMA CIRCUITS

Apollo Cinemas
Apollo Leisure (UK)
11 Arkwright Office Suite
Mill Lane
Coppull
Lancs PR7 5AN
Tel: 0257 471012
Now includes the Unit Four circuit and operates 49 screens on 16 sites. Apollo's Theatre Division operates the Dominion, London, and Futurist, Scarborough, which occasionally show films

CAC Leisure
PO Box 21
23-25 Huntly Street
Inverness IV1 1LA
Tel: 0463 237611
Operates 19 screens on 9 sites, all in Scotland

Metro Goldwyn Mayer Cinemas
76 Hammersmith Road
London W14 8YR
Tel: 071 603 4555
Operated 396 screens on 134 sites in May 1991

National Amusements (UK)
200 Elm Street
Dedham
Massachusetts
02026-9126
USA
Tel: 0101 617 461 1600
Operators of seven Showcase multiplexes with 85 screens, with a new 12-screen multiplex announced for Coventry

Panton Films
Coronet Cinema
Notting Hill Gate
London W11
Tel: 071 221 0123
Operates the Coronet circuit of 11 screens on 5 sites, comprising former circuit cinemas of Rank and Cannon

Rank Theatres
439-445 Godstone Road
Whyteleafe
Surrey CR3 0YG
Tel: 0883 623355
Operates the Odeon chain totalling 270 screens on 76 sites in May 1991, with many additional screens under construction

Robins Cinemas
13 New Row
London WC2N 4LF
Tel: 071 497 3320
Operates 12 screens at 9 locations in May 1991 including The Prince Charles in the West End

Tatton Group
Davenport Theatre
Buxton Road
Stockport
Greater Manchester
Tel: 061 483 3801
Operates 8 screens on 4 sites in the Manchester area

UCI (UK)
Parkside House
51-53 Brick Street
London W1Y 7DU
Tel: 071 409 1346
Formerly CIC/UA. Operators of 19 purpose-built multiplexes with 181 screens in spring 1991, with 3 more scheduled to open shortly

Warner Bros Theatres (UK)
135 Wardour Street
London W1V 4AP
Tel: 071 437 5600
In addition to the 5-screen Warner West End in Leicester Square, operated 5 multiplexes with 48 screens at Bury, Newcastle, York, Basingstoke and West Thurrock in spring 1991, with at least 5 more to follow

LONDON WEST END – PREMIERE RUN

Astral
Brewer Street
Tel: 071 734 6387
Seats: 1:89, 2:159

Barbican ♿
Silk Street
Tel: 071 638 8891/638 4141
Seats: 1:288, 2:255

Camden Parkway
Parkway
Tel: 071 267 7034

Seats: Kings: 946, Regency: 90

Camden Plaza ♿
Camden High Street
Tel: 071 485 2443
Seats: 340

Cannon Baker Street
Marylebone Road
Tel: 071 935 9772
Seats: 1:171, 2:169

Cannon Chelsea
King's Road
Tel: 071 352 5096/351 1026
Seats: 1:233, 2:264, 3:151, 4:119

Cannon Fulham Road
Tel: 071 370 0265/2636/2110
Seats: 1:416 ♿ 2:374 ♿ 3:223 ♿ 4:223 ♿ 5:222

Cannon Haymarket
Tel: 071 839 1527/1528
Seats: 1:448, 2:200, 3:201

Cannon Oxford Street
Tel: 071 636 0310/3851
Seats: 1:334, 2:227, 3:195, 4:225, 5:47

Cannon Panton Street
Tel: 071 930 0631/2
Seats: 1:127 ♿ 2:144 ♿ 3:138, 4:136

Cannon Piccadilly Circus
Tel: 071 437 3561
Seats: 1:124, 2:118

Cannon Premiere
Swiss Centre
Tel: 071 439 4470/437 2096
Seats: 1:97, 2:101, 3:93, 4:108

Cannon Shaftesbury Avenue
Tel: 071 836 6279/379 7025
Seats: 1:616, 2:581

Cannon Tottenham Court Road
Tel: 071 636 6148/6749
Seats: 1:328, 2:145, 3:137

Cannon Trocadero
Trocadero Centre
Piccadilly Circus
Seats: 1,300 (7 screens)

Centre Charles Peguy ♿ ⋆
Leicester Square
Tel: 071 437 8339
Seats: 100

Chelsea Cinema
King's Road
Tel: 071 351 3742
Seats: 713

Coronet
Notting Hill Gate
Tel: 071 727 6705
Seats: 396

Curzon Mayfair
Curzon Street
Tel: 071 499 3737/465 8865
Seats: 542

Curzon Phoenix
Phoenix Street
Tel: 071 240 9661
Seats: 212

Curzon West End
Shaftesbury Avenue
Tel: 071 439 4805
Seats: 624

Design Museum ♿ ⋆
Butler's Wharf, Shad Thames
Tel: 071 403 6933
Seats: 70

Dominion ♿ ⋆
Tottenham Court Road
Tel: 071 580 9562/3
Seats: 2,000

Electric ♿
Portobello Road
Tel: 071 792 2020
Seats: 437

Empire Leicester Square
Tel: 071 497 9999/437 1234
Seats: 1:1,330 ♿ 2:353, 3:80

French Institute ⋆
Queensberry Place SW7
Tel: 071 589 6211
Seats: 350

Gate ♿
Notting Hill Gate
Tel: 071 727 4043
Seats: 241

Goethe Institute ⋆
Princes Gate SW7
Tel: 071 581 3344
Seats: 170

bfi ***ICA Cinema*** ♿
The Mall
Tel: 071 930 0493
Seats: 208, C'thèque: 50

Imperial War Museum ♿ ⋆
Lambeth Road
Tel: 071 735 8922
Seats: 216

bfi ***London Film Makers' Co-op*** ⋆
Gloucester Avenue NW1
Tel: 071 586 8516
Seats: 100

Lumière ♿
St Martin's Lane
Tel: 071 836 0691/379 3014
Seats: 737

Metro ♿
Rupert Street
Tel: 071 437 0757
Seats: 1:195, 2:85

Minema
Knightsbridge
Tel: 071 235 4225
Seats: 68

Museum of London ♿ ⋆
London Wall EC2
Tel: 071 600 3699/1058
Seats: 270

bfi ***National Film Theatre/ Museum of the Moving Image*** ♿ ☑
South Bank, Waterloo
Tel: 071 928 3232
Seats: 1:466, 2:162, MOMI:130

Odeon Haymarket ♿ ☑
Tel: 071 839 7697
Seats: 600

Odeon High Street Kensington
Tel: 071 602 6644/5
Seats: 1:657, 2:301 ♿ 3:193 ♿ 4:234 ♿

Odeon Leicester Square
Tel: 071 930 6111/4250/4259
Seats: 1,965 ♿
Mezzanine: 291 (5 screens)

Odeon Marble Arch ☑
Tel: 0426 914501
Seats: 1,360

Odeon Swiss Cottage
Finchley Road
Tel: 0426 914098
Seats: 1:736, 2:152 ♿ 3:155 ♿

Odeon West End
Leicester Square
Tel: 071 930 5252/3
Seats: 1:830, 2:450 (approx)

Plaza Piccadilly Circus
Lower Regent Street
Tel: 071 497 9999/437 1234
Seats: 1:732, 2:367 ♿ 3:161, 4:187

Prince Charles ♿
Leicester Place
Tel: 071 437 8181
Seats: 487

Queen Elizabeth Hall ♿ ⋆
South Bank, Waterloo
Tel: 071 928 3002
Seats: 906

Renoir
Brunswick Square
Tel: 071 837 8402
Seats: 1:251, 2:251

Royal Festival Hall ♿ ⋆
South Bank, Waterloo
Tel: 071 928 3002
Seats: 2,419

Scala Kings Cross
Pentonville Road
Tel: 071 278 8052/0051
Seats: 350

Screen on Baker Street
Tel: 071 935 2772
Seats: 1:95, 2:100

Screen on Islington Green ♿
Upper Street
Tel: 071 226 3520
Seats: 300

Screen on the Hill
Haverstock Hill
Tel: 071 435 3366/9787
Seats: 339

UCI Whiteleys 8 ♿
Queensway, Bayswater
Tel: 071 792 3332/3303
Seats: 1:333, 2:281, 3:196, 4:178, 5:154, 6:138, 7:147, 8:125

Warner West End
Leicester Square
Tel: 071 439 0791
Seats: 1:132, 2:890, 3:246, 4:434, 5:105

OUTER LONDON

Barking
Odeon Longbridge Road
Tel: 0426 910596
Seats: 1:806, 2:83, 3:131 ♿ 4:130, 5:132, 6:162

Barnet
Odeon Great North Road
Tel: 0426 911167
Seats: 1:543, 2:140 ♿ 3:140 ♿

Battersea
Arts Centre Old Town Hall Lavender Hill ♿ ★
Tel: 071 223 2223
Seats: 180

Beckenham
Cannon High Street
Tel: 081 650 1171/658 7114
Seats: 1:478, 2:228, 3:127 ♿

Borehamwood
Hertsmere Hall Elstree Way ★
Tel: 081 953 9872
Seats: 664

Brentford
Watermans Arts Centre High Street ♿
Tel: 081 568 1176
Seats: 240

Brixton
Ritzy Brixton Oval
Tel: 071 737 2121
Seats: 420

Bromley
Odeon High Street
Tel: 0426 910468
Seats: 1:402, 2:125 ♿ 3:98 ♿ 4:273

Catford
Cannon Central Parade
Tel: 081 698 3306/697 6579
Seats: 1:519 ♿ 2:259

Croydon
Cannon London Road
Tel: 081 688 0486/5775
Seats: 1:650, 2:399, 3:187
Fairfield Hall/Ashcroft Theatre Park Lane ★
Tel: 081 688 9291
Seats: Fairfield: 1,552 ♿
Ashcroft: 750 ♿ ▣

Dalston
Rio Kingsland High Street ♿ ▣
Tel: 071 254 6677/249 2722
Seats: 400

Ealing
Cannon Northfields Avenue
Tel: 081 567 1075
Seats: 1:155, 2:149
Cannon Uxbridge Road
Tel: 081 567 1333/579 4851
Seats: 1:764, 2:414 ♿ 3:210

East Finchley
Phoenix High Road ♿
Tel: 081 883 2233
Seats: 300

Edgware
Cannon Station Road
Tel: 081 952 2164/951 0299
Seats: 1:705, 2:207 ♿ 3:146 ♿

Elephant & Castle
Coronet Film Centre New Kent Road
Tel: 071 703 4968/708 0066
Seats: 1:546, 2:271 ♿ 3:211 ♿

Enfield
Cannon Southbury Road
Tel: 081 363 4411/367 4909
Seats: 1:700, 2:356, 3:217 ♿ 4:140 ♿

***Ewell** Surrey*
Cannon Kingston Road
Tel: 081 393 2211/0760
Seats: 1:606, 2:152 ♿

Golders Green
Cannon Ionic Finchley Road
Tel: 081 455 1724/4134

Greenwich
Cinema High Road ♿ ▣
Tel: 081 853 0053
Seats: 1:350, 2:288, 3:144

Hackney
Drive In Homerton High Road
Tel: 071 254 4336
Cars: 2,000

Hammersmith
Cannon King Street
Tel: 081 748 0557/2388
Seats: 1:955, 2:455, 3:326
Odeon Queen Caroline Street ♿ ★
Tel: 081 748 4081/2
Seats: 3,485
Riverside Studios Crisp Road
Tel: 081 748 3354
Seats: 200

Hampstead
Cannon Pond Street
Tel: 071 794 4000/435 3307
Seats: 1:474, 2:197 ♿ 3:191 ♿
Everyman Holly Bush Vale ♿
Tel: 071 435 1525
Seats: 285

Harrow
Cannon Station Road
Tel: 081 427 1743/863 4137
Seats: 1:612, 2:133
Cannon Sheepcote Road
Tel: 081 863 7261/427 1946
Seats: 1:628, 2:207 ♿ 3:204 ♿

Hayes
Beck Theatre Grange Road ♿ ▣ ★
Tel: 081 561 8371
Seats: 536

Hendon
Cannon Central Circus
Tel: 081 202 7137/4644
Seats: 1:572, 2:346 ♿ 3:320 ♿

Holloway
Odeon Holloway Road
Tel: 0426 914042
Seats: 1:388, 2:198, 3:270, 4:391, 5:361

Ilford
Odeon Gants Hill
Tel: 0426 939518
Seats: 1:768, 2:225 ♿ 3:315 ♿ 4:180

Kingston
Cannon Options Richmond Road
Tel: 081 546 0404
Seats: 1:303, 2:287, 3:208

Muswell Hill
Odeon Fortis Green Road
Tel: 0426 911885
Seats: 1:610, 2:134 ♿ 3:130 ♿

Purley
Cannon High Street
Tel: 081 660 1212/668 5592
Seats: 1:438, 2:135 ♿ 3:120 ♿

Putney
Cannon High Street
Tel: 081 788 2263/3003
Seats: 1:434, 2:312 ♿ 3:147

Richmond
Odeon Hill Street
Tel: 081 940 5759
Seats: 1:478, 2:201 ♿ 3:201 ♿
Filmhouse Water Lane ♿
Tel: 081 332 0030
Seats: 150

Romford
Cannon South Street
Tel: 0708 43848/47671
Seats: 1:652, 2:494 ♿ 3:246 ♿
Odeon Mercury Gardens
Tel: 0426 910609
Seats: 1:410, 2:255, 3:150, 4:181, 5:181, 6:150, 7:335, 8:253

Sidcup
Cannon High Street
Tel: 081 300 2539/309 0770
Seats: 1:516 ♿ 2:303

Staples Corner
Cannon Geron Way
Tel: 081 208 4488
Seats: 1:455, 2:362, 3:214, 4:210, 5:166, 6:166

Streatham
Cannon High Road
Tel: 081 769 1928/6262
Seats: 1:630, 2:432 ♿ 3:231 ♿
Odeon High Road
Tel: 0426 912977
Seats: 1:1095, 2:267 ♿ 3:267 ♿

Sutton
Cannon Cheam Road
Tel: 081 642 8927/0855
Seats: 1:260 ♿ 2:120, 3:120
Secombe Centre Cheam Road ♿ ▣ ★
Tel: 081 661 0416
Seats: 330

Turnpike Lane
Coronet Turnpike Parade
Tel: 081 888 2519/3734
Seats: 1:624, 2:417 ♿ 3:269 ♿

Walthamstow
Cannon Hoe Street
Tel: 081 520 7092
Seats: 1:960, 2:181 ♿ 3:181 ♿

Well Hall
Coronet Well Hall Road
Tel: 081 850 3351
Seats: 1:450, 2:131 ♿

Wimbledon
Odeon The Broadway
Tel: 0426 919227
Seats: 1:702, 2:90, 3:190 ♿ 4:175, 5:218 ♿

Woodford
Cannon High Road
Tel: 081 989 3463/4066
Seats: 1:562, 2:199 ♿ 3:131 ♿

Woolwich
Coronet John Wilson Street
Tel: 081 854 2255
Seats: 1:678, 2:370 ♿

ENGLAND

Aldeburgh Suffolk
Aldeburgh Cinema High Street ♿
Tel: 072 885 2996
Seats: 286

Aldershot Hants
Cannon High Street
Tel: 0252 317223/20355
Seats: 1:313, 2:187, 3:150

Alnwick Northumberland
Corn Exchange Bondgate Within
Tel: 0665 602230
Seats: 288

Alton Hants
Palace Normandy Street
Tel: 0420 82303
Seats: 111

Ambleside Cumbria
Zeffirelli's Compston Road
Tel: 0966 33845
Seats: 180

Andover Hants
Savoy London Street
Tel: 0264 52624
Seats: 350

Ardwick Greater Manchester
Apollo Ardwick Green ⋆
Tel: 061 273 6921
Seats: 2,641

Ashford Kent
Picture House Beaver Road
Tel: 0233 620124
Seats: 1:280, 2:250, 3:81

Ashington Northumberland
Picture House Station Road ⋆
Tel: 0670 520237
Seats: 102

Ashton-under-Lyne Greater Manchester
Metro Old Street
Tel: 061 330 1993
Seats: 987

Aylesbury Bucks
Odeon Cambridge Street
Tel: 0296 82660
Seats: 1:450, 2:108, 3:113

Banbury Oxon
Cannon The Horsefair
Tel: 0295 62071
Seats: 1:432, 2:225

Barnsley South Yorks
Odeon Eldon Street
Tel: 0226 205494
Seats: 1:419, 2:636

Barnstaple Devon
Astor Boutport Street
Tel: 0271 42550
Seats: 360

Barrow Cumbria
Astra Abbey Road
Tel: 0229 825354
Seats: 1:640, 2:260, 3:260

Basildon Essex
Cannon Great Oaks
Tel: 0268 27421/27431
Seats: 1:644, 2:435, 3:101(V)
Towngate ⋆
Tel: 0268 23953
Seats: 459

Basingstoke Hants
Warner
Tel: 0256 818739/818448
Seats: 1:427, 2:238, 3:223, 4:154, 5:157, 6:157, 7:154, 8:223, 9:238, 10:427

Bath Avon
Cannon Westgate Street ♿
Tel: 0225 461730/462959
Seats: 733
Robins St John's Place
Tel: 0225 461506
Seats: 1:126, 2:151 ♿ 3:49
Little Theatre St Michael's Place
Tel: 0225 466822
Seats: 1:222, 2:78

Bedford Beds
Civic Theatre Horne Lane ⋆
Tel: 0234 44813
Seats: 266
Cannon Aspect Leisure Park Barkers Lane ♿
Tel: 0234 212844
Seats: 1:340, 2:300, 3:300, 4:300, 5:200, 6:200

Belper Derbyshire
Ritz
Tel: 0773 827284
Two screens

Berwick Northumberland
Playhouse Sandgate
Tel: 0289 307769
Seats: 650

Beverley East Yorks
Playhouse Market Place
Tel: 0482 881315
Seats: 310

Bexhill-on-Sea East Sussex
Curzon Western Road
Tel: 0424 210078
Seats: 216

Billingham Cleveland
Forum Theatre Town Centre ⋆
Tel: 0642 552663
Seats: 494

Birmingham West Mids
Cannon Arcadian Centre
Nine screens
Cannon John Bright Street
Tel: 021 643 0292/2128
Seats: 1:699, 2:242
Capitol Alum Rock Road Ward End
Tel: 021 327 0528
Seats: 1:340, 2:250, 3:130
Midlands Arts Centre Cannon Hill Park
Tel: 021 440 3838
Seats: 1:202, 2:144
Odeon New Street
Tel: 0426 855103
Seats: 1:238, 2:387, 3:308, 4:239, 5:204, 6:190, 7:126, 8:80
Tivoli Station Street
Tel: 021 643 1556
Two screens
bfi **Triangle Gosta Green** ♿
Tel: 021 359 4192/2403
Seats: 180
Warwick Westley Road Acocks Green
Tel: 021 706 0766
Seats: 462

Blackburn Lancs
Unit Four King William Street
Tel: 0254 51779
Seats: 1:315, 2:256, 3:186

Blackpool Lancs
Cannon Church Street
Tel: 0253 27207/24233
Seats: 1:717, 2:330, 3:231
Odeon Dickson Road
Tel: 0253 26211
Seats: 1:1,404, 2:190, 3:190
Royal Pavilion Rigby Road
Tel: 0253 25313
Seats: 347

Blyth Northumberland
Wallaw Union Street
Tel: 0670 352504
Seats: 1:850, 2:150, 3:80

Bognor Regis West Sussex
Cannon Canada Grove
Tel: 0243 823138
Seats: 1:391, 2:96

Bolton Greater Manchester
Cannon Bradshawgate
Tel: 0204 25597
Seats: 1:275, 2:329, 3:100

Boston Lincs
Regal West Street
Tel: 0205 50553
Seats: 182

Bournemouth Dorset
Cannon Westover Road
Tel: 0202 28433/290345
Seats: 1:652, 2:585, 3:223
Odeon Westover Road
Tel: 0202 552402
Seats: 1:757, 2:359, 3:267, 4:119, 5:121

Bovington Dorset
Globe Bovington Camp Wool
Tel: 0929 462666
Seats: 396

Bowness-on-Windermere Cumbria
Royalty Lake Road
Tel: 09662 3364
Seats: 399

Bracknell Berks
South Hill Park Arts Centre ♿
Tel: 0344 427272
Seats: 1:60, 2:200 ⋆
UCI The Point
Tel: 0344 868181/868100
Seats: 1:177, 2:205, 3:205, 4:177, 5:316, 6:316, 7:177, 8:205, 9:205, 10:177

Bradford West Yorks
bfi **National Museum of Photography, Film and TV Prince's View** ♿
Tel: 0274 732277/727488
Seats: 340
Odeon Prince's Way
Tel: 0274 726716/722442
Seats: 1:467, 2:1,190, 3:244
bfi **Playhouse and Film Theatre Chapel Street** ♿ ☑
Tel: 0274 720329
Seats: 1:295, 2:45

Brentwood Essex
Cannon Chapel High
Tel: 0277 212931/227574
Seats: 1:300, 2:196

Bridgnorth Shropshire
Majestic Whitburn Street
Tel: 0746 761815/761866
Seats: 1:500, 2:200

Bridgwater Somerset
Film Centre Penel Orlieu
Tel: 0278 422383
Seats: 1:230, 2:240

Bridport Dorset
Palace South Street
Tel: 0308 22167
Seats: 420

Brierfield Lancs
Unit Four Burnley Road
Tel: 0282 698030
Seats: 1:70, 2:70, 3:61, 4:66

Brierley Hill West Mids
UCI Merry Hill 10
Tel: 0384 78244/78282
Seats: 1:175, 2:254, 3:226, 4:254, 5:350, 6:350, 7:254, 8:226, 9:254, 10:175

Brighton East Sussex
Cannon East Street
Tel: 0273 27010/202095
Seats: 1:345, 2:271, 3:194
Duke of York's Preston Circus
Tel: 0273 602503
Seats: 359
MGM Marina Village
Tel: 0273 818114
Seats: 2,000 (8 screens)
Odeon West Street
Tel: 0426 941661
Seats: 1:388, 2:883, 3:504, 4:275, 5:242, 6:103

Bristol Avon
Arnolfini Narrow Quay ♿ ☑
Tel: 0272 299191
Seats: 176
Arts Centre Cinema King Square ♿
Tel: 0272 422110
Seats: 124
Cannon Frogmore Street
Tel: 0272 262848/9
Seats: 1:411, 2:301
Cannon Northumbria Drive Henleaze
Tel: 0272 621644
Seats: 1:186, 2:124, 3:129
Cannon Whiteladies Road
Tel: 0272 730679/733640
Seats: 1:372, 2:253, 3:135
Gaiety Wells Road
Tel: 0272 776224
Seats: 650
Odeon Union Street
Tel: 0272 290882
Seats: 1:399, 2:224, 3:215
bfi **Watershed** ♿ ☑
Tel: 0272 276444
Seats: 1:200, 2:50

Broadstairs Kent
Windsor Harbour Street ◐
Seats: 100

Bungay Suffolk
Mayfair Broad Street
Tel: 0986 2397
Seats: 400

Burgess Hill West Sussex
Robins Take Two Cyprus Road
Tel: 0444 232137/248972
Seats: 1:150, 2:121

Burnham-on-Crouch Essex
Rio Station Road
Tel: 0621 782027
Seats: 200

Burnham-on-Sea Somerset
Ritz Victoria Street
Tel: 0278 782871
Seats: 260

Burton-on-Trent Staffs
Odeon Guild Street
Tel: 0283 63200
Seats: 1:502, 2:110, 3:110

Bury Greater Manchester
Warner 12
Tel: 061 766 2440/1121
Seats: 1:559, 2:322, 3:278, 4:434, 5:208, 6:166, 7:166, 8:208, 9:434, 10:278, 11:322, 12:573

Bury St Edmunds Suffolk
Cannon Halter Street
Tel: 0284 754477
Seats: 1:196, 2:117

Camberley Surrey
Cannon London Road
Tel: 0276 63909/26768
Seats: 1:441, 2:114, 3:94
Globe Hawley ⋆
Tel: 0252 876769
Seats: 200

Cambridge Cambs
bfi **Arts Market Passage** ♿ ☑
Tel: 0223 352001/462666
Seats: 275
Cannon St Andrews Street
Tel: 0223 354572/645378
Seats: 1:736, 2:452
Corn Exchange Wheeler Street
Tel: 0223 357851
Seats: 453

Cannock Staffs
Cannon Walsall Road
Tel: 05435 2226
Seats: 1:363, 2:178

Canterbury Kent
Cannon St Georges Place
Tel: 0227 462022/453577
Seats: 1:536, 2:404
bfi **Cinema 3 University of Kent** ♿ ⋆
Tel: 0227 764000
Seats: 300

Carlisle Cumbria
Lonsdale Warwick Road
Tel: 0228 25586
Seats: 1:410, 2:220, 3:50

Chatham Kent
Cannon High Street
Tel: 0634 42522/46756
Seats: 1:520, 2:360, 3:170

Chelmsford Essex
Cramphorn Theatre Fairfield Road ⋆
Tel: 0245 495028
Seats: 190
Select New Whittle Street
Tel: 0245 352724
Seats: 400

Cheltenham Glos
Odeon Winchcombe Street
Tel: 0426 914551
Seats: 1:756, 2:129, 3:104, 4:90, 5:204

Chester Cheshire
Cannon Greyhound Park Sealand Road
Tel: 0224 380459
Seats: 1,600 (6 screens)
Odeon Northgate Street
Tel: 0244 324930
Seats: 1:406, 2:151, 3:151, 4:122, 5:122

Chesterfield Derbyshire
Regal Cavendish Street
Tel: 0246 73333
Seats: 484

Chichester East Sussex
Minerva Studio Theatre New Park Film Centre ⋆
Tel: 0243 784881

Chippenham Wilts
Cannon Marshfield Road
Tel: 0249 652498
Seats: 1:215, 2:215

Chipping Norton Oxon
The Theatre Spring Street ⋆
Tel: 0608 2349/2350
Seats: 195

Christchurch Hants
Regent Centre High Street ⋆
Tel: 0202 499148
Seats: 370

Cirencester Glos
Regal Lewis Lane
Tel: 0285 658755
Seats: 1:100, 2:100

Clacton Essex
Coronet Century Pier Avenue
Tel: 0255 429627
Seats: 1:600, 2:187

Clevedon Avon
Curzon Old Church Road
Tel: 0272 872158
Seats: 425

Clitheroe Lancs
Civic Hall York Street
Tel: 0200 23278
Seats: 400

Colchester Essex
Odeon Crouch Street
Tel: 0206 572294
Seats: 1:482, 2:208, 3:120, 4:135

Coleford Glos
Studio High Street
Tel: 0594 333331
Seats: 1:200, 2:80

Consett Co Durham
Empire Front Street ♿ ▣
Tel: 0207 506751
Seats: 535

Corby Northants
Forum Queens Square
Tel: 0536 203974
Seats: 1:339, 2:339

Cosford Staffs
Astra RAF Cosford ⋆
Tel: 090 722 2393
Seats: 460

Cosham Hants
Cannon High Street
Tel: 0705 376635
Seats: 1:441, 2:118, 3:107

Coventry West Mids
bfi **Arts Centre University of Warwick** ♿
Tel: 0203 417417/417314
Seats: 1:250
Odeon Jordan Well
Tel: 0203 222042
Seats: 1:712, 2:155, 3:172, 4:390, 5:121
Theatre One Ford Street
Tel: 0203 224301
Seats: 1:230, 2:140, 3:135

Cranleigh Surrey
Regal High Street
Tel: 0483 272373
Seats: 268

Crawley West Sussex
Cannon High Street
Tel: 0293 27497/541296
Seats: 1:297, 2:214, 3:110
Hawth, Hawth Avenue ♿ ▣ ⋆
Tel: 0293 553636
Seats: 800

Crewe Cheshire
Apollo High Street
Tel: 0270 255708
Seats: 1:110, 2:110, 3:95
Lyceum Theatre Heath Street ⋆
Tel: 0270 215523
Seats: 750
Victoria Film Theatre West Street ◐
Tel: 0270 211422
Seats: 180

Cromer Norfolk
Regal Hans Place
Tel: 0263 513311
Seats: 1:129, 2:136

Crookham Hants
Globe Queen Elizabeth Barracks
Tel: 0252 876769
Seats: 340

Crosby Merseyside
Apollo Crosby Road North
Tel: 051 928 2108
Seats: 1:671, 2:103, 3:103

Darlington Co Durham
Arts Centre Vane Terrace ♿ ▣ ⋆
Tel: 0325 483168/483271
Seats: 100
Cannon Northgate
Tel: 0325 62745/484994
Seats: 1:590, 2:218, 3:148

Dartford Kent
Orchard Theatre Home Gardens ♿ ▣ ⋆
Tel: 0322 343333
Seats: 930

Dartington Devon
bfi **Barn Theatre** ♿ ⋆
Tel: 0803 862224
Seats: 203

Deal Kent
Flicks Queen Street
Tel: 0304 361165
Seats: 173

Derby Derbyshire
Assembly Rooms Market Place ⋆
Tel: 0332 255800
Seats: 998
bfi **Metro Green Lane** ♿ ▣
Tel: 0332 40170
Seats: 126
Showcase Cinemas Outer Ring Road
Osmarton Park Road at Sinfin Lane
Tel: 0332 270300
Seats: 2,600 (11 screens)
UCI Meteor Centre 10 Mansfield Road
Tel: 0332 295010/296000
Seats: 1:192, 2:189, 3:189, 4:192, 5:278, 6:278, 7:192, 8:189, 9:189, 10:192

Dereham Norfolk
CBA Dereham Entertainment Centre Market Place
Tel: 0362 3261
Seats: 210

Devizes Wilts
Palace Market Place
Tel: 0380 722971
Seats: 253

Dewsbury West Yorks
Apollo Market Place
Tel: 0924 464949
Seats: 1:315, 2:151

Didcot Oxon
New Coronet The Broadway ⋆
Tel: 0235 812038
Seats: 490

Doncaster South Yorks
Cannon Cleveland Street
Tel: 0302 67934/66241
Seats: 1:477, 2:201, 3:135
Civic Theatre Waterdale ⋆
Tel: 0302 62349
Seats: 547
Odeon Hallgate
Tel: 0302 344626
Seats: 1:1,003, 2:155, 3:155

Dorchester Dorset
Plaza Trinity Street
Tel: 0305 262488
Seats: 1:100, 2:320

Dorking Surrey
Grand Hall Dorking Halls ⋆
Tel: 0306 889694
Seats: 851

Dover Kent
Silver Screen White Cliffs Experience Gaol Lane
Tel: 0304 228000
Seats: 110

Durham Co Durham
Robins North Road
Tel: 091 384 3434
Seats: 1:312 ♿ 2:98, 3:98, 4:74

Eastbourne East Sussex
Cannon The Crumbles Pevensey Bay Road
Tel: 0323 470070/470071
Six screens
Curzon Langney Road
Tel: 0323 31441
Seats: 1:530, 2:236, 3:236

Elland Yorks
Rex
Tel: 0422 372140

Ellesmere Cheshire
Arts Centre ⋆
Tel: 0691 622828
Seats: 220

Ely Cambs
The Maltings ⋆
Tel: 0353 666388
Seats: 212

Epsom Surrey
Playhouse ⋆
Tel: 03727 42555/6

Erith Kent
Academy Sports Centre Avenue Road ⋆
Tel: 0322 350271
Seats: 160

Esher Surrey
Cannon High Street
Tel: 0372 65639/63362
Seats: 1:918, 2:117

Evesham Hereford & Worcs
Regal Port Street
Tel: 0386 6002
Seats: 540

Exeter Devon
Northcott Theatre Stocker Road ⋆
Tel: 0392 54853
Seats: 433
Odeon Sidwell Street
Tel: 0392 54057
Seats: 1:744, 2:119, 3:105, 4:344

Exmouth Devon
Savoy Market Street
Tel: 0395 268220
Seats: 1:230, 2:110

Fawley Hants
Waterside Long Lane
Tel: 0703 891335
Seats: 355

Felixstowe Suffolk
Top Rank Crescent Road
Tel: 0394 282787
Seats: 1:150, 2:90

Filey Yorks
Grand Union Street ◐
Tel: 0723 512129

Folkestone Kent
Silver Screen Guildhall Street
Tel: 0303 221230
Seats: 1:423, 2:114

Frome Somerset
Westway Cork Street
Tel: 0373 65685
Seats: 304

Gainsborough Lincs
Trinity Arts Centre Trinity Street ⋆
Tel: 0427 617 242
Seats: 210

Gateshead Tyne & Wear
UCI Metro 10 Metro Centre
Tel: 091 493 2022/3
Seats: 1:196, 2:196, 3:227, 4:252, 5:364, 6:364, 7:252, 8:227, 9:196, 10:196

Gatley Greater Manchester
Tatton Gatley Road
Tel: 061 491 0711
Seats: 1:648, 2:247, 3:111

Gerrards Cross Bucks
Cannon Ethorpe Crescent
Tel: 0753 882516/883024
Seats: 1:350, 2:212

Gloucester Glos
Cannon Peel Centre Bristol Road
Tel: 0452 331181/5
Seats: 1:354, 2:354, 3:238, 4:238, 5:219, 6:219
Guildhall Arts Centre Eastgate Street ⋆
Seats: 125

Godalming Surrey
Borough Hall ⋆
Tel: 0483 861111
Seats: 250

Gosport Hants
Ritz Walpole Road
Tel: 0705 501231
Seats: 1,136

Grantham Lincs
Paragon St Catherine's Road
Tel: 0476 70046
Seats: 1:270, 2:160

Gravesend Kent
Cannon King Street
Tel: 0474 356947/352470
Seats: 1:576, 2:320, 3:107

Grays Essex
Thameside Orsett Road ⋆
Tel: 0375 382555
Seats: 303

Great Yarmouth Norfolk
Cinema Royal Aquarium
Tel: 0493 842043/842707
Seats: 1:1,180, 2:264
Empire Marine Parade ◐ ⋆
Tel: 0493 843147
Seats: 967
Windmill Marine Parade ◐
Tel: 0493 843504
Seats: 140

Grimsby Humberside
Cannon Freeman Street
Tel: 0472 42878/49368
Seats: 1:419, 2:251, 3:130
bfi **Whitgift Crosland Road** ♿ ⋆
Tel: 0472 887117
Seats: 206

Guildford Surrey
Odeon Epsom Road
Tel: 0426 941049
Seats: 1:452, 2:135, 3:144, 4:250

Halifax West Yorks
Cannon Ward's End
Tel: 0422 52000/46429
Seats: 1:670, 2:199, 3:172

Halstead Essex
Empire Butler Road
Tel: 0787 477001
Seats: 320

Halton Bucks
Astra RAF Halton
Tel: 0296 623535
Seats: 570

Hanley Staffs
Cannon Broad Street
Tel: 0782 22320/268970
Seats: 1:573, 2:233, 3:162

Harlow Essex
Cannon Queensgate Centre
Tel: 0279 433333
Seats: 1,500 (6 screens)
Odeon The High
Tel: 0279 426989
Seats: 1:450, 2:243, 3:201
Playhouse The High ♿ ⋆
Tel: 0279 424391
Seats: 435

Harrogate North Yorks
Odeon East Parade
Tel: 0423 503626
Seats: 1:532, 2:108, 3:75, 4:259

Harwich Essex
Electric Palace King's Quay Street ⋆
Tel: 0255 553333
Seats: 204

Haslemere Surrey
Haslemere Hall Bridge Road ⋆
Tel: 0428 2161
Seats: 350

Hastings East Sussex
Cannon Queens Road
Tel: 0424 420517
Seats: 1:376, 2:176, 3:128

Hatfield Herts
Forum ⋆
Tel: 07072 71217
Seats: 210

Haywards Heath Sussex
Clair Hall Perrymount Road ⋆
Tel: 0444 455440/454394
Seats: 350

Heaton Moor Greater Manchester
Savoy Heaton Manor Road
Tel: 061 432 2114
Seats: 496

Hebden Bridge West Yorks
Cinema New Road
Tel: 0422 842807
Seats: 498

Hemel Hempstead Herts
Odeon Marlowes ⋆
Tel: 0442 64013
Seats: 785

Henley-on-Thames Oxon
Kenton Theatre ⋆
Tel: 0491 575698

Hereford Hereford & Worcs
Cannon Commercial Road
Tel: 0432 272554
Seats: 378

Hexham Northumberland
Forum Market Place
Tel: 0434 602896
Seats: 207

High Wycombe Bucks
UCI Wycombe 6 Crest Road Cressex
Tel: 0494 463333/464309/465565
Seats: 1:390, 2:390, 3:285, 4:285, 5:200, 6:200

Hinckley Leics
Cannon Trinity Lane
Tel: 0455 637523
Seats: 1:350, 2:206, 3:224

Hoddesdon Herts
Broxbourne Civic Hall High Road ⋆
Tel: 0992 441946/31
Seats: 564

Holbury Hants
Waterside Long Lane
Tel: 0703 891335
Seats: 355

Hollinwood Greater Manchester
Roxy Hollins Road
Tel: 061 681 1441
Seats: 1:470, 2:130, 3:260, 4:260, 5:320

Hordern Co Durham
Fairworld Sunderland Road
Tel: 0783 864344
Seats: 1:156, 2:96

Horsham Sussex
Arts Centre (Ritz Cinema and Capitol Theatre) North Street
Tel: 0403 68689
Seats: 1:126, 2:450 ⋆

Horwich Lancs
Leisure Centre Victoria Road ⋆
Tel: 0204 692211
Seats: 400

Hoylake Merseyside
Cinema Alderley Road
Tel: 051 632 1345

Hucknall Notts
Byron High Street
Tel: 0602 636377
Seats: 430

Huddersfield West Yorks
Cannon Queensgate Zetland Street
Tel: 0484 530874
Seats: 1:495, 2:214

Hull Humberside
Cannon Anlaby Road
Tel: 0482 224981
Seats: 1:308, 2:308, 3:165
bfi **Film Theatre Central Library Albion Street** ♿
Tel: 0482 224040 x 30
Seats: 247
Odeon Kingston Street ♿
Tel: 0482 586420
Seats: 1:170, 2:170, 3:150, 4:172, 5:418, 6:206, 7:132, 8:150

UCI St Andrew's Quay Clive Sullivan Way ♿
Tel: 0482 587525
Seats: 1:166, 2:152, 3:236, 4:292, 5:292, 6:236, 7:152, 8:166

Hunstanton Norfolk
Princess Theatre The Green ⋆
Tel: 0485 532252
Seats: 467

Huntingdon Cambs
Cromwell Cinema Centre Princes Street
Tel: 0480 411575
Seats: 264

Hyde Greater Manchester
Royal Corporation Street
Tel: 061 368 2206
Seats: 1:800, 2:224

Ilfracombe Devon
Pendle Stairway High Street
Tel: 0271 63484
Seats: 460

Ilkeston Derbyshire
Scala Market Place
Tel: 0602 324612
Seats: 500

Ipswich Suffolk
bfi **Film Theatre Corn Exchange** ♿ ☑
Tel: 0473 55851
Seats: 1:221, 2:40
Odeon Majors Corner
Tel: 0426 915622
Seats: 1:506, 2:318, 3:290, 4:218, 5:218

Kendal Cumbria
Brewery Arts Centre Highgate ♿ ☑
Tel: 0539 725133
Seats: 148

Keswick Cumbria
Alhambra St John Street ◐
Tel: 0596 72195
Seats: 313

Kettering Northants
Ohio Russell Street
Tel: 0536 515130
Seats: 1:145, 2:206

King's Lynn Norfolk
Arts Centre King Street ⋆
Tel: 0553 774725/773578
Seats: 359
Majestic Tower Street
Tel: 0553 772603
Seats: 1:450, 2:130, 3:400

Kirkby-in-Ashfield Notts
Regent
Tel: 0623 753866

Kirkham Lancs
Empire Birley Street
Tel: 07722 684817
Seats: 256

Knutsford Cheshire
bfi **Civic Centre Toft Road**
Tel: 0565 3005
Seats: 400

Lake Isle of Wight
Screen De Luxe Sandown Road
Tel: 0983 406056
Seats: 150

Lancaster Lancs
Cannon King Street
Tel: 0524 64141/841149
Seats: 1:250, 2:250
bfi **Duke's Playhouse Moor Lane** ♿ ☑ ⋆
Tel: 0524 66645/67461
Seats: 307

Leamington Spa Warwicks
Regal Portland Place
Tel: 0926 26106/27448
Seats: 904
Robins Spa Centre Newbold Terrace
Tel: 0926 887726/888997
Seats: 208

Leatherhead Surrey
Thorndike Theatre Church Street ⋆
Tel: 0372 376211/377677
Seats: 526

Leeds West Yorks
Cannon Vicar Lane
Tel: 0532 451013/452665
Seats: 1:670, 2:483, 3:227
Cottage Road Cinema Headingley
Tel: 0532 751606
Seats: 468
Hyde Park Brudenell Road
Tel: 0532 752045
Seats: 360
Lounge North Lane Headingley
Tel: 0532 751061/58932
Seats: 691
Odeon The Headrow
Tel: 0532 430031/2
Seats: 1:982, 2:441, 3:200, 4:174, 5:126
Showcase Gelderd Road Birstall ♿
Tel: 0924 420071
Seats: 3,400 (12 screens)

Leicester Leics
Cannon Belgrave Gate
Tel: 0533 24346/24903
Seats: 1:616, 2:408, 3:232
Odeon Queen Street
Tel: 0533 622892
Seats: 1:872, 2:401, 3:111, 4:142
bfi **Phoenix Arts Newarke Street** ♿ ☑ ⋆
Tel: 0533 559711/555627
Seats: 270

Leiston Suffolk
Film Theatre High Street
Tel: 0728 830549
Seats: 350

Letchworth Herts
Broadway Eastcheap
Tel: 0462 684721
Seats: 1,410

Lichfield Staffs
Civic Hall Castle Dyke ⋆
Tel: 0543 254021
Seats: 278

Lincoln Lincs
Ritz High Street
Tel: 0522 46313
Seats: 1,400

Littlehampton West Sussex
Windmill Church Street⋆
Tel: 09064 6644
Seats: 252

Liverpool Merseyside
Bluecoat Arts Centre (Merseyside Film Institute) ⋆
Tel: 051 709 4260
Cannon Allerton Road
Tel: 051 709 6277/708 7629
Seats: 493
Cannon Edge Lane Retail Park Binns Road
Ten screens
Cannon Lime Street
Tel: 051 709 6277/708 7629
Seats: 1:697, 2:274, 3:217
bfi **Cinema 051 Mount Pleasant Meteor Centre** ♿
Tel: 051 707 0257
Seats: 1:122, 2:116, 3:108
Odeon London Road
Tel: 0426 950072
Seats: 1:976, 2:597, 3:167, 4:148, 5:148
Showcase West Derby
Tel: 051 549 2021
Seats: 3,400 (12 screens)

Woolton Mason Street
Tel: 051 428 1919
Seats: 256

Long Eaton Notts
Screen Market Place
Tel: 0602 732185
Seats: 253

Longridge Lancs
Palace Market Place
Tel: 0772 785600
Seats: 212

Looe East Cornwall
Cinema Higher Market Street
Tel: 05036 2709
Seats: 95

Loughborough Leics
Curzon Cattle Market
Tel: 0509 212261
Seats: 1:420, 2:303, 3:199, 4:186, 5:140, 6:80

Louth Lincs
Playhouse Cannon Street
Tel: 0507 603333
Seats: 218

Lowestoft Suffolk
Hollywood London Road South
Tel: 0502 564567
Seats: 1:200, 2:170
Marina Theatre The Marina
Tel: 0502 573318/514274
Seats: 751

Ludlow Shropshire
Picture House Castle Square ⋆
Tel: 0584 875363

Luton Beds
Cannon George Street
Tel: 0582 27311/22537
Seats: 1:615, 2:458, 3:272
St George's Theatre Central Library ⋆
Tel: 0582 21628
Seats: 238

Lyme Regis Dorset
Regent Broad Street
Tel: 0297 442053
Seats: 400

Lymington Hants
Community Centre New Street ⋆
Tel: 05907 2337
Seats: 110

Mablethorpe Lincs
Bijou Quebec Road
Tel: 0521 77040
Seats: 264

CINEMAS

Macclesfield Cheshire
Majestic Mill Street
Tel: 0625 22412
Seats: 687

Maghull Merseyside
Astra Northway
Tel: 051 526 1943
Seats: 1:200, 2:200, 3:300, 4:300

Maidstone Kent
Cannon Lower Stone Street
Tel: 0622 52628
Seats: 1:260, 2:90, 3:260

Malton North Yorks
bfi **Palace The Lanes** ▣
Tel: 0653 600008
Seats: 140

Malvern Hereford & Worcs
Cinema Grange Road
Tel: 0684 892279/892710
Seats: 407

Manchester Greater Manchester
bfi **Cornerhouse Oxford Street** ♿ ▣
Tel: 061 228 7621
Seats: 1:300, 2:170, 3:58
Odeon Oxford Street
Tel: 061 236 8264
Seats: 1:629, 2:737, 3:203
Showcase Hyde Road Belle Vue
Tel: 061 220 8765
Seats: 3,400 (14 screens)

Mansfield Notts
Cannon Leeming Street
Tel: 0623 23138/652236
Seats: 1:367, 2:359, 3:171
Studio Leeming Street
Tel: 0623 653309
Seats: 75

March Cambs
Hippodrome Dartford Road ⋆
Tel: 0354 53178
Seats: 150

Margate Kent
Dreamland Marine Parade
Tel: 0843 227822
Seats: 1:378, 2:376, 3:66(V)

Marple Greater Manchester
Regent Stockport Road
Tel: 061 427 5951
Seats: 285

Matlock Derbyshire
Ritz Causeway Lane
Tel: 0629 2121
Seats: 1:176, 2:100

Melton Mowbray Leics
Regal King Street
Tel: 0664 62251
Seats: 226

Middlesbrough Cleveland
Odeon Corporation Road
Tel: 0642 242888
Seats: 1:616, 2:98, 3:122, 4:246

Middleton Greater Manchester
Palace Manchester Middleton Gardens
Tel: 061 643 2852
Seats: 234

Midsomer Norton Somerset
Palladium High Street
Tel: 0761 413266
Seats: 482

Millom Cumbria
Palladium Horn Hill ◐
Tel: 0657 2441
Seats: 400

Milton Keynes Bucks
UCI The Point 10 Midsummer Boulevard
Tel: 0908 661662
Seats: 1:156, 2:169, 3:248, 4:220, 5:220, 6:220, 7:220, 8:248, 9:169, 10:156

Minehead Somerset
Regal The Avenue
Tel: 0643 702439

Mirfield West Yorks
Vale Centre Huddersfield Road
Tel: 0924 493240
Seats: 1:98, 2:96

Monkseaton Tyne & Wear
Cannon Caldwell Lane
Tel: 091 252 5540
Seats: 1:351, 2:116

Monton Greater Manchester
Princess Monton Road
Tel: 061 789 3426
Seats: 580

Morpeth Northumberland
New Coliseum New Market
Tel: 0670 516834
Seats: 1:132, 2:132

Nantwich Cheshire
Civic Hall Market Street ⋆
Tel: 0270 628633
Seats: 300

Nelson Lancs
Grand Market Street
Tel: 0282 692860
Seats: 391

Newark Notts
Palace Theatre Appleton Gate ⋆
Tel: 0636 71636
Seats: 351

Newbury Berks
Cannon Park Way
Tel: 0635 41291/49913
Seats: 484

Newcastle-under-Lyme Staffs
Savoy High Street
Tel: 0782 616565
Seats: 200

Newcastle upon Tyne Tyne & Wear
Jesmond Cinema Lyndhurst Avenue
Tel: 091 281 0526/2248
Seats: 626
Odeon Pilgrim Street
Tel: 091 232 3248
Seats: 1:1,228, 2:159, 3:250, 4:361
bfi **Tyneside Pilgrim Street** ♿ ▣
Tel: 091 232 8289/5592
Seats: 1:400, 2:155
Warner Manors
Tel: 091 221 0202/0545
Seats: 1:404, 2:398, 3:236, 4:244, 5:290, 6:657, 7:509, 8:398, 9:248

Newport Isle of Wight
Cannon High Street
Tel: 0983 527169
Seats: 377

Newquay Cornwall
Camelot The Crescent
Tel: 063 73 874222
Seats: 812

Newton Abbot Devon
Alexandra Market Street
Tel: 0626 65368
Seats: 360

Northallerton North Yorks
Lyric Northend
Tel: 0609 2019
Seats: 305

Northampton Northants
Cannon Abingdon Square
Tel: 0604 35839/32862
Seats: 1:1,018, 2:275, 3:210
bfi **Forum Weston Favell Centre** ⋆
Tel: 0604 401006/407544
Seats: 250

Northwich Cheshire
Regal London Road
Tel: 0606 3130
Seats: 1:797, 2:200

Norwich Norfolk
Cannon Prince of Wales Road
Tel: 0603 624677/623312
Seats: 1:524, 2:343, 3:186, 4:105
bfi **Cinema City St Andrews Street** ♿
Tel: 0603 625145
Seats: 230
Noverre Theatre Street
Tel: 0603 626402
Seats: 272
Odeon Anglia Square ▣
Tel: 0603 621903
Seats: 1:442, 2:197, 3:195 ♿

Nottingham Notts
Cannon Chapel Bar
Tel: 0602 45260/418483
Seats: 1:764, 2:437, 3:280
bfi **Broadway, Nottingham Media Centre Broad Street**
Tel: 0602 410053
Seats: 1:500, 2:75
Odeon Angel Row
Tel: 0602 417766
Seats: 1:924, 2:581, 3:141, 4:153, 5:114, 6:96
Savoy Derby Road
Tel: 0602 472580
Seats: 1:386, 2:128, 3:168
Showcase Redfield Way
Lenton
Tel: 0602 866766
Seats: 3,200 (13 screens)

Nuneaton Warwicks
Nuneaton Arts Centre Abbey Theatre Pool Bank Street
Tel: 0203 382706

Okehampton Devon
Carlton St James Street
Tel: 0822 2425
Seats: 380

Oswestry Shropshire
Regal Salop Road
Tel: 0691 654043
Seats: 1:261, 2:261, 3:66

Oxford Oxon
Cannon George Street
Tel: 0865 244607/723911
Seats: 1:626, 2:326, 3:140
Cannon Magdalen Street
Tel: 0865 243067
Seats: 866
Penultimate Picture Palace
Jeune Street
Tel: 0865 723837
Seats: 185
Phoenix Walton Street
Tel: 0865 54909/512526
Seats: 1:200, 2:95
Playhouse Beaumont Street
Tel: 0865 247134/798600
Seats: 638

Oxted Surrey
Plaza Station Road West
Tel: 0883 712567
Seats: 442

Padstow Cornwall
Capitol Lanadwell Street ◐
Tel: 0841 532344
Seats: 210

Paignton Devon
Torbay, Torbay Road ◐
Tel: 0803 559544
Seats: 484

Penistone South Yorks
Town Hall
Tel: 0226 767532/205128
Seats: 450

Penrith Cumbria
Alhambra Middlegate
Tel: 0768 62400
Seats: 202

Penzance Cornwall
Savoy Causeway Head
Tel: 0736 3330
Seats: 450

Peterborough Cambs
Odeon Broadway
Tel: 0733 343319
Seats: 1:544, 2:110, 3:110
Showcase Mallory Road Boongate ♿
Tel: 0733 558498
Seats: 2,600 (11 screens)

Pickering North Yorks
Castle Burgate
Tel: 0751 72622
Seats: 250

Plymouth Devon
Arts Centre Looe Street ♿
Tel: 0752 660060
Seats: 73
Cannon Derry's Cross
Tel: 0752 63300/25553
Seats: 1:583, 2:340, 3:115
Odeon Derry's Cross
Tel: 0752 668825/227074
Seats: 1:420, 2:166, 3:166, 4:220, 5:120

Pocklington East Yorks
Ritz Market Place
Tel: 0759 303420
Seats: 250

Pontefract West Yorks
Crescent Ropergate
Tel: 0977 703788
Seats: 412

Poole Dorset
Ashley Arts Centre Kingsland Road ⋆
Seats: 143
UCI Tower Park 10
Tel: 0202 715040
Seats: 1:192, 2:186, 3:186, 4:192, 5:270, 6:270, 7:192, 8:186, 9:186, 10:192

Portsmouth Hants
Cannon Commercial Road
Tel: 0705 823538/839719
Seats: 1:542, 2:255, 3:203
Odeon London Road
Tel: 0705 661539
Seats: 1:524, 2:225, 3:173, 4:259
Rendezvous The Hornpipe Kingston Road ◐
Tel: 0705 833854
Seats: 90

Potters Bar Herts
Wyllyotts Dark Lane ♿
Tel: 0707 45005
Seats: 345

Preston Lancs
Odeon Church Street
Tel: 0772 823298/555122
Seats: 1:1,166, 2:112
UCI Riversway 10 ♿
Tel: 0772 728888/722322
Seats: 290 (2 screens), 180 (8 screens)

Quinton West Mids
Cannon Hagley Road West
Tel: 021 422 2562/2252
Seats: 1:300, 2:236, 3:232, 4:121

Ramsey Cambs
Grand Great Whyte
Tel: 0487 813777
Seats: 173

Ramsgate Kent
Granville Victoria Parade ⋆
Tel: 0843 591750
Seats: 861

Rawtenstall Lancs
Picture House
Tel: 0706 226774
Seats: 120
Unit Four Bacup Road
Tel: 0706 23123
Seats: 1:121, 2:118, 3:165, 4:118

Reading Berks
Cannon Friar Street
Tel: 0734 573907
Seats: 1:532, 2:226, 3:118
Film Theatre Whiteknights ⋆
Tel: 0734 868497/875123
Seats: 409
Odeon Cheapside
Tel: 0426 915484
Seats: 1:410, 2:221, 3:221

Redcar Cleveland
Regent The Esplanade
Tel: 0642 482094
Seats: 381

Redditch Hereford & Worcs
Cannon Unicorn Hill
Tel: 0527 62572
Seats: 1:208, 2:155, 3:155

Redruth Cornwall
Regal Film Centre Fore Street
Tel: 0209 216278
Seats: 1:200, 2:128, 3:600, 4:95

Reigate Surrey
Screen Bancroft Road
Tel: 0737 223213
Seats: 1:139, 2:142

Retford Notts
Majestic Coronation Street
Tel: 0777 709405
Seats: 1:444, 2:136

Rickmansworth Herts
Watersmeet Theatre High Street ⋆
Tel: 0923 771542
Seats: 390

Ripley Derbyshire
Hippodrome High Street
Tel: 0773 746559
Seats: 350

Rochdale Greater Manchester
Cannon The Butts
Tel: 0706 524362/45954
Seats: 1:538, 2:276, 3:197

Royston Herts
Priory, Priory Lane
Tel: 0763 43133
Seats: 305

Rugeley Staffs
Plaza Horse Fair
Tel: 0889 574856
Two screens

Rushden Northants
Ritz College Street
Tel: 0933 312468
Seats: 822

St Albans Herts
Alban Arena Civic Centre ♿ ⊡ ⋆
Tel: 0727 44488
Seats: 800
Odeon London Road
Tel: 0426 911842
Seats: 1:452, 2:115, 3:128, 4:145

St Austell Cornwall
Film Centre Chandos Place
Tel: 0726 73750
Seats: 1:276, 2:134, 3:133, 4:70, 5:70

St Helens Merseyside
Cannon Bridge Street
Tel: 0744 51947/23392
Seats: 1:494, 2:284, 3:179

St Ives Cornwall
Royal, Royal Square
Tel: 0736 796843
Seats: 682

Salford Quays Lancs
Cannon Quebec Drive Trafford Road
Tel: 061 873 7155/7279
Seats: 1:265, 2:265, 3:249, 4:249, 5:213, 6:213, 7:177, 8:177

Salisbury Wilts
Odeon New Canal
Tel: 0722 322080
Seats: 1:471, 2:120, 3:120

Scarborough North Yorks
Futurist Forshaw Road ⋆
Tel: 0723 365789
Seats: 2,155
Hollywood Plaza North Marine Road ◐
Tel: 0723 365119
Seats: 275
Opera House St Thomas Street ⋆
Tel: 0723 369999
Seats: 225

Scunthorpe Humberside
Majestic Oswald Road
Tel: 0724 842352

Seats: 1:177, 2:162, 3:193
bfi Film Theatre Central Library Carlton Street ♿ ★
Tel: 0724 860161 x30
Seats: 249

Sevenoaks Kent
Stag Theatre London Road
Tel: 0732 450175/451548
Seats: 1:455 ★, 2:102, 3:102

Sheffield South Yorks
Fiesta Flat Street
Tel: 0742 723981
Seats: 1:141, 2:189
Odeon Barker's Pool
Tel: 0742 767962
Seats: 1:500, 2:324
UCI Crystal Peaks 10 Eckington Way Sothall
Tel: 0742 480064/470095
Seats: 1:200, 2:200, 3:228, 4:224, 5:312, 6:312, 7:224, 8:228, 9:200, 10:200

Sheringham Norfolk
Little Theatre Station Road ◐
Tel: 0263 822347
Seats: 198

Shipley West Yorks
Unit Four Bradford Road
Tel: 0274 583429
Seats: 1:89, 2:72, 3:121, 4:94

Shrewsbury Shropshire
Cannon Empire Mardal
Tel: 0743 62257
Seats: 573
The Cinema in the Square Music Hall
Tel: 0743 50763
Seats: 100

Sidmouth Devon
Radway, Radway Place
Tel: 039 55 3085
Seats: 400

Sittingbourne Kent
Cannon High Street
Tel: 0795 23984
Seats: 1:300, 2:110

Skegness Lincs
Tower Lumley Road
Tel: 0754 3938
Seats: 401

Skelmersdale Lancs
Premiere Film Centre
Tel: 0695 25041
Seats: 1:230, 2:248

Skipton North Yorks
Plaza Sackville Street
Tel: 0756 3417
Seats: 320

Sleaford Lincs
Sleaford Cinema Southgate
Tel: 0529 30 3187
Seats: 60

Slough Berks
Gallery High Street
Tel: 0753 692233/692492
Seats: 2,058 (10 screens)

Solihull West Mids
UCI 8 Stratford Road
Tel: 021 733 3696
Seats: 286 (2 screens), 250 (2 screens), 210 (2 screens), 180 (2 screens)

South Woodham Ferrers Essex
Flix Market Street
Tel: 0245 329777
Seats: 249

Southampton Hants
Cannon Ocean Village
Tel: 0703 330666
Seats: 1:421, 2:346, 3:346, 4:258, 5:258
bfi **The Gantry Off Blechynden Terrace** ♿
Tel: 0703 229319/330729
Seats: 194
Mountbatten Theatre East Park Terrace★
Tel: 0703 221991
Seats: 515
Odeon Above Bar Street
Tel: 0703 333243
Seats: 1:476, 2:756, 3:127

Southend Essex
Cannon Alexandra Street
Tel: 0702 344580
Seats: 1:665, 2:498
Odeon Elmer Approach
Tel: 0702 344434
Seats: 1:455, 2:1235

Southport Merseyside
Arts Centre Lord Street★
Tel: 0704 40004/40011
Seats: 400
Cannon Lord Street
Tel: 0704 30627
Seats: 1:494, 2:385

Spilsby Lincs
Phoenix Reynard Street
Tel: 0790 53675/53621
Seats: 264

Stafford Staffs
Apollo New Port Road
Tel: 0785 51277
Seats: 1:305, 2:170, 3:168
Picture House Bridge Street
Tel: 0785 58291
Seats: 483

Staines Surrey
Cannon Clarence Street
Tel: 0784 53316/59140
Seats: 1:586, 2:361, 3:173

Stalybridge Greater Manchester
New Palace Market Street
Tel: 061 338 2156
Seats: 414

Stanley Co Durham
Civic Hall★
Tel: 0207 32164
Seats: 632

Stevenage Herts
Cannon St Georges Way
Tel: 0438 313267/316396
Seats: 1:340, 2:182
Gordon Craig Theatre Lytton Way★
Tel: 0438 354568/316291
Seats: 507

Stockport Greater Manchester
Davenport Buxton Road
Tel: 061 483 3801/2
Seats: 1:1,794 ◐, 2:170
Cannon Grand Central
Ten screens

Stockton Cleveland
Cannon Dovecot Street ♿
Tel: 0642 676048
Seats: 1:242, 2:110, 3:125
Dovecot Arts Centre Dovecot Street
Tel: 0642 611625/611659
Seats: 100

Stoke-on-Trent Staffs
bfi **Film Theatre College Road**
Tel: 0782 411188
Seats: 212
Odeon 8 Etruria Road
Tel: 0782 215311
Seats: 1:177, 2:177, 3:309, 4:150, 5:160, 6:160, 7:521, 8:150

Stowmarket Suffolk
Movieland Church Walk
Tel: 0449 672890
Seats: 234
Regal Ipswich Street★
Tel: 0449 612825
Seats: 234

Stratford-upon-Avon Warwicks
Waterside
Tel: 0789 69285
Seats: 140

Street Somerset
bfi **Strode Theatre Church Road** ♿ ★
Tel: 0458 42846
Seats: 400

Sudbury Suffolk
Quay Theatre Quay Lane
Tel: 0787 74745
Seats: 129

Sunderland Tyne & Wear
Cannon Holmeside
Tel: 091 567 4148
Seats: 1:550, 2:209
Empire High Street West★
Tel: 0783 42517
Seats: 1,000
Studio High Street West
Tel: 0783 42517
Seats: 150

Sunninghill Berks
Novello Theatre High Street★
Tel: 0990 20881
Seats: 160

Sutton Coldfield West Mids
Odeon Birmingham Road
Tel: 021 354 2714
Seats: 1:598, 2:132, 3:118, 4:307

Swanage Dorset
Mowlem Shore Road
Tel: 0929 422229
Seats: 400

Swindon Wilts
MGM Multiplex Shaw Ridge Leisure Park
Tel: 0793 877727
Seats: 1,800 (7 screens)
Wyvern Theatre Square★
Tel: 0793 24481
Seats: 617

Tamworth Staffs
Palace Lower Gungate
Tel: 0827 57100
Seats: 325
UCI

Seats: 203 (8 screens), 327 (2 screens)

Teignmouth Devon
Riviera Den Crescent
Tel: 0626 774624
Seats: 417

Telford Shropshire
UCI Telford Centre 10 Forgegate
Tel: 0952 290606/290126
Seats: 1:192, 2:189, 3:189, 4:192, 5:278, 6:278, 7:192, 8:189, 9:189, 10:192

Tenbury Wells Hereford & Worcs
Regal Teme Street
Tel: 0584 810235
Seats: 260

Tewkesbury Glos
Roses Theatre
Tel: 0684 295074
Seats: 375

Thirsk North Yorks
Studio One
Tel: 0845 24559
Seats: 238

Tiverton Devon
Tivoli Fore Street
Tel: 0884 252157
Seats: 364

Toftwood Norfolk
CBA Shipham Road
Tel: 0362 3261
Seats: 30

Tonbridge Kent
Angel Centre Angel Lane⋆
Tel: 0732 359588
Seats: 306

Torquay Devon
Odeon Abbey Road
Tel: 0803 292324
Seats: 1:309, 2:346

Torrington Devon
Plough Fore Street
Tel: 0805 22552/3
Seats: 108

Truro Cornwall
Plaza Lemon Street
Tel: 0872 72894
Seats: 1:849, 2:102, 3:160

Tunbridge Wells Kent
Cannon Mount Pleasant
Tel: 0892 41141/23135
Seats: 1:450 ♿ 2:402, 3:124

Uckfield East Sussex
Picture House High Street
Tel: 0825 763822
Seats: 1:150, 2:100

Ulverston Cumbria
Laurel & Hardy Museum Upper Brook Street⋆ ◐
Tel: 0229 52292/86614
Seats: 50 (free)
Roxy Brogden Street
Tel: 0229 53797/56211
Seats: 310

Urmston Greater Manchester
Curzon Princess Road
Tel: 061 748 2929
Seats: 1:400, 2:134

Uttoxeter Staffs
Elite High Street
Tel: 08893 3348
Seats: 120

Uxbridge Middx
Odeon High Street
Tel: 0426 931395/0895 813139
Seats: 1:230, 2:439

Wadebridge Cornwall
Regal The Platt
Tel: 020 881 2791
Seats: 1:250, 2:120

Wakefield West Yorks
Cannon Kirkgate
Tel: 0924 373400/365236
Seats: 1:532, 2:233, 3:181

Walkden Greater Manchester
Unit Four Bolton Road
Tel: 061 790 9432
Seats: 1:118, 2:108, 3:86, 4:94

Wallasey Merseyside
Unit Four Egremont
Tel: 051 639 2833
Seats: 1:181, 2:127, 3:177, 4:105, 5:91, 6:92

Wallingford Oxon
Corn Exchange⋆
Tel: 0491 39336
Seats: 187

Walsall West Mids
Cannon Townend Bank
Tel: 0922 22444/644330
Seats: 1:506, 2:247, 3:143
Showcase Bentley Mill Lane Darlaston
Tel: 0922 22123
Seats: 2,800 (12 screens)

Waltham Cross Herts
Cannon High Street
Tel: 092 761160
Seats: 1:460, 2:284, 3:103, 4:83

Wantage Oxon
Regent Newbury Street
Tel: 02357 71155/67878
Two screens

Wareham Dorset
Rex West Street
Tel: 092 95 2778
Seats: 239

Warrington Cheshire
Odeon Buttermarket Street
Tel: 0426 950170
Seats: 1:576, 2:291, 3:196
UCI Westbrook 10 Westbrook Centre Cromwell Avenue
Tel: 0925 416677
Seats: 1:192, 2:189, 3:189, 4:192, 5:278, 6:278, 7:192, 8:189, 9:189, 10:192

Washington Tyne & Wear
Fairworld Victoria Road
Tel: 091 416 2711
Seats: 1:227, 2:177

Watford Herts
Cannon Merton Road
Tel: 0923 24088/33259
Seats: 1:356, 2:195

Wellingborough Northants
Palace Gloucester Place
Tel: 0933 222184
Two screens

Wellington Somerset
Wellesley Mantle Street
Tel: 0823 272291
Seats: 429

Welwyn Garden City Herts
bfi **Campus West**⋆
Tel: 0707 332880
Seats: 365

West Bromwich West Mids
Kings Paradise Street
Tel: 021 553 7605/0030
Seats: 1:326, 2:287, 3:462

Westgate-on-Sea Kent
Carlton St Mildreds Road
Tel: 0843 32019
Seats: 303

Weston-super-Mare Avon
Odeon The Centre
Tel: 0426 950499
Seats: 1:875, 2:110, 3:133
Playhouse High Street⋆
Tel: 0934 23521/31701
Seats: 658

West Thurrock Essex
UCI Lakeside 10 Waterglade Park Centre ♿
Tel: 0708 869920
Seats: 270 (2 screens), 192 (4 screens), 186 (4 screens)
Warner Lakeside Shopping Centre
Tel: 0708 891010
Seats: 1:382, 2:184, 3:177, 4:237, 5:498, 6:338, 7:208

Weymouth Dorset
Cannon Gloucester Street
Tel: 0305 785847
Seats: 412

Whitby North Yorks
Coliseum Victoria Square⋆
Tel: 0947 604641
Seats: 226

Whitefield Lancs
Mayfair Bury Old Road
Tel: 061 766 2369
Seats: 1:578, 2:232

Whitehaven Cumbria
Gaiety Tangier Street
Tel: 0946 3012
Seats: 330

Whitley Bay Tyne & Wear
Playhouse Park Road
Tel: 0632 523505
Seats: 860

Wigan Greater Manchester
Ritz Station Road
Tel: 0942 323632
Seats: 1:485, 2:321, 3:106
Unit Four Ormskirk Road
Tel: 0942 214336
Seats: 1:99, 2:117, 3:88

Wilmslow Cheshire
Rex Alderley Road⋆
Tel: 0625 522145
Seats: 838

Wincanton Somerset
Plaza South Street⋆
Seats: 346

Winchester Hants
Theatre Royal Jewry Street★
Tel: 0962 843434
Seats: 405

Withington Greater Manchester
Cine-City Wilmslow Road
Tel: 061 445 3301
Seats: 1:150, 2:150, 3:150

Woking Surrey
QEII Cinema★
Tel: 0483 755855

Wolverhampton West Mids
Cannon Garrick Street
Tel: 0902 22917/11244
Seats: 1:590, 2:127, 3:94
Light House Lichfield Street
Tel: 0902 312033
Seats: 120

Woodbridge Suffolk
Riverside Theatre Quay Street
Tel: 039 43 2174
Seats: 280

Woodhall Spa Lincs
Kinema in the Woods Coronation Road
Tel: 0526 52166
Seats: 365

Worcester Hereford & Worcs
Northwick Ombersley Road★
Tel: 0905 755141
Seats: 700
Odeon Foregate Street
Tel: 0905 24733
Seats: 1:650, 2:205, 3:109, 4:109, 5:66

Worksop Notts
Regal Carlton Road
Tel: 0909 482896
Seats: 1:326★, 2:154

Worsley Greater Manchester
Unit Four Bolton Road
Tel: 061 790 9432
Seats: 1:118, 2:108, 3:86, 4:94

Worthing West Sussex
Connaught Theatre Union Place★
Tel: 0903 31799/35333
Seats: 400
Dome Marine Parade
Tel: 0903 200461
Seats: 650

Wymondham Norfolk
Regal Friarscroft Lane
Tel: 0953 602025
Seats: 300

Yeovil Somerset
Cannon Court Ash Terrace
Tel: 0935 23663
Seats: 1:575, 2:239, 3:247

York North Yorks
bfi **City Screen Tempest Anderson Hall** ♿ ★
Yorkshire Museum
Tel: 0904 612940
Seats: 300
bfi **Film Theatre Central Hall York University** ♿ ★
Tel: 0904 612940
Seats: 750
Odeon Blossom Street
Tel: 0904 623040
Seats: 1:834, 2:111, 3:111
Warner Clifton Moor ♿
Tel: 0904 691199/691094
Seats: 1:128, 2:212, 3:316, 4:441, 5:185, 6:251, 7:251, 8:185, 9:441, 10:316, 11:212, 12:128

CHANNEL ISLANDS AND ISLE OF MAN

Douglas Isle of Man
Palace Cinema
Tel: 0624 76814
Seats: 1:319, 2:120
Summerland Cinema
Tel: 0624 25511
Seats: 200

St Helier Jersey
Odeon Bath Street
Tel: 0534 24166
Seats: 1:719, 2:171, 3:213

St Peter Port Guernsey
Beau Sejour Centre
Tel: 0481 26964
Seats: 398

St Saviour Jersey
Cine de France St Saviour's Road
Tel: 0534 71611
Seats: 291

SCOTLAND

A number of BFI-supported cinemas in Scotland also receive substantial central funding and programming/ management support via the Scottish Film Council

Aberdeen Grampian
Cannon Union Street
Tel: 0224 591477/587458
Seats: 1:566, 2:153, 3:146
Capitol Union Street
Tel: 0224 583141
Seats: 2,010
Odeon Justice Mill Lane
Tel: 0224 586050
Seats: 1:400, 2:123, 3:123, 4:216, 5:216

Annan Dumfries & Gall
Ladystreet, Lady Street ◐
Tel: 046 12 2796
Seats: 450

Arbroath Tayside
Palace James Street
Tel: 0241 73069
Seats: 900

Aviemore Highland
Speyside Aviemore Centre
Tel: 0479 810627
Seats: 721

Ayr Strathclyde
Odeon Burns Statue Square
Tel: 0292 264048
Seats: 1:388, 2:166, 3:135, 4:366

Bathgate Lothian
Regal Northbridge Street ♿
Tel: 0506 634152
Seats: 467

Brechin Tayside
Kings High Street
Tel: 035 62 2140
Seats: 754

Campbeltown Strathclyde
Picture House Hall Street★
Tel: 0586 2264
Seats: 265

Castle Douglas Dumfries & Gall
Palace St Andrews Street ◐
Tel: 0556 2141
Seats: 400

Clydebank Strathclyde
UCI Clydebank 10 Clyde Regional Centre Britannia Way
Tel: 041 951 1949/2022
Seats: 1:200, 2:200, 3:228, 4:252, 5:385, 6:385, 7:252, 8:228, 9:200, 10:200

Cumnock Strathclyde
Picture House Glaisnock Street
Tel: 0290 20160
Seats: 652

Dumfries Dumfries & Gall
Cannon Shakespeare Street
Tel: 0387 53578
Seats: 532
Robert Burns Centre Film Theatre Mill Road★
Tel: 0387 64808
Seats: 67

Dundee Tayside
Cannon Seagate
Tel: 0382 26865/25247
Seats: 1:618, 2:319
bfi **Steps Theatre The Wellgate** ♿ ★
Tel: 0382 24938/23141
Seats: 250

Dunfermline Fife
Orient Express East Port
Tel: 0383 721934
Seats: 1:212, 2:157, 3:97(V)

Dunoon Strathclyde
Studio John Street
Tel: 0369 4545
Seats: 1:188, 2:70

East Kilbride Lanarkshire
UCI Olympia Mall 9 Town Centre
Tel: 03552 49022
Seats: 319, 217 (3 screens), 209, 206 (4 screens)

Edinburgh Lothian
Cameo Home Street Tollcross ♿
Tel: 031 228 4141
Seats: 1:398, 2:78, 3:68
Cannon Lothian Road
Tel: 031 228 1638/299 3030
Seats: 1:868, 2:738 ♿ 3:318 ♿
Dominion Newbattle Terrace
Tel: 031 447 2660
Seats: 1:584, 2:296, 3:50

bfi **Filmhouse Lothian Road** ♿ ▣
Tel: 031 228 2688/6382
Seats: 1:285, 2:101
Odeon Clerk Street
Tel: 031 667 7331/2
Seats: 1:695, 2:293 ♿
3:201 ♿ 4:259, 5:182
Playhouse Leith Walk★
Tel: 031 557 2692
Seats: 3,131
UCI Craig Park Newcraighall Road
Tel: 031 669 0777
Seats: 168 (6 screens), 208 (4 screens), 308 (2 screens)

Elgin Grampian
Moray Playhouse High Street
Tel: 0343 542680
Seats: 1:330, 2:220

Eyemouth Berwicks
Cinema Church Street
Tel: 0390 50490
Seats: 220

Falkirk Central
Cannon Princess Street
Tel: 0324 31713/23805
Seats: 1:704, 2:128 ♿
3:128

Fort William Highlands
Studios 1 and 2
Tel: 0397 5095

Galashiels Borders
Kingsway Market Street
Tel: 0896 2767
Seats: 395

Girvan Strathclyde
Vogue Dalrymple Street ◐
Tel: 0465 2101
Seats: 500

Glasgow Strathclyde
Cannon Clarkston Road Muirend ♿
Tel: 041 637 2641
Seats: 1:482, 2:208
Cannon Grand Jamaica Street
Tel: 041 248 4620
Seats: 326
Cannon The Forge Parkhead ♿ ▣
Tel: 041 554 1483
Seats: 1:434, 2:434, 3:322, 4:262, 5:208, 6:144, 7:132
Cannon Sauchiehall Street
Tel: 041 332 1592/9513
Seats: 1:970, 2:872 ▣ (rear), 3:384, 4:206 ▣ 5:194 ▣

bfi **Film Theatre Rose Street** ♿ ▣
Tel: 041 332 6535
Seats: 1:404, 2:144
Grosvenor Ashton Lane Hillhead
Tel: 041 339 4298
Seats: 1:277, 2:253
Odeon Renfield Street ♿
Tel: 041 332 8701/3413
Seats: 1:1,138, 2:208, 3:227, 4:240, 5:288, 6:222
Salon Vinnicome Street Hillhead ♿
Tel: 041 339 4256
Seats: 406

Glenrothes Fife
Kingsway Church Street
Tel: 0592 750980
Seats: 1:294, 2:223

Hamilton Strathclyde
Odeon Townhead Street
Tel: 0698 283802/422384
Seats: 1:466, 2:224, 3:310

Inverness Highland
Eden Court Bishops Road
Tel: 0463 221718/239841
Seats: 1:797, 2:70
La Scala Strothers Lane
Tel: 0463 233302
Seats: 1:438, 2:255

Inverurie Grampian
Victoria West High Street
Tel: 0467 21436
Seats: 473

Irvine Strathclyde
Magnum Harbour Street
Tel: 0294 78381
Seats: 323
WMR Film Centre Bank Street
Tel: 0294 79900/76817
Seats: 252

Kelso Borders
Roxy
Tel: 0573 24609
Seats: 260

Kilmarnock Strathclyde
Cannon Titchfield Street
Tel: 0563 25234/37288
Seats: 1:602, 2:193, 3:149

Kirkcaldy Fife
bfi **Adam Smith Theatre Bennochy Road** ♿ ▣ ★
Tel: 0592 260498/202855
Seats: 475
Cannon High Street
Tel: 0592 260143/201520
Seats: 1:547, 2:287 ♿
3:235 ♿

Kirkwall Orkney
Phoenix Junction Road
Tel: 0856 4407
Seats: 500

Livingston Lothian
Caledonian Almondvale Centre ♿
Tel: 0506 33163
Seats: 1:168, 2:165

Lockerbie Dumfries & Gall
Rex Bridge Street ◐
Tel: 05762 2547
Seats: 195

Millport Strathclyde
The Cinema (Town Hall) Clifton Street ◐
Tel: 0475 530741
Seats: 250

Motherwell Lanarkshire
Civic Theatre★
Tel: 0698 66166

Newton Stewart Dumfries & Gall
Cinema Victoria Street
Tel: 0671 2058
Seats: 412

Oban Strathclyde
Highland Theatre George Street★
Tel: 0631 62444
Seats: 420

Paisley Strathclyde
Kelburnie Glasgow Road
Tel: 041 889 3612
Seats: 1:249, 2:248

Perth Tayside
Playhouse Murray Street
Tel: 0738 23126
Seats: 1:590, 2:227, 3:196

Peterhead Grampian
Playhouse Queen Street
Tel: 0779 71052
Seats: 731

Pitlochry Tayside
Regal Athal Road ◐
Tel: 0796 2560
Seats: 400

St Andrews Fife
New Picture House North Street
Tel: 0334 73509
Seats: 1:739, 2:94

Saltcoats Strathclyde
La Scala Hamilton Street
Tel: 0294 63345/68999
Seats: 1:301, 2:142

Stirling Central
Allanpark, Allanpark Road
Tel: 0786 74137
Seats: 1:321, 2:287
bfi **MacRobert Arts Centre University of Stirling** ♿ ▣ ★
Tel: 0786 73171
Seats: 500

WALES

Aberaman Aberdare
Grand Theatre Cardiff Road★
Tel: 0685 872310
Seats: 950

Aberystwyth Dyfed
Commodore Bath Street
Tel: 0970 612421
Seats: 410

Bala Gwynedd
Neuadd Buddig★
Tel: 0678 520 800
Seats: 372

Bangor Gwynedd
Plaza High Street
Tel: 0248 362059
Seats: 1:306, 2:163
Theatr Gwynedd Deiniol Road
Tel: 0248 351707/351708
Seats: 343

Bargoed Mid Glam
Cameo High Street
Tel: 0443 831172
Seats: 302

Barry South Glam
Theatre Royal Broad Street
Tel: 0446 735019
Seats: 496

Brecon Powys
Coliseum Film Centre Wheat Street
Tel: 0874 2501
Seats: 1:164, 2:164

Brynamman Dyfed
Public Hall Station Road

Tel: 0269 823232
Seats: 838

Brynmawr Gwent
Market Hall
Market Square
Tel: 0495 310576
Seats: 320

Builth Wells Powys
Wyeside Arts Centre
Castle Street
Tel: 0982 552555
Seats: 210

Cardiff South Glam
Cannon Queen Street
Tel: 0222 31715
Seats: 1:616, 2:313, 3:152
bfi **Chapter Market Road** ♿
Tel: 0222 396061
Seats: 1:195, 2:78
Monico Pantbach Road
Tel: 0222 691505
Seats: 1:500, 2:156
Monroe Globe Centre Albany Road
Seats: 216
Odeon Queen Street
Tel: 0222 227058
Seats: 1:448, 2:643
Odeon Capitol Shopping Centre Queen Street
Seats: 1,227 (5 screens)
bfi **Sherman Theatre Senghennydd Road** ♿ ☑ ⋆
Tel: 0222 30451/396844
Seats: 474
St David's Hall The Hayes⋆
Tel: 0222 371236/42611
Seats: 1,600

Carmarthen Dyfed
Lyric King's Street⋆
Tel: 0267 232632
Seats: 800

Cwmbran Gwent
Scene The Mall
Tel: 063 33 66621
Seats: 1:115, 2:78, 3:130

Denbigh Powys
Futura
Tel: 0745 715210
Seats: 112

Fishguard Dyfed
Studio West Street
Tel: 0348 873421/874051
Seats: 252

Gilfach Goch Mid Glam
Workmen's Hall Glenarvon Terrace
Tel: 044 386 231
Seats: 400

Haverfordwest Dyfed
Palace Upper Market Street
Tel: 0437 2426
Seats: 538

Holyhead Gwynedd
Empire Stanley Street
Tel: 0407 2093
Seats: 1:350, 2:159

Llandudno Gwynedd
Palladium Gloddaeth Street
Tel: 0492 76244
Seats: 355

Llanelli Dyfed
Entertainment Centre Station Road
Tel: 0554 774057/752659
Seats: 1:516, 2:310, 3:122

Merthyr Tydfil Mid Glam
Studio Castle Street
Tel: 0685 3877
Seats: 1:98, 2:198

Milford Haven Dyfed
Torch Theatre
St Peters Road
Tel: 064 62 4192/5267
Seats: 297

Mold Clwyd
bfi **Theatr Clwyd Civic Centre** ♿
Tel: 0352 56331
Seats: 1:530, 2:129

Monmouth Gwent
Magic Lantern Church Street
Tel: 0600 3146
Seats: 124

Neath Glam
Windsor
Tel: 0639 646019
Seats: 470

Newport Gwent
Cannon Bridge Street
Tel: 0633 54326
Seats: 1:572, 2:190, 3:126

Newtown Powys
Regent Broad Street
Tel: 0686 25917
Seats: 210

Pontypool Gwent
Scala Osborne Road
Tel: 049 55 56038
Seats: 197

Pontypridd Mid Glam
bfi **Muni Screen Municipal Hall Gelliwasted Road** ♿ ☑ ⋆
Tel: 0443 485934
Seats: 400

Porthcawl Mid Glam
Regent Trecco Bay ◐
Tel: 065 671 2103
Seats: 168

Portmadoc Gwynedd
Coliseum Avenue Road
Tel: 0766 2108
Seats: 582

Port Talbot West Glam
Plaza Theatre Talbot Road
Tel: 0639 882856
Seats: 1:846, 2:196, 3:111

Prestatyn Clwyd
Scala High Street
Tel: 07456 4365
Seats: 314

Pwllheli Gwynedd
Town Hall Cinema
Tel: 0758 613371
Seats: 450

Resolven West Glam
Welfare Hall Cinema
Tel: 0269 592395
Seats: 541

Rhyl Clwyd
Apollo High Street
Tel: 0745 353856
Seats: 1:250, 2:225

St Athan South Glam
Astra Llantwit Major RAF St Athan
Tel: 04465 3131 x4124
Seats: 350

Swansea West Glam
Filmcenta Worcester Place
Tel: 0792 653433
Seats: 650
Odeon Kingsway
Tel: 0792 652351
Seats: 1:708, 2:242, 3:172
UCI Parc Tawe 10
Tel: 0792 644980
Seats: 277 (2 screens), 174 (4 screens), 156 (4 screens)

Taibach West Glam
Entertainment Taibach
Seats: 200

Tenby Dyfed
Royal Playhouse White Lion Street
Tel: 0834 4809
Seats: 479

Treorchy Mid Glam
Parc and Dare Hall Station Road
Tel: 0443 773112
Seats: 794

Tywyn Gwynedd
The Cinema
Tel: 0654 710260
Seats: 368

Wrexham Clwyd
Hippodrome Henblas Street
Tel: 0978 364479
Seats: 613

NORTHERN IRELAND

Antrim Antrim
Cinema Castle Street
Tel: 084 94 3136
Seats: 400
Coltworthy House Arts Centre Louth Road

Ballymena Antrim
State Ballymoney Road
Tel: 0266 2306
Seats: 1:215, 2:166

Banbridge Down
Iveagh Huntley Road
Tel: 082 06 22423
Seats: 930

Bangor Down
Cineplex
Tel: 0247 271360
Four screens

Belfast Antrim
Cannon Fisherwick Place
Tel: 0232 222484/248110
Seats: 1:551, 2:444, 3:281, 4:215
Curzon 300 Ormeau Road
Tel: 0232 491071/641373
Seats: 1:453, 2:360, 3:200, 4:104
bfi **Queen's Film Theatre University Square Mews** ♿
Tel: 0232 244857/667687
Seats: 1:250, 2:150
The Strand Hollywood Road
Tel: 0232 673500
Four screens

Coleraine Londonderry
Palladium Society Street
Tel: 0265 2948
Seats: 538

Cookstown Tyrone
Ritz Studio Burn Road
Tel: 06487 65182
Seats: 1:192, 2:128

Downpatrick Down
Grand Market Street
Tel: 0396 2104
Seats: 450

Dungannon Tyrone
Astor George's Street
Tel: 08687 23662

Dungiven Derry
St Canice Hall
Main Street

Enniskillen
Fermanagh
Ritz Forthill Street
Tel: 0365 22096
Seats: 450
Ardhowen Centre
Dublin Road
Tel: 0365 23233
Seats: 296

Glengormley Antrim
Moviehouse Glenville Road
Tel: 0232 833424
Seats: 1:309, 2:243, 3:117, 4:110, 5:76, 6:51

Keady Armagh
Scala Cinema
Granemore Road
Tel: 0861 531547
Seats: 200

Kilkeel Down
Vogue Newry Street
Seats: 413

Londonderry
Londonderry
Strand, Strand Road
Tel: 0504 262084
Seats: 1:293, 2:178

Magherafelt
Londonderry
Cinema Queen Street
Tel: 0648 33172
Seats: 230

Newry Down
Savoy 2 Merchant's Quay
Tel: 0693 67549
Seats: 1:197, 2:58

Portrush Antrim
Playhouse
Tel: 0265 823917

♿ – Accessible to people with disabilities (advance arrangements sometimes necessary – please phone cinemas to check)

– Induction loop for the hard of hearing

bfi – Supported by the BFI through finance, programming assistance or occasional programming/publicity services

⋆ – Part-time or occasional screenings

◐ – Cinema open seasonally

(V) – Video

Acknowledgements: Artsline, London's information and advice centre on arts and entertainment for disabled people; Artlink Lincolnshire/ Humberside; Shape East; Equal Arts (Northern Shape); Project Ability Glasgow; East Midlands Shape; Disability Scotland; Artlink Edinburgh and the Lothians; Artshow Avon; Artlink West Yorkshire; Artability

COURSES

Film and TV study courses generally fall into two categories: academic and practical. Listed here are the educational establishments which offer film and television as part of a course or courses. Where a course is mainly practical, this is indicated with a P next to the course title. In the remaining courses, the emphasis is usually on theoretical study; some of these courses include a minor practical component as described. The information here is drawn from two BFI Education booklets – 'Film and television training: A guide to courses' and 'Studying film and tv: A list of courses in higher education'. More information about listed courses can be found in these booklets, along with information on certain further education courses not included here

Advancement of Film Education Charitable Trust

4 Stanley Buildings
Pancras Road
London NW1 2TD
Tel: 071 837 5473
The purpose of this organisation is to make professional-level, practical film education available on a part-time basis to those who may have neither the means nor the time to attend a full-time film course

P Part-time course in practical 16mm filmmaking
Both Beginner and Intermediate courses integrate learning with production. The bias is that of traditional narrative, and despite limitations of scale the course allows students to realise personal, artistic, social and cultural expression in this medium
a) One year Beginners course. Storyboarding leading to 35mm stills exercise. Instruction and practicals in camera, lenses, lighting, lightmeter and editing, leading to 16mm sequence which will be edited. Scripting and shooting group film with individual sequences, production and crewing of these, rotating jobs. Editing films, introduction to sound, then scripting and shooting individual film for each student
b) One year Intermediate course. This course provides a five-minute sync-sound film for each student

Barking College of Technology

General Education Department
Dagenham Road
Romford RM7 0XU
Tel: 0708 766841

P B/TEC National Diploma in Media
Two year full-time course in video, radio and print. Facilities include 3 camera colour television studio, S-VHS and VHS editing facilities, sound recording studios and full desktop publishing and print workshops

University of Bath

School of Modern Languages and International Studies
Claverton Down
Bath BA2 7AY
Tel: 0225 826826

BA (Hons) Modern Languages and European Studies
First year lectures and seminars on the language and theory of film, whilst the second and fourth years offer a wide range of options on French films between the wars, the films of the Nouvelle Vague, film and television in German speaking countries and film in Italy and the Soviet Union. There is a final year option dealing with European cinema in the 70s and 80s. No practical component

MPhil and PhD
Part-time or full-time research degrees in French cinema

Bedford College of Higher Education

Polhill Avenue
Bedford MK41 9EA
Tel: 0234 351671

Modular BA/BSc Programme (Arts Pathway)
Dance and Drama in Contemporary Culture
Two modules in Year: Film, Television and Realism. Each module 3 hours per week for 15 weeks. One and a half hours theory in Dance and Drama; one and a half hours practical video production focusing on either Dance or Drama

University of Birmingham

Department of Cultural Studies
Faculty of Commerce and Social Sciences
PO Box 363
Birmingham B15 2TT
Tel: 021 414 6060/6061

B Soc Sc. (Hons) Media and Cultural Studies
A wide-ranging analytic degree concerned with contemporary social and cultural issues, of which media are a part. Course (brochure available) includes media history; year's course on contemporary media, particularly press and TV; option of specialist dissertation on media; some practical SLR photography (Year 1), video (Year 2), plus short period of placement in local media organisations

BA (Combined Hons) Media and Cultural Studies
A half degree, either combined with another Arts subject or as base for a General degree. Because the department is small, the single honours degree includes courses outside the department. In practice the half degree omits little of the full degree. All modes of entry are heavily oversubscribed: standard offer BBC. Mature/access candidates especially welcome

Department of French Studies

BA (Hons) French
Four-year course which includes options on French cinema (Year 1), documentary film (Year 2) and the practice of transposing works of fiction to the screen (Year 4). Also options on French television: Reading television (Year 1), television and ideology (Year 2), and television genres (Year 4). The third year of the course is spent at a French university. Students are encouraged to follow courses in Cinema and/or TV as preparation for Year 4 studies

Bournemouth and Poole College of Art and Design

School of Film, Television and Audio Visual Production
Wallisdown Road
Poole
Dorset BH12 5HH
Tel: 0202 538204

P B/TEC National Diploma in Audio Visual Design
A new course, offering tape-slide, video production and audio recording at a practical level. Facilities include 9 projector Multivision rig, 4 track and 8 track music studios, VHS and S-VHS cameras and edit suite and full photographic rostrum. Supported by design studies, creative writing, music and word processing

P B/TEC Higher National Diploma in Design (Film and Television)
An extensive and intensively practical two-year course based on the production process. All areas of film and television production are covered, with an emphasis on drama and documentary. The majority of work is student originated, with an equal emphasis on film and tape processes. The course has a substantial input from, and contact with, working professionals within the industry. The course has full BECTU accreditation. Facilities include: Arriflex SR and BL Film cameras, Nagra 4.2 recorders, Steenbeck, pic-syncs, PAG dubbing suite, 2 fully spec'd (multicamera) studios, 2 Hitachi FP60 cameras, 2 FP21 and 1 FP40 cameras, Sony 4800 recorders, Sony 5 series edit suites, Quantel paintbox, video and film rostra, 4 and 8 track music studios. Now added full Betacam SP Sony BVP 7 camera, BVW 35 recorder, 3 machine (BVW 60, 65, 70) Betacam SP edit suite

P Advanced Diploma in Media Production
Film/television option. One-year production opportunity for post B/TEC, postgraduate and mid-career students. Application through personal statement of intent and interview. Runs in tandem with HND course, as above

Bournemouth Polytechnic

Department of Communication and Media
Wallisdown Road
Poole
Dorset BH1 5BB
Tel: 0202 524111

P BA (Hons) Media Production
A three-year course covering the academic, practical, aesthetic, technical and professional aspects of work in the media. The course is equally divided between practical and theoretical studies. After Year 1 students can specialise in audio, video or computer graphics, leading to a major production project in Year 3. In addition students complete a piece of individual research in the area of Communication Processes. Facilities include 4-colour CCTV studio with DVE equipment, 6 U-Matic edit suites, 6 U-Matic O/B units, 5 sound studios (including a radio studio linked directly to BBC Radio Solent), 21 computer graphics workstations including Iris 2400 Turbo, DG MV400 and 3 Sony SMC 70s

P Postgraduate Diploma/MA in Video Production
A one-year full-time course for graduates wishing to acquire the skills of producing and directing television and video. It is based on practical project work in the studio and on location, using Betacam SP

University of Bristol

Department of Drama
29 Park Row
Bristol BS1 5LT
Tel: 0272 303030

BA Drama
Three-year course, includes introduction to critical and theoretical approaches to film and television in year 1; core seminar courses in film history, with additional academic and practical options in year 2, and a number of optional extras in film and television in year 3. Practical courses extend the critical and practical work using multi-camera studio and single camera OB video resulting in the production of original works in the most appropriate format

P Postgraduate Certificate in Radio, Film and Television
One-year practical course. It offers a grounding in practical skills in film and tv production, centring on group exercises in studio television, location and studio film and video projects, and fiction and non-fiction productions for public exhibition and/or broadcast. Production equipment includes a broadcast-standard television studio, U-Matic video production and post-production facilities, 16mm Arriflex/Nagra production outfits, and 4 film cutting rooms with Steenbeck and Prevost tables. Additional video, sound and photographic facilities are available for students' preparatory work. In addition the Drama department has a fully equipped professional theatre whose resources and technical support are available to students. The course is BECTU accredited

Brunel University

Department of Human Sciences
Uxbridge
Middx UB8 3PH
Tel: 0895 56461

BSc Communication and Information Studies
Four-year inter-disciplinary course which aims to give an understanding of the social, intellectual and practical dimensions of the new technologies. Includes practical courses in computing and in video production and technology. All students undertake three periods (five months) of work placement
MA in Communications and Technology
Offers an advanced training in the social study of new technology in relation to issues of communications and cultural policy and technological and social change. It is structured around a programme of formal lectures, directed reading and participation in seminars and class discussion. Students take a core course in Communications and Technology, a research course resulting in a dissertation and two optional courses. The course is completed in one year (full-time) or two years (part-time)

College of Cardiff
University of Wales
PO Box 908
French Section
EUROS
Cardiff
Tel: 0222 875000
BA French
Study of French cinema included as part of optional courses. Small practical component
BA German
Study of contemporary German cinema forms part of both compulsory and optional courses

Polytechnic of Central London
School of Communication
18-22 Riding House Street
London W1P 7PD
Tel: 071 486 5811
P BA (Hons) Film, Video and Photographic Arts
Gives equal emphasis to filmmaking and to film theory and criticism. This modular degree has two pathways: Film and Television, and Photography and Multimedia. Film and TV students combine theoretical study with practical productions. The film course is BECTU-accredited. Facilities include a photographic studio suite, a film studio and television studio with all the associated control rooms, changing rooms and stores, a dubbing theatre, transfer room, editing rooms, animation room, radio and recording studios, design studio, black and white and colour processing and printing areas, loading rooms, full computing and desk top publishing facilities, tape/slide room, workshops and labs. Film equipment includes self-blimped and non-synchronous film cameras (all film-making is done on 16mm), tape-recorders, 12 motorised editing machines, 7-track 'rock and roll' dubbing system, 10-channel mixing desk, animation stand, 3 U-Matic ENG systems, VHS portapack systems and 3 U-Matic/VHS edit suites
P BA (Hons) Media Studies
This degree studies the social context in which the institutions of mass communications operate, including film and television, and teaches the practice of print and broadcasting journalism and video production. On levels 2 and 3 students choose one of the following pathways: radio, journalism or video production. The course gives equal emphasis to theory/criticism and practice. The video pathway is accredited by BECTU
Linked MA and Postgraduate Diploma in Film and Television Studies
Advanced level part-time course (evenings and study weekends) concerned with theoretical aspects of film and TV. Modular credit and accumulation scheme, with exemption for work previously done. Postgraduate Diploma normally awarded after two years (70 credits), MA after three years (120 credits). Modules offered in 1991/92: Authorship, Structuralism, Realism and Anti-Realism, the Film and TV Audience, Problems of Method, Hollywood, Psychoanalysis, Third World Cinema, Issues in British Film Culture, Public Service Broadcasting, TV Genres and Gender, the Documentary Tradition, British TV Drama, Soviet Cinema, Production Studies. No practical component
MPhil and PhD Film and Television Studies (CNAA)
Research degrees in film and television history, theory and criticism. Applicants should have the Postgraduate Diploma and the MA in Film and Television Studies or equivalent qualifications and be able to submit a detailed research proposal
Short Courses in Film and Television
A range of introductory and specialist courses in film and TV skills, and in theory

Polytechnic of Central London
Centre for Communication and Information Studies
235 High Holborn
London WC1V 7DN
Tel: 071 911 5157
M.Phil and PhD research degrees in Communication and Information studies

Christ Church College
North Holmes Road
Canterbury
Kent CT1 1QU
Tel: 0227 762444
Fax: 0227 470442
P BA or BSc (Hons) in Radio, Film and Television with one other subject
RFTV is one-half of a three-year joint honours degree and may be combined with Art, English, Geography, History, Mathematics, Movement Studies, Music, Religious Studies and Science. The course introduces students to an understanding and appreciation of radio, film and TV as media of communication and creative expression, stressing their relevance to the individual and to society. It also offers an opportunity to develop and practice production skills in each of the three media. Production facilities include: a television studio, hi-band video production facilities, a film workshop with Super 8mm and 16mm film equipment
P MA in Media Production
A one-year taught MA which concentrates on production in radio, film and TV. Part I of the course introduces relevant production skills; in Part II members will fulfil a measurable major role in a production project in either radio, film or TV. Course members with practical experience can update their skills and concentrate on one medium in Part I. All course members will attend theory seminars through the course. Assessment will be based on the major piece of practical work and an extended essay

City of London Polytechnic
Department of Fine and Applied Art
Sir John Cass Faculty
59-63 Whitechapel High Street
London E1 7PF
Tel: 071 283 1030 x221
BA (Hons) Art, Design and Visual Communication
This part-time degree is designed to meet the needs and aspirations of mature students (twenty-one and over). It provides an opportunity to work with a variety of media across three related fields of study: Fine Art, Design and Communications media

Coventry Polytechnic

Coventry School of Art and Design
Gosford Street
Coventry CV1 5RZ
Tel: 0203 838540

BA (Hons) Communication Studies
Three-year course which includes optional modules in a range of aspects of communication, including a European exchange. Students must undertake a major project and may include practical/field work. This has included making video pieces. This course may be studied part-time

P BA (Hons) Fine Art
BA (Hons) Graphic Design
Students may work in film and video within the Fine Art and Graphic Design degrees

P MA/PgD Electronic Graphics
The course offers full-time students the choice of a three-term postgraduate diploma, or four-term MA. All students register initially for the postgraduate diploma and may, on successful completion, progress to the MA. This course may also be studied part-time. The course is essentially a practical one and the majority of students' time is spent using the computing equipment for the generation of electronic images. There is a significant theoretical component which is integrated with the practical activities. The school has purpose built computer studios which are interfaced to the video post-production facilities. There are also video studio facilities, film and mainframe computing

MPhil/PhD programmes
Researchers registered for MPhil/PhD awards conduct investigations into aspects of computer animation and multimedia

Derby School of Art and Design

Kedleston Road
Derby DE3 1GB
Tel: 0332 47181

P BA (Hons) Photographic Studies
Three-year course divided into two parts of five and four terms. The course offers students the ability to specialise in film/video practice in addition to the normal photographic and academic routes. Part 1 concentrates on development of ideas and investigation of ways they may be carried out. In Part 2 students are expected to assume considerable responsibility for their own work programmes. Academic studies form 30% of the course. Creative and inventive use of the media is encouraged from conception to projection. The Film and Video route on this course will be separate from 1992. Facilities include: Super 8mm sound and silent cameras, editing and projection; 16mm Bolex, Pathe, Auricon, Beaulieu, Eclair NPR, time lapse and rostrum cameras; Uhers, Nagra, Revox and 40-track Teac recorders; 6-plate flat-bed and pic sync editing; animation stand for 16mm and QAR video animation; VHS and U-Matic portable video recorders; U-Matic edit suite; studio; cinema with 35mm, 16mm and video projection

BA/BSc Modular Scheme with intermediate awards of Certificate and Diploma in Higher Education
Film and Television studies may be taken as a Major (75%), Joint (50%) or Minor (25%) option. Courses offered include Hollywood (authorship and genre), Hollywood (stars and ideology), Institutions and National Cinema, TV and Popular Culture, Race and Ethnicity in Film and TV, Realist Film and TV, Narration in Film and Television Fiction, Third Cinema, Classical Hollywood Cinema, Independent Cinema and Black Film-making, Women and Film, Science-Natural History-TV, Melodrama and Soaps, Weimar Cinema, Early Cinema (Europe), Early Cinema (GB and US), Soviet Cinema, Surrealism and Film, Film-Music-Sound, and News Gathering, New Technologies and National Boundaries. Students may complete a dissertation of 5,000 words in film and/or television studies

Linked Postgraduate Diploma/MA in Film Studies
Advanced level full-time or part-time (three year) concerned with theoretical and historical issues in the study of film and television. From 1992 the course will be offered on a modular basis with exemption for work previously completed. Modules offered at Postgraduate Diploma level: Classical Hollywood Cinema, Melodrama and Soaps, Realist Film and TV, Narration in Film and Television Fiction, Third Cinema, Spectatorship and Gender, Independent Cinema and Black Film-making, Early Cinema (Europe), Early Cinema (USA & GB), Weimar Cinema, Soviet Cinema, News Gathering, New Technologies and National Boundaries Modules offered at MA level: Advanced Narrative Theory, Film Historiography, and an independently researched dissertation. No practical component

MPhil and PhD
Students are accepted for MPhil or PhD by thesis. Particular expertise is offered in the area of early film and research is supported by the Centre for Early Film

Dewsbury College

Halifax Road
Dewsbury
West Yorkshire WF13 2AS
Tel: 0924 465916
Fax: 0924 457047

P B/TEC National Diploma in Design (Communications) Video Production and Related Studies
Two-year course in video production in which some role specialisation is possible in the second year. Students are placed in industry for a minimum of four weeks during Year 2. Facilities include: VHS and U-Matic Portapacs; 2 U-Matic lo-band edit suites with TBCs and FX generator; 2-camera studio with full mixing and Chromakey; computer graphics with animation, frame grab and video interface; computer tapeslide production; 16mm cameras; animation rostrum; still photography studios and darkrooms. Yearly intake: 20 students

University of East Anglia

School of English and American Studies
Norwich NR4 7TJ
Tel: 0603 56161

BA (Hons) Film and English Studies
A Joint Major programme which integrates Film and Television study with Literature, History and Cultural Studies. Course includes formal instruction in use of 8mm film and VHS video equipment, and either a practical project on film or video or an independent dissertation on a film or television topic

BA (Hons) in Literature, History, Linguistics, Drama or American Studies
Film can be taken as a substantial Minor programme (up to 40% of degree work) in combination with any of these Major subjects. There is no formal practical element in these programmes, but students have access to instruction in the use of 8mm film and VHS video equipment

MA Film Studies
One-year full-time taught programme. MA is awarded 50% on coursework, 50% on individual dissertation. Courses include: Early Cinema, Theories of narrative and representation in classical and post-classical cinema, Anglo-American film relations, National cinema: contemporary British cinema. There is scope for work on television as well as on other aspects of cinema. This MA includes a new specialist option, offering training in the operations and use of film archives
MPhil and PhD
Students are accepted for research degrees

Polytechnic of East London
Department of Art and Design
Greengate Street
London E14 0BG
Tel: 081 590 7722
P **BA (Hons) Fine Art**
During the first year of the course students can experiment with each of the disciplines that are available but can also specialise in film and video throughout the three years. Facilities include studio, U-Matic colour cameras and edit suite, Sony portapacks, 16mm and Super 8mm film cameras, Revox and Teac tape-recorders

Department of Cultural Studies
Livingstone House
Livingstone Road
London E15 2LL
BA (Hons) Cultural Studies
Three-year course offering options on media, film and photography in Years 2 and 3. Also includes a practical component (20%) in video, tape-slide and photography over all three years
BSc (Hons) New Technology (Interdisciplinary Studies)
This new degree examines the development, applications and implications of new technologies. The Media option involves the study and practice of video, computer graphics and newspaper production

Edinburgh College of Art
Visual Communications Department
School of Design and Crafts
Lauriston Place
Edinburgh EH3 9DF
Tel: 031 229 9311
P **BA (Hons) in Design**
Film/TV students enter the Visual Communications Dept at second year level following a foundation year in Art and Design (at ECA or elsewhere) or other relevant course or experience. Applications close on 15th March annually. Some interest in a related discipline (Illustration, Animation, Photography, Graphic Design) is expected, as the first part of the course is general. After this, Film/TV students do a combination of individual projects (eg animated sequences, TV graphics, music videos, small scale documentary) and group projects (eg live-action drama). Postgraduate applications are also welcome for the Diploma in Design (three terms) or the M.Des (four terms). Facilities include: 16mm rostrum camera, 16mm sync-sound shooting facilities, 16mm editing, super 8 equipment, video animation rostrum, computer graphics facilities, three camera TV studio, 8 track sound mixing, and video portable VCRs and edit suites in VHS, S-VHS, lo-band and hi-band SP formats

University of Exeter
American and Commonwealth Arts
School of English
Queen's Building
The Queen's Drive
Exeter EX4 4QH
Tel: 0392 264263
Fax: 0392 263108
BA (Hons) American and Commonwealth Arts
BA (Combined Hons) American and Commonwealth Arts and English
BA (Combined Hons) American and Commonwealth Arts and Music
BA (Combined Hons) American and Commonwealth Arts and Italian
Students can take up to a third of their degree in Film Studies, with the emphasis on American film. Combined Hons with Italian also include a course on Italian cinema and culture. No practical component
MA, MPhil and PhD
Students wishing to take an MA degree by coursework and dissertation or an MPhil or PhD by thesis alone can be accommodated and candidates with proposals in any aspect of American or Commonwealth cinema will be considered. Applications for postgraduate study in American Film History will be particularly welcome

School of Modern Languages
Italian Department
BA (Single and Combined Hons) Italian
Italian either on its own or combined with another subject. One of the six courses that students take is Italian cinema and culture. In general, Neo-realism to the present day

School of Education
Media and Resources Centre
St Luke's
Exeter EX1 2LU
Tel: 0392 76311
Includes subsidiary courses in Media Education at undergraduate, post-graduate and Advanced Course level. The TV facilities in the Media and Resources Centre include a three colour camera studio, control gallery and 4 machine editing suite with S-VHS and hi-band SP. The courses are both academic (award bearing) and practical (video/programme production)

Farnborough College of Technology
Boundary Road
Farnborough
Hampshire GU14 6SB
Tel: 0252 515511
P **Higher National Diploma Media Production and Business Studies**
Two year full-time course to study media production techniques with business studies. Course includes TV and video production, video and audio systems, radio, journalism and finance in the media. Principal facilities available: TV and Video studio professionally lit and equipped with three colour cameras (Sony DXC 3000); control room fully equipped with Chromakey vision effect generator and wipe facility, audio mixer, CD, tape recorders and record player, microphones and talk-back system. Edit room with 1 U-Matic SP hi-band 3-machine edit and 2 S-VHS 2 machine edit systems. An Amiga computer-generated graphics facility. Audio studio fully equipped with 12 channel mixer, 2 Revox reel-to-reel recorders, cartridge machine, CD and cassette player, record decks, microphones and professional studio console

Glasgow Polytechnic
Department of Communication
Cowcaddens Road
Glasgow G4 0BA
Tel: 041 331 3000
Fax: 041 331 3005
BA Communication Studies
Four-year course (unclassified and honours) examining the place of mass communication in contemporary society.

Includes practical studies in print, television, advertising and public relations

University of Glasgow

Department of Theatre, Film and TV Studies
Glasgow G12 8QQ
Tel: 041 330 5162
Fax: 041 330 4808

MA Joint Honours in Film and Television Studies
Four-year undergraduate course. Film/TV Studies represents 50% of an Honours degree or 30% of an Ordinary degree. Year 1 is concerned with Film and TV as 'languages', the institutional structures of British TV, and the implications of recent developments in technology and programming. Year 2 is structured under two headings: Genre in Film and Television and Film, Television and British National Culture. Years 3 and 4 consist of a range of Honours courses, four to be taken in each year. There is also a compulsory practical course, involving the production of a video

Department of French
Glasgow G12 8QQ
Tel: 041 339 8855

MA (Hons) French
Study of French Cinema is a one-year special subject comprising one two-hour seminar per fortnight plus weekly screenings. No practical component

Goldsmiths' College, University of London

Lewisham Way
London SE14 6NW
Tel: 081 692 7171

P **BA Communications**
This new course brings together theoretical analyses in social sciences and cultural studies with practical work in creative writing (fiction), electronic graphics and animation, photography, print journalism, radio, script writing and TV (video and film) production. The practical element constitutes 50% of the total degree course. The theoretical element includes media history and sociology, textual and cultural studies, personal and interpersonal contexts of communication and media management

BA Anthropology and Communication Studies
Half of this course constitutes Communication Studies. The course is mainly theoretical but does include a short practical course of ten weeks in length in one of the practice areas. These include TV, videographics and animation, radio, print journalism, photography, creative writing and script writing. The theory component is concerned with media history, sociology, psychology, textual and cultural studies

BA Communication Studies/Sociology
Communication studies constitutes half this course and is split into theoretical studies and a ten week practical course. Practical options include TV, videographics and animation, radio, print journalism, photography, creative writing and script writing. The theory component is concerned with psychology, media sociology, cultural studies, semiotics and media history

P **Diploma in Communications**
One-year full-time course with practical work in one of the following: TV and video, film, radio, photography, electronic graphics and creative writing. Students complete a 10,000-word dissertation (or three 3,000-word essays) which counts for 30% at final assessment. Equipment includes 8mm, 16mm, VHS and U-Matic editing facilities, multi-camera TV studio, Paintbox, computer graphics laboratory and video animator, photographic studio, colour and black and white darkrooms

Department of Continuing and Community Education
A programme of evening courses are offered which include video production and editing

Gwent College of Higher Education

Faculty of Art and Design
Clarence Place
Newport
Gwent NP9 0UW
Tel: 0633 259984

P **B/TEC Higher National Diploma in Film and Video Production: Live Action and Animation**
Two-year intensive vocational course. Two strands: Live Action: lighting camera operating, sound recording, film and video editing, scriptwriting, directing and art directing and producing; and Animation: scripting and storyboarding, 2 and 3D animation techniques and theory, and post production skills. All students go on placement with BBC, ITV or other production companies. Facilities include: Arriflex, Eclair and Bolex cameras, Nagra tape recorders, Steenbeck editors, Neilson Hordell rostrum camera, and VHS and lo-band U-Matic production and editing

Harrogate College of Arts and Technology

Hornbeam Park
Hookstone Road
Harrogate HG1 8QT
Tel: 0423 879466

P **B/TEC Diploma in Design (Communications)**
Two-year course providing training in a range of high tech arts subjects. Options include video production, TV graphics, computer imaging and animation, DTP, basic design, animation and model-making, sound creation, radio and tape/slide. Research and scripting are included in all areas. Course is 80% practical and vocationally based. Entry requirements: four GCSE or equivalent plus folder of relevant work. Equipment includes: 3 U-Matic edit benches, 3 portable packs, TV studio with 6 colour cameras, TV graphics, Chromakey and SEG/TBC computer graphics, 19 Amigas/Macs with laser and colour printers, purpose-built sound, radio and TV rooms and portable recorders. Also available for course use: 16mm film and darkrooms

Harrow College of the Polytechnic of Central London

Harrow School of Design and Media
Northwick Park
Harrow
Middlesex HA1 3TP
Tel: 071 911 5000

P **BA (Hons) in Contemporary Media Practice**
A practical course within a unique media environment providing students with a range of experience in photography, film and electronic imaging integrated with theoretical, historical and critical studies. After a first year which is both fundamental and experimental, students may specialise or continue using a variety of media. 60% practical, 40% theoretical. Equipment includes Arriflex and Bolex 16mm cameras; Bolex, Nalcom, Canon and Eumig Super 8mm cameras; portable hi- and lo-band U-Matic and S-VHS cameras; Nagra, Uher, Philips, Revox, Tanberg, Ferrograph and Teac tape-recorders; 8mm, 16mm, VHS and U-Matic editing facilities; specialist AV facility; computer image generators with video interface; video animation

Hatfield Polytechnic

School of Humanities and Education
Wall Hall Campus
Aldenham
Watford
Herts WD2 8AT

Tel: 0923 852511
BA (Hons) Contemporary Studies
Full-time and part-time degree for mature students. Media Studies is a half-year introductory course for first year students followed by a one-year optional course for second year students. They involve study of media practices and institutions/apparatuses. No practical component
BA (Hons) Humanities
Full or part-time degree. Includes courses on sociology of media/media studies. Within the Historical Studies Major/Minor a one year optional course available in the second year, Film and History, examines the inter-war period through film. Focuses on the historian's use of film. No practical component
BA (Hons) Social Sciences
Final year dissertation may involve studies of analyses of TV arts programming

Havering College of Further and Higher Education

Department of Art & Design
Ardleigh Green Road
Hornchurch
Essex RM11 2LL
Tel: 04024 55011
P B/TEC National Diploma Media
Full-time two year course. Options include Film and Video, Radio, AV and Print Production. Also Film and Communication Studies A Levels, plus a range of short practical courses available in scriptwriting, animation and video editing. Facilities include: two full eng kits (lo-band), various format camcorders, three editing suites (VHS and lo-band, 2 and 3 machine), 8 track audio studio, computer graphics suite

University of Hull

Department of Drama
Cottingham Road
Hull HU6 7RX
Tel: 0482 46311
P BA Joint and Special Honours
Introduction to film and TV studies in Year 1. Honours students may opt for practical courses in TV, radio and filmmaking in subsequent years. Equipment includes 16mm cameras, TV and radio studios, film and U-Matic editing

Humberside Polytechnic

School of Art, Architecture and Design
Queens Gardens
Hull HU1 3DQ
Tel: 0482 440550
Fax: 0482 586721
P BA (Hons) Graphic Design
Students may specialise in animation/film/video or graphic design or illustration. After an introductory period, animation and film primers are located in Terms 1 and 2. Full specialisation begins at the start of term 3. The course is essentially practical, with a strong theoretical/critical element and a programme of visiting animators and filmmakers. The course has strong components in scriptwriting, cinematography, direction, animation and production competence. Films are initiated by students in narrative fiction, animation, and include sponsored public-information film and videotape productions, computer animation and much experimental work. Equipment includes Bolex and Eclair cameras, Uher, Nagra Stellavox and Tandberg recorders, Steenbecks, Pic-syncs, PAG mini-rack with 16-4 2 mixing desk and effects, Neilson-Hordell 212 rostrum with bi-pack camera; JK optical printer; VHS and U-Matic portapacks and Series V editing suites; film/video studio; 3 animation stands (16mm); 2 video rostra; Rotoscope

projector/drawing table; Apple Mac DTP and animation systems, Spaceward systems; darkrooms; 16mm processing/printing; post-production and dubbing rooms; TV and sound studios; library, slide library, film/videotape collection

P BA (Hons) Fine Art
Time-based media: 8mm and 16mm film; VHS and U-Matic video; sound photography; and related live work. Course is essentially practical (80%), projects being student-initiated following the first general introductory term. Work frequently crosses disciplines including printmaking, painting and sculpture. Supported by a programme of visiting tutors, artists, film/videomakers, screenings and critical/theoretical studies (20%). Equipment as for BA (Hons) Graphic Design

P BA (Hons) Documentary Communication
This is a mixed mode honours degree with three production pathways: still photography/text; sound/radio; and video. The course provides the context within which individuals acquire the knowledge and skills pertinent to communicating in documentary forms, their understanding and interpretation of the nature and variety of human society. The course seeks to produce graduates who are able to operate professionally in a variety of contexts, and who have developed the interpersonal skills necessary to working with others in a co-operative manner. The minimum and maximum periods of study are normally 3 and 6 years respectively for the full and part-time modes of attendance. Equipment as for the other courses plus additional camcorders etc

Institute of Education, University of London
Department of English, Media and Drama
20 Bedford Way
London WC1H 0AL
Tel: 071 636 1500
Fax: 071 436 2186

PGCE English and Media Studies
One-year full-time teacher training course, including practical component. Additional PGCE Further Professional Option in Film, TV and Media Studies available within general PGCE framework (equivalent to approx 20% of qualification)

MA Media Education
One-year full-time or two-year part-time. Three elements: 1) Mandatory module in The Theory and Practice of Media Education, assessed by final examination; 2) Optional module, assessed by course work, from the following: Childhood, Youth and Popular Culture; Media Education, Race and Gender; The Theory and Practice of Media Education; Ideology and the Media; British and European Media; Hollywood Cinema: Text and Context; Television and its Audiences; 3) Dissertation

MA Media Studies
One year full-time, two years part-time, with three elements: 1) Mandatory Module in Ideology and the Media (assessed by final examination); 2) Optional module, assessed by course-work, drawn from those listed under MA Media Education above; 3) Dissertation

MPhil and PhD
Supervision of research theses in the area of Film Studies, TV Studies, Media Studies and Media Education

Institute Associateship
Individualised one-year courses for mature educationalists wishing to study pedagogic and intellectual developments in the field of Media Education and Media Studies

Kent Institute of Art and Design
Rochester upon Medway College
(formerly Medway College of Design)
Fort Pitt
Rochester
Kent ME1 1DZ
Tel: 0634 830022

P B/TEC Higher National Diploma in Advertising and Editorial Photography
Two-year course which includes the possibility of specialising in film and video

Kent Institute of Art and Design at Maidstone
(formerly Maidstone College of Art)
Oakwood Park
Oakwood Road
Maidstone
Kent ME16 8AG
Tel: 0622 757286
Fax: 0622 692003

P BA (Hons) Communication Media Pathway in Time-Based Studies
Full-time production and theory centred and mainly video based, seeking to explore new creative developments in moving imagery as well as linking to other pathways through such areas as animation and computer generated imagery

University of Kent
Rutherford College
Canterbury
Kent CT2 7NX
Tel: 0227 764000

BA Combined Hons
A Part 1 course on Narrative Cinema is available to all Humanities students in Year 1. The Part 2 component in Film Studies in Years 2 and 3 can vary from 25% to 75% of a student's programme. Courses include Film Theory, British Cinema, Early Film Form, and Sexual Difference and Cinema. The rest of a student's programme consists of courses from any other Humanities subject. No practical component

MA and PhD
There are no courses at postgraduate level but students are accepted for MA or PhD by thesis

King Alfred's College of Higher Education
Sparkford Road
Winchester SO22 4NR
Tel: 0962 841515
Fax: 0962 842280

P BA (Hons) (CNAA) in Drama, Theatre and TV
Three-year course that relates theories of contemporary television and drama to practical work in both media. The course looks at both the institutions and the practices of the two media from the perspectives of the psychology and critical ideologies, including women's studies, of the twentieth century. It includes 3 major TV projects in which students work together to produce documentaries or drama documentaries. Facilities include: purpose built 3-machine editing suites for S-VHS and lo-band U-Matic, 10 S-VHS camcorders, and 3 Sony M3 cameras. The TV studio has a control room equipped with broadcast standard vision mixer and 8 channel audio sound mixer. Uhers, stills cameras and other ancillary equipment available. Course also has access to a 3 camera outside broadcast unit

MA/Post-graduate Diploma Documentary Production (Television and Video)
This one-year course aims to be of value to students who are currently working in specific non-broadcast contexts as well as to those who wish to work in broadcast media in Britain or abroad. Through relating the practical production project of the course to the needs of a specific client group, company or organisation, the course proposal takes account of the particular difficulties

students are currently experiencing in undertaking postgraduate study. The form of the course therefore aims to give students some flexibility in studying from the workbase of their current employers, or by raising funding for specific projects from client groups

Kingston Polytechnic

School of Three Dimensional Design
Knights Park
Kingston-upon-Thames
Surrey KT1 2QJ
Tel: 081 549 6151

CNAA Post-Graduate Diploma in Design for Film and Television
One-year course in scenic design tailored to the needs of those who wish to enter the industry with the eventual aim of becoming production designers or art directors. The course is constructed as a series of design projects to cover different types of film and television production

School of Art and Design History
BA (Hons) Architecture
Options in History of Film. No practical component
BA (Hons) Fine Art
Two-year Complementary Studies course. First year is an 18-week introductory course. Second year is a 12-week course on Modernism in the cinema. No practical component
BA (Hons) Three Dimensional Design
Second year Complementary Studies: one-term option on scenography
BA (Hons) Graphic Design
First year Complementary Studies: History of Animation and History of Documentary. No practical component

School of Graphic Design
P BA (Hons) Graphic Design
The course aims to give students a technical and practical understanding of animation and moving image on film and video. Students learn to research, script and storyboard ideas, prepare sound tracks and take their projects through to shooting and post-production. Facilities consist of the following: 16mm Neilson Hordell rostrum camera and 16mm editing equipment including 16mm Steenbeck. Full sound recording and transfer facility onto 16mm magnetic track or video. EOS video animation single frame rostrum system with three machine U-Matic hi-band editing suite. 16mm projection. Film/video studio with overhead lighting

School of Languages
Penrhyn Road
Kingston-upon-Thames
Surrey KT1 2EE
BA (Hons) Modern Arts
Two-term option course in Year 2 on French Cinema since 1930. No practical component

Kingsway College

Grays Inn Centre
Sidmouth Street
Grays Inn Road
London WC1H 8JB
Tel: 071 837 8185

P B/TEC National Diploma in Design Communications (Media Studies)
Two-year full-time course for those interested in pursuing a career in the media industry. The course covers an integrated programme of practical training in photography, video, film and computer technology, and theoretical studies relating to the analysis of media texts.
Facilities include: VHS video studio/cameras/recorders etc, VHS two machine edit with Time Base Correction, Super-8 film equipment (cameras and editors), rostrum camera for animation, computer graphics facilities and studios, photographic workshops, cinema, sound recording facilities

Leicester Polytechnic

School of Arts
PO Box 143
Leicester LE1 9BH
Tel: 0533 551551 x2119

P BA (Hons) Arts and Humanities: Media Studies (Single, Joint or Combined Honours Degrees)
As a Single Honours degree, Media Studies offers a range of courses which focus specifically on Film, Television/Video, Photography and Media institutions. It offers courses in both theoretical and practical work which provide students with the opportunity to develop their skills and learning through detailed analysis of media texts, through understanding the social and political processes of media industries and institutions and through practical work in video, photography and time-based arts. As Joint Honours, it is possible to take Media Studies in conjunction with one other arts discipline; for Combined Honours, with two other disciplines

University of Leicester

Centre for Mass Communication Research
104 Regent Road
Leicester LE1 7LT
Tel: 0533 523863
Fax: 0533 523874

MA Mass Communications
One-year taught course studying the organisation and impact of the mass media both nationally and internationally and providing practical training in research methods

Liverpool Polytechnic

School of Art, Media and Design
Hope Street
Liverpool L1 9HW
Tel: 051 207 3581
Fax: 051 709 0172

P BA (Hons) Graphic Design
Film/Animation is a specialised option within the Graphic Design degree. After a general first year a number of students may specialise in Film/Animation in their second and third years
BA (Hons) Media and Cultural Studies
Some practical components within this degree are integrated into a theoretical study of television, film, video and radio. First year courses in reading and producing the media lead to specialist options in film studies, video, photography and newspaper and broadcast journalism

University of Liverpool

Department of Communication Studies
Chatham Street
Liverpool L69 3BX
Tel: 051 794 2890

BA Combined Hons (Arts)
BA Combined Hons (Social and Environmental Studies)
BA Joint Hons (English and Communication Studies)
BA Joint Hons (Politics and Communication Studies)
In all these programmes, students combine work in the Communication Studies Department with largely non media-related work in other Departments; Communication Studies forms up to 50% of their programme
Year 1: Communication: a programme of introductory work on communication and cultural analysis
Year 2: courses on Broadcasting, Film Studies and Drama
Year 3: courses available include 'Documentary', exploring a range of work in literature, photography, film and TV. No practical component

London College of Printing

The Media School
School of Film and Video
6 Back Hill
Clerkenwell Road
London EC1R 5EN
Tel: 071 278 7445

Fax: 071 833 8842

P BA (Hons) Film Video and Animation

An autonomous course in Film and Video, part of a degree scheme in Communication Media courses, leading to the award of BA (Hons) degree. Main concerns are Women's Cinema, Third World Cinema, Popular Culture and Film. Stress on experimentation and innovation, education, independent filmmakers. Practice/Theory ratio is 70:30. Course stresses integration of theory and practice. Since 1988 the course has included an option in Animation. Facilities include 16mm film and VHS/S-VHS, U-Matic lo- and hi-band video, production and postproduction facilities. This course is accredited by BECTU

The London Institute

Central St Martins College of Art and Design
Southampton Row
London WC1B 4AP
Tel: 071 753 9090 x414

P BA (Hons) Fine Art, Film and Video

Three years full-time. Students are recruited directly into the Film and Video subject of the Fine Art course. The first four terms are designed to develop technical and conceptual skills with a series of projects which explore image, sound, animation, video and 16mm film production. During the first year of the course there will be opportunities to spend some time in another area of Fine Art and during the second year there will be a Placement experience. As the course progresses, students work towards a more self-directed course of study. There is ample opportunity for both individual and group activity. The Fine Art context strongly encourages experimental enquiry, and the course is 80% practical and 20% theoretical. Equipment includes: 16mm facilities (Aaton, Arriflex, Bolex cameras, Nagras, 10 editing areas – Steenbecks and pic-syncs), U-Matic and S-VHS video formats (4 edit suites, 2 and 3 machines), 2 sound rooms, 2 16mm rostrums, video rostrum, lighting studio, a viewing theatre and seminar spaces

P Advanced Diploma in Film and Video

This is a one year full-time course which is taught as a practical subject. Students are asked to design and submit an outline of a year's programme of study which they will be encouraged to realise through tutorial guidance and technical assistance. Students will be expected to participate in a weekly critical seminar with 3rd year BA undergraduates, and to present work at the final Degree shows. They will have full access to the equipment and facilities which are outlined in the text for the BA (Hons) Fine Art Film and Video course. Application to the Advanced Course in Film and Video is made directly to the: Registrar, School of Art, Central St Martins College of Art and Design
Details of the BA (Hons) Fine Art Film and Video course are obtainable from the same office, although applications are made through the: Art and Design Registry, Penn House, 9 Broad Street, Hereford HR4 9AP

London International Film School

Department F15
24 Shelton Street
London WC2H 9HP
Tel: 071 836 9642

P Two-year Diploma course in the Art and Technique of Filmmaking

A practical course teaching skills necessary for professional employment in the industry, recognised by LEAs and BECTU. Courses commence in January, April and September. Each student works on one or more films in every term. Approximately half of each term is spent in filmmaking, half in practical tuition, lectures, tutorials, film analysis and scriptwriting. Facilities include two viewing theatres, two fully-equipped studios, a video rehearsal studio, and comprehensive editing and sound departments. Equipment includes 35mm Panavision, 16mm and 35mm Arriflex cameras, Nagra sound recorders and Steenbeck and Hollywood Magnasync editing tables

University College London

Department of Spanish and Latin American Studies
Gower Street
London WC1 6BT
Tel: 071 380 7121

BA (Hons) Spanish

One MA course in Women in Latin American Film and Narrative. No practical component. One course in Latin American Film for undergraduates. No practical component

Manchester Polytechnic

Department of Communication Arts and Design
Capitol Building
School Lane
Didsbury
Manchester M20 0HT
Tel: 061 247 2000 x7143

P BA (Hons) Design for Communication Media

Television Production is a main area of study offering a three year full-time course. The normal intake is 12 students per year. The course is organised around group-based, practical projects. Typically these will include documentaries, dramas, music programmes and commercials. Research and scripting are important elements of the course and emphasis is placed on the organisation and development of programme content. An initial grounding in a range of production skills (direction, camerawork, sound-recording, editing etc) is provided and students will then specialise in one of these disciplines. Facilities include a fully equipped, four camera studio with hi-band recording, Sony and JVC portable cameras with hi-band and VHS recording and editing, a sound studio and scenic workshop

Department of English and History
Lower Ormond Street
Manchester M15 6BX
Tel: 061 247 1730

BA (Hons) Modern Studies

Film/TV small component. A mixed course of English, Film and Current TV News. Mass Media: a multi-disciplinary course which applies the methodologies of the social sciences and the humanities to the mass media. May run as one-year course for students with Dip HE, or as three-year BA. No practical component

BA (Hons) English Studies/Historical Studies

Film/TV small component. A mixed course including documentary film, TV soap opera and TV news. No practical component

Department of Interdisciplinary Studies
Cavendish Street
Manchester M15 6BG
Tel: 061 247 3027

Dip HE

Two-year course which includes an introduction to film and film theory in Year 1 and a course on film as propaganda in Year 2. No practical component

University of Manchester

Department of Drama
Oxford Road
Manchester M13 9PL
Tel: 061 275 3347
Fax: 061 275 3519

BA Single and Joint Honours in Drama
Normally an optional course in film studies in Year 3 with a compulsory course for Single Honours in Year 2 (optional for Joint). No practical component
MLitt
Possibility for research theses on aspects of film and TV drama

Department of Education
Oxford Road
Manchester M13 9PL
Tel: 061 275 3463
MEd in Education and the Mass Media
Course offered on a full or part-time basis, which enables teachers and youth and community workers to explore effective communication techniques within their fields of work. Some practical work. Visits to media organisations and contributions from media specialists are arranged
Diploma in Advanced Study in Education and the Mass Media
Designed for educators from the UK and overseas, this full or part-time course provides an introduction to the study of mass media systems and the use of audiovisual material for teaching and learning

Middlesex Polytechnic

Modular Scheme
Combined Studies
Trent Park
Cockfosters Road
Barnet
Herts EN4 0PT
Tel: 081 368 1299
BA (Hons) Combined Studies
Modular system degree. In years 2 and 3 students take twelve modules. From the range on offer a student may take five on film or TV
BA (Hons) History of Art, Design and Film
Modular system degree. First two years as combined studies. Third year allows greater specialisation and includes dissertation which could be in film or TV studies. The modules are: British Cinema; National Cinemas; Popular Cinema: Genre and Pleasure; Realisms; Art and the Mass Media; Independent Film; Postmodernist Culture; Hollywood. No practical component

Faculty of Art and Design
Cat Hill
Barnet
Herts EN4 8HT
Tel: 081 368 1299
BA (Hons) Contemporary Cultural Studies
One-year course (or 2/3 years part-time) designed for students who possess a Dip HE or equivalent (2 years full-time degree-level work). Film and television are studied as aspects of cultural practice. No practical component
P MA in Video
A one year full-time course (48 weeks) emphasising the creative aspects of professional video production in the independent sector. Intended for graduate students with considerable lo-band video experience. The course covers all aspects of the production cycle, with an emphasis on scriptwriting. 50% practical; 50% theoretical

Napier Polytechnic

Department of Photography, Film and Television
61 Marchmont Road
Marchmont
Edinburgh EH9 1HU
Tel: 031 444 2266
Fax: 031 452 8532
P BA/BA Hons Photography, Film and TV
With option of specialising in Film and TV production from middle of second year
P MSc Film and TV Production
Post graduate/experience one year full-time course in Film and TV production

National Film and Television School

Beaconsfield Studios
Station Road
Beaconsfield
Bucks HP9 1LG
Tel: 0494 671234
Fax: 0494 674042
P The School offers a three-year, full-time professional course leading to an Associateship (ANFTS) with specialisation in the training of producers, directors, directors of photography, editors, animators, art directors, sound recordists, documentary and film composers. A 12-15 month course is also available for Screen Writers. Students are encouraged to interchange roles in any practical activity at the same time as developing their specialisation. Approximately 35 students are admitted annually, with six or seven places reserved for overseas students. Average age is 27 years. Previous experience in film or a related field is expected. Facilities include three studios, fully equipped to professional standards, hi-band and lo-band U-Matic video editing suites, 20 film editing rooms, professional cameras and tape recorders, lighting equipment for studio and location work, 35mm/16mm Oxberry rostrum camera with 3-D facility, viewing facilities. The school is funded by a partnership of Government and industry (film and TV). Its graduates occupy leading roles in all aspects of film and TV production. It is a full member of CILECT (Centre International de Liaison des Ecoles de Cinéma et de Télévision) and actively co-operates with professional bodies in the UK and abroad

Newcastle upon Tyne Polytechnic

Faculty of Art and Design
Squires Building
Sandyford Road
Newcastle upon Tyne
NE1 8ST
Tel: 091 232 6002
P BA (Hons) Media Production
Three-year course, started in September 1986. Practical course with fully integrated theoretical and critical components in which students are offered the opportunity to specialise in individual programmes of work. Organised into three stages with the Media Theory programme continuing throughout. Facilities include computer workstations, a sound studio, U-Matic cameras, studio, edit suites, 16mm cameras and rostra
BA (Hons) History of Modern Art, Design and Film
Offered as a three-year full-time course or as a five-year part-time course (over two evenings a week). Film Studies is given equal weighting with painting and architecture/design in the first two years of both the full and part-time courses. Thereafter a student can spend up to 75% of his or her time involved with the study of film
MPhil
There are possibilities for research degrees in either film theory or practice

University of Newcastle upon Tyne

School of English
Newcastle upon Tyne
NE1 7RU
Tel: 091 222 6000
BA (Hons) English Literature
Third year optional course: Theoretical Introduction and special areas of study (classical and contemporary Hollywood). No practical component
MA in Twentieth Century Studies: English and American Literature and Film
Modules in film and television are available in one-year, full-time, two year part-time course

Combined Honours Centre
Newcastle upon Tyne
NE1 7RU
Tel: 091 222 6000
BA (Hons) Combined Studies

Two-year course, available in the second year of the degree. Year 1 covers British and American film, and Theory and History of Film; Year 2 Studies in European film and a dissertation

School of Modern Languages
Newcastle upon Tyne
NE1 7RU
Tel: 091 232 8511

BA (Hons) Modern Languages
Optional final year course: studies in European film. Optional final year course in French: French Film in the 1980s

Department of Spanish and Latin-American Studies
Old Library Building
Newcastle upon Tyne
NE1 7RU
Tel: 091 222 6000

BA (Hons) Spanish
Undergraduate special subject Hispanic Drama and Film. Option in European Film Studies

MA Hispanic Drama and Film
MA in film is in two parts: Buñuel and post-50s Spanish Film. No practical component

Northbrook College

Littlehampton Road
Goring-by-Sea
Worthing
West Sussex BN12 6NU
Tel: 0903 830057

P B/TEC Higher National Diploma Design (Audio Visual Production)
Two year, full-time creative video production course including sound, computer graphics and access to 16mm film and animation. The programme includes business, technical and visual studies. History and theory of film and work experience also feature in the course. During the second year students have the opportunity to specialise in aspects of pre-production/production/post-production. Equipment includes: hi-band U-Matic ENG kits, hi- and lo-band edit suites; Pluto, De Grafe and Gee Systems computer graphics on-line terminals; rostrum; VHS and Video 8 equipment with edit facilities; Atari sound tools equipment, 16mm film, camera and editing; photo, supporting location and studio equipment

North Cheshire College

Padgate Campus
Fearnhead Lane
Fearnhead
Warrington WA2 0DB
Tel: 0925 814343

P BA (Joint Hons) Media with Business Management and Information Technology
A modular system degree. The media component combines practical production work in video, sound recording, photography, graphics and print media, with academic analysis of the media through modules on Forms, Representations, Institutions and Audiences. The course structure enables students to relate their business and information technology studies to their work in media. Years 2 and 3 call for specialisation in one medium of production, combined with a choice of options in the theory course. The programme includes one term in Year 2 devoted to work experience in the media industry and institutions. Facilities include well-equipped graphics and photography studios, multi-track sound studio and desk-top publishing. There is a three colour-camera TV studio with extensive post-production facilities, Chromakey, U-Matic and VHS edit suites, U-Matic and VHS location cameras and equipment

BA (Hons) Mature Student Programme
A modular system degree, designed specifically for mature student entry. A broad range of modules is available, and students can choose some or all of the media modules, theoretical and practical

Diploma in Media Education
A part-time postgraduate Diploma designed for serving teachers in the primary, secondary and further education sectors who are, or who wish to be, involved in teaching some aspect of media education. The course calls for analysis of key theoretical issues, consideration of issues of curriculum and pedagogy, together with practical work in video, sound and photography. Attendance is either one evening a week over two years or day release over one year

Northern School of Film and Television

This is a joint venture between Leeds Polytechnic, Sheffield City Polytechnic and Yorkshire Television providing postgraduate level professional training in practical film production. At present two courses are offered

NSFTV
Leeds Polytechnic
Calverley Street
Leeds LS1 3HE
Tel: 0532 832600

P MA/Postgraduate Diploma in Scriptwriting for Film and Television (Fiction)
This is an intensive one-year practical course running from January to January, based at Leeds Polytechnic. Staffed largely by working professional writers, it covers the various forms of fiction scriptwriting for film and TV – short film, feature film, TV drama, soap opera, series etc. The course has a strong emphasis on professional presentation, and aims to help graduates to set up a credible freelance practice. After a first term of instruction and short projects, the course proceeds to a short film script in term two and a TV script in term three. The major project, in the third term and over the summer, is a 10,000 word script, either feature film or TV drama

NSFTV
Sheffield City Polytechnic
School of Cultural Studies
Psalter Lane
Sheffield S11 8UZ
Tel: 0742 556101

P MA/Postgraduate Diploma in Film Production (Fiction)
This is an intensive one-year practical course running from October to October, and is based at Sheffield City Polytechnic. Students are admitted into specialist areas: Direction (6 students per year), Production (3), Camera (3), Art-Direction (3), Editing (3) and Sound (3). Students work in teams to produce six short films, in two batches of three. The resulting films may be broadcast on Yorkshire Television, who provide the base production funding and some facilities. Scripts are normally drawn from the product of the Script-writing Course at NSFTV and the emphasis is on team working and joint creativity under pressure. It is not a course for 'author' film makers. There is also a theoretical studies component. Full professional equipment is available, and each film has its own cutting room for the length of production

Polytechnic of North London

School of Literary and Media Studies
Prince of Wales Road
London NW5 3LB
Tel: 071 607 2789

Humanities Scheme
Three-year full-time course. Six-year part-time course by day or evening study. Film Studies is one of 14 subject components and may be taken as a Major, Joint or Minor. One practical component

MA Modern Drama Studies
Two-year part-time

evening course with optional Film Studies. No practical component
MA Theories of Representation
Two-year part-time evening modular course. Core courses in Mimesis/Anti-mimesis and Signification and the subject. Optional unit in Film Studies

Nottingham Polytechnic
Faculty of Art & Design
Department of Visual Arts
Burton Street
Nottingham NG1 4BU
Tel: 0602 418418 x6404
P BA (Hons) Fine Art
BA (Hons) Creative Arts
Film-making and video are available as options on these degree courses. These options, separately or in combination, can be taken as the main area of study. Equipment includes Arriflex and Bolex 16mm cameras, 16mm Rostrum camera, Nagra and Uher tape recorders, Super 8 cameras, film editing facilities, video studio and lo-band U-Matic edit suite, EOS/U-Matic video animation rostrum, sound recording and mixing facilities

Nottingham University
School of Education
Nottingham NR7 2RD
Tel: 0602 506101
MEd/BEd/Diploma/ Certificate Options in Mass Media Communication
Particular emphasis on TV and media studies in schools. Opportunities are provided for a good deal of practical work, though the major emphasis is upon analysis and criticism
PGCE
Second area option in media studies
MPhil and PhD
Research can be supervised for higher degrees by thesis

Plymouth College of Art and Design
Department of Photography, Film and Television
Tavistock Place
Plymouth
Devon PL4 8AT
Tel: 0752 385959
Fax: 0752 385972
P B/TEC Higher National Diploma in Photography, Film and Television
A two year course with options in Combined Media and Film and Television. All areas of film, video and television production are covered and the course is well supported by visiting lecturers and workshops. Strong links with the industry have been developed and work based experience forms an important part of the course. The course has BKSTS accreditation. Facilities include Arriflex SR and BL film cameras, Nagra recorders, 4 Steenbeck edit tables, pic syncs, TV studio, Sondor Film Dubbing Suite, 4 Sony CCD cameras, 2 machine edit suites, Sony 3 machine edit suite with Eric Digital video effects generator, Vista Tips 2D, Panorama, Topas 3D, Corel Draw and Autocad Computer facilities
P Advanced Diploma in Photography, Film and Television leading to the BIPP Professional Qualifying Exam
A one year course post HND and post graduate. The film and television option allows students to plan their own line of study, including practical work, dissertation and an extended period of work based experience. Students from both courses have had considerable success in film and video scholarships and competitions

Portsmouth Polytechnic
School of Social and Historical Studies
Kings Rooms
Bellevue Terrace
Southsea PO5 3AT
Tel: 0705 827681
BA (Hons) Cultural Studies

Year 1: 10 one-hour introductory lectures, five seminars. Year 2 options: 10 lectures – the Studio system. Options on Popular Texts, including Melodrama. Year 3 options on British Cinema 1933-70, British TV Drama, Avant-Garde Films and Feminism. Options are 2 hours a week for 25 weeks

Department of Design
Lion Terrace
Portsmouth PO1 3HF
Tel: 0705 827681

P BA (Hons) in Media and Design
Three-year course. In the first year students experience four main resource areas, one of which is video. By the second year, students concentrate on one specialism plus other supporting studies including design and media history and theory. The course combines professional practice with an innovative approach to multi-disciplinary design. Emphasis is placed on documentary and narrative video production. There are also 'live' projects and occasional student placements in the UK and Europe. There is also a close link with the Polytechnic Television Centre and projects take place throughout the course. Historical, cultural and theoretical analysis form an important part of the degree and are integrated into practical teaching. Equipment includes lo- and hi-band U-Matic video shooting and editing facilities, 16mm sound cameras and editing. Nagra. Sound studio. Computer and film animation equipment. 16mm and 35mm projection

Ravensbourne College of Design and Communication

School of Television
Walden Road
Chislehurst
Bromley
Kent BR7 5SN
Tel: 081 468 7071

P B/TEC Higher National Diploma in Engineering Communications (for Television and Broadcasting)
Two-year full-time vocational course designed in consultation with the TV broadcasting industry leading to employment opportunities as technician-engineers

P B/TEC Higher National Diploma in Design Communication (Television Programme Operations)
Two-year full-time vocational course designed in consultation with the TV broadcasting industry leading to employment opportunities as programme operators in lighting, camera operators, sound, video recording and editing, vision-mixing, telecine, and audio-recording. Facilities include two TV studios each with production, lighting and sound control rooms. Each studio has its own vision apparatus room and shares a central apparatus room, telecine and video recording and editing facilities

University of Reading

Faculty of Letters and Social Sciences
Whiteknights
Reading RG6 2AA
Tel: 0734 875123

BA Film and Drama (Single Subject)
After the first two terms in which three subjects are studied, students work wholly in film and drama. The course is critical but with significant practical elements which are designed to extend critical understanding. It does not provide professional training

BA Film and Drama with English, French, German, Italian or Sociology
Students in general share the same teaching as Single Subject students but the course does not include practical work

Department of English

BA (Hons) English
Second year optional course on literature, film and television. Third year optional course in media semiotics

PhD
Research can be supervised on the history of the British Broadcasting Corporation and other mass media topics

Department of German

BA (Hons) German
Two-term Finals option: The German Cinema. Course covers German cinema from the 1920s to the present, with special emphasis on the Weimar Republic, the Third Reich, and the 'New German Cinema'. No practical component. Six-week module: The German Mass Media. Course covers history of broadcasting and the press and current issues in media. No practical component. One of ten modules in two-year core course

Department of Italian Studies

BA (Hons) Italian/French and Italian with Film Studies
First year introductory course: Post-War Italian Cinema (one half-term). Second year course: Italian Cinema (three terms). Final year course: European Cinema (two terms). Dissertation on an aspect of Italian cinema. These courses available to students reading other subjects in the Faculty. No practical component

MA Italian Cinema
One-year full-time or two-year part-time course on Italian Cinema: compulsory theory course, options on film and literature, Bertolucci, Italian industry and genre – the Spaghetti Western. No practical component

MPhil and PhD
Research can be supervised on Italian cinema for degree by thesis

Richmond upon Thames College

Egerton Road
Twickenham TW2 7SJ
Tel: 081 892 6656

P B/TEC Diploma in Communication Design (Media Studies)
This two year full-time course offers an introduction to media studies and production skills in photography, video and desk top publishing, with specialisation in the second year

College of Ripon and York St John

Lord Mayor's Walk
York YO3 7EX
Tel: 0904 56771

BA Combined Hons
Honours degree students take 17 courses in three years. Of these, seven are drama/film/TV courses. The practical component includes some off-campus work and can include experience in related industries

Roehampton Institute

Department of Drama
Digby Stuart College
Roehampton Lane
London SW15 5PU
Tel: 081 876 8273

BA Drama and Theatre Studies
The Drama and Theatre Studies modular programme (Major, Equal or Minor) is combined with one other subject. Year One includes a one term module in Film Analysis with some practical work in portable video. A double module in Contemporary Television Drama and a practical double module in Television Drama Production are offered in Year Three. Other modules, such as Representing Women and Shakespeare in Contemporary Performance, contain substantial study of film and television production. Students may also specialise in areas of film and television for research dissertations. Technical facilities include a professionally staffed multi-camera

colour TV studio, VHS and U-Matic editing suites and VHS portable cameras

Royal College of Art

School of Film and Television
Kensington Gore
London SW7 2EU
Tel: 071 584 5020
Fax: 071 225 1487

P MA in Film and Television Direction
Two years. Practical craft course including production of narrative fiction and documentary film. Emphasis is placed on pre-production development, scripting and planning. Professional workshops, accompanied by seminars covering development and history of cinema and television. Inter-related with film and television production and design for film and television courses. Assessment by submission of practical work and interview

P MA Film and Television Production
Inter-related with film and television direction and design for film and television courses. Students responsible for complete practical production of film and television projects from idea and script development through production processes to completed product. Seminars cover raising finance, budgeting, script selection, company law, contracts, insurance and copyright. Assessment by submission of evidence of production experience and interview

P Design for Film and Television
Course based on all aspects of 3-dimensional production design in film and television including history, aesthetics and techniques. Covers redesigning from a 'classic' film or television script and design of a television advertising campaign. Inter-related with film and television design and production courses. Assessment by submission of practical work and interview

Department of Animation
Kensington Gore
London SW7 2EU
Tel: 071 584 5020
Fax: 071 225 1487 x343

P MA in Animation
Two-year full-time course with work divided roughly into 80% practical and 20% theoretical. Equipment includes 2 16mm cameras, 2 video scanners and video edit suite. Also 16mm Steenbeck, editing and sound recording equipment

Royal Holloway and Bedford College, University of London

Department of Drama and Theatre Studies
Egham Hill
Egham
Surrey TW20 0EX
Tel: 0784 34455

BA (Hons) Drama and Theatre Studies
History of Film: a two-year course for second and third-year students, constituting one paper at Finals. Principally a historical and critical account of the development of cinema and the use of film for entertainment and art. Film – mainly film theory – is also taught as a special subject. Examination includes a dissertation. No practical component

P Television Drama
A two-year studio production course for second and third-year students. Largely practical with some critical analysis of television and television drama. By the end of the course all students direct their own short production

St Helens College

Faculty of General and Community Education
Brook Street
St Helens
Merseyside WA10 1PZ
Tel: 0744 33766 x221

P B/TEC National Diploma in Media
Two years full-time, the course aims to provide a foundation in basic skills relevant to many areas of the media industry and the opportunity, through option selection, to examine one or more sectors in detail

Salford College of Technology

Adelphi
Peru Street
Salford M3 6EQ
Tel: 061 834 6633

P B/TEC National Diploma in Media and Communication Techniques
Two years full-time. A first-level course designed for those wishing to work or progress onto higher education in television, radio, sound recording and non-broadcast video. Practical and production based

P B/TEC Higher National Diploma in Media Production
Two years full-time. A creative and vocational programme of study in the technology and techniques of audio and video production, reflecting the industrial need for creative and versatile people. Students work with professionals from the BBC, Granada TV and a number of independent companies

BA (Hons) Television and Radio
Three years full-time. New course comprising a common core of three major fields of study extending throughout the three years: Media, Culture and Society; Production Theory and Practices; Projects: Production and Analysis. Final year allows greater specialisation and an individual choice of study with emphasis on student-led project work

University of Salford

Department of Modern Languages
Salford M5 4WT
Tel: 061 745 5000

BA (Hons) Modern Languages
One of the Final Year options is in French Cinema. One hour per week out of a total of 15 hours of language work. No practical component

MA Modern Languages
Includes modules on French Cinema

Sandwell College of Further and Higher Education

High Street Campus
High Street
West Bromwich
West Midlands B70 8DW
Tel: 021 556 6000 x8611

P B/TEC National Diploma in Electronics and Television Studio Operations
Two-year course for those seeking a career in the broadcast media and associated industries. Offers a sound foundation in electronics and computer awareness. Course consists of the following components: vision and sound principles and operations; micro-electronics systems; computer graphics and assignments; transmission principles; radio and TV systems; programme production; communications and media studies; electrical and electronic principles; electronics; mathematics; industry and society

Sheffield City Polytechnic

Division of Communication Studies and English
36 Collegiate Crescent
Sheffield S10 2BP
Tel: 0742 665274

BA (Hons) Communication Studies
Course covers all aspects of communications, one area being Mass Communication. Option course in TV Fictions in Year 3. Some practical work

Collegiate Crescent
Sheffield S10 2BP
Tel: 0742 730911

MA Communication Studies
Part-time course over six terms, followed by the completion of a dissertation by the end of term eight. Aims to

develop theoretical understandings and analytical skills in relation to the processes and practices of communication in modern society. Students attend for two sessions of 2+ hours each week

Faculty of Cultural Studies
Psalter Lane
Sheffield S11 8UZ
Tel: 0742 556101

BA (Hons) History of Art, Design and Film
Film studies is a major component of this course. Year 1: introduction to film analysis and history. Year 2: special study on Hollywood. Year 3: critical and theoretical studies in Art, Design and Film and Contemporary Film Theory and Practice. No practical component

MA Film Studies
Two-year part-time course; two evenings per week, plus dissertation to be written over two terms in a third year. Main areas of study: Problems of Method; The Classical Narrative Tradition; British Cinema 1927-45; British Independent Cinema 1966-84. No practical component

Faculty of Art and Design
Psalter Lane
Sheffield S11 8UZ
Tel: 0742 556101

P BA (Hons) Fine Art (Combined and Media Arts)
After initial work with a range of media, students can specialise in film and/or video. Film productions can range from short 8mm films, through 16mm documentaries or widescreen features, to small 35mm productions. There are professional facilities for shooting, processing, editing, recording and dubbing 16mm films, and good animation equipment. Also well-equipped video and sound studios, with studio cameras, portable units, automatic colour edit suites, multi-track sound recording and mixing, disc tape-cassette transfer and synthesisers

University of Sheffield

Department of English Literature
Shearwood Mount
Shearwood Road
Sheffield S10 2TD
Tel: 0742 768555 x6043/6276

BA (Hons) English Literature
Students may study one or two Special Subjects in Film in their second or third years

MA Theatre and Film
One-year course on elements of both theatre and film studies. Work on all topics is assessed at the conclusion of the course

South Manchester College

Arden Centre
Sale Road
Northenden
Manchester M23 0DD
Tel: 061 998 5511 x165

P B/TEC National Diploma in Audio Visual Design
Multi-disciplinary integrated, group-based course working between graphics, video, film/animation, sound recording, photography and tape/slide production. Assessment is continuous, based on practical projects linked to theoretical studies. Equipment includes 4 VHS portapacks and cameras, VHS Camcorder, 2 JVC KY1900 cameras, VHS and lo-band U-Matic edit suites, 16mm Bolex camera, VHS effects generator plus supporting studio/ portable sound, lighting equipment and computer graphics

South Thames College

Department of Design and Media
Wandsworth High Street
London SW18 2PP
Tel: 081 870 2241
Fax: 081 874 6163

P B/TEC Higher National Certificate in Design (Communication) – Television Production
Two-year part-time course. All students experience every aspect of making both portable single camera (location) and multi-camera (studio) television programmes, starting with discussion of a brief with a 'client' and submitting a programme proposal, through the implementation of the programme production to the submission of the finished product. In Year 1 every student produces and directs one studio programme and in Year 2 one single camera programme, plus a final production in a form chosen by the student. In addition to the practical work there are lectures, tutorials and visits to production companies. Facilities include: 3-camera colour studio with telecine, caption generator, source and record VCRs and a microprocessor controlled lighting rig, plus 8-channel sound mixing with usual sources. On location there are single tube or 3-CCD colour cameras, portable U-Matic recorders, a range of microphones, ENG lighting. Computer graphics and audio laboratories are bookable by arrangement

University of Southampton

Faculty of Educational Studies
Southampton SO9 5NH
Tel: 0703 595000

Postgraduate Certificate in Education
This one-year initial training course for secondary/6th form teachers offers specialist work in Media Studies as an integral part of English Drama and Media Studies

MA (Ed) Media Education
The MA in Education is run on a modular basis in this full- or part-time taught course. The course as a whole requires the completion of six modules and a supervised dissertation. Included are television studies, media and communication, video in education, and others

MPhil and PhD
Research degrees in any area of Media Education, Media Studies, Educational Broadcasting and Educational Technology are available

School of Modern Languages
Southampton SO9 5NH
Tel: 0703 592256/592389
Fax: 0703 593939

MA Culture and Society in Contemporary Europe
A core course of weekly lectures and seminars examines a series of issues in contemporary European culture and society. Accompanied by an option course chosen from three topics including Contemporary European Cinema

Staffordshire Polytechnic

Department of History of Art and Design and Complementary Studies
College Road
Stoke on Trent ST4 2DE
Tel: 0782 744531

BA (Hons) History of Design and the Visual Arts
An introductory course in film studies is compulsory in Year 1. Film studies courses are optional in Years 2 and 3. Second year course emphasises the study of Hollywood and European cinema. Third year course focuses on Gender and Representation, Czechoslovak Cinema, Responses to and Representations of Empire. There is a practical element in Year 2. Dissertation in Year 3

P BA (Hons) Film, Television and Radio Studies
An academic course with a practical content focusing on the histories of the three media, mass media institutions (including law and economics), formal and critical analysis, and writing for the mass media. Specialist studies include Documentary and Current Affairs, British

Popular Film and Broadcast Drama, Culture and Imperialism in the Developing World, Politics and the Media in East/Central Europe. Studio project in Year 1, Placement and Production Project in Year 2, Dissertation or Script Writing Project in Year 3

University of Stirling

Stirling FK9 4LA
Tel: 0786 73171
Fax: 0786 51335

BA (Hons) in Film and Media Studies (Single and Joint Honours)
Four-year degree in which students follow courses in the theory and analysis of all the principal media. All students take courses in the theories of mass communication and in cultural theories, as well as problems of textual analysis and then select from a range of options, including practical courses in the problems of news reporting in radio and TV and in TV documentary. As a joint honours degree Film and Media Studies can be combined with a variety of other subjects

BA General Degree
Students can build a component of their degree in film and media studies ranging from as much as eight units (approximately 50% of their degree) if they take a major in the subject, down to as little as three if they wish merely to complete a Part 1 major. For the most part students follow the same units as do Film and Media Studies Honours students

MLitt and PhD
Applications are considered for research in a number of areas of film and media studies

Suffolk College of Higher and Further Education

School of Art and Design
Rope Walk
Ipswich
Suffolk IP4 1LT
Tel: 0473 55885

P B/TEC Higher National Diploma in Design Communication
A two-year course with options in film/TV graphics, animation and art direction. Students complete a period of work experience with employers in film and TV companies. Facilities include two colour TV studios, post-production facilities for film and video, and a film animation unit

P CNAA BA (Hons) in Design Studies
A one year follow on from the above B/TEC in Design Communications. Options in Advanced TV Graphic Design, Animation, TV Set Design

Sunderland Polytechnic

School of Humanities
Forster Building
Chester Road
Sunderland SR1 3RL
Tel: 091 515 2188/9
Fax: 091 515 2105

BA (Hons) Communication Studies
Study of linguistics, psychology and sociology in relation to inter-personal communications and mass communi-cation. The course is primarily academic, but includes practical study of radio, video and computing. Options include: Perspectives on Visual Communications, The Languages of Film and Representations of Women in Painting and Film

MA in Cultural and Textual Studies
One year (full-time) or two year (part-time) MA. Postgraduate courses are constructed from a wide range of modules, two of which are compulsory. These compulsory modules provide students with a flexible theoretical foundation, and a multi-media and comparative study of verbal and visual forms of cultural communication, representing both 'high' and 'popular' culture. Students are then asked to choose three other modules, two of which must be in film studies, and to write a dissertation on a film-studies topic leading to the entitlement to the award of **MA in Cultural, Textual and Film Studies**

University of Sussex

Arts Building
Brighton BN1 9QN
Tel: 0273 606755

BA English with Media Studies
A three-year full-time degree course which includes analysis of television, film and the press, together with some opportunity (unassessed) to be involved in practical television and video production

BA Media Studies
The degree course in Media Studies enables students to develop a critical understanding of the press, cinema, radio and television and of the particular character of media communications. The media are studied in their historical develop-ment, as social and economic institutions, as technologies and techniques of communi-cation, and as inter-locking with other social circuits for the relay of meanings and values. The Major in Media Studies is taught in two Schools of Studies – Cultural and Community Studies (CCS) and European Studies (EURO): different School Courses accompany it according to the School. The course in EURO also involves study of a modern European language and an additional year abroad in Europe

Educational Development Building
Institute of Education
University of Sussex
Brighton BN1 9RG
Tel: 0273 606755

MA Language, the Arts and Education
Full-time and two-year part-time course, for both art-makers and for teachers in schools, FE and HE. Though work on film/TV forms only a small part of the taught seminar courses, students can specialise in the film/TV area for all written and practical work

Trinity and All Saints College

Faculty of Academic Studies
Brownberrie Lane
Horsforth
Leeds LS18 5HD
Tel: 0532 584341
Fax: 0532 581148

BA (Hons) Communications and Cultural Studies
Three-year course in combination with a professional study in either Public Media or Business Management and Administration. Film and TV Studies is a major component within the course, which includes some practical work

University of Ulster

Coleraine
Co Londonderry
Northern Ireland BT52 1SA
Tel: 0265 44141

BA (Hons) Media Studies
Three-year course integrating theoretical, critical and practical approaches to film, TV, radio and the press. Film and TV Studies constitutes over 60% of the course. Important practical component. Facilities include: TV studio; portable VHS and S-VHS, hi-band and lo-band; post-production COX 58, Gemini 2; hi-band video animation suite; 16mm Frezzolini; 4-plate Steenbeck; Super 8; professional 8-track sound studio; Uher and Marantz portables; Apple Mac computer lab; Amiga graphics generator

Faculty of Art and Design

BA (Hons) Fine Art
BA (Hons) Design
BA (Hons) Combined Studies in Art and Design
B/TEC Higher National Diploma in Design Communication
Minor component units

in theoretical and some practical elements of film, video and media studies as part of the core studies of all BA courses. Combined Studies students undertake a greater Media Studies input. Fine Art students may specialise in Fine Art video as part of their final studio work. Design students may take video production as part of their graphic design studio work. Design Communication students all take video production project work in Year 1 and as a major option in Year 2

University of Warwick

Joint School of Film and Literature
Faculty of Arts
Coventry CV4 7AL
Tel: 0203 523523

BA Joint Degree in Film and Literature
Four courses offered each year, two in film and two in literature. Mainly film studies but some TV included. No practical component

BA French or Italian with Film Studies
This degree puts a particular emphasis on film within and alongside its studies of French or Italian language, literature and society. No practical component

Various Degrees
Options in film studies can be taken as part of undergraduate degrees in other departments. No practical component

MA in Film and Television Studies
Taught courses on Textual Analysis, methods in Film History, Modernity and Innovation, and Issues of Representation

MA, MPhil and PhD
Students are accepted for research degrees

West Glamorgan Institute of Higher Education

Townhill Road
Swansea SA2 0UT
Tel: 0792 203482

P **BA (Hons) Combined Studies**
Three year degree with several options. The Art in Society option includes a substantial amount of practical work, of which video and tape-slide form a major element. Facilities include: a Sony Series 5 animation unit, a sound studio based on a Tascam Portastudio, a Fairlight Computer Video Instrument, U-Matic editing suite and portable U-Matic unit dedicated to the course. Additional facilities include U-Matic and VHS editing suites and 3-camera studio. The Modern English Studies option includes Film and TV Studies (no practical component)

BEd Primary
This course includes a Literature and Media Studies main subject option.

Polytechnic of West London

Department of Humanities
St Mary's Road
Ealing
London W5 5RF
Tel: 081 579 4111

BA (Hons) Humanities
Students take 10 units as part of degree, of which six may be in media studies, including one practical video unit

MA Cultural Studies
Part-time taught evening course of six units plus dissertation. Topics include film and television, popular culture. No practical component

West Surrey College of Art and Design

Department of Fine Art and Audio-Visual Studies
Falkner Road
The Hart
Farnham
Surrey GU9 7DS
Tel: 0252 722441

P **BA (Hons) Photography**
BA (Hons) Film and Video
BA (Hons) Animation
The approach in each course is essentially practical, structured to encourage a direct and fundamental appraisal of photography, film, video and animation through practice and by theoretical study. 70% practical, 30% theoretical. Equipment includes 16mm Arriflex, Bolex, Canon Scopic and CP16 cameras; sound studio with Neve 12 channel mixer; 10 edit rooms; 4-camera TV studio; Ikegami 3-tube camera; portable 3-tube video camera; U-Matic record and edit suites; range of VHS equipment; three animation rostra; aerial image faculty; NAC quick action recorder; Image Artist and Picasso computer graphics systems; 3 photographic studios; full range of flash and tungsten lighting, all camera formats, B & W and colour processing and printing. Courses are ACTT accredited

BA (Hons) Media Studies
A range of theoretical approaches to the mass media are examined. Emphasis is placed on the critical application of such theories to the actual production and consumption of media, primarily visual, culture. Units on professional practice, the European context of media production, and the learning of a modern European language prepare students for a career in the media industry. (Course subject to approval)

Weymouth College

Cranford Avenue
Weymouth
Dorset DT4 7LQ
Tel: 0305 208856

P **B/TEC National Diploma in Media**
Two year full-time course designed as a solid foundation in a range of media skills but which allows for some specialisation in either television and video or sound and radio. Facilities available are VHS and S-VHS camcorders, lo-band portable U-Matic cameras, Sony 3CCD cameras, videographics and full edit suites

Wimbledon School of Art

Merton Hall Road
London SW19 3QA
Tel: 081 540 0231

P **BA (Hons) Fine Art**
Students enrol in either Painting or Sculpture. It is more usual for Painting students to study Film and/or Video. Equipment includes Super 8mm sync sound and editing facilities; 16mm Bolex with post-sync sound; ½" b/w video and colour U-Matic with editing

P **BA (Hons) Theatre Design**
There are substantial opportunities for Super 8 filmmaking within the course of Theatre Design. Equipment include Beaulieu and Nizo cameras; Schmidt 4-plate sound mixing/editing suite; Uher, Revox, Teac, Soundcraft, MXR, Lexicon, Greengate and Casio sound facilities

Wolverhampton Polytechnic

School of Humanities and Social Sciences
Dudley DY1 3HR
Tel: 0902 3121000

Diploma in Higher Education
Two-year course for formally unqualified students. Work on film and television is situated within a cultural studies perspective, and students are offered four modules over two years in combination with other study areas

BA (Hons) Theme Studies
One-year degree programme open to those who have completed a DipHE. Film and TV emphasis dependent upon subject of the Independent Study paper (50% of the final assessment)
A three-year modular degree programme offering a Cultural Studies theme in Years 2 and 3. Film and TV are also components of complementary modules in History, French and Drama. No practical component

BA (Hons) Humanities
BA Combined Studies
Offer a range of subject programmes which include critical and historical work in Film, TV and the Media, including History of Art and Design, Media and Communication, French and Drama

DISTRIBUTORS (NON-THEATRICAL)

Companies here control UK rights for non-theatrical distribution (for domestic and group viewing in schools, hospitals, airlines and so on). For an extensive list of titles available non-theatrically with relevant distributors' addresses, see the 'British National Film & Video Catalogue', available for reference from BFI Library Services and major public reference libraries. Other sources of film and video are listed under Archives and Libraries (p72) and Workshops (p316)

ABC Films
via Glenbuck Films

Academy Television
104 Kirkstall Road
Leeds LS3 1JS
Tel: 0532 461528
Fax: 0532 429522
Geoff Foster

Air India
Publicity Dept
17-18 New Bond Street
London W1Y 0BD
Tel: 071 493 4050

Albany Video Distribution
Battersea Studios
Television Centre
Thackeray Road
London SW8 3TW
Tel: 071 498 6811
Fax: 071 498 1494
Val Martin
Julia Knight
Education videos

Amber Films
5 Side
Newcastle upon Tyne
NE1 3JE
Tel: 091 232 2000
Fax: 091 230 3217

Argus Film Library
15 Beaconsfield Road
London NW10 2LE
Tel: 081 451 1127

Artificial Eye Film Co
via Glenbuck Films

Arts Council of Great Britain
via Concord Video and Film Council

Association of British Insurers
via Multilink Film Library

Audience Planners
4 Beadles Lane
Oxted
Surrey RH8 9JJ
Tel: 0883 717194
Fax: 0883 714480

Australia Tourist Commission
and

Austrian Tourist Office
via Audience Planners

Avon Distributors
Everyman Cinema
Holly Bush Vale
London NW3 6TX
Tel: 071 485 4326

BBC Enterprises Video Sales
Woodlands
80 Wood Lane
London W12 0TT
Tel: 081 743 5588/576 2000
Fax: 081 749 0538

BBC Training Videos
Woodlands
80 Wood Lane
London W12 0TT
Tel: 081 576 2361
Fax: 081 749 8766

bfi ***BFI Film + Video Library***
21 Stephen Street
London W1P 1PL
Tel: 071 255 1444
Fax: 071 436 7950

bfi ***BFI Production***
via BFI Film + Video Library

BP Film Library
15 Beaconsfield Road
London NW10 2LE
Tel: 081 451 1129

Bahamas Tourist Office
via Audience Planners

Banking Information Service
via Multilink Film Library

Barclays Bank Film Library
via Multilink Film Library and Training Communications

Belgian National Tourist Office
via Audience Planners

Big Bear Records
PO Box 944
Birmingham B16 8UT
Tel: 021 454 7020/8100
Fax: 021 454 9996

Birmingham Film and Video Workshop
The Bond
180/182 Fazeley Street
Birmingham B5 5SE
Tel: 021 766 7635
Alan Lovell

Black Audio Film Collective
89 Ridley Road
London E8 2NH
Tel: 071 254 9527/9536

Lina Gopaul
Avril Johnson
David Lawson
Black independent films

Blue Dolphin Films
via Glenbuck Films

Boulton Hawker Films
Hadleigh
near Ipswich
Suffolk IP7 5BG
Tel: 0473 822235
Fax: 0473 824519
Educational films and videos, specialising in health education, biology, and social welfare

Brent Walker Films
via Glenbuck Films

British Cement Association Film Library
and
British Gas Film Library
via Viscom

British Home Entertainment
via Glenbuck Films

British Steel Films
via Viscom

British Telecom Film Library
via Training Communications and Education Distribution Service

British Transport Films
via Film Archive Management and Entertainment, and SCFVL

British Universities Film and Video Council
55 Greek Street
London W1V 5LR
Tel: 071 734 3687
Fax: 071 287 3914

Bryanston Films
via Filmbank

Bulgarian Tourist Office
via Audience Planners

John Burder Films
7 Saltcoats Road
London W4 1AR
Tel: 081 995 0547
Fax: 081 995 3376

Training and safety programmes. Also via Training Communications

CBS Broadcast
via Glenbuck Films

CFL Vision
PO Box 35
Wetherby
Yorks LS23 7EX
Tel: 0937 541010
Fax: 0937 541083

CTVC Video
Beeson's Yard
Bury Lane
Rickmansworth
Herts WD3 1DS
Tel: 0923 777933
Fax: 0923 896368
Christian, moral and social programmes. Free catalogue available

Caledonian MacBrayne
via Audience Planners

Canada House Film and Video Library
Canada House
Trafalgar Square
London SW1Y 5BJ
Tel: 071 629 9492 x2215
Fax: 071 321 0025
Features, animation, wildlife and documentaries from Canada on free loan to film societies, educational institutions, etc

Castle Target
via Glenbuck Films

Castrol Video and Film Library
Athena Avenue
Swindon
Wiltshire SN2 6EQ
Tel: 0793 693402
Fax: 0793 511479
Motorsport films

Cayman Islands Tourist Office
via Audience Planners

Central Independent Television
Video Resource Unit
Broad Street
Birmingham B1 2JP
Tel: 021 643 9898

Central Office of Information
via CFL Vision

Channel Four Television
Sales Department
60 Charlotte Street
London W1P 2AX
Tel: 071 927 8541
Fax: 071 580 2622
Stephen Mowbray

Children's Film and Television Foundation
via Glenbuck Films. For further details, see under Organisations

Cinema Action
27 Winchester Road
London NW3 3NR
Tel: 071 586 2762
Fax: 071 722 5781
Features and documentaries "provoking the bourgeoisie"

Cinenova (Women's Film and Video Distribution)
(formerly Circles)
113 Roman Road
London E2 0HU
Tel: 081 981 6828
Distribution of new films and videos by women filmmakers from around the world

Cinema of Women
via Glenbuck Films

Columbia Tri-Star Films (UK)
via Filmbank

Concord Video and Film Council
201 Felixstowe Road
Ipswich
Suffolk IP3 9BJ
Tel: 0473 715754/726012
Videos and films for hire/sale on domestic and international social issues – counselling, development, education, the arts, race and gender issues, disabilities, etc – for training and discussion

Connoisseur Films
and
Contemporary Films
via Glenbuck Films

DS Information Systems
See National Audio Visual Aids Library (NAVAL)

Danish Embassy
55 Sloane Street
London SW1X 9SR
Tel: 071 333 0200

Danish Tourist Board
via Audience Planners

Darvill Associates
280 Chartridge Lane
Chesham
Bucks HP5 2SG
Tel: 0494 783643
Fax: 0494 784873
Available through Glenbuck Films

Derann Film Services
99 High Street
Dudley
W Midlands DY1 1QP
Tel: 0384 233191
Fax: 0384 456488
8mm package movie distributors

The Walt Disney Co
via Filmbank

Walt Disney Educational Media
via Viewtech Audio Visual Media

Duke of Edinburgh Awards
via Glenbuck Films

Dutch Embassy Films
via National Audio Visual Aids Library (NAVAL)

Eastern Arts Board
Cherry Hinton Hall
Cherry Hinton Road
Cambridge CB1 4DW
Tel: 0223 215355

Educational and Television Films
247a Upper Street
London N1 1RU
Tel: 071 226 2298
Documentary films from USSR and Eastern Europe. Archive film library

Educational Media, Film & Video
235 Imperial Drive
Rayners Lane
Harrow
Middx HA2 7HE
Tel: 081 868 1908/1915
Fax: 081 868 1991

Health, safety, educational, and business/management training material

Education Distribution Service
85b North Street
Milton Regis
Sittingbourne
Kent ME10 2HJ
Tel: 0795 427614
Fax: 0795 429565

Electric Pictures
via Glenbuck Films and BFI Film + Video Library

Electricity Association Film Library
30 Millbank
London SW1P 4RD
Tel: 071 834 2333 x5456
Fax: 071 931 0356

Enterprise Pictures
via Glenbuck Films

Entertainment Films
via Filmbank

Essential (16mm) Films
via Concord Video and Film Council

Esso Film & Video Library
via Viscom

Euro-London Films
via Glenbuck Films

Filmbank Distributors
Grayton House
498-504 Fulham Road
London SW6 5NH
Tel: 071 386 9909/5411
Fax: 071 381 2405
Handles 16mm film on behalf of major, and some other, UK distributors

Films of Israel
via Viscom

Films of Poland
Polish Cultural Institute
34 Portland Place
London W1N 4HQ
Tel: 071 636 6032/3/4
Fax: 071 637 2190

Films of Scotland
via SCFVL

Finnish Embassy
via Audience Planners

First Independent Films (formerly Vestron (UK))
via Glenbuck Films

Ford Film and Video Library
Audio Visual Services
Ford Motor Company
Room 1/469
Eagle Way
Brentwood
Essex CM13 3BW
Tel: 0277 252766
Fax: 0277 260168
Tom Malcolm

French Scientific Film Library
via SCFVL

David Furnham Films
39 Hove Park Road
Hove
Sussex BN3 6LH
Tel: 0273 559731

GTO
and
Gala Film Library
via Glenbuck Films

Gas Council
see ***British Gas Film Library***

German Film and Video Library
via Viscom

Glenbuck Films
Glenbuck House
Glenbuck Road
Surbiton
Surrey KT6 6BT
Tel: 081 399 0022/5266
Fax: 081 399 6651
Handles non-theatrical 16mm, 35mm and video

Gower
Gower House
Croft Road
Aldershot
Hants GU11 3HR
Tel: 0252 331551
Fax: 0252 317446
Training videos and packages

Sheila Graber Animation
50 Meldon Avenue
South Shields
Tyne and Wear
NE34 0EL
Tel/Fax: 091 455 4985
Over 60 animated shorts available on 16mm and VHS

Granada Television Film Library
via Concord Video and Film Council

Greater London Arts
Coriander Building
20 Gainsford Street
London SE1 2NE
Tel: 071 403 9013
Fax: 071 403 9072

Greek National Tourist Office
via Audience Planners

HandMade Films
and
Hobo Films Enterprises
via Glenbuck Films

Honda UK Film Library
via Viscom

IAC (Institute of Amateur Cinematographers)
63 Woodfield Lane
Ashtead
Surrey KT21 2BT
Tel: 03722 76358

ICA Video
Institute of Contemporary Arts
Nash House
The Mall
London SW1Y 5AH
Tel: 071 930 0493
Fax: 071 873 0051
Video series of writers in conversation

India Government Tourist Office
via Audience Planners

India House Information Service
India House
Aldwych
London WC2B 4NA
Tel: 071 836 8484 x147
Video documentaries

Intercontinental Films
via Glenbuck Films

International Defence and Aid Fund for Southern Africa
Canon Collins House
64 Essex Road
London N1 8LR
Tel: 071 359 9181

Irish Tourist Board
via Viscom

Jamaica Tourist Board
via Audience Planners

Japan Tourist Organisation
and
Japanese Embassy Films
via Viscom

Robert Kingston Films
via Glenbuck Films

Leeds Animation Workshop
(A Women's Collective)
45 Bayswater Row
Leeds LS8 5LF
Tel: 0532 484997
Producers and distributors of animated films on social issues

London Film Makers' Co-op
42 Gloucester Avenue
London NW1 8JD
Tel: 071 586 4806
Experimental/art-based films: 2,000 classic and recent titles for hire from 1920s to current work

London Video Access (LVA)
23 Frith Street
London W1A 4XD
Tel: 071 437 2786
Fax: 071 734 2003
LVA is Britain's national centre for video and new media art

Longman Training (formerly Rank Training Films)
Cullum House
North Orbital Road
Denham
Uxbridge
Middx UB9 5HL
Tel: 0895 834142
Fax: 0895 833616

Luxembourg National Tourist Office
via Audience Planners

MTV Finland
via Darvill Associates

Mainline Pictures
via Glenbuck Films and BFI Film + Video Library

Medusa Communications
via Glenbuck Films

Mediacraft
via Training Communications

Melrose Film Productions
16 Bromells Road
Clapham Common
London SW4 0BL
Tel: 071 627 8404

Mercedes Benz Film Library
via Viscom

Multilink Film Library
12 The Square
Vicarage Farm Road
Peterborough PE1 5TS
Tel: 0733 67622
Distributors of films/videos to the education sector

Mushroom Growers Association
via Viscom

National Audio Visual Aids Library (NAVAL)
(DS Information Systems)
George Building
Normal College
Bangor
Gwynedd LL57 2PZ
Tel: 0248 370144
Fax: 0248 351415
Educational audio visual aids consisting of videotapes, 16mm films, slides and overhead projector transparencies available for hire or purchase

National Film and Television School
Beaconsfield Studios
Beaconsfield
Bucks HP9 1LG
Tel: 0494 671234
Fax: 0494 674042

National Society for the Prevention of Cruelty to Children
67 Saffron Hill
London EC1N 8RS
Tel: 071 242 1626
Fax: 071 831 9562

National Westminster Bank Video Unit
Phase 2
Kings Cross House
200 Pentonville Road
London N1 9HL
Tel: 071 239 8000
Fax: 071 239 8903
Ernie Fowles

Netherlands Information Service
and

Netherlands PD Films
via Darvill Associates

Northern Arts
via Amber Films

Norwegian Embassy Films
via National Audio Visual Aids Library (NAVAL)

Oasis (UK) Films
(formerly Recorded Releasing)
via Filmbank and Glenbuck Films

Open University Educational Enterprises
12 Cofferidge Close
Stony Stratford
Milton Keynes
MK11 1BY
Tel: 0908 261662
Fax: 0908 261002
Diana Ruault

Palace Pictures
via Glenbuck Films

Pathé Cannon
via Filmbank

Edward Patterson Associates
Treetops
Cannongate Road
Hythe
Kent CT21 5PT
Tel: 0303 264195
Fax: 0303 264195
Health, safety and education video programming

Pedigree Pet Foods Film Library
via Viscom

Peru Tourist Board
via Audience Planners

Polytechnic of Central London (Film Section)
School of Communications
18-22 Riding House Street
London W1P 7PD
Tel: 071 911 5000 x2726

Post Office Video and Film Library
PO Box 145
Sittingbourne
Kent ME10 1NH
Tel: 0795 426465

RNLI
via Viscom

RoSPA
Film Library
Head Office
Cannon House
Priory Queensway
Birmingham B4 6BS
Tel: 021 200 2461
Fax: 021 200 1254
Safety films

RSPCA
Causeway
Horsham
West Sussex RH12 1HG
Tel: 0403 64181
Fax: 0403 41048

Radio Netherlands Television
and

Radio Sweden International
via Darvill Associates

Rank Film Distributors
via Filmbank

Retake Film and Video Collective
19 Liddell Road
London NW6 2EW
Tel: 071 328 4676

Royal College of Art
Department of Film and Television
Kensington Gore
London SW7 2EU
Tel: 071 584 5020 x337
Fax: 071 225 1487

Royal Society for the Protection of Birds
Film Hire Library
15 Beaconsfield Road
London NW10 2LE
Tel: 081 451 1127

Save the Children Fund
via Viscom

Scottish Central Film and Video Library (SCFVL)
74 Victoria Crescent Road
Dowanhill
Glasgow G12 9JN
Tel: 041 334 9314
Fax: 041 334 6519
Educational, training and general interest titles

Scottish Television
via Academy Television

Scottish Tourist Board Films
via SCFVL

Shell Film Library
via Education Distribution Service and Viscom

Southbrook Film Productions (formerly Palladium Media)
via Glenbuck Films

South West Arts Board
Bradninch Place
Gandy Street
Exeter EX4 3LS
Tel: 0392 218188
Fax: 0392 413554

Spastic Society Film Library
via Viscom

Steel Bank Film Co-op
Brown Street
Sheffield S1 2BS
Tel: 0742 721235
TV documentaries, drama features, arts programmes

Supreme Films
via Glenbuck Films

Swedish Embassy (Cultural Dept)
via Darvill Associates and Glenbuck Films

Swiss National Tourist Office/Swiss Federal Railways
Swiss Centre
Swiss Court

London
W1V 8EE
Tel: 071 734 1921
Fax: 071 437 4577

TSW – Television South West
via Academy Television

TTT PlayBack Communications
via Video Arts

TV Choice
80-81 St Martin's Lane
London WC2N 4AA
Tel: 071 379 0873

Tate & Lyle Sugars
and

The Tea Council
via Viscom

Team Video Productions
Canalot
222 Kensal Road
London W10 5BN
Tel: 081 960 5536

Television History Centre
42 Queen Square
London WC1N 3AJ
Tel: 071 405 6627
Fax: 071 242 1426
Programmes for hire or purchase about work, health, women, community action, particularly suitable for educational discussion groups 16 plus
See also under Production Companies

Texaco Film Library
Public & Government Affairs Department
Texaco
1 Knightsbridge Green
London SW1X 7QJ
Tel: 071 225 3351
Fax: 071 584 6310
Neil van Coevorden

Thames Television Video Sales
via Academy Television

Touchstone Pictures
via Filmbank

Training Communications
Brooklands House
29 Hythegate
Werrington
Peterborough PE4 6ZP
Tel/Fax: 0733 327337
Christine Tipton

Transatlantic Films
Blythe Hall
100 Blythe Road
London W14 0HE
Tel: 071 727 0132
Fax: 071 603 0668

Twentieth Century Fox
via Filmbank

Tyne Tees Television
via Academy Television

UIP (UK)
via Filmbank

UK Atomic Energy Authority Film Library
via Viscom

United States Travel and Tourism Administration
via Audience Planners

Video Arts
Dumbarton House
68 Oxford Street
London W1N 9LA
Tel: 071 637 7288
Fax: 071 580 8103
Distributes the John Cleese training films; 'Take It from the Top' – the David Frost interviews; 'In Search of Excellence' and other films from the Nathan/Tyler Business Video Library and the Harvard Business School Video Series

Viewtech Audio Visual Media
161 Winchester Road
Brislington
Bristol BS4 3NJ
Tel: 0272 773422/717030
Fax: 0272 724292

Virgin Films
via Glenbuck Films

Viscom
Unit B11
Park Hall Road Trading Estate
London SE21 8EL
Tel: 081 761 3035
Fax: 081 761 2698

Waldegrave Films
via Training Communications

Warner Bros Films
via Filmbank

Weintraub Entertainment
via Glenbuck Films and Filmbank

Welsh Arts Council
Film, Video & TV Dept.
Museum Place
Cardiff CF1 3NX
Tel: 0222 394711
Fax: 0222 221447

West Derbyshire Tourist Office
via Audience Planners

Westbourne Film Distribution
1st Floor
17 Westbourne Park Road
London W2 5PX
Tel: 071 221 1998
Classic children's films
The Singing Ringing Tree

Workers Film Association
9 Lucy Street
Manchester M15 4BX
Tel: 061 848 9782

World Gold Council
via Viscom

York MDM
via Training Communications

Yorkshire Television
Video Sales Department
The Television Centre
Leeds LS3 1JS
Tel: 0532 438283 x4060
Fax: 0532 429522
Also via Academy Television

Yugoslavian Tourist Board
via Audience Planners

DISTRIBUTORS (THEATRICAL)

These are companies which acquire the UK rights to films for distribution to cinemas and, in many cases, also for sale to network TV, satellite, cable and video media. Listed is a selection of features certificated by the censor for those companies in 1990 and the first quarter of 1991, and some past releases or re-releases available during this period

Albany Video Distribution
Battersea Studios
Television Centre
Thackeray Road
London SW8 3TW
Tel: 071 498 6811
Fax: 071 498 1494
Films and video art

All American Leisure Group
6 Woodland Way
Petts Wood
Kent BR5 1ND
Tel: 0689 871535/871519
Fax: 0689 871519

Apollo Film Distributors
14 Ensbury Park Road
Bournemouth BH9 2SJ
Tel: 0202 520962

Arrow Film Distributors
18 Watford Road
Radlett
Herts WD7 8LE
Tel: 0923 858306
Fax: 0923 859673
63 Poland Street
London W1V 3DF
Tel: 071 734 0727
Fax: 071 434 1528
Meet the Feebles
The Monk
Welcome Home Roxy Carmichael

Artificial Eye Film Co
211 Camden High Street
London NW1 7BT
Tel: 071 267 6036/
482 3981
Fax: 071 267 6499
An Angel at My Table
Bye Bye Blues
La Captive du Désert
Cyrano de Bergerac
The Garden
Golden Braid
Night Sun
A Tale of Springtime
Tilaï
A World Without Pity

Arts Council of Great Britain
See under Organisations

Atlantic Film Distributors
Premier House
77 Oxford Street
London W1R 1RB
Tel: 071 437 4415
French Massage Parlour
Hot Bodies
Hot Desires
Luscious
St Tropez Vice

BFI Film & Video Distribution
21 Stephen Street
London W1P 1PL
Tel: 071 255 1444
Fax: 071 436 7950
See also p8
Fellini's $8^1/_2$
In the Realm of the Senses
The Naked Kiss
Noi Tre (The Three of Us)
Riff-Raff
Rocco and his Brothers
Shock Corridor
and several films by Pier Paolo Pasolini, including
The Gospel According to St Matthew
Oedipus Rex
Pigsty
Theorem

BFI Production
29 Rathbone Street
London W1P 1AG
Tel: 071 636 5587
Fax: 071 580 9456
See also p12
Caravaggio
December Bride
Distant Voices, Still Lives
Draughtsman's Contract
Fellow Traveller
Melancholia
New Directors Shorts
On the Black Hill
Play Me Something
Silent Scream
Young Soul Rebels

Black Audio Film Collective
89 Ridley Road
London E8 2NH
Tel: 071 254 9527/9536
Testament
See under Distributors (Non-Theatrical) for further details

Blue Dolphin Films
15-17 Old Compton Street
London W1V 6JR
Tel: 071 439 9511
Fax: 071 287 0370
Beautiful Dreamers
Dick
Explorers
The Holy Innocents
Kamikaze
La Vie est Belle
The Last of England
Mr. Frost
McCabe and Mrs Miller
Roger Corman's Frankenstein Unbound
What Happened to Kerouac?
Vincent and Theo

Bordeaux Films International
22 Soho Square
London W1V 5FJ
Tel: 081 959 8556
See under Production Companies for list of films

BratPack Programme Distribution Co
Canalot Studios
222 Kensal Road
London W10 5BN
Tel: 081 969 7609
Fax: 081 969 2284
Animated Alphabet
Bump
Fingerprint Farm
Puppydog Tales
Tiko's Adventures in Kash Koosh

Brent Walker Film Distributors
19 Rupert Street
London W1V 7FS
Tel: 071 465 0111
Fax: 071 465 8101

John Burder Films
7 Saltcoats Road
London W4 1AR
Tel: 081 995 0547
Fax: 081 995 3376
Broadcast TV programmes
See also under Distributors (Non-Theatrical)

Castle Premier Releasing
Premier House
77 Oxford Street
London W1R 1RB
Tel: 071 493 0440
Fax: 071 491 9040
Buddy's Song
Bullseye
Captain America
First Power
Meet the Applegates
Rainbow Drive
Welcome Home Roxy Carmichael

Cavalcade Films
Regent House
235-241 Regent Street
London W1R 8JU
Tel: 071 734 3147
Fax: 071 734 2403

Chain Production
11 Hornton Street
London W8 7NP
Tel: 071 937 1981
Fax: 071 376 0556
Specialist in Italian films: library of 1,000 titles available for UK exploitation. Releasing *Mignon has Left* theatrically through Metro Pictures. *Casablanca Express* on video

Cinenova (Women's Film and Video Distribution)
113 Roman Road
London E2 0HU
Tel: 081 981 6828
Castles of Sand
Cover Up: Behind the Iran Contra Affair
Nice Coloured Girls
Rabbit on the Moon
Shadow Panic
A Song of Ceylon
Surname Viet Given Name Nam
See also under Distributors (Non-Theatrical)

Columbia Tri-Star Films (UK)
19-23 Wells Street
London W1P 3FP
Tel: 071 580 2090
Fax: 071 528 8980
Feature releases from the Columbia and Tri-Star companies, Orion Pictures and Weintraub Screen Entertainment
Avalon
Awakenings
Flatliners
The Freshman
I Love You to Death
Look Who's Talking
Look Who's Talking Too
Postcards from the Edge
Revenge
She's Out of Control

Contemporary Films
24 Southwood Lawn Road
Highgate
London N6 5SF
Tel: 081 340 5715
Fax: 081 348 1238
Piravi
Also co-distribute product with Electric Pictures
Celia
C'est la vie
The Company of Strangers
The Match Factory Girl
Max Mon Amour
The Plot against Harry
Sweetie
The Unbelievable Truth
Please contact Contemporary Films for bookings, and Electric Pictures for publicity material

Crawford Films
15-17 Old Compton Street
London W1V 6JR
Tel: 071 734 5298
Fax: 071 287 0370

Curzon Film Distributors
38 Curzon Street
London W1Y 8EY
Tel: 071 465 0565
Fax: 071 499 2018
Au Revoir Les Enfants
Dark Eyes
Henry V
La Lectrice
Milou in May
Pelle the Conqueror

Darvill Associates
280 Chartridge Lane
Chesham
Bucks HP5 2SG
Tel: 0494 783643
Fax: 0494 784873

Dee & Co
Suite 204
Canalot
222 Kensal Road
London W10 5BN
Tel: 081 960 2712
Fax: 081 960 2728
See under International Sales

The Walt Disney Co
31-32 Soho Square
London W1V 6AP
Tel: 071 734 8111
Fax: 071 734 5619
Television distribution and European production arm of major US studio. See under Warner Bros for theatrical release information

Electric Pictures
22 Carol Street
London NW1 0HU
Tel: 071 267 8418/284 0524/0583
La Bête Humaine
Dr Petiot
Henry, Portrait of a Serial Killer
I Hired a Contract Killer
Co-distributed with Contemporary
C'est la vie
The Company of Strangers
The Match Factory Girl
The Plot Against Harry
The Unbelievable Truth

Elephant Entertainments
Tivoli Cinema
Station Street
Birmingham B5 4DY
Tel: 021 616 1021
Fax: 021 616 1019
City of the Living Dead
House by the Cemetery
The Last Hunter

English Film Co
6 Woodland Way
Petts Wood
Kent BR5 1ND
Tel: 0689 71535
Fax: 0689 71519

Entertainment Film Distributors
27 Soho Square
London W1V 5FL
Tel: 071 439 1606
Fax: 071 734 2483
Bad Influence
Creator
Dark Angel
Kickboxer 2
Kid
Men at Work
Stockade
Waiting for the Light
Why Me?
Wild Orchid

Film and Video Umbrella
Top Floor, Chelsea Reach
79-89 Lots Road
London SW10 0RN
Tel: 071 376 3171
Fax: 071 351 6479
Promoting experimental film and electronic arts
Art & Science
The Body in Extremis
The Cinema of Andy Warhol
Dance Film Dance
Electric Eyes
Inside the Pleasure Dome – The Magickal World of Kenneth Anger
Mortal Signs
A Thoughtful Gaze – The Video Tapes of Bill Viola

First Independent Films (formerly Vestron UK)
69 New Oxford Street
London WC1A 1DG
Tel: 071 379 0406
Fax: 071 528 7772
Blue Steel
Catchfire
Communion
Fear
Love Hurts
Misery
Over Her Dead Body
Sibling Rivalry

Gala Films
26 Danbury Street
Islington
London N1 8JU
Tel: 071 226 5085
Le Cop II
Milou in May
Noce Blanche
Romuald and Juliette
These Foolish Things
Three Sisters
Wings of Fame
Women on the Roof

Glenbuck Films
Glenbuck House
Glenbuck Road
Surbiton
Surrey KT6 6BT
Tel: 081 399 0022/5266
Fax: 081 399 6651

The Samuel Goldwyn Company
St George's House
14-17 Wells Street
London W1P 3FP
Tel: 071 436 5105
Fax: 071 580 6520
My Heroes Have Always Been Cowboys
The Object of Beauty
The Tapes of Dexter Jackson
Truly, Madly, Deeply

Guild Film Distribution
Kent House
14-17 Market Place
Great Titchfield Street
London W1N 8AR
Tel: 071 323 5151
Fax: 071 631 3568
Air America
Dances With Wolves
The Doors
Hamlet
L.A. Story
Narrow Margin
Terminator 2 – Judgement Day

HandMade Films (Distributors)
26 Cadogan Square
London SW1X 0JP
Tel: 071 584 8345
Fax: 071 584 7338

Hemdale Film Distribution
21 Albion Street
London W2 2AS
Tel: 071 724 1010
Fax: 071 724 9168
Blood Red
The Boost
Chattahoochee
Criminal Law
Miracle Mile
Staying Together
Vampire's Kiss
War Party

Hobo Film Enterprises
9 St Martin's Court
London WC2N 4AJ
Tel: 071 895 0328
Fax: 071 895 0329
The Ballad of the Sad Cafe
The Big Picture
The Big Steal
The Fool
Howard's End
Paper Marriage
Rosencrantz and Guildenstern are Dead

Hollywood Pictures
see **Warner Bros**

ICA Projects
12 Carlton House Terrace
London SW1Y 5AH
Tel: 071 930 0493
Fax: 071 873 0051
Akira
Alice
La Amiga
Berlin Jerusalem
Circus Boys
The Enchantment
Heavy Petting
Ju Dou
Life is Cheap...but Toilet Paper is Expensive
Rouge

Ideal Communications Films and Television
40-41 Great Marlborough Street
London W1V 1DA
Tel: 071 287 4082
Fax: 071 287 4083
See under Production Companies for list of titles

Ideal-Opix Sales
40-41 Great Marlborough Street
London W1V 1DA
Tel: 071 287 4082
Fax: 071 287 4083
Television programming. For further details, see under International Sales

Kruger Leisure Organisation
see **TKO Films and TV**

MCEG Virgin Vision
Atlantic House
1 Rockley Road
Shepherds Bush
London W14 0DL
Tel: 081 740 5500
Fax: 081 967 1360/1
American Friends
Cold Feet
Diamond Skulls
The Handmaid's Tale
The Mahabharata
Q & A
The Reflecting Skin
Salute of the Jugger
Teenage Mutant Ninja Turtles
Windprints

MGM/UA
see **United International Pictures (UK)**

Mainline Pictures
37 Museum Street
London WC1A 1LP
Tel: 071 242 5523
Fax: 071 430 0170
Apartment Zero
Bagdad Cafe
Let's Get Lost
Metropolitan
The Music Teacher
The Nasty Girl
Rosalie Goes Shopping
Salaam Bombay
Santa Sangre
3 Women in Love

Medusa Communications
Regal Chambers
51 Bancroft
Hitchin
Herts SG5 1LL
Tel: 0462 421818
Fax: 0462 420393
See also under Video Labels

Metro Pictures
79 Wardour Street
London W1V 3TH
Tel: 071 734 8508/9
Fax: 071 287 2112
Coming Out
Dark Habits
Icicle Thief
Kamikaze Hearts
Lady of the Shanghai Cinema
Matador
To Sleep with Anger
The Vanishing

Miracle Communications
69 New Oxford Street
London WC1A 1DG
Tel: 071 379 5006

Nelson Entertainment International
8 Queen Street
London W1X 7PH
Tel: 071 493 3362
Fax: 071 409 0503

New Realm Entertainments
2nd Floor
80-82 Wardour Street
London W1V 3LF
Tel: 071 437 9143
Fax: 0372 469816

Oasis (UK) Films
66-68 Margaret Street
London W1N 7FL
Tel: 071 734 7477
Fax: 071 734 7470
A Bout de Souffle
Drowning by Numbers
Manhunter
Sidewalk Stories
Speaking Parts
True Love
Venus Peter
We Think the World of You
Wings of Desire
Withnail and I
Yaaba

Orbit Films
14 Campden Hill Gardens
London W8 7AY
Tel: 071 221 5548
Fax: 071 727 0515
The Adventures of Buckaroo Banzai
The Golden Years of Television: vintage product from the first decade of American TV, including features and serials

Palace Pictures
16-17 Wardour Mews
London W1V 3FF
Tel: 071 734 7060
Fax: 071 437 3248
The Grifters
The Hairdresser's Husband
Life is Sweet
Longtime Companion
Mr & Mrs Bridge
Monsieur Hire
Nikita
Nuns on the Run
The Sheltering Sky
Wild At Heart

Paramount
see **United International Pictures (UK)**

Poseidon Film Distributors
Hammer House
113 Wardour Street
London W1V 3TD
Tel: 071 734 4441
Fax: 071 437 0638
Autism
Dyslexia
Lysistrata

Rank Film Distributors
127 Wardour Street
London W1V 4AD
Tel: 071 437 9020
Fax: 071 434 3689
Alice
Ambition
Drop Dead Fred
Everybody's Fine
King of New York
The Linguini Incident
Mannequin on the Move
Mermaids
Navy Seals
Pyrates
Rock-a-Doodle
Scorchers
Silence of the Lambs
State of Grace
Under Suspicion

River First
First Floor
84 Wardour Street
London W1V 3LF
Tel: 071 287 9390
Fax: 071 287 1246
Black Magic Woman
Cold Justice
Cold Light of Day
Cresta Run

Sovereign Pictures
11-13 Soho Street
London W1V 5DA
Tel: 071 494 1010
Fax: 071 494 3939

Squirrel Films Distribution
119 Rotherhithe Street
London SE16 4NF
Tel: 071 231 2209
Fax: 071 231 2119
Biddy
The Nightingale
Tales of a Flying Trunk
The Tales of Beatrix Potter

Supreme Film Distributors
Premier House
77 Oxford Street
London W1R 1RB
Tel: 071 437 4415

TCB Releasing
Stone House, Rudge, Frome
Somerset BA11 2QQ
Tel: 0373 830769
Fax: 0373 831028
Television and video programming

TKO Films and TV (formerly Kruger Leisure Organisation)
PO Box 130, Hove
East Sussex BN3 6QU
Tel: 0273 550088
Fax: 0273 540969
Adventures of Scaramouche
Catch Me a Spy
Diamond Mercenaries
Gallavants
The Mark of Zorro

Touchstone Pictures
see **Warner Bros**

Twentieth Century Fox Film Co
20th Century House
31-32 Soho Square
London W1V 6AP
Tel: 071 437 7766
Fax: 071 437 1625
Come See the Paradise
Desperate Hours
Die Hard II
Exorcist III
Home Alone
Leviathan
Miller's Crossing
Nightbreed
Pacific Heights
Young Guns II

UA (United Artists)
see **United International Pictures (UK)**

United International Pictures (UK)
Mortimer House
37-41 Mortimer Street
London W1A 2JL
Tel: 071 636 1655
Fax: 071 636 4118
Releases product from Paramount, Universal, and MGM/UA
Back to the Future Part III
Bird on a Wire
Days of Thunder
Ghost
The Godfather part III
Havana
Internal Affairs
Kindergarten Cop
Rocky V
The Russia House

Universal
see **United International Pictures (UK)**

Vestron UK
see **First Independent Films**

Virgin Vision
see **MCEG Virgin Vision**

Warner Bros Distributors
135 Wardour Street
London W1V 4AP
Tel: 071 734 8400
Fax: 071 437 5521
Feature releases from Warner Bros and Disney/ Touchstone/Hollywood Pictures
Arachnophobia
Dick Tracy
GoodFellas
Gremlins 2
The Little Mermaid
Memphis Belle
The Never Ending Story 2
Presumed Innocent
Pretty Woman
Three Men and a Little Lady

Westbourne Film Distribution
First Floor
17 Westbourne Park Road
London W2 5PX
Tel: 071 221 1998
Classic children's films
The Singing Ringing Tree

Weintraub Screen Entertainment
Distributed through Columbia Tri-Star Films and Hobo Film Enterprises

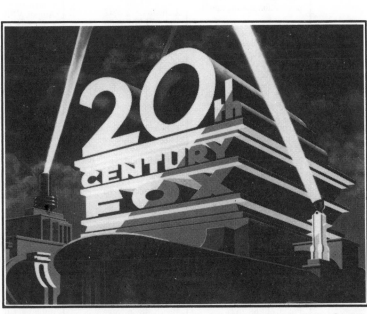

Winstone Film Distributors
80-82 Wardour Street
London W1V 3LF
Tel: 071 439 4525
Sub-distributors for Palace, Oasis, Hemdale and Pacific Television

FACILITIES

AIRtv Facilities
Hawley Crescent
London NW1 8NP
Tel: 071 485 4121
Fax: 071 485 3667
Video formats: C, BVU, Betacam
Standards Conversion, component and composite editing, voice over booths, VHS Duplication, NTSC 1″, NTSC Betacam SP, NTSC VHS, lines working, transmission services, studios
Vision effects: ADO, Aston 3, colour caption cameras
Graphics: 5 workstations Super Nova/Matisse
Telecine: Rank Cintel Mk3

AKA
Film and Television Services
60 Farringdon Road
London EC1R 3BP
Tel: 071 251 3885
Fax: 071 253 2045
Editing: Three machine Betacam SP component with 1″, Zeno, Aston 3, Nagra T$^1/_4$″, and colour caption camera, Charisma, 16mm cutting room; sound transfer; equipment hire incl Aaton 16mm, Betacam SP
Studios: 2 sound proof stages, 180° cyc, overhead rigging. Full crewing and production management

ARTA
Lancaster House
583 High Road
Tottenham
London N17 6SB
Tel: 081 885 3982
Fax: 081 365 0755
Cameras: Sony DXC-325, M3
Format: hi-band SP
Editing: hi-band SP/ lo-band U-Matic suite; 2/3 machine
Special Effects: GML DVP
Apple Macintosh computer captions/ graphics
Full production personnel
Training workshops

Abbey Road Studios
3 Abbey Road
London NW8 9AY
Tel: 071 286 1161
Fax: 071 289 7527
Four studios; music to picture; film sound transfer facilities; audio post-production; audio sweetening for video and TV; Sonic Solutions computer sound enhancement system
Residential accommodation, restaurant and bar

Abbey Video
Holly Bank
Hollington
Derbyshire DE6 3GA
Tel: 0335 60531
Mobile: 0860 855936
Betacam SP location shooting
ENG/Corporate

Advision Studios
1 Montague Place
Kemptown
Brighton BN2 1JE
Tel: 0273 677375
Fax: 0273 672597
Digital/analogue 24/48-track studio; pre-production studio; wide range of outboard gear; fully residential
Two state-of-the-art mobile studios for location recording, post-production and audio for video; Lexicon Opus Digital Post-Production System

After Image Facilities
32 Acre Lane
London SW2 5SG
Tel: 071 737 7300
Fax: 071 326 1850
Cameras: Sony 330P, M3
Studios: broadcast studio A: 2000 sq ft Ultimatte/packshot studio B: 27 x 27 x 11ft with cyc
Editing: Grass Valley 200, Sony BVE 5000, Charisma DVE, Ultimatte and Chromakey
Video formats: 1″C, Beta SP and BVU

Air Recording Studios
214 Oxford Street
London W1N 9DF
Tel: 071 637 2758
Fax: 071 636 5001
Studio 1: 65 musicians, 72Ch Neve/Focusrite; Studio 2: 30 musicians, 56Ch SSL, G series computer; Studio 3: O/D Booth, 48Ch Neve V series, GML automation; Studio 4: O/D Booth, 48Ch SSL, G series computer
Sony 48tk and 24tk, Mitsubishi 32tk, Studer; A800 24tk/48tk, U-Matic on site available in any room

Angel Recording Studios
311 Upper Street
London N1 2TU
Tel: 071 354 2525
Fax: 071 226 9624
2 x 100-musician studio complex with mixing to 35mm and 16mm film
Customised Neve desks

Anner Communications
T4 Stillorgan Industrial Park
Blackrock
Co Dublin
Tel: (353) 952221
Fax: (353) 952193
Studio: 3,000 sq ft drive-in studio with Ultimatte and White Cyclorama
Four Betacam SP ENG crews
Film: Rank Cintel MkIII Telecine with 'Colour Grade' Film post-production
Editing: CMX 3600, GVG 200, Dual Channel Abekas A53 with Key-channels, Aston 3 Character Generator Ampex VPR-3 1″ C-formats and Bosch 1″ B-format Betacam SP and Nagra T; CMX 3600, GVG 100 component, Dual Channel Abekas A53 with key-channels, Aston 3 Character Generator, Betacam SP and Nagra T
Duplication: 250 VHS PAL Slaves

Anvil Film and Recording Group
Denham Studios
North Orbital Road
Denham
Uxbridge
Middx UB9 5HH
Tel: 0895 833522
Fax: 0895 835006
35/16mm film and video production; studio re-recording, ADR, post-sync FX recording, transfers, foreign version dubbing; cutting rooms, neg cutting

Avolites Production Co
184 Park Avenue
London NW10 7XL
Tel: 081 965 8522
Fax: 081 965 0290
Manufacture, sale and hire of dimming systems, memory and manual lighting control consoles and chain hoist control systems
Sales of relevant cabling and connectors
Distributors for SL series Socapex connectors in UK

Geoff Axtell Associates
16a Newman Street
London W1P 3HD
Tel: 071 637 9321
Fax: 071 637 2850
Harry/Paintbox/Encore digital suite, Cypher XL, film opticals, titles and effects, computerised motion control, film and video rostrum cameras

BBRK
Shepperton Studio Centre
Studios Road
Shepperton
Middx TW17 0QB
Tel: 0932 564922
Fax: 0932 560598
Art direction and construction, building services, prop hire, catering services

BTS Television
115 Portland Street
Manchester M1 6DW
Tel: 061 236 6911
Fax: 061 236 6914
Transfers 1″, Beta SP, BVU SP, VHS, Betamax, standards conversions, off-line editing, A/V to video transfers

BUFVC
55 Greek Street
London W1V 5LR
Tel: 071 734 3687
Fax: 071 287 3914
16mm cutting room and viewing facilities

Jim Bambrick and Associates
10 Frith Street
London W1V 5TZ
Tel: 071 434 2351
Fax: 071 734 6362
16mm, 35mm cutting rooms, off-line video edit suite

Barcud
Cibyn
Caernarfon
Gwynedd
Tel: 0286 3458
Fax: 0286 5330
Video formats: 1″C, Beta SP
2-7 camera OB unit, Betacam units
Studios: 6,500 sq ft studio with audience seating and comprehensive lighting rig; 1,500 sq ft studio with vision/ lighting control gallery and sound gallery
Editing: Sony 9000 full-effects suite with GVG 200; Sony 5000 full-effects suite with GVG 100, Sony 900 cut suite
Graphics: Paintbox, Rank-Cintel Artfile, Chyron Infinite etc
DVE: 3 channels Charisma, 2 channels Cleo
Sound: 2 suites each with AMS Audiofile, V/O booth and CD fx and music library
BT lines
VHS off-line

CTS Studios
The Music Centre
Engineers Way
Wembley
Middlesex HA9 0DR
Tel: 081 903 4611
Fax: 081 903 7130
Largest of 4 studios holds 130 musicians with three alternatives between 10 and 40
Synchronised film projection available with Telecine or video facilities for recording music to picture
Digital or analog available, restaurant, large car park

CTV
PO Box 1098
Gerrards Cross
Bucks SL9 8DY
Tel: 02407 71513
Fax: 02407 71086
Video production cassette duplication; standards conversions; film to video transfers; edit suite hire

Canalot Production Studios
222 Kensal Road
London W10 5BN
Tel: 081 960 6985/8580
Fax: 081 968 6020
Glennis Wybrow
Media business complex housing over 70 companies, involved in television, film, video and music production

Capital FX (formerly Mike Uden Opticals)
21a Kingly Court
off Beak Street
London W1R 5LE
Tel: 071 439 1982
Fax: 071 734 0950
Opticals; special effects and titling

Capital Group Studios
13 Wandsworth Plain
London SW18 1ET
Tel: 081 874 0131
Fax: 081 871 9737
Studios: 3,000 sq ft, 2,000 sq ft; separate galleries, 8 cameras, 2 x Ampex mixers each with 3 ME decks; Charisma digital effects; Aston caption
Video formats: D2,1″C, Quad, Beta SP
Editing: Ampex Ace, Grass Valley, Cox mixers, Charisma and ADO digital effects. Aston 3, Aston caption and caption camera.
Sound: 24(with SR)/4/2 track to picture, Calrec 48 input/Trident 32 input desks, CD effects
Telecine with TOPSY, caption camera, canteens, car park

Capital Television Facilities
22 Newman Street
London W1P 4AJ
Tel: 071 636 3663
Fax: 071 436 3989
Video formats: Quad, 1″C, BVU, Betacam, U-Matic, Betacam SP
Editing: Datatron, 3 machine lo-band U-Matic off-line
Vision effects: Ampex ADO, Gemini 3
Graphics: Quantel Paintbox
Standards conversion; cassette duplication

Carlton Television
St John's Wood Studios
St John's Wood Terrace
London NW8
Tel: 071 722 8111/9255
Fax: 071 483 4264
ENG/Multi Camera OB
Units: two 4-10 camera OB units, 1-4 camera OB unit, 3-8 VTR/editing truck, 2-4 VTR recording truck, single and multi-camera units
Post production: two 4x1″ edit suites with Abekas A64, ADO and Abekas A53 digital effects, colour caption camera, Aston 4 and Aston 3 character generator, Beta and BVU play-in machines, vertical interval time code and disc conform editing; 1x4 Beta SP component edit suite with A53, VistaVision mixer, Aston 3 and colour correctors

Chamberlain Film Studio
16-20 Wharfdale Road
London N1 9RY
Tel: 071 837 3855
Stage: 80 sq metres
Construction facilities

Chatsworth Television
97-99 Dean Street
London W1V 5RA
Tel: 071 734 4302/3/4
Fax: 071 437 3301
Transportable Sony edit suite with RM440 controller

Roger Cherrill
65-66 Dean Street
London W1V 6PL
Tel: 071 437 7972
Fax: 071 437 6411
High speed dubbing theatre, Dolby A, SR and SVA; High speed ADR and FX recording; Digital suite with Synclavier 9600; Transfer Bay, all formats; 25 cutting rooms (16mm, 35mm); Film/video editors

Cherry Video
65-66 Dean Street
London W1V 6PL
Tel: 071 437 7972
Fax: 071 437 6411
Video formats: 1″C, PAL and NTSC, Beta SP, BVU, lo-band and VHS
Telecine: Rank Cintel MkIIIC, in PAL and NTSC with computerised colour grading.
35mm, 16mm and 8mm with autoshot, varispeed and XYZoom ADAC digital standards conversion

Chess Valley Films and Video
Film House
Little Chalfont
Bucks HP7 9PY
Tel: 0494 762222
Fax: 0494 763333
Video formats: Betacam SP, BVU SP, 1"; 35mm, 16mm film; all equipment/lighting/ viewing; off-line edit facilities; corporate TV and films for marketing/ sales/promos/training etc
Established 1961

Chromaco!our
16 Grangemills
Weir Road
London SW12 0NE
Tel: 081 675 8422
Fax: 081 675 8499
Animation supplies and equipment

Chrysalis TV Mobiles (formerly Recording and Production Services)
3 Chrysalis Way
Langley Bridge
Eastwood
Nottingham NG16 3RY
Tel: 0773 718111
Fax: 0773 716004
4 x OB units, component and PAL; component edit suite with A53D DVE and Aston 4

Cinecontact
175 Wardour Street
London W1V 3AB
Tel: 071 434 1745
Fax: 071 494 0405
3x16mm film cutting rooms, each fitted with 1901s; 2xVHS off-line suites; 16mm film gear and Sony Betacam for hire

Cine-Europe
7 Silver Road
Wood Lane
London W12 7SG
Tel: 081 743 6762
Fax: 081 749 3501
16mm, 35mm and full range of grip equipment hire

Cinefocus
1 Pavilion Parade
Wood Lane
London W12 0HQ
Tel: 081 743 2552
Fax: 081 743 0822
Unit 9, Orchard Street Industrial Estate
Salford
Manchester M6 6FL
Tel: 061 745 8146
Film, video, grip; Arriflex 16/35mm, Sony SP, Chapman, cranes, full equipment rental service

Cine-Lingual Sound Studios
27-29 Berwick Street
London W1V 3RF
Tel: 071 437 0136
Fax: 071 439 2012
3 sound studios, 16/35mm computerised ADR; Foley recording; Dolby stereo mixing; sound transfers; cutting rooms

Cinequip Lighting Co
Units 6-8 Orchard Street Industrial Estate
Salford
Manchester M6 6FL
Tel: 061 736 8034
Fax: 061 745 8023
Lighting equipment hire

Cinevideo
Broadcast Television Equipment Hire
7 Silver Road
White City Industrial Park
Wood Lane
London W12 7SG
Tel: 081 743 3839
Fax: 081 743 8417
Video formats: 1", Beta SP, MII
Cameras: Ikegami HL355, HL-55, Sony range, PAL and NTSC

Colour Film Services Group
22-25 Portman Close
London W1A 4BE
Tel: 071 486 2881
Fax: 071 486 4152
Videotape to film transfer specialists, direct from broadcast video to 35mm and 16mm negative; Telecine mastering and tape dubbing all formats; Betacam SP component edit suite and 'Alphabet' video assembly from A+B cut neg; 16mm sound dubbing studios; bulk cassette duplication; full film laboratory services; equipment hire; conference centre; media management

Compass Production Associates
3rd Floor
18-19 Warwick Street
London W1R 5RB
Tel: 071 439 2581
Fax: 071 439 1865
Production offices; 16mm cutting rooms; U-Matic off-line edit suite

Complete Video Facilities
Slingsby Place
London WC2E 9AB
Tel: 071 379 7739
Fax: 071 497 9305
Telecom lines
Video formats: 1"C, D1, D2, BVU, U-Matic, SP Betacam
Editing: Sony BVE 9000, Grass Valley 200 Vision Mixer, Harry, Abekas A64, Aston 3
Vision effects: Grass Valley DVE, ADO 100, Quantel Mirage, Encore, Paintbox, Abekas A60, Symbolics 3-D Computer Graphics System
Sound: SSL 32 channel and DDA 16 channel consoles, voiceover and sound library
Telecine: 35mm/16mm 4:2:2 telecine, Steadifilm, Colourist colour corrector, pin registration gate

Corinthian and Synchro-Sonics
5 Richmond Mews
Richmond Buildings
London W1V 5AG
Tel: 071 734 3325
Fax: 071 437 3502
16mm cutting rooms; sound transfer, video transfer; equipment hire; 16mm or video commentary to picture studio; rough dubs; sound fx library

Crow Film and Television Services
12 Wendell Road
London W12 9RT
Tel: 081 749 6071
Fax: 081 740 0795
Video formats: 1", Betacam SP, Betacam, BVU
Cameras: Sony BVP 50/7 P, Arriflex SR2, BVU 300
Edit suite 1: Sony 9000 Edit controller, Grass Valley 200 vision mixer, 2 Channel Charisma, Aston Caption Character Generator, Sony 1/4" tape recorder with time code, rostrum camera
Edit suite 2: 900 edit controller, Grass Valley 1800 vision mixer, Questech 6101 DVE, Aston 3, Revox 1/4" play in, rostrum camera
1", Beta SP and BVU editing machines also available
Offline editing, hi-/lo-band, VHS
16mm cutting room

Crystal Film and Video
50 Church Road
London NW10 9PY
Tel: 081 965 0769
Fax: 081 965 7975
Aatons, Arriflex, Nagras Radio mics, lights and transport; Sony Beta SP; studio 50' x 30'; crews

Cygnet
The Studios
Communication Business Centre
14 Blenheim Road
High Wycombe
Bucks HP12 3RS
Tel: 0494 450541
Fax: 0494 462154
Full production facilities for 16mm and video; editing suites; sound department

DATS Video
Nicholford Hall
Norland Lane
Widnes WA8 9AX
Tel: 051 423 4040
Fax: 051 423 6955
Selling U-matic, VHS edit suites, cameras, monitors
Equipment repairs
Tape duplication – all formats

DBA Television
21 Ormeau Avenue
Belfast BT2 8HD
Tel: 0232 231197
Fax: 0232 333302
Crew hire and 16mm edit facilities, off-line and sound transfers; Aaton, Steenbeck
Studio: 600 sq ft

Dateline Productions
79 Dean Street
London W1V 5HA
Tel: 071 437 4510
Fax: 071 287 6544
16mm, 35mm film editing, off-line editing, negative cutting

De Lane Lea Sound Centre
75 Dean Street
London W1V 5HA
Tel: 071 439 1721
Fax: 071 437 0913
2 high speed 35mm Dolby stereo dubbing theatres (inc 1 x 16/35mm) with Dolby SR; high speed ADR and FX

theatre (16/35mm and video); Synclavier digital FX suite; digital sound FX suite with audition room inc video; sound rushes and transfers; video transfers to VHS and U-Matic; 13x35mm cutting rooms

Dean Street Studio
75 Dean Street
London W1V 5HA
Tel: 071 494 0735
Fax: 071 734 2519

Delta Sound Services
Lee Shepperton Studios Centre
Squires Bridge Road
Shepperton
Middx TW17 0QD
Tel: 0932 562045
Fax: 0932 568989
16mm, 35mm and video dubbing theatre; post-sync and footsteps; effects work; in-house sound transfers

Denman Productions
60 Mallard Place
Strawberry Vale
Twickenham TW1 4SR
Tel: 081 891 3461
Fax: 081 891 6413
Video and film production, ENG crews and equipment

Diverse Production
6 Gorleston Street
London W14 8SX
Tel: 071 603 4567
Fax: 071 603 2148
VHS, lo-band, hi-band, Beta and 1″ editing, Abekas DVE, image processing and computer graphics

Document Films
8-12 Broadwick Street
London W1V 1FH
Tel: 071 437 4526
Film and video cutting rooms; 16mm Aaton/Nagra and video crews, 16mm, 35mm sound transfer bay, mono and stereo
Production offices

Dolby Laboratories
346 Clapham Road
London SW9 9AP
Tel: 071 720 1111
Fax: 071 720 4118
Cinema processors for replay of Dolby Stereo and Dolby Stereo SR encoded soundtracks
Audio noise reduction equipment

Dubbs
25-26 Poland Street
London W1V 3DB
Tel: 071 629 0055
Fax: 071 287 8796
Videotape duplication
Standards conversion

Joe Dunton Cameras
see **Panavision UK**

ECO
9-10 Westgate Street
Cardiff CF1 1DA
Tel: 0222 373321
Fax: 0222 341391
Studio 1: 16-track Dolby U-Matic video sound dubbing
Studio 2: film dubbing; 8-track U-Matic with AMS audiofile; transfer suite

ENG Video
see **Headline Video**

Edinburgh Film and Video Productions
Edinburgh Film and TV Studios
Nine Mile Burn by Penicuik
Midlothian EH26 9LT
Tel: 0968 72131
Fax: 0968 72685
Stage: 50 sq metres; 16mm, 35mm cutting rooms; 16mm, 35mm transfer facilities; preview theatre; sound transfer; edge numbering; lighting grip equipment hire; scenery workshops

Edinburgh Film Workshop Trust
29 Albany Street
Edinburgh EH1 3QN
Tel: 031 557 5242
Facilities include lo-band edit suite, rostrum camera; VHS off-line suite; film cutting room (16mm)

Edit 142
20 St Anne's Court
London W1V 3AW
Tel: 071 439 7934
Fax: 081 751 1119
16mm and 35mm cutting rooms; video off-line

The Edit Works
Units 1-6, 2nd Floor
Chelsea Garden Market
Chelsea Harbour
London SW10 0XE
Tel: 071 352 5244
Fax: 071 376 8645
Video formats: 1″C, D2 SP Betacam
Editing: Component – Sony 5000, Grass Valley 200 vision mixer
Composite: Sony 5000, Grass Valley 300 vision mixer; off-line: Sony 5000, 4 x U-Matic
Vision effects: ADO100, Abekas A72
Sound: voiceover booth available to all suites

Edric Audiovisual Hire
Unit 3
Chalfont Industrial Park
Chiltern Hill
Chalfont St Peter
Bucks SL9 9UQ
Tel: 0753 884646
Fax: 0753 887163
Audiovisual and video production facilities

Elstree Studios (formerly Goldcrest Elstree Studios)
Shenley Road
Borehamwood
Herts WD6 1JG
Tel: 081 953 1600
Fax: 081 207 0860
Post-production department part of major redevelopment of studios and will include ultra-modern viewing, dubbing and re-recording theatres; cutting rooms; sound transfer

Eye Film and Television
The Guildhall
Church Street
Eye
Suffolk IP23 7BD
Tel: 0379 870083
Fax: 0379 870987
Betacam SP production crew; component Betacam SP editing suite

Faction Films
28-29 Great Sutton Street
London EC1V 0DU
Tel: 071 608 0654/3
Fax: 071 608 2157
For hire; 6 plate 16mm Steenbeck edit suite; sound transfer; VHS edit suite with 6 channel mixer; U-Matic and VHS viewing and transfer; production office space; Nagra 4.2 and redhead lighting kit.
Spanish/English translation service

Fantasy Factory Video
42 Theobalds Road
London WC1X 8NW
Tel: 071 405 6862
Video formats: U-Matic, hi-band SP, hi-band and lo-band, Hi 8, video 8
Editing: three machine hi-band SP and lo-band with listing, automated vision mixer, EDIS DVE, with full timecode system using VITC and LTC and Quanta Cap Gen
2-machine BVU SP/lo-band with a caption camera, CEL DVE, For-A Cap Gen and timecode reader/generator, 6-channel audio mixer; training courses in video editing on the above suites

SG Fenner Lighting
Unit 5a
1-5 Standard Road
London NW10 6EX
Tel: 081 961 1935
Fax: 081 961 8595
Lighting equipment hire

FinePoint Broadcast
The Red Lodge
Brighton Road
Tadworth
Surrey KT20 6UQ
Tel: 0737 833099
Fax: 0737 833743
Broadcast facilities hire in PAL and NTSC; VTRs in 1″, Beta SP and BVU
Sony CCD cameras; Abekas A53, Charisma, Paintbox, Aston etc; editing, dubbing, standards conversion; 6 camera, 4VTR outside broadcast vehicles

Flintdown – Channel Five Television
339 Clifton Drive South
St Annes on Sea
Lancashire FY8 1LP
Tel: 0253 725499
Fax: 0253 713094
Cintel Telecine 9.5/8/16/35mm
Video formats: C, BVU, U-Matic
Cameras: IVC

Fox Television
10-12 Fitzroy Mews
London W1P 5DQ
Tel: 071 387 3308
Fax: 071 388 6265
Video formats: Betacam SP – PAL and NTSC
Cameras: Sony BVP 7 and BVW 400
Editing: 3-machine Betacam SP with 3-D DVE, Inscriber, CD, Grams

Mike Fraser
225 Goldhawk Road
London W12 8ER
Tel: 081 749 6911
Neg cutting, rubber numbering, computer logging, videotape recycling, post production supervision through OSC/R

Frontline Television Services
44 Earlham Street
London WC2H 9LA
Tel: 071 836 0411
Fax: 071 379 5210
2 x Betacam/BVU to 1″ and 3-machine computerised editing with Abekas A53D, Grass Valley 200 vision mixer, Z6000 edit controller and Aston 4 graphics generator; tape duplication, standards conversion, all formats, telecine

Fundamental Films and Video
15 Wardour Mews
D'Arblay Street
London W1V 3FF
Tel: 071 437 9475
Film and video production
Editing: 16mm/35mm, computerised lo-band U-Matic

GBS Film Lighting
169 Talgarth Road
London W14 9DA
Tel: 081 748 0316
Fax: 081 563 0679
Lighting equipment hire

General Screen Enterprises
Highbridge Estate
Oxford Road
Uxbridge
Middx UB8 1LX
Tel: 0895 231931
Fax: 0895 235335
Studio: 100 sq metres
16mm, 35mm opticals including matting, aerial image work, titling; editing, trailers, promos, special effects, graphics, VistaVision; computerised rostrum animation; video suite; preview theatre

Goldcrest Elstree Studios
see ***Elstree Studios***

Grip House Facilities and Studios
5-11 Taunton Road
Metropolitan Centre
Greenford
Middx UB6 8UQ
Tel: 081 578 2382
Fax: 081 578 1536
Grip equipment and studio hire
Also: Grip House North
Unit E20 Eleventh Avenue
Team Valley Trading Estate
Gateshead
Tyne & Wear NE11 0JY
Tel: 091 491 1220
Fax: 091 491 1221
Grip equipment hire only

Hall Place Studios
4 Hall Place
Leeds LS9 8JD
Tel: 0532 405553
16mm/U-Matic/VHS production units, lighting, cutting rooms, lo-band and S-VHS edit suites, rostrum camera, film/video studio, 16-track sound studio with SMPTE video dubbing, 4-track 16mm dubbing, sound transfer, sound effects library
See also under Workshops for information on training courses

Hammonds Audio Visual and Video Services
Presentation Division
60-64a Queens Road
Watford
Herts WD1 2LA
Tel: 0923 39733 (7 lines)
Fax: 0923 221134
ENG crews; Betacam SP, BVU, SVHS, Hi-8, Professional editing, multiformat. DVE, computer graphics (animation), separate full recording studio, audio and video studio facilities. S-VHS off-line; duplication and STDS conversion via AVS systems

Headline Video (formerly ENG Video)
3 Nimrod Way
Elgar Road
Reading
Berks RG2 0EB
Tel: 0734 751555
Fax: 0734 861482
Video formats: 1″, Betacam SP, BVU SP
Two fully component multi-format broadcast edit suites with 2 channels DVE. 2 Paintboxes, Harriet, DGS 3.2 3D system.
Duplication and Standards conversion

Hillside Studios
Merry Hill Road
Bushey
Herts WD2 1DR
Tel: 081 950 7919
Fax: 081 950 1437
Jacqui Summers
Production and post-production facilities
Betacam, BVU, 1″C and Betacam SP plus component shooting
Two studios: 1,500 sq ft – drive in access and 384 sq ft
On-line and off-line editing suites – composite and component
Audio pre-production and post-production studios
Audience seating for 100, set design, construction, 3 conference rooms and licensed restaurant

Holborn Studios
Herbal House
10 Back Hill
London EC1R 5EN
Tel: 071 278 4311
Fax: 071 833 1377
Three film stages, set building

Humphries Video Services
Unit 2, The Willow Business Centre
17 Willow Lane
Mitcham
Surrey CR4 4NX
Tel: 081 648 6111
Fax: 081 648 5261
Evershed House
71 Chiltern Street
London W1M 1HT
Tel: 071 636 3636
Videocassette duplication, standards conversion, mastering, dubbing facilities; full packaging and distribution service

ITN
200 Gray's Inn Road
London WC1X 8XZ
Tel: 071 833 3000
Video dubbing and transfer – all formats
Standards conversion
Helicopter hire
IDF Graphic design service
Harry/Paintbox dry hire and training
2 and 3 machine edit suites with or without staff
Sound dubbing suites
Tape recycling
OB unit

International Broadcast Facilities
12 Neal's Yard
London WC2H 9DP
Tel: 071 497 1515
Fax: 071 379 8562
Copying: 1″ - Betacam SP etc
PAL-NTSC-PAL standards conversion
Cassette duplication all formats

In-Video Productions
16 York Place
Edinburgh EH1 3EP
Tel: 031 557 2151
Fax: 031 557 5465
Four Ampex 1″ VTRs, Sony 9000 edit controller, Grass Valley 300 switcher with Kaleidoscope digital effects unit, Quantel digital effects unit, Dubner character generator, Abekas A64 digital recorder, Matisse Paint and 3-D
Cameras: Ampex CVC 50 (2), Ampex CVC 7
Off-line edit suite; video studio; voiceover booth

André Jacquemin Recording
68a Delancey Street
London NW1 7RY
Tel: 071 485 3733
Fax: 071 284 1020
24 track post-production suite; large screen projection; computer mixing. Large sound effects and music library; array of keyboards, samplers, special effects; 35/16mm triple track

sound transfer machine with Dolby SR/A

Terry Jones Post Productions
The Hat Factory
16-18 Hollen Street
London W1V 3AD
Tel: 071 434 1173
Fax: 071 494 1893
35mm, 16mm post-production facilities

LTM (UK) Cinebuild
Studio House
Rita Road
London SW8 1JU
Tel: 071 582 8750
Fax: 071 793 0467
Special effects: rain, snow, fog, mist, smoke, fire, explosions; lighting and equipment hire
Studio: 200 sq metres

Ladbroke Films (Dubbing)
4 Kensington Park Gardens
London W11 3HB
Tel: 071 727 3541
Fax: 071 727 3632
16mm/35mm Film dubbing, (12 track Dolby Stereo, SR and A); sound transfer and cutting rooms

Lane End Productions
63 Riding House Street
London W1P 7PP
Tel: 071 637 2794
Fax: 071 580 0135
Video formats: 1″C, Betacam SP, BVU, U-Matic, VHS
Vision effects: Grass Valley mixer, colour camera, Aston 3, Abacus A53D, off-line and 525 editing
Transfer and standards conversion

Lazer F.I.L.M.S.
Building No 1
GEC Estate
East Lane
Wembley
Middx
Tel: 081 904 1448
Film/video editing and other post-production facilities

Lee Lighting
Wycombe Road
Wembley
Middx HA0 1QD
Tel: 081 900 2900
Fax: 081 902 5500
Lighting equipment hire

Lee International Studios
Studios Road
Shepperton
Middx TW17 0QD
Tel: 0932 562611
Fax: 0932 568989
Cutting rooms; 16mm, 35mm viewing theatres

Light House Media Centre
Art Gallery
Lichfield Street
Wolverhampton WV1 1DU
Tel: 0902 312033
Fax: 0902 26644
Video production with 3-machine edit, computer graphics/animation

Lighthouse Film and Video
19 Regent Street
Brighton BN1 1UL
Tel: 0273 686479
Video cameras: Panasonic F70, F15 and S-VHS camcorder
Video editing: Series 5 two machine or S-VHS to U-Matic two machine; JVC KM-1200 effects generator, Fostex 8 track mixer, video typewriter
16mm Film: Arriflex BL, Nagra III, O'Connor tripod, 4 plate Steenbeck and pic-sync
Lights: 4 x 800W kit, 2kW kit
Dry hire, crews and training

Limehouse Television
The Trocadero
19 Rupert Street
London W1V 7FS
Tel: 071 287 3333
Fax: 071 287 1998
Live transmission centre with studios, edit suites and graphics

London Fields Film and Video
10 Martello Street
London E8 3PE
Tel: 071 241 2997
Computer graphics; video editing; 16mm editing

London Film Makers' Co-op
42 Gloucester Avenue
London NW1 8JD
Tel: 071 722 1728
Houses a wide range of 16mm and Super 8 production equipment and facilities including B & W printing and processing (service or DIY), optical printer, rostrum camera, Steenbecks (both 16mm and Super 8), sound dubbing and transfer facilities

London Video Access (LVA)
23 Frith Street
London W1A 4XD
Tel: 071 734 7410
Fax: 071 734 2003
Three machine hi-band SP mastering (lo-band/hi-band SP source) suite; 3 off-line suites (VHS and lo-band); computer graphics suite; viewing; duplication; equipment hire

Lynx Video
Lynx House
7 High Road
Ickenham
Uxbridge
Middx UB10 8LE
Tel: 0895 676221
Fax: 0895 621623
Video formats: Digital, 1″C, Betacam SP, BVU
Cameras: Ikegami, Sony – CCD and tube
Vision effects: Charisma and graphics

MAC Sound Hire
1-2 Attenburys Park
Park Road
Altrincham
Cheshire WA14 5QE
Tel: 061 969 8311
Fax: 061 962 9423
Hire of professional sound equipment

Margaret Street Studio
79-80 Margaret Street
London W1N 7HB
Tel: 071 636 4444
Fax: 071 436 9872
1,300 sq ft 3 camera component broadcast studio, 3 x Sony BVP7, Ace T8 component vision mixer, Aston 3B cap gen; Editing: component on-line edit suites, Sony BVW75, 2 x Sony BVW65, Grass Valley 100CV vision mixer, Aston cap gen, Sony 900 edit controller; BT lines; graphics facilities; video crews; production offices

Austin Martin Film and Video Services
87 Wardour Street
London W1V 3TS
Tel: 071 439 4397
Editing rooms

Mayflower Sound Studios
3 Audley Square
Mayfair
London W1Y 5DR
Tel: 071 493 0016
Fax: 071 355 4071
Complete foreign version service, any language or film/video format; voice over, dubbing/lip sync; Automated Dialogue Replacement (ADR); Digital sound effects and music library

Media Arts
Town Hall Studios
Regent Circus
Swindon SN1 1QF
Tel: 0793 493454
Video cameras: F10s, KY1900s, M3
Video editing: VHS 2-machine, Series 5 2/3-machine, 3-machine lo-/hi-/SP and effects; sound studio and effects, interview studio
8mm/16mm cutting rooms
B/W and colour photography; lighting: Reds and 2000W; dry hire, crews, training

Mercury Studio Sound
see **Studiosound**

Merseyside Film and Video Resource
110 Bold Street
Liverpool L1 4HY
Tel: 051 708 5259
Fax: 051 709 3059
2/3 Machine lo-band and VHS editing; lo-band and 16mm production equipment; lo-band and VHS exhibition equipment; Amiga 2000 computer graphics; Lights, microphones etc

Metropolis Video
8-10 Neal's Yard
London WC2H 9DP
Tel: 071 240 8423
Fax: 071 379 6880
Off-line editing: 4 suites
1 x 3 machine computerised lo-band giving 8″CMX Disc for autoconform
2 x 2 machine lo-band
1 x 2 machine VHS
Video duplication: all formats, large or small

runs. Overnight Betacam rushes service. Rushes transferred with BITC, VITC overnight for off-line next day

Metrovideo
The Old Bacon Factory
57-59 Great Suffolk Street
London SE1 0BS
Tel: 071 928 2088
Fax: 071 261 0685
Metro Mansions
6-7 Great Chapel Street
London W1V 3AG
Tel: 071 439 3494
Fax: 071 437 3782
Video formats: Betacam SP, D2, MII, BVU SP, Hi-8, SVHS, lo-band
Cameras: BVP7/70, BVW 300/400/507/570, DXC-M7, DXC3000, EVW325
ADAC standards conversion, duplication, Videowalls, Prowalls, video projectors, large screen monitors

Molinare
34 Fouberts Place
London W1V 2BH
Tel: 071 439 2244
Fax: 071 734 6813
Video formats: D1, D2, 1″ C PAL, NTSC, SECAM, 1″ B format – BCN, Beta sp PAL + NTSC, Betacam, BVU, U-Matic, VHS
Editing: 1 x U-Matic off-line suite. 4 x on-line edit suites: 2 x component with Grass Valley 200 mixers, 2 x composite with Grass Valley 300 mixers. All with Grass Valley 151 edit controllers. 3 channels A53, 4 channels ADO. Aston 3, Aston Caption + A72 character generators. Abekas A64 digital disc store
Graphics: Harry with Paintbox Encore HUD and D1, separate Quantel Paintbox, Abekas A64, Abekas A72
Telecine: Rank Cintel III with 4.2.2 digital output, Digigrade 3 and secondary colour correction – 35mm and 16mm
Audio: 3 x 24 track audio dubbing suites, 2 x radio suites, sound effects library
Duplication: all formats
Other: BT landlines, satellite downlink, transmission capability

Morgan Laboratories
Unit 4.16
Wembley Commercial Centre
East Lane
Wembley
Middx HA9 7XD
Tel: 081 908 3856
Fax: 081 908 4211
Post-production facilities

Tom Morrish Films
171 Wardour Street
London W1V 3TA
Tel: 071 437 2136
Fax: 071 734 5295
16mm, 35mm post-production

Motion Control Studio
CNN House
19-22 Rathbone Place
London W1P 1DF
Tel: 071 436 5544
Fax: 071 734 2519
Studio with overhead motion control rig

The Moving Picture Company
25 Noel Street
London W1V 3RD
Tel: 071 434 3100
Fax: 071 437 3951/734 9150
Video formats: D1, D2, 1″C, MII, Beta SP, Betacam, hi-/lo-band, S-VHS
Cameras: Sony BVP 330 portable and Sony DXC 3000 CCD
Editing: five editing suites (three fully digital), using CMX editors
Vision effects: ADO, Mirage, Abekas A53-D, A64, A84
Telecine: two Rank Cintel – two URSAs, one MKIII 4.2.2 Digiscan with Pogle, for 16mm or 35mm film, each with Register Pin and Steadiguide gates, digital noise reduction, Matchbox, Ultimatte 5
Graphics: 3 x Paintbox/Harrys, with Encore HUD and A53D; 3 x Alias 3-D computer animation systems, with 4-D 220 renderers; Aston 3 and 4 character generators
Studios: motion control studio (with 35mm Apogee/Lynx system) main studio: 47′ x 30′ x 13′, L cyc
Video rostrum studio
Cutting rooms
16mm/35mm and off-line editing suite

Mr Lighting
2 Dukes Road
Western Avenue
London W3 0SL
Tel: 081 993 9911
Fax: 081 993 9533
Lighting equipment and studio hire

Nant Films
Moreia
Penrallt Isaf
Caernarfon
Gwynedd L55 1NS
Tel: 0286 5722
Fax: 0286 5159
Production company with two 16mm cutting rooms, off-line facilities

National Screen Productions
2nd Floor
2 Wedgwood Mews
12-13 Greek Street
London W1V 5LW
Tel: 071 437 2783
Fax: 071 494 1811
Creative and technical services for production of promos, documentaries, trailers, teasers and TV spots. Logo and main title design and animation. All aspects of on-screen promotion and presentation for feature films, TV, cable and video. In-house film/video editing, design and art studio. Videowall programming

Northern Light
39-41 Assembly Street
Leith
Edinburgh EH6 7RG
Tel: 031 553 2383
Lighting equipment hire

Numo Productions
The Hat Factory
16-18 Hollen Street
London W1V 3AD
Tel: 071 437 2877
Fax: 071 437 8706
Stop-frame, live-action special effects
Mitchell S35R with b & w flicker-free video assist

The OBE Partnership
16 Kingly Street
London W1R 5LD
Tel: 071 734 3028
Fax: 071 734 2830
Film Editors

Omnititles
37 Ripplevale Grove
London N1 1HS
Tel: 071 607 9047
Fax: 071 704 9594
Spotting and subtitling services for film, telecine, video, satellite and cable. Subtitling in most world languages and for the deaf

Roger Owen and Associates
24-25 Foley Street
London W1P 7LA
Tel: 071 436 2268
Fax: 071 436 7936
Film and videotape editing services; Videotape to film transfers

Oxford Film and Video Makers
The Stables
North Place
Headington
Oxford OX3 9HY
Tel: 0865 60074
Cameras: Sony DXC-325, Panasonic F10, Arriflex 16mm and Super 8
Recorders: Sony 8800SP (w. T/c), Sony 4800
Editing: Sony lo-band U-Matic, 16mm Steenbecks

PMPP Facilities
69 Dean Street
London W1V 5HB
Tel: 071 437 0979
Fax: 071 434 0386
Editing: on-line, multi-format, Component Betacam SP, 1″, BVU, D2 with Charisma DVE and Aston 3
Off-line: U-Matic, VHS, S-VHS, BVU-SP, Shotlister, JVC Editmaster, 3 machine computerised lo-band with effects
Matisse 2D and Rodin 3D computer graphics; Sound dubbing studio, AudioFile, DAT, 24 track, voice over to picture; transmission dubbing, hi-fi stereo duplication, standards conversion

The Palace (Video Editing Centre)
8 Poland Street
London W1V 3DG
Tel: 071 439 8241
Fax: 071 287 1741

Video formats: 1″, Beta SP, Beta, BVU
Editing: three 5-machine suites, 3-machine component suite
Digital effects: 3 ADO 3000 with infinity and digimatte, Quantel digital effects
Off-line editing: multimachine U-Matic and VHS
Graphics: Spaceward Matisse system

Panavision UK (formerly Joe Dunton Cameras)
Wycombe Road
Wembley
Middx HA0 1QN
Tel: 081 903 7933
Fax: 081 902 3273
Camera equipment hire; services many major feature productions

Picardy Television
Picardy House
4 Picardy Place
Edinburgh EH1 3JT
Tel: 031 558 1551
Fax: 031 558 1555
Facilities include: dry/crewed camera hire; multi format editing including Betacam SP component, DVE and graphics; full broadcast standard studio for single/multi camera shoots and casting; EVS video paint system with 2 and 3D animation

Picture Post-Productions
13 Manette Street
London W1V 5LB
Tel: 071 439 1661
Fax: 071 494 1661
35/16mm film editing; off-line editing

Pinewood Studios
Iver
Bucks SL0 0NH
Tel: 0753 656301
Fax: 0753 656844
Two large high-speed stereo dubbing theatres with automated consoles; small general purpose recording theatre; large ADR and sound effects theatre; preview theatre: 115 seats, 70/35/16mm, all formats stereo sound; four-bay sound transfer area; mono/stereo sound negative transfer; 60 fully-serviced cutting rooms

Prominent Facilities (formerly Prominent Studios)
68a Delancey Street
London NW1 7RY
Tel: 071 284 0242
Fax: 071 284 1020
Cutting rooms; edit suites; production offices; sound transfers; preview theatre

Q Studios
Queniborough Industrial Estate
1487 Melton Road
Queniborough
Leicester LE7 8FP
Tel: 0533 608813
Fax: 0533 608329
Video formats: Betacam SP, BVU, 1″
Component editing with Charisma DVE, off-line edit, 24 track sound, original music production, computer graphics; two drive-in studios (1,350 and 754 sq ft), black and chromakey drapes, computer controlled lighting. Full production services available including crews, set construction, on-line and off-line editing

Rank Video Services
Phoenix Park
Great West Road
Brentford
Middx TW8 9PL
Tel: 081 568 4311
Fax: 081 847 4032
10,500 realtime slaves, all hi-fi capable and 36 Hi-speed Sony Sprinters; specialist corporate duplication department including standards conversion

Recording and Production Services
see **Chrysalis TV Mobiles**

Redapple
Orchard House
The Street
Albury, Nr Guildford
Surrey GU5 9AG
Tel: 048641 3797
Fax: 048641 3781
Video formats: 1″C, Beta, Beta SP, BVU, NTSC/PAL
Cameras: Sony BVP50, Sony BVP7/400, ENG/EFP units
Film: 16mm Arriflex unit
Transport: 5 estate cars, pressurised twin engine aircraft
Two lighting vehicles

Richmond Film Services
The Old School
Park Lane
Richmond
Surrey TW9 2RA
Tel: 081 940 6077
Fax: 081 948 8326
Sound equipment available for hire, sales of tape and batteries, and UK agent for Ursta recordists' trolleys and Denecke timecode equipment

Rockall Data Services
320 Western Road
London SW19 2QA
Tel: 081 640 6626
Fax: 081 640 1297
Safe storage of documents, film, video and audio material

Rostrum Cameras
11 Charlotte Mews
off Tottenham Street
London W1P 1LN
Tel: 071 637 0535
Fax: 071 323 3892
16/35mm Rostrum computerised cameras

Rushes
66 Old Compton Street
London W1V 5PA
Tel: 071 437 8676
Fax: 071 734 2519
Post production: digital, analogue editing; Harry, 3-D animation; Motion Control Studio; CIS compositing; telecine; Nicam playouts

SVC Television
142 Wardour Street
London W1V 3AU
Tel: 071 734 1600
Fax: 071 437 1854
7 x edit suites including 1 x multiformat, 2 x Beta SP, 2 x 1″, 1 x offline, 1 x fully digital with A84; Mirage, Encore, A53, A72, Harry Symbolics, Paintbox, Motion Control, rostrum camera; 3 x telecine including Ursa and Mastergrade colour grading facility

Salon Post-Productions
13-14 Archer Street
London W1V 7HG
Tel: 071 437 0516
Fax: 071 437 6197
35/16mm Steenbecks and editing equipment hire; cutting rooms; 35/16mm Steenbeck, telecine, U-Matic and VHS edit suites

Sammy's – Samuelson Film Service London
21 Derby Road
Metropolitan Centre
Greenford
Middx UB6 8UJ
Tel: 081 578 7887
Fax: 081 578 2733
Cameras: Panavision, Moviecam, Arriflex
Lenses: Canon, Cooke, Nikon, Leitz, Zeiss, Hasselblad
Video assist, sound, editing, stock, consumables and transport. 24hrs

Michael Samuelson Lighting
Pinewood Studios
Iver Heath
Bucks SL0 0NH
Tel: 0753 631133
Fax: 0753 630485
10 Back Hill
Clerkenwell Road
London EC1R 5EN
Tel: 071 833 8719
Fax: 071 833 8721
Milford Place
Lennox Road
Leeds LS4 2BL
Tel: 0532 310770
Lighting equipment hire

Screenworks
Portsmouth Media Trust
The Hornpipe
143 Kingston Road
Portsmouth PO2 7EB
Tel: 0705 861851/833854
Video hire and post-production; 90-seat auditorium with 35mm and 16mm, video and slide projection; VHS edit suite; U-Matic to VHS

Sheffield Independent Film
Avec
Brown Street
Sheffield S1 2BS
Tel: 0742 720304
16mm Aaton LTR/XTR, Arriflex BL, Beaulieu R16, 6-plate Steenbeck

and Picsyncs, Nagra IS, Nagra 3, Revox B77, Fostex 350 mixer, Sony U-Matic type 5 including TBC mixer and captions, National Panasonic VHS, M5 VHS camcorder, Sony portapaks VO 8800 and VO 6800, Sony DXC 3000 and 3 machine edit suite
Lighting equipment and studio facilities hire

Signal Vision
Parkgate Industrial Estate
Knutsford
Cheshire WA16 8DX
Tel: 0565 755678
Fax: 0565 634164
2 edit suites (D2/1″/Betacam SP)
Paintbox computer graphics
1,600 sq ft studio
VHS duplication
Standards conversion

Sound House
14 Livonia Street
London W1V 3TH
Tel: 071 434 2928/437 7105
Fax: 071 287 9110
Sound transfer; 16/35mm 1/4″ DAT; FX library; Video sync recording; FX/voice-over booth; Beta rushes transfer to U-Matic, SP U-Matic, SVHS and VHS

Brian Stevens Animated Films
11 Charlotte Mews
off Tottenham Street
London W1P 1LN
Tel: 071 637 0535
Fax: 071 323 3892
Studio specialising in graphic, technical and cartoon animation

Studio Film and Video
Video Facilities
Royalty House
72-73 Dean Street
London W1V 5HB
Tel: 071 437 4161
Fax: 071 734 9471
Video formats: 1″C, Betacam SP, BVU SP, BVU, U-Matic, VHS, S-VHS, Betamax, Video 8
Telecine: 35mm, 16mm and Super 8, Rank Cintel MkIII with Digigrade. Also 8mm and 9.5mm
Editing: U-Matic suite, standards conversion, NTSC, PAL, SECAM via ADAC or AVS

Studio Operation SW
The Old Chapel
Abbey Hill
Lelant
Cornwall TR26 3EG
Tel: 0736 753538/071 379 6724
Fax: 0736 756744
1,500 sq ft studio with production office, cam, lighting, sound, special effects, pyrotechnics, post production film/video and digital sound suite

Studio Sound (formerly Mercury Studio Sound)
84-88 Wardour Street
London W1V 3LF
Tel: 071 734 0263
Fax: 071 434 9990
Film and video recording, dubbing and transfer facilities

TSI Video
10 Grape Street
London WC2H 8DY
Tel: 071 379 3435
Fax: 071 379 4589
Video formats: 1″ x 9, Betacam SP x 9, plus BVU, D2
Editing: 3 suites – Sony 5000, edit controllers in component and composite with any combination of above, Grass Valley vision mixer, 4 channels of Charisma DVE with key channels and CLEO, caption camera, Aston 3 B character generators
Computer graphics: Quantel VE Series Paintbox and Harriet, digital library store, Matisse with Frame 3-D and traditional animation
Sound: Q Lock/Eclipse synchronisers, 24 track dubbing and voiceover recording with Opus Digital Audio post production. Four BT lines (vision and sound), BT control lines (2 in, 2 out), colour caption camera, Sony BVH 2500 single frame recorder, Honeywell Matrix camera

TVi
Film House
142 Wardour Street
London W1V 3AU
Tel: 071 434 2141
Fax: 071 439 3984
Video formats: PAL/625 and NTSC/525: D1, D2, 1″B, 1″C, Betacam SP, BVU SP, BVU, U-Matic, VHS, S-VHS with PAL/625 2″ Quad
Editing: six stereo edit suites with D2, 1″C, Betacam SP, BVU VTRs – A53 with warp and dimension or ADO digital effects, A64 digital disc recorder for multi-layering, colour caption camera, Aston III or A72 character generator. VHS and U-Matic off-lines
Sound: Post production dubbing to picture (D2, 1″, Beta, BVU or U-Matic) with TS 24 channel mixer, voiceover booth and DAR hard disc digital recorder – PAL/NTSC operation
Telecine: 16mm/35mm to 625/PAL/SECAM or 525/NTSC Rank Cintel 4:2:2 telecines with wetgate
Graphics: Matisse and A72

TWTV
20 Kingly Street
London W1R 5LD
Tel: 071 437 4706
Fax: 071 437 5992
Video editing and graphics. Online with Beta SP and 1″. Offline with Shotlister. Graphics from Quantel Paintbox and Harriet. Full rushes transfer, standards conversion and duplication services

Tattooist International
3 Centro House
20 Mandela Street
London NW1 0DU
Tel: 071 380 0488
Fax: 071 388 8890
16mm cutting room, Super 16 and stereo options, lo-band U-Matic off-line, Aaton camera hire specialists, Steadicam, time lapse equipment, production offices

Team Television
The Exchange Buildings
Mount Stuart Square
Cardiff CF1 6EA
Tel: 0222 484080
Fax: 0222 494210
Edit 1 Multiformat: 1″C, Beta SP, BVU, 2 Channel Charisma, Quantel DLS; Edit 2: fully component Beta SP; Telecine 16mm/35mm Quantel V series Paintbox; duplicating and standards conversion

Tele-Cine
48 Charlotte Street
London W1P 1LX
Tel: 071 637 3253
Fax: 071 631 3993
Multiformat editing, transfer and standards conversion; digital audio post-production; Bosch CCD telecines with DA Vinci; all digital and analogue VTR formats; BT land lines

Third Eye Productions
Unit 210 Canalot Studios
222 Kensal Road
London W10 5BN
Tel: 081 969 8211
Fax: 081 960 8790
Fully equipped 16mm cutting room and S-VHS off-line edit suite

Tiny Epic Video Co
138-140 Wardour Street
London W1V 3AU
Tel: 071 437 2854/434 2377
Fax: 071 434 0211
14 suites of off-line editing 24 hours a day, 7 days a week. 9 x Sony 5 series U-Matic (and Shotlister); 2 x Panasonic 6500 VHS (and Shotlister); 2 x Panasonic 7500 S-VHS (and Shotlister); 1 x 3 machine Sony series 9 U-Matic with GVG100 (with vision mixer and edit master controller)
Music and sound effects; EDL generation; EDL translation; dubbing; autoconforming (Beta, Beta SP)

Transworld TV Productions
Whitecrook Centre
Whitecrook Street
Clydebank
Glasgow G81 1QS
Tel: 041 952 4816
Fax: 041 951 1537
Film and editing on BVUSP and Betacam SP

Roy Turk Opticals
57 Rupert Street
London W1V 7HW
Tel: 071 437 8884

Fax: 071 734 6579
Titles and opticals

Twickenham Studios
St Margaret's
Twickenham
Middlesex TW1 2AW
Tel: 081 892 4477
Fax: 081 891 0168
Two dubbing theatres, ADR effects theatre, 41 cutting rooms, Dolby installation

Mike Uden Opticals
see **Capital FX**

VMTV
1st Floor
34 Fouberts Place
London W1V 2BH
Tel: 071 439 4536
Fax: 071 437 0952
OBs: Four units with 2-12 cameras, 1″ or Beta SP record format, full complement ancillary equipment
Studios: Two West End broadcast studios
Dry hire: Betacam SP and 16mm equipment with/without crews

The Video Duplicating Co
VDC House
South Way
Wembley
Middx HA9 0EH
Tel: 081 903 3345
Fax: 081 900 1427
Comprehensive video services in all formats, tape to tape, bulk cassette duplication

Video Time
22-24 Greek Street
London W1V 5LG
Tel: 071 439 1211
Fax: 071 439 7336
Standards conversion; duplication; dubbing; mastering; foreign version track laying; telecine 16/35mm; laser disc video; editing; FACT approved

Videola
171 Wardour Street
London W1V 3TA
Tel: 071 437 5413
Fax: 071 734 5295
Video formats: 1″, BVU, U-Matic
Cameras: Sony, Ikegami
Computer rostrum camera
Editing: hi-band to 1″, BVU

Videolondon Soundstudios
16-18 Ramillies Street
London W1V 1DL
Tel: 071 734 4811
Fax: 071 494 2553
5 sophisticated sound recording studios, 3 with overhead TV projection systems. 16mm, 35mm and video post-synch recording and mixing. NED digital audio suite. All sound facilities for film or video post-production including 1″ PAL and Betacam SP

Videoscope
Ty-Cattwg Cottage
Llancarfan
Barry
South Glamorgan CF6 9AG
Tel: 0446 710963
Fax: 0446 710023
Video format: hi-band U-Matic, Betacam, 1″
Cameras: Sony 3000
Timecode transfer, 3-machine, hi-band editing, SP editing; copying bank

VisCentre
66-67 Newman Street
London W1P 3LA
Tel: 071 436 5692
Fax: 071 580 9676
Three-camera broadcast interview studio; ENG crews worldwide; video formats: 1″, Betacam, BVU; 3-machine Betacam SP PAL; 2-machine Betacam SPBVU 525/625; standards conversion: AVS; telecine: Rank Cintel enhanced MkIII 4:2:2 digital telecine 35/16 and 8mm with Da Vinci colour corrector; satellite transmissions

Visnews
Cumberland Avenue
London NW10 7EH
Tel: 081 965 7733
Fax: 081 965 0620
Video formats: 1″C, 1″B, 2″, MII, Betacam SP, BVU SP, Betacam, BVU, Video 8, U-Matic, VHS, Betamax
Standards conversion: Ace, Quantel and AVS
Transcoding: PAL-SECAM-PAL
Post production: BVE 3000, Grass Valley, Quantel 5001, Aston 3
Telecine: Rank Cintel Enhanced MkIIIC 4:2:2 digital telecine, 35/16 and 8mm with da Vinci colour corrector
Satellite transmissions

Warwick Dubbing Theatre
WFS (Film Holdings)
151-153 Wardour Street
London W1V 3TB
Tel: 071 437 5532
Sound recording and mixing to video and film; sound transfer, magnetic stereo/mono optical; ADR post sync; FV dubbing; edge numbering

Wembley Studios
10 Northfield Industrial Estate
Beresford Avenue
Wembley
Middlesex HA0 1RT
Tel: 081 903 4296
Studios: 78′ x 40′ x 15′
CVC: 52′ x 40′ x 15′
Power: 900 amps 3 phase
Production offices, dressing rooms

West One Television
10 Bateman Street
London W1V 5TT
Tel: 071 437 5533
Fax: 071 287 8621
Post production

Whitelion Facilities
Bradley Close
White Lion Street
London N1 9PN
Tel: 071 837 4836
Fax: 071 833 0013
Locations units: Sony BVP7 cameras recording onto Betacam SP
Graphics: Quantel Paintbox with Abekas A60 digital disc recorder
Editing: main suite equipped with D2, 1″, Beta SP, Abekas A53-D, Abekas A60, Sony 9000, rostrum camera and Aston
On-line: 2 equipped with D2, 1″, Beta SP, Abekas A53-D, Sony 910, rostrum camera and Aston
Off-line: two 3 machine computer controlled U-Matic suites

Windmill Lane Pictures
4 Windmill Lane
Dublin 2
Tel: 0001 713444
Fax: 0001 718413/718898
Film, video, news, graphics, recording and production facilities

Wiseman
27-35 Lexington Street
London W1R 3HQ
Tel: 071 439 8901
Fax: 071 437 2481
Editing: 1 – Abekas A84, A64, A53, A72, caption camera, 2 x Bosch D1 DVTR, 2 x Betacam SP, CMX Controller; 2 – GVG 200CV, A72, ADO, caption camera, 4 x VPR3, 2 x Betacam SP, ACE controller; 3 – GVG 2000CV, A72, ADO, Caption camera, 3 x Betacam SP, ACE controller; 4 – GVG 100CV, 4 x Betacam SP, ACE controller
Offline: Ediflex 12 x VHS; disc driven offline with video and audio edit lister; lo-band U-Matic 2MCH
Telecine: 1 – Rank Cintel 4:2:2 XYZoom, digigrade, Steadigate, secondary colour correction, Matchbox, digislate and Aaton timecode readers; 2 – Rank Cintel Jumpscan, Amigo grading
Harry: Harry LP, VE series Paintbox, Encore HUD, D1 DVTR, caption camera: VE series Paintbox, Quantel carousel, colour video printer, caption camera
Rostrum: IMC computer controlled camera
Video transfer formats available: 1″C, 2″ Quad, Betacam SP and most cassette formats
Standards conversion: ADAC, AVS6500; Fostex DAT, Nagra T, Aston 3 and Telecom lines
Audio: Lexicon Opus digital audio suite with V/O record facilities

Wolff Productions
6a Noel Street
London W1V 3RB
Tel: 071 439 1838/734 4286
35mm/16mm rostrum camera work; animation production

Workhouse
Granville House
St Peter Street
Winchester
Hants SO23 9AF

Tel: 0962 863449
Fax: 0962 841026
3 x SP Beta Editing and 1″ and BVU Vista Vision Mixer, ADO 100 digital effects, 2 x edit teams; lo-band, VHS offlining transfer from any format to VHS

World Wide Sound
21-25 St Anne's Court
London W1V 3AW
Tel: 071 434 1121
Fax: 071 734 0619
16/35mm High-speed rock'n'roll dubbing theatres; four track Dolby stereo; effects recording; post synchronisation; translation facilities; caligraphy band writing; cutting rooms

Worldwide Television News Corporation
The Interchange
Oval Road
Camden Lock
London NW1
Tel: 071 410 5200
Fax: 071 413 8302/3/8327
BVU editing (PAL and NTSC); multi-machine editing with digital effects and colour captioning; Betacam record/replay; 1″C editing; digital standards conversion; PAL/SECAM transcoding; duplication; local and international feeds, studio facilities; Matisse graphics

FESTIVALS

Listed below by country of origin are the main international film, TV and video festivals with contact addresses and brief synopses

AUSTRALIA

Australian International Video Festival (Oct-Dec)
PO Box 661
Glebe NSW 2021
Tel: (61) 2 552 4220
Fax: (61) 2 552 4229
Competitive for video art, graphics, music, documentary and drama/narrative. Also includes a student section

Melbourne International Film Festival (June)
PO Box 12367
A'Beckett Street
Melbourne 3000
Victoria
Tel: (61) 3 663 1395
Fax: (61) 3 662 1218
Non-competitive section for feature films (60 mins and over) and a competitive section for short films (less than 60 mins). Films should not previously have been shown in Melbourne

Sydney Film Festival (June)
PO Box 25
Glebe NSW 2037
Tel: (61) 2 660 3844
Fax: (61) 2 692 8793
Non-competitive for feature films and shorts not previously shown in Australia

AUSTRIA

Viennale (Oct)
Uraniastrasse 1
1010 Vienna
Tel: (43) 1 75 32 84
Fax: (43) 1 75 32 85
Non-competitive for features and documentaries

BELGIUM

Brussels International Film Festival (Jan)
Chaussée de Louvain 30
B-1030 Brussels
Tel: (32) 2 218 10 55
Fax: (32) 2 218 66 27
Competitive for feature films

Brussels International Festival of Fantasy, Thriller and Science Fiction Films (March)
144 avenue de la Reine
B-1210 Brussels
Tel: (32) 2 242 17 13
Fax: (32) 2 216 21 69
Competitive for features and shorts (less than 20 mins)

International Flanders Film Festival (Oct)
1104 Kortrijkse Steenweg
B-9051 Ghent
Fax: (32) 91 21 90 74
Competitive film festival with official selection on 'The impact of music on film'

Movie Art '92 (Feb)
1104 Kortrijkse Steenweg
B-9051 Ghent
Fax: (32) 91 21 90 74
International festival of films about art

BRAZIL

Mostra Banco Nacional de Cinema (Sep)
Rua Voluntarios do Patria 88
Botafogo
CEP 22270
Rio de Janeiro RJ
Tel: (55) 21 286 6149
Fax: (55) 21 537 1112
Non-competitive festival, promoting films that would not otherwise get to Brazilian screens

São Paulo International Film Festival (Oct-Nov)
Alameda Lorena 937
Suite 302
01424 São Paulo
Tel: (55) 11 883 5137
Fax: (55) 11 853 7936
Non-competitive for features/shorts/ documentary/animation and experimental films which must have been produced during 2 years preceding the festival

BULGARIA

Bulgarian International Festival of Comedy and Satirical Films (May)
PO Box 104
Gabrovo
Tel: (359) 66 27229

Varna World Animated Film Festival (Oct odd years)
1 Bulgaria Square
Sofia 1414
Tel: (359) 2 586 014/589 159/586 167
Competitive for animated films produced in previous two years, including children's animation, animation for TV, student films, first films. (NB Films awarded prizes at Annecy or Zagreb not accepted)

BURKINA FASO

Ouagadougou International Film Festival (Feb-March alternate years)
Secretariat Général des Festivals Ciñematographiques
BP 2505 Ouagadougou
Tel: (226) 307 538
Festival featuring African filmmakers whose work must have been produced during the three years preceding the festival and not shown before at FESPACO

Panafrican Film Festival (FESPACO)
(Feb-March alternate years)
BP 2505 Ouagadougou
Tel: (226) 307 538

CANADA

Atlantic Film Festival (Sept-Oct)
1571 Argyle Street
Halifax
Nova Scotia, B3J 2B2
Tel: (1) 902 426 5936
Competitive for feature films, animation, experimental, documentary, educational and industrial. Also includes student section, first film/video, short drama, news/current affairs, TV variety and commercials. All work must have been made during two years preceding festival

Banff Television Festival (June)
PO Box 1020
Banff
Alberta T0L 0C0
Tel: (1) 403 762 3060
Fax: (1) 403 762 5357
Competitive for films made for television, including features, drama specials, limited series, continuing series, documentaries, children's programmes and comedy which were broadcast for the first time in the previous year

International Festival of New Cinema and Video
(Oct)
3726 Boulevard Saint-Laurent
Montreal
Quebec H2X 2V8
Tel: (1) 514 843 4725
Fax: (1) 514 843 4631
Non-competitive for innovative films produced during previous two years which have not been screened in Canada

Montreal World Film Festival (+ Market) (Aug)
1455 de Maisonneuve Blvd West
Montreal
Quebec H3G IM8
Tel: (1) 514 848 3883
Fax: (1) 514 848 3886
Competitive for feature films and shorts (up to 30 mins), produced in previous year, which have not been screened outside country of origin or been entered in other competitive festivals

Ottawa International Animation Festival
(Sept-Oct even years)
2 Daly Avenue
Ottawa
Ontario K1N 6E2
Tel: (1) 613 232 6727
Fax: (1) 613 232 6315

Toronto Annual International Festival of Festivals (Sept)
70 Carlton Street
Toronto
Ontario M5B 1L7
Tel: (1) 416 967 7371
Fax: (1) 416 967 9477
Non-competitive for feature films and shorts not previously shown in Canada. Also includes some American premieres, retrospectives and national cinema programmes. Films must have been completed within the year prior to the festival to be eligible

Vancouver International Film Festival (Oct)
788 Beatty Street
Suite 303
Vancouver
BC V6B 2M1
Tel: (1) 604 685 0260
Fax: (1) 604 688 8221

COLOMBIA

Cartagena International Film Festival (March)
Apartado Aéreo 1834
Cartagena
Tel: (57) 53 653 952
Fax: (57) 53 655 608
Competitive for films produced in Colombia, Spain, Portugal, Latin and South America. Also non-competitive section for feature films, shorts and documentaries, and a Film Market. Films must be subtitled in Spanish and not previously screened in Colombia

CUBA

International Festival of New Latin American Cinema (Dec)
Calle 23
1155 Vedado (E/10 y 12)
Havana 4
Tel: (53) 7 400 4711
Competitive films produced in or about America. Market for features, documentaries, animation

CZECHOSLOVAKIA

Golden Prague International TV Festival (June)
Czechoslovak Television
Gorkého nám 29
11150 Prague 1
Tel: (42) 2 2364760
Fax: (42) 2 2321342
The 'Golden Prague' TV Festival competition is in two categories: TV drama works and TV music works and programmes with music themes

DENMARK

Odense Film Festival (Aug odd years)
Vindegade 18
DK-5000 Odense C
Tel: (45) 66 13 13 72 x4294
Fax: (45) 65 91 43 18
Competitive festival for fairy-tale and experimental-imaginative films

EGYPT

Cairo International Film Festival (Dec)
17 Kasr El Nil Street
Cairo
Tel: (20) 2 392 3562/392 3962/393 3832
Fax: (20) 2 393 8979
Competitive film festival for feature films, plus a Film, TV and Video market

Cairo International Film Festival for Children (Oct)
17 Kasr El Nil Street
Cairo
Tel: (20) 2 392 3562/392 3962/393 3832
Fax: (20) 2 393 8979
Competitive festival for children's films: features, shorts, documentaries, educative, cartoons, TV films and programmes for children up to 14 years old

FINLAND

Midnight Sun Film Festival (June)
Box 305
33101 Tampere
Tel: (358) 31 130034
Fax: (358) 31 230121
Held in Sodankylä, Finnish Lapland, in 1991

Tampere International Short Film Festival (March)
PO Box 305
33101 Tampere 10
Tel: (358) 31 130034/235681
Fax: (358) 31 230121
Competitive films with themes promoting peace and social equality. Films must have been released on or after Jan 1st of the preceding year

FRANCE

Annecy International Festival of Animation (+ Market) (June)
JICA/MIFA
BP 399
74013 Annecy Cedex
Tel: (33) 50 57 41 72
Fax: (33) 50 67 81 95
Competitive for animated short films, feature-length films, TV films, commercials, produced in the previous 26 months

Avoriaz International Fantasy Film Festival (Jan)
33 Avenue MacMahon
75017 Paris
Tel: (33) 1 42 67 71 40
Fax: (33) 1 46 22 88 51
Competitive for science fiction, horror, supernatural and fantasy feature films, which have not been commercially shown in France or

participated in festivals in Europe

Cannes International Film Festival (May)
71 rue du Faubourg St Honoré
75008 Paris
Tel: (33) 1 42 66 92 20
Fax: (33) 1 42 66 68 85
Competitive section for feature films and shorts (up to 30 mins) produced in the previous year, which have not screened outside country of origin nor been entered in other competitive festivals, plus non-competitive section: Un Certain Regard
Other non-competitive events:
Directors Fortnight (Quinzaine des Réalisateurs)
215 rue du Faubourg St Honoré
75008 Paris
Tel: (33) 1 45 61 01 66
Critic's Week (Semaine de la Critique)
90 rue d'Amsterdam
75009 Paris
Tel: (33) 1 40 16 98 30/(33) 1 45 74 53 53
Programme of French Cinema (Perspective du Cinéma Français)
Palais de Tokyo
2 rue de la Manutention
75116 Paris
Tel: (33) 1 47 23 73 00
Fax: (33) 1 47 23 78 07

Cinéma du Réel (International Festival of Visual Anthropology)
(March)
Bureau du Festival
Cinéma du Réel
19 rue Beaubourg
Bibliothèque Publique d'Information
75197 Paris Cedex 04
Tel: (33) 1 42 77 12 33
Fax: (33) 1 42 77 72 41
Competitive – must not have been released in France, released commercially or been awarded a prize at an international festival in France. Must have been made in the 2 years prior to the Festival

Cognac International Film Festival of the Thriller (March-April even years)
33 avenue MacMahon
75017 Paris
Tel: (33) 1 42 67 71 40
Fax: (33) 1 46 22 88 51

Créteil International Festival of Women's Films (+ Market) (March-April)
Maison des Arts
Place Salvador Allende
94000 Créteil
Tel: (33) 1 49 80 38 98
Fax: (33) 1 43 99 04 10
Competitive for feature films, documentaries, shorts, retrospectives directed by women and produced in the previous 23 months and not previously shown in France

Deauville European Festival of American Film (Sept)
33 avenue MacMahon
75017 Paris
Tel: (33) 1 42 67 71 40
Fax: (33) 1 46 22 88 51
Non-competitive festival of American feature films, not yet released in Europe (except UK), or shown in other French film festivals

FIFREC (International Film and Student Directors Festival)
(April)
FIFREC
BP 7144
30913 Nîmes Cedex
Tel: (33) 66 21 80 63
Fax: (33) 66 76 08 00
Official film school selections (3 per school) and open selection for directors from film schools, either students or recent graduates. Films to be under 40 mins. Golden Crocodile awards are presented

French-American Film Workshop
(July)
10 Montée de la Tour
30400 Villeneuve-les-Avignon
Tel: (33) 90 25 93 23
Fax: (33) 90 25 93 24
For independent film-makers, offering the 'Tournage Award' to one French and one American film-maker to enable them to make another film

MIPCOM (Oct)
179 avenue Victor Hugo
75116 Paris
Tel: (33) 1 45 05 14 03
Fax: (33) 1 47 55 91 22

MIP-TV International TV Programme Market
(April)
179 avenue Victor Hugo
75116 Paris
Tel: (33) 1 45 05 14 03
Fax: (33) 1 47 55 91 22
Market for television programmes, TV films and video.
Non-competitive

Montbéliard International Video and TV Festival
(June even years)
Centre International de Création Vidéo
Montbéliard Belfort
Chateau Peugeot, BP5
25310 Herimoncourt
Tel: (33) 81 30 90 30
Fax: (33) 81 30 95 25
Competitive for documentaries, news, fiction, art, animation, music, computer graphics produced during 18 months preceding festival

Nantes Festival of Three Continents
(Nov-Dec)
BP 3306
44033 Nantes Cedex 01
Tel: (33) 40 69 09 73/40 69 74 14
Fax: (33) 40 73 55 22
Films from Africa/Asia/Latin America with competitive section

Rouen Festival du Cinéma Nordique
(March)
91 rue Crevier
76000 Rouen
Tel: (33) 35 98 28 46
Fax: (33) 35 70 92 08
Competitive festival of Scandinavian films

GERMANY

Berlin International Film Festival (Feb)
International Filmfestspiele Berlin
Budapester Strasse 50
D-1000 Berlin 30
Tel: (49) 30 254 890
Fax: (49) 30 254 89249
Competitive for feature films and shorts (up to 15 mins), plus a separate competition for children's films – feature length and shorts – produced in the previous year and not entered for other festivals. Also has non-competitive programme consisting of forum of young cinema, film market and an information show

Dokfestival Leipzig
(Nov)
Festivalbüro
Springerstrasse 22-24
D-7022 Leipzig
Tel: (37) 41 51456
Fax: (37) 41 592421
Documentary film festival

European Film Forum (Sep)
Friedensallee 7
D-2000 Hamburg 50
Tel: (49) 40 390 4040
Fax: (49) 40 390 0142

Kinderfilmfestival
(Feb)
Jugendinformations-zentrum
Rottstrasse 24
D-4300 Essen 1
Tel: (49) 201 884512
Fax: (49) 201 885109
Children's film festival

Lübeck Nordic Film Days (Nov)
Postfach 2132
D-2400 Lübeck 1
Tel: (49) 451 122 4105
Fax: (49) 451 122 10 90
Festival of Scandinavian films

Mannheim Film Festival (Oct)
Collini-Center, Galerie
D-6800 Mannheim 1
Tel: (49) 621 10 29 43
Fax: (49) 621 29 15 64
The competition is dedicated to the slogan 'One World', referring to the dialogue in film art between 'East' and 'West' and of both with the 'South'. Features and documentaries by new and established directors are eligible

Munich Film Festival (June-July)
Internationale Münchner Filmwochen
Türkenstrasse 93
D-8000 München 40
Tel: (49) 89 38 19 04 0
Fax: (49) 89 38 19 04 61
Non-competitive for feature films, shorts and documentaries which have not previously been shown in Germany

No-Budget Short Film Festival (May-June)
LAG FILM Hamburg e V
NO-BUDGET-Büro
Glashüttenstrasse 27
D-2000 Hamburg 36
Tel: (49) 40 439 27 10/43 44 99
Fax: (49) 430 27 03
Competitive for short films produced on a low budget – section for films and videos under 15 mins

Oberhausen International Short Film Festival (April)
Christian-Steger Strasse 10
D-4200 Oberhausen 1
Tel: (49) 208 825 2652
Fax: (49) 208 852 591
Competitive for documentaries (up to 60 mins), animation, experimental and short features (up to 35 mins), student films, which have been produced in the previous 16 months and not previously shown in Germany; national section and side programme

Prix Futura Berlin
International Radio and TV Contest (April odd years)
Sender Freies Berlin
Masurenallee 8-14
D-1000 Berlin 19
Tel: (49) 30 3031 1610
Fax: (49) 30 3031 1619
Competitive for documentary and drama both on radio and TV. One entry per category in TV, 2 per category in radio for day competition. Evening competition has similar categories, but is for young people and newcomers. One entry per category per organisation

Prix Jeunesse International Television Competition (May-June even years)
Bayerischer Rundfunk
Rundfunkplatz 1
D-8000 Munich 2
Tel: (49) 89 5900 2058
Fax: (49) 89 5900 3053
Competitive for TV animation, drama, documentaries and light entertainment programmes, produced in the previous two years. Only one entry per category accepted

Stuttgart International Animated Film Festival (March even years)
Stuttgarter Trickfilmtage
Teckstrasse 56
(Kulturpark Berg)
D-7000 Stuttgart 1
Tel: (49) 2 62 26 99
Fax: (49) 2 62 49 80
Competitive for animated short films of an artistic and experimental nature, which have been produced in the previous two years and not exceeding 35 mins

HONG KONG

Hong Kong International Film Festival (April)
Level 7, Admin Building
Hong Kong Cultural Centre
10 Salisbury Road
Tsimshatsui
Kowloon
Hong Kong
Tel: (852) 734 2903
Fax: (852) 366 5206
Non-competitive for feature films, documentaries and invited short films, which have been produced in the previous two years

INDIA

Bombay International Film Festival for Documentary and Short Films (March)
c/o Ministry of Information & Broadcasting
Film Bhavan
24-Dr G Deshmukh Marg
Bombay 400 026
Tel: (91) 22 361461
Fax: (91) 22 4949751
Non-competitive festival devoted to the promotion of the Indian documentary film

International Film Festival of India (+ Market) (Jan)
Directorate of Film Festivals
Lok Nayak Bhavan
Fourth Floor
Khan Market
New Delhi 110 003
Tel: (91) 11 697167
Fax: (91) 11 694920
Non-competitive festival held in different Indian cities by rotation, including New Delhi, Bangalore, Bombay, Calcutta, Hyderabad, Trivandrum and most recently Madras

IRELAND

Cork Film Festival (Oct)
15 Tobin Street
Cork
Tel: (353) 21 271711
Fax: (353) 21 275945
Non-competitive for features, documentaries and short films. Competitive for European short films (up to 30 mins) and films in black and white, produced in the previous two years

Dublin Film Festival (Feb-March)
1 Suffolk Street
Dublin 2
Tel: (353) 1 6792937
Fax: (353) 1 6792939
An international film festival showcasing a wide range of world cinema with a special emphasis on Irish films

ISRAEL

Jerusalem Film Festival (July)
PO Box 8561
Jerusalem 91083
Tel: (972) 2 724 131
Fax: (972) 2 733 076
Non-competitive for features, shorts, documentaries, video and animation, for films not previously screened in Israel

ITALY

Florence International Festival of Independent Cinema (May)
Via Martiri dei Popolo 27
50122 Florence
Tel: (39) 55 24 58 69/24 36 51
Non-competitive for recent quality feature-length fiction films

Florence International Festival of Social Documentary Films – Festival dei Popoli (Nov-Dec)
Via dei Castellani 8
50122 Florence
Tel: (39) 55 475 5672
Fax: (39) 55 213 698
Competitive for documentaries on sociological, political, anthropological, economic, folklore and ethnographic subjects. Plus a non-competitive information section. Entries must not have been released previously in Italy and produced during 2 years preceding the festival

International Children's Film Festival (July-Aug)
84100 Giffoni Valle Piana
Salerno
Tel: (39) 89 868 544
Fax: (30) 89 868 544
Fiction, animated, documentary, experimental features both medium-length and short films for children 6-12 years and 12-18 years. Entries must have been produced within 2 years preceding the festival

MIFED (Milan) (Oct)
Largo Domodossola 1
CP 1270
20145 Milan
Tel: (39) 2 499 7267
Fax: (39) 2 499 77020
Indian summer cinema and television international multimedia market

Mystfest – International Mystery Festival (June)
Via dei Coronari 44
00186 Rome
Tel: (39) 6 683 3844
Fax: (39) 6 686 7902
Competitive film festival held in Viareggio for thrillers between 30-180 mins length, which have been produced in the previous year and not released in Italy

Pesaro Film Festival (Mostra Internazionale del Nuovo Cinema) (June)
Via Yser 8
00198 Rome
Tel: (39) 6 844 2453/841 3596
Fax: (39) 6 884 0531
Non-competitive for films from new directors, film groups and national cinemas

Pordenone Silent Film Days (Le Giornate del Cinema Muto) (Oct)
c/o La Cineteca del Friuli
Via Osoppo 26
33014 Gemona (UD)
Tel: (39) 432 98 04 58
Fax: (39) 432 97 05 42
Non-competitive silent film festival. Annual award for restoration and preservation of the silent film heritage

Prix Italia (Sept)
RAI Radiotelevisione Italiana
Via del Babuino 9
00187 Rome
Tel: (39) 6 312 782
Fax: (39) 6 322 5270
Competitive for television and radio productions from national broadcasting organisation. In the three categories (arts and music, drama, documentaries) each broadcasting organisation may submit: Radio – maximum 4 entries; Television – in case of 1 channel max. 2 entries; in case of more than 1 channel max. 3 entries

Salerno International Film Festival (Oct)
Casella Postale 137
84100 Salerno
Tel: (39) 89 231953
Fax: (39) 89 223632
Competitive for scientific, medical, educational, animation, sponsored feature and documentary films

Taormina International Film Festival (July)
Palazzo Firenze
Via Pirandello 31
98039 Taormina
Tel: (39) 942 21142
Fax: (39) 942 23348
Competitive for directors of first and second feature films. Emphasis on new directors and cinema from developing countries

Turin International Film Festival (Nov)
Piazza San Carlo 161
10123 Turin
Tel: (39) 11 547 171/513 703/513 287
Fax: (39) 11 519 796
Competitive sections for feature and short films. Italian Space section (videos and films) open solely to Italian work. All works must be completed during 13 previous months, with no prior release in Italy

Venice Film Festival (Sept)
La Biennale di Venezia
Settore Cinema e Televisione
Ca' Giustinian
San Marco
30124 Venice
Tel: (39) 41 521 8711
Fax: (39) 41 522 7539
Competitive for feature films which have not been shown at other festivals or released outside the country of origin. By invitation only

JAPAN

Hiroshima International Animation Festival
(Aug every 2 or 3 years)
4-17 Kako-machi
Naka-ku
Hiroshima 730
Tel: (81) 82 245 0245
Fax: (81) 82 245 0246
The festival programme consists of competition, panorama, retrospective, homage, tributes etc

Tokyo International Film Festival (Sept-Oct)
Organising Committee
Asano Building No 3, 2-14-19
Ginza, Chuo-Ku
Tokyo 104
Tel: (81) 3 3563 6305
Fax: (81) 3 3563 6310
Competitive international festival. Young cinema section for films by young or new directors; best of Asian films section, and Nippon Cinema now: masterpieces by contemporary Japanese directors

Tokyo Video Festival (Nov)
c/o Victor Co of Japan
2-4, 3-Chome
Kasumigaseki
Chiyoda-Ku
Tokyo 100
Tel: (81) 3 581 5715
Fax: (81) 3 581 4702
Competitive for videos; one division for general videos, another for compositions which explore the possibilities of video as a means of communication

MALTA

Golden Knight International Amateur Film & Video Festival (Nov)
Malta Amateur Cine Circle
PO Box 450
Valletta
Tel: (356) 222345/236173
Fax: (356) 225047
Three classes: amateur, student, professional – not exceeding 30 minutes

MARTINIQUE

Images Caraïbes (Caribbean Film and Video Festival)
(June even years)
77 route de la Folie
97200 Fort-de-France
Tel: (596) 63 43 20/60 21 42
Fax: (596) 64 11 30
Competitive for all film and video makers native to the Caribbean Islands – features, shorts and documentary

MONACO

International TV Festival of Monte Carlo (+ Market)
(Jan-Feb)
CCAM Boulevard Louis II
98000 Monte Carlo
Tel: (3393) 304944
Fax: (3393) 507014

THE NETHERLANDS

Dutch Film Days
(Sept)
Stichting Nederlandse Filmdagen
Hoogt 4
3512 GW Utrecht
Tel: (31) 30 322684
Fax: (31) 30 313200

International Documentary Filmfestival Amsterdam (Dec)
Kleine-Gartmanplantsoen 10
1017 RR Amsterdam
Tel: (31) 20 6273329
Fax: (31) 20 6385388
35mm or 16mm documentaries of any length. Joris Ivens award

Stichting Film Festival Rotterdam
(Jan-Feb)
PO Box 21696
3001 AR Rotterdam
Tel: (31) 10 411 8080
Fax: (31) 10 413 5132
Non-competitive for feature films. Retrospective programmes

NEW ZEALAND

Auckland International Film Festival (July)
PO Box 1411
Auckland
Tel: (64) 850 0162
Fax: (64) 801 7304
Non-competitive for shorts (up to 45 mins)

and feature films (up to 180 mins) which have been screened at festivals outside New Zealand

Wellington Film Festival (July)
PO Box 9544
Te Aro
Wellington
Tel: (64) 4 850 162
Fax: (64) 4 801 7304
Non-competitive for feature and short films. By invitation only

NORWAY

Norwegian International Film Festival (August)
PO Box 145
5501 Haugesund
Tel: (47) 428422
Fax: (47) 721347
Non-competitive film festival

POLAND

International Festival of Short Films in Cracow (May-June)
Ul Mazowiecka 6/8
PO Box 127
00950 Warsaw
Tel: (48) 22 26 40 51/22 45 40 41
Competitive for short films (up to 45 mins), including documentaries, fiction, animation, popular science and experimental subjects, produced in the previous 15 months and not awarded prizes in other international festivals

PORTUGAL

Algarve International Film Festival (May)
Festival de Amigos
PO Box 8091
1801 Lisboa Codex
Tel: (351) 1 851 36 15
Held at Praia da Rocha in the Algarve. Competitive for films not exceeding 30 mins in length. Open to all amateur filmmakers

Cinanima (International Animated Film and Video Festival) (Nov)
Organising Committee 'Cinanima'
Apartado 43
4501 Espinho Codex
Portugal
Tel: (351) 2 72 16 21/72 46 11
Fax: (351) 2 72 60 15
Competitive for features, advertising, children, youth, experimental, first work and didactic films. Also includes work by student directors. Entries must have been completed in the two years preceding the festival

Figueira da Foz (Sept)
Rua Luis de Camoes 106
2600 Vila Franca de Zira
Competitive for fiction and documentary films, preferably on social themes. Includes a retrospective of Portuguese cinema, films for children and shorts under 12 minutes. Entries must have been produced during $3^1/_2$ years preceding the festival

Oporto Fantasporto (Feb)
Rua Diogo Brandao 87
4000 Oporto
Tel: (351) 2 32 07 59
Fax: (351) 2 38 36 79
Competitive section for feature films and shorts, produced in the previous three years. Also holds retrospectives, an information section and a programme of Portuguese cinema. Films must have been produced during 3 years preceding the festival

Troia International Film Festival (Festroia) (June)
2902 Setúbal Codex
Troia
Tel: (351) 65 44121/44124
Fax: (351) 65 44162
Film/TV/video festival and market. Competitive for features/ documentaries/shorts dealing with the subject 'Man and Nature' on topics reflecting concerns of an environmental/ ecological nature. Films must not have been screened previously in Portugal and must have been produced during 32 months preceding the festival

PUERTO RICO

Ciné San Juan (Festival of Film and Video from the Caribbean Countries) (Oct)
Festival Ciné San Juan
Apartado 4543
San Juan PR 00905
Tel: (809) 721 5676
Competitive for recent features, documentaries, shorts and animated films from the Caribbean

SINGAPORE

International Film Festival (Jan biennial)
17-A Cecil Street
Singapore 0104
Tel: (65) 223 5109
Fax: (65) 223 5116

SPAIN

Barcelona Film Festival (Nov)
Passeig de Gracia 47
08007 Barcelona
Tel: (34) 3 487 1090/0264
Fax: (34) 3 215 2966
1991 festival postponed

Bilbao International Festival of Documentary and Short Films (Nov-Dec)
Colón de Larreátegui 37-40
48009 Bilbao
Tel: (34) 4 24 8698/16 5429/24 7860
Fax: (34) 4 42 3045
Competitive for documentary, animation, drama and experimental short films (up to 60 mins, except documentaries), produced in the previous two years, which have not won awards at other European festivals

Huesca International Short Film Festival (June)
Cortos – Ciudad de Huesca
Ricado de Arco 6
22003 Huesca
Tel: (34) 7 422 70 58
Competitive for short films (up to 30 mins) on any theme except tourism and promotion. Films which have won awards at other festivals are not eligible. Entries must have been produced in the previous two years

International Film Festival for Young People (July)
Apartado de Correos 76
Calle Gral. Vigon 4
33206 Gijon
Tel: (34) 85 34 37 39
Fax: (34) 85 35 41 52
Competitive for features and shorts made for children and young people. Must have been produced during 18 months preceding the festival and not awarded a prize at any other major international film festival

Madrid International Film Festival – Imagfic (April)
Gran Via 62-8
28013 Madrid
Tel: (34) 1 541 3721/541 5545
Fax: (34) 1 542 5495
Competitive festival which promotes 'Cinema of the Imagination', expressed in a wide variety of styles (eg SF, horror, thriller and mystery films). Films must not have been shown publicly or participated in other Spanish festivals or won prizes at any other festivals. Must have been produced during the 2 years preceding the festival

Murcia International Festival of Short Films (April)
Centro Cultural
Salzillo 7
30001 Murcia
Tel: (34) 68 21 7751/21 7752

Competitive for fiction, news, animation and documentaries

Donostia – San Sebastián International Film and Video Festival
(Sept)
PO Box 397
PZ Oquendo S/N
Donostia 20080
San Sebastian
Tel: (34) 43 481 212
Fax: (34) 43 285 979
Competitive for feature films produced in the previous year and not released in Spain or shown in any other festivals.
Non-competitive for creative documentaries, new directors/independent cinema. Also retrospective section

Sitges International Festival of Fantastic Cinema
(Oct)
Calle Diputacion 279
08007 Barcelona
Tel: (34) 3 317 35 85
Fax: (34) 3 301 22 47
Competitive for fantasy and horror films and shorts. Plus information section and retrospective programmes

Valencia Mediterranean Cinema Exhibition
(Oct)
Pl del Arzobispo 2acc
46003 Valencia
Tel: (34) 6 332 1506
Fax: (34) 6 331 5156
Competitive film festival and market for films made in the Mediterranean countries. Includes 'mostra' for children, Spanish cinema, retrospectives and film archives. Films must be completed after Jan 1st of preceding year

Valladolid International Film Festival (Oct)
Calle Angustias 1
Teatro Calderon
Apartado-646
Valladolid 47003
Tel: (34) 83 30 55 88/30 57 00
Fax: (34) 83 30 98 35
Competitive for features, documentaries and shorts not previously screened at any festival in Spain

SWEDEN

Gothenburg Film Festival (Jan-Feb)
Box 7079
S-402 32 Gothenburg
Tel: (46) 31 41 05 46
Fax: (46) 31 41 00 63
Non-competitive festival for features, documentaries and shorts not released in Sweden

Uppsala International Film Festival (Oct)
Kulturföreningen
Uppsala Filmfestival
Box 1746
S-751 47 Uppsala
Tel: (46) 18 50 30 10
Fax: (46) 18 50 15 10
Competitive for shorts (up to 60 mins), features and children's films, fiction, documentaries, animation and experimental. No advertising or tourist films

SWITZERLAND

Festival International de Films de Fribourg
(Jan-Feb)
Rue de Locarno 8
CH-1700 Fribourg
Tel: (41) 37 22 22 32
Fax: (41) 37 22 79 50
Films from Africa, Asia and Latin America

Geneva International Video Week (Nov odd years)
Maison des Jeunes et de la Culture
5 rue du Temple
CH-1201 Geneva
Tel: (41) 22 732 20 60
Fax: (41) 22 738 42 15
Competitive for original work displaying an individual approach and made during two years before festival

Golden Rose of Montreux TV Festival (May)
Giacomettistrasse 1-3
CH-3000 Berne 15
Tel: (41) 31 43 92 11
Fax: (41) 31 43 94 74
Competitive for TV productions (24-60 mins) of light entertainment, music and variety, first broadcast in the previous 14 months

Locarno International Film Festival (+ Market)
(Aug)
Via della Posta 6
CP 465
CH-6600 Locarno
Tel: (41) 93 32 02 32
Fax: (41) 93 31 74 65
Competitive for fiction films by new directors, produced in the previous year, which have not won prizes at other festivals. Plus information and retrospective programmes

Nyon International Documentary Film Festival (Oct)
PO Box 98
CH-1260 Nyon
Tel: (41) 22 61 60 60
Fax: (41) 22 61 70 71
Competitive documentary film festival

Vevey International Comedy Film Festival (Aug)
Place de la Gare 5
1800 Vevey
Tel: (41) 21 921 2292
Fax: (41) 21 921 1065
Competitive for features/short films only (no video). Films must not have been shown in Switzerland or have won a prize in another IFFPA festival

TUNISIA

International Film Festival of Carthage (Oct-Nov even years)
The JCC Managing Committee
PO Box 1029-1045
Tunis RP
Tel: (216) 1 260 323
Official competition open to African and Arab short and full-length films. Entries must have been made within two years before festival and not have been awarded first prize at any previous international festival in an African or Arab country. Also has an information section, a childhood and youth film section and an international film market

TURKEY

Istanbul International Film Festival (March-April)
Istanbul Foundation for Culture and Arts
Yıldız Kültür ve Sanat Merkezi
Beşiktaş 80700
Istanbul
Tel: (90) 1 160 45 33
Fax: (90) 1 161 88 23
Two competitive sections, international and national. The International Competition for feature fims on art (literature, theatre, cinema, music, dance and plastic arts) is judged by an international jury and the 'Golden Tulip Award' is presented as the Grand Prix. Entry by invitation

UNITED KINGDOM

BP Expo '92
(Jan-Feb)
Riverside Studios
Crisp Road
London W6 9RL
Tel: 081 741 2251
Fax: 081 563 0336
Competitive festival of British and international new short film and video: fiction, documentary, animation, experimental, focusing on student and low-budget work

Birmingham International Film and Television Festival (Sept-Oct)
The Bond
180-182 Fazeley Street
Digbeth
Birmingham B5 5SE
Tel: 021 766 6707
Fax: 021 766 7038
Non-competitive for features and shorts, plus retrospective and tribute programmes. The Festival hosts

conferences debating topical issues in film and television production

Brighton Festival Media Programme (May)
Duke of York's Cinema
Preston Circus
Brighton BN1 4AA
Tel: 0273 602503
Non-competitive thematic film festival with seminars/ discussions with visiting directors and other professionals, screening retrospectives, previews, new releases and films directly from production companies abroad. Special interest in political and cultural issues

Cambridge Film Festival (July)
Arts Cinema
Market Passage
Cambridge CB2 3PF
Tel: 0223 462666
Fax: 0223 462555
Non-competitive for feature films; some selected from other festivals, original choices, short retrospectives and revived classics

Edinburgh International Film Festival (Aug)
Filmhouse
88 Lothian Road
Edinburgh EH3 9BZ
Tel: 031 228 4051
Fax: 031 229 5501
Competitive for best: new British animation, British feature, student film, and first time feature produced in previous two years (except Britain, produced in previous year). Programme strands include retrospectives, documentaries, features and shorts, special events and lectures

Edinburgh International Television Festival (Aug)
1-4 Langley Court
London WC2E 9JY
Tel: 071 379 4519
Fax: 071 836 0702
Conference discussing current issues in television, accompanied by screenings of television programmes grouped according to the themes/topics under discussion

IVCA Film and Video Festival (Nov)
International Visual Communications Association
Bolsover House
5-6 Clipstone Street
London W1P 7EB
Tel: 071 580 0962
Fax: 071 436 2606
Competitive for industrial/training films and videos, covering all aspects of the manufacturing and commercial world, plus categories for non-broadcast, educational, environmental, leisure and communications subjects

The International Animation Festival, Cardiff (formerly the Bristol Animation Festival)
(March even years)
Festival Office
79 Wardour Street
London W1V 3PH
Tel: 071 287 1194
Fax: 071 287 2112
Non-competitive thematic festival. Entry by invitation only

International Festival of Film and TV in the Celtic Countries (Scotland, Wales, Ireland, Brittany – March-April peripatetic)
The Library
Farraline Park
Inverness IV1 1LS
Scotland
Tel: 0463 226189
Competitive for films whose subject matter has particular relevance to the Celtic nations

Leeds International Film Festival (Oct)
19 Wellington Street
Leeds LS1 4DG
Tel: 0532 478389
Fax: 0532 426761
Non-competitive for feature films and shorts, plus thematic retrospective programme. Lectures, seminars, exhibitions and children's festival

London International Film Festival (Nov)
National Film Theatre
South Bank
London SE1 8XT
Tel: 071 928 0536
Non-competitive festival for feature films and shorts, by invitation only, which have not previously been released in Great Britain. Films are selected from other festivals, plus some original choices

London Latin American Film Festival (Sep)
Metro Pictures
79 Wardour Street
London W1V 3TH
Tel: 071 434 4457
Fax: 071 287 2112
Non-competitive, bringing to London a line up of contemporary films from Latin American and surveying currents and trends

London Lesbian and Gay Film Festival (Mar)
Festivals Office
National Film Theatre
South Bank
London SE1 8XT
Tel: 071 928 3535
Fax: 071 633 9323
Non-competitive for film and videos of special interest to lesbian and gay audiences. Some entries travel to regional film theatres as part of a national tour from April to June

Southampton Film Festival (June)
Special Events Unit
Civic Centre
Southampton SO9 4XF
Tel: 0703 832515
Fax: 0703 631437
Non-competitive festival for feature films and shorts. Open to all categories

Tyneside International Film Festival (Oct)
Tyneside Cinema
10-12 Pilgrim Street
Newcastle upon Tyne
NE1 6QG
Tel: 091 232 8289
Fax: 091 221 0535
Non-competitive festival for feature films and shorts, by invitation only. Special seasons, including an annual celebration of Spanish cinema, presentations and on-stage interviews, plus retrospective programmes

UK Horror Film Festival (biannual)
51 Thatch Leach Lane
Whitefield
Manchester M25 6EN
Tel: 061 766 2566
Non-competitive for horror and horror-related pre-release features with some shorts, produced in the previous year. Special guests. Plus retrospective programmes

Video Positive '91
(April-May odd years)
International Video Art Festival
Moviola
Bluecoat Chambers
Liverpool L1 3BX
Tel: 051 709 2663
Non-competitive for video art produced world-wide in the two years preceding the festival. Includes community and education programme, workshops and seminars. Some commissions available

Welsh International Film Festival, Aberystwyth (Nov)
c/o Premiere Cymru Wales Cyf
Unit 8c
Cefn Llan
Aberystwyth
Dyfed SY23 2AH
Tel: 0970 617995
Fax: 0970 623311
Non-competitive festival for international feature films, together with films from Wales in Welsh and English. Also short retrospectives and seminars

Wildscreen: International Wildlife Film and Television Festival
(Oct)
Bristol and West Building Society

PO Box 27
Broad Quay
Bristol BS99 7AX
Tel: 0272 292656
Competitive for film and TV programmes made during 14 months preceding the festival

USA

American Film Institute (AFI) European Film Festival (June)
2021 N Western Avenue
Los Angeles CA 90027
Tel: (1) 213 856 7707
Fax: (1) 213 462 4049
Features only, non-competitive.
Co-sponsored by the European Community.
Screenings in New York, Washington, Los Angeles, Minneapolis

AFI Los Angeles Film Festival (April)
2021 N Western Avenue
Los Angeles CA 90027
Tel: (1) 213 856 7707
Fax: (1) 213 462 4049
Non-competitive, FIAPF accredited. Features, documentaries, shorts by invitation

AFI National Video Festival (Oct)
2021 N Western Avenue
Los Angeles CA 90027
Tel: (1) 213 856 7707
Fax: (1) 213 462 4049
Screenings in Los Angeles, Washington.
Accepts: VHS, $^{3}/_{4}''$, NTSC/PAL/SECAM (No Beta, no 1″)

American Film Market – AFM (Feb-March and Oct)
12424 Wilshire Blvd
Suite 600
Los Angeles CA 90025
Tel: (1) 213 447 1555
Fax: (1) 213 447 1666
Twice-yearly market for international film, TV and video

Asian American International Film Festival (June)
c/o Asian CineVision
32 East Broadway, 4th Floor
New York, NY 10002
Tel: (1) 212 925 8685
Fax: (1) 212 925 8157

Athens International Film and Video Festival (April-May)
PO Box 388
Athens OH 45701
Tel: (1) 614 593 1330
Competitive for film and video including art, narrative, documentary, education, animation and experimental. Entries must have been produced in two years preceding festival

Chicago International Film Festival (Oct-Nov)
415 North Dearborn Street
Chicago IL 60610
Tel: (1) 312 644 3400
Fax: (1) 312 644 0784
Competitive for feature films, shorts, animation, TV productions, student films and commercials

Cleveland International Film Festival (April)
6200 SOM Center Road #C20
Cleveland OH 44139
Tel: (1) 216 349 0270
Fax: (1) 216 349 0210
Non-competitive for feature, narrative, documentary, animation and experimental films

Denver International Film Festival (Oct)
999 Eighteenth Street
Suite 247
Denver CO 80202
Tel: (1) 303 298 8223
Fax: (1) 303 298 0209
Non-competitive mainly for independent material – features, shorts, documentary, animation and children's films

Hawaii Film Festival (Nov)
East/West Center
Institute of Culture and Communications
1777 East/West Road
Oahu
Honolulu HA 96848
Tel: (1) 808 944 7007
Fax: (1) 808 944 5578

Houston International Film and Video Festival – Worldfest-Houston (+ Market) (April)
PO Box 56566
Houston TX 77256-6566
Tel: (1) 713 965 9955
Fax: (1) 713 965 9960
Competitive for features, shorts, documentary, TV production and TV commercials.
Independent & major studios, experimental and video with inclusive film market

Miami Film Festival (Feb)
Film Society of Miami
444 Brickell Avenue
Suite 229
Miami FL 33131
Tel: (1) 305 377 3456
Fax: (1) 305 577 9768
Non-competitive film festival

National Educational Film and Video Festival (May)
655 Thirteenth Street
Oakland CA 94612
Tel: (1) 415 465 6885
Festival of educational media. Competitive for documentaries, dramatic features and shorts, animation, classroom programmes, medical/health programmes, training/instructional tapes, special interest tapes, made-for-TV programmes, public service announcements, film and video art and student made programmes. Includes producer's market

New York Film Festival (Sept-Oct)
140 West 65th Street
New York NY 10023
Tel: (1) 212 877 1800
Non-competitive for feature films, shorts (up to 30 mins), including drama, documentary, animation and experimental films. Films must have been produced in the 15 months prior to festival

New York International Film and TV Festival (Nov)
IFTF of New York Inc
5 West 37th Street
New York NY 10018
Tel: (1) 914 238 4481
Fax: (1) 914 238 5040
Competitive for industrial and educational films, filmstrips, shorts and commercials which have been produced in the previous year

PHILAFILM (July)
121 North Broad Street
Suite 618
Philadelphia PA 19107
Tel: (1) 215 977 2831
Fax: (1) 215 977 2856
International film and video competition and marketplace. Product prizes, trophies, certificates and cash awards given

San Francisco International Film Festival (April-May)
1560 Fillmore Street
San Francisco CA 94115
Tel: (1) 415 567 4641
Fax: (1) 415 921 5032
Feature films, by invitation, shown non-competitively. Shorts, documentaries, animation, experimental works and TV productions eligible for Golden Gate Awards competition section

San Francisco Lesbian and Gay Film Festival (June)
Frameline
PO Box 14792
San Francisco CA 94114
Tel: (1) 415 861 5245
Fax: (1) 415 861 1404
Features, documentary, short film and video

Seattle International Film Festival (May)
801 East Pine
Seattle WA 98122
Tel: (1) 206 324 9996
Fax: (1) 206 324 9998

US Industrial Film & Video Festival

(June)
841 North Addison Avenue
Elmhurst IL 60126-1291
Tel: (1) 312 834 7773
Fax: (1) 312 834 5565
Competitive for films and videos produced during previous year

USSR

Moscow International Film Festival

(July odd years)
Sovinterfest
Management of International Film Festival & Exhibitions
10 Khokholovsky per.
Moscow 109028
Tel: (7) 095 227 54 17
Fax: (7) 095 227 01 07
Competitive for feature films produced in the 2 years prior to the festival and not shown in competition in other international festivals. Also includes out of competition screenings and retrospectives

YUGOSLAVIA

Belgrade International Film Festival

(Jan-Feb)
Sava Centar
Milwnrija Popovica 9
11070 Novi Beograd
Tel: (38) 11 60 94 63
Fax: (38) 11 22 11 56
Non-competitive for features/shorts reflecting high aesthetic and artistic values and contemporary trends

Zagreb World Festival of Animated Films

(June even years)
Nova Ves 18
41000 Zagreb
Tel: (38) 41 271 355
Fax: (38) 41 275 994
Competitive for animated films (up to 30 mins), educational children's films and first films categories. Films must have been completed in two years prior to festival and not have been awarded prizes at Annecy or Varna in the previous year

FILM SOCIETIES

Listed below are UK film societies which are open to the public, and those based in educational establishments and private companies and organisations. Addresses are grouped in broad geographical areas, along with the regional officers who can offer specific local information. There is a constant turnover of society officers, so if you are not certain whom to contact or your enquiry goes astray, you should contact the Film Society Unit at the BFI ***(see p9)***

BFFS CONSTITUENT GROUPS

The Film Society Unit exists to service the British Federation of Film Societies. The BFFS is divided into Constituent Groups which usually follow the borders of Regional Arts Boards, but sometimes include more than one RAB area

Eastern
Bedfordshire, Cambridgeshire, Essex, Hertfordshire, Lincolnshire, Norfolk, Suffolk

London
32 London Boroughs and the City of London

Midlands
Derbyshire (excluding High Peak District), Leicestershire, Northamptonshire, Nottinghamshire, Hereford and Worcester, Shropshire, Staffordshire, Warwickshire, Metropolitan districts of Birmingham, Coventry, Dudley, Sandwell, Solihull, Walsall, Wolverhampton

North West
Cheshire, High Peak district of Derbyshire, Lancashire, Metropolitan districts of Bolton, Bury, Knowsley, City of Liverpool, Manchester, Oldham, Rochdale, St Helens, Salford, Sefton, Stockport, Tameside, Trafford, Wigan, Wirral, Northern Ireland

Northern
Cleveland, Cumbria, Durham, Northumberland, Metropolitan districts of Gateshead, Newcastle, North Tyneside, South Tyneside, Sunderland

Scotland

South East
Kent, Surrey, East Sussex, West Sussex

South West
Avon, Channel Islands, Cornwall, Devon, Dorset (except districts of Bournemouth, Christchurch and Poole), Gloucestershire, Somerset

Southern
Berkshire, Buckinghamshire, Hampshire, Isle of Wight, Oxfordshire, Wiltshire, Districts of Bournemouth, Christchurch, Poole

Wales

Yorkshire
Humberside, North Yorkshire, Metropolitan districts of Barnsley, Bradford, Calderdale, Doncaster, Kirklees, Leeds, Rotherham, Sheffield, Wakefield

EASTERN

BFFS Eastern Group
Mr Gerry Dobson
Kennel Cottage
Burton
Nr Lincoln
Lincs

Bedford Film Society
Mr Derek Ebden
59 Greenshields Road
Bedford
Beds MK40 3TU

Berkhamsted Film Society
Dr C J S Davies
Seasons
Gardenfield Lane
Berkhamsted
Herts HP4 2NN

British Telecom Film Society
Mr A P Martin
Research Dept RT52
Rm 40B/MLB4
Martlesham Heath
Ipswich
Suffolk
IP5 7RE

Bury St Edmunds Film Society
Mr J W Garbutt
Sharon, Livermere Road
Conyers Green
Bury St Edmunds
Suffolk IP31 2QG

CCAT Film Society
Mr S Davies
Ents and Publicity Officer
CCAT Student Union
East Road
Cambridge CB1 1PT

Cambridge Union Film Society
Chairman
Film Committee
Bridge Street

Cambridge
CB2 1DB

Chelmsford Film Club
Mr Lawrence Islip
11 Sunningdale Road
Chelmsford
Essex CM1 2NH

Coopers' Company & Coborn School Film Society
Mr David Wynne-Jones
Coopers' Company & Coborn School
St Mary's Lane
Upminster
Essex

University of East Anglia SU Film Society
Mr N Rayns
University of East Anglia
The Plain
Norwich
Norfolk NR4 7TJ

Ely Film Society
Mr Clive Jeffries
33 Langham Way
Ely
Cambs CB6 1DZ

Epping Film Society
Mr A R Carr
58 Centre Drive
Epping
Essex CM16 4JE

University of Essex Film Society
Mandy Charles
Students' Union Building
Wivenhoe Park
Colchester CO4 3SQ

Great Yarmouth Film Society
Mr E C Hunt
21 Park Lane
Norwich
Norfolk NR2 3EE

Hatfield Polytechnic Film Society
Mr David Cowan, Drama Tutor
Wall Hall Campus
Aldenham
Watford
Herts WD2 8AZ

ICI (Welwyn) Film Society
Mr B M Chick
ICI Advanced Materials
PO Box 6, Bessemer Road
Welwyn Garden City
Herts AL7 1HD

International University Film Society
Mr D B Rogalski
The Avenue
Bushey
Herts WD2 2LN

Ipswich Film Society
Mr Terry Cloke
4 Burlington Road
Ipswich
Suffolk IP1 2EU

Leighton Buzzard Library and Arts Centre
Mr Stuart Antrobus
Lake Street
Leighton Buzzard
Beds LU7 8RX

Letchworth Film Society
Mr Sean Boughton
29 Norton Road
Letchworth
Herts SG6 1AA

Lincoln Film Society
Mr M Bingham
27 Breedon Drive
Lincoln
Lincs LN1 3XA

Long Road Sixth Form College Film Society
Ms Julie Lindsay
Long Road
Cambridge CB2 2PX

Maldon Cinema Club
Administrator
Oakwood Arts Centre
Market Place
Maldon
Essex CM9 6UA

Old Town Hall Film Society
Jackie Alexander
Old Town Hall Arts Centre
High Street
Hemel Hempstead
Herts HP1 3AE

Peterborough Film Society
Mr A J Bunch
196 Lincoln Road
Peterborough
Cambs PE1 2NQ

Playhouse Co-operative Film Society (Harlow)
Mrs S Herbert
72 Broadfields
Harlow
Essex CM20 3PT

Saint John's College Film Society
Mr Martin John Turner
St John's College
Cambridge CB2 1TP

Stamford Schools' Film Society
Dr J P Slater
Stamford School
St Paul's Street
Stamford
Lincs PE9 2BS

Towngate Theatre
Mr Peter Neville-Hadley
Pagel Mead
Basildon
Essex SS14 1DW

Welwyn Garden City Film Society
Mr Michael Massey
3 Walden Place
Welwyn Garden City
Herts AL8 7PG

LONDON

BFFS London Group
Mr Mark Sullivan
7 Contour House
663 London Road
North Cheam
Surrey SM3 9DF

Aquila Film Society
Mr M A Lever
Block 4, DGDQA
'Aquila', Golf Road
Bromley
Kent BR1 2JB

Australian Film Society
Mr S Hughes
'Eagle', 33 Delius Way
Stanford-le-Hope
Essex SS17 8RG

Avant-Garde Film Society
Mr C White
9 Elmbridge Drive
Ruislip
Middlesex HA4 7XD

BBC Film Club
Mr D Charlton
Room 2084
BBC TV Centre
Wood Lane
London W12 7RJ

BCC Sport and Social Club Film Society
Miss Janice Bullen
CIN Management
PO Box 10
London SW1X 7AD

Barclays Bank Film Society
The Secretary
Fleetway House
25 Farringdon Street
London EC4A 4LP

The Biograph Film Society
Ms Carol Swords
Pimlico Arts and Media
St James the Less School
Moreton Street
London SW1V 2PT

Bowring Film Society
Ms D Woods
58 Beehive Lane
Redbridge
Ilford
Essex IG1 3RS

Brunel Film Society
The President
Brunel University
Uxbridge
Middlesex UB8 3PH

Channel 4 Film Society
Ms Sally Brown
Channel 4 Television
60 Charlotte Street
London W1P 2AX

Durning Hall Film Society
Nim Njuguna
Durning Hall
Earlham Grove
Forest Gate
London E7 9AB

Gothique Film Society
Mr R James
75 Burns Avenue
Feltham
Middlesex TW14 9LX

Holborn Film Society
Ms Janet McCabe
84d West End Lane
London NW6 2LX

ICRF Film Club
Ms Marie Fleetwood
Tissue Antigen Laboratory

ICRF
PO Box 123
Lincoln's Inn Fields
London WC2A 3PX

Imperial College Union Film Society
Mr Martin Gans
c/o Dept of Civil Engineering
Imperial College
Exhibition Road
London SW7 2AZ

Institut Français Film Society
The Secretary (Cinema Dept)
17 Queensberry Place
London SW7 2DT

John Lewis Partnership Film Society
Mr P Allen
Social Secretary
8th Floor
171 Victoria Street
London SW1E 5NN

Kino Club
Katia Rossini
Fine Art, Film and Video Dept
Central St Martin's School of Art
Long Acre
London WC2

Lensbury Film Society (Shell Oil)
Mrs A Catto
Shell Centre
Room Y1085, York Road
Waterloo
London SE1 7NA

London Film Makers' Co-operative
Ms Moira Sweeney
The Cinema
42 Gloucester Avenue
London NW1

Middlesex Polytechnic SU Film Society
Ms Clare Squire
104w Gubbay Hall
Trent Park
Cockfosters Road
Barnet
Herts EN4 0PT

Mullard House Film Society
Ms L S Denny
Chairman
Mullard House
Torrington Place
London WC1E 7HD

NPL Film Society
Mr R Townsend
National Physical Laboratory
Queens Road
Teddington
Middlesex TW11 0LW

North London Film Theatre
Miss B Underwood
7 Hillary Rise
Barnet
Herts EN5 5AZ

PNL Film Society
Ms Dena Blakeman
73 Warner Road
Camberwell
London SE5 9NE

Polish Social and Cultural Association
Mr A Ostaszewski
238-246 King Street
London W6 0RF

RCA Film Society
Ms Clare Sprawson
Royal College of Art
Kensington Gore
London SW7 2EU

Richmond College Film Society
Mr B Nevitt
Richmond College
Queen's Road
Richmond
Surrey TW10 6JP

Richmond Film Society
Mr Richard Howarth
49 Selwyn Avenue
Richmond
Surrey TW9 2HB

Scandinavian Film Society
Mrs Françoise Cowie
111 Old Brompton Road
London SW7 3LE

School of Oriental and African Studies Film Society
Mr Nigel Boyd
Thornhaugh Street
Russell Square
London WC1H 0XG

South Bank Poly Film Society
Mr Thierry Gondal
3 Granville Square
Peckham
London SE15 6YD

South London Film Society
Dr M Essex-Lopresti
14 Oakwood Park Road
Southgate
London N14 6QG

Southwark Arts Film Club
Ms Valerie Chang
Southwark Arts
186 Walworth Road
London SE17 1JJ

St George's Hospital Medical School
Mr Matthew Clarke
Cranmer Terrace
Tooting
London SW17 0RE

John Stanley Media Management
John Stanley
28 Nottingham Place
London W1M 3FD

Thames Polytechnic Film Society
Ms Sally Baldry
Students Union
Thomas Street
London SE18 6HU

University College Union Film Society
Mr N McAlpine
University College London Union
25 Gordon Street
London WC1H 0AH

Waltham Forest (Libs) Film Society
Mrs V Bates
William Morris Gallery
Lloyd Park
Forest Road
Walthamstow E17 4PP

Woolwich and District Co-op Film Society
Mr P Graham
10 Harden Court
Tamar Street
Charlton
London SE7 8DQ

MIDLANDS

BFFS Midland Group
Mr Robert Johnson
The Villas
86 School Lane
Cookshill, Caverswall
Stoke-on-Trent

BGS Film Society
Dr D Savage
Fluid Processes Research Group
British Geological Survey
Nottingham NG12 5GG

Bablake School Film Society
Mr J R Lawrence
Coventry School, Bablake
Coundon Road
Coventry CV1 4AU

Bishops Castle Film Society
Ms J Parker
4 Lavender Bank
Bishops Castle
Shropshire SY9 5BD

Bromsgrove Film Society
Mr Chris Page
80 New Road
Bromsgrove
Worcs B60 2LA

Central Television SSC Film Society
Mr G Lee
Central House
Broad Street
Birmingham B1 2JP

University of Keele Film Society
Mrs D Steele
Accounts Office
Students Union
Keele
Staffs ST5 5BJ

Kinver Film Society
Ms Pat Adams
38 Vicarage Road
Amblecote
Stourbridge
W Midlands DY8 4JD

Lion Street Cultural Centre Film Society
Richard Seabury
Lion Street
Oakengates
Telford
Shropshire TF2 6AQ

Loughborough Students Union Film Society
Union Building
Ashby Road
Loughborough
Leics LE11 3EA

Ludlow and District Film Society
J Sydenham
2 Rectory Court
Clungunford
Shropshire SY7 0PH

Malvern Film Society
Mr George Wells
42 North Malvern Road
Malvern
Worcs WR14 4LT

New Kettering Film Society
Mr C J E Owen
4 Church Street
Cottingham
Market Harborough
Leics LE16 8XG

Nottingham Polytechnic SU Film Society
Simon Paul Barber
66A Peveril Street
Radford
Nottingham NG7 4AH

Oundle School Snr Film Society
Mr David Sharp
North Street
Oundle
Northants PE8 4AL

Ross Film Society
Mrs B Laws
Meadow Cottage
Broad Oak
Hereford HR2 8QX

Shrewsbury Film Society
Mr B Mason
Pulley Lodge
Lower Pulley Lane
Bayston Hill
Shrewsbury
Shropshire SY3 0DW

Solihull Film Society
Mr M Bryanston
34 Silhill Hall Road
Solihull
W Midlands B91 1JU

Stafford Film Society
Mr M Whalley
10 Park Street
Stafford
Staffs ST17 4AL

Stourbridge Film Society
Mrs M J Keightley
1A Pargeter Street
Stourbridge
W Midlands DY8 1AU

University of Warwick Film Society
The Secretary
Students Union
University of Warwick
Coventry CV4 7AL

Weston Coyney and Caverswall Film Society
Mr R Johnson
86 School Lane
Cookshill, Caverswall
Stoke-on-Trent
ST11 9EN

NORTH WEST

BFFS North West Group
Mr A Payne
18 Cecil Street
Lytham St Annes
Lancs FY8 5NN

Birkenhead Library Film Society
Mr H G Mortimer
Music Dept
Borough Road
Birkenhead
Merseyside L41 2XB

Black Sunday Horror Film Society
Mr David Bryan
51 Thatch Leach Lane
Whitefield
Manchester M25 6EN

Blackburn and District Film Society
Mr Alan Cottam
8 Cabin End Row
Knuzden
Blackburn
Lancs BB1 2DP

Chester Film Society
Mr G Mayled
19 Crofters Way
Saughall
Chester
Cheshire CH1 6AA

Chorley Film Society
Mr C Collison
21 Weldbank Lane
Chorley
Lancs PR7 3NG

Citadel Arts Centre Film Society
Paul Hogan/Robert Cave
Citadel Arts Centre
Waterloo Street
St Helens WA10 1PX

Deeside Film Society
Mr Ramsey Hewson
44 Albion Street
Wallasey
Merseyside L45 9JG

Ellesmere Port Library Film Society
Mr J G Fisher
Ellesmere Port Library
Civic Way
Ellesmere Port
Cheshire L65 0BG

Forum Film Society
Mrs M Holleran
Central Library
Wythenshawe
Manchester M22 5RT

Frightnite Horror Film Society
Mr Stephen Faragher
35 Hilberry Avenue
Tuebrook
Liverpool L13 7ES

Frodsham Film Society
Mr M F Donovan
58 The Willows
Frodsham
Cheshire WA6 7QS

Heswall Film Society
Mr Alvin Sant
18 Fairlawn Court
Bidston Road
Birkenhead L43 6UX

University of Lancaster Film Society
The President
Bowland Annexe
Bailrigg
Lancaster LA1 4GT

Lytham St Annes Film Society
Mr A Payne
18 Cecil Street
Lytham St Annes
Lancs FY8 5NN

Manchester and Salford Film Society
Mr H T Ainsworth
64 Egerton Road
Fallowfield
Manchester M14 6RA

Manchester University Film Society
Hon Secretary
Union Building
Oxford Road
Manchester M13 9PR

Manchester Women's Film Group
Ms E Gent
27 Thorpe Street
Old Trafford
Manchester M16 9PR

The Media Centre Film Society
Ms C Dahl
Leigh College
Railway Road
Leigh WN7 7AH

Merseyside Film Institute
Mr G Donaldson
45 Bluecoat Chambers
School Lane
Liverpool L1 3BX

Preston Film Society
Mr M Lockwood
14 Croftgate
Highgate Park, Fulwood
Preston
Lancs PR2 4LS

Runcorn Library Film Society
Mrs S Davies
Runcorn Library
Shopping City
Runcorn
Cheshire WA7 2PF

Saddleworth Film Society
Sue Haslam
2 Oldham Road
Delph
Oldham OL3 5EB

The Society of Fantastic Films
Mr H Nadler
5 South Mesnefield Road
Salford
Lancs M7 0QP

Southport Film Guild Film Society
Mr A Macdonald
69 Queens Road
Southport
Merseyside PR9 9JF

Turnpike Film Society
Wendy Heaton
c/o Leigh Library
Civic Square
Leigh WN7 1EB

UMIST Union Film Society
Hon Secretary
PO Box 88

Sackville Street
Manchester M60 1QD

University of Ulster Film Society
Mrs J Rushton
c/o Estates Dept
Cromore Road
Coleraine
County Londonderry
N Ireland BT52 1SA

Winnington Hall Club Film Society
Mr C Riemer
15 Hadrian Way
Sandiway
Northwich
Cheshire CW8 2JR

Workers' Film Association Film Society
F Johnson
WFA
9 Lucy Street
Old Trafford
Hulme
Manchester M15 4BX

NORTHERN

BFFS Northern Group

Bede Film Society
The President
College of St Hild and St Bede
Durham DH1 1SE

Centre Film Club
Mr R A Smith
20 Stanhope Grove
Acklam
Middlesbrough
Cleveland TS5 7SG

Cleveland Film Group
Mr Steven D Moses
45 Oxford Road
Linthorpe
Middlesbrough
Cleveland TS5 5DY

Durham University Film Unit
The President
Dunelm House
New Elvet
Durham DH1 3LH

Elvet Film Society
Mrs M Bryden
Durham University
Dunelm House
New Elvet
Durham DH1 3HP

Film Club at the Roxy
Gwyneth Walker
13 Conishead House
Priory Road
Ulverston
Cumbria LA12 9QQ

Hartlepool Film Society
Mr A Gowing
6 Warkworth Drive
Hartlepool
Cleveland TS26 0EW

Newcastle Polytechnic SU Film Society
Mrs M Bennett
Union Building
2 Sandyford Road
Newcastle-upon-Tyne
NE1 8SB

Penrith Film Club
Mr B R Jimack
1 Beacon Edge
Penrith
Cumbria CA11 7SE

Tullie House Film Society
Ms Norma Rutherford
Tullie House
Castle Street
Carlisle
Cumbria CA3 8TP

201 Film Society (Durham)
Mr D Boffey
Van Mildert College
University of Durham
Durham DH1 3LH

SCOTLAND

BFFS Scottish Group
Mr Eric Sykes
64 Castle Street
Duns
Berwickshire TD11 3BE

Aberdeen University Film Society
The President
Aberdeen University Union
Broad Street
Aberdeen AB9 1AW

Avondale Film Society
Mr Tom Goodwillie
3 Kirkhill Road
Strathaven
Lanarkshire ML10 6HN

Ayr & Craigie Film Society
Mr R J Currie
15A Carrick Road
Ayr KA7 2RA

Bank of Scotland Film Society
Mr H Boyd
Tax Department
PO Box 41
101 George Street
Edinburgh EH2 3JH

The Barony Film Society
G Harrower
68 Grange Terrace
Bo'ness
West Lothian EH51 4LP

Berwickshire Film Society
Mr Eric Sykes
64 Castle Street
Duns
Berwickshire TD11 3BE

Broughton High School Film Society
Mr R Armstrong
Broughton High School
Carrington Road
Edinburgh EH4 1EG

Broughton High School Junior Film Society
Mr L Timson
Broughton High School
Carrington Road
Edinburgh EH4 1EG

Callander Film Society
Benmore House
19 Bridgend
Callander
Perthshire FK17 8AG

Crieff Film Society
Ms M Thomson
Glenshira
Drummond Terrace
Crieff
Perthshire PH7 4AF

Duncan of Jordanstone Film Society
Mr Alan Woods
Duncan of Jordanstone College of Art
Perth Road
Dundee DD1 4LP

University of Dundee Film Society
Films Convener
Students Association
Airlie Place
Dundee DD1 4HN

East Kilbride Film Society
Mr Robert Jenkins
13 St Leonards Road
East Kilbride
Strathclyde G74 2JB

Edinburgh Film Guild
Ms Helene Telford
Secretary
Filmhouse
88 Lothian Road
Edinburgh EH3 9BZ

Edinburgh University Film Society
Societies' Centre
60 The Pleasance
Edinburgh EH8 9TJ

Haldane Film Society
Mr T G Crocket
62 Cardross Road
Dumbarton
Dunbartonshire G82

Lanarkshire Schools Film Society
Robert Stewart
Brannock High School
Loanhead Road
Motherwell
Lanarkshire ML1 5AU

Lewis Film Society
Mr D Leadbitter
14 Builnacraig Street
Stornoway
Isle of Lewis PA87 2RY

Linlithgow Film Society
Mr G Shinwell
90 Deanfield Road
Bo'ness
West Lothian EH51 0ER

Lloyds Bowmaker Film Club
Helen Watson
Finance House
Orchard Brae
Edinburgh EH4 1PF

North Ayrshire Film Society
Mrs N Yuill
Sanox
Ardrossan Road
Seamill
West Kilbride
Ayrshire KA23 9LX

North West Skye Film Society
Di Gilpin
9 Lower Milovaig

SONY

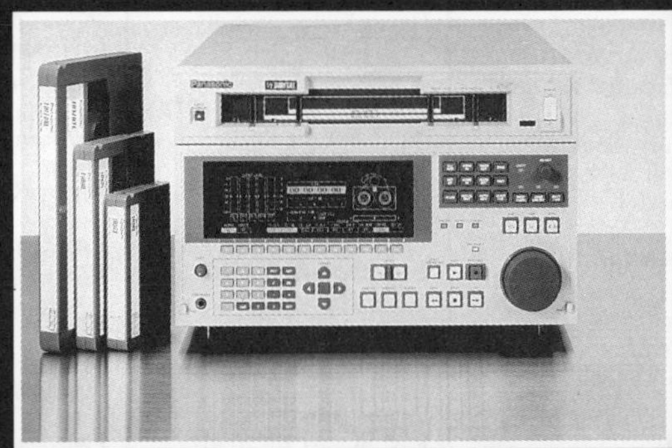

Glendale
Isle of Skye IV56 8FE

Robert Burns Centre Film Theatre
Kenneth Eggo
Dumfries Museum
The Observatory
Dumfries DG2 7SW

Scottish Office Film Society
H MacKenzie
10 Ormelie Terrace
Joppa
Edinburgh EH15 2EX

Shetland Film Club
Mr S Hubbard
Secretary
The Manse, Bridge Road
Burra Isle
Shetland Isles ZE2 9LE

Standard Life Film Society
Mrs Nancy Moore
59 High Street
Cockenzie
East Lothian EH32 0DG

University of Stirling Film Circle
The Secretary
Film/Media Department
Stirling FK9 4LA

Strathclyde University S A Film Society
Michael Daly
Strathclyde University
Students Association
90 John Street
Glasgow G1 1AU

Trinity Academy Film Society
Mr T Ablett
c/o Trinity Academy
Craighall Avenue
Edinburgh EH6 4RT

Tweeddale Film Club
Mrs Jeanette Carlyle
23 Marchmont Road
Edinburgh EH9 1HY

SOUTH EAST

BFFS South East Group

Arundel Festival Film Society
Mr D A Edginton
1 Tower House Gardens
Arundel
West Sussex BN18 9BH

Charterhouse Film Society
Christopher O'Neill
Brooke Hall
Charterhouse
Godalming
Surrey GU7 2DX

Chertsey Film Society
Mr H Lawes
29 Sayes Court
Addlestone
Surrey KT15 1NA

Chichester City Film Society
Mr R Gibson
Westlands, Main Road
Hunston
Chichester
West Sussex PO20 6AL

Cranbrook Film Society
Mrs C Williams
St Helens
Moor Hill
Hawkhurst
Kent TN18 4NY

Cranleigh Film Society
Mr H B Hemingway
9 Hitherwood
Cranleigh
Surrey GU6 8BN

Ditchling Film Society
Mr G Hinckley
11 The Fieldway
Lewes Road
Ditchling
Hassocks
West Sussex BN6 8UA

Dover Film Society
Mr D Antony Pratt
19 Bramley Avenue
Canterbury
Kent CT1 3XW

Eastbourne Film Society
Miss B Wilson
2 Chalk Farm Close
Willingdon
Eastbourne
East Sussex BN20 9HY

Farnham Film Society at the Maltings
Mrs P Woodroffe
c/o The Maltings
Bridge Square
Farnham
Surrey GU9 7QR

Faversham Film Society
Mrs V Cackett
15 South Road
Faversham
Kent ME13 7LR

Hastings Arts Film Society
Mr Robert Brook
4 Martineau Lane
Hastings
East Sussex TN35 5DS

Hastings College Film Society
Helen Dessent
Department of Art & Design
Hastings College of Art & Technology
Archery Road
St Leonards-on-Sea
East Sussex TN38 0HX

Havant College Film Society
Mr P Turner
New Road
Havant
Hants PO9 1QL

Havant Film Society
Mrs P Stallworthy
The Old Town Hall
East Street
Havant
Hants PO9 1BS

Horsham Film Society
Mr Norman Chapman
Farthings
King James Lane
Wenfield
Sussex BN5 9ER

Intimate Cinema Film Society
Mr A Henk
10 Aston Way
Epsom
Surrey KT18 5LZ

Lancing College Film Society
Mr G Jones
Lancing College
Lancing
West Sussex BN15 0RW

Lewes Film Society
Ms Mary Burke
6 Friars Walk
Lewes
East Sussex BN7 2LE

Maidstone Film Society
Libby Bernard
2 White Rock Court
Maidstone
Kent ME16 8HX

Oscar Film Unit
Students Union
University of Surrey
Guildford
Surrey GU2 5XH

Reigate and Redhill Film Society
Mrs A Spice
17 Parkgate Road
Reigate
Surrey RH2 7JL

Royal Holloway and Bedford New College Film Society
Laura Corkell
70 Hythe Park Road
Egham
Surrey TW20 8DA

Stables Film Society
Mr Fred Nash
32 Vale Road
Silverhill
St Leonards-on-Sea
East Sussex TN37 6PS

Steyning Film Society
Mr Tony Golding
3 Clyde Terrace
Station Road
Steyning BN44 3YN

Walton and Weybridge Film Society
Joan Westbrook
28 Eastwick Road
Walton-on-Thames
Surrey KT12 5AD

West Hoathly Film Society
Mrs W Cole
2 Fern Cottage, Sandy Lane
West Hoathly
West Sussex RG19 4QQ

West Kent College Film Society
Mr D B Davies
West Kent College of FE
Brook Street
Tonbridge
Kent TN9 2PN

Woking's New Cinema Club
Mr A Rozelaar
67 Lansdown Close
St Johns
Woking
Surrey GU21 1TG

Worthing Film Society
Karen French
Flat 5, 2 Georges Road
Worthing
West Sussex BN11 2DS

SOUTH WEST

BFFS South West Group
Mr Brian Clay
1 Arbutus Close
Dorchester
Dorset DT1 1PZ

Bath Film Society
Ms Carole Sartain
c/o Royal Photographic Society
Milsom Street
Bath
Avon BA1 1DN

Bath Schools' Film Society
Mrs J Wheals
Oldfield Girls School
Kelston Road
Bath
Avon BA1 9AB

Bath University Film Society
BUFS Secretary
Students Union
University of Bath
Claverton Down
Bath
Avon BA2 7AY

Bideford Film Club
Mr A Whittaker
Factory Cottage
Rope Walk
Bideford
Devon EX39 2NA

Blandford Forum Film Society
Mr J E England
6 Kings Road
Blandford Forum
Dorset DT11 7LD

Bridport Film Society
Mrs M Wood
Greenways
9 Bowhayes
Bridport
Dorset DT6 4EB

Bristol Student Films
The Chairman
University of Bristol
Students Union
Queens Road
Clifton
Bristol BS8 1LN

Cheltenham Film Society
Mrs G Sage
35 Bookway Road
Charlton Kings
Cheltenham
Glos GL53 8HF

The Cinema at the Warehouse
Malcolm Young
33 East Street
Ilminster
Somerset TA19 0AN

Dartington Arts Film Society
The Arts Officer
Dartington Arts Society
Dartington Hall
Totnes
Devon TQ9 6EJ

Dorchester Film Society
Catherine Dyer
12 Victoria Road
Dorchester
Dorset DT1 1SB

Exeter Film Society
Ms H James
16 Pavilion Place
Exeter
Devon EX2 4HR

Exeter University CinSoc
The President
Devonshire Houses
Stocker Road
Exeter
Devon EX4 4PZ

Falmouth School of Art and Design Student Union Film Club
Mr W Flint
Woodlane
Falmouth TR11 4RA

Gloucester Film Society
Mr C Toomey
8 Garden Way
Longlevens
Gloucester GL2 9UL

Holsworthy Film Society
Ms C Wade
Belmont
Trewyn Road
Holsworthy
Devon EX22 9ER

Jersey Film Society
Mr John Christensen
Brooklands
Old Road, Gorey
Jersey
Channel Isles JE3 9EX

Lyme Regis Film Society
Ms Selima Hill
Sundial House
Marine Parade
Lyme Regis
Dorset DT7 3JQ

PSW (Exmouth) Film & Video Society
Mr Peter Powell
34 Morton Road
Exmouth
Devon

Real to Reel Film Society
Athos Piltordou
The Beaford Arts Centre
Beaford
Nr Winkleigh
Devon EX19 8LU

Rolle College Community Arts Group Film Society
Mr J Collins
Rolle College
2 Douglas Avenue
Exmouth
Devon EX8 2AT

Sherborne School Film Society
Mr A Swift
Abbey Road
Sherborne
Dorset DT9 3AP

Stroud and District Film Society
Mrs M G Allington
'Camelot', East Drive
Ebley
Stroud
Glos GL5 4QF

Thornbury Film Society
Mr Gerald Clarke
15 Hyde Avenue
Thornbury
Bristol BS12 1JA

Yeovil Cinematheque
Ms Nina Gilman
42 Bowden Road
Templecombe
Somerset BA8 0LF

SOUTHERN

BFFS Southern Group
Mr Timothy Ffrench-Lynch
32 Wyndham Road
Chatham
Kent

Abingdon College and District Film Society
Mr M Bloom
Abingdon College of FE
Northcourt Road
Abingdon
Oxon 0X14 1NH

Amersham and Chesham Film Society
A W Burrows
Hon Treasurer
73 Lye Green Road
Chesham
Bucks HP5 3NB

The Ashcroft Arts Centre
Mr Richard Finch
Fareham and Gosport Drama Centre
Osborn Road
Fareham
Hants PO16 7DX

Aylesbury Vale Film Society
Mr D M Harding
29 Stock Lane
Aylesbury
Bucks HP21 7RR

Banbury Film Club
Matthew Holder
Laurel Cottage
North Newington
Nr Banbury
Oxon OX15 6AD

Barton Peveril College 6th Form Film Society
Mr T C Meaker
Cedar Road
Eastleigh
Hants SO5 5ZA

Bournemouth and Poole College of Further Education Film Society
Mr T Baber
Learning Resources
Bournemouth and Poole FE College
The Lansdowne
Bournemouth BH1 3JJ

Bournemouth and Poole Film Society
Mrs C Stevenson
15 Milestone Road
Oakdale
Poole
Dorset BH15 3DR

Bracknell Film Society
Mrs Shelagh Barnett
35 Spinis
Roman Wood
Bracknell
Berks RG12 4XA

Bradford on Avon Film Society
Neil McDougall
4 Wine Street
Bradford on Avon
Wiltshire BA15 1NS

Eton College Film Society
Mr Adam Pettitt
2 Common Lane
Eton College
Windsor
Berks

Harwell Film Society
Ms J Allan
B150 AERE
Harwell
Didcot
Oxon OX11 0RA

Henley-on-Thames Film Society
Mr P Whitaker
10 St Andrews Road
Henley-on-Thames
Oxon RG9 1HP

Newbury Film Society
Miss Anne Marshall
11 Falkland Garth
Wash Common
Newbury
Berks RG14 6PA

Open Film Society
Mr D J Pimm
c/o Maths Department
Open University
Walton Hall
Milton Keynes
Bucks MK7 6AA

Radley College Film Society
Mr C R Barker
Radley College
Abingdon
Oxon OX14 2HR

Rewley House Film Theatre Club
M J Shallis
Rewley House (Dept Ext Studies)
1 Wellington Square
Oxford OX1 2JA

Salisbury Film Society
Mrs S Collier
45 St Ann's Street
Salisbury
Wilts SP1 2DX

Shaftesbury Arts Centre Film Society
Mr P Schilling
Sheepwash Cottage
Burton, Mere
Warminster
Wilts BA12 6BR

Slough Co-operative Film Society
Dr Jo Hughes
1 Vanstone Cottages
Bagshot Road
Englefield Green
Egham
Surrey TW20 0RS

Southampton Film Theatre - The Phoenix
Dr Peter Street
24 The Parkway
Bassett
Southampton SO2 3PQ

Union Films, Southampton University
Southampton University Students' Union
Highfield
Southampton SO9 5NH

Swindon Film Society
Ms Carolyn Hardy
35 Greywethers Avenue
Swindon
Wilts SN3 1QG

Trowbridge College Film Society
Ms Antoinette Midgley
Dept of General and Social Studies
Trowbridge College
College Road
Trowbridge
Wilts BA14 0ES

West End Centre (Aldershot) Film Society
Ms J Bowden
West End Centre
Queens Road
Aldershot
Hants GU11 3JD

Winchester College Film Society
Mr P J M Roberts
Winchester College
Winchester
Hants SO23 9NA

Winchester Film Society
Ms A Rushworth
2 Chilbolton Avenue
Winchester
Hants SO22 5HH

Windsor Arts Centre Film Society
Mr C Brooker
St Leonards Road
Windsor
Berks SL4 3DB

Wolfson College Film Society
Ms Kathy Whittaker
Wolfson College
Oxford OX2 6UD

WALES

BFFS Welsh Group
Bryn Roberts
52 Radyr Avenue
Mayals
Swansea
West Glamorgan

Canton Film Appreciation Group
Mr Dennis C Pope
c/o 235 Cowbridge Road
East Canton
Cardiff CF1 9AL

Fishguard Film Society
Ms J Worsley
Church Hill House
Treffgarne
Haverfordwest
Dyfed SA62 5PH

Gweithdy Fidio Cymunedol Scrin
Robin Williams
Gweithdy Scrin
Safle ATS
Ffordd Bangor
Caernarfon
Gwynedd LL55 1AR

Haverfordwest Film Society
Mrs J Evans
25 Greenhill Crescent
Merlins Bridge
Haverfordwest
Dyfed SA61 1LX

Phoenix Film Club
Ms S Hallam
48 Barrack Hill
Newport
Gwent NP9 5FY

Presteigne Film Society
Mr R Scadding
Llugw Farm
Llanbister Road
Llandrindod Wells
Powys

Theatr Mwldan Film Society
Ms Helen Steel
Theatr Mwldan
Cardigan
Dyfed SA43 1JY

Trinity Film Society
Mr Jeremy Webb
Brynhyfryd
Talog
Carmarthen
Dyfed SA33 6NZ

YORKSHIRE

BFFS Yorkshire Group
Mr Richard Fort
Yorkshire Group
8 Bradley Grove
Silsden
Keighley
West Yorks BD20 9LX

Ampleforth Film Society
Rev S P Wright
Junior House
Ampleforth College
York YO6 4EN

Bradford Film Society
Ms Fiona Bradford
29 Northdale Road
Frizinghall
Bradford
West Yorks

University of Bradford Union Film Society
The Secretary
Richmond Road
Bradford
West Yorks BD7 1DP

Friends of the Grange Film Society for the Disabled
Mrs Joan Goldsack
23 Scarborough Terrace
York YO3 6UL

Giggleswick School Film Society
Mr J R Pennell
Giggleswick School
Settle
North Yorks BD24 0DE

Halifax Playhouse Film Club
Mr Paul S Cairns
23 Plane Tree Nest
Halifax
West Yorks HX2 7PR

Harrogate Film Society
Mr P Caunt
19 Keats Walk
Harrogate
North Yorks HG1 3LN

Hebden Bridge Film Society
Ms Sue Bower
4 Cornholme Terrace
Cornholme
Todmorden
Lancs OL14 8NH

Ilkley Film Society
Mr R J Fort
8 Bradley Grove
Silsden
Keighley
West Yorks BD20 9LX

Lynchpin Film Society
Doj Graham
2 Sunnybank Court
Sunnybank
Denby Dale
West Yorks HD8 8TJ

Scarborough Film Society
Mr A E Davison
29 Peasholm Drive
Scarborough
North Yorks Y012 7NA

Sheffield University SU Film Unit
The Chair
Student Union
Sheffield University
Western Bank
Sheffield S10 2TG

York University Film Society
Mr Jason Stratford
Students' Union
Goodricke College
Heslington
York Y01 5DD

FUNDING

The list below is representative of the schemes available at any current time, but not definitive since the volatile nature of funding, both public and private, means that schemes emerge and fall by the wayside unpredictably. These funding schemes cover development, distribution, exhibition etc as well as production. The funds available fall into three main categories: direct grants, production finance and reimbursable loans. Where possible approximate closing dates are given, however it is advisable to check directly with the institution. In almost all cases these schemes are not open to students

Access for Disabled People to Arts Premises Today (ADAPT)

45 Harrington Gardens
London SW7 4JV
Tel: 071 373 8121
Contact: Derek Lodge
A charitable trust which provides matching funds to arts venues who are trying to make themselves accessible to at least one class of disabled person. Grants made between £1,000 and £25,000. All work, be it the installation of sound loops or lifts, to be carried out to British standards. Venues must be in England, Scotland or Wales. A Northern Ireland scheme is being set up. To date two cinemas have been in receipt of funds. Rolling scheme; no closing date

Arts Council of Great Britain

14 Great Peter Street
London SW1P 3NQ
Tel: 071 333 0100
Fax: 071 973 6590
Under the umbrella department of Film, Video and Broadcasting, the Arts Council supports three areas of arts film and video production:
Documentaries on the Arts: professionally made arts documentaries by independent production companies, and primarily intended for TV distribution. Any arts activity eligible for Arts Council support is within the terms of reference, plus related subjects such as architecture, crafts, popular culture etc. The committee meets four times a year. Dates available on request
Black Arts Video Project Awards: made to video makers for the production of non-broadcast videos on Black arts subjects. Awards are given on the basis of an agreed budget with a ceiling figure of £10,000 at the time of writing. Awards are made annually
The Artists Film & Video Committee: supports the production, promotion and exhibition of experimental, innovative and avant-garde film and video. It currently supports production in the following ways: Arts Council/Channel 4 11th Hour Production Awards (budget range of £10,000-£20,000), advertised nationally, next deadline likely to be 31 January 1992; Arts Council/Channel 4 Animation Production Awards (budget range of £10,000-£20,000) for innovative animation projects, deadline likely to be 15 February 1992; Regional Commissions: funds are made available to regionally based organisations such as galleries on a one-off basis for the commissioning of film and video installations. Calls for applications from artists appear in the art press throughout the year, details on request; Artists Film & Video Committee Awards: Large Awards for film & video artists' major projects (£3,000-£9,000), Small Awards supporting low-budget productions (£1,000-£4,000) for recent graduates or artists new to Arts Council funding. Large and Small Awards open to artists resident in England only, closing date likely to be beginning of October

Association of Black Film and Video Workshops

Unit 215
22 Highbury Grove
London N5 2EA
Tel: 071 359 0302
Contact: Geoff Morris
Advises on funding. For other areas of work see under Organisations

BBC Animation Fund

BBC Bristol
Production Office
Whiteladies Road
Bristol BS8 2LR
Tel: 0272 732211

Producer: Colin Rose
New commissions or bought-in work of adult animation by experienced animators. No closing date

BBC Bristol Television Features

Production Office
BBC South & West
Whiteladies Road
Bristol BS8 2LR
Tel: 0272 732211
Producer: Colin Rose
10 x 10 is an initiative to encourage and develop new and innovative film making talent through the provision of limited production finance for 10-minute films, combined with unlimited practical guidance from experienced producer-directors. The scheme is open to any director with no previous credit on broadcast TV, this includes film school students. No closing date

BFI Exhibition and Distribution Division

21 Stephen Street
London W1P 1PL
Tel: 071 255 1444
Fax: 071 436 7950
Head of Division: Ian Christie
Deputy/Head of Exhibition Services: Jayne Pilling
Administers direct grant funding of around £550,000 (1991-2) to a range of exhibition clients mainly within the regional film theatre network. Also offers one-off and short-term funding to applicants from the cultural film exhibition sector through the Regional Project Fund (approx. £30,000 in 1991-92)

BFI Planning Unit

21 Stephen Street
London W1P 1PL
Tel: 071 255 1444
Fax: 071 436 7950
Head of Division: Irene Whitehead
The Planning Unit is responsible for 60% of the Institute's external funding: £1,584,507 in the form of 3-year 'block grants' to Regional Arts Boards (see separate heading below) mainly used to support ongoing revenue expenditure by their clients and schemes such as production, exhibition etc; a Development Budget of £435,000 operates on incentive funding rules and mainly by invitation. Projects funded include media centres, production and training resource centres etc. £50,000 of this sum is reserved for equal opportunities (priority for people with disabilities)

BFI Production

29 Rathbone Street
London W1P 1AG
Tel: 071 636 5587
Fax: 071 780 9456
Head of Production: Ben Gibson
Three areas of production finance:

Low budget features, theatrical documentaries and script development
Application on a script or treatment basis. Unsolicited manuscripts and general applications are responded to within 4-6 weeks. The Production Board, a collection of industry representatives, meets every two months to consider shortlisted applications. Features are not generally fully financed by the BFI, every feature project taken on will involve a fund-raising element. The BFI offers a wide range of production relationships and holds legal and financial control once a project is taken on. Films on Super 16 or 35mm only. Two to three features produced in any one year

New Directors Scheme
Executive Producer: Kate Ogborn
For film and video makers who are in the early stages of their careers or for people changing careers. Aims to produce 6-8 productions a year with a budget ceiling of £27,500, all productions to be made under Equity and ACTT agreements. Advertised annually in November; submissions accepted in January with final selection made by May

Production Projects Fund
Director: Steve Brookes
Offers grant support to innovative, low budget film and video production in Scotland, Wales, London and English regions. The Fund emphasises development and is unlikely to fully fund projects. Applicants are encouraged to seek other funders (public sector or industry). Open for applications for development, completion, equipment (up to £5,000), and production (up to £30,000). Small amounts of money are also available for cultural projects not directly production based. (At time of writing Production Projects is set up for once yearly application. A rolling format of 3 times a year is planned, details from the Director). In addition there is a Sales and Distribution arm which sells BFI produced films to foreign territories and launches or distributes them in the UK

British Council

11 Portland Place
London W1N 4EJ
Tel: 071 389 3065
Fax: 071 389 3199
Contacts: Jo Morris & Robert Turnock
Does not provide direct funds to filmmakers but can assist in the coordination and shipping of films to festivals, and in some cases can provide funds for the filmmaker to attend when invited

British Screen Finance

37-39 Oxford Street
London W1R 1RE
Tel: 071 434 0291
Fax: 071 434 9933
Contact: Annette Caulkin
Invests in British films or films made under co-production treaties with other countries. Scripts should be submitted with full background information to Annette Caulkin. All scripts are read. Scripts that are part of production package are preferred, and the project must have commercial potential as a theatrical release. Total budget should not exceed £3,000,000. British Screen's contribution rarely exceeds £500,000

Channel 4/MOMI Animation Award

Museum of the Moving Image
South Bank
London SE1 8XT
Tel 071 928 3535
Contact: Animation Coordinator
Four Professional Residencies are awarded to young or first time animators. A fee of £2,250 plus a budget of up to £1,000 towards materials. At the end of residency at MOMI, project will be considered for commission by Channel 4. (Likely deadline end of August 1992)

Department of Trade & Industry (DTI)

2nd Floor Grey
151 Buckingham Palace Road
London SW1W 9SS
Tel: 071 215 1761
Fax: 071 215 1971
For Co-productions: Les Mondry (071 215 1723)
For Media/Eureka: Angela Knell (071 215 1730)
For ECPF: Pauline Givens (071 215 1757)
Carries out Government policy concerning the commercial and business aspects of the film, video and cinema industries, and the administration of the UK's Co-Production agreements. The DTI helps fund the UK contribution to the MEDIA programme and provides funding for the European Co-Production Fund, administered by British Screen Finance

EUROCREATION UK see under ***European and Pan-European Sources*** below

First Film Foundation
Canalot Production Studios
222 Kensal Road
London W10 5BN
Tel: 081 969 5195
Fax: 081 960 6302
Administrator: Deborah Burton
A non-profit making organisation which has charitable status, First Film supports new film makers by advising on specific projects, offering development funding or seeking funding from other sources, and eventually seeking finance for production. Acts as the umbrella organisation for First Film Europe (see under European and Pan-European Sources below)

Fulbright Awards
The Fulbright Commission
6 Porter Street
London W1M 2HR
Tel: 071 486 7697
Programme director: Catherine Boyle
Open to all (including film and video makers) intending to undertake postgraduate work at an American educational establishment. Details of closing date on application

MEDIA 95
see under ***European and Pan-European Sources*** below

The Nicholl Fellowships
Academy of Motion Picture Arts and Sciences
Dept K, 8949 Wilshire Boulevard
Beverly Hills
CA 90211
USA
Annual screen writing fellowship awards. Up to five fellowships of $20,000 each to new screenwriters. Write for rules and application form

Sarah Noble Memorial Fund
29 Albany Street
Edinburgh EH1 3QN
Set up in 1987 to commemorate the life and work of filmmaker Sarah Noble by supporting video, photography, slide-tape and film projects in the following areas: women's issues, peace and the environment, health and Third World development. Annual award

The Prince's Trust
8 Bedford Row
London WC1R 4BA
Contact: Anne Engel
The Richard Mills Travel Fellowship, offered in association with the Gulbenkian Foundation and the Peter S Cadbury Trust. It offers 3 grants of £1,000 for people working in community arts in the areas of housing, minority arts, special needs, or arts for young people, especially the unemployed. One grant is applicable to people up to 35, the others up to 30

Scottish Film Council
Dowanhill
74 Victoria Crescent Road
Glasgow G12 9JN
Tel: 041 334 4445
Fax: 041 334 8132
Director: David Bruce
Deputy Director: Erica King
Annual production awards scheme (4 categories from £100-£5,000). Project grants are available to SFC revenue clients. Projects grants are also made for developing exhibition opportunities in Scotland

Scottish Film Production Fund
74 Victoria Crescent Road
Glasgow G12 9JN
Tel: 041 337 2526
Contact: Ivan Mactaggart
The fund aims to foster and develop film and video production in Scotland. Production fund committee meets quarterly to consider applications ranging from documentaries through to feature films. All productions must have particular connection with and relevance to Scotland. Total resources this financial year £230,000

REGIONAL ARTS BOARDS

Arts Board: North West
12 Harter Street
Manchester M1 6HY
Tel: 061 228 3062
Fax: 061 236 5361

Eastern Arts Board
Cherry Hinton Hall
Cherry Hinton Road
Cambridge CB1 4DW
Tel: 0223 215355
Fax: 0223 248075

East Midlands Arts Board
Mountfields House
Forest Road
Loughborough
LE11 3HU
Tel: 0509 218292
Script development up to £500; Production bursaries up to £500; Production grants up to £10,000; Biennial grants of £25,000 or more. Small awards made for exhibition, group and individual training and distribution. Details on application

London Arts Board
Coriander Building
20 Gainsford Street
London SE1
Tel: 071 403 9013
At time of going to press, no details were available as to the continuance or otherwise of LAB's film and video schemes. Those living in the Greater London region should consult the entries for BFI Production and The Arts Council

Northern Arts Board
9-10 Osborne Terrace
Jesmond
Newcastle-upon-Tyne
NE2 1NZ
Tel: 091 281 6334
Fax: 091 281 3276
Northern Arts has established a Media Investment Fund in order to encourage and support film and video projects within the Northern Arts region. All activities supported by the fund must: be of benefit to the region; contribute to the development of media in the region; use the region's skills and facilities where possible. Applications can be made to the fund under 5 categories:
Script development up to £3,000 (if taken up by a commercial company grant is paid back in full by the first day of principal shoot)
Pilot projects up to £2,000: short tapes which give the style and feel of a production in order to attract further funding
Production: the full amount will be considered for short experimental productions up to £3,000 or productions up to £10,000. Part funding up to £10,000 will be given to productions over £10,000 or completion monies for post-production on work not funded by Northern Arts
Time Limited Development projects: rotation funding of projects on a two, sometimes three year basis
Capital: the fund will consider applications from non-profit distribution organisations for capital support but not more than 50% of the total cost. The fund is normally available twice yearly, closing dates in February and September. Full details of all the above on application

South-East Arts Board
10 Mount Ephraim
Tunbridge Wells
Kent TN4 8AS
Tel: 0892 515210
Take One (for information see Southern Arts entry below). Production grants of up to £10,000 awarded for full or part funding of films or videos from

makers who have previous work to show. Production grants for beginners with no film or video to show in support of application. Training budget of £5,000 earmarked for organisations in the region mounting courses. Applications are also accepted from individuals wishing to attend courses not available in the region, max. £500. Full details given on application

South West Arts Board

Bradninch Place
Gandy Street
Exeter EX4 3LS
Tel: 0392 218188
Two categories of annual production awards:
Individual 'first time' – materials only projects (usually up to £500)
Production groups and co-operatives towards their on-going production programme (usually up to £2,000)
Occasional one-off major awards are made for collaborations with regionally based ITV or BBC companies; these are widely advertised. Financial support is offered for exhibition of independent 'art-house', historic, experimental and community films and videos

Southern Arts Board

13 St Clement Street
Winchester
Hants SO23 9DQ
Tel: 0962 855099
Workshop production grants up to £500; individual film and video production grants up to £3,000. Annual David Altshul award of £1,000 for excellence in film and video, open to young film and video makers (under 30 on 1st Dec 1991) in the Southern Arts region. Take One TVS/Southern Arts/South East Arts production scheme open to film and video makers in the early stages of their career (including students in higher education). A script appraisal service offers an objective opinion from a professional writer or critic for £5.00 and is open to writers living in the region. Full details on all the above on application

Welsh Arts Council

Holst House
Museum Place
Cardiff CF1 3NX
Tel: 0222 394711

West Midlands Arts Board

82 Granville Street
Birmingham B1 2LH
Tel: 021 631 3121
Two main schemes in operation:
Materials: only designed for beginners or first time film and video makers, pre-production development up to £500 or materials post-production up to £3,000
Salaried production: pre-production script development up to £7,000; Low Budget Production Fund £15,000-£20,000 and post-production up to £10,000
Other areas of cultural film and video work supported include marketing, training, exhibition and education. Co-productions in the area of script development and productions are also being developed. Details of all the above on application

Yorkshire and Humberside Arts Board

Glyde House
Glydegate
Bradford BD5 0BQ
Tel: 0274 723051
(future location to be decided)
Two schemes in operation:
Film and Video Production Awards (1992-93): awards from £4,000 to £7,000 from a total budget of £11,500. Applications welcome from experienced directors for videos and 16mm films (under Code of Practice). Application forms and deadline details available from the Media Secretary
Community Video Scheme: grants of around £500 for community groups seeking to redress exclusion from or misrepresentation in the mass media, using video (or 8mm) to articulate concerns and interests. Rolling scheme with no deadlines. Application forms available from Media Secretary

EUROPEAN AND PAN-EUROPEAN SOURCES

Audio-Visual EUREKA

Avenue des Arts 44
1040 Brussels
Belgium
Tel: (32) 2 511 06 40
Fax: (32) 2 512 91 66
Industry-led and financed project to encourage collaboration between European firms on EUREKA projects. More information available from Angela Knell at the DTI (071 215 1730)

Carat Espace Academy

La Grande Arche
1 place du Parvis
Cedex 41
92044 Paris La Défense
France
Tel: (33) 1 40 90 32 50
Fax: (33) 1 40 90 33 12
Grants of 200,000FFr over 10 month period available to applicants under 30 to assist specific TV projects (programming, marketing, law, production). Attendance at European TV events and seminars is also arranged, and personal expenses covered. Closing date May 1992

EURIMAGES

B.P. 431 R6
67006 Strasbourg
France
Tel: (33) 88 61 49 61
Fax: (33) 88 36 70 57
Executive Secretary: Ryclef Rienstra
Supports co-productions through advances on box-office receipts up to 20% of cost, ceiling of 5,000,000FFr. Information and applications for assistance available from the Executive Secretary. Four deadlines a year

EUROCREATION (Paris)

rue Debelleyme 3
75003 Paris
France
Tel: (33) 1 48 04 78 79
Fax: (33) 1 40 29 92 46
Eurocreation: Anne-Marie Autissier
Venture Capital: Eric Grimaldi
Eurocreation Conseil: Gilles Roussel
A French agency for young (18-30) European creators to assist innovative and experimental projects in sciences, technology, communications and audio-visuals, cultural production, distribution, tourism and environment. Finance up to 40% through venture capital investment (up to 700,000FFr) and through co-production (up to 300,000FFr).
Eurocreation Conseil is a consultancy service in areas of technological innovation, programme definition, training and youth

EUROCREATION UK

c/o The Prince's Trust
8 Bedford Row
London WC1R 4BA
Tel: 071 430 0524
Fax: 071 831 7289
Contact: Anne Engel
Two non-repayable grants available ('Go and See' up to £500, and 'Go Ahead' up to £10,000) for young people under 26 with ideas for European partnerships in arts, crafts, design, tourism, communications, technology and the environment. Application is direct to Eurocreation UK. Larger project ideas should be sent to Eurocreation Paris

European Co-Production Association

c/o ZDF
Essenheimerstrasse
PO Box 4040
6500 Mainz

Germany
Tel: (49) 6131 705168
Fax: (49) 6131 78060
A consortium of European public service TV networks for the co-production of TV fiction series. Can offer complete finance. Development funding is also possible. Proposals should consist of full treatment, financial plan and details of proposed co-production partners. Projects are proposed directly to Secretariat or to member national broadcasters (Channel 4 in UK)

European Co-Production Fund

c/o British Screen Finance
37-39 Oxford Street
London W1R 1RE
Tel: 071 434 0291
Fax: 071 434 9933
The aim of the ECF is to enable UK producers to collaborate in the making of films which the European market wishes to see made but which could not be made without its involvement. The ECF offers commercial loans, up to 30% of the total budget, for full length feature films intended for theatrical release. Producers who are citizens or residents of an EC member state and who have companies incorporated in the EC may apply. The film must be a co-production involving at least two production companies, with no link of common ownership, established in two separate EC states

European Fellowship Awards

Awards Department
CRE
10 Conseil-Général
1211 Geneva 4
Switzerland
Tel: (41) 22 29 26 44
Contact: Dr Andris Barblan
A scheme by the Standing Conference of Rectors, Presidents and Vice-Chancellors of the European Universities and the Times Higher Educational Supplement. It promotes academic exchanges amongst Europe's universities. Staff (academic and administrative) and advanced students engaged in teaching or research are eligible for awards. The fellowship must be used to study or do research in another European country. The award could be made for the attachment of a member of staff to another university; for a short study tour; a staff exchange between universities; an attachment of an advanced student to another university for research projects or training programmes

Film Fonds Hamburg

Friedensallee 14-16
2000 Hamburg 50
Germany
Tel: (49) 40 390 5883
Fax: (49) 40 390 62 49
Contacts: Eva Hubert, Dieter Kosslick
Producers of cinema films can apply for a subsidy of up to 2 million German marks – amounting to at most 30% of the overall production costs of the finished film. Foreign producers can also apply for this support, whether for German co-productions or entirely foreign productions. Financial support provided by the Film Fonds can be used in combination with other private or public funding, including that of TV networks

First Film Europe

Canalot Studios
222 Kensal Road
London W10 5BN
Tel: 081 969 5195
Coordinator: Angeli Macfarlane
The First Film Foundation operates a development fund for its pan-European feature film programme First Film Europe. Sponsored by Kodak it helps new writers and directors through critical stages in the development of films by employing a 'godfather' system where new directors are advised by senior directors

The MEDIA 95 Programme

Ten projects dealing with various aspects of the film and television industries

BABEL (Broadcasting Across the Barriers of European Language)

c/o European Broadcasting Union
Case Postale 67
1218 Grand Saconnex
Geneva
Switzerland
Tel: (41) 22 717 21 11
Fax: (41) 22 798 58 97
Chairman: Michael Johnson
Coordinator: Frank Naef
Promotes multi-lingual approaches to post-production and distribution of European audio-visual productions. Non-reimbursable grants of up to 50% of post-production budget. Priority given to completed productions in less widely spoken languages. Eligible projects: cultural documentaries, magazines, series pilots, dramas (especially for children or young people), research projects into post-production techniques, training schemes. Details of application deadlines available from BABEL's offices, along with application forms which should be submitted with synopsis, confirmation of broadcaster interest and VHS cassette of production

CARTOON (European Association for Animated Film)

Rue Franz Merjay 127
1060 Brussels
Belgium
Tel: (32) 2 347 2870
Fax: (32) 2 347 2347
General Secretary: Marc Vandeweyer
Director: Corinne Jenart
Promotes major animation productions in European studios. Reimbursable loans are available for near-funded projects (at least 66%), pre-production and series pilots and development of training. Provides a data base on European animation (access free of charge). Open to professionals on a national membership basis, though non-members may also apply. National membership details from Jayne Pilling, BFI, 21 Stephen Street, London W1P 1PL
Tel: 071 255 1444.
Fax: 071 436 7950

EAVE (European Audio-visual Entrepreneurs)

Rue de la Presse 14
1000 Brussels
Belgium
Tel: (32) 2 511 9032
Fax: (32) 2 511 0279
Managing Director: Raymond Ravar
EAVE (UK)
c/o Blake Friedmann
37-41 Gower Street
London WC1E 6HH
Tel: 071 631 4331
UK Coordinator: Julian Friedmann
Development of European productions and creation of network of producers through three one-week workshops over a year. Attending producers must cover costs, though some assistance is available through national coordinators

EFDO (European Film Distribution Office)

Europäisches Film Büro
Friedensallee 14-16
2000 Hamburg 50
Germany
Tel: (49) 40 390 9025
Fax: (49) 40 390 6249
Assists European distribution of low-budget European features through reimbursable interest-free loans. Eligibility: groups of distributors from no less than 3 European countries. Application deadlines available from EFDO offices

EURO-AIM (Audio-visual Market for Independent Producers)
Rue des Minimes 26
1000 Brussels
Belgium
Tel: (32) 2 518 1460
Fax: (32) 2 512 8657
President: Karol Kulik
Supports independent production companies in the festival market place, and seeks to attract international buyers to European independent productions. Access to a data-bank and legal, technical and commercial assistance are provided. Application forms available from EURO-AIM or from:
Lori Keating
The Producers' Association
Paramount House
162-170 Wardour Street
London W1V 4LA
Tel: 071 437 7700
Fax: 071 734 4464

EVE (Espace Vidéo Européen)
c/o Irish Film Institute
6 Eustace Street
Dublin 2
Ireland
Tel: (353) 1 679 5744
Fax: (353) 1 679 9657
Chief Executive: John Dick
EVE's main purpose is to increase the supply of European product onto the video market, by offering advances on receipts to European publishers (up to 40%, ceiling of ECU 20,000). EVE also provides a database for video publishers. Application forms for loans are available from EVE offices, along with deadline details

Euro Media Garanties
66 Rue Pierre Charron
75008 Paris
France
Tel: (33) 1 43 59 88 03
Fax: (33) 1 45 63 85 58
President: Georges Prost
Offers guarantees of bank loans through a fund to financial operators involved in European film and audiovisual productions. Projects to involve two other member countries of the Council of Europe. Credit required for financing can be guaranteed by EMG up to 70%. Applications to be submitted in French to the EMG offices.

European Script Fund
39c Highbury Place
London N5 1QP
Tel: 071 226 9903
Fax: 071 354 2706
Applications Coordinator: Karen Street
Assists the development of scripts that are of European interest, through loans reimbursable on production. Applications welcome from producer/writer, director/writer teams, and from individual writers. For team applications awards of 20-80% may be made. Next application deadline: 30 November 1991. Forms available by post

MAP-TV (Memory Archives Programmes)
c/o INA
Avenue de l'Europe 4
94366 Bry-sur-Marne Cedex
France
Tel: (33) 1 49 83 27 20/ 49 83 27 44/5
Fax: (33) 1 49 83 25 97
Chairman: Jean Cherasse
Assists the production and broadcast of archive-based work, of interest to European audiences and dealing with questions of their respective identities. Loans will not exceed 50% of development budget (ceiling fixed at ECU 40,000). Applications welcome from any independent European producer with an agreement in principle from 2 potential co-producers from 2 other countries and from at least 1 broadcaster or video-tape distributor. Forms available by post. Next application deadlines: 15 November 1991, 15 February 1992

Media Investment Club
Avenue de l'Europe 4
94366 Bry-sur-Marne Cedex
France
Tel: (33) 1 49 83 32 72/ 49 83 23 22
Fax: (33) 1 49 83 25 82
President: Ian Maxwell
Secretary General: Patrick Madelin
The Club (whose members include industrial companies, communications groups and financial organisations) acts as co-producer for audio-visual productions in pioneering areas of new technology, through reimbursable loans (up to 50% of total budget). Application is by proposal, including precise technical description of project, detailed cost estimate, financial plan, potential partners and the conditions under which it will take place (time limits, participating parties, rights required). Applications may be submitted at any time

Media Venture
SEFI – EFEG
10 Boulevard Royal
2449 Luxembourg
Tel: (352) 46 07 10
Fax: (352) 46 07 11
Contact: J P Bouillot
Investment in commercial film and TV projects and selected production companies, for major feature films, large budget TV series and soap opera. Further information available directly from Media Venture

INTERNATIONAL SALES

These companies acquire the rights to audiovisual product for sale to foreign distributors in all media (see also Distributors (Theatrical) and (Non-Theatrical) p134)

All American Leisure Group UK
6 Woodland Way
Petts Wood
Kent BR5 1ND
Tel: 0689 871535/871519
Fax: 0689 871519

Allied Vision
Avon House
360 Oxford Street
London W1N 9HA
Tel: 071 409 1984
Fax: 071 493 4286
Peter McRae
Catherine Peak

Arts Council of Great Britain
14 Great Peter Street
London SW1P 3NQ
Tel: 071 333 0100
Fax: 071 973 6590
Distributes Arts Council funded films such as *Science and Light: Joseph Wright of Derby, Hidden Heritage* and *Word of Mouth.* Also distributes films by independent producers including *Haydn's Creation, Hoppla* and *Brian Eno: Imaginary Landscapes.*
See also under Organisations

August Entertainment
10 Arminger Road
London W12 7BB
Tel: 081 742 9099
Fax: 081 742 9311
Eleanor Powell
Emma Crawford
International sales agent for independent producers. Films include *The Lawnmower Man, Isabelle Eberhardt, Dingo, Where Sleeping Dogs Lie, Strawberry Fields, The Closer*

Australian Film Commission
2nd Floor
Victory House
99-101 Regent Street
London W1R 7HB
Tel: 071 734 9383
Fax: 071 434 0170
Sue Murray
UK representative for Beyond International, Australia

BBC Enterprises
Woodlands
80 Wood Lane
London W12 0TT
Tel: 081 743 5588/ 576 2000
Fax: 081 749 0538
Paul Holland
Commercial exploitation and export of BBC product, including books, records and programmes edited as videograms for consumer and educational markets. Also responsible for BBC television co-productions and BBC magazines ('Radio Times', 'BBC Wildlife', 'Fast Forward', 'BBC Good Food' and 'World')

bfi BFI Production
29 Rathbone Street
London W1P 1AG
Tel: 071 636 5587
Fax: 071 580 9456
Sue Bruce-Smith
Sales and distribution of own BFI Production films *Young Soul Rebels, Silent Scream, Melancholia, Distant Voices, Still Lives, On the Black Hill, New Directors Shorts* and Peter Greenaway Shorts

Jane Balfour Films
Burghley House
35 Fortess Road
London NW5 1AD
Tel: 071 267 5392
Fax: 071 267 4241
Jane Balfour
Mary Barlow
Ashley Luke
Distribution agent for Channel 4 and independent producers, handling drama, documentaries and specialised feature films

The Box Office
3 Market Mews
London W1Y 7HH
Tel: 071 499 3968
Fax: 071 491 0008
Paul Shields
International film and television consultancy.

British Home Entertainment
20 High Street
Walton on Thames
Surrey KT12 1DA
Tel: 0932 228832
Fax: 0932 247759
Clive Williamson

CBC TV Programme Sales
43-51 Great Titchfield Street
London W1P 8DD
Tel: 071 580 0336
Fax: 071 323 5658
Susan Hewitt Jolley
Sabine Kanngiesser
Yvonne Body
Véronique Vergès
The marketing division of Canadian Broadcasting Corporation and Société Radio-Canada

CBS Broadcast International Europe
1 Red Place
London W1Y 3RE
Tel: 071 355 4422
Fax: 071 355 4429
Sonja Mendes
Anne Hirsch
Wide range of US TV product

CTVC
Beeson's Yard
Bury Lane
Rickmansworth
Herts WD3 1DS
Tel: 0923 777933
Fax: 0923 896368
Peter Leeming
Programmes that explore human values, including dramas, documentaries and children's programming

Castle Target International
29 Barwell Business Park
Leatherhead Road
Chessington
Surrey KT9 2NY

Tel: 081 974 1021
Fax: 081 974 2674
Ric Phillips
An international distributor of quality feature films. Currently involved with *Buddy's Song, The Monk, That Summer of White Roses* and *Conspiracy*

Central Television Enterprises
43-45 Portman Square
London W1H 9FG
Tel: 071 486 6688
Fax: 071 486 1707
Philip Jones
Anthony Utley
Evi Nicoupolis
Sale of all Central TV-produced films and TV programmes, amounting currently to a 2,000-hour catalogue

Channel 4 International
60 Charlotte Street
London W1P 2AX
Tel: 071 631 4444
Fax: 071 580 2622
Frances Berwick
Where Channel 4 retains sales rights in its programmes, they are handled either through this in-house programme sales operation or through its approved distributors and sales agents. For film sales, see Film Four International

Chatsworth Television
97-99 Dean Street
London W1V 5RA
Tel: 071 734 4302
Fax: 071 437 3301
Halina Stratton
Extensive library of documentary and special interest films. Also Chatsworth-produced light entertainment, drama and adventure series

Colstar Communications and Entertainment
11 Wythburn Place
London W1H 5WL
Tel: 071 437 5725
Fax: 071 706 1704
International distributors of broadcast programming for all media; documentaries, short films, drama, programme specials and series. Library includes films and series on art, the sciences, history, sport and nature. Titles include *The National Gallery – A Private View* series, *Kenneth Clark's Romantic Classic Art* series, *The Wandering Company, The Life and Times of Lord Mountbatten* series, *The Monkey's Paw, The Man Who Loves Giants, Journey to Australia's Inland Sea, The Most Dangerous Animal, Australian Tales of Mystery and Treasure, Beyond Reach, The Contortionist, The Snow Queen, A Portait of James Ensor, Codename Schlier, Ixok – Woman*

Columbia Pictures Television
19 Wells Street
London W1P 3FP
Tel: 071 637 8444
Fax: 071 528 8849
Nick Bingham
Production and co-production of TV product and international distribution of Columbia's and Tri-Star's feature films and TV product

CORI Distribution Group
19 Albemarle Street
London W1X 3HA
Tel: 071 493 7920
Fax: 071 493 8088
Marie Hoy
Fiona Mitchell
Bob Jenkins
Involved in international sales and co-production funding, with offices in London and Los Angeles. Recent acquisitions include American Playhouse, including the titles *André's Mother, Another Place, Sunset Gang;* the features *Paper Marriage, Waiting* and *Dr. M;* children's special *Klondike Christmas* and the cartoon series *Wicked Willie*

Dee & Co
Suite 204
Canalot
222 Kensal Road
London W10 5BN
Tel: 081 960 2712
Fax: 081 960 2728
Drew Ellicott
Specialists in the distribution of nature and environmental programmes. Catalogue contains selected award winning films

The Walt Disney Company
31-32 Soho Square
London W1V 6AP
Tel: 071 734 8111
Fax: 071 734 5619
Etienne de Villiers
Ed Borgerding
Worldwide television distribution arm of a major US production company

English Film Co (Exports)
6 Woodland Way
Petts Wood
Kent BR5 1ND
Tel: 0689 871535/871519
Fax: 0689 871519

Film Four International
60 Charlotte Street
London W1P 2AX
Tel: 071 631 4444
Fax: 071 580 2622
Bill Stephens
Heather Playford-Denman
Film sales arm of Channel 4, set up in 1984 to sell feature films which it finances or part-finances. Recent titles include *Secret Friends, The Long Day Closes, Best Intentions* and *Hear My Song*

Glinwood Films
Swan House
52 Poland Street
London W1V 3DF
Tel: 071 437 1181
Fax: 071 494 0634
Terry Glinwood
Marie Vine
Sale of feature films such as *Insignificance, Merry Christmas Mr Lawrence, The Last Emperor, When The Wind Blows, Erik the Viking, Everybody Wins* and *The Sheltering Sky*

Global Television Services
see **Portman Entertainment**

Goldcrest Films and Television
36-44 Brewer Street
London W1R 3HP
Tel: 071 437 8696
Fax: 071 437 4448
John Quested
Richard Hellman
Jo Deakin
Major feature film production, sales and finance company. Recent films include *All Dogs go to Heaven, Black Rainbow, Rock-A-Doodle* and *Scorchers*

Golden Communications (Overseas)
47 Greek Street
London W1V 5LQ
Tel: 071 439 1431
Fax: 071 287 2348
David Shepperd
Responsible for sales co-ordination of: *High Road to China, Cannonball Run, Cannonball Run II, Teenage Mutant Ninja Turtles, Lassiter, The Protector, Flying, Armour of God 2* and other projects including Jackie Chan and Bruce Lee pictures from an extensive library

The Samuel Goldwyn Co
St George's House
14-17 Wells Street
London W1P 3FP
Tel: 071 436 5105
Fax: 071 580 6520
Diana Hawkins
Liz Elton
Gary Phillips
Offices in Los Angeles, London, New York. Acquisition, sales, distribution and marketing of films and television product worldwide. Recent film titles include *The Object of Beauty; Truly, Madly, Deeply; My Heroes Have Always Been Cowboys* and *The Tapes of Dexter Jackson.* Television product includes Goldwyn Classics Library and the Rogers and Hammerstein Film Library

Grampian Television
Queen's Cross
Aberdeen AB9 2XJ
Tel: 0224 646464
Fax: 0224 635127
Michael J McLintock
North Scotland ITV station producing a wide range of product including documentaries

Portrait of the Wild; Scotland's Larder; The Energy Alternative and *Scotland the Grave.* Children's animation *James the Cat* is available, as is extensive footage on the world's oil industry with large library of offshore material. Represented by ITEL

Granada Television International
36 Golden Square
London W1R 4AH
Tel: 071 734 8080
Fax: 071 494 6280
Vivien Wallace

HIT Communications
The Pump House
13-16 Jacob's Well Mews
London W1H 5PD
Tel: 071 224 1717
Fax: 071 224 1719
Peter Orton
Sophie Turner Laing
Jane Smith
Charles Caminada
Distributors of children's and family programming including *Where's Wally, Shakespeare the Animated Tales, We All Have Tales, Mystery of the Keys, Dream Patrol, Brum, Fiddley Foodle Bird, Dance of Polar Bears, The Winjin' Pom, Mother Goose Rock 'n' Rhyme, Harvey Library of Classic Cartoons, RARG, Postman Pat, Metronome HIT Collection,* and *Bush Beat*

Hemdale
21 Albion Street
London W2 2AS
Tel: 071 724 1010
Fax: 071 724 9168
Roy Votier
UK sales office of US production company. Titles include *Terminator, Platoon, The Last Emperor* and *Return of the Living Dead*

ITC Entertainment
24 Nutford Place
London W1H 4YN
Tel: 071 262 3262
Fax: 071 724 0160
Lynden Parry
Distributors of *Night of the Fox, People Like Us, Aftermath, The Last to Go, UFO Cafe, Stepfather II, Poor Little Rich Girl – The Barbara Hutton Story, Billionaire Boys Club, Windmills of the Gods, Without a Clue,* and many other titles

Ideal Communications Films and Television
40-41 Great Marlborough Street
London W1V 1DA
Tel: 071 287 4082
Fax: 071 287 4083
Carey Fitzgerald
Mike Allaway
Co-production and sales company. For list of product, see under Production Companies

Ideal-Opix Sales
40-41 Great Marlborough Street
London W1V 1DA
Tel: 071 287 4082
Fax: 071 287 4083
Carey Fitzgerald
Mike Allaway
Distributes television programmes internationally, covering areas such as TV drama, feature films, music, light entertainment, arts and sport. Recent programmes include *David Jensen's Canadian Crossing, Calvi – God's Banker,* and *Champions – Where Are They Now?*

International Television Enterprises (ITEL)
48 Leicester Square
London WC2H 7FB
Tel: 071 491 1441
Fax: 071 493 7677
Andrew Macbean
Distribution and production development company based in London and Los Angeles. Active in all areas of international television – investment in initial concepts, programmme development, sales and marketing. Represents Anglia TV, Anglia Films, Survival, Grampian, Little Bird and programming from Home Box Office, Roadshow, Coote and Carroll

J & M Entertainment
2 Dorset Square
London NW1 6PU
Tel: 071 723 6544
Fax: 071 724 7541
Julia Palau
Michael Ryan
Michael Brawley
Anthony Miller
Specialise in sales of all media, distribution and marketing of independent feature films. Recent films are *Mistress, Freddie as F.R.O.7, Iron Maze, Year of the Gun* and *Homicide*

Liberty Films
The Forum
74-80 Camden Street
London NW1 0JL
Tel: 071 387 5733
Fax: 071 383 5368
John Kelleher
Teresa Kelleher
Distribution of films, video and television programmes to all media worldwide

Link Licensing
7 Baron's Gate
33-35 Rothschild Road
Chiswick
London W4 5HT
Tel: 081 995 5080
Fax: 081 747 9452
Claire Derry
David Hamilton
Peter Woodhead
Specialists in children's programmes for worldwide distribution and character licensing. New properties include: *Spider!, Barney, Salad Days, What-a-Mess, Morph, Tiny Tales, Penny Crayon* and many classic children's programmes

London Film Productions
44a Floral Street
London WC2E 9DA
Tel: 071 379 3366
Fax: 071 240 7065
Sheila Berry
Independent production and distribution company, with offices in London and LA. London Films offers a distribution and sales service to independent producers as well as selling its own productions

London Television Service
Hercules Road
London SE1 7DU
Tel: 071 261 8592
Fax: 071 928 5037
Distributors and producers of documentaries worldwide including science and technology series *Perspective*

London Weekend Television International
South Bank Television Centre
London SE1 9LT
Tel: 071 620 1620
Fax: 071 928 8476
Sydney Perry
Sue Lytle
Colin Jarvis
Programme sales and distribution arm of London Weekend Television. Leading programmes include *Agatha Christie's Poirot, Forever Green, A Perfect Hero, London's Burning* and *Hale & Pace*

MCA TV
1 Hamilton Mews
London W1V 9FF
Tel: 071 491 4666
Fax: 071 493 4702
Roger Cordjohn
Penny Craig
UK operation for the major US corporation which owns Universal Pictures

MCEG Virgin Vision
Atlantic House
1 Rockley Road
London W14 0DL
Tel: 081 740 5500
Fax: 081 967 1360/1
Music and special programmes. Film and TV international sales. *After Dark My Sweet, Peter Gabriel Live in Athens – P.O.V., Soul II Soul – 1990 A New Decade Live*

MGM/UA Television
see **Turner International**

McCann International Programme Marketing
68 Gloucester Place
London W1H 3HL
Tel: 071 224 4748
Fax: 071 487 5071
Andrew Luff
International distributors of drama series, TV movies, music, light

entertainment, documentaries and children's programmes to broadcasters, cable and satellite operators and home-video distributors worldwide

Majestic Films International
Gloucester Mansions
Cambridge Circus
London WC2H 8HD
Tel: 071 836 8630
Fax: 071 836 5819
Guy East
Organises finance, sales, distribution and marketing of feature films throughout the world. Recent titles include *Driving Miss Daisy, Henry V, Dances with Wolves, Until the End of the World, The Thief & the Cobbler, K-2* and *City of Joy*

Manifesto Film Sales
1 Water Lane
Kentish Town Road
London NW1 8NZ
Tel: 071 911 6100
Fax: 071 911 6151
Wendy Palmer
John Durie
Caroline Burton
PolyGram, Working Title and Propaganda Films have been joined by A&M Films in their international Sales and Marketing venture. Titles include *Map of the Human Heart, High Heels, Close to Eden, Drop Dead Fred, Barton Fink, Looking for Billy, Love Field, Red Rock West, London Kills Me* and *Wild at Heart.*

Manifesto TV Sales
1 Water Lane
Kentish Town Road
London NW1 8NZ
Tel: 071 911 6100
Fax: 071 911 6151
Marten Rabarts
An offshoot of Manifesto Film Sales, Manifesto TV Sales handles worldwide distribution of PolyGram, Island Visual Arts and some Propaganda Music Programming. Artists include Elton John, Dire Straits, Tears for Fears, Van Morrison, Sinéad O'Connor and David Lynch directing Julee Cruise

NBD Pictures
Remo House
310-312 Regent Street
London W1R 5AJ
Tel: 071 499 9701
Nicky Davies
Caroline McGee
Company specialising in music and entertainment programming, but broadening into features and drama. Clients include The Elvis Presley Estate, Warner Bros Records, Lightyear, CBS Records International and Island Visual Arts

NVC Arts
The Forum
74-80 Camden Street
London NW1 0JL
Tel: 071 388 3833
Fax: 071 383 5332
John Kelleher
Hazel Wright
Barbara Bellini-Witkowski
Producers and distributors of opera, ballet, dance, music specials and documentaries for television broadcast. Recent productions include the Kirov Ballet's *Swan Lake* and Deutsche Oper Berlin's *Salome*

National Film Board of Canada
1 Grosvenor Square
London W1X 0AB
Tel: 071 629 9492 x3482
Fax: 071 495 8085
Jane Taylor
European sales office for documentary, drama and animation productions from Canada's National Film Board

Nelson Entertainment International
8 Queen Street
London W1X 7PH
Tel: 071 493 3362
Fax: 071 409 0503
International sales for *City Slickers, Eve of Destruction, Late for Dinner, Misery, Sibling Rivalry,* and *The Taking of Beverly Hills*

Orbit Films
14 Campden Hill Gardens
London W8 7AY
Tel: 071 221 5548
Fax: 071 727 0515
Chris Ranger
Gordon Pilkington
Specialises in vintage product from the first decade of American TV: *The Golden Years of Television*

Paramount Television
23 Berkeley House
Hay Hill
London W1X 8JB
Tel: 071 629 1150
Fax: 071 491 2086
Peter Cary

Perfect Features
78a Santos Road
London SW18 1NS
Tel: 081 877 9563
Fax: 081 877 0690
Grace Carley
Financing and sales of low-budget cult-type movies, including *Meet the Feebles, Deadline* and *Brain Dead*

Photoplay Productions
21 Princess Road
London NW1 8JR
Tel: 071 722 2500
Fax: 071 722 6662
Kevin Brownlow
David Gill
Patrick Stanbury
European dealer for the Blackhawk 16mm library of silent and early sound films

Picture Music International
20 Manchester Square
London W1A 1ES
Tel: 071 486 4488
Fax: 071 465 0748
Dawn M Stevenson
Itzhak Perlman's *Perlman in Russia,* Nigel Kennedy's performance of Bruch's Violin Concerto No. 1, Robert Palmer's *Don't Explain,* Jools Holland's *Mr Roadrunner*

Playpont Films
1-2 Ramillies Street
London W1V 1DF
Tel: 071 734 7792
Fax: 071 734 9288
Don Getz
Ellen Trost
International sales representatives for feature films and TV series. Titles include *Enemy, Man Eaters, Five Card Stud* and *Flying Dutchman*

Portman Entertainment
Pinewood Studios
Iver Heath
Bucks SL0 0NH
Tel: 0753 630366
Fax: 0753 630332
Pam Mackenzie
Gary Mitchell

Richard Price Television Associates (RPTA)
Seymour Mews House
Seymour Mews
Wigmore Street
London W1H 9PE
Tel: 071 935 9000
Fax: 071 487 3975
Richard Price
RPTA distributes for over 100 producers

The Production Line Sales Co
41-42 Berners Street
First Floor
London W1P 3AA
Tel: 071 323 0656
Fax: 071 637 1407
Idi Toth-Davy
Film sales division of Medusa Communications. Recent titles include *The Grand Tour* and *Maniac Cop 2*

RM Associates
46 Great Marlborough Street
London W1V 1DB
Tel: 071 439 2637
Fax: 071 439 2316
Sally Fairhead
In addition to handling the exclusive distribution of programmes produced/co-produced by Reiner Moritz's company RM Arts, RM Associates works closely with numerous broadcasters and independent producers to bring together a comprehensive catalogue of music and arts programming

Radio Vision International
Avon House
360 Oxford Street
London W1N 9HA
Tel: 071 493 0439
Fax: 071 493 0421
Stefan Ericson
Leading contemporary music distributors, specialising in live and recorded concerts including: *Pavarotti, Rock In Rio II, Prince, Sinéad O'Connor, Billy*

Joel, Billy Idol and many others

Rank Film Distributors
127 Wardour Street
London W1V 4AD
Tel: 071 437 9020
Fax: 071 434 3689
Nicole Mackey
A library of 500 feature films plus TV series. Also 200 hours of colour programming from the Children's Film and Television Foundation. New product includes *Mannequin on the Move, Ambition, The Linguini Incident, Pyrates* and *Under Suspicion*

Red Rooster Film & Television Entertainment
11-13 Macklin Street
London WC2B 5NH
Tel: 071 405 8147
Fax: 071 831 0679
Linda James
Mary Ann Simmons
Feature film production and producers and distributors of quality television fiction and feature films: *Joni Jones, And Pigs Might Fly, The Works, The Flea and the Giant, Hazel's Children, Coming Up Roses, Equinox: Earthquake Country, Just Ask for Diamond, Travelling Hopefully, Kersplat!, The Diamond Brothers – South by Southeast* and *The Gift*

S4C Enterprises
Parc Ty Glas
Llanishen
Cardiff
CF4 5DU
Tel: 0222 747444
Fax: 0222 754444
Christopher Grace
Teleri Roberts
Distributing programmes commissioned by S4C from independent producers and from HTV Cymru/Wales – animation, drama, documentaries

Safir Films
22 Soho Square
London W1V 5FJ
Tel: 071 734 5085
Fax: 071 734 1329
Lawrence Safir
Sidney Safir
Holds rights to a number of Australian, US and British pictures, including Sam Spiegel's *Betrayal*, Steve Jodrell's *Shame*, and the Romulus Classics comprising more than 30 titles such as *The African Queen, Moulin Rouge, Room at the Top* and *Beat the Devil*

The Sales Company
62 Shaftesbury Avenue
London W1V 7AA
Tel: 071 434 9061
Fax: 071 494 3293
Carole Myer
Alison Thompson
Penny Rigby
Formed in 1986 by British Screen, Palace and Zenith to represent their feature productions worldwide in all media. Recent films include *American Friends, The Miracle, The Garden, Perfectly Normal, Trust, The Pope Must Die, The Bridge, Waterland, Prague, Edward II* and *Dust Devil*. Also represent outside product such as *La Captive du Désert* and *Luba*

Scottish Television International
Cowcaddens
Glasgow G2 3PR
Tel: 041 332 9999
Fax: 041 332 6982
Anita Cox
Sales of all programmes from Scottish Television

Screen Ventures
49 Goodge Street
London W1P 1FB
Tel: 071 580 7448
Fax: 071 631 1265
Dominic Saville
Christopher Mould
Specialise in international TV and video licensing of music specials with artists such as John Lennon, Jimi Hendrix, Chuck Berry, Jerry Lee Lewis, Otis Redding, B B King and Lou Reed. Worldwide television sales agents for BMG Video International and The Jimi Hendrix Estate

Silverbach-Lazarus
Utopia Village
7 Chalcot Road
London NW1 8LX
Tel: 071 722 6080
Fax: 071 586 1552
George Blaug
UK base of SLG, Los Angeles. Properties include six TV movies and six mini-series from PBL Australia, *The Littlest Hobo* (114 half hours), and *The March of Time* (60 half hours) plus wildlife documentaries

Smart Egg Pictures
62 Brompton Road
London SW3 1BW
Tel: 071 581 1841
Fax: 071 581 8998
Tom Sjoberg
Independent foreign sales company. Titles include *Spaced Invaders, Cameron's Closet, Dinosaurs, Montenegro, The Coca-Cola Kid* and *Fatal Inheritance*

D L Taffner (UK)
10 Bedford Square
London WC1B 3RA
Tel: 071 631 1184
Fax: 071 636 4571
Specialising in entertainment programming; *Talkabout* (ITV game show), *Winter with Flowers* (BBC sit-com), and *The Saint* (LWT drama series). Also operates a joint venture with the Theatre of Comedy at the Shaftesbury Theatre. The parent company is a well-known producer and distributor based in New York, Los Angeles and Sydney

Talbot Television
Greendon House
7c/d Bayham Street
London NW1 0EY
Tel: 071 380 1189
Fax: 071 383 5369
David Champtaloup
London arm of NY-based Fremantle Int. Produces and distributes game shows and light entertainment

Television Entertainment
65 Blandford Street
London W1H 3AJ
Tel: 071 486 6626
Fax: 071 224 5385
Rod Allen
Noel Copley
Lynn James
Represents HTV, RTE, Channel Television, TSW, Mentorn Films, Partridge Films, Brook Productions, The Vision Group, Leo Dickinson and a number of independent producers worldwide

Telso International
84 Buckingham Gate
London SW1E 6PD
Tel: 071 976 7188
Fax: 071 976 7113/4
Wendy Hallam
Ann Harris
Bernard Macleod
Properties include: *The Diamond Brothers – South by South East*, a family drama series and *Skeletons Have Names – So Have the Guilty*, an investigative documentary about how the Chileans are trying to come to terms with the horrors of their past under military dictatorship

Thames Television International
149 Tottenham Court Road
London W1P 9LL
Tel: 071 387 9494
Fax: 071 388 6073
Mike Phillips
Roger Miron
Represents largest programme producer in ITV network and its subsidiaries Euston Films and Cosgrove Hall Productions in programme sales, co-productions, the non-theatrical and home video markets, publishing and merchandising. Also represents major UK independent, Tyburn Productions

Trans World International
TWI House
23 Eyot Gardens
London W6 9TN
Tel: 081 846 8070
Fax: 081 746 5334
Eric Drossart
Buzz Hornett
Chris Guinness
TV and video arm of Mark McCormack's International Management Group, specialising in sports programming – from live coverage and event highlights to made-for-TV programming and sports documentaries

Turner International
25 Old Burlington Street
London W1X 1LB
Tel: 071 434 4341
Fax: 071 434 9727
Howard Karshan
US production and distribution company. Distributor of MGM, pre-1950 Warner Bros features and Turner series

Twentieth Century Fox Television
31-32 Soho Square
London W1V 6AP
Tel: 071 437 7766
Fax: 071 439 1806/437 1625
Malcolm Vaughan
Sales of all Twentieth Century Fox product to TV worldwide

Tyne Tees Enterprises
15 Bloomsbury Square
London WC1A 2LJ
Tel: 071 405 8474
Fax: 071 242 2441
Ann Gillham
International sales division of Tyne Tees TV. Also represents the catalogue of Border TV and other independent producers

United Media Film Sales
United House
20 Wells Mews
London W1P 3FJ
Tel: 071 580 5586
Fax: 071 323 0464
Vic Bateman
Acquisition, sales and marketing worldwide of quality feature films, including *The Krays*

VATV
60-62 Margaret Street
London W1N 7FJ
Tel: 071 636 9421
Fax: 071 436 7426
David Llewellyn-Jones
Jane Lighting
VATV represents over 45 independent companies in the international market and is an approved distributor for Channel 4 documentary and factual programmes, and for the BBC and ITN

VCI Programme Sales
Strand VCI House
Caxton Way
Watford
Herts WD1 8UF
Tel: 0923 55558
Fax: 0923 817969
Kevin J Lagden
Lisa Gamble
A wholly owned subsidiary of the Video Collection International, responsible for all overseas activities. Distributes a wide variety of product from music, sport, educational, fitness, documentary and features. Has a joint venture partnership with Thames Television and ITN and distributes its product for video internationally

Viacom International
40 Conduit Street
London W1R 9FB
Tel: 071 434 4483
Fax: 071 439 0858
Peter Press
UK-based distribution operation for the US independent company. Current product includes *The Cosby Show* (seventh year), *Different World* (fourth year), *Roseanne* (third year), *Jake and the Fatman* (fourth year), *Matlock* (fifth year), *Father Dowling* (third year), *Perry Mason* TV movie specials, *Superboy, Superforce* plus an extensive library of theatrical and made-for-TV movies

Visnews
Cumberland Avenue
London NW10 7EH
Tel: 081 965 7733
Fax: 081 965 0620
Syndication of international TV news, sport, library footage and complete programmes

Warner Bros Television
(a division of Warner Bros Distributors)
135 Wardour Street
London W1V 4AP
Tel: 071 494 3710
Fax: 071 287 9086
Includes Lorimar Telepictures product

Weintraub Screen Entertainment
167-169 Wardour Street
London W1V 3TA
Tel: 071 439 1790
Fax: 071 734 1509
Richard Milnes
A library of over 1500 titles from classic to contemporary: *Brighton Rock, The Third Man, The Deerhunter, The Elephant Man* and *Highlander*

Worldwide Television News Corporation (WTN)
The Interchange
Oval Road
Camden Lock
London NW1
Tel: 071 410 5200
Fax: 071 413 8327 (library)
Keith Reynolds
Gerry O'Reilly
International TV news, features, sport, entertainment, documentary programmes, *Earthfile* (an environmental programme series), *Healthfile,* weather, archive resources. Camera crews in major global locations, plus in-house broadcasting and production facilities

Bucks Motion Picture Laboratories
714 Banbury Avenue
Slough
Berks SL1 4LH
Tel: 0753 576611
Fax: 0753 691762
West End pick up and delivery at Roger Cherrills
65-66 Dean Street
London W1
Comprehensive lab services in 35mm and 16mm. West End rushes pick up until 11pm
Chromakopy: 35mm low-cost overnight colour reversal dubbing prints
Photogard: European coating centre for negative and print treatment
Chromascan: 35mm and 16mm video to film transfer

Colour Film Services Group
10 Wadsworth Road
Perivale
Greenford
Middx UB6 7JX
Tel: 081 998 2731
Fax: 081 997 8738
Full 35mm, 16mm and Super 16mm 24-hour laboratory services, handling all aspects of film work from feature films and TV programming to industrial shorts and commercials. In-house sound transfer and telecine mastering. Tape to film transfer to 35mm and 16mm. Bulk cassette duplication. Conference centre, equipment hire

Colour Tone Film Laboratories
PO Box 1098
Gerrards Cross
Bucks SL9 8DY
Tel: 02407 71513/4
Fax: 02407 71086
Film duplication for specialised distributors

Film and Photo Design
13 Colville Road
South Acton Industrial Estate
London W3 8BL
Tel: 081 992 0037
Fax: 081 993 2409
Leading European lab for 16/35mm colour & b/w reversal workprints. Specialists in nitrate preservation. Full lab facilities

Film Clinic
8-14 Meard Street
London W1V 3HR
Tel: 071 734 9235/6
Fax: 071 734 9471
Scratch treatment, reconditioning and restoration of 16/35mm film. Archive specialists

Filmatic Laboratories/ Filmatic Television
16 Colville Road
London W11 2BS
Tel: 071 221 6081
Fax: 071 229 2718
Complete film processing laboratory and sound transfer service with full video post production facility including Digital Telecines, 1″ VTRs, Betacam SP and other video formats. On-line editing, duplication and standard conversion. A + B Roll Negative to Tape Transfers. Electronic Film Conforming (EFC), the system that produces the highest quality video masters from any original source, with frame accurate editing from a film or off-line video edit

Henderson Film Laboratories
18-20 St Dunstan's Road
South Norwood
London SE25 6EU
Tel: 081 653 2255
Fax: 081 653 9773
Full b/w laboratory service in 35mm and 16mm including b/w reversal processing in 16mm and Super 8. Blow-up to 16mm from 9.5mm and Std 8mm. Specialists in the handling of archive material, especially shrunken and nitrate film

London Film Makers' Co-operative
42 Gloucester Avenue
London NW1 8JD
Tel: 071 722 1728
16mm b/w processing

Metrocolor London
91-95 Gillespie Road
London N5 1LS
Tel: 071 226 4422
Fax: 071 359 2353
Full 16mm, Super 16mm and 35mm processing services, handling a range from 16mm short films through pop promos, commercials, BBC and ITV programmes to feature films, video mastering, sound transfer and stereo-optical camera

Rank Film Laboratories
North Orbital Road
Denham
Uxbridge
Middx UB9 5HQ
Tel: 0895 832323
Fax: 0895 833617
Principal laboratories at Denham in the UK, Deluxe in Los Angeles and Film House in Toronto, with satellite laboratories in Manchester and Leeds. Full optical facilities available from General Screen Enterprises at Uxbridge. Experienced sales and servicing personnel able to provide a complete worldwide film processing service

Studio Film and Video Group
8-14 Meard Street
London W1V 3HR
Tel: 071 437 0831
Fax: 071 734 9471
Full film processing day and night plus telecine transfer, mastering and video duplication. Film restoration and preservation (Film Clinic)

Technicolor
PO Box 7
Bath Road
West Drayton
Middx UB7 0DB
Tel: 081 759 5432
Fax: 081 759 6270
24-hour laboratory service, adjacent to London Heathrow Airport. Modern high speed plant caters for all formats: 16mm, Super 16mm, 35mm, 70mm. Laboratories in Rome, Hollywood and New York

LEGISLATION

***The principal acts affecting the operation of the film and television industries in the UK are listed chronologically below with a brief explanation of their provisions. The list does not include statutory instruments by which the measures may be modified or implemented. All the items listed are published by HMSO and available in public reference libraries or through BFI Library Services. The more important measures are marked by* ***

CINEMA LEGISLATION

* Cinematograph Act, 1909

Provisions for licensing of exhibition premises and the safety of audiences. (The first Act of Parliament relating to cinema)

Celluloid and Cinematograph Film Act, 1922

Provisions for the prevention of fire in premises where raw celluloid or cinematograph film is stored or used

* Cinematograph Films Act, 1927

(repealed by Cinematograph Films Act, 1948)
Restrictions on blind booking and advance booking of films. Registration of films exhibited to the public. Provisions for securing a 'quota' of British films for renting by exhibitors

Sunday Entertainment Act, 1932

(amended by Sunday Cinema Act 1972)
Permits and regulates the opening and use of premises on Sundays for certain entertainments. Establishment of the Sunday Cinematograph Fund for 'encouraging the use and development of the cinematograph as a means of entertainment and instruction'. (This is the means by which the BFI was originally funded)

The Cinematograph Films (Animals) Act, 1937

Designed to prevent exhibition or distribution of films in which suffering may have been caused to animals

Cinematograph Films Act, 1938

(repealed by and consolidated in Films Act, 1960)
Renters' and exhibitors' quotas. Restrictions on blind and advance booking. Registration of films for public exhibition. Wages and conditions of people employed in production

Cinematograph Films Act, 1948

(repealed and consolidated in Films Act, 1960)
Provisions on quotas. Composition of Cinematograph Films Council

* Cinematograph Film Production (Special Loans) Act, 1949

Establishment of the National Film Finance Corporation

* British Film Institute Act, 1949

Provides for payment of grants to BFI from the Treasury as well as from the (Sunday) Cinematograph Fund (see also Sunday Cinema Act, 1972)

Cinematograph Film Production (Special Loans) Act, 1950

(repealed by Films Act, 1970)
Amends the 1949 Act

Cinematograph Film Production (Special Loans) Act, 1952

(repealed by Films Act, 1980)
Empowers the NFFC to borrow otherwise than from the Board of Trade

* Cinematograph Act, 1952

Extends the 1909 Act to cover exhibition premises using non-flam film and television. Control of cinema exhibition for children. Exemptions for non-commercial exhibition Music and dancing licences not required for cinematograph exhibitions

Cinematograph Film Production (Special Loans) Act, 1954

Extended the period during which loans and advances may be made under The Cinematograph Film Productions (Special Loans) Acts, 1949 and 1952 and authorised the NFFC to enter into special arrangements on certain loans

* Cinematograph Films Act, 1957

(amended by Films Act, 1960)
Provides for a statutory levy on exhibitors to be collected by Customs and Excise and paid to the British Film Fund Agency (to be established by Statutory Instrument). The BFFA to pay the resulting funds to makers of British films and to the Children's Film Foundation. This put the formerly voluntary levy, known as 'Eady Money' on a statutory footing. Amends law relating to National Film Finance Corporation, laying down its duty to pay its way and providing for its eventual dissolution under certain specified conditions

Cinematograph Films Act, 1960

(repealed by and consolidated in Films Act, 1960)
Extension of existing legislation with minor variations

* Films Act, 1960

(consolidates The Cinematograph Film Acts, 1938-1960. Repealed by Films Act, 1985)
Includes the up-to-date legislation on: quota; registration: conditions for registration as British or foreign, renters' and exhibitors' licences; restrictions on blind and advance booking; registration of newsreels; wages and conditions of employment; powers of Board of Trade; constitution of The Cinematograph Films Council, amends the Copyright Act, 1956 as it relates to film; amends references to previous legislation in Cinematograph Films Act, 1957

Films Act, 1964

(repealed by Films Act, 1985)
Amends the Films Act, 1960 in its relation to newsreels

Films Act, 1966

(repealed by Films Act, 1985)
Extends and adjusts provisions of previous measures. Much of it subsequently repealed by Films Act, 1970

Films Act, 1970

(repealed by Films Act, 1985)
Extends functions of the National Film Finance Corporation. Imposes time limit of 1980 on all loan arrangements. Repeals various provisions of previous Acts

Sunday Cinema Act, 1972

Repeals certain sections of The Sunday Entertainments Act, 1932 and The British Film Institute Act, 1949. Winds up the Cinematograph Fund. Ends restrictions on Sunday opening of cinemas

European Communities Act, 1972

Community films not to be classed as foreign but as quota films under The Films Acts, 1960-1970

Cinematograph Films Act, 1975

(repealed by Films Act, 1980)

Films Act, 1979

(repealed by Films Act, 1985)
Amends Films Act, 1960 in relation to foreign films shown for at least eight weeks

* Films Act, 1980

(repealed by Films Act, 1985)
Extends functions of NFFC. Provides for Government grant of £1 million and write-off of accumulated outstanding capital and interest repayments. NFFC may borrow up to £5 million at any time. Extends levy and quota periods. Provides for aggregation of screen time for quota when more than one cinema in a building. Provides power to suspend quota by Statutory Instrument. (Note: Quota ended 1982)

National Film Finance Corporation Act, 1981

Consolidates The Cinematograph Film Production (Special Loans) Acts, 1949-1980 and makes certain changes in the operation of the NFFC

Film Levy Finance Act, 1981

Consolidates The Cinematograph Films Acts, 1957-1980. Contains provisions for a certain proportion of Eady Levy to be paid to the NFFC

Cinematograph (Amendment) Acts 1982

Extends the provisions of the 1909 Act to 'all exhibitions of moving pictures for private gain'. This brings pornographic cinema and video 'clubs' within the licensing requirements. Bona fide film societies and 'demonstrations' such as those used in video shops are excluded. Also excluded are exhibitions to provide information, education or instruction

Cinema Act, 1985

This consolidates the Cinematograph Acts 1909 to 1982. Licences are required for exhibition, and the Act lays down the procedure for application for and renewal of licences. Exempted exhibition includes exhibition in private dwelling houses, non-commercial shows and premises used only occasionally. The Act also specifies the conditions for Sunday opening

* Films Act, 1985

This Act repeals the Films Acts 1960 to 1980, abolishes the Cinematograph Films Council, ends Eady Levy and dissolves the National Film Finance Corporation. It makes provision for future Government financial assistance to the film industry – should Government decide to provide such assistance. (In fact, the Government has agreed to provide £1.5 million for five years to the loan fund of the British Screen Finance Consortium which takes over from the NFFC and whose members include Screen Entertainment, Rank and Channel 4). The Register of Films, started by the Board of Trade in 1928, is to be discontinued

Copyright, Designs & Patents Act 1988

This Act updates the Act of 1956. The duration of copyright for sound recordings and films is set at 50 years from the release date or from the date they were made if unreleased, and 50 years for broadcast or cable programmes from the date of first transmission. The rest of the Act consists of exceptions to the general principles of copyright

TELEVISION LEGISLATION

The rapid development of the new medium was foreseen in the Wireless Telegraphy Act, 1904 which reserved wide powers to the State for the regulation of wireless telegraphy. It was the first Wireless Act in the world and gave the Postmaster General the duty to license all wireless-telegraphy apparatus. The BBC was originally registered as a company (The British Broadcasting Co Ltd) in 1922 and received a licence from the Post Office in 1923. The present Corporation has never been a

LEGISLATION

statutory body but has operated under a Royal Charter since 1926. The present Charter came into force on 1 August 1981 for 15 years. Subsequently developments in television have been covered by statutory measures and the principal ones are listed below

Television Act, 1954
Provides for a commercial television service from companies supervised by the Independent Television Authority (the ITA, later the IBA). Advertising was to be separated from programming, and requirements were laid down on the content of programmes

Copyright Act, 1956
Provides for copyright protection of broadcasting for the first time

Television Act, 1963
Extends the period for which the ITA should provide services until 1976

Television Act, 1964
Consolidates the 1954 and 1963 Acts

Sound Broadcasting Act, 1972
Extends the functions of the Independent Television Authority (ITA) to cover provision of local sound broadcasting services and renames it the Independent Broadcasting Authority (IBA)

Independent Broadcasting Authority Act, 1973
Consolidates the Television and Sound Broadcasting Acts, 1964 and 1972. Its provisions are essentially the same as those two Acts

Independent Broadcasting Authority Act, 1974
Makes further provision on payments to be made to the IBA by television programme contractors. The 'Exchequer Levy' payments are changed to a tax on profits instead of advertising revenue only

Independent Broadcasting Authority (No 2) Act, 1974
Extends the date until which IBA provides television and sound broadcasting services to 31 July 1979

Independent Broadcasting Authority Act, 1978
Extends the above functions to 31 December 1981. Removes prohibition on certain specified people from broadcasting opinions where opinion is expressed in proceedings of parliament or local authorities

Independent Broadcasting Authority Act, 1979
Confers power on IBA to transmit a fourth channel

Broadcasting Act, 1980
Extends IBA's functions to provision of programmes, but not advertisements, for the fourth channel. Extends IBA's function to 31 December 1996. Establishes a Broadcasting Complaints Commission

Broadcasting Act, 1981
Consolidates the Independent Broadcasting Authority Acts, 1973, 1974 and 1978 and the Broadcasting Act, 1980

Copyright (Amendment) Act, 1983
This act increases significantly the penalties for trading in and making pirate videocassettes, with heavier fines and possible prison sentences

Video Recordings Act, 1984
This Act requires the certification of all new video releases. In view of the large number of titles to be classified, the work is to be done in six phases, beginning on 1 September 1985 – from which date any new release on video has to have a certificate – and finishing on 1 September 1988, by which time the backlog of titles should have been classified

Cable and Broadcasting Act, 1984
This Act set up the new Cable Authority, following a second reading of the Cable and Broadcasting Bill, introduced in 1983. The Cable Authority has the job of selecting operators for particular areas on the basis of the range of services which they intend to offer, and of seeing that they then live up to their promises

Copyright, Designs & Patents Act 1988
This Act updates the Act of 1956. The duration of copyright for broadcast or cable programmes becomes 50 years from the date of first transmission. Amongst the most important changes are the permission of fair dealing of films and TV material for purposes of review or reporting current events, the legalisation of domestic video recording for time-shift viewing and the introduction of moral rights. Sections dealing with off-air video recording for educational and archival purposes were introduced following lobbying by the BFI

* *Broadcasting Act 1990*
This Act repeals the Broadcasting Acts of 1981 and 1987. It sets up the Independent Television Commission to regulate commercial television originated in Britain, replacing the IBA and the Cable Authority, and creates the Radio Authority to regulate commercial sound programme services. The Act changes the method of awarding franchises for terrestrial commercial television services on Channel 3 and introduces a similar system for the prospective Channel 5, whereby the franchises will in general be awarded by the ITC to the highest bidder. Channel 4 becomes a Corporation operating as a licensed service with charge of its own advertising sales. Independent production quotas are imposed on commercial channels and the BBC. The Broadcasting Standards Council is created to monitor broadcasting standards. Following lobbying by the BFI, statutory support for a National Television Archive will be required from Channel 3 and 5 licence holders

ORGANISATIONS

Listed below are the main trade/government organisations and bodies relevant to the film and television industry. A separate list of the Regional Arts Boards is included at the end of this section

APRS – The Professional Recording Association

2 Windsor Square
Silver Street
Reading RG1 2TH
Tel: 0734 756218
Fax: 0734 756216
Represents the interests of the professional recording industry, including radio, TV and video studios and companies providing equipment and services in the field. It runs the international APRS Exhibition held at Olympia, London each year

Advertising Association

Abford House
15 Wilton Road
London SW1V 1NJ
Tel: 071 828 2771 (business)
Tel: 071 828 4831 (general)
Fax: 071 931 0376
Contact: Information Officer
The Advertising Association is a federation of 30 trade associations and professional bodies representing advertisers, agencies, the advertising media and support services. It is the central organisation for the UK advertising business, on British and European legislative proposals and other issues of common concern, both at national and international levels, and as such campaigns actively to maintain the freedom to advertise and to improve public attitudes to advertising. It publishes UK and European statistics on advertising expenditure, instigates research on advertising issues and organises seminars and courses for people in the communications business. Its Information Centre is one of the country's leading sources for advertising and associated subjects

Advertising Film and Videotape Producers' Association (AFVPA)

26 Noel Street
London W1V 3RD
Tel: 071 434 2651
Fax: 071 434 9002
Contact: Cecilia Garnett
The Association represents most producers of TV commercials. It negotiates with recognised trade unions, with the advertisers and agencies and also supplies a range of member services

Arts Council of Great Britain

Film, Video and Broadcasting
14 Great Peter Street
London SW1P 3NQ
Tel: 071 333 0100
Fax: 071 973 6590
Director: Rodney Wilson
Film and Video Officer: David Curtis
Education Officer: Will Bell
Film Sales Executive: Richard Gooderick
The Arts Council is funded by the Office of Arts and Libraries to encourage and support the arts. One of the means of achieving its objectives is the funding of documentary films on the arts intended for broad public use, particularly television and education. As an extension of its support for the visual arts, funds are available for the production, distribution and exhibition of artists' film and video

Arts Council of Northern Ireland

181a Stranmillis Road
Belfast BT9 5DU
Tel: 0232 381591
Fax: 0232 661715
Contact: Brian Ferran
The Northern Irish Arts Council is funded from the Department of Education for Northern Ireland and promotes film culture in the region by supporting the Queen's Film Theatre, assisting film societies and occasionally commissioning films on arts subjects

Association of Black Film and Video Workshops

Unit 215
22 Highbury Grove
London N5 2EA
Tel: 071 359 0302
The Association aims to represent and advance the interests of the black grant-aided sector in all areas of film and video production, distribution, training and exhibition, to initiate discussion and where relevant, policies on film and television culture, training and matters related to black cultural industries primarily in the UK but also in the EEC

Association of Cinematograph, Television and Allied Technicians (ACTT)

see ***Broadcasting Entertainment and Cinematograph Technicians Union (BECTU)***

Association of Professional Composers (APC)

34 Hanway Street
London W1P 9DE
Tel: 071 436 0919

Fax: 071 436 1913
Contact: Rosemary Dixson
APC represents composers from all sides of the profession – concert music, film, television, radio, theatre, electronic media, library music, jazz and so on. Its aims are to further the collective interests of its members and to inform and advise them on professional and artistic matters

Association of Professional Video Distributors
PO Box 25
Godalming
Surrey GU7 1PL
Tel: 0483 423429
Contact: Charles Potter MBE
Formed to improve the standards of the video industry with regard to the hardware by imposing professional discipline and controlling quality

Audio Visual Association
46 Manor View
London N3 2SR
Tel: 081 349 2429
Sandy Boyle
Terry Bowles, Chairman
Tel: 081 398 8060
The Audio Visual Association is the only professional body which protects and enhances the interests of all parties involved in non-broadcast visual and audio media and communications within the UK, whether creative, technical, administrative or supply

Australian Film Commission (AFC)
European Marketing Branch
2nd Floor, Victory House
99-101 Regent Street
London W1
Tel: 071 734 9383
Fax: 071 434 0170
Contact: Sue Murray
The AFC is a statutory authority established in 1975 to assist the development, production and distribution of Australian films. The European marketing branch services producers and buyers, advises on co-productions and financing, and promotes the industry at markets and through festivals

British Academy of Film and Television Arts (BAFTA)
195 Piccadilly
London W1V 9LG
Tel: 071 734 0022
Fax: 071 734 1792
BAFTA was formed in 1946 by Britain's most eminent filmmakers as a non-profit making company. It aims to advance the art and technique of film and television and encourage experiment and research. Membership is restricted to those who have made a substantial contribution to the industry. BAFTA has facilities for screenings and discussion meetings, and makes representations to parliamentary committees. Its awards to the industries (Craft Awards and Production and Performance Awards) are annual televised events. The Academy has branches in Manchester, Glasgow, Cardiff, Los Angeles and New York. See also under Awards and Preview Theatres

British Academy of Songwriters, Composers and Authors (BASCA)
34 Hanway Street
London W1P 9DE
Tel: 071 436 2261
Fax: 071 436 1913
Represents its members interests within the music industry. It issues standard contracts between publisher and songwriter

British Amateur Television Club (BATC)
Grenehurst
Pinewood Road
High Wycombe
Bucks HP12 4DD
BATC publish a quarterly technical publication 'CQTV', which is only available via subscription, and covers television engineering at a constructional and practical level. The BATC also produce printed circuit boards for their projects which range from a simple fade to black to electronic test cards, SPGs and vision switchers

British Board of Film Classification (BBFC)
3 Soho Square
London W1V 5DE
Tel: 071 439 7961
Fax: 071 287 0141
The 1909 Cinematograph Films Act forced public cinemas to be licensed by their local authority. Originally this was a safety precaution against fire risk but was soon interpreted by the local authorities as a way of censoring cinema owners' choice of films. In 1912, the British Board of Film Classification was established to impose a conformity of viewpoint: films cannot be shown in public in Britain unless they have the BBFC's certificate or the relevant local authorisation. The Board finances itself by charging a fee for the films it views. When viewing a film, the Board attempts to judge whether a film is liable to break the law, for example by depraving and corrupting a significant proportion of its likely audience. It then assesses whether there is material greatly and gratuitously offensive to a large number of people. The Board seeks to reflect contemporary public attitudes. There are no written rules but films are considered in the light of the above criteria, previous decisions and the examiners' personal judgement. It is the policy of the Board not to censor anything on political grounds. Five film categories came into effect in 1982, with the introduction of a '12' category in August 1989:

Universal: Suitable for all

Parental Guidance: Some scenes may be unsuitable for young children

Passed only for persons of 12 years and over

Passed only for persons of 15 years and over

Passed only for persons of 18 years and over

For Restricted Distribution only, through segregated premises to which no one under 18 years is admitted

The final decision, however, still lies with the local authority. In 1986 the GLC ceased to be the licensing authority for London cinemas, and these powers devolved to the Borough Councils. Sometimes films are passed by the BBFC and then banned by local authorities (*Straw Dogs, Caligula*). Others may have their categories altered (*Monty Python's Life of Brian, 9½ Weeks*). Current newsreels are exempt from censorship. In 1985 the BBFC was designated by the Home Secretary as the authority responsible for classifying video works under the Video Recordings Act 1984. The film categories listed above are also the basis for video classification

British Broadcasting Corporation (BBC)
Portland Place
London W1A 1AA
Tel: 071 580 4468
Fax: 071 636 9786
The BBC provides its radio and TV services under the auspices of the Home Office, which deals with legislative and constitutional aspects of broadcasting. See also under Television Companies

British Copyright Council
29-33 Berners Street
London W1P 4AA

Provides liaison between societies which represent the interest of those who own copyright in literature, music, drama and works of art, making representation to Government on behalf of its member societies

British Council

10 Spring Gardens
London SW1A 2BN
Contacts: John Cartwright, Rosemary Hood
11 Portland Place
London W1N 4EJ
Tel: 071 389 3065
Fax: 071 389 3041
As part of its work of promoting understanding of Britain in other countries, the British Council purchases films for showing by its offices in around 80 countries. It also selects the films for British film weeks and film festivals overseas. The British Council has a Film, TV and Video Advisory Committee chaired by Lord Brabourne. The British Council receives funds from the Foreign and Commonwealth Office and from the Overseas Development Administration

British Equity

8 Harley Street
London W1N 2AB
Tel: 071 636 6367/ 637 9311
Fax: 071 580 0970
Equity was formed in 1930 by professional performers to achieve solutions to the problems of casual employment and short-term engagements. Equity has over 45,000 members, an increase by 35,000 since the 1950s. It represents performers (other than musicians), stage managers, stage directors, stage designers and choreographers in all spheres of work from variety and circus to television. It negotiates agreements on behalf of its members with producers' associations and other employers. In certain areas of work it has agreements with employers which regulate entry into the profession. In some fields of work only artists with previous professional experience are normally eligible for work. Membership of Equity is treated as evidence of professional experience under these agreements. It publishes a quarterly *Equity Journal*

bfi British Federation of Film Societies (BFFS)

British Film Institute
21 Stephen Street
London W1P 1PL
Tel: 071 255 1444
Fax: 071 436 7950
The BFFS exists to promote the work of some 300 film societies in the UK. In 1982 the BFI set up the Film Society Unit to service the BFFS. See also p9

bfi British Film Institute (BFI)

21 Stephen Street
London W1P 1PL
Tel: 071 255 1444
Fax: 071 436 7950
Founded in 1933, the BFI was incorporated by Royal Charter in 1983; its aim is to encourage the development of the art of film and TV. It is funded largely by a grant from the OAL. The BFI is involved in almost every aspect of film and television in Britain, through the Regional Film Theatre network including the National Film Theatre, a Distribution library, the preservation work of the National Film Archive, and a Production arm which makes both feature-length and short low-budget films. The BFI also publishes books and the monthly magazine 'Sight and Sound' and acts as a centre for original research. The BFI Library and Stills, Posters and Designs Collection are unparalleled sources for the documentation of film and television history; highlights of these collections are on display in the prize-winning Museum of the Moving Image where the development of film and television is displayed from its earliest beginnings. For a full description of BFI activities, see pages 5-14

British Kinematograph, Sound and Television Society (BKSTS)

547-549 Victoria House
Vernon Place
London WC1B 4DJ
Tel: 071 242 8400
Fax: 071 405 3560
Contact: Ray Mobsby
British technicians formed this society in 1931 to keep in touch with major technical developments. The Society arranges regular meetings, where new equipment and techniques are demonstrated and discussions held. It also provides training courses and seminars for the industry and organises a biennial International Conference and Exhibition attended by delegates from all over the world. The monthly BKSTS journal, 'Image Technology', includes technical articles and reviews. Corporate members must hold responsible positions in film or TV. There is also an associate membership and a third membership for students

British Radio and Electronic Equipment Manufacturers' Association

Landseer House
19 Charing Cross Road
London WC2H 0ES
Tel: 071 930 3206
Fax: 071 839 4613
Trade association for British consumer electronics industry

British Screen Advisory Council

13 Bateman Street
London W1V 6EB
Tel: 071 437 9617/8
Fax: 071 734 7143
Fiona Clarke-Hackston
The BSAC is a non-statutory advisory body set up to replace the statutory-based Cinematograph Films Council and the non-statutory Interim Action Committee which were respectively abolished and wound up on the passing of the Films Act 1985. The Council is a broadly based industry body embracing film, television and video, meeting every month under the Chairmanship of Sir Richard Attenborough to consider a number of industry questions

British Screen Finance (British Screen)

37-39 Oxford Street
London W1R 1RE
Tel: 071 434 0291
Fax: 071 434 9933
Since January 1986, British Screen, a private company aided by Government grant, has taken over the role and the business of the National Film Finance Corporation which was dissolved following the Films Act 1985. The Department of Trade and Industry has pledged support until the end of 1993. British Screen aims to support new talent in commercially viable productions which might find difficulty in attracting mainstream commercial funding. Between 1986 and 1990 it supported 57 productions, and hopes to support a further 10 in 1991. Through the National Film Development Fund it also runs a programme of 11 minute short films for first time writers, directors and producers

British Tape Industry Association

Carolyn House
22-26 Dingwall Road
Croydon CR0 9XF
Tel: 081 681 1680
Trade association for the manufacturers of audio and videotape

British Universities Film and Video Council (BUFVC)

55 Greek Street
London W1V 5LR
Tel: 071 734 3687
Fax: 071 287 3914
Contact: Murray Weston
The BUFVC is an organisation with members in many institutions of higher education. It provides a number of services in the general area of production and use of film, television and other audiovisual materials for teaching and research and receives a grant from the Department of Education and Science for its work in the higher education sector. It operates a comprehensive Information Service, produces a regular magazine 'Viewfinder', catalogues and other publications, such as the 'Researchers' Guide to British Film and Television Collections', organises conferences and seminars and distributes specialised film and video material. It maintains a preview service called the Audiovisual Reference Centre where visitors may see a wide range of items, mainly on videocassette. Researchers in history come to the Council's offices to use the Slade Film History Register, with its information on British newsreels

British Videogram Association (BVA)

22 Poland Street
London W1V 3DD
Tel: 071 437 5722
Fax: 071 437 0477
Contact: N C B Abbott
The BVA represents the interests – with particular regard to copyright – of British producers and distributors of pre-recorded videocassettes and videodiscs

Broadcasters' Audience Research Board (BARB)

5th Floor, North Wing
Glenthorne House
Hammersmith Grove
London W6 0ND
Tel: 081 741 9110
Fax: 081 741 1943
Succeeding the Joint Industries' Committee on Television Audience Research (JICTAR), BARB commissions audience research on behalf of the BBC and ITV

Broadcasting and Entertainment Trades Alliance (BETA)

see **Broadcasting Entertainment and Cinematograph Technicians Union (BECTU)**

Broadcasting Complaints Commission (BCC)

Grosvenor Gardens House
35-37 Grosvenor Gardens
London SW1W 0BS
Tel: 071 630 1966
Fax: 071 828 7316
A statutory body set up by the Home Secretary under the Broadcasting Act 1981 (and now operating under the 1990 Act) to consider complaints of unjust or unfair treatment or unwarranted infringement of privacy in television and radio programmes broadcast by the BBC, television programmes broadcast by the ITC, radio programmes broadcast by the Radio Authority and programmes included in a licensed cable service

Broadcasting Entertainment and Cinematograph Technicians Union (BECTU)

ACTT-section:
111 Wardour Street
London W1V 4AY
Tel: 071 437 8506
BETA-section:
181-185 Wardour Street
London W1V 4BE
Tel: 071 439 7585
Contacts: D A Hearn, General Secretary, R Lockett, Deputy General Secretary
BECTU is the UK trade union for workers in film, broadcasting and the arts. Formed in 1991 by the merger of the ACTT and BETA, the union is 60,000 strong and represents permanently employed and freelance staff in television, radio, film, cinema, theatre and entertainment.
BECTU provides a comprehensive industrial relations service based on agreements with the BBC, ITV companies, Channel 4, the Producers' Association, AFVPA and MFVPA, the Theatrical Management Association, the Society of West End Theatres and others

Broadcasting Press Guild

c/o Harvey Lee
25 Courthouse Gardens
Finchley
London N3 1PU
Tel: 081 346 0643
An association of journalists who write about TV and radio in national, regional and trade press. Membership by invitation

Broadcasting Standards Council

5-8 The Sanctuary
London SW1P 3JS
Tel: 071 233 0544
Fax: 071 233 0397
Chairman: Lord Rees-Mogg
Deputy Chairman: Jocelyn Barrow OBE
Director: Colin Shaw
The Broadcasting Standards Council monitors the portrayal of violence, of sex and matters of taste and decency (such as bad language or the treatment of disasters), in television or radio programmes or broadcast advertisements. The Council publishes a Code of Practice, carries out research and deals with complaints about these matters. The Council may also make complaints of its own. The BSC is a statutory body under the Broadcasting Act 1990

CFL Vision

PO Box 35
Wetherby
Yorkshire LS23 7EX
Tel: 0937 541010
Fax: 0937 541083
CFL Vision began in 1927 as part of the Imperial Institute and is reputedly the oldest non-theatrical film library in the world. It is part of the COI and is the UK distributor for their audiovisual productions as well as for a large number of programmes acquired from both public and private sectors. Over 750 titles are available for loan or purchase by schools, film societies and by industry

Cable Authority

see **Independent Television Commission**

The Cable Television Association

50 Frith Street
London W1V 5TE
Tel: 071 437 0549
Represents the interests of cable operators, installers, programme providers and equipment suppliers. For further information on cable, see under Cable and Satellite

Campaign for Press and Broadcasting Freedom

96 Dalston Lane
London E8 1NG
Tel: 071 923 3671
Fax: 071 923 3672
A broad-based membership organisation campaigning for more diverse, accessible and accountable media in Britain, backed by the media unions. Established in 1979, it now incorporates the Campaign Against Racism in the Media (CARM), the Television Users Group (TUG) and is developing regional structures. Specialist groups deal with women's issues and media studies. CPBF publications cover all aspects of the media from broadcasting policy to sexism; its bi-monthly journal 'Free Press' watches ethical, industrial and political developments, with regular supplements on topical issues; its video

library includes Open Door films *It Ain't Half Racist, Mum, Why Their News is Bad News, Making News* and *Wapping Lies*. CPBF organises conferences, offering the public assistance in obtaining a right of reply against media bias or misrepresentation

Celtic Film and Television Association

The Library
Farraline Park
Inverness IV1 1LS
Tel: 0463 226189
Fax: 0463 237001
Development of film, TV and video production relevant to the languages of the Celtic nations and regions. Organises an annual competitive festival/conference, itinerant Scotland/ Ireland/Wales/Brittany in March/April

Central Office of Information (COI)

Films and Television Division
Hercules Road
London SE1 7DU
Tel: 071 261 8500
Fax: 071 928 5037
Contact: Malcolm Nisbet
COI Films and Television Division is responsible for government filmmaking on informational themes as well as the projection of Britain overseas. The COI organises the production of a wide range of documentary films, television programmes, video programmes and audiovisual presentations including videodisc production. It uses staff producers and draws on the film and video industry for production facilities. It provides help to visiting overseas television teams

Centre for the Study of Communication and Culture

221 Goldhurst Terrace
London NW6 3EP
Tel: 071 328 2868
Fax: 071 372 1193
A Jesuit-founded centre which promotes inter-disciplinary applied research on the problems of modern communication. Particular attention is paid to issues affecting the Third World and to the field of religious communication

Children's Film and Television Foundation

Elstree Studios
Borehamwood
Herts WD6 1JG
Tel: 081 953 0844
Fax: 081 207 0860
In 1944 Lord Rank founded the Children's Entertainment Film Division to make films specifically for children. In 1951 this resulted in the setting up of the Children's Film Foundation (now CFTF), a non-profit making organisation which, up to 1981, was funded by an annual grant from the BFFA (Eady money). The CFTF no longer makes films from its own resources but, for suitable children's/family cinema/television projects, is prepared to consider financing script development for eventual production by commercial companies. Films from the Foundation's library are available for hiring at nominal charge in 35mm, 16mm and video format from Glenbuck Films, with overseas sales handled by Rank Film Distributors (see under Distributors and International Sales)

Church of England Communications Unit

Church House
Great Smith Street
London SW1P 3NZ
Tel: 071 222 9011 x356/7
Fax: 071 222 6672
(Out of office hours: 071 222 9233)
Contact: Rev Patrick Forbes
Responsible for liaison between the Church of England and the broadcasting and film industries. Advises the C of E on all matters relating to broadcasting

The Cinema Advertising Association (CAA)

127 Wardour Street
London W1V 4AD
Tel: 071 439 9531
Fax: 071 439 2395
Paul Butler
The Cinema Advertising Association is a trade association of cinema advertising contractors operating in the UK and Eire. First established as a separate organisation in 1953 as the Screen Advertising Association, its main purpose is to promote, monitor and maintain standards of cinema advertising exhibition including the pre-vetting of commercials. It also commissions and conducts research into cinema as an advertising medium and is a prime sponsor of the CAVIAR annual surveys

Cinema and Television Benevolent Fund (CTBF)

Royalty House
72 Dean Street
London W1V 6LT
Tel: 071 437 6567
Fax: 071 437 7186
The CTBF helps those in need who have worked in cinema and/or ITV industries

Cinema and Television Veterans

166 The Rocks Road
East Malling
Kent ME19 6AX
Tel: 0732 843291
An association open to all persons employed in the film or television industries in their distribution, exhibition, or any of their production departments for at least thirty years

Cinema Exhibitors' Association (CEA)

1st Floor
Royalty House
72-73 Dean Street
London W1V 5HB
Tel: 071 734 9551
Fax: 071 734 6147
The first branch of the industry to organise itself was the cinema owners, who formed the CEA in 1912 and, following the merger with the Association of Independent Cinemas (AIC), is the only association representing cinema exhibition. CEA members account for the vast majority of all UK commercial cinemas, including independents, Regional Film Theatres and those cinemas in local authority ownership. The Association represents members' interests both within the industry, and to Government – European, national and local. It has been closely involved with all recent and proposed legislation affecting exhibition coming from both the UK Government and the European Commission

Cinema Theatre Association

40 Winchester Street
London SW1V 4NF
Tel: 071 834 0549
Contact: Richard Gray
The Cinema Theatre Association was formed in 1967 to promote interest in Britain's cinema building legacy, in particular the magnificent movie palaces of the 1920s and 1930s. It is the only major organisation committed to cinema preservation in the UK. It campaigns for the protection of architecturally important cinemas and runs a comprehensive archive. The CTA publishes a bi-monthly bulletin and the magazine 'Picture House'

Commonwealth Broadcasting Association

Broadcasting House
London W1A 1AA
Tel: 071 927 5022
An association of 58 public service broadcasting organisations in 51 Commonwealth countries

Composers' Guild of Great Britain
34 Hanway Street
London W1P 9DE
Tel: 071 436 0007
The Guild represents composers of serious music, covering the stylistic spectrum from jazz to electronics. Although its main function is to safeguard and assist the professional interests of its members, it also provides information for those wishing to commission music and will put performers or societies in touch with composers

Confederation of Entertainment Unions (CEU)
see ***Federation of Entertainment Unions (FEU)***

Critics' Circle
Film Section
31 Hampstead Lane
London N6
Tel/Fax: 081 340 0003
Chairman: William Hall
Vice-Chairman: George Perry
Honorary Secretary: Virginia Dignam
Honorary Treasurer: Peter Cargin
The film section of the Critics' Circle brings together most national and regional critics for meetings, functions and the presentation of annual awards

Deaf Broadcasting Council (DBC)
592 Kenilworth Road
Balsall Common
Coventry CV7 7DQ
Tel: 0203 832076
Fax: 0203 832150
Contact: Austin Reeves
An umbrella voluntary group working as a link between deaf people/organisations working for the deaf and the TV broadcasters – aiming for increased access to TV programmes

Defence Press and Broadcasting Committee
Room 2235
Ministry of Defence
Main Building
Whitehall
London SW1A 2HB
Tel: 071 218 2206
This committee is responsible for D notices. These give guidance on the publication of information which it regards as sensitive for reasons of national security

Department of Education and Science (DES)
Elizabeth House
York Road
London SE1 7PH
Tel: 071 934 9000
Fax: 071 934 9082
The DES is responsible for: policies for education in England; the Government's relations with universities in England, Scotland and Wales; fostering civil science

Department of Trade and Industry (DTI)
2nd Floor, Grey Core
151 Buckingham Palace Road
London SW1W 9SS
Tel: 071 215 5000
Fax: 071 215 1971
The DTI is responsible for carrying out Government policy concerning the commercial aspects of the film, video and cinema industries including the film facilities sector; UK and EEC films legislation; Council of Europe, OECD (Organisation for Economic Co-operation and Development) and GATT (General Agreement on Tariff and Trade) films interest. It is also responsible for the administration of co-production agreements and the certification of British films

Designers and Art Directors' Association
Nash House
12 Carlton House Terrace
London SW1Y 5AH
Tel: 071 839 2964
A professional association, registered as a charity, which publishes an annual of the best of British design, advertising, television commercials, pop promos/videos and organises travelling exhibitions. Membership is selected and only those who have had work accepted are eligible

Directors' Guild of Great Britain
1st Floor
Suffolk House
1-8 Whitfield Place
London W1P 5SF
Tel: 071 383 3858
Fax: 071 383 5175
Represents interests and concerns of directors in all media

Educational Broadcasting Services, BBC
BBC White City
201 Wood Lane
London W12 7TS
Tel: 081 752 5252
Contact: Brian Wright
EBS supports the work of BBC Education radio and television production departments. It services the Educational Broadcasting Council representing professional users

Educational Television Association
The King's Manor
Exhibition Square
York YO1 2EP
Tel: 0904 433929
Fax: 0904 433949
Contact: Josie Key
An umbrella organisation of institutions and individuals using TV for education and training. Award scheme and conference held annually. Membership enquiries welcome

Electrical Electronic Telecommunication and Plumbing Union (EETPU)
Hayes Court
West Common Road
Bromley BR2 7AU
Tel: 081 462 7755
Fax: 081 462 4959
A trade union representing – among others – people employed in film and TV lighting/electrical/electronic work

European Film Awards
General Secretariat
Münchener Strasse 6
D-1000 Berlin 30
Germany
Tel: (49) 30 261 1888/89
Fax: (49) 30 243 545

European Script Fund
39c Highbury Place
London N5 1QP
Tel: 071 226 9903
Fax: 071 354 2706
Contact: Renee Goddard
MEDIA 91-95 Script Development Fund based in London and supported by the BFI

The Federation Against Copyright Theft (FACT)
7 Victory Business Centre
Worton Road
Isleworth
Middlesex TW7 6ER
Tel: 081 568 6646
Fax: 081 560 6364
An organisation founded in 1982 by the legitimate film and video industry, dedicated to stamping out copyright piracy in the UK

Federation of Broadcasting Unions (FBU)
see ***Federation of Entertainment Unions***

Federation of Commercial Audio-Visual Libraries (FOCAL)
PO Box 422
Harrow
Middx HA1 3YN
Tel: 081 423 5853
Fax: 081 423 5853
Administrator: Anne Johnson
An international, non-profit making professional trade association representing commercial film/audiovisual libraries and interested individuals. Among other activities, it organises regular meetings, maximises copyright information, and

produces a directory of libraries

Federation of Entertainment Unions (FEU)

79 Redhill Wood
New Ash Green
Longfield
Kent DA3 8QP
Fax: 0474 874277
Secretary: John Morton
The Federation comprises British Actors' Equity Association, Broadcasting Entertainment and Cinematograph Technicians' Union (incorporating ACTT and BETA), Film Artistes' Association, Musicians' Union, National Union of Journalists and Writers' Guild of Great Britain. It has two standing committees covering Film and Electronic Media and Live Entertainment. It provides liaison and co-ordination between the constituent unions and makes joint representations on agreed matters

Feminist Library and Information Centre (formerly WRRC)

5 Westminster Bridge Road
London SE1 7XW
Tel: 071 928 7789
Has a large collection of fiction and non-fiction including books, pamphlets, papers etc. It also keeps an index of research by and on women and women's issues and information on women's studies courses. It holds a wide selection of journals and newsletters from all over the world and publishes its own newsletter. Open Tuesday (11.00-20.00) and Saturday and Sunday (14.00-17.00)

Ffilm Cymru

33 Castle Arcade
Cardiff CF1 2BW
Tel: 0222 340868
Fax: 0222 342235
Artistic Director: John Hefin
An organisation founded in 1988 by S4C and BBC Cymru to fund low budget feature films in Welsh, English and other European languages. Films completed: two 90-minute features *White Hall* and *Un Nos Ola Leuad (One Moonlit Night)*. Three further theatrical feature films in production

Film and Television Lighting Contractors Association

20 Darwin Close
New Southgate
London N11 1TA
Tel: 081 361 2122
Contact: A W Jacques
Set up in 1983 to negotiate with the EETPU on behalf of individual lighting contractors

Film Artistes' Association (FAA)

61 Marloes Road
London W8 6LE
Tel: 071 937 4567
General Secretary: Michael Reynel
The FAA represents extras, doubles, stand-ins and small part artistes. Under an agreement with the Producers Association and IPPA, supplies all background artistes in the major film studios and within a 40 mile radius of Charing Cross on all locations

Film Education

37-39 Oxford Street
London W1R 1RE
Tel: 071 434 9932
Fax: 071 287 5047
Ian Wall
Film Education is a film industry sponsored body. Its aims are to promote the use of film across the school curriculum and to further the use of cinemas by schools. To this end it publishes a variety of teaching materials – including study guides on individual films – and organises visits, lectures and seminars

First Film Foundation

Canalot Studios
222 Kensal Road
London W10 5BN
Tel: 081 969 5195
Fax: 081 960 6302
Contact: Deborah Burton
Set up to work with first time filmmakers in film and TV

German Film Board

Century House
4th Floor
100 Oxford Street
London W1N 9FB
Tel: 071 580 4422
Fax: 071 631 3049
Contact: Dina Lom
UK representative of the German Film Board, the official government organisation, and the German Film Export Union, concerned with distribution and to a growing extent co-production

Guild of British Animation

26 Noel Street
London W1V 3RD
Tel: 071 434 2651
Fax: 071 434 9002
Contact: Cecilia Garnett
Represents interests of producers of animated films. The AFVPA acts as secretariat for this association

Guild of British Camera Technicians

5-11 Taunton Road
Metropolitan Centre
Greenford
Middlesex UB6 8UQ
Tel: 081 578 9243
Fax: 081 575 5972
Contact: Julie Curran
Editor, 'Eyepiece': Kevin Desmond
Advertising Consultant: Ron Bowyer
The Guild exists to further the professional interests of technicians working with motion picture cameras. Membership is restricted to those whose work brings them into direct contact with motion picture cameras and who can demonstrate competence in their particular field of work. They must also be members of the appropriate union. By setting certain minimum standards of skill for membership, the Guild seeks to encourage its members, especially newer entrants, to strive to improve their art. Through its publication, 'Eyepiece', The Magazine of Moving Images, disseminates information about both creative and technical developments, past and present, in the motion picture industry

Guild of British Film Editors

c/o Alfred E Cox
Travair
Spurlands End Road
Great Kingshill
High Wycombe
Bucks HP15 6HY
Tel: 0494 712313
Fax: 02406 3563
To ensure that the true value of film and sound editing is recognised as an important part of the creative and artistic aspects of film production

Guild of Television Cameramen

1 Churchill Road
Whitchurch
Tavistock
Devon PL19 9BU
Tel/Fax: 0822 614405
Sheila Lewis
The Guild was formed in 1972 'to ensure and preserve the professional status of the television cameramen and to establish, uphold and advance the standards of qualification and competence of cameramen'. The Guild is not a union and seeks to avoid political involvement

Home Office

50 Queen Anne's Gate
London SW1H 9AT
Tel: 071 273 3000
The Home Office deals with questions of policy on broadcasting, classification of videos, cinema licensing and obscenity, and issues exemption certificates under the Cinemas Act 1985. It also sponsors publicity and training films

Imperial War Museum

Department of Film
Lambeth Road
London SE1 6HZ
Tel: 071 416 5000
Fax: 071 416 5379
The Imperial War Museum is the national

museum of twentieth century conflict, illustrating and recording all aspects of modern war, whether military, political, diplomatic, social or cultural. The Department of Film reflects these terms of reference with an extensive archive of film and video material. The Museum offers public screenings in its own cinema, and its viewing and research facilities are extensively used by historians and by film and television companies. It also promotes seminars and conferences and other activities relating to the study of history through film

Incorporated Society of British Advertisers (ISBA)

44 Hertford Street
London W1Y 8AE
Tel: 071 499 7502
Fax: 071 629 5355
Contact: Deborah Morris
The ISBA was founded in 1900 as an association for advertisers, both regional and national. Subscriptions are based on advertisers' expenditure and the main objective is the protection and advancement of the advertising interests of member firms. This involves organised representation, co-operation, action and exchange of information and experience, together with conferences, workshops and publications

Incorporated Society of Musicians

10 Stratford Place
London W1N 9AE
Tel: 071 629 4413
Fax: 071 408 1538
Contact: Neil Hoyle
A professional association for all musicians: teachers, performers and conductors. The ISM produces various publications, including the monthly 'Music Journal', and gives advice to members on professional issues

Independent Broadcasting Authority

see ***Independent Television Commission***

Independent Film Distributors' Association (IFDA)

c/o Glenbuck Films
Glenbuck Road
Surbiton
Surrey KT6 6BT
Tel: 081 399 0022
Fax: 081 399 6651
Contact: Sid Brooks
IFDA was formed in 1973, and its members are mainly specialised film distributors who deal in both 16mm and 35mm from 'art' to 'popular music' films. They supply to many users including schools, hospitals, prisons, hotels etc

Independent Programme Producers' Association (IPPA)

50-51 Berwick Street
London W1A 4RD
Tel: 071 439 7034
Fax: 071 494 2700
Contact: Margaret Wyndham Heffernan
IPPA is the trade association for British independent television producers, representing over 700 production companies based throughout the UK. Services to members include a specialist industrial relations unit and advice on all matters relating to independent production for television. Having led the successful campaign for 25% of all new British TV programmes to be made by independents, IPPA maintains an active lobby to ensure that the needs of the sector are heard and understood by Government in Britain and Europe. Merging late 1991 with The Producers Association to form The Producers Alliance for Cinema and Television (PACT)

Independent Television Association (ITVA)

Knighton House
56 Mortimer Street
London W1N 8AN
Tel: 071 636 6866
Fax: 071 580 7892
Contact: Margaret Bassett
Incorporated as a company limited by guarantee, the ITVA is the organisation which provides a Central Secretariat to service the needs of the industry requiring a co-ordinated and centralised approach. The governing body is the Council, comprising all the Managing Directors, and its main task is to determine the joint policy of the companies over a wide range of industry matters. Several committees – Network Programme, Industrial Relations, Marketing, Finance, Rights and Technical, supported by specialised sub-committees and working groups – undertake the detailed work

Independent Television Commission

70 Brompton Road
London SW3 1EY
Tel: 071 584 7011
Fax: 071 589 5533
The ITC operates under the Broadcasting Act 1990. It is the controlling body for Channels 3 (ITV), 4 and the proposed Channel 5, cable, satellite and 'additional services'. The ITC will license a variety of services and regulate these through its various codes on programme content, advertising sponsorship and technical standards

Institute of Amateur Cinematographers

63 Woodfield Lane
Ashtead
Surrey KT21 2BT
Tel: 03722 76358
Encouraging amateurs interested in the art of making moving pictures and supporting them with a variety of services

Institute of Practitioners in Advertising (IPA)

44 Belgrave Square
London SW1X 8QS
Tel: 071 235 7020
Fax: 071 245 9904
The IPA is the representative body for UK advertising agencies and the people who work in them. It represents the collective views of its member agencies in liaison with Government departments, the media and industry and consumer organisations

International Association of Broadcasting Manufacturers (IABM)

4b High Street
Burnham
Slough SL1 7JH
Tel: 0628 667633
Fax: 0628 665882
Administrator: Alan Hirst
IABM aims to foster the interests of manufacturers of broadcast equipment from all countries. Areas of interest include liaison with broadcasters, standardisation and exhibitions. All companies active in the field of broadcast equipment manufacturing are welcome to join

International Federation of the Phonographic Industry (IFPI)

IFPI Secretariat
54 Regent Street
London W1R 5PJ
Tel: 071 434 3521
Fax: 071 439 9166
President: Sir John Morgan
An international association of over 950 members in 64 countries, representing the copyright interests of the sound recording and music video industries

International Institute of Communications

Tavistock House South
Tavistock Square
London WC1H 9LF
Tel: 071 388 0671
Fax: 071 380 0623
Contact: Carol Joy
The IIC provides a centre for the analysis of social, economic, political, cultural and legal issues

related to media and electronic communication. It carries out research projects and consultancy, holds conferences and seminars and publishes books. UK members include BBC, ITC, C4 and many individuals. Its journal is 'InterMedia' which appears bi-monthly

International Visual Communications Association (IVCA)

Bolsover House
5-6 Clipstone Street
London W1P 7EB
Tel: 071 580 0962
Fax: 071 436 2606
Contact: Stuart Appleton
IVCA is the professional association representing the interests of the users and suppliers of visual communications. In particular it pursues the interests of the producers, commissioners and manfacturers involved in the non-broadcast and independent facilities industries. It represents all sizes of company and freelance individuals, offering information and advice services, publications, a professional network, special interest groups, a magazine and a variety of events including the UK's Film and Video Communications Festival

London Screenwriters' Workshop

1 Greek Street
London W1V 6NQ
Tel: 081 551 5570
Ray Frensham
Promotes contact between screenwriters and producers, agents, development executives and other film and TV professionals through a wide range of seminars. Practical workshops provide training in all aspects of the screenwriting process. Membership is open to anyone interested in writing for film and TV, and to anyone in these and related media

Mechanical-Copyright Protection Society (MCPS)

Elgar House
41 Streatham High Road
London SW16 1ER
Tel: 081 769 4400
Fax: 081 769 8792
Contact: General Licensing Department
MCPS licenses the recording of its members' copyright musical works in all areas of television, film and video production

Media Team of the Volunteer Centre UK

29 Lower Kings Road
Berkhamsted
Herts HP4 2AB
Tel: 0442 873311
Contact: James Ford Smith, Liz Schofield
The Media Team provides information, training and support for volunteers and voluntary organisations using broadcast media

Mental Health Media Council

380 Harrow Road
London W9 2HU
Tel: 071 286 2346
Contact: Sylvia Hines
An independent charity founded in 1965, the MHMC provides information, advice and consultancy on film/video use and production relevant to mental health education. Resource lists, quarterly magazine 'Mediawise'. Also regular screenings and occasional video production

Music Film and Video Producers' Association (MFVPA)

26 Noel Street
London W1V 3RD
Tel: 071 434 2651
Contact: Cecilia Garnett
The MFVPA was formed in 1985 to represent the interests of pop/music promo production companies. It negotiates agreements with bodies such as the BPI and ACTT on behalf of its members. Secretariat support is run through AFVPA

Music Publishers' Association

7th Floor
Kingsway House
103 Kingsway
London WC2B 6QX
Tel: 071 831 7591
Fax: 071 242 0612
The only trade association representing UK music publishers. List of members available at £3.50

Musicians' Union (MU)

60-62 Clapham Road
London SW9 0JJ
Tel: 071 582 5566
Fax: 071 582 9805
Contact: Don Smith
The MU represents the interests of performing musicians in all areas

National Association for Higher Education in Film and Video

c/o London International Film School
24 Shelton Street
London WC2H 9HP
Tel: 071 836 9642/240 0168
Contact: Martin Amstell
The Association's main aims are to act as a forum for debate on all aspects of film, video and TV education and to foster links with industry, the professions and Government bodies. It was established in 1983 to represent all courses in the UK which offer a major practical study in film, video or TV at the higher educational level. Some 40 courses are currently in membership

National Campaign for the Arts

Francis House
Francis Street
London SW1P 1DE
Tel: 071 828 4448
Fax: 071 828 5504
Director: Simon Mundy
Administrator: Stephanie McKennell
Campaigns and Information Officer: Charles Morgan
The NCA specialises in lobbying, campaigning (eg running the 'I Vote for the Arts' events at the last election, or the National Arts Advocacy Day), research and information. It provides up-to-the-minute facts and figures for politicians, journalists and any other interested parties. The NCA is independent of any political party or government agency and is funded solely by membership subscriptions and donations from arts organisations and individuals

National Council for Educational Technology (NCET)

Sir William Lyons Road
Science Park
University of Warwick
Coventry CV4 7EZ
Tel: 0203 416994
Fax: 0203 411418
The Department of Education and Science engages NCET to monitor and evaluate technology on behalf of educators, trainers, and learners. NCET has the strategic role of introducing appropriate equipment and methods, and spreading knowledge about them to key people

National Film and Television School

Beaconsfield Studios
Station Road
Beaconsfield
Bucks HP9 1LG
Tel: 0494 671234
Fax: 0494 674042
Director: Colin Young
The National Film and Television School provides advanced training and retraining in all major disciplines to professional standards. Graduates are entitled to ACTT/BECTU membership on gaining employment. It is an autonomous non-profit making organisation funded by the Office of Arts and Libraries and the film and television industries. See also under Courses

National Film Development Fund (NFDF)

37-39 Oxford Street
London W1R 1RE
Tel: 071 434 0291
Fax: 071 434 9933

Administrator: Tessa Ross
The NFDF was set up in 1976 to make loans for the development of British cinema feature films. Funded originally from the Eady Levy, it has helped to develop such films as *Defence of the Realm, Dance with a Stranger, A Room with a View, Tree of Hands, Joyriders, A Very British Coup* and *Soursweet.* Under the 1985 Films Act, the fund receives £500,000 annually from the Department of Trade and Industry – £350,000 for the development of scripts and £150,000 for the production of short films. The NFDF is managed by British Screen Finance (the semi-privatised successor of the NFFC), but has a separate administrator and panel of independent consultants

National Film Trustee Company (NFTC)

37-39 Oxford Street
London W1R 1RE
Tel: 071 434 0291
Fax: 071 434 9933
Contact: Alun Tyers
An independent revenue collection and disbursement service for producers and financiers. The NFTC has been in business since 1971. It is a subsidiary of British Screen

National Union of Journalists

314 Grays Inn Road
London WC1X 8DP
Tel: 071 278 7916
Fax: 071 837 8143
National Broadcasting Organiser: John Fray
NUJ represents all journalists working in broadcasting in the areas of news, sport, current affairs and features. It has agreements with all of the broadcasting companies and the BBC. It also has agreements with the main broadcasting agencies, WTN and Visnews with approximately 5,000 members in broadcasting

National Viewers' and Listeners' Association (NVALA)

Ardleigh
Colchester
Essex CO7 7RH
Tel: 0206 230123
Contact: Mary Whitehouse
General Sec: John Beyer
Concerned with moral standards in the media, particularly the role of TV in the creation of social and cultural values

Network of Workshops

c/o The Video Workshop
Chapter Arts Centre
Market Road
Canton
Cardiff CF5 1EQ
Tel: 0222 342755
Contact: Ruth Scofield
The Network of Workshops is a membership organisation which is open to all independent collective film and video groups who are committed to the cultural aims stated in the ACTT workshop declaration

Office of Arts and Libraries (OAL)

Horse Guards Road
London SW1P 3AL
Tel: 071 270 3000
Fax: 071 270 5776
Contact: J C Mole
Within its wider concern with matters affecting the arts, museums and libraries, the OAL is the major source of government finance for film. It funds – among other bodies – the BFI and the Arts Council

Office of Fair Trading

Field House
Bream's Buildings
London EC4A 1PR
Tel: 071 242 2858
Fax: 071 269 8800
The Office of Fair Trading has an interest in the film industry following two reports on the supply of films for exhibition in cinemas – by the Monopolies Commission in October 1966 and by the Monopolies and Mergers Commission in 1983

Performers' Alliance

Consists of British Equity, Musicians' Union, Writers' Guild of Great Britain. Contact through member organisations above

Performing Right Society (PRS)

29-33 Berners Street
London W1P 4AA
Tel: 071 580 5544
Fax: 071 631 4138
The PRS is a non-profit making association of composers, authors and publishers of musical works. It collects and distributes royalties for the use, in public performances, broadcasts and cable programmes, of its members' copyright music and has links with other performing right societies throughout the world. Explanatory literature and/or a film explaining the Society's operations is available from the Public Relations Department

Phonographic Performance

Ganton House
14-22 Ganton Street
London W1V ILB
Tel: 071 437 0311
Fax: 071 734 2986
Formed by the British recording industry for the collection and distribution of revenue in respect of the UK public performance and broadcasting of sound recordings

The Producers Association

162-170 Wardour Street
London W1V 4LA
Tel: 071 437 7700
Fax: 071 734 4564
Contact: John Woodward
The Producers Association was formed out of a merger between the British Film and Television Producers' Association (BFTPA) and the Association of Independent Producers (AIP) in 1990. The Producers Association is the leading British trade association representing UK-based feature film and television producers in Britain and abroad. It works to secure the future for film and TV production in the UK ensuring liaison with BBC, ITV and Channel 4. It runs an industrial relations service with IPPA which negotiates and maintains trade union agreements and provides detailed information to producers on the interpretation of agreements etc. It provides a wide range of information services, publishes handbooks and the magazine 'Producer', and offers international marketing advice, British Overseas Trade Board subvention schemes and acts as the UK contact for the EEC-backed Euro-Aim distribution network. Merging late 1991 with IPPA to form The Producers Alliance for Cinema and Television.

Radio, Electrical and Television Retailers' Association (RETRA)

Retra House
St John's Terrace
1 Ampthill Street
Bedford MK42 9EY
Tel: 0234 269110
Fax: 0234 269609
Contact: Paula Greening
The Association was founded in 1942 to represent the interests of electronic retailers to all those who make decisions likely to affect the selling and servicing of electrical and electronic products

Reel Women

57 Holmewood Gardens
London SW2 3NB
Tel: 081 678 7404
Jini Rawlings
A networking organisation for all women in film, video and television. It places particular emphasis on the creative interaction between women from the broadcast, non-broadcast and independent sectors, aiming to provide a forum for debate around issues affecting women in all areas of production and training, as well as around broader concerns about the representation and position of women in the industry and on screen. Seminars,

screenings and workshops are held as well as regular 'nights out'

Royal Television Society (RTS)

Tavistock House East
Tavistock Square
London WC1H 9HR
Tel: 071 387 1970
Fax: 071 387 0358
Contact: Tracey Dyer
The Royal Television Society, founded in 1927, has over 3,000 members in the UK and overseas, half of which are serviced by the Society's 14 regional centres. The Society aims to bring together all the disciplines of television by providing a forum for debate on the technical, cultural and social implications of the medium. This is achieved through the many lectures, conferences, symposia and training courses organised each year. A monthly journal 'Television' is published by the RTS as well as monographs, television engineering textbooks, career broadsheets and a number of topical papers relating to Society events. The RTS Television Journalism Awards are presented every year in February and the Programme Awards in May. There are also Design and Educational Television Awards. See also under Awards

Scottish Film Council

Dowanhill
74 Victoria Crescent Road
Glasgow G12 9JN
Tel: 041 334 4445
Fax: 041 334 8132
The Scottish Film Council is the national body with a remit to promote all aspects of film, television and video throughout Scotland. In particular it aims to make viewing films and film making accessible throughout the community and encourages the development of Scotland's film and television industries

Scottish Film Production Fund

74 Victoria Crescent Road
Glasgow G12 9JN
Tel: 041 337 2526
Fax: 041 334 8132
The Fund was set up in 1982 with a brief to foster and promote film and video production in Scotland. The Production Fund committee meets quarterly to consider applications for finance for projects which must have a particular connection with and relevance to Scotland. The Fund's annual budget now stands at £200,000

Scottish Film Training Trust

74 Victoria Crescent Road
Glasgow G12 9JN
Tel: 041 337 2526
Fax: 041 334 8132
A charitable trust set up in 1982 and financed by the Scottish Film Council, the Scottish Arts Council, the European Social Fund, Scottish Television plc and BAFTA/Shell. It aims to assist in the training of young Scots entering the film and TV industries

The Shape Network

c/o Shape London
1 Thorpe Close
London W10 5XL
Tel: 081 960 9245
A federation of around 18 independent local services which work to improve and increase the involvement of disabled, elderly and other under-represented groups in the arts. The Network currently works mainly as an information-sharing forum, but has also held a nationally funded, regionally diverse training programme. Details of regional Shape groups can be obtained from the above address

Society of Authors' Broadcasting Committee

84 Drayton Gardens
London SW10 9SB
Tel: 071 373 6642
Fax: 071 373 5768
Contact: Kathryn Dymoke
Specialities: Radio, television and film scriptwriters

Society of Cable Television Engineers (SCTE)

10 Avenue Road
Dorridge
Solihull
West Midlands B93 8LD
Tel: 0564 774058
Fax: 0564 779032
Contact: T H Hall MBE
Aims to raise the standard of cable TV engineering to the highest technical level and to elevate and improve the status and efficiency of those engaged in cable TV engineering

Society of Film Distributors (SFD)

Royalty House
72-73 Dean Street
London W1V 5HB
Tel: 071 437 4383
Fax: 071 734 0912
General Secretary: D C Hunt
SFD was founded in 1915 and membership includes all the major distribution companies and several independent companies. It promotes and protects its members' interests and co-operates with all other film organisations and Government agencies where distribution interests are involved

Society of Television Lighting Directors

46 Batchworth Lane
Northwood
Middlesex HA6 3HG
The Society provides a forum for the exchange of ideas in all aspects of the TV profession including techniques and equipment. Meetings are organised throughout the UK and abroad. Technical information and news of members' activities are published in the Society's magazine. The Society has no union or political affiliations

Sovexport Film

103 Swains Lane
Highgate
London N6 6RG
Tel: 081 348 5812
Fax: 081 348 1390
Contact: Sergei Kuzmenko
Exports Soviet films to different countries and imports films to Soviet Union. Provides facilities to foreign companies wishing to film in Soviet Union. Co-production information for producers

Telefilm Canada

4th Floor
55-59 Oxford Street
London W1R 1RD
Tel: 071 437 8308
Fax: 071 734 8586
Contact: Robert Linnell, Director
Canadian government organisation financing film and television productions. The London office advises on co-productions between Canada and the UK

Variety Club of Great Britain

32 Welbeck Street
London W1M 7PG
Tel: 071 935 4466
The greatest children's charity in the world

Video Trade Association

54d High Street
Northwood
Middlesex HA6 1BL
Tel: 0927 429122
Fax: 0923 835980
Trade association set up to improve trading standards and customer service offered by the video software retailer

Voice of the Listener

101 King's Drive
Gravesend
Kent DA12 5BQ
Tel: 0474 564676
An independent non-profit making association working to ensure high standards in broadcasting. Membership is open to all concerned for the future quality and range

of British radio and television

Welsh Arts Council

Film, Video & Television Department
Holst House
9 Museum Place
Cardiff CF1 3NX
Tel: 0222 394711
Fax: 0222 221447
Director: T A Owen
Film Director: Mike Sweet
Advises the Arts Council on matters in Wales. Like the English Regional Arts Associations and Boards, it is eligible to receive funds from the BFI

Wider Television Access (WTVA)

c/o Flashbacks
6 Silver Place
London W1R 3LJ
A pressure group and publisher of 'Primetime' magazine, seeking to stimulate interest in old UK and US TV programmes and promote greater use of TV archives

Women in Film (UK)

Garden Studios
11-15 Betterton Street
London WC2H 9BP
Tel: 071 379 0344
Fax: 071 379 0801
Chairman: Lynda Myles
Administrator: Janet Fielding
A membership organisation for women with a minimum of three years experience in the film and television industry. It is closely modelled on and affiliated to the American groups of the same name. Its aims are to provide information and career support for members, offer an educational forum for all media professionals, promote and safeguard the interests of women and champion and recognise women's achievements and contributions to the industry

Writers' Guild of Great Britain

430 Edgware Road
London W2 1EH
Tel: 071 723 8074
Fax: 071 706 2413
The Writers' Guild is the recognised TUC-affiliated trade union for writers working in film, television, radio, theatre and publishing. It has negotiated industrial agreements in all the areas mentioned above. These agreements set the minimum rates and conditions for each field of writing

REGIONAL ARTS BOARDS

Council of Regional Arts Associations

13a Clifton Road
Winchester SO22 5BP
Tel: 0962 851063
Fax: 0962 842033
Executive Officer: Christopher Gordon
Administrator: Nicola Gunn

Arts Board: North West

comprising Merseyside Arts and North West Arts Board
12 Harter Street
Manchester M1 6HY
Tel: 061 228 3062
Fax: 061 236 1257
Regional arts board for Merseyside and the North West

East Midlands Arts Board

Mountfields House
Forest Road
Loughborough
Leicestershire LE11 3HU
Tel: 0509 218292
Fax: 0509 262214
Director: John Buston
Derbyshire (excluding High Peak District), Leicestershire, Northamptonshire, Nottinghamshire

Eastern Arts Board

Cherry Hinton Hall
Cherry Hinton Road
Cambridge CB1 4DW
Tel: 0223 215355
Director: Jeremy Newton
Bedfordshire, Cambridgeshire, Essex, Hertfordshire, Lincolnshire, Norfolk and Suffolk

London Arts Board

Coriander Building
20 Gainsford Street
London SE1 2NE
Tel: 071 403 9013
Fax: 071 403 9072
The area of the 32 London Boroughs and the City of London

Northern Arts Board

9-10 Osborne Terrace
Jesmond
Newcastle upon Tyne NE2 1NZ
Tel: 091 281 6334
Fax: 091 281 3276
Director: Peter Stark
Cleveland, Cumbria, Durham, Northumberland, Tyne and Wear

South East Arts Board

10 Mount Ephraim
Tunbridge Wells
Kent TN4 8AS
Tel: 0892 515210
Fax: 0892 549383
Director: Chris Cooper
East Sussex, Kent, Surrey and West Sussex

South West Arts Board

Bradninch Place
Gandy Street
Exeter EX4 3LS
Tel: 0392 218188
Fax: 0392 413554
Director: Christopher Bates
Avon, Cornwall, Devon, Dorset (except Bournemouth, Christchurch and Poole DCs), Gloucestershire and Somerset

Southern Arts Board

13 St Clement Street
Winchester
Hampshire SO23 9DQ
Tel: 0962 855099
Director: Bill Dufton
Berkshire, Buckinghamshire, East Dorset, Hampshire, Isle of Wight, Oxfordshire and Wiltshire

West Midlands Arts Board

82 Granville Street
Birmingham B1 2LH
Tel: 021 631 3121
Fax: 021 643 7239
Director: Mick Elliot
Hereford and Worcester, Shropshire, Staffordshire, Warwickshire, West Midlands

Yorkshire and Humberside Arts Board

Glyde House
Glydegate
Bradford BD5 0BQ
Tel: 0274 723051
(future location to be decided)
Director: Roger Lancaster
North, South, West Yorkshire and Humberside

ORGANISATIONS (EUROPE)

This new section of the Handbook comprises a representative list of the main pan-European film and television organisations (whose offices may be located outside the EC), including the MEDIA projects, followed by entries for each of the UK's eleven partner countries of the EC

PAN-EUROPEAN ORGANISATIONS

AGICOA (Association de Gestion internationale collective des oeuvres audiovisuelles)
25 route de Fernay
1202 Geneva
Switzerland
Tel: (41) 22 734 45 80
Fax: (41) 22 734 47 62
Contacts: Rodolphe Egli, Luigi Cattaneo
AGICOA ensures the protection of the rights of producers worldwide when their works are retransmitted by cable. By entering their works in the AGICOA Registers, producers can claim royalties collected for them

Association Internationale de la Distribution par Câble (AID)
Boulevard Anspach 1
Box 28
1000 Brussels
Belgium
Tel: (32) 2 211 94 49
Fax: (32) 2 211 99 07
Contact: M de Sutter
International Alliance of Cable Distribution Organisations in the different European countries. It defends the interests of the different member countries

Audiovisual EUREKA
see ***DTI Films Branch – European Initiatives*** and ***The EUREKA Programme***

BABEL (Broadcasting Across the Barriers of European Language)
c/o European Broadcasting Union
Ancienne Route 17a
PO Box 67
1218 Grand-Saconnex
Geneva
Switzerland
Tel: (41) 22 717 2111
Fax: (41) 22 798 5897
Contact: Frank Naef
MEDIA project. BABEL was set up to provide financial support for mainly European multilingual audiovisual production. It is aimed at assisting dubbing and subtitling, the development of new post-production techniques (eg multilingual news) and professional training in this sphere. Preference is given to productions in less widely spoken languages; drama productions (especially those aimed at children and young people, including animation); European cultural magazines; pilots for television series; documentaries on culture, music, arts, etc

Bureau de Liaison Européen du Cinéma
c/o Fédération Internationale des Associations de Distributeurs de Films (FIAD)
43 boulevard Malesherbes
75008 Paris
France
Tel: (33) 1 42 66 05 32
Fax: (33) 1 42 66 96 92
Grouping of cinema trade organisations to pursue goals of common interest

Bureau Internationale des Sociétées gérant les Droits d'Enregistrement (BIEM)
rue Kepler 56
75016 Paris
France
Tel: (33) 1 47 04 57 04
Contact: A Vacher-Desvernais
Copyright register for musicians. Handles negotiations and royalty payments over recordings

The Business School of Film
Velazquez 12
28001 Madrid
Spain
Tel: (34) 1 431 4246
Fax: (34) 1 435 5994
MEDIA project, still in the planning stages. Should run as umbrella for various types of training

CARTOON (European Association of Animation Film)
127 rue Franz Merjay
1060 Brussels
Belgium
Tel: (32) 2 347 28 70
Fax: (32) 2 347 23 47
Contacts: Marc Vandeweyer, Corinne Jenart
Part of MEDIA umbrella. Supports European animation industry. Grants aid for script and adaptation, graphic research and pilot film

Centre for Cultural Research
Am Hofgarten 17
5300 Bonn 1
and
Wallstrasse 61-65
1020 Berlin
Germany
Tel: (49) 228 211058
Fax: (49) 228 217493

Contact: Professor A J Wiesand
Research, documentation, advisory tasks in all fields of the arts and media, especially with 'European' perspectives. Participation in arts and media management courses at university level. Produces publications

Centre Internationale de Liaison des Ecoles de Cinéma et de Télévision (CILECT)

rue Thérésienne 8
1000 Brussels
Belgium
Tel: (32) 2 511 98 39
Fax: (32) 2 511 02 79
Contact: Henry Verhasselt
CILECT was formed at Cannes in 1955 and is the oldest association in the field of film and television training in the world. It is represented in 41 countries in the five continents and has a membership of 79 institutions. CILECT is a Non-Governmental Association, Status B, recognised by UNESCO. The aim of the association is to promote co-operation among higher teaching and research institutes and among their staff and students, to raise standards of teaching and to improve the education of future creative film and television programme makers and scholars throughout the world

Comité des Industries Cinématographiques et Audiovisuelles des Communautés Européennes et de l'Europe Extracommunautaire (CICCE)

5 rue du Cirque
75008 Paris
France
Tel: (33) 1 42 25 70 63
Fax: (33) 1 42 25 94 27
Contact: Pascal Rogard
European committee of film and audiovisual industry associations, including producers, distributors and technical industries. It represents the industry to European governmental bodies, advises them on audiovisual policy and how to implement it

Coordination of European Independent Producers (CEPI)

59 rue de Châteaudun
75009 Paris
France
Tel: (33) 1 44 53 03 03
Fax: (33) 1 49 95 99 80
Contact: Alain Modot
Network of the European associations of TV producers

Department of Trade and Industry – Films Branch

Room 2/165 Grey Core
151 Buckingham Palace Road
London SW1W 9SS
Tel: 071 215 1761
Fax: 071 215 1971
Contacts:
For MEDIA/EUREKA: Angela Knell 071 215 1730
For ECPF: Pauline Givans 071 215 1757
For Co-Productions: Les Mondry 071 215 1723
DTI carries out UK Government policy concerning the commercial and business aspects of the film, video and cinema industries and the administration of the UK's Co-production Agreements. It co-ordinates the EUREKA initiative within the UK, making information available so that industry can suggest projects for inclusion. DTI also collaborates with OAL on MEDIA 95. DTI helps fund the UK contribution to the MEDIA programme and provides funding for the European Co-Production Fund, administered by British Screen Finance (see Organisations)

EAVE (European Audiovisual Entrepreneurs)

Rue de la Presse 14
1000 Brussels
Belgium
Tel: (32) 2 219 09 20
Fax: (32) 2 223 00 34
Contact: Raymond Ravar
MEDIA project. Over the last three years EAVE has provided the only top-level professional training in development and co-production of European film and television projects. EAVE's objectives are to develop genuine European co-productions, to create a pan-European network for producers and to disseminate its expertise as widely as possible

EFDO

Friedensallee 14-16
2000 Hamburg 50
Germany
Tel: (49) 40 390 90 25
Fax: (49) 40 390 54 95
Contact: Dieter Kosslick
MEDIA project. It assists the theatrical distribution of low/mid budget European feature films by providing conditionally re-payable, interest-free loans to groups of European distributors from no less than 3 different countries

EGAKU (European Committee of Trade Unions in Arts, Mass Media and Entertainment)

15 avenue de Balexert
1219 Châtelaine-Geneva
Switzerland
Tel: (41) 22 796 27 33
Fax: (41) 22 796 53 21
Contact: Irène Robadey
Addresses the concerns of unions whose members are engaged in the arts and all types of entertainment. It circulates information on wages and working conditions, maintains relations with other concerned international bodies, and reinforces its affiliated unions' activities at an international level

EUTELSAT (European Telecommunications Satellite Organisation)

Tour Maine-Montparnasse
33 avenue du Maine
75755 Paris Cedex 15
France
Tel: (33) 1 45 38 47 47
Fax: (33) 1 45 38 37 00
Contact: Philippe Binet
EUTELSAT is an intergovernmental organisation of 28 European Member states, all represented by their telecommunications organisations. EUTELSAT provides the satellites for carrying their national and international services for telephony, television, radio and business and mobile communication throughout Europe

EVE (Espace Vidéo Européen)

c/o Irish Film Institute
6 Eustace Street
Dublin 2
Ireland
Tel: (353) 1 679 5744
Fax: (353) 1 679 9657
Contacts: John Dick, Norma Cairns
MEDIA project, co-ordinated by the Irish Film Institute and the Médiathèque de la Communauté Française de Belgique to promote European film on video

EUREKA Programme

DTI
Room 2/165 Grey Core
151 Buckingham Palace Road
London SW1 9SS
Contacts:
For HDTV: Brian Aldiss
Tel: 071 215 1737
For Technology: Nick Kaspar
Tel: 071 215 1617
A co-operation mechanism which makes information available to industry and encourages collaborative projects and programme exchanges in audiovisual wares, with a view to opening up a bigger domestic European market and using it as a firm base to tackle the world market. There is no dedicated UK or European project funding though specific projects might qualify for public funding

Eurimages

BP 431 R6
F-67006 Strasbourg
France
Tel: (33) 88 61 49 61

Fax: (33) 88 36 70 57
Contact: Ryclef Rienstra
Founded in 1988 by a group of Council of Europe member states. Its objective is to stimulate film and audiovisual production by partly financing the co-production and distribution of European cinematographic and audiovisual works

EuroAim
rue des Minimes 26
1000 Brussels
Belgium
Tel: (32) 2 518 14 60
Fax: (32) 2 512 86 57
Contact: Karol Kulik
MEDIA project. It provides a range of technical, legal and commercial advice to European TV producers at the MIP and MIPCOM markets for a reduced entry fee. Preference is given to producers new to markets and to companies making 'culturally based' programmes

Eurocreation
c/o The Prince's Trust
8 Bedford Row
London WC1R 4BA
Fax: 071 831 7280
Contact: Anne Engel
They operate the 'Pépinières Programme', where a network of European cities offer work facilities to people under 30. In 1991 they offered: scriptwriting in Barcelona and Angers; new media digital arts in Frankfurt; contemporary music in Bologna

Eurocreation Production
3 rue Debelleyme
75003 Paris
France
Tel: (33) 1 48 04 78 79
Fax: (33) 1 40 29 92 46
Contact: Anne-Marie Autissier
Eurocreation Production was formed in February 1989 to discover young European talents in the audiovisual fields and has built upon a network of European film and audiovisual professionals

Eurodience
c/o Institut National de l'Audiovisuel
avenue de l'Europe 4
94360 Bry-sur-Marne
Cedex
France
Tel: (33) 1 49 83 20 00
The first European television programming and audience rating newsletter, published monthly by the INA Research Department and Médiamétrie, in association with several European audience rating institutes

Euro Media Garanties
GEFCA
66 rue Pierre Charron
75008 Paris
France
Tel: (33) 1 43 59 88 03
Fax: (33) 1 45 63 85 58
Contact: Georges Prost
MEDIA project. Guarantee fund geared towards large budget production and distribution on a commercial basis

Europäisches Dokumentarfilm Institut
c/o Filmbüro N W eV
In der Alten Post
Postfach 100534
4330 Mühlheim a/d Ruhr
Germany
European Documentary Institute

European Broadcasting Union
Ancienne Route 17a
PO Box 67
1218 Grand-Saconnex
Geneva
Switzerland
Tel: (41) 22 717 2111
Fax: (41) 22 798 5897
Contact: Michael Type
The EBU's aim is to promote co-operation between its members and broadcasting organisations of the entire world and to represent the interests of its Members in the programme, legal, technical and other fields. It organises Eurovision and Euroradio news and programme exchanges. There are currently 97 members in 66 countries

European Co-Production Fund (ECF)
c/o British Screen Finance
37-39 Oxford Street
London W1R 1RE
Tel: 071 434 0291
Fax: 071 434 9933
The £5m ECF, which will be provided over the next three years, will be available for investment in feature films made by European co-producers and for investment in film development work. This is intended to result in feature films made by European co-producers. British Screen Finance will be responsible for disbursing the Fund to producers and writers in the form of loans on commercial terms. The Fund aims to improve the opportunity for UK producers to co-produce with an EC partner

European Television and Film Forum
see **European Institute for the Media**

European Institute for the Media (EIM)
University of Manchester
Manchester M13 9PL
Tel: 061 273 2754
Fax: 061 273 8788
Contacts: George Wedell, Pierre Yves Lochon
The EIM is a forum for research and documentation in the field of media in Europe. Its activities include: research into the media in Europe with a political, economic and juridical orientation; the organisation of conferences and seminars like the Annual European Forum for Television and Film; the management of a European satellite Educational Channel, Channel E; the development of an advanced studies programme for students and media managers

European Production Group
c/o ZDF
Essenheimerstrasse
PO Box 4040
D-6500 Mainz
Germany
Tel: (49) 6131 705168
Fax: (49) 6131 78060
A consortium of European public service TV networks for the co-production of TV fiction series. Can offer complete finance or development funding

European Script Fund
39c Highbury Place
London N5 1QP
Tel: 071 226 9903
Fax: 071 354 2706
Contact: Renee Goddard
MEDIA project. Provides development money for film and television fiction with European appeal. Applications are taken from individual scriptwriters, or writer/producer/director teams

European Scriptwriting and Film Analysis Certificate
Université Libre de Bruxelles
Faculty of Philosophy and Letters
CP 175
50 Avenue Roosevelt
1050 Brussels
Belgium
Tel: (32) 2 650 24 04
Fax: (32) 2 650 24 50
Contacts: Dominique Nasta, Natalie Tricnot
Two year European programme (MEDIA pilot initiative) which started in October 1988. Aims to provide academic training in scriptwriting, film criticism, teaching, film-club animation, research. Scriptwriting workshops dealing with many genres (adaptations, originals, TV series) and weekend script doctoring seminars. Links with EC and non EC countries. Admission conditions: candidates need a degree or proven involvement in screenwriting or film-making

FIAF (International Federation of Film Archives)
rue Franz Merjay 190
1080 Brussels

Belgium
Tel: (32) 2 343 06 91
Fax: (32) 2 514 58 10
Though not itself an archive, FIAF has over 50 member archives and many observers from 58 countries

FIAT (International Federation of Television Archives)
c/o Centro Documentation RTVE
Calle Saturno 10
E-28023 Madrid
Spain
Tel: (34) 1 715 44 32
Fax: (34) 1 715 51 00

Fédération Européenne des Industries Techniques du Cinéma
50 Avenue Marceau
75008 Paris
France
Tel: (33) 1 47 23 75 76
Formed by a group of technical professional organisations to develop the technical and artistic potential of cinema

Fédération Internationale des Associations de Distributeurs de Films (FIAD)
43 boulevard Malesherbes
75008 Paris
France
Tel: (33) 1 42 66 05 32
Fax: (33) 1 42 66 96 92
Contacts: Gilbert Grégoire, Antoine Virenque
Represent the interests of film distributors

Fédération Internationale des Producteurs de Films Indépendants (FIPFI)
50 avenue Marceau
75008 Paris
Tel: (33) 1 47 23 70 30
Fax: (33) 1 47 20 78 17
Contact: René Thevenet
Federation of independent film producers, currently with members in 21 countries. It is open to all independent producers, either individual or groups, provided they are legally registered as such. FIPFI aims to promote the distribution of independent films, to increase possibilities for co-production, to share information between member countries and seeks to defend freedom of expression

Fédération Internationale des Syndicats des Travailleurs de l'Audiovisuel
1 rue Janssen
75019 Paris
France
Tel: (33) 1 42 45 72 14
Federation of audiovisual workers' unions

Fondation Européenne des Métiers de l'Image et du Son (FEMIS)
avenue du Président Wilson 13
75116 Paris
France
Tel: (33) 1 47 23 36 53
Fax: (33) 1 40 70 17 03
High level technical training in the audiovisual field for French applicants and those from outside France with a working knowledge of French. Organises regular student exchanges with other European film schools

IVENS Project
Skindergade 29
1159 Copenhagen K
Denmark
Tel: (45) 3 315 0099
Fax: (45) 3 315 7676
Ebbe Preisler
c/o Fonds voor de Nederlandse Film
Jan Luykenstraat 2
1071 CM Amsterdam
Netherlands
Tel: (31) 20 664 7838
Fax: (31) 20 675 03 98
Hans Klap
MEDIA project to stimulate creative documentaries both before and after production. Loans may be given for project development (via the Danish office) to an independent producer who has produced a documentary with the participation of two countries or two

European distributors, with priority given to a first-time documentary director or one who has recently obtained an award in an international festival. The Dutch office of IVENS may give loans to finished films and programmes in order to establish a promotional package of a video master, VHS preview prints, a press book, posters, stills etc. Applications from European countries with little documentary activity are given priority

Institut Robert Schuman – European Media Studies

rue de l'Association 32-34
1000 Brussels
Belgium
Tel: (32) 2 217 2355
Fax: (32) 2 219 5764
Contact: Anne de Daecker
Post-graduate training in journalism. Drawing students from all over Europe, it offers a 9-month intensive training in journalism for press, radio and television. A residential college, it is based on three principles: Professional, European and Christian

International Federation of Actors (FIA)

31a Thayer Street
London W1M 5LH
Tel: 071 487 4699
Fax: 071 487 5809
Contact: Rolf Rembe
Trade union federation founded in 1952 and embracing 58 performers' trade unions in 43 countries. It organises solidarity action when member unions are in dispute, researches and analyses problems affecting the rights and working conditions of film, television and theatre actors as well as singers, dancers, variety and circus artistes. It represents members in the international arena on issues such as cultural policy and copyright and publishes twice-yearly news-sheet FOCUS and occasional women's bulletin FEMINA. Has observer status with UNESCO and WIPO

International Federation of Film Producers Associations (FIAPF)

33 avenue des Champs-Elysées
75008 Paris
France
Tel: (33) 1 42 25 62 14
Fax: (33) 1 42 56 16 52
Contact: André Chaubeau
FIAPF gathers at an international level national associations of film producers (23 member countries). It represents the general interests of film producers in worldwide forums (WIPO, UNESCO, GATT) and with European authorities (EC, Council of Europe, Audiovisual EUREKA). It lobbies for better international legal protection of film and audiovisual producers

MAP-TV

c/o INA
Avenue de l'Europe
94366 Bry-sur-Marne Cedex
Tel: (33) 1 49 83 27 20
Fax: (33) 1 49 83 25 97
Contact: Jean Cherasse
MEDIA project. A professional association of production and audio-visual archive organisations. It pools resources and expertise to encourage the knowledge, production and broadcast of archive-based works

MEDIA

c/o British Film Institute
21 Stephen Street
London W1P 1PL
Tel: 071 255 1444
Fax: 071 436 7950
Contact: Wilf Stevenson
MEDIA is the media programme of the European Commission. It consists of projects dealing with various aspects of the film and television industries. At the time of going to press, these included: BABEL, CARTOON, EFDO, EAVE, EURO-AIM, the Media Investment Club, the European Script Fund, MAP-TV, EVE, MEDIA Venture, Euro Media Garanties, the Business School of Film and IVENS. The MEDIA desk at the BFI provides written and oral information on Community audiovisual policy, particularly on the MEDIA '95 programme, to professionals operating in the field of film, video and television

Media Investment Club

c/o INA
4 avenue de l'Europe
94366 Bry-sur-Marne
France
Tel: (33) 1 49 83 23 22/ 32 72/28 63
Fax: (33) 1 49 83 25 82
Contacts: Patrick Madelin, Veronique Damien
MEDIA project. It unites European businesses with financial institutions to fund projects made in or using new technologies. It supports production of audiovisual programmes using advanced technology; training of individuals in advanced audiovisual techniques; circulation and transfer of information and knowledge; export of EC products to countries outside the Community and exchange within the Community

Media Venture

SEFI – EFEC
10 Boulevard Royal
2449 Luxembourg
Tel: (352) 46 07 10
Fax: (352) 46 07 11
Contact: Jean-Pierre Bouillot
MEDIA project. Media Venture is a venture capital fund to be created in Luxembourg. It aims to co-finance the production and distribution of feature films and television series with a high commercial potential. Some equity investments in the capital of European production and distribution companies are also contemplated

The Prince's Trust European Programme

8 Bedford Row
London WC1R 4BA
Fax: 071 831 7280
Contact: Anne Engel
Offer grants (max £500) towards partnership projects in Europe and 3 others per year for travel (see Funding)

Université Radiophonique et Télévisuelle Internationale (URTI)

Maison de Radio France
116 avenue du Président Kennedy
75786 Paris
France
Tel: (33) 1 42 30 39 98
Fax: (33) 1 40 50 89 99
Contacts: Roland Fauré, Jacques Matthey-Doret
Non-governmental organisation recognised by UNESCO and founded in 1949. It is an umbrella group of some 50 radio and TV organisations, to exchange and broadcast several hundred cultural programmes per year

BELGIUM

Belgische Radio en Televisie-Nederlandse Uitzendingen (BRT)

Boulevard Reyerslaan 52
1040 Brussels
Tel: (32) 2 737 3111
Fax: (32) 2 735 3704
Contact: C Goossens
Public service station serving Dutch speaking Flemish community in Belgium

Cinémathèque Royale de Belgique/Royal Film Archive

Rue Ravenstein 23
1000 Brussels
Tel: (32) 2 507 83 70
Fax: (32) 2 513 12 72
Contact: Gabrielle Claes
Film preservation. The collection can be consulted on the Archive's premises for research purposes. Edit

the annual of Belgian film

Commission du Film/Filmcommissie
Ministère des Affaires Economiques
Rue de Mot 24-26
1040 Brussels
Tel: (32) 2 233 61 11
Film commission

Commission de contrôle des films cinématographiques
Place Poelaert 4
1000 Brussels
Tel: (32) 2 511 42 00

Commission de sélection du film
Galerie Ravenstein 28
1000 Brussels
Tel: (32) 2 513 94 40

Direction d'administration de l'audiovisuel
Galerie Ravenstein 27
1000 Brussels
Tel: (32) 2 513 94 40

Film Museum Jacques Ledoux
Rue Baron Horta 9
1000 Brussels
Tel: (32) 2 507 83 70
Fax: (32) 2 513 12 72
Contact: Gabrielle Claes
Permanent exhibition of the pre-history of cinema. 5 screenings per day – 3 sound, 2 silent. Organises 2 mini-festivals a year: l'Age d'Or and Cinédécouvertes

Radio-Télévision Belge de la Communauté Française (RTBF)
Blvd Auguste Reyers 52
1040 Brussels
Tel: (32) 2 737 2111
Fax: (32) 2 737 2885
Contact: Robert Stephane
Public broadcaster responsible for French language services

UPPT (Union professionnelle des producteurs de programmes de télévision)
21 rue Rasson
1040 Brussels
Tel: (32) 2 736 54 37
Fax: (32) 2 736 52 39
Contact: Pierre Levie
Trade association for TV producers

DENMARK

Danmarks Radio (DR)
Morkhojvej 170
2860 Soborg
Tel: (45) 31 671 233
Fax: (45) 39 661 233
Contact: Henrik Antonsen
Public service television and radio network

DFI (Danish Film Institute)
Store Søndervoldstraede 4
1419 Copenhagen K
Tel: (45) 31 57 65 00
Fax: (45) 31 57 67 00
Contact: Bo Christensen
An autonomous self-governing institution under the auspices of the Ministry of Cultural Affairs, financed through the state budget. It offers support and funding to Danish feature films, import of international features, distribution and exhibition. Promotes Danish films abroad, and finances two community access workshops

Det Danske Filmmuseum
Store Søndervoldstraede 4
PO Box 2158
1419 Copenhagen K
Tel: (45) 31 57 65 00
Fax: (45) 31 57 67 00
Contact: Ib Monty
The Film Museum, founded in 1941, is one of the world's oldest film archives. It has a collection of 13,000 titles from almost every genre and country, and has daily screenings. There is also an extensive library of books and pamphlets, periodicals, clippings, posters and stills

Filmarbejderforeningen
Kongens Nytorv 21
Baghuset 3.sal
1050 Copenhagen K
Tel: (45) 33 14 33 55/30 58
Fax: (45) 33 14 33 03
Contact: Asger Boertmann
Trade union, which organises film, video and television workers, and maintains the professional, social, economic and artistic interests of its members. Negotiates collective agreements for feature films, documentaries, commercials, negotiating contracts, copyright and authors' rights. Also protection of Danish film production

Producenterne (Association of Film, TV, Video and AV Producers)
Vesterbrogade 37
1620 Copenhagen V
Tel: (45) 31 22 16 36
Fax: (45) 31 22 06 47
Contact: Ole John
Tel: (45) 31 96 62 30
Producers' trade association

Statens Filmcentral
Vestergade 27
1456 Copenhagen K
Tel: (45) 33 13 26 86
Fax: (45) 33 13 02 03
Contact: Tue Steen Müller
Statens Filmcentral is the National Film Board of Denmark, created in 1939. It is regulated by the Ministry of Culture and produces, purchases and rents out shorts and documentaries on 16mm and video to educational institutions and libraries

FRANCE

Antenne 2 (A2)
22 Avenue Montaigne
75387 Paris Cedex 07
Tel: (33) 1 44 21 42 42
Fax: (33) 1 44 21 54 11
Contact: Jean-Michel Gaillard
One of France's two public service terrestrial channels (in direct competition with TF1)

The British Council
11 rue de Constantine
75007 Paris
Tel: (33) 1 49 55 73 00
Fax: (33) 1 47 05 77 02
Contact: Barbara Dent
British cultural representation overseas. It promotes British film, video and television in France through provision of information and documentation, screening British films and TV product at the British Cultural Centre in Paris

CNC (Le Centre National de la Cinématographie)
12 rue de Lübeck
75784 Paris Cedex 16
Tel: (33) 1 45 05 14 40
Fax: (33) 1 47 55 04 91
Contact: Dominique Wallon
A government institution, under the auspices of the Ministry of Culture. Its areas of concern are: the economics of cinema and the audiovisual industries; film regulation; the promotion of the cinema industries and the protection of cinema heritage. Offers financial assistance in all aspects of French cinema (production, exhibition, distribution etc)

La Cinémathèque Française
29 rue du Colisée
75008 Paris
Tel: (33) 1 45 53 21 86
Fax: (33) 1 42 56 08 55
Contact: Jean Saint-Geours
Founded in 1936 by Henri Langlois, Georges Franju and Jean Mitry to save and conserve film, it now also includes a cinema museum, screening theatres, library and stills and posters library

National Federation of Technical Industries for Film and Television (FNITCA)
50 avenue Marceau
75008 Paris
Tel: (33) 1 47 23 75 76
Fax: (33) 1 47 23 70 47
Contact: Jean Fleurent-Didier
A federation of technical trade associations which acts as intermediary between its members and their market. Maintains a database on all technical aspects of production, and helps French and European companies find suitable partners for research and development or commercial ventures

Fédération de la Production Cinémato-graphique Française

5 rue du Cirque
75008 Paris
Tel: (33) 1 42 25 70 63
Fax: (33) 1 42 25 94 27
Contacts: Alain Poiré, Pascal Rogard
Federation of French Cinema Production

Fédération Nationale des Distributeurs de Films

43 boulevard Malesherbes
75008 Paris
Tel: (33) 1 42 66 05 32
Fax: (33) 1 42 66 96 92
Contact: M. Grégoire
National federation of film distributors

IFCIC (Institut pour le Financement du Cinéma et des Industries Culturelles)

55 rue Pierre Charron
75008 Paris
Contact: Madame Grenier
Credit guarantees for a variety of cultural industries

Institut National de l'Audiovisuel (INA)

4 avenue de l'Europe
94366 Bry-sur-Marne Cedex
Tel: (33) 1 49 83 21 12
Fax: (33) 1 49 83 25 84
Contact: Yann Cotten
Television and radio archive; research into new technology; research and publications about broadcasting; production of over 130 first works for television and 15 major series and collections. INA initiates major documentaries and cultural series involving partners from Europe and the rest of the world

Service des Archives du Film

7 bis rue Alexandre Turpault
78390 Bois d'Arcy
Tel: (33) 1 34 60 20 50
Fax: (33) 1 34 60 52 25
Contact: Michelle Aubert
The department of Film Archives was set up to preserve and restore the heritage of the French Film industry. Since the 1950s, its priority has been to stop the destruction of films on nitrate backing and it restores the equivalent of 400 feature films each year

Télévision Française 1 (TF1)

1-19 rue Cognacq-Jay
75330 Paris Cedex 07
Tel: (33) 1 42 75 12 34
Fax: (33) 1 42 75 20 23
Contact: Patrick Le Lay
Recently privatised national television channel

Union Syndicale de la Production Audiovisuelle (USPA)

59 rue de Châteaudun
75009 Paris
Tel: (33) 1 44 53 03 03
Fax: (33) 1 49 95 99 80
Contact: Alain Modot
An association of French television producers, representing them on a national and international level. Also offers advice, information, seminars etc to members

GERMANY

ARD (Arbeitsgemein-schaft der öffentlich-rechtlichen Rundfunkanstalten der Bundesrepublik Deutschland)

Arnulfstrasse 42
Postfach 20 06 22
8000 München 2
Tel: (49) 89 5900 01
Fax: (49) 89 5900 3249
Contact: Dietrich Schwarzkopf
One of the two public service broadcasters in Germany, made up of 9 regional TV stations

Bundesministerium des Innern (Federal Ministry of the Interior)

Postfach 170290
5300 Bonn 1
Tel: (49) 228 681 5566/5569
Fax: (49) 228 681 4665
Contacts: Detlef Flotho, Rainer Novak
Awards prizes, grants funds for scripts for German feature films, short films, films for children and young people and documen-taries. Keeps a library of national film production, promotes film institutes, festivals, specific events

BVDFP (Bundesverband Deutscher Fernseh-produzenten)

Widenmayerstrasse 32
8000 München 22
Tel: (49) 89 22 35 35
Fax: (49) 89 228 55 62
Contact: Claus Hardt
Trade association for independent television producers

Deutsches Institut für Filmkunde

Schaumainkai 41
6000 Frankfurt 70
Tel: (49) 69 617 045
Fax: (49) 69 620 060
Contacts: Gerd Albrecht, Eberhard Spiess
The German Institute for Film Studies is a non-profit making organisation and its remit includes amassing culturally significant films and publications and documents about film; to catalogue them and make them available for study and research. It also supports and puts on screenings of scientific, cultural and art films. The Institute's top priority is to provide as comprehensive a documentation of German film as possible

Deutsches Filmmuseum

Schaumainkai 41
6000 Frankfurt 70
Tel: (49) 69 21 23 33 69
Fax: (49) 69 21 23 78 81
Contact: Walter Schobert
Incorporates the Komunales Kino, the municipal cinémathèque. Permanent and temporary exhibitions. It also has an archive; equipment, documentation, stills, posters and designs, music and sound collections; a library and a videothèque

FFA (Filmförderungs-anstalt)

Budapester Strasse 41
1000 Berlin 30
Tel: (49) 30 261 60 06
Fax: (49) 30 262 89 76
Contact: Kirsten Niehuus
Federal Film Fund of Germany, subsidising national projects in film production and the film industry generally. Based on the FFG (Law for German film funding), its tasks are to promote the quality of German films and to improve the economic structures of the film industry. The FFA subsidises script development, the production of features, documentaries and short films for the cinema. Other tasks include assistance for distribution, modernisation of cinemas, continuing education for film professionals etc

FSK (Freiwillige Selbstkontrolle der Filmwirtschaft)

Langenbeckstrasse 9
Postfach 5129
6200 Wiesbaden
Tel: (49) 6121 172 70
Fax: (49) 6121 172 739
Film industry voluntary self-regulatory body

Film Fonds Hamburg

Friedensallee 14-16
2000 Hamburg 50
Tel: (49) 40 390 5883
Fax: (49) 390 62 49
Contact: Eva Hubert, Dieter Kosslick
The Film Fonds is a facility of the Free and Hanseatic City of Hamburg aimed at promoting full-length 35mm theatrical film productions. It provides advice on film financing and on shooting in Hamburg. In conjunction with other film and media institutions, the Film Fonds is also responsible for the organisation of the co-production conference ECCO. It also provides subsidy and financial

support (see Funding). Other regional offices around Germany offer similar facilities

Focus Germany
Location Berlin
Senatsverwaltung für Kulturelle Angelegenheiten
Europa-Center
1000 Berlin 30
Tel: (49) 30 2123 3339
Fax: (49) 30 2123 3288
Focus Germany has four offices in various parts of Germany: Hamburg, Berlin, Potsdam and Düsseldorf. It offers information and contacts on development, co-production, locations and subsidies

ZDF (Zweites Deutsches Fernsehen)
PO Box 4040
6500 Mainz 1
Tel: (49) 61 31 70-1
Fax: (49) 61 31 702 157
Contact: Prof. Dieter Stolte
Germany's largest single public service broadcaster

GREECE

ERT (Elleniki Radiophonia Tileorassi SA)
Messoghion 402
15342 Aghia Parasekvi
Athens
Tel: (30) 1 639 0772/0383
Fax: (30) 1 639 0652
Contact: Irene Gavala-Chardalia
National public TV and radio broadcaster

GCC (Greek Cinema Centre)
10 Panepistimiou Avenue
10671 Athens
Tel: (30) 1 363 1733
Fax: (30) 1 361 4346
Contact: Manos Zacharias
Governmental organisation under the auspices of the Ministry of Culture. Grants subsidies for production

Ministry of Culture
Cinema Department
14 Aristidou Street
Athens 10559
Tel: (30) 1 322 4737

SPET (Association des Producteurs de la Television Hellenique)
c/o Dionyssis Samiotis
39 Solonos Street
10672 Athens
Tel: (30) 1 364 7878
Fax: (30) 1 360 1328
Contact: George Sgourakis
Trade association for independent television producers

IRELAND

The Arts Council
70 Merrion Square
Dublin 2
Tel: (353) 1 611840
Fax: (353) 1 761302
Contact: Paul Freaney
Statutory body for the promotion of the arts. The Arts Council funds the Irish Film Institute, Film Base, Federation of Film Societies, Dublin and Cork Film Festivals etc. Also provides Ir£100,000 per annum for film and video awards

Film Censor's Office
16 Harcourt Terrace
Dublin 2
Tel: (353) 1 676 1985
Fax: (353) 1 676 1898
Contact: Sheamus Smith
The Official Film Censor is appointed by the Irish Government to consider and classify all feature films and videos distributed in Ireland

Irish Film Institute
6 Eustace Street
Dublin 2
Tel: (353) 1 679 5744
Fax: (353) 1 679 9657
Contacts: David Kavanagh, Mary Scally
The Irish Film Institute is the national organisation with responsibility for the promotion of film culture in Ireland, responsible for the Irish Film archive, developing policies on Media Education, providing information on all aspects of the local and international audio-visual industry and for co-ordinating MEDIA initiatives within Ireland

RTE (Radio Telefis Éireann)
Donnybrook
Dublin 4
Tel: (353) 1 643 111
Fax: (353) 1 643 082
Contact: Vincent Finn
Ireland's public service broadcaster

ITALY

ANICA (Associazione Nazionale Industrie Cinematografiche e Audiovisive)
Viale Regina Margherita 286
00196 Rome
Tel: (39) 6 884 1271
Fax: (39) 6 440 4128
Trade association for TV producers

ANCCI (Associazione Nazionale Circoli Cinematografici Italiani)
Via Nomentana 251
00161 Rome
Tel: (39) 6 440 2273
Fax: (39) 6 440 2280

Cineteca Italiana
Villa Communale
Via Palestro 16
20120 Milan
Tel: (39) 2 799 224

Cineteca Nazionale Centro Sperimentale di Cinematografia
Via Tuscolana 1524
00173 Rome
Tel: (39) 6 722 941
Fax: (39) 6 721 1619

Fininvest Television
Palazzo dei Cigni
20090 Segrate Milan
Tel: (39) 2 216 218880
Contact: Adriano Galliano
Major competitor to RAI, running television channels Canale 5, Italia Uno and Rete Quattro

Istituto Luce
Via Tuscolana 1055
00173 Rome
Tel: (39) 6 722 931
Fax: (39) 6 722 2493
Contact: Antonio Manca
Created to spread culture and education through cinema. It invests in film, distributes films of cultural interest and holds Italy's largest archive

Ministero del Turismo e Spettacolo
Ufficio Cinema
Via Ferratella 55
00184 Rome
Tel: (39) 6 773 2492
Contact: Mario Ligeri
Subsidises and supports production, distribution and exhibition

Museo Nazionale del Cinema
Palazzo Chiablese
Piazza San Giovanni 2
10122 Turin
Tel: (39) 11 436 1365/436 1148
Fax: (39) 11 521 2341
Contact: Paolo Bertetto
The museum represents photography, pre-cinema and cinema history. Its collections include films, books and periodicals, posters, photographs and cinema ephemera

RAI (Radiotelevisione Italiana)
Viale Mazzini 14
00195 Rome
Tel: (39) 6 3878
Fax: (39) 6 361 2012
Contact: Gianni Pasquarelli
Italian state broadcaster

LUXEMBOURG

Cinémathèque Municipale – Ville de Luxembourg
Rue de la Chapelle 19
1325 Luxembourg
Tel: (352) 4796 2644
Fax: (352) 45 93 75
Contact: Fred Junck
Official Luxembourg film archive. Holds 2 screenings daily per weekday, every year 'Live Cinema' performances – silent films with music. Member of FIAF

CLT/RTL
Villa Louvigny
2830 Luxembourg

Tel: (352) 47661
Contact: Gaston Thorn
Private company entrusted with TV and radio – no state broadcaster

THE NETHERLANDS

Ministry of Welfare, Health and Cultural Affairs (WVC)
PO Box 5406
2280 HK Rijswijk
Tel: (31) 70 340 6148/6150
Fax: (31) 70 340 7834
Contacts: Camila Ylstra, Seamus Cassidy
The film department of the Ministry is responsible for the development and maintenance of Dutch film policy. Various different organisations for production, distribution, promotion and conservation of film are subsidised by this department

Nederlandse Omroep-programma Stichting (NOS)
Postbus 444
1200 JJ Hilversum
Tel: (31) 35 779 222
Contact: Louis Heinsman
Public corporation responsible for co-ordinating three-channel public television

Netherlands Filmmuseum
Vondelpark 3
1071 AA Amsterdam
Tel: (31) 20 589 1400
Fax: (31) 20 683 3401
Contact: Hoos Blotkamp
Film museum with three public screenings each day, permanent and temporary exhibitions, library, film-cafe and film distribution

OTP (Vereniging van Onafhankelijke Televisie Producenten)
Vaartweg 66
1217 SV Hilversum
Tel: (31) 35 218 241
Fax: (31) 35 218 984
Contact: Han Peekle
Trade association for independent television producers

PORTUGAL

Cinemateca Portuguesa
Rua Barata Salgueiro 39
1200 Lisbon
Tel: (351) 1 54 62 79/ 54 75 09
Fax: (351) 1 352 3180
Contact: João Benard da Costa
National film archive, preserving, restoring and showing films. Includes a public documentation centre, a stills and posters archive and a small museum

IPC (Instituto Portugues de Cinema)
Rua São Pedro de Alcantara 45 (1H)
1200 Lisbon
Tel: (351) 1 346 66 34
Fax: (351) 1 37 27 77
Contact: Manuel Falcão
Governmental organisation; supports production and exhibition and helps promotion and distribution of Portuguese films abroad. Negotiates national and international agreements connected with film

RTP (Radiotelevisão Portuguesa)
Avenida 5 de Outubro 197
1094 Lisbon Cedex
Tel: (351) 1 793 1774
Fax: (351) 1 766 226
Contact: Maria Manuela Furtado
State-owned public television service

Secretariado Nacional para o Audiovisual (SNA)
Rua São Pedro de Alcantara 45
1200 Lisbon
Tel: (351) 1 347 86 44/346 88 19/847 30 77
Fax: (351) 1 347 86 43/80 81 70
Contact: Antonio-Pedro Vasconcelos
SNA has two aims: the definition of a coherent global audiovisual policy and a coordinated and integrated policy to increase the value of Portuguese culture and language

SPAIN

Academia de las Artes y de las Ciencias Cinematográficas de España
General Oraá 68
28006 Madrid
Tel: (34) 1 563 33 41
Fax: (34) 1 563 26 93
Contact: Antonio Gimenez Rico

Asociacion de Distribuidores e Importadores Cinematográficos de Ambito Nacional (ADICAN)
Blanca de Navarra 7
28010 Madrid
Tel: (34) 1 308 01 20
Fax: (34) 1 319 00 36
Contact: Antonio Recoder
Association of theatrical distributors

British Council
Arts Department
Plaza de Santa Barbara 10
28004 Madrid
Tel: (34) 1 337 3562
Fax: (34) 1 337 35 73
Contact: Tim Pearce
Co-ordination with Spanish 'Filmotecas' film festivals, providing them with films from the British Council and BFI film libraries

Delegació de Cinematografia i Video
Direcció General de Promoció Cultural
Calle Diputació 279-283
08007 Barcelona
Tel: (34) 3 317 35 85
Fax: (34) 3 301 22 47
Contact: Antonio Kirchner
Film institute for the Catalan government

Filmoteca Española
Carretera de la Dehesa de la Villa s/n
28040 Madrid
Tel: (34) 1 549 00 11
Fax: (34) 1 549 73 48
Spanish national archive recognised by FIAF, with a Library and a Stills Department

ICAA (Instituto de la Cinematografia y de las Artes Audiovisuales)
Ministerio de Cultura
Plaza del Rey 1
28071 Madrid
Tel: (34) 1 532 50 89/ 12 22/00 89
Fax: (34) 1 531 92 12/ 522 93 77
Contact: Enrique Balmaseda Arias-Davila
The promotion, protection and diffusion of cinema and audiovisual activities in production, distribution and exhibition. Gives financial support in these areas to Spanish companies. Also involved in the promotion of Spanish cinema and audiovisual arts, and their cultural communication between the different communities within Spain

RTVE (Radiotelevisión Española)
Prado del Rey
28023 Madrid 1
Tel: (34) 1 711 9921
Fax: (34) 1 711 2562
Contact: Juan Rueda Villen
National public service broadcaster

MEDIA

THE MEDIA PROGRAMME SUPPORTS THE EUROPEAN CINEMA AND THE AUDIOVISUAL INDUSTRY

COMMISSION OF THE EUROPEAN COMMUNITIES
DIRECTORATE-GENERAL AUDIOVISUAL, INFORMATION, COMMUNICATION, CULTURE
200, RUE DE LA LOI B-1049 BRUSSELS BELGIUM
TEL: 32-2/236 07 18 FAX: 32-2/236 42 77

PR COMPANIES

These are companies which handle all aspects of promotion and publicity for film and video production companies and/or individual productions

Tony Brainsby PR
16b Edith Grove
London SW10 0NL
Tel: 071 834 8341
Fax: 071 352 9451
Tony Brainsby

Byron Advertising, Marketing and PR
Byron House
Wallingford Road
Uxbridge
Middx UB8 2RW
Tel: 0895 52131
Fax: 0895 52137
Les Barnes

Cantor Wise Publicity
2 Reynolds Close
London NW11 7EA
Tel: 081 905 5250
Fax: 081 905 5383
Melanie Cantor

Jacquie Capri Enterprises
c/o Floreat Productions
46 St James's Place
London SW1A 1MS
Tel: 071 499 1996
Fax: 071 499 6727

Max Clifford Associates
109 New Bond Street
London W1Y 9AA
Tel: 071 408 2350
Fax: 071 409 2294
Max Clifford

Corbett and Keene
122 Wardour Street
London W1V 3LA
Tel: 071 494 3478
Fax: 071 734 2024
Ginger Corbett
Sara Keene

Dennis Davidson Associates
Royalty House
72-74 Dean Street
London W1V 5HB
Tel: 071 439 6391
Fax: 071 437 6358
Dennis Davidson
Dennis Michael

Daniel J Edelman
Kingsgate House
536 King's Road
London SW10 0TE
Tel: 071 835 1222
Fax: 071 351 7676
Rosemary Brook

Clifford Elson (Publicity)
1 Richmond Mews
Off Dean Street
London W1V 5AG
Tel: 071 437 4822
Fax: 071 287 6314
Clifford Elson
Patricia Lake-Smith
Howard Elson

FEREF Associates
14-17 Wells Mews
London W1A 1ET
Tel: 071 580 6546
Fax: 071 631 3156
Peter Andrews
Ken Paul
Robin Behling
David Kemp

Soren Fischer Associates
37 Ollgar Close
London W12 0NF
Tel: 081 740 9059/0202 393033
Soren Fischer

Foresight Communications
48 Lexington Street
London W1R 3LH
Tel: 071 734 6691
Fax: 071 734 2359
Nicola Lockey
Tim Smith

Lynne Franks PR
6-10 Frederick Close
Stanhope Place
London W2 2HD
Tel: 071 724 6777
Fax: 071 724 8484

Good Relations
59 Russell Square
London WC1B 4HJ
Tel: 071 631 3434
Fax: 071 631 1399
Jeffrey Lyes

Gruber Public Relations
5 Dryden Street
Covent Garden
London WC2E 9NW
Tel: 071 829 8498/9
Fax: 071 240 5600
Christiana Gruber
Michael Bee Slade

HPR Publicity
22 Mount View Road
London N4 4HX
Tel: 071 263 7736
Fax: 081 341 0748
Gwyn Headley

Ray Hodges Associates
Unit 6 Kings Grove
Maidenhead
Berks SL6 4DX
Tel: 0628 75171
Fax: 0628 781301
Maureen Ward

Sue Hyman Associates
70 Chalk Farm Road
London NW1 8AN
Tel: 071 485 8489/5842
Fax: 071 267 4715
Sue Hyman

JAC Publicity
Hammer House
113 Wardour Street
London W1
Tel: 071 734 6965
Fax: 071 439 1400
Claire Forbes

Carolyn Jardine Publicity
3 Richmond Buildings
Off Dean Street
London W1V 5EA
Tel: 071 287 6661
Fax: 071 437 0499

Richard Laver Publicity
3 Troy Court
Kensington High Street
London W8 7RA
Tel: 071 937 7322
Fax: 071 937 8670
Richard Laver

Lay & Partners
Citybridge House
235-245 Goswell Road
London EC1V 7JD
Tel: 071 837 1475
Fax: 071 833 4615
Nick Oldham

Namara Cowan Associates
45 Poland Street
London W1V 3DF
Tel: 071 434 3871
Fax: 071 439 6489
Theo Cowan
Laurie Bellew
Jane Harker

Optimum Communications
31 Bedford Square
London WC1B 3SG
Tel: 071 436 6681
Fax: 071 436 1694
Nigel Passingham

PSA Rogers & Cowan International
49 Whitehall
London SW1A 2BX
Tel: 071 839 7198
Fax: 071 930 1823
Philip Symes
Terry Pritchard
Brian Daly
Michelle Sewell

Premier Relations
18 Exeter Street
Covent Garden
London WC2E 7DU
Tel: 071 497 2055
Fax: 071 497 2117
Victoria Franklin

Stone Hallinan McDonald
100 Ebury Street
London SW1W 9QD
Tel: 071 730 9009
Fax: 071 730 7492
Charles McDonald

Judy Tarlo
125 Old Brompton Road
London SW7 3RP
Tel: 071 835 1000
Fax: 071 373 0265
Media Relations

Taylor and New
1 Northolme Road
London N5 2UZ
Tel: 071 354 8125
Fax: 071 354 8126
Annie Taylor
Janie New

Peter Thompson Associates
134 Great Portland Street
London W1N 5PH
Tel: 071 436 5991/2
Fax: 071 436 0509
Peter Thompson
Amanda Malpass

Town House Publicity
45 Islington Park Street
London N1 1QB
Tel: 071 226 7450
Fax: 071 359 6026
Mary Fulton

Tristan Whalley Publicity
46C Handforth Road
London SW9 0LP
Tel: 071 582 8767
Tristan Whalley

Alan Wheatley Associates
12 Poland Street
London W1V 3DE
Tel: 071 734 1290
Fax: 071 734 1289
Alan Wheatley

Stella Wilson Publicity
130 Calabria Road
London N5 1HT
Tel: 071 354 5672
Fax: 071 354 2242
Stella Wilson

Winsor Beck Public Relations
Network House
29-39 Stirling Road
London W3 8DJ
Tel: 081 993 7506
Fax: 081 993 8276
Geri Winsor

Zakiya and Associates
13 Tottenham Mews
London W1P 9PJ
Tel: 071 323 4050
Fax: 071 580 0397
Zakiya Powell

PRESS CONTACTS

Below are magazine and newspaper critics and journalists who write about film, TV and video. Circulation figures may have altered since going to press. Also listed are the news and photo agencies which handle media news syndication, and TV and radio programmes concerned with the visual media

Arena (bi-monthly)
The Old Laundry
Ossington Buildings
London W1M 3JD
Tel: 071 935 8232
Fax: 071 935 2237
Editor: Dylan Jones
Magazine for men covering general interest, celebrities, film, music and fashion
Lead time: 4-5 weeks
Circulation: 64,000

Art Monthly
36 Great Russell Street
London WC1B 3PP
Tel: 071 580 4168
Jack Wendler
Peter Townsend
Aimed at artists, arts administrators, teachers, collectors, amateurs directly connected with the visual arts
Lead time: 4 weeks
Circulation: 4,000

Blitz Magazine
(monthly)
40-44 Newman Street
London W1P 3PA
Tel: 071 436 5211
Fax: 071 436 5290
Editorial Director: Simon Tesler
Editor: Bonnie Vaughan
Essential coverage in film, photography, fashion, print and the arts
Lead time: 6 weeks
Circulation: 50,000

Broadcast
(weekly, Fri)
7 Swallow Place
London W1R 7AA
Tel: 071 491 9484
Fax: 071 355 3177
Publisher: Martin Jackson
Editor: Marta Wohrle
Broadcasting industry news magazine with coverage of TV, radio, cable and satellite, corporate production and international programming and distribution in a monthly section 'Worldwatch'.
Press day: Wed
Lead time: 2 weeks
Circulation: 10,400

The Business of Film (monthly)
24 Charlotte Street
London W1P 1HJ
Tel: 071 580 0141
Fax: 071 225 1264
Publisher/executive editor: Elspeth Tavares
Editor: Lloyd Shepherd
Aimed at film industry professionals – producers, distributors, exhibitors, investors, financiers
Lead time: 2 weeks

Capital Gay
(weekly, Fri)
38 Mount Pleasant
London WC1
Tel: 071 278 3764
Fax: 071 278 3250
Film/TV Editor: David White
Newspaper for lesbians and gay men in the South East combining news, features, arts and entertainment, what's on guide
Lead time: 1 week (Mon)
Circulation: 18,000

Caribbean Times incorporating African Times
(weekly)
139-149 Fonthill Road
London N4 3HF
Tel: 071 281 1191
Fax: 071 263 9656
Editor: Arif Ali
Tabloid dealing with issues pertinent to community it serves. 'Asian Times' (circ. 15,000) is also at this address
Press day: Thur
Circulation: 25,000

City Limits
(weekly, Thur)
66/67 Wells Street
London W1P 3RB
Tel: 071 636 4444
Fax: 071 637 2471
Film: Nick James
TV: Antonia Foster
Video: Stevan Keane
London listings magazine with cinema section and TV coverage
Press day: Mon
Lead time: 8-11 days
Circulation: 31,000

Company (monthly)
National Magazine House
72 Broadwick Street
London W1V 2BP
Tel: 071 439 5372
Arts/style editor: Dee Pilgrim
Assistant editor: Sarah Kennedy
Glossy magazine for women aged 18-30
Lead time: 10 weeks
Circulation: 193,459

Cosmopolitan
(monthly)
National Magazine House
72 Broadwick Street
London W1V 2BP
Tel: 071 439 7144
Fax: 071 439 5016
Film: Derek Malcolm
TV: Sue Summers
Arts/General: Vanessa Raphaely
Aimed at women aged 18-35
Lead time: 12 weeks
Circulation: 426,665

Creative Review
(monthly)
50 Poland Street
London W1V 4AX
Tel: 071 439 4222
Fax: 071 734 6748
Editor: Lewis Blackwell
Assistant editor: Dominic Murphy
Publisher: Annie Swift
Trade paper for creative people covering film, advertising and design. Film reviews, profiles and technical features
Lead time: 4 weeks
Circulation: 20,000

Daily Express
245 Blackfriars Road
London SE1 9UX
Tel: 071 928 8000
Fax: 071 922 7970
Showbusiness: David Wigg, Annie Leask, Ian Lyness
National daily newspaper
Circulation: 1,700,000

Daily Mail
Northcliffe House
2 Derry Street
London W8 5TT
Tel: 071 938 6000
Fax: 071 937 3745
Showbusiness: Corinna Honan
Film: Shaun Usher
TV: Peter Paterson
National daily newspaper
Circulation: 1,720,000

Daily Mirror
Holborn Circus
London EC1P 1DQ
Tel: 071 353 0246
Film: Pauline McLeod
TV: Tony Purnell
National daily newspaper
Circulation: 3,775,180 incorporating The Daily Record (Scottish daily newspaper)

The Daily Star
Ludgate House
245 Blackfriars Road
London SE1 9UX
Tel: 071 928 8000
Film: Pat Codd, Alec Lom
TV: Michael Burke, Ollie Wilson
Video: Julia Westlake
National daily newspaper

Daily Telegraph
Peterborough Court at South Quay
181 Marsh Wall
London E14 9SR
Tel: 071 538 5000
Fax: 071 538 6242
Arts: Miriam Gross
TV: Penny McDonald
National daily newspaper
Circulation: 1,075,000

The Economist
(weekly)
25 St James's Street
London SW1A 1HG
Tel: 071 839 7000
Books and Arts Editor: Caroline Robinson
Film/video/TV (cultural): Ann Wroe
Film/video/TV (business): John Heilemann
International coverage of major political, social and business developments with arts section
Press day: Wed
Circulation: 450,000

Elle (monthly)
Rex House
4-12 Lower Regent Street
London SW1Y 4PE
Tel: 071 930 9050
Fax: 071 839 2762
Editor: Maggie Alderson
Features editor: Carl Hindmarch
Glossy magazine aimed at 18-35 year old working women
Lead time: 8 weeks

Empire (monthly)
42 Great Portland Street
London W1N 5AH
Tel: 071 436 5430
Fax: 071 631 0781
Editor: Barry McIlheney
Quality film monthly incorporating features, interviews and movie news as well as reviews of all new movies and videos
Lead time: 2 weeks
Circulation: 70,000

The European
(weekly, Fri)
Orbit House
5 New Fetter Lane
London EC4A 1AP
Tel: 071 822 2002
Fax: 071 377 4773
Arts editor: Derwent May
In-depth coverage of European politics and culture
Press day: Tues
Circulation: 330,000

European Cable and Pay TV/ European Television/ International Co-Productions
(monthly)
Shackleton House
4 Battle Bridge Lane
London SE1 2HR
Tel: 071 403 8786
Managing editor: Jay Stuart
Business and financial information on companies and markets broadcasting television and producing television programming and film
Lead time: 10 days

Evening Standard
(Mon-Fri)
New Northcliffe House
2 Derry Street
London W8 5EE
Tel: 071 938 6000
Fax: 071 937 3745
Arts: Brian Sewell
Film: Alexander Walker
TV: Geoffrey Phillips
London weekday evening newspaper

Everywoman
(monthly)
34a Islington Green
London N1 8DU
Tel: 071 359 5496
Editor: Barbara Rogers
Arts editor: Barbara Norden
A current affairs magazine for women
Lead time: 6 weeks
Circulation: 15,000

The Face (monthly)
Third Floor Block A
Exmouth House
Pine Street
London EC1R 0JL
Tel: 071 837 7270
Fax: 071 837 3906
Film/TV: Sheryl Garratt, John Godfrey
Visual-orientated youth culture magazine: emphasis on music, fashion and films
Lead time: 4 weeks
Circulation: 66,000

Fact (monthly)
Producers Alliance for Cinema and Television
Paramount House
162-170 Wardour Street
London W1V 4LA
Tel: 071 437 7700
Editor: John Murray
PACT members monthly

bfi ***Film***
(10 issues a year)
Film Society Unit
BFI, 21 Stephen Street
London W1P 1PL
Tel: 071 255 1444
Editor: Peter Cargin
Non-commercial aspects of film
Lead time: 2 weeks

Film and Television Technician
(10 issues a year)
111 Wardour Street
London W1
Tel: 071 437 8506
Fax: 071 437 8268
Editor: Janice Turner
BECTU members' journal
Circulation: 58,000

Film Review
(monthly)
4th Floor Centro House
Mandela Street
London NW1 0DU
Tel: 071 387 3848
Fax: 071 388 8532
Editor: David Aldridge
Reviews of films on cinema screen and video; articles; star interviews and profiles; book reviews
Incorporates Films and Filming
Lead time: 8 weeks
Circulation: 34,000

Financial Times
1 Southwark Bridge
London SE1 9HL
Tel: 071 873 3000
Fax: 071 873 3076
Arts: J D F Jones
Film: Nigel Andrews
TV: Christopher Dunkley
National daily newspaper
Circulation: 300,000

Gay Times
(monthly)
283 Camden High Street
London NW1 7BX
Tel: 071 482 2576
Fax: 071 284 0329
Film: Stephen Bourne
TV: Jonathan Sanders
Britain's leading Gay magazine. Regular film and television coverage
Lead time: 6 weeks
Circulation: 35,000

The Glasgow Herald
195 Albion Street
Glasgow G1 1QP
Tel: 041 552 6255
Chelsea Bridge House
Queenstown Road
London SW8 4NN
Tel: 071 738 8000
Fax: 071 738 8159
London editor/film critic: William Russell
Scottish daily newspaper
Circulation: 124,715

The Guardian
119 Farringdon Road
London EC1R 3ER
Tel: 071 278 2332
Fax: 071 837 2114
Arts: Helen Oldfield
Film: Derek Malcolm
TV: Nancy Banks-Smith
Media editor: Georgina Henry
PR manager: Camilla Nicholls
Weekend Editor: Roger Alton
National daily newspaper
Circulation: 428,000

Harpers & Queen
(monthly)
National Magazine House
72 Broadwick Street
London W1V 2BP

Tel: 071 439 7144
Fax: 071 439 5506
Art/reviews: Janine Di Giovanni
Glossy magazine for women
Lead time: 12 weeks
Circulation: 86,000

The Hollywood Reporter
(daily; weekly international, Tues)
23 Ridgmount Street
London WC1E 7AH
Tel: 071 323 6686
Fax: 071 323 2314/16
European bureau chief: Rich Zahradnik
European news editor: Adam Dawtrey
Showbusiness trade paper

i-D Magazine
(monthly)
3rd Floor
134-146 Curtain Road
London EC2A 3AR
Tel: 071 729 7305
Fax: 071 729 7266
Film: Matthew Collin
Youth/fashion magazine with items on film
Lead time: 8 weeks
Circulation: 40,000

Illustrated London News
(6 issues a year)
20 Upper Ground
London SE1 9PP
Tel: 071 928 2111
Fax: 071 620 1594
Editor: James Bishop
Film listings: Roger Sabin
News, pictorial record and commentary, and a guide to coming events
Lead time: 8-10 weeks
Circulation: 53,970

Impact (bi-monthly)
Producers Alliance for Cinema and Television
Paramount House
162-170 Wardour Street
London W1V 4LA
Tel: 071 437 7700
Fax: 071 734 4564
Editor: Peter Goodwin
PACT magazine

The Independent
40 City Road
London EC1Y 2DB
Tel: 071 253 1222
Fax: 071 956 1435
Arts: Thomas Sutcliffe
Film: Sheila Johnston
Media: Maggie Brown
National daily newspaper
Circulation: 406,000

The Independent on Sunday
40 City Road
London EC1Y 2DB
Tel: 071 253 1222
Fax: 071 415 1333
Arts: Michael Church
National Sunday newspaper
Circulation: 386,000

Interzone (monthly)
217 Preston Drove
Brighton BN1 6FL
Tel: 0273 504710
Fax: 0273 29703
Film: Nick Lowe
TV: Wendy Bradley
Science-fiction magazine
Lead time: 8 weeks
Circulation: 10,000

The Jewish Chronicle (weekly)
25 Furnival Street
London EC4A 1JT
Tel: 071 405 9252
Fax: 071 405 9040
Editor: Edward J Temko
Film critic: Pamela Melnikoff
Arts editor: David Sonin
Press day: Wed
Circulation: 50,000

The List
(fortnightly, Thur)
14 High Street
Edinburgh EH1 1TE
Tel: 031 558 1191
Editor: Robin Hodge
Film/video: Trevor Johnston
TV: Tom Lappin
Glasgow and Edinburgh events guide
Lead time: 1 week
Circulation: 12,000

London Weekly Diary of Social Events (weekly, Sun)
25 Park Row
Greenwich
London SE10 9NL
Tel: 081 305 1274/1419
Fax: 081 853 2355
Editor/film critic: Denise Silvester-Carr
Arts-oriented subscription magazine with weekly film column
Lead time: 8 days
Circulation: 18,000

Mail on Sunday
Northcliffe House
2 Derry Street
London W8 5TS
Tel: 071 938 6000
Fax: 071 937 3745
Film critic: Tom Hutchinson
Media correspondent: Paul Nathanson
National Sunday newspaper
Press day: Fri/Sat
Circulation: 1,940,000

Marie Claire
(monthly)
Mercury House
195 Knightsbridge
London SW7 1RE
Tel: 071 261 6939
Fax: 071 261 5277
Film/TV: Sean French
Features: Michele Lavery
Lead time: 2-3 months
Circulation: 182,230

Marxism Today
(monthly)
6 Cynthia Street
London N1 9JF
Tel: 071 278 4430
Fax: 071 278 4427
Arts: Matt Ffytche
Lively current affairs and cultural magazine
Lead time: 8 weeks
Circulation: 17,500

Media Week
(weekly, Thur)
City Cloisters
188-196 Old Street
London EC1V 9BP
Tel: 071 490 5500
Fax: 071 490 0957
Editor: Liz Roberts
News Editor: Richard Gold
Broadcast Editor: Steven Armstrong
News magazine aimed at the advertising and media industries
Press day: Wed
Circulation: 18,700

Melody Maker
(weekly, Tues)
King's Reach Tower
Stamford Street
London SE1 9LF
Tel: 071 261 6228
Fax: 071 261 6706
Film: Steve Sutherland
Rock music newspaper
Press day: Wed
Circulation: 71,000

Midweek
(weekly, Thur)
7-9 Rathbone Street
London W1P 1AF
Tel: 071 636 6651
Fax: 071 872 0806
Arts/Film: Bill Williamson
Free magazine with film section
Press day: Tues
Circulation: 124,000

Morning Star
1-3 Ardleigh Road
London N1 4HS
Tel: 071 254 0033
Fax: 071 254 5950
Film: Jeff Sawtell
TV: Jeffrey James
The only national daily owned by its readers as a co-operative. Weekly film and TV reviews
Circulation: 28,000

Moving Pictures International
(weekly, Thur)
26 Soho Square
London W1V 5FJ
Tel: 071 494 0011
Fax: 071 287 9637
Editorial director: Nick Roddick
Worldwide coverage of television, film, video and cable
Press day: Tues
Circulation: 9,500

Ms London
(weekly, Mon)
7-9 Rathbone Street
London W1P 1AF
Tel: 071 636 6651
Fax: 071 872 0805
Free magazine with drama, video, film and general arts section
Press day: Fri
Circulation: 138,238

New Musical Express
(weekly, Wed)
25th Floor
King's Reach Tower
Stamford Street
London SE1 9LS
Tel: 071 261 5000
Fax: 071 261 5185
Film/TV: Gavin Martin
Rock music newspaper
Press day: Mon
Circulation: 121,001

New Scientist
(weekly, Thur)
King's Reach Tower
Stamford Street
London SE1 9LS
Tel: 071 261 5000
Fax: 071 261 6162
Editor: David Dickson
Audio-visual: Barry Fox
Contains articles and reports on the progress of science and technology in terms which the non-specialist can understand
Press day: Mon
Circulation: 105,000

New Statesman and Society
(weekly, Fri)
Foundation House
Perseverance Works
38 Kingsland Road
London E2 8DQ
Tel: 071 739 3211
Fax: 071 739 9307
Editor: Stuart Weir
Arts editor: Boyd Tonkin
Independent radical journal of investigation, revelation and comment
Press day: Mon
Circulation: 35,000

News of the World
(weekly, Sun)
News International
1 Virginia Street
London E1 9BD
Tel: 071 782 4000
Editor: Patsy Chapman
TV: Charles Catchpole
National Sunday newspaper
Press day: Sat
Circulation: 4,863,208

Nine to Five (weekly)
9a Margaret Street
London W1
Tel: 071 631 3708
Fax: 071 636 4694
Film/entertainments editor: John Symes
Free magazine
Press day: Mon & Wed
Circulation: 125,000

19 (monthly)
IPC Magazines
King's Reach Tower
London SE1 9LS
Tel: 071 261 6360
Fax: 071 261 6032
Film/Arts: Maureen Rice
Magazine for young women
Lead time: 12 weeks
Circulation: 173,000

The Observer
(weekly, Sun)
Chelsea Bridge House
Queenstown Road
London SW8 4NN
Tel: 071 627 0700/350 3546
Fax: 071 627 5570
Arts editor: Gillian Widdicombe
Film: Philip French
TV: John Naughton
National Sunday newspaper
Press day: Fri
Circulation: 675,000

Observer Magazine
(Sun)
Editor: Angela Palmer
Supplement to 'The Observer'

Options (monthly)
IPC
King's Reach Tower
Stamford Street
London SE1 9LS
Tel: 071 261 5000
Fax: 071 261 6023
Film: David Pirie
TV: Daniela Soave
Magazine for women
Lead time: 12 weeks
Circulation: 178,000

The People
Holborn Circus
London EC1P 1DQ
Tel: 071 353 0246
Fax: 071 822 2193
Film critics: Kate Molloy, Christopher Tookey
National Sunday newspaper
Press day: Fri
Circulation: 2,405,000

Punch (weekly, Wed)
Ludgate House
245 Blackfriars Road
London SE1 9UZ
Tel: 071 921 5900
Features editor/TV: Sean Macaulay
Film: Dilys Powell
A combination of topical satire, comment and wide-ranging arts coverage
Lead time: 10 days
Circulation: 58,250

Q (monthly)
42 Great Portland Street
London W1N 5AH
Tel: 071 436 5430
Fax: 071 631 0781
Editor: Mark Ellen
Specialist music magazine for 18-45 year olds. Includes reviews of new albums, films and books
Lead time: 14 days
Circulation: 160,000

Radio Times
35 Marylebone High Street
London W1M 4AA
Tel: 071 937 4262 (editorial)
Weekly guide to all UK television, BBC Radio and satellite programmes
Circulation: 2,891,831

Scotland on Sunday
20 North Bridge
Edinburgh EH1 1YT
Tel: 031 225 2468
Fax: 031 220 2443
Arts Editor: Richard Mowe
Film critic: Allan Hunter
Scottish Sunday newspaper

The Scotsman
20 North Bridge
Edinburgh EH1 1YT
Tel: 031 225 2468
Fax: 031 226 7420
Arts Editor: Allen Wright
Scottish daily newspaper

Screen Digest
(monthly)
37 Gower Street
London WC1E 6HH
Tel: 071 580 2842
Fax: 071 580 0060
Editorial chairman: John Chittock
Editor: David Fisher
Executive editor: Ben Keen
An international industry news digest and research report covering film, TV, cable, satellite, video and other multimedia information. Has a centre page reference system every month on subjects like law, statistics or sales. Now also available on a computer data base via fax at 071 580 0060 under the name Screenfax
Lead time: 10 days

Screenfax (database)
Available on-line via Dialog, Predicasts or by fax: 071 580 0060. Provides customised print-outs on all screen media subjects with summaries of news developments, market research. See entry under Screen Digest

Screen International
(weekly, Fri)
7 Swallow Place
249-259 Regent Street
London W1R 7AA
Tel: 071 491 9484
Fax: 071 355 3337
Editor: Oscar Moore
International trade magazine for the film, TV, video, cable and satellite industries. Regular news, features, production information from around the world
Press day: Thur
Circulation: 15,000

bfi Sight and Sound
(monthly)
British Film Institute
21 Stephen Street
London W1P 1PL
Tel: 071 255 1444
Fax: 071 436 2327
Editor: Philip Dodd
Relaunched in May 1991, incorporating 'Monthly Film Bulletin'. Includes regular columns, feature articles, a book review section and review/synopsis/credits of every feature film theatrically released plus a brief listing of every video
Copy date: 15th of each month
Circulation: 35,000

Spare Rib (monthly)
27 Clerkenwell Close
London EC1R 0AT
Tel: 071 253 9792
Film: Esther Bailey
TV: Jennifer Mourin
Progressive women's magazine, collectively produced
Lead time: 3-6 weeks
Circulation: 25,000

The Spectator
(weekly, Thur)
56 Doughty Street
London WC1N 2LL
Tel: 071 405 1706
Fax: 071 242 0603
Arts editor: Jenny Naipaul
Film: Gabriele Annan
TV: Martyn Harris
Independent review of politics, current affairs, literature and the arts
Press day: Wed
Circulation: 40,000

The Sun
PO Box 481
1 Virginia Street
London E1 9BD
Tel: 071 782 4000
Fax: 071 488 3253
Film critic: Peter Cox
TV: Garry Bushell
National daily newspaper
Circulation: 3,732,175

Sunday Express
Ludgate House
245 Blackfriars Road
London SE1 9UX
Tel: 071 928 8000
Fax: 071 620 1656
Film/Theatre: Clive Hirschhorn
National Sunday newspaper
Circulation: 1,880,000

Sunday Express Magazine
Ludgate House
245 Blackfriars Road
London SE1 9UX
Tel: 071 928 8000
Editor: Sue Peart
Deputy editor: Hilary Smith
Film/TV: Gill Morgan
Supplement to 'Sunday Express' newspaper
Lead time: 6 weeks
Circulation: 1,720,000

Sunday Magazine
1 Virginia Street
London E1 9BD
Tel: 071 782 7000
Fax: 071 782 7474
Editor: Sue Carroll
Features editor: Jonathan Worsnip
Supplement to 'News of the World'
Lead time: 8 weeks

Sunday Mirror
33 Holborn Circus
London EC1P 1DQ
Tel: 071 353 0246
Fax: 071 822 3405
Film: Charles Golding
TV: Jean Carr
National Sunday newspaper
Circulation: 2,999,000

Sunday Telegraph
Peterborough Court
at South Quay
181 Marsh Wall
London E14 9SR
Tel: 071 538 5000
Fax: 071 538 1330
Arts: John McEwan
Film: Christopher Tookey
TV: A.N. Wilson
National Sunday newspaper
Circulation: 648,000

Sunday Times
News International
1 Virginia Street
London E1 9BD
Tel: 071 782 5000
Film reviews: George Perry
TV reviews: Patrick Stoddart
National Sunday newspaper
Press day: Fri
Circulation: 1,188,373

Sunday Times Magazine
News International
1 Virginia Street
London E1 9BD
Tel: 01 782 7000
Editor: Philip Clarke
Films editor: George Perry
Supplement to 'Sunday Times'
Lead time: 6 weeks
Circulation: 1,310,000

TV Quick
(weekly, Mon)
25-27 Camden Road
London NW1 9LL
Tel: 071 284 0909
Film/TV editor: Adrian Turner
Mass market television magazine
Lead time: 3 weeks

TV Times
(weekly, Tues)
ITV Publications
247 Tottenham Court Road
London W1P 0AU
Tel: 071 323 3222
Weekly guide to all UK television, BBC Radio and satellite programmes
Circulation: c 3,000,000

TV World
(7 issues a year)
7 Swallow Place
249-259 Regent Street
London W1R 7AA
Tel: 071 491 9484
Fax: 071 355 3182
Editor: Marta Wohrle
Features Editor: Susan Eardely
International magazine for executives in programming industry – buyers, distributors, producers
Lead time: 5 days
Circulation: 10,433

Tatler (10 issues a year)
Vogue House
1-2 Hanover Square
London W1R 0AD
Tel: 071 499 9080
Fax: 071 409 0451
Arts: Jessamy Calkin
Smart society magazine favouring profiles, fashion and the arts
Lead time: 12 weeks
Circulation: 57,000

The Teacher
(8 issues a year)
National Union of Teachers
Hamilton House
Mabledon Place
London WC1H 9BD
Tel: 071 388 6191
Fax: 071 387 8458
Editor: Mitch Howard
Circulation: 250,000 mailed direct to all NUT members and to educational instutions

Telegraph Weekend Magazine
Editor: Nigel Horne
Supplement to Saturday edition of the 'Daily Telegraph'
Lead time: 6 weeks
Circulation: 1,008,000

Television
(bi-monthly)
Royal Television Society
Tavistock House East
Tavistock Square
London WC1H 9HR
Tel: 071 387 1970
Fax: 071 387 0358
Editor: Harvey Lee
The magazine of the Royal Television Society now incorporating 'Talkback'

Television Today
(weekly, Thur)
47 Bermondsey Street
London SE1 3XT
Tel: 071 403 1818
Fax: 071 403 1418
Editor: Peter Hepple
'Television Today' constitutes the middle section of 'The Stage' and is a weekly trade paper

Television Week
(weekly, Thur)
67 Clerkenwell Road
London EC1R 5BH
Tel: 071 251 6222
Fax: 071 831 4607
Editor: Charles Brown
Press day: Tuesday
Circulation: 15,000

Televisual (monthly)
50 Poland Street
London W1V 4AX
Tel: 071 494 0300
Fax: 071 287 0768
Editor: Mundy Ellis
Monthly business magazine for production professionals in the business of moving pictures
Circulation: 8,900

Time Out
(weekly, Wed)
Tower House
Southampton Street
London WC2E 7HD
Tel: 071 836 4411
Fax: 071 836 7118
Film: Geoff Andrew
Film listings: Wally Hammond
Films on TV: Brian Case
TV: Alkarim Jivani
London listings magazine with cinema and TV sections
Listings lead time: 8 days
Features lead time: 1 week
Circulation: 82,764

The Times
News International
1 Virginia Street
London E1 9BD
Tel: 071 782 5000
Fax: 071 488 3242
Film: Geoff Brown
Video: Peter Waymark
Arts (TV): Richard Morrison
Saturday editor: Andrew Harvey
National daily newspaper
Circulation: 413,244

The Times Educational Supplement
(weekly, Fri)
Priory House
St John's Lane
London EC1M 4BX
Tel: 071 253 3000
Fax: 071 608 1599
Arts: Heather Neill
Film critic: Robin Buss
Broadcasting: Gillian Macdonald
Video: Sean Coughlan
Press day: Wed
Circulation: 116,833

The Times Higher Education Supplement
(weekly, Fri)
Priory House
St John's Lane
London EC1M 4BX
Tel: 071 253 3000
Arts & Features: Jon Turney
Press day: Wed
Lead time for reviews: copy 10 days before publication
Circulation: 16,500

The Times Literary Supplement
(weekly, Fri)
Priory House
St John's Lane
London EC1M 4BX
Tel: 071 253 3000
Fax: 071 251 3424
Arts editor: Anna Vaux
Press day: Tues
Circulation: 30,000

The Times Scottish Education Supplement
(weekly, Fri)
37 George Street

Edinburgh EH2 2HN
Tel: 031 220 1100
Fax: 031 220 1616
Editor: Willis Pickard
Press day: Wed

Today

News International
1 Virginia Street
London E1 9BS
Tel: 071 782 4600
Film: Sue Heal
TV: Pam Francis
Showbusiness editor: Lester Middlehurst
National daily newspaper
Circulation: 505,423

Tribune (weekly, Fri)

308 Gray's Inn Road
London WC1X 8DY
Tel: 071 278 0911
Reviews editor: Paul Anderson
Political, literary newspaper with socialist and feminist approach

Variety (weekly, Mon)

34-35 Newman Street
London W1P 3PD
Tel: 071 637 3663
Fax: 071 580 5559
London bureau chief: Terry Ilott
International showbusiness newspaper
Press day: Fri

Vogue (monthly)

Vogue House
Hanover Square
London W1R 0AD
Tel: 071 499 9080
Editor: Elizabeth Tilberis
Features: Eve MacSweeney, Kathy O'Shaughnessy, Sarah Mower
Glossy magazine for women
Lead time: 12 weeks

The Voice (weekly)

370 Coldharbour Lane
London SW9 8PL
Tel: 071 737 7377
Fax: 071 274 8994
Editor: Winsome Grace Cornish
Film: Sharon Martin
Britain's leading black newspaper with mainly 18-35 age group readership. Regular film, TV and video coverage
Press day: Fri
Circulation: 50,000

Western Mail

Thomson House
Cardiff CF1 1WR
Tel: 0222 223333
Features editor: Gareth Jenkins
Film: Mario Basini
TV: Terry Hurst
Arts Correspondent: Nicol Socher
Welsh daily newspaper
Circulation: 75,874

What's On in London

(weekly, Tues)
182 Pentonville Road
London N1 9LB
Tel: 071 278 4393
Fax: 071 837 5838
Editor: David Parkes-Bristow
Film editor: Michael Darvell
Film correspondent: Phillip Bergson
London based weekly covering cinema, theatre, music, arts, entertainment, books and fashion
Press day: Mon
Lead time: 10 days
Circulation: 50,000

What's on TV

(weekly, Mon)
247 Tottenham Court Road
London W1P 0AU
Tel: 071 323 3222
Fax: 071 323 2957
Film/TV editor: Peter Genower
TV listings magazine
Lead time: 3 weeks

Yorkshire Post

Wellington Street
Leeds
West Yorkshire LS1 1RF
Tel: 0532 432701
Fax: 0532 443430
Regional daily morning newspaper
Deadline: 10.00 pm
Circulation: 94,000

NEWS AND PHOTO AGENCIES

Associated Press

12 Norwich Street
London EC4A 1BP
Tel: 071 353 1515

Central Office of Information

Hercules Road
London SE1
Tel: 071 928 2345

Central Press Features

20 Spectrum House
32-34 Gordon House Road
London NW5 1LP
Tel: 071 284 1433

Fleet Street News Agency

68 Exmouth Market
London EC1R 4RA
Tel: 071 278 5661
Fax: 071 278 8480

Knight Ridder Unicom News Service

72-78 Fleet Street
London EC4Y 1HY
Tel: 071 353 4861

London News Service

68 Exmouth Market
London EC1R 4RA
Tel: 071 278 5661/1223
Fax: 071 278 8480

More News

Dalling House
132 Dalling Road
London W6 0EP
Tel: 081 741 7000

Press Association

85 Fleet Street
London EC4P 4BE
Tel: 071 353 7440
Fax: 071 583 6082 (Photo), 071 936 2400 (News)

Reuters

85 Fleet Street
London EC4P 4AJ
Tel: 071 250 1122

United Press International

Meridian House
2 Greenwich View
Millharbour
London E14 9NN
Tel: 071 538 5310
Fax: 071 538 1051

BBC TELEVISION

BBC

Television Centre
Wood Lane
London W12 7RJ
Tel: 081 743 8000
BBC1
Omnibus; Film '91; Breakfast Time
BBC2
Arena; The Late Show

INDEPENDENT TELEVISION

Anglia Television

Anglia House
Norwich NR1 3JG
Tel: 0603 615151
Anglia News East; Anglia News West; Anglia Reports; Folio; Wideangle - weekly listings programme

Border Television

Television Centre
Carlisle CA1 3NT
Tel: 0228 25101
Lookaround

Central Independent Television

Central House
Broad Street
Birmingham B1 2JP
Tel: 021 643 9898
East Midlands Television Centre
Nottingham NG7 2NA
Tel: 0602 863322
Unit 9, Windrush Court
Abingdon Business Park
Abingdon
Oxon OX14 1SA
Tel: 0235 554123
Central News (separate bulletins prepared for east, south and west); *Central Lobby; Central Weekend; First Night; Earth Dwellers' Guide; The Works*

Channel 4 Television

60 Charlotte Street
London W1P 2AX
Tel: 071 631 4444
Channel 4 News c/o ITN; *Right to Reply*

Channel Television

The Television Centre
La Pouquelaye
St Helier
Jersey
Channel Islands
Tel: 0534 68999
Television Centre
St George's Place
St Peter Port
Guernsey
Channel Islands
Tel: 0481 723451

Grampian Television

Queen's Cross
Aberdeen AB9 2XJ
Tel: 0224 646464
North Tonight; Crossfire; Crann Tara; Criomagan

Granada Television

Quay Street
Manchester M60 9EA
Tel: 061 832 7211
Bridgegate House
5 Bridge Place

Lower Bridge Street
Chester CH1 1SA
Tel: 0244 313966
White Cross Estate
South Road
Lancaster LA1 4XQ
Tel: 0524 60688
Albert Dock
Liverpool L3 4BA
Tel: 051 709 9393
Daisyfield Business Centre
Appleby Street
Blackburn BB1 3BL
Tel: 0254 690099
Granada Tonight

HTV Wales
Television Centre
Culverhouse Cross
Cardiff CF5 6XJ
Tel: 0222 590590
Primetime

HTV West
Television Centre
Bath Road
Bristol BS4 3HG
Tel: 0272 778366
Press Officer: 0272 722214
Fax: 0272 722400
HTV News; The West This Week; Police Five; HTV Newsweek; Crimestoppers; Sportsweek

Independent Television News
200 Gray's Inn Road
London WC1X 8XZ
Tel: 071 833 3000

LWT
South Bank Television Centre
London SE1 9LT
Tel: 071 620 1620
South Bank Show

S4C
Sophia Close
Cardiff CF1 9XY
Tel: 0222 747444
Fax: 0222 341643
Head of Press, Publicity and International Affairs: Ann Benyon

Scottish Television
Cowcaddens
Glasgow G2 3PR
Tel: 041 332 9999
The Gateway
Edinburgh EH7 4AH
Tel: 031 557 4554
Chief Press Officer: Stephen McCrossan

TV-am
Hawley Crescent
London NW1 8EF
Tel: 071 267 4300/4377
Good Morning Britain; After Nine; Wacaday; David Frost on Sunday

TVS Television
Television Centre
Vinters Park
Maidstone
Kent ME14 5NZ
Tel: 0622 691111
Television Centre
Northam
Southampton SO9 5HZ
Tel: 0703 634211

Television South West
Derry's Cross
Plymouth
Devon PL1 2SP
Tel: 0752 663322
Compass; Consumer File; Business South West

Thames Television
365 Euston Road
London NW1 3AR
Tel: 071 911 0033
Fax: 071 911 0242
01; Video View

Tyne Tees Television
The Television Centre
City Road
Newcastle upon Tyne
NE1 2AL
Tel: 091 261 0181
Fax: 091 261 2302

Ulster Television
Havelock House
Ormeau Road
Belfast BT7 1EB
Tel: 0232 328122
Six Tonight; Spectrum; Preview

Yorkshire Television
The Television Centre
Leeds LS3 1JS
Tel: 0532 438283
Calendar

BBC RADIO

BBC
Broadcasting House
London W1A 1AA
Tel: 071 580 4468
Fax: 071 636 9786
RADIO 1
Steve Wright, Simon Bates, Dave Lee Travis, Mark Goodier
RADIO 2
Radio 2 Arts Programme; Cinema 2; Gloria Hunniford Show
RADIO 3
Third Ear; Third Opinion
RADIO 4
Kaleidoscope
RADIO 5
Morning Edition; On Your Marks
WORLD SERVICE
Bush House
Strand
London WC2B 4PH
Tel: 071 240 3456
Meridian

BBC LOCAL RADIO STATIONS

BBC Hereford & Worcester
Hylton Road
Worcester WR2 5WW
Tel: 0905 748485
Fax: 0905 748006
Manager: John Pickles
Programme Organiser: Denzil Dudley

Greater London Radio (GLR)
35c Marylebone High Street
London W1A 4LG
Tel: 071 224 2424
Fax: 071 487 2908

Greater Manchester Radio (GMR)
PO Box 90
New Broadcasting House
Oxford Road
Manchester M60 1SJ
Tel: 061 200 2000
What's On – Andrea Nilsen

Radio Bedfordshire
PO Box 476
Hastings Street
Luton
Bedfordshire LU1 5BA
Tel: 0582 459111
Fax: 0582 401467
Programme organiser: Jeff Winston

Radio Bristol
PO Box 194
Bristol BS99 7QT
Tel: 0272 741111
Fax: 0272 732549
What's On; Events West; Tea-Time Show

Radio CWR
25 Warwick Road
Coventry CV1 2WR
Tel: 0203 559911
Fax: 0203 520080
Manager: Andy Wright
Programme Organiser: Charles Hodkinson

Radio Cambridgeshire
PO Box 96
Cambridge CB2 1LD
Tel: 0223 315970
Rowland Myers

Radio Cleveland
PO Box 95FM
Broadcasting House
Newport Road
Middlesbrough TS1 5DG
Tel: 0642 225211
Ann Davies

Radio Cornwall
Phoenix Wharf
Truro TR1 1UA
Tel: 0872 75421
Fax: 0872 40679
TV/Film/Arts: Tim Hubbard
Seen and Heard; Cornwall Daily; Saturday Breakfast Show

Radio Cumbria
Hilltop Heights
London Road
Carlisle CA1 2NA
Tel: 0228 31661
Fax: 0228 511195/512228
What's On; Cumbria Today

Radio Derby
PO Box 269
Derby DE1 3HL
Tel: 0332 361111
Fax: 0332 290794
Sound and Vision; Chris Baird Show; Peter Gore

Radio Devon
PO Box 100
Exeter EX4 4DB
Tel: 0392 215651
Arts: John Lilley
PO Box 5
Catherine Street
Plymouth PL1 2AD
Tel: 0752 260323
The Arts Programme

Radio Essex
198 New London Road
Chelmsford
Essex CM2 9XB
Tel: 0245 262393
Fax: 0245 492983

Radio Foyle
PO Box 927
8 Northland Road
Londonderry BT48 7NE
Tel: 0504 262244
Fax: 0504 260067
The Afternoon Show; AM on Foyle

Radio Guernsey
Commerce House
Les Banques
St Peter Port
Guernsey
Tel: 0481 728977
Manager: Bob Bufton
News editor: Kay Langlois

Radio Humberside
9 Chapel Street
Hull HU1 3NU
Tel: 0482 23232
Fax: 0482 226409
Steve Massam

Radio Jersey
Broadcasting House
Rouge Bouillon
St Helier
Jersey
Tel: 0534 70000
Fax: 0534 32569
Manager: Bob Bufton

Radio Kent
Sun Pier
Chatham
Kent ME4 4EZ
Tel: 0634 830505
Soundtrack

Radio Lancashire
Darwen Street
Blackburn
Lancs BB2 2EA
Tel: 0254 62411
Fax: 0254 680821
Arts producer: Joe Wilson
Film specialist: Wendy Howard

Radio Leeds
Broadcasting House
Woodhouse Lane
Leeds LS2 9PN
Tel: 0532 442131
Fax: 0532 420652
Richard Rudin

Radio Leicester
Epic House
Charles Street
Leicester LE1 3SH
Tel: 0533 516688
Fax: 0533 511463

Radio Lincolnshire
PO Box 219
Newport
Lincoln LN1 3XY
Tel: 0522 511411
Fax: 0522 511058
Arts producer: Alan Stennett
What's On Diary; Gallery

Radio Merseyside
55 Paradise Street
Liverpool L1 3BP
Tel: 051 708 5500
Fax: 051 709 2394
Film critic: Ramsey Campbell

Radio Newcastle
Broadcasting Centre
Fenham
Newcastle upon Tyne
NE99 1RN
Tel: 091 232 4141
Fax: 091 232 5082
Senior producer: Simon Pattern

Radio Norfolk
Norfolk Tower
Surrey Street
Norwich NR1 3PA
Tel: 0603 617411
Fax: 0603 633692
Arts producer: Stewart Orr

Radio Northampton
PO Box 1107
Northampton NN1 2BE
Tel: 0604 239100
Fax: 0604 230709
Arts producers: David Saint, Laurence Culhane

Radio Nottingham
PO Box 222
Nottingham NG1 3NZ
Tel: 0602 415161
Fax: 0602 481482
Programme organiser: Nick Brunger

Radio Oxford
269 Banbury Road
Oxford OX2 7DW
Tel: 0865 311444
Fax: 0865 311996
Stewart Woodcock

Radio Peterborough
PO Box 957
Peterborough PE1 1YT
Tel: 0733 312832
Fax: 0733 343768
Senior producer: Steve Somers

Radio Sheffield
Ashdell Grove
60 Westbourne Road
Sheffield S10 2QU
Tel: 0742 686185
Fax: 0742 664375
Programme organiser: Chris van Schaick
On Screen

Radio Solent
Broadcasting House
10 Havelock Road
Southampton SO1 0XR
Tel: 0703 631311
Fax: 0703 339648
Programme organiser: John Smith

Radio Stoke
Cheapside
Hanley
Stoke-on-Trent ST1 1JJ
Tel: 0782 208080
Fax: 0782 289115
First Edition; Glyn Johnson Show

Radio Sussex
1 Marlborough Place
Brighton BN1 1TU
Tel: 0273 680231
Fax: 0273 601241
Programme organiser: Jim Beaman

Radio WM
PO Box 206
Birmingham B5 7SD
Tel: 021 414 8484

Somerset Sound
14-16 Paul Street
Taunton
Somerset
Tel: 0823 251641
Fax: 0823 332539
Senior producer: Richard Austin

Wiltshire Sound
Broadcasting House
Prospect Place
Swindon SN1 3RN
Tel: 0793 513626
Fax: 0793 513650
Arts producer: Chris Highton

INDEPENDENT LOCAL RADIO

BRMB-FM
Radio House
PO Box 555
Aston Road North
Birmingham B6 4BX
Tel: 021 359 4481
Fax: 021 359 1117
Head of programmes: Nick Meanwell

Beacon Radio
267 Tettenhall Road
Wolverhampton
WV6 0DQ
Tel: 0902 757211
Fax: 0902 745456
Programme director: Pete Wagstaff

Beacon Radio Shropshire
Thorn's Hall
28 Castle Street
Shrewsbury SY1 2BQ
Tel: 0743 232271
Fax: 0743 231944

Breeze AM
PO Box 3000
Southend-on-Sea
Essex SS1 1SY
Tel: 0702 333711
Head of features: Romilly Paradine

CN.FM 103
PO Box 1000
The Vision Park
Chivers Way
Histon
Cambridge CB4 4WW
Tel: 0223 235255
Fax: 0223 235161
Programme controller: Adrian Crookes
Film and TV reviews: Mark Simpson

Capital Radio
Euston Tower
Euston Road
London NW1 3DR
Tel: 071 388 1288
Fax: 071 387 2345
Nicholas Wheeler
The Way It Is; The David Jensen Show

Chiltern Radio
Chiltern Road
Dunstable LU6 1HQ
Tel: 0582 666001
Fax: 0582 661725
Programme controller: Paul Chantler

City Talk
PO Box 1548
Liverpool L69 7DQ
Tel: 051 227 5100
Fax: 051 255 1143
Programme controller: Tony Ingham

Classic Gold
PO Box 777
Sheffield S1 1GP
Programme controller: Dean Pepall

County Sound
93 Chertsey Road
Woking
Surrey GU21 5XY
Tel: 0483 740066
Fax: 0483 740753
Paul Owens

DevonAir Radio
35-37 St David's Hill
Exeter EX4 4DA
Tel: 0392 430703
Fax: 0392 411893

Downtown Radio
Newtownards BT23 4ES
Tel: 0247 815555

Fax: 0247 817878
Film/video: John Daly

Essex Radio
Radio House
Clifftown Road
Southend-on-Sea SS1 1SX
Tel: 0702 333711
Head of Features: Romilly Paradine

GEM-AM
29/31 Castle Gate
Nottingham NG1 7AP
Tel: 0602 581731
Fax: 0602 588614
Programme Controller: Chris Hughes

GWR
Lime Kiln Studios
Wootton Bassett
Swindon
Wilts SN4 7EX
Tel: 0793 853222
Station Director: Simon Cooper

Great North Radio
Swalwell
Newcastle upon Tyne
NE99 1BB
Tel: 091 496 0377
Fax: 091 488 9222
Programme Controller: Giles Squire

Hereward Radio
PO Box 225
Queensgate Centre
Peterborough PE1 1XJ
Tel: 0733 346225
Fax: 0733 896400
Programme controller: Adrian Crookes

Jazz FM
The Jazz House
26-27 Castlereagh Street
London W1H 5YR
Tel: 071 706 4100
Fax: 071 723 9742
Film critic: George Perry

Invicta Radio
Radio House
John Wilson Business Park
Whitstable
Kent CT5 3QX
Tel: 0227 772004
Fax: 0227 771558
Sue Flipping

IRN
Crown House
72 Hammersmith Road
London W14 8YE
Tel: 071 603 2400
Editor: John Perkins

LBC News Talk
Crown House
72 Hammersmith Road
London W14 8YE
Tel: 071 603 2400
Fax: 071 371 1515
Film/TV: Carol Allen, Rebecca Nicholson

London Talkback Radio
Crown House
72 Hammersmith Road
London W14 8YE
Tel: 071 333 0003
Fax: 071 371 2456

Leicester Sound
Granville House
Granville Road
Leicester LE1 7RW
Tel: 0533 551616
Fax: 0533 550869
Programme controller: David Lloyd
Film and media programmes: Mark Hayman

Marcher Sound
The Studios
Mold Road
Gwersyllt
Wrexham
Clwyd LL1 4AF
Tel: 0978 752202
Fax: 0978 759701
Programme Controller: Paul Mewies

MAX AM
PO Box 1548
Forth House
Forth Street
Edinburgh EH1 3LF
Tel: 031 556 9255
Fax: 031 558 3277
Programme Controller: Ken Haynes

Mercia-FM
Hertford Place
Coventry CV1 3TT
Tel: 0203 633933
Fax: 0203 258206
Managing director/programme controller: Stuart Linnell
News editor: Alan Turner

Metro FM
Newcastle upon Tyne
NE99 1BB
Tel: 091 488 3131
Fax: 091 488 8611
Programme manager: Steve Martin

Midlands Radio
29/31 Castle Gate
Nottingham NG1 7AP
Tel: 0602 503020
Fax: 0602 582606
Managing director: R J Coles
Incorporating BRMB-FM, GEM-AM, Mercia-FM, Trent-FM (Derby), Trent-FM (Nottingham), Sound-FM and Xtra-AM

Moray Firth Radio
PO Box 271
Inverness IV3 6SF
Tel: 0463 224433
Fax: 0463 243224

Northsound Radio
45 King's Gate
Aberdeen AB2 6BL
Tel: 0224 632234
Fax: 0224 637289
Head of news: Mark Coyle

Orwell FM
Electric House
Lloyds Avenue
Ipswich IP1 3HZ
Tel: 0473 216971
Fax: 0473 230350
Mike Stewart

Pennine-FM
PO Box 235
Pennine House
Forster Square
Bradford
W Yorks BD1 5NP
Tel: 0274 731521
Fax: 0274 392031
News Editor: Charles Lees

Piccadilly Gold/ Piccadilly Key
127-131 The Piazza
Piccadilly Plaza
Manchester M1 4AW
Tel: 061 236 9913
Fax: 061 228 1503
Programme controller: Mark Story

Plymouth Sound
Earl's Acre
Alma Road
Plymouth PL3 4HX
Tel: 0752 227272
Fax: 0752 670730
Head of News and Current Affairs: Malcolm Carroll

Radio Aire FM/ Magic 828
PO Box 2000
Leeds LS3 1LR
Tel: 0532 452299
Fax: 0532 421830
Programme controller: Paul Faiburn

Radio Broadland
47-49 St Georges Plain
Colegate
Norwich NR3 1DB
Tel: 0603 630621
Fax: 0603 666353
Programme Director: Mike Stewart

Radio Clyde
Clydebank Business Park
Glasgow G81 2RX
Tel: 041 306 2345
Fax: 041 306 2265
Andy Dougan

Radio Forth RFM
PO Box 4000
Forth House
Forth Street
Edinburgh EH1 3LF
Tel: 031 556 9255
Fax: 031 558 3277
Films: Colin Somerville

Radio Hallam FM
PO Box 194
Hartshead
Sheffield S1 1GP
Tel: 0742 766766
Programme controller: Steve King

Radio Tay
PO Box 123
Dundee DD1 9UF
Tel: 0382 200800
Fax: 0382 24549
Station manager: A J Wilkie

Radio Wyvern
5-6 Barbourne Terrace
Worcester WR1 3JZ
Tel: 0905 612212
Fax: 0905 29595
Managing director/Programme controller: Norman Bilton
Programme co-ordinator: Stephanie Denham

Red Dragon Radio
Radio House
West Canal Wharf
Cardiff CF1 5XJ
Tel: 0222 384041
Fax: 0222 384014
Programme director: Peter Milburn
Film/video: John Dash

Red Rose Radio
PO Box 301
St Paul's Square
Preston PR1 1YE
Tel: 0772 556301
Fax: 0772 201917
Programme controller: Mark Matthews

Saxon-FM
Long Brackland
Bury St Edmunds
Suffolk IP33 1JY
Tel: 0284 701511

Fax: 0284 706446
Nigel Rennie

Severn Sound
Old Talbot House
67 Southgate Street
Gloucester GL1 2DQ
Tel: 0452 423791
Fax: 0452 29446
Keith Francis

Signal Radio
Stoke Road
Stoke-on-Trent ST4 2SR
Tel: 0782 747047
Fax: 0782 744110
Arts: Terry Underhill, Judith Franklin
The Weekly Review

Sound-FM
Granville House
Granville Road
Leicester LE1 7RW
Tel: 0533 551616
Fax: 0533 550869
General manager: David Lloyd

South Coast Radio
Whittle Avenue
Segensworth-West
Fareham
Hants PO15 5PA
Tel: 04895 89911
Fax: 04895 89453

Film reviews: Guy Hornsby

Southern Radio
Radio House
PO Box 99
Fareham
Hampshire PO15 5TA
Tel: 0489 589911
Fax: 0489 589453
Alexis Cooper

Southern Sound FM
PO Box 2000
Brighton BN41 2SS
Tel: 0273 430111
Fax: 0273 430098
Richard Gwynn

Swansea Sound
Victoria Road
Gowerton
Swansea SA4 3AB
Tel: 0792 893751
Fax: 0792 898841
Head of programmes: Andrew Armitage (news, features), Rob Pendry (music)

TFM 96.60
74 Dovecot Street
Stockton-on-Tees
Cleveland TS18 1HB
Tel: 0642 615111
Fax: 0642 606300
Heather Raw

Trent FM (Derby)
The Market Place
Derby DE1 3AA
Tel: 0332 292945
Fax: 0332 292229
Programme controller: Chris Hughes

Trent FM (Nottingham)
29-31 Castle Gate
Nottingham NG1 7AP
Tel: 0602 581731
Fax: 0602 588614
Programme controller: Chris Hughes

210 FM
PO Box 210
Reading RG3 5RZ
Tel: 0734 413131
Fax: 0734 431215
Programme controller: Phil Coope

2CR FM
5-7 Southcote Road
Bournemouth BH1 3LR
Tel: 0202 294881
Fax: 0202 299314
Programme controller: Phil Coope
News editor: Mel Bray

WABC
267 Tettenhall Road
Wolverhampton WV6 0DQ
Tel: 0902 757211
Fax: 0902 745456
Programme director: Pete Wagstaff

West Sound
Radio House
54A Holmston Road
Ayr KA7 3BE
Tel: 0292 283662
Fax: 0292 283665
Programme controller: John McCauley
Arts producer: Gordon McArthur

Xtra-AM (Birmingham)
PO Box 555
Aston Road North
Birmingham B6 4BX
Tel: 021 359 4481
Fax: 021 359 1117

Xtra-AM (Coventry)
West End House
Hertford Place
Coventry CV1 3TT
Tel: 0203 633933
Fax: 0203 258206

PREVIEW THEATRES

Alva Films
16 Brook Street
Alva
Clackmannanshire
FK12 5JL
Tel: 0259 60936
Fax: 0259 69436
Formats: 16mm double-head, U-Matic, VHS
Seats: 24

BAFTA
195 Piccadilly
London W1V 9LG
Tel: 071 734 0022
Fax: 071 734 1792
Formats: Twin 16mm and Super 16mm double-head stereo, 35mm double-head Dolby stereo at all aspect ratios, U-Matic and VHS stereo. General Electric Talaria projector
Seats: Princess Anne: 213, Run Run Shaw: 30, Function Room: up to 200
Catering by Roux Restaurants

BFI
21 Stephen Street
London W1P 1PL
Tel: 071 255 1444
Fax: 071 436 7950
Formats: 35mm double-head/Dolby stereo optical, 16mm double-head/optical, U-Matic hi-/lo-band/triple standard, VHS triple standard, PAL S VHS
Seats: 1 (film): 36, 2 (video): 12, 3 (film): 36

Baronet Theatre
84 Wardour Street
London W1V 3LF
Tel: 071 437 2233
Fax: 071 434 9990
Formats: 16mm, 35mm double-head
Large screen video
U-Matic, VHS
Seats: 25

Bijou Theatre
113 Wardour Street
London W1V 3LF
Tel: 071 437 2233
Fax: 071 434 9990
Formats: 16mm and 35mm, Dolby stereo, double-head, U-Matic, VHS
Large screen video
Seats: 88

British Universities Film and Video Council (BUFVC)
55 Greek Street
London W1V 5LR
Tel: 071 734 3687
Fax: 071 287 3914
Formats: 16mm double-head, VHS, U-Matic
Seats: 15-20

CFS Conference Centre
22 Portman Close
London W1A 4BE
Tel: 071 486 2881
Fax: 071 486 4152
Formats: 16mm and 35mm film projection, video projection
Full bar and in-house catering
Seats: 110

Cannon Cinemas
Preview Theatre
Ground Floor
Pathé House
76 Hammersmith Road
London W14 9YR
Tel: 071 603 4555
Fax: 071 603 4277
Formats: 16mm mag and optical. 16mm double head edge and centre
35mm Dolby Stereo optical
SVA Magnetic Dolby stereo
35mm Triple Track
35mm Mono
Video: U-matic, VHS
Triple standard, Betamax projection system
35mm projection FP20
16mm projection FP18
Cinemascope 2.35,
Widescreen 1.85
Standard 1.37
Seats: 36

Century Preview Theatres
31-32 Soho Square
London W1V 6AP
Tel: 071 437 7766
Fax: 071 437 1625
Formats: Century Theatre: 35mm Dolby optical and magnetic stereo, Dolby A & SR noise reduction, 2,000′ double-head capacity; Executive Theatre: Dolby stereo optical and magnetic, A type noise reduction, 2,000′ double-head capacity
Seats: Century: 61, Executive: 38

Chapter Cinema
Market Road
Canton
Cardiff CF5 1QE
Tel: 0222 396061
Formats: 35mm optical, 16mm double-head, high quality video projection, U-Matic/VHS. Reception space and restaurant
Seats: 78

Columbia Tri-Star Films UK
19-23 Wells Street
London W1P 3FP
Tel: 071 580 2090
Fax: 071 580 8980
Formats: 16mm, 35mm double-head Dolby SR stereo and full video projection, induction loop system. Catering and reception facilities
Seats: 65

Coronet Theatre
84 Wardour Street
London W1V 3LF
Tel: 071 437 2233
Fax: 071 434 9990
Formats: 35mm double-head, large screen video
U-Matic, VHS
Seats: 15

Crawford Preview Theatre
15-17 Old Compton Street
London W1V 6JR
Tel: 071 734 5298
Fax: 071 287 0370
Formats: 16mm, 35mm
Triple standard U-Matic, VHS, Beta
Seats: 1 (film): 15, 2 (video): 15

Crown Theatre
86 Wardour Street
London W1V 3LF
Tel: 071 437 2233
Fax: 071 434 9990
Formats: 16mm, 35mm double-head, Dolby stereo
Large screen video
Seats: 45

De Lane Lea Sound Centre
75 Dean Street
London W1V 5HA
Tel: 071 439 1721
Fax: 071 437 0913
Formats: 35mm and 16mm, Dolby stereo SR & A with double-head capacity. 3/4″ hi- and lo-band video and VHS
Bar and catering available
Seats: 30

Edinburgh Film Studios
Nine Mile Burn
Penicuik EH26 9LT

Tel: 0968 72131
Fax: 0968 72685
Formats: 16mm and 35mm double-head stereo, U-Matic, VHS
Seats: 100

Elstree Studios
Shenley Road
Borehamwood
Herts WD6 1JG
Tel: 081 953 1600
Fax: 081 207 0860
New preview theatres are part of major redevelopment of Elstree Studios. Please telephone for details and information on completion date

Grip House Preview Theatre
5-11 Taunton Road
Metropolitan Centre
Greenford
Middx UB6 8UQ
Tel: 081 578 2382
Fax: 081 578 1536
Formats: 16mm and 35mm, optical and magnetic double-head projection
Seats: 40

King's Lynn Arts Centre
27 King Street
King's Lynn
Norfolk PE30 1HA
Tel: 0553 774725
Formats: 16mm, 35mm
Seats: 349

The Metro
11 Rupert Street
London W1V 7FS
Tel: 071 434 3357/734 1506
Fax: 071 287 2112
Formats: 16mm and 35mm double-head. Two screens available until 2pm only
Seats: 195, 86

The Minema
45 Knightsbridge
London SW1X 7NL
Tel: 071 235 4225
Fax: 071 235 4330
Formats: 35mm and 16mm, full AV systems
Seats: 68

Mr Young's
First Floor
1-6 Falconberg Court
London W1V 5FG
Tel: 071 437 1771
Fax: 071 734 4520
Formats: 16mm, Super 16mm, 35mm, Super 35mm, U-Matic, VHS, Betamax, Dolby stereo double-head optical and magnetic Dolby SR. Catering by request
Seats: 35 (extended to 40 on request)

Pinewood Studios
Iver
Bucks SL0 0NH
Tel: 0753 656296
Fax: 0753 656844
Formats: 16mm, 35mm, 70mm, U-Matic
Seats: Five theatres with 12 to 115 seats

Prominent Facilities THX Preview Theatre
68a Delancey Street
London NW1 7RY
Tel: 071 284 0242
Fax: 071 284 1020
Formats: 35mm Dolby optical and magnetic, 2,000′ double-head, rock 'n' roll. All aspect ratios, and Super 35, 24-25-30 fps, triple-track, interlock, Dolby A & SR. Large screen video projection. Fully air conditioned, kitchen and reception area. Wheelchair access
Seats: 26

Rank Preview Theatre
127 Wardour Street
London W1V 4AD
Tel: 071 437 9020 x257
Fax: 071 434 3689
Formats: U-Matic, 16mm, 35mm double-head, Dolby stereo, VHS, U-Matic, slides
Seats: 58

Richmond Filmhouse
3 Water Lane
Richmond
Surrey TW9 1TG
Tel: 081 332 0030
Fax: 081 332 0316
Formats: 35mm, 70mm, 35mm double-head, Dolby 6-track Stereo
Seats: 150

Royal Society of Arts
8 John Adam Street
London WC2N 6EZ
Tel: 071 930 5115
Fax: 071 839 5805
Formats: VHS triple standard, Super VHS, Sony Video 8, data projection. Catering available
Seats: 60

Scottish Council for Educational Technology
Dowanhill
74 Victoria Crescent Road
Glasgow G12 9JN
Tel: 041 334 9314
Fax: 041 334 6519
Formats: Video, 16mm, 35mm, double band
A variety of catering facilities available
Seats: 173

Shepperton Studios
Shepperton
Middx TW17 0QD
Tel: 0932 562611
Fax: 0932 568989
Formats: 35mm, 16mm
Seats: 1 (35mm): 40, 2 (16mm): 20

Sherman Theatre
Senghenydd Road
Cardiff CF2 4YE
Tel: 0222 396844
Formats: 16mm, 35mm, Dolby stereo, U-Matic
Seats: 474

Twickenham Studios
St Margaret's
Twickenham
Middx TW1 2LT
Tel: 081 892 4477
Fax: 081 981 0168
Formats: 16mm, 35mm
Seats: 31

Warner Bros Preview Theatre
135 Wardour Street
London W1V 3TD
Tel: 071 734 8400
Fax: 071 437 5521
Formats: 16mm, 35mm double-head, Dolby stereo. VHS/U-Matic video projection
Seats: 33

Watershed Media Centre
1 Canons Road
Bristol BS1 5TX
Tel: 0272 276444
Fax: 0272 213958
Formats: Super 8mm, 16mm double-head, 35mm, U-Matic, VHS
Seats: 1: 200, 2: 50

Weintraub House Preview Theatre
167-169 Wardour Street
London W1V 3TA
Tel: 071 439 1790
Fax: 071 734 1509
Formats: 35mm Dolby stereo, U-Matic, VHS
For bookings contact: Soulla Thomas or Ken Ward
Seats: 35-40

PRODUCTION COMPANIES

These are UK companies which are currently active in financing and/or making audiovisual product for UK and international media markets. Also making audiovisual product are film and video workshops (see p316). Not listed below are the numerous companies making TV commercials, educational and other non-broadcast material, nor those companies set up to facilitate the production of particular films (see Facilities p144)

Aardman Animations
14 Wetherell Place
Clifton
Bristol BS8 1AR
Tel: 0272 744802
Fax: 0272 736281
Peter Lord
David Sproxton
Made 'Lip Synch', a series of films for Channel 4. A full-length model animation feature is in development. Aardman is committed to adult animation with the emphasis on character and movement

Acacia Productions
80 Weston Park
London N8 9TB
Tel: 081 340 2619/341 9392
Fax: 081 341 4879
J Edward Milner
Nikki Milner
Documentary, news, current affairs: environmental, social and political issues. Recent productions include: *Greening of Thailand, Channel 4 News Report: Amazon Indians: Colombia and Tigray* under TPLF

After Image
32 Acre Lane
London SW2 5SG
Tel: 071 737 7300
Fax: 071 326 1850
Jane Thorburn
Mark Lucas
After Image is best known for the long-running arts series *Alter Image* featuring artists and performers. Recent productions include *The Greatest Show on Earth,* two short operas jointly called *Tales of Faith and Foxes* and *Les Ballets Africaines.* Currently working on two television operas called *Camera* and *The Empress of Newfoundland*

Alive Productions
37 Harwood Road
London SW6 4QP
Tel: 071 384 2243
Fax: 071 384 2026
Television programme production, currently *Star Test* for Channel 4

All American Leisure Group
6 Woodland Way
Petts Wood
Kent BR5 1ND
Tel: 0689 871535/871519
Fax: 0689 871519

Allied Vision
Avon House
360 Oxford Street
London W1N 9HA
Tel: 071 409 1984
Fax: 071 493 4286
Edward Simons
Peter McRae
Completed *Howling VI – The Freaks* in 1990. Due to produce Stephen King's *The Lawnmower Man* and *Howling VII* in 1991

Alomo Productions
Elstree Studios
Shenley Road
Borehamwood
Herts WD6 1JG
Tel: 081 953 1600
Fax: 081 905 1427
Birds of a Feather II and a Christmas Special, *Taking the Floor* and *Love Hurts*

Amy International Productions
2a Park Avenue
Wraysbury
Middx TW19 5ET
Tel: 0784 483131/483288
Fax: 0784 483812
Susan George
Simon MacCorkindale
Odds End, Lucan

Andor Films
8 Ilchester Place
London W14 8AA
Tel: 071 602 2382
Fax: 071 602 1047
Production of theatrical motion pictures

Anglia Films
48 Leicester Square
London WC2H 7FB
Tel: 071 321 0101
Graeme McDonald
Brenda Reid
David FitzGerald
The filmmaking and drama production arm of Anglia TV. Current projects include *The Chief* Series 2, *Chimera* (in association with Zenith Productions), *Frankie's House, Growing Rich, Riders, Starlight* and *A Dangerous Man*

Anglo/Fortunato Films
170 Popes Lane
London W5 4NJ
Tel: 081 840 4196
Fax: 081 840 0279
Luciano Celentino
Feature film production company

Anglo-International Films
21a Kingly Court
London W1R 5LE
Tel: 071 734 5747
Fax: 071 734 5784
Don Boyd
Mary Davies
Robert McCrum
Polly Leys

Continuing in the tradition established with such films as *The Tempest, The Great Rock 'n' Roll Swindle, An Unsuitable Job for a Woman, Scum, Honky Tonk Freeway, Captive, The Last of England* and the multi-directional *Aria,* in 1988 Boyd produced *War Requiem* starring Laurence Olivier. In 1989 he returned to his directorial career with *Goldeneye* and in 1990 *Twenty-One*

Animation City/AC Live

69 Wells Street
London W1P 3RB
Tel: 071 494 3084
Fax: 071 436 8934
Ammie Purcell
Company currently producing animated and live action commercials, pop promos, designs and TV and film titles and optical effects

Antelope Films

3 Fitzroy Square
London W1P 5AH
Tel: 071 387 4454
Fax: 071 388 9935
Peter Montagnon
Mick Csaky
Productions undertaken for various broadcast television companies including BBC, ITV and Channel 4: *Testament, Global Rivals, Fonteyn – Story of a Dancer, The Midas Touch, Childhood, Terror, Nureyev, Carols from Prague* and *Spaceship Earth.* In production: *The Royal Collection, Tina Modotti, Fire and Friendship, Parallel Bars* and *French Family Robinson*

Arena Films

Twickenham Film Studios
St Margaret's
Twickenham
Middlesex TW1 2AW
Tel: 081 892 4477
Fax: 081 891 0168
Specialising in European co-production. Produced: *Coup de Foudre,* 27 half-hour films for television, for Telecip and Reteitalia. Also made *Vincent and Theo* released theatrically UK and USA, and for UK and US television *Magic Moments*

Ariel Productions

93 Wardour Street
London W1V 3TE
Tel: 071 494 2169
Fax: 071 494 2695
Otto Plaschkes
Produced *Shadey,* written by Snoo Wilson, directed by Philip Saville and starring Anthony Sher, for Film Four International. In development are *Changing Places,* scripted by Peter Nichols, *The Well* by Marc Zuber and *A Hero of our Time,* adapted by Derek Marlowe

Artifax

17 Clifford Street
London W1X 1RG
Tel: 071 734 4584
Fax: 071 287 1947
Elizabeth Queenan
Documentaries, arts, music, drama and light entertainment. Recent productions: the 1987 Prix Italia prize-winning *Behind the Mask – Perspectives on the Music of Harrison Birtwistle. Big, Big Country* with Hank Wangford, and a second series of *The Secret Life of Machines,* with Tim Hunkin. In production, for BBC Music and Arts: *Not Mozart,* five half-hour programmes for the bi-centenary year

Aspect Film and Television Production

36 Percy Street
London W1P 9FG
Tel: 071 636 5303
Fax: 071 436 0666
Mark Chapman
Producers of documentaries, comedies and drama

BFI Production

29 Rathbone Street
London W1P 1AG
Tel: 071 636 5587
Fax: 071 580 9456
Young Soul Rebels, Silent Scream, Fellow Traveller, Melancholia, New Directors Shorts, Play Me Something, La Deuda Interna, Distant Voices, Still Lives, On the Black Hill, Caravaggio, The Draughtsman's Contract

BJE

Home Farm
Church Hill
High Littleton
Bristol BS18 5HF
Tel: 0761 471055
John King
Current productions include: *Kali the Lion, Countryfile* weekly series, *Telly Addicts, EuroArchers, Puy Du Fou* and *Walk on the Wild Side*

Badger Films

Badger Studios
249-251 Kensal Road
London W10 5DB
Tel: 081 968 1446
Fax: 081 968 1318
Tony Coggans
Independent company producing documentaries

Banner Film and TV

11 Swaledale Road
Sheffield S7 2BY
Tel: 0742 556875
David Rea
Broadcast documentaries and drama

Peter Batty Productions

Claremont House
Renfrew Road
Kingston
Surrey KT2 7NT
Tel: 081 942 6304
Fax: 081 336 1661
Peter Batty
Recent Channel 4 productions include *Swastika Over British Soil, A Time for Remembrance, The Divided Union, Fonteyn and Nureyev, The Algerian War, Swindle* and *Il Poverello.* Previous independent productions include *The Story of Wine, Battle for Warsaw, Battle for Dien Bien Phu, Birth of the Bomb, Search for the Super, Battle for Cassino, Operation Barbarossa* and *Farouk: Last of the Pharaohs*

Bedford Productions

6th Floor
6 Vigo Street
London W1X 1AH
Tel: 071 287 9928
Fax: 071 287 9870
Mike Dineen
Francis Megahy
Television, documentary, drama production, and business to business programming

Bevanfield Films

22 Soho Square
London W1V 5FJ
Tel: 071 287 0628
Fax: 071 439 0138
Producers of animated and feature films

Bordeaux Films International

22 Soho Square
London W1V 5FJ
Tel: 081 959 8556
Recent projects include *Caravans, Double Jeopardy, Giselle, Guns and the Fury, Laura, Mr Wrong* and *The Witch*

Britannia Entertainment

Pinewood Studios
Iver
Bucks SL0 0NH
Tel: 0753 651700
Fax: 0753 656844
David Nicholas Wilkinson
Long established independent production company specialising in international co-production. Also raises finance for and acts as consultant to other independent producers. Recent productions the company has been involved with include: *Le Cirque Imaginaire, I Is a Long Memoried Woman, Dylan Thomas – Return Journey, 7001 Nights* and *The Wanderer*

British Lion

Pinewood Studios
Iver Heath
Bucks SL0 0NH
Tel: 0753 651700
Peter Snell
As Britannic Films, first project was the telemovie *Squaring the Circle,* co-financed with TVS and Metromedia Producers Associates. *Lady Jane* for Paramount Pictures and *Turtle Diary,* in association with United British Artists. *A Man for All Seasons* for Turner Network Television and *Treasure Island* also for TNT. Recent productions: *A*

Prayer for the Dying for Samuel Goldwyn Company and *The Crucifer of Blood* for TNT

Britt Allcroft Group
61 Devonshire Road
Southampton
SO1 2GR
Tel: 0703 331661
Fax: 0703 332206
Cathy Service
Production company, videos, film strip video; animation/children/ television. Specialising in family and children's programming, international merchandising. Recent works: *Thomas the Tank Engine and Friends,* 52 episodes based on The Railway Series by the Rev W Awdry. *Shining Time Station,* the award winning children's series, 20 half-hour US TV programmes networked PBS

Broadcast Communications (Corporate)
14 King Street
London WC2E 8HN
Tel: 071 240 6941
Fax: 071 379 5808
Michael Braham
Michael Braham is currently executive producer of the Channel 4 *Business Programme* and *Business Daily*

Broadside Productions
17b Finsbury Park Road
London N4 2LA
Tel: 071 354 2276
Ruth Pantoleon
Recent productions: *By Word of Mouth,* Channel 4 series on story-telling, *Five Women Photographers,* also for Channel 4, *Female Focus* and Broadside current affairs series

Brook Productions
21-24 Bruges Place
Randolph Street
London NW1 0TF
Tel: 071 482 6111
Fax: 071 284 0626
Anne Lapping
Udi Eichler
Philip Whitehead
Produced *Three of a Kind* (discussion series) and *The Session* for the BBC and the following for Channel 4: *The Thatcher Factor, Reagan on Reagan* (documentary series), *Prisoners of Childhood* (psychological drama), *Goodbye Russia, Brewing Trouble, Under the Influence, Street Doctors* (documentaries), *A Strike Out of Time* (drama-documentary), *A Week In Politics* (current affairs series), *Incident in Judaea* (drama). Works in progress for the BBC include *Museums of Madness*

Buena Vista Productions
31-32 Soho Square
London W1V 6AP
Tel: 071 734 8111
Fax: 071 287 6338
David Simon
European television production arm of The Walt Disney Company

Burrill Productions
19 Cranbury Road
London SW6 2NS
Tel: 071 736 8673
Fax: 071 731 3921
Petra Willoughby de Broke
Timothy Burrill
Burrill Productions co-produced *Return of the Musketeers* and *Valmont, the Lover.* Produced *The Rainbow Thief*

Busy Hands Productions
18-20 Rosendale Road
Dulwich
London SE21 8DX
Tel: 081 442 4930
A recently formed Black production company comprised of a variety of experienced media and production individuals. Busy Hands aims to produce educational videos, a Black video magazine programme and documentary features dealing with Black and Third World issues

Cabachon Films
16 Brechin Place
London SW7 4QA
Tel: 071 373 6453
Celestino Coronado
Productions include: *Smoking Mirror, The Lindsay Kemp Circus, Miroirs, Le Belle Indifferent, Hamlet, A Midsummer Night's Dream*

Camden Productions
20 Jeffreys Street
London NW1 9PR
Tel: 071 482 0527
Theresa FitzGerald
Small company consisting of two writers who develop their own work for film and TV

Carnival (Films and Theatre)
(formerly Picture Partnership Productions)
12 Raddington Road
Ladbroke Grove
London W10 5TG
Tel: 081 968 1818
Fax: 081 968 0155
Brian Eastman
Recently completed second series of *Jeeves and Wooster* for Granada, *Forever Green* and *Agatha Christie's Poirot* (third series) for LWT. Further series are planned. Currently in production with the feature film *Under Suspicion* for Columbia/Rank/ LWT. Future projects include a six part drama series for Channel 4, *The Big Battalions.* Previous productions include feature films *Wilt, Whoops Apocalypse, Traffik* and *Porterhouse Blue* (Channel 4), *Words of Love* and *Blott on the Landscape* (BBC)

Cartwn Cymru
Model House
Bull Ring
Llantrisant
Mid Glamorgan
Tel: 0443 222316
Fax: 0443 229242
Naomi Jones
Animation production
ITV Network: *Toucan 'Tecs*

Celador Productions
39 Long Acre
London WC2E 9JT
Tel: 071 240 8101
Fax: 071 836 1117
Paul Smith
Jackie Tyler
Television: primarily entertainment programming for all broadcast channels. Includes game shows, variety, with selected factual and drama output

Celtic Films
1-2 Bromley Place
London W1
Tel: 071 637 7651
Fax: 071 436 5387
Muir Sutherland
The Monk

Centre Films
118 Cleveland Street
London W1P 5DN
Tel: 071 387 4045
Fax: 071 388 0408
Jeffrey Taylor
Derek Granger
Kent Walwin

Chain Production
11 Hornton Street
London W8 47ND
Tel: 071 937 1981
Fax: 071 376 0556
Garwin Davison
Roberta Licurgo
Distribution/production specialist in Italian films. Theatrical release of *Mignon Has Left* through Metro cinema. UK production co-ordinators on: *Casablanca Express, Plague Sower* and *Across the Red Night*

Champion Television
TWI House
23 Eyot Gardens
London W6
Tel: 081 846 8088
Fax: 081 746 5381
Alan Bushell
Champion Television, a wholly owned subsidiary of Trans World International, the British subsidiary of Mark McCormack's International Management Group, has been contracted to produce The Sports Channel for British Sky Broadcasting. Launched in March 1990 Champion TV produces up to 16 hours a day of British and international sports programming every day of the year

Channel X
Middlesex House
34-42 Cleveland Street
London W1P 5SB
Tel: 071 436 2200

Charisma Films
4th Floor
Russell Chambers

London WC2E 8AA
Tel: 071 379 4267
Fax: 071 836 7216
James Atherton

Chatsworth Television
97-99 Dean Street
London W1V 5RA
Tel: 071 734 4302
Fax: 071 437 3301
Malcolm Heyworth
Sister company to Chatsworth distribution and merchandising companies. Producers of light entertainment and drama. *Operation Julie* for Tyne Tees. *Interceptor* for Thames ITV and *The Crystal Maze* for Channel 4

Cheerleader Productions
62 Chiswick High Road
London W4 1SY
Tel: 081 995 7778
Fax: 081 995 7779
Charles Balchin
Producers of sports programmes (American football, sumo wrestling, motor racing, three day eventing, karting, arena ball etc) for Channel 4, BBC, British Sky Broadcasting

Children's Film and Television Foundation
Elstree Studios
Borehamwood
Herts WD6 1JG
Tel: 081 953 0844
Fax: 081 207 0860
The CFTF does not make films from its own resources but, for suitable children's/family cinema/television projects, is prepared to consider financing script development for eventual production by commercial companies. For further information, see under Organisations

The Children's Film Unit
Unit 4
Berrytime Studios
192 Queenstown Road
London SW8 3NR
Tel: 071 622 7793
Fax: 071 498 0593
A registered Educational Charity, the CFU makes low-budget films for television and PR on subjects of concern to children and young people. Crews and actors are trained at regular weekly workshops in Battersea. Work is in 16mm and video and membership is open to children from 8-16. Latest films for Channel 4 *Hard Road, Doombeach, Survivors*. For the Samaritans *Time to Talk*

Childsplay Productions
8 Lonsdale Road
London NW6 6RD
Tel: 071 328 1429
Fax: 071 328 1416
Television producers specialising in children's and family programming. Recent productions include two series of *Streetwise,* an action drama made for TVS and ITV. Also produced two series of *All Change,* a comedy drama for Yorkshire TV. *Picture Box,* the long running educational series is an ongoing production for Granada and ITV

Chrysalis Television Productions
(formerly Chrysalis Visual Programming)
The Chrysalis Building
Bramley Road
London W10 6SP
Tel: 071 221 2213
Fax: 071 221 6286
Mark Sharman
Specialising in news, sport and current affairs; producers of *LWT News* and *ITV Snooker*

Cinema Verity
The Mill House
Millers Way
1a Shepherds Bush Road
London W6 7NA
Tel: 081 749 8485
Fax: 081 743 5062
Verity Lambert
Ann Weir
Currently in production with fourth series of *May to December*. Produced *GBH* 7 x 90 min drama series written by Alan Bleasdale for Channel 4; *Sleepers,* 4 x 1 hour comedy spy thriller with Nigel Havers and Warren Clarke, *Boys from the Bush,* 10 x 1 hour comedy drama for BBC Television and *Coasting,* 7 x 1 hour comedy drama for Granada with Peter Howitt and James Purefoy

Colstar Communications and Entertainment
11 Wythburn Place
London W1H 5WL
Tel: 071 437 5725
Fax: 071 706 1704
Producers of art, history, sport, biography and wildlife documentaries for video sales and international broadcast markets

Columbia Pictures
19-23 Wells Street
London W1P 3FP
Tel: 071 580 2090
Lester McKellar

The Comic Strip
43a Berwick Street
London W1V 3RE
Tel: 071 439 9509
Fax: 071 734 2793
Lolli Kimpton
Nira Park

Compass Film Productions
3rd Floor
18-19 Warwick Street
London W1R 5RB
Tel: 071 439 6456
Fax: 071 439 1865
Simon Heaven
Involved since 1974 in cultural, educational and sponsored programmes for television. 1990/1 work includes *Violent Lives* a series of four programmes for Channel 4

Cosgrove Hall Productions
8 Albany Road
Chorlton-cum-Hardy
Manchester M21 1BL
Tel: 061 881 9211
Fax: 061 881 1720
A subsidiary of Thames Television

Creative Law
Media Legal
Burbank House
75 Clarendon Road
Sevenoaks
Kent TN13 1ET
Tel: 0732 460592
John Wheller
Production arm of Media Legal developing legal projects for film and TV

Crystalvision
Communications House
5 Factory Lane
Croydon CR9 3RA
Tel: 081 781 6444
Fax: 081 681 2340
Specialist sports programming together with children's programmes and drama. Produced the 8 part series *The Complete Skier* for Channel 4, *World Invitation Club Basketball* for Screensport and *The Royal Dublin Horseshow* for American TV, as well as several smaller OB's for ITV and satellite channels

DBA Television
21 Ormeau Avenue
Belfast BT2 8HD
Tel: 0232 231197
Fax: 0232 333302
David Barker
Northern Ireland's leading production company. Wide range of documentary programmes for Channel 4 and BBC. Just completed: *Heart on the Line, Nothing to Fear* (Channel 4), *Two Villages* (BBC2) and *Gordonall* (BBC). In production: *Hobo* and *Drink Talking* (BBC) and *The Mass* (Channel 4)

Debonair Productions
40-44 Clipstone Street
London W1P 7EA
Tel: 071 323 3220
Fax: 071 637 2590
Toni Strasburg
Mike Rossiter
Ivan Strasburg
Productions include *Chain of Tears, The Other Bomb, The Wasted Hand, Fog of War* and *Fragile Earth: South Africa – The Wasted Land*

Deptford Beach Productions
79 Wardour Street
London W1V 3TH
Tel: 071 734 8508
Fax: 071 287 2122
Tony Kirkhope

Distant Horizon
5-6 Portman Mews South
London W1H 9AU
Tel: 071 493 1625
Fax: 071 493 3429

Paul Janssen
Recent productions include *The Fever, American Kickboxer 1, American Kickboxer 2, Terminal Bliss, Reason to Die, Sarafina* and *Cry the Beloved Country*

Diverse Production
Gorleston Street
London W14 8XS
Tel: 071 603 4567
Fax: 071 603 2148
Philip Clarke
Company with commitment to innovative television. Producers of *Check Out, Europe Express, Obsessions, Not on Sunday, Rough Guide to Careers* and a number of other broadcast series

Domino Films
8 Stockwell Terrace
London SW9 0QD
Tel: 071 582 0393
Fax: 071 582 0437
Joanne Mack
Steve Humphries
Producers of *Lost Children of the Empire* for Granada, *A Secret World of Sex* for the BBC, *Breadline Britain – 1990s* for LWT, *A Century of Childhood, Soviet Citizens, Return of the Death Squads, The Travelling Talkshow,* all for Channel 4 and *The West at War* for HTV. In production a three part series on the social history of disability and a 1 hour documentary on propaganda and the Third Reich, both for Channel 4. In development a major series on the Soviet Union for Granada

Double Exposure
Unit 24
63 Clerkenwell Road
London EC1M 5PS
Tel: 071 490 2499
Fax: 071 490 2556
Production and distribution of broadcast and educational documentaries in the UK and abroad

Dramatis Personae
122 Kennington Road
London SE11 6RE
Tel: 071 735 0831
Maria Aitken
Nathan Silver
Completed production of second TV series on *Acting,* co-produced with the BBC. Series *Boom Architecture* and two others in preparation. This company is concerned primarily with features on artistic skills and human development having broad cultural or social interest

Driftwood Films
192 Sutton Court Road
London W4 3HR
Tel: 071 742 2886
Fax: 071 747 8198
Made *Dark River* and *Les Bikes.* In development *Looking On.* Also make comedy and drama corporate films

Edinburgh Film and Video Productions
Edinburgh Film and TV Studios
Nine Mile Burn
by Penicuik
Midlothian EH26 9LT
Tel: 0968 72131
Fax: 0968 72685
Robin Crichton
Major Scottish production company. Currently in production *Torch,* a TV drama series

Endboard Productions
114a Poplar Road
Bearwood
Birmingham B66 4AP
Tel: 021 429 9779
Fax: 021 429 9008
Yugesh Walia
Sunandan Walia
Producers of TV programmes and information videos. In 1990/91 produced *Kabaddi* a new Asian sports series for Channel 4. A second series is planned

Enigma Productions
Pinewood Studios
Pinewood Road
Iver
Bucks SL0 0NH
Tel: 0753 630555
Fax: 0753 630393
David Puttnam
Film and television production

Equal Media
1 Wakeman Road
London NW10 5BJ
Tel/Fax: 081 960 1832
Sarah Hobson
Parminder Vir
A production company working particularly with filmmakers from Africa, Asia, Latin America and the Black diaspora. Recent productions include *Cinemama* (Channel 4), *Investing in Women* (WomenKind) and *Behind the Cocaine War* (Channel 4). Consultant to the BBC for a series on African Cinema

Euston Films
365 Euston Road
London NW1 3AR
Tel: 071 387 0911
Fax: 071 388 2122
John Hambley
Andrew Brown
The filmmaking subsidiary of Thames TV. Recent projects include: *Minder, Dealers, Capital City, The Fear,* and *Shrinks*

Mary Evans Productions
115 Goldhawk Road
London W12 8EJ
Tel: 081 740 5319/749 3877

Eye Film and Television
The Guildhall
Church Street
Eye
Suffolk IP23 7BD
Tel: 0379 870083
Fax: 0379 870987

Faction Films
28-29 Great Sutton Street
London EC1V 0DU
Tel: 071 608 0654/3
Fax: 071 608 2157
Sylvia Stevens
Dave Fox
Group of independent filmmakers. Titles include: *Irish News: British Stories, Year of the Beaver, Picturing Derry, Trouble the Calm* and *Provocation or Murder* (C4 Dispatches). Production facilities for hire – see under Workshops

Fairwater Films
68 Vista Rise
Llandaff
Cardiff CF5 2SD
Tel: 0222 554416
Fax: 0222 578488
Car: 0836 732810
Tony Barnes
Award winning animation and video producers. Recent work includes *Billy the Fish* for Channel 4, *Roger Mellie* for Comic Relief, *Transylvania Pet Shop* and *Botsworth and Co* for BBC1. Promotional video for Cardiff Marketing *Just Capital.* In development *The Toenail Folk, Y Squad, The Royals* and *Propellerhead & Pals*

Falkman Communications
33 Gresse Street
London W1 1PN
Tel: 071 636 1371
Fax: 071 631 1492
John Finnis
Independent television production company set up by BBC presenter Bernard Falk. Produced *Travelog* for Channel 4 and *The Waltons Meet Mickey Mouse* for ITV. Corporate video clients include ICI, Lucas Industries, Memorex Telex, Whitbread Inns and Lex Service

The Film Company
see **Mary Evans Productions**

Film Form Productions
64 Fitzjohn's Avenue
London NW3 5LT
Tel: 071 794 6967
Fax: 071 794 6967
Susi Oldroyd
Tony Harrild
Film/video production, drama and documentary for television and video distribution. We offer full crewing, writers, producers and directors

Film Four International
60 Charlotte Street
London W1P 2AX
Tel: 071 631 4444
Fax: 071 580 2622
International film sales and distribution arm of Channel 4, often credited as a co-production partner for UK and international productions. Decisions on programming and finance relating to these

productions are initiated by Film on Four, the film programming strand of Channel 4's drama department. For a list of recent product, see under Channel 4 in Television Companies. See also under International Sales

FilmFair
1-4 Jacobs Well Mews
London W1
Tel: 071 935 1596
Lewis Rudd
Prolific producers of cartoon and puppet animation series for children, including *Huxley Pig, Bangers and Mash, Paddington Bear,* and *The Wombles*

The Filmworks
65 Brackenbury Road
Hammersmith
London W6 0BG
Tel: 081 741 5631
Fax: 081 748 3198
Recent productions: *On the Trail of the Chinese Wildman, Struggle for the Pole – In the Footsteps of Scott, A Day in the Life of a Medical Officer, Antarctic Challenge* and *Anything's Possible*

The First Film Company
38 Great Windmill Street
London W1V 7PA
Tel: 071 439 1640
Fax: 071 437 2062
Feature film, television and commercial production. *Dance with a Stranger, Soursweet, The Commitments, The Railway Station Man*

Flamingo Pictures
47 Lonsdale Square
London N1 1EW
Tel: 071 607 9958
Christine Oestreicher
James Scott
Produced *Loser Takes All,* based on Graham Greene's novel. Future plans include *Dibs,* based on a true story by Virginia M Axline

Flashback Productions
22 Kildare Terrace
London W2 5LX
Tel: 071 727 9904
Stephen Wegg-Prosser
Producers of *Flashback,* a 20-part series for Channel 4 which won a BFI Award and *The Games in Question, Fifties Features, Tales Out of School* and 60 programmes on *The March of Time.* Makers of documentaries for Channel 4, the BBC and overseas co-producers. Commmitted to public service broadcasting

Flashback Television
2/3 Cowcross Street
London EC1M 6DR
Tel: 071 490 8996
Fax: 071 490 5610
Taylor Downing
Producers of a wide range of factual programming for broadcast and non-broadcast. We specialise in historical documentaries, *Civil War* for Channel 4; drama documentaries, *Adoption* for Thames; sports programmes for the International Olympic Committee; arts documentaries, *Beyond the Forest* for Arts Council/Channel 4. Several projects in development

Focus Films
Rotunda Studios
Rear of 116-118 Finchley Road
London NW3 5HT
Tel: 071 435 9004
Fax: 071 431 3562
David Pupkewitz
Marsha Levin
Most recent productions include Janet Suzman's critically acclaimed *Othello* for Channel Four and Gad Hollander's film *Diary of a Sane Man* selected for Berlin International Film Festival 1990. Now also financing international co-productions

Folio Productions
(formerly Independent Film Production Associates (IFPA))
87 Dean Street
London W1V 5AA
Tel: 071 734 3847/439 3795
Fax: 071 734 0776
Charles Thompson
Film, video, TV production in the areas of documentary, light entertainment, music and the arts

Mark Forstater Productions
8A Trebeck Street
London W1Y 7RL
Tel: 071 408 0733
Fax: 071 499 8772
Mark Forstater Productions 1990: *Separation* for BBC/American Playhouse directed by Barry Davis with Rosanna Arquette and David Suchet
Productions 1991: *The Gift* for Canal Plus directed by Cheryl Johnson with Helen Mirren, *Paper Marriage* directed by Krzysztof Lang and *The Touch* directed by Krzysztof Zanussi

Fourth Wall Productions
1 Little Argyll Street
London W1R 5DB
Tel: 071 437 2222
Fax: 071 734 0663
Lino Ferrari
Bob Marsland
Broad based television production company. Productions in 1990 included *The Frank Bough Interview* for Sky News and a 12 part series *The Astrology Show* for Channel 4. Current productions include documentaries and a comedy series

Freeway Films
67 George Street
Edinburgh EH2 2JG
Tel: 031 225 3200
Fax: 031 225 3667
John McGrath
Susie Brown

Front Page Films
Twickenham Film Studios
St Margaret's
Twickenham TW1 2AW
Tel: 081 892 4477
Fax: 081 891 0168
Produced *The Mini Sagas,* six theatrical shorts which were released by UIP alongside *A Fish Called Wanda, Parenthood* and *The Naked Gun.* Owners of the Richmond Filmhouse. 1990 production *Get Back,* a feature with Paul McCartney directed by Richard Lester as well as two TV dramas for Channel 4. A number of feature films are currently in development/pre-production

Frontroom Films
79 Wardour Street
London W1V 3TH
Tel: 071 734 4603
Fax: 071 287 0849
John Davies
Robert Smith
Now involved in the production of drama and commercials. Produced the 1983 feature *Acceptable Levels* directed by John Davies. Short features include: *Intimate Strangers* directed by Robert Smith, and *Ursula and Glenys* devised and directed by John Davies in 1985. 1987 feature *The Love Child* directed by Robert Smith. 1989 feature *Wild Flowers* written by Sharman Macdonald, directed by Robert Smith. Planned for 1992: a feature *The Golondrina* written by Tom Murphy, directed by John Davies and *Beast Turns in its Sleep,* a European TV horror series

Fugitive Features
Unit 1
14 William Road
London NW1 3EN
Tel: 071 383 4373
Fax: 071 383 5681
Makers of *The Krays* and *The Reflecting Skin*

Fulcrum Productions
254 Goswell Road
London EC1V 7EB
Tel: 071 253 0353
Fax: 071 490 0206
Involved in making investigative, financial and arts documentaries for Channel 4 and the BBC. Recent productions: *Empire,* an analysis of Rupert Murdoch's media empire, *Act of Union,* the British role in South Africa, *Bad Meat Trail* for Channel 4 Dispatches and *Out on Tuesday,* Channel 4's lesbian and gay magazine show

David Furnham Films
39 Hove Park Road
Hove

East Sussex BN3 6LH
Tel: 0273 559731
New developments: *Harriet and Her Harmonium,* a new musical; *South Coast Jazz,* a series; *The David Heneker Collection,* a performance documentary; and *Our Lady of Good Counsel* for BBC TV

Gainsborough (Film and TV) Productions

8 Queen Street
London W1X 7PH
Tel: 071 409 1925
Fax: 071 408 2042
John Hough
Made *Hazard of Hearts, The Lady and the Highwayman, A Ghost in Monte Carlo* and *Duel of Hearts*

John Gau Productions

Burston House
1 Burston Road
London SW15 6AR
Tel: 081 788 8811
Fax: 081 789 0903
John Gau
Susan Gau
Television documentary production

Noel Gay Television

143 Charing Cross Road
London WC2H 0EE
Tel: 071 287 0087
Bill Cotton
Paul Jackson
Light entertainment/ documentaries, including: *Juke Box Jury, The Happening, La Triviata*

General Entertainment Investments

65-67 Ledbury Road
London W11 2AD
Tel: 071 221 3512
Fax: 071 792 9005
John Oakley
Feature film producers/financiers. Recent work includes *Tropic of Ice,* Anglo-Finnish co-production, *Soweto,* African music feature, *Olympus Force,* Anglo-Greek co-production. Currently preparing *Extreme Remedies* and *Living Evidence,* Anglo-European productions and *Lorenzo the Magnificent,* Anglo-German production

Gibb Rose Organisation (GRO)

Pinewood Studios
Pinewood Road
Iver Heath
Bucks SL0 0HN
Tel: 0753 651700
Fax: 0753 630372
Sydney Rose
Company formed by Sydney Rose and Bee Gee Maurice Gibb to make international film and TV productions

Nick Gifford

Street Farmhouse
Woodnesborough
Nr Sandwich
Kent CT13 ONF
Tel: 0304 612631
Fax: 0304 614949
Nick Gifford
c/o Hope and Lyne
Work includes two films on violence/probation for Channel 4/Compass, together with a project on a Sudanese refugee camp and a year long study of a village school

Global Features

49 Hornton Street
London W8 7NT
Tel: 071 937 1039
Fax: 071 937 1039
Documentary and drama-documentary programme makers, specialising in social and religious themes. Last credit *Shadow on the Cross*

Bob Godfrey Films

199 Kings Cross Road
London WC1X 9DB
Tel: 071 278 5711
Fax: 071 278 6809
Bob Godfrey
Mike Hayes
Prominent studio, titles including: Childrens: *Henry's Cat*
Commercials: *Trio, Angel's Delight, Oracle*
Entertainment: *Revolution, Happy Birthday Switzerland, Wicked Willie*

Goldcrest Films and Television

36-44 Brewer Street
London W1R 3HP
Tel: 071 437 8696
Fax: 071 437 4448
John Quested
Richard Hellman
Jo Deakin
Major feature film production, sales and finance company. Recent films include *All Dogs Go To Heaven, Black Rainbow, Rock-a-Doodle,* and *Scorchers*

The Grade Company

7 Queen Street
Mayfair
London W1X 7PH
Tel: 071 409 1925
Fax: 071 408 2042
Lord Grade
Company recently completed production on fourth TV film based on Barbara Cartland novels and developing other potential film projects

Granada Film

36 Golden Square
London W1R 4AH
Tel: 071 734 8080
Fax: 071 494 6360
Steve Morrison
Pippa Cross
Feature film production. Following on the success of *My Left Foot* and *The Field* Granada Film is actively developing quality films for the international market

Grand Slam Sports

120 Long Acre
London WC2E 9PA
Tel: 071 836 8741
Fax: 071 836 4823
Ron Allison
Derek Brandon
Simon Reed
John Watts
Nick Sharrard
Productions: *World Wide Soccer, Channel 4 Daily International Sports News* with over 200 hours and 25 sports covered

Grapevine TV

Hebron House
Sion Road
Bedminster
Bristol BS3 3BD
Tel: 0272 637973/637634
Fax: 0272 631770
Jayne Cotton
Lynne Harwood
Adrian Mack

Grasshopper Productions

50 Peel Street
London W8 7PD
Tel: 071 229 1181
Fax: 071 229 1181
Joy Whitby
Productions to date: for children *Grasshopper Island, Emma and Grandpa* and *East of the Moon,* film series based on the Terry Jones fairy tales with music by Neil Innes; *The Angel and the Soldier Boy,* 25 minute animation by Alison de Vere and family telefilm *A Pattern of Roses*

Greenpoint Films

5a Noel Street
London W1V 3RB
Tel: 071 437 6492
Fax: 071 437 0644
Ann Scott
Patrick Cassavetti
Simon Relph
A loose association of eight filmmakers: Simon Relph, Christopher Morahan, Ann Scott, Richard Eyre, Stephen Frears, Patrick Cassavetti, John Mackenzie and Mike Newell. Projects have included Eyre's *The Ploughman's Lunch* and *Laughterhouse,* Morahan's *In The Secret State,* Hare's *Wetherby* and *Paris by Night,* Newell's *The Good Father,* Giles Foster's *Tree of Hands,* Mike Bradwell's *Chains of Love* and Peter Barnes' *Nobody Here But Us Chickens*

Griffin Productions

Balfour House
46-54 Great Titchfield Street
London W1P 7AE
Tel: 071 636 5066
Fax: 071 436 3252
Adam Clapham
Drama and factual programmes. Produced *Act of Betrayal,* mini-series for TVS and ABC Australia, *Secret Weapon* for TVS and Turner Network Television, *Painting with Light* for BBC, *Club X* and *Odyssey* for Channel 4. Co-produced *Captain James Cook* with Revcom for ITV

Reg Grundy Productions

Enterprise House
59-65 Upper Ground

London SE1 9PQ
Tel: 071 928 8942
Fax: 071 928 8417
Television production company

HTV International
126 Baker Street
London W1M 1FH
Tel: 071 224 4048
Fax: 071 486 0615
A wholly owned subsidiary of the HTV Group, HTV International was set up in 1988 to specialise in theatrical and television production for world markets. Productions to date are *King of the Wind, Eminent Domain* and *The Last Butterfly.* Currently in production are *Dylan* and *Lucky Lucan*

Hammer Film Productions
Elstree Studios
Borehamwood
Herts WD6 1JG
Tel: 081 953 1600
Fax: 081 905 1127
Richelle Wilder
The company responsible for many classic British horror films was revived under new management in 1983 to start work on 13 films under the title *Hammer House of Mystery and Suspense,* to be released worldwide by 20th Century Fox. Nine projects in current feature film production programme

HandMade Films (Productions)
26 Cadogan Square
London SW1X 0JP
Tel: 071 584 8345
Fax: 071 584 7338
George Harrison
Denis O'Brien
Producers of *Monty Python's Life of Brian, The Long Good Friday, Time Bandits, Privates on Parade, The Missionary, A Private Function, Mona Lisa, Withnail and I, Five Corners, Bellman and True, Track 29, The Lonely Passion of Judith Hearne,* and *The Raggedy Rawney.* Recent releases include *Powwow Highway, Nuns on the Run. T.V.P.* filming in 1991

Harcourt Films
58 Camden Square
London NW1 9XE
Tel: 071 267 0882
Fax: 071 267 1064
Jeremy Marre
Producer and director of documentaries for Channel 4, BBC and ITV. In production: A film for BBC's *Under the Sun* series shot in Mexico and four one-hour programmes on the theme of musical improvisation for Channel 4 and RM Arts. Most recent productions: two films for BBC's *Under the Sun; The Nature of Music,* three films for Channel 4/RM Arts; *Beats of the Heart,* 14 part music series; *Chasing Rainbows,* 7 part series for Channel 4 and *Ourselves and Other Animals,* 12 part wildlife series for Primetime

Hartswood Films
Shepperton Studios
Studios Road
Shepperton
Middlesex TW17 0QD
Tel: 0932 562611
Fax: 0932 68989
Independent production company for film and television, owned and run by producer Beryl Vertue. Producing in 1991 *Men Behaving Badly* for Thames Television

Hat Trick Productions
10 Livonia Street
London W1V 3PH
Tel: 071 434 2451
Fax: 071 287 9791
Denise O'Donoghue
Jimmy Mulville
Rory McGrath
Geoffrey Perkins
Specialising in comedy, current productions include; *Round the Bend* for YTV, *Whose Line Is It Anyway USA, Paul Merton – The Series, Drop the Dead Donkey, S & M, The Big One, Clive Anderson Talks Back* for Channel 4 and for the BBC new series of *The Harry Enfield Television Programme* and *Have I Got News For You*

Hawkshead
3 Fitzroy Square
London W1P 5AH
Tel: 071 388 1234
Fax: 071 387 5789
Nigel Houghton
Carol Haslam
Angela Law
Fiona Nunn
Productions include: *Fat Man in Argentina* (Channel 4, S4C, WGBH, Channel 7 Australia), *Remember, Remember* (BBC2), *Roux Brothers* (BBC2), *The Manager* (Channel 4)

Hemdale Holdings
21 Albion Street
London W2 2AS
Tel: 071 724 1010
Fax: 071 724 9168
Produced *Terminator, Return of the Living Dead, Body Slam, River's Edge, Vampire's Kiss, Shag, Staying Together, Chattahoochee, Salvador, Platoon* and *The Last Emperor*

Jim Henson Productions
Elstree Film Studios
Shenley Road
Borehamwood
Herts WD6 1JG
Tel: 081 935 1600
Fax: 081 905 1324
Messages: 081 905 1412
Moving 1991
Duncan Kenworthy
Peter Coogan
Producers with TVS of *The Storyteller,* and *Greek Myths.* Producers of Warners' 1990 feature *The Witches,* directed by Nic Roeg from the novel by Roald Dahl. Produced series of 13 half-hour episodes of *The Ghost of Faffner Hall* for Tyne Tees and 39 8-minute episodes of *Mother Goose* for TSW

Jim Henson's Creature Shop
1b Downshire Hill
Hampstead
London NW3 1NR
Tel: 071 431 2818
Fax: 071 431 3737
John Stephenson
William Plant
John Geraghty
Creators of animatronic, puppet and prosthetic designs for feature films, television and commercials. Outstanding examples can be seen on *Teenage Mutant Ninja Turtles, The Witches* and *The Bear.* Previous work includes characters for *Dark Crystal, Labyrinth, Dreamchild* and fantasy characters in *The Storyteller*

Hightimes Productions
5 Anglers Lane
Kentish Town
London NW5 3DG
Tel: 071 482 5202
Fax: 071 485 4254
Al Mitchell
Tony Humphreys
The company specialises in developing, packaging and producing light entertainment and comedy ideas for television. It has recently expanded its activities to include drama and has a variety of projects at different stages of development. Hightimes packaged *Me and My Girl* (five series) for LWT and *The Zodiac Game* (two series) for Anglia. Recently completed thirteen episodes of *Guys N' Dolls,* which was licensed to BSB, and *Trouble in Mind,* a new situation comedy for LWT

Holmes Associates
10-16 Rathbone Street
London W1P 1AH
Tel: 071 637 8251
Fax: 071 637 9024
Andrew Holmes
Adrian Bate
Stephen Taylor
Recent work: *Signals* Channel Four's weekly arts series; *Rock Steady* Channel Four's live rock concert roadshow and *Piece of Cake* major film mini-series for LWT

Hyndland Television
Kelvingrove House
54 Kelvingrove Street
Glasgow G3 7SA
Tel: 041 332 1005
Fax: 041 332 1009
David Kemp
Company specialising in story-based journalism. The 1991 output included *Making History Pay* in the Scottish Eye series and *The Movement* for Dispatches (both for Channel 4). Also *Night Flyte,* a series of ten late-night talk shows for Scottish Television

Iambic Productions
The Production House
147a St Michael's Hill
Bristol BS2 8DB
Tel: 0272 237222
Fax: 0272 238343
8 Warren Mews
London W1P 5DJ
Tel: 071 388 3323
Fax: 071 388 7121
Music, arts and drama television productions for UK network and world TV. Regular producers of South Bank Show programmes (LWT) and rock and classical music programmes for BBC and Channel 4

Ideal Communications Films and Television
40-41 Great Marlborough Street
London W1V 1DA
Tel: 071 287 4082
Fax: 071 287 4083
Productions include *Money Talks* (aka *Loser Takes All*) co-produced with Miramax, BBC and British Screen. *Medium Rare* co-produced with Limelight. Currently in pre-production *Calvi – God's Banker*

The Ideas Factory
Maxron House
Green Lane
Romiley
Stockport SK6 3JG
Tel: 061 406 6685
Fax: 061 406 6672
Produce sports series for Channel 4 *Don't Just Sit There* and are to introduce wheelchair basketball to Channel 4

Illuminations
19-20 Rheidol Mews
Rheidol Terrace
London N1 8NU
Tel: 071 226 0266
Fax: 071 359 1151
John Wyver
Linda Zuck
Producers of cultural programmes for Channel 4, BBC Television and others. Recent projects include *1001 Nights of TV*, an evening of archive television; *Doing the Dishes*, a documentary about satellite dishes – and *Shooting Star* – a film about the American artist Jean Michel Basquiat – both for Channel 4's Without Walls, and *Amis K. – The Memoirs* for BBC 2's Bookmark. Several projects in development about aspects of contemporary culture and new technologies

Illuminations Interactive
19-20 Rheidol Terrace
London N1 8NU
Tel: 071 226 0266
Fax: 071 359 1151
Terry Braun
John Wyver
Company developing and producing Interactive Video projects about the visual and performing arts. Productions include *Ways of Looking* for the Arts Council of Great Britain

Illustra Communications
13-14 Bateman Street
London W1V 6EB
Tel: 071 437 9611
Fax: 071 734 7143
Douglas Kentish

Independent Film Production Associates (IFPA)
see **Folio Productions**

Independent Producers
5 Elm Quay Court
Nine Elms Lane
London SW8 5DE
Tel: 071 498 6822
Fax: 071 498 6517
Jan Martin
Corporate programmes and live events: the big screen live transmission from The Royal Opera House to the Covent Garden Piazza, now in its fourth year

Infovision
63 White Lion Street
London N1 9PP
Tel: 071 837 0012
Fax: 071 278 1632
Fergus Hall
Infovision is a corporate and employee communications consultancy providing live event, print, media training and video production services. Clients include British Steel, the Water Companies, Electricity Distribution Companies

Initial Film and Television
10-16 Rathbone Street
London W1P 1AH
Tel: 071 637 8251
Fax: 071 436 0151
Eric Fellner
Malcolm Gerrie

Insight Productions
Gidleigh Studio
Gidleigh
Chagford
Newton Abbot
Devon TQ13 8HP
Tel: 0647 432686
Fax: 0647 433141
Brian Skilton
TV production in arts, drama, entertainment, environment and documentary. Recent work includes the documentary series *Dartmoor the Threatened Wilderness* and *Camargue*, environment documentaries. In pre-production *Omnibus* with Ted Hughes and *Zambia National Park*

International Broadcasting Trust
2 Ferdinand Place
London NW1 8EE
Tel: 071 482 2847
Fax: 071 284 3374
Paddy Coulter
A consortium of some 80 organisations, including development agencies, churches, trade unions and environmental organisations, formed to make programmes about the Third World, development and the environment, both for TV and non-broadcast. Recent productions include *The Global Environment*, 10 part series for BBC Schools and *Portraits of Change* on women in the Third World for Channel 4

Interprom
7a Tythings Court
Minehead
Somerset TA24 5NT
Tel: 0643 706774
Fax: 0643 702698
Clive Woods
Producers and distributors of various music programmes, specialising in jazz and blues

Island World Productions
12-14 Argyll Street
London W1V 1AB
Tel: 071 734 3536
Fax: 071 734 3585
Margaret Matheson
Tony Garnett
Founded in June 1990 to finance and produce theatrical films and television programmes for international distribution. Part of the Island World Group with offices in Los Angeles and New York. Their first theatrical production is *Juice*, a rap movie set in New York, due for release early 1992. Forthcoming television productions include a six-part adaptation of John Le Carre's *The Secret Pilgrim* and *Century*, a 26 hour documentary series about the history of the Twentieth century

Isolde Films
4 Kensington Park Gardens
London W11 3HB
Tel: 071 727 3541
Fax: 071 727 3632
Recent productions include *Testimony, The Children* and *Menuhin*

Jennie & Co
3 Duck Lane
London W1V 1FL
Tel: 071 437 0600
Fax: 071 439 2377
Gower Frost
Terry Bedford
Kate Symington

Kai Productions
1 Ravenslea Road
London SW12 8SA
Tel: 081 673 4550
George Haggerty
Mike Wallington
Channel 4 productions: *Malltime* (1987), *Robotopia* (1989)

Kestrel Films
11 Landford Road
London SW15 1AQ
Tel: 081 788 6244
Bill Shapter

King Rollo Films
Dolphin Court
High Street
Honiton
Devon EX14 8LS
Tel: 0404 45218
Fax: 0404 45328
Clive Juster

Producers and distributors of the animated series: *Mr Benn, King Rollo, Victor and Maria, Towser, Watt the Devil, The Adventures of Spot, The Adventures of Ric, Any Time Tales* and *Art*

Kohler
16 Marlborough Road
Richmond
Surrey TW10 6JR
Tel: 081 940 3967
Fax: 071 287 3779
Michael Kohler
Cabiri, The Experiencer

Koninck
175 Wardour Street
London W1V 3AB
Tel: 071 734 4943
Fax: 071 494 0405
Keith Griffiths and The Brothers Quay
Specialists in puppet animation and producers of cultural documentaries and fiction. Latest projects include: *The Comb – from the Museums of Sleep; De Artificialia Perspectiva; Secret Joy; Suburbs in the Sky; Karl Kraus*. In development: *Faust; The Sleepwalkers of Daylight; The Institute; The Presence; Abstract Film*

Kruger Leisure Organisation
see **TKO Film and TV**

Lambeth Productions
Twickenham Studios
St Margaret's
Twickenham TW1 2AW
Tel: 081 892 4477
Fax: 081 891 0168
Sir Richard Attenborough
Terry Clegg
Diana Hawkins
Feature *Charlie* in preparation for shooting in 1991

Landseer Film and Television Productions
140 Royal College Street
London NW1 0TA
Tel: 071 485 7333
Fax: 071 485 7573
Documentary, drama, music and arts. Productions include: *Sex, Politics & Alan Ayckbourn* (BBC Omnibus); *Out of Line*, a profile of Kenneth MacMillan (BBC); *Not Pots* (Channel 4); *Will Apples Grow on Mars?* (Central TV); *La Stupenda*, a profile of Dame Joan Sutherland (RM Arts); *Galway at 50* (BBC NI) and *Don Giovanni* with Opera Factory (Channel 4)

Langham Productions
10 Abbeville Road
London SW4 9NJ
Tel: 081 675 3326
Fax: 081 675 3326
Michael Johnstone
New company, formerly the production arm of VATV

Helen Langridge Associates of London
75 Kenton Street
London WC1N 1NN
Tel: 071 833 2955
Fax: 071 837 2836
Helen Langridge
Juliet Naylor
Feature development, television, commercials and music videos

Brian Lapping Associates
21-24 Bruges Place
Randolph Street
London NW1 0TF
Tel: 071 482 5855
Fax: 071 284 0626
Producers of TV programming, including *Countdown to War* (Granada/ITV) with Ian McKellen as Hitler, *Hypotheticals* (BBC2) – the 1990 award-winning series of 3 one-hour programmes dealt with media, government and the law, the 1991 series with crisis management in war, ecological disaster and a prison occupation, and *The Second Russian Revolution* (BBC2), six one hour documentaries on politics inside the Kremlin

Large Door
41-45 Beak Street
London W1R 3LE
Tel: 071 439 1381
Fax: 071 439 0849
John Ellis
Simon Hartog
Producers of current affairs and media documentaries, including the award-winning *This Food Business, New Chinese Cinema, Distilling Whisky Galore, TV Globo* and Channel 4's *Visions* series (1982-85). Future projects include series on British movie actors, Asian cinema and domestic technologies

Lazer Entertainments (UK)
86-88 Wardour Street
London W1V 3LF
Tel: 071 437 9910
Fax: 071 734 6312
Feature production company. Editing and other post-production facilities

Leda Serene
66 Crownstone Court
London SW2 1LT
Tel: 071 733 2861
Ingrid Lewis
Frances-Anne Solomon

Limehouse Productions
62 Chiswick High Road
London W4 1SY
Tel: 081 995 7789
Fax: 081 995 7791
Susi Hush
Chris Gormley
Drama, light entertainment and documentaries

Limelight Films
3 Bromley Place
London W1P 5HB
Tel: 071 255 3939
Fax: 071 436 4334
Steve Barron
Simon Fields
Producers of pop promos, TV commercials, TV programming and feature films, with offices in London and LA

Little Bird Co
91 Regent Street
London W1R 7TA
Tel: 071 434 1131
Fax: 071 434 1803
James Mitchell
Jonathan Cavendish
Company has made three series of *The Irish RM*, four hour mini-series *Troubles*. Feature films *Joyriders* and *December Bride*. Television films *The Lilac Bus* and *In the Border Country*

Living Tape Productions
Ramillies House
1-2 Ramillies Street
London W1V 1DF
Tel: 071 439 6301
Fax: 071 439 0731
Nick Freethy
Stephen Bond
Producers of educational and documentary programmes for TV and video distribution. Currently completed major new TV series *Oceans of Wealth*

Euan Lloyd Productions
Pinewood Studios
Iver Heath
Bucks SL0 0NH
Tel: 0753 651700
Fax: 0753 656844
Euan Lloyd
Chris Chrisafis
Since 1968, Lloyd has made nine major action adventures including *The Wild Geese, Who Dares Wins* and *The Sea Wolves*. In development are *Centrifuge* and *Okavango*

London Film Productions
44a Floral Street
London WC2E 9DA
Tel: 071 379 3366
Fax: 071 240 7065
Steven North
Founded in 1932 by Alexander Korda. Many co-productions with the BBC, including *I, Claudius, Poldark* and *Testament of Youth*. Produced *The Country Girls* for Channel 4. In receipt of a direct drama commission from a US network for *Scarlet Pimpernel* and *Kim*. Renowned for productions of classics, now developing more contemporary fiction work

Lusia Films
7-9 Earlham Street
London WC2 1HL
Tel: 071 240 2350
Fax: 071 497 0446
Mark Karlin
Karlin made *For Memory*, a BFI/BBC co-production, and a four-part series of documentaries on Nicaragua. Also a two-hour film called *Utopias* for Channel 4. Currently in production: a film on the last ten years of the Nicaraguan revolution

Jo Lustig

PO Box 472
London SW7 4NL
Tel: 071 937 6614
Fax: 071 937 8680
Jo Lustig
Represents Mel Brooks and Managing Director of Brooksfilms (UK). Co-producer *84 Charing Cross Road* (Brooksfilms and Columbia), producer of TV documentaries: *Maria Callas – Life and Art* (Channel 4); *The Unforgettable Nat 'King' Cole* (BBC TV); *John Cassavetes* (BBC TV); *Hollywood Babylon* (Arena BBC). In production: drama for BBC *Q* with Ian Holm, directed by Jack Gold

Magic Hour Films and Television

143 Chatsworth Road
London NW2 5QT
Tel: 081 459 8987
Fax: 081 459 3074
Bianka Ford
Producer and distributor of TV movies, mini-series, drama series and reality/magazine programming. Specialises in international co-productions

Malachite Productions

East Kirkby House
Spilsby
Lincolnshire PE23 4BX
Tel: 07903 538/
071 487 5451
Fax: 07903 409
Charles Mapleston
Nancy Thomas
Producers of people-based documentary programmes on music, design, painting, photography, arts, anthropology and environmental issues for broadcast TV. Recent productions include: *The Invisible Recorder, Cambridge Darkroom* and *Fiore – Sculpting Tuscany*

Malone Gill Productions

Canaletto House
39 Beak Street
London W1R 3LD
Tel: 071 287 3970
Fax: 071 287 8146
Michael Gill
Georgina Denison
Lita Yong
Hugh Newsam
Mandy Field
Currently in production: *Nomads* four hours for Channel 4 and ITEL; *Nature Perfected* twelve half-hours for Channel 4, WETA (US) and the Io Corporation (Japan); *The Buried Mirror: Reflections of Spain and the New World* for the Smithsonian Institution, Sociedad General de Television and BBC TV. Recent productions include *Claude Monet: Legacy of Light* for WGBH (US); *Vintage: A History of Wine by Hugh Johnson* for WGBH and Channel 4 and *Paul Gauguin: The Savage Dream* for the National Gallery of Art, Washington and WETA

Manhattan Films

217 Brompton Road
London SW3 2EJ
Tel: 071 581 2408
Robert Paget
Directed and wrote *The Choice* in Switzerland. Currently preparing *Persona Non Grata* to be shot in England and *Mistakes* to be shot in London

Mike Mansfield Television

5-7 Carnaby Street
London W1V 1PG
Tel: 071 494 3061
Fax: 071 494 3057
Sportsmasters, Comedy Store, The Party, The Entertainers, Jean-Michel Jarre: Paris – A City in Concert all for ITV, *Royal Appointment* for the BBC, *Animal Country* for Anglia TV, and *Calypso,* a music video for Jean-Michel Jarre

Marble Arch Productions

Twickenham Studios
St Margaret's
Twickenham TW1 2AW
Tel: 081 892 4477
Fax: 081 891 0168
Sir Richard Attenborough
Terry Clegg
Diana Hawkins
Preparing feature on the life on Thomas Paine

Maya Vision

43 New Oxford Street
London WC1A 1BH
Tel: 071 836 1113
Fax: 071 836 5169
1990/91 productions have included several full length documentaries plus magazine items for Channel 4's *Out on Tuesday* series; travel documentaries for BBC, Central and Channel 4, and *Nocturne,* a 56 min drama for Channel 4. In development: a 90 min feature and a 13 part ecological drama

Medialab

Unit 8 Chelsea Wharf
15 Lots Road
London SW10 0QH
Tel: 071 351 5814
Fax: 071 351 7898
John Gaydon
Kevin Godley
Geoff Foulkes
Producers of commercials, music videos, documentaries and videolas. Also run *Exposed Films* and *The Videolabel*

Meditel Productions

Bedford Chambers
The Piazza
Covent Garden
London WC2 8HA
Tel: 071 836 9216/9364
Fax: 071 836 9461
Joan Shenton
Provides medical and science-based documentaries for TV. Made *HRT – Pause for Thought, This Week* for Thames TV, *Impotence – One in Ten Men* for Channel 4, and *The AIDS Catch,* Dispatches for Channel 4

Mendoza Productions

22 Soho Square
London W1V 5FJ
Tel: 071 434 9641
Fax: 071 439 1226
Debby Mendoza

Mentorn Films

Mentorn House
140 Wardour Street
London W1V 3AV
Tel: 071 287 4545
Fax: 071 287 3728
Tom Gutteridge
Arts, entertainment, children's and drama. *Challenge Anneka, 01, Box Office, Early Bird, 1st Night* (with subsidiary Mentorn Midlands), *Wide Angle* and *Never the Sinner.* Currently developing drama projects

Merchant Ivory Productions

46 Lexington Street
London W1
Tel: 071 437 1200
Fax: 071 734 1579
Ismail Merchant
Paul Bradley
Producer Ismail Merchant and director James Ivory together made *Shakespeare Wallah, Heat and Dust, The Bostonians, A Room with a View, Maurice, Slaves of New York* and *Mr & Mrs Bridge. The Ballad of the Sad Cafe* released during 1991 will be followed by E M Forster's *Howard's End* in production for release in 1992

Mersey Television

Campus Manor
Childwall Abbey Road
Liverpool L16 0JP
Tel: 051 722 9122
Fax: 051 722 6839
Phil Redmond
Independent production company responsible for Channel 4 thrice-weekly drama series, *Brookside.* Also produce *Waterfront Beat* for BBC1. Mersey Music and Mersey Casting are subsidiary companies

Mersham Productions

41 Montpellier Walk
London SW7 1JH
Tel: 071 589 8829
Fax: 071 584 0024
Lord Brabourne
Lord Brabourne, a Fellow and a Governor of the BFI, is Chairman of Thames Television. Amongst other films, he has produced in conjunction with Richard Goodwin four films based on stories by Agatha Christie and *A Passage to India* directed by David Lean. During 1986, co-produced *Little Dorrit.* In 1988/9, co-produced the TV series *Leontyne*

Midnight Films

4th Floor
Ramillies House
1/2 Ramillies Street

London W1V 1DF
Tel: 071 494 0926
Fax: 071 494 2676
Michael Hamlyn
Features, promos and television. Produced the full-length feature film *U2 Rattle and Hum* – part concert film, part cinema verité documentary. Currently developing future feature projects

Milesian Film Productions
10 Selwood Place
London SW7 3QQ
Tel: 071 373 8858
Fax: 071 373 8858
Christopher Miles

Mirus Productions
3rd Floor
9 Carnaby Street
London W1V 1PG
Tel: 071 439 7113/494 2399
Howard Johnson
Mike Wallington
Produced *Songs of Freedom; C L R James* in 1986. *Colonial Madness; This Joint is Jumpin'* in 1987. *One Love* and *Art Tatum* in 1988. *Black Faith* in 1990 and *Us* in 1991

Montage Films
81 Berwick Street
London W1P 3PS
Tel: 071 439 8113
Fax: 071 287 1983
Revenge of Billy the Kid

Moonlight Films
31 Healey Street
London NW1 8SR
Tel: 071 284 4104
Fax: 071 284 4075
Terence Francis
Moonlight Films is an independent film company specialising primarily in documentaries exploring new perspectives on the international black community and creating innovative programme strands which adequately reflect today's multi-cultural society in Britain

Moving Picture Productions
179 Wardour Street
London W1V 3FB
Tel: 071 434 3100
Fax: 071 734 9150
Lauren Campbell
Commercials production – UK, Europe, USA. Corporate and interactive communications

Multivision Communications
Bradley Close
off White Lion Street
London N1 9PN
Tel: 071 837 5588
Fax: 071 278 8733
Clive Delamain
Film and television producers/co-producers/ consultants. Projects for 1991/92 include series *Video View* for Thames. Projects in active development include a sell-thru video show, children's video, a film series and a quiz show

NVC Arts
The Forum
74-80 Camden Street
London NW1 0JL
Tel: 071 388 3833
Fax: 071 383 5332
Produces recordings of live opera and ballet from the world's leading international venues and companies. Recent recordings include *Swan Lake* from the Kirov Ballet, *Salome* from the Deutsche Oper Berlin and the four Brahms symphonies with Kurt Masur and the Leipzig Gewandhaus Orchestra

Nelson Entertainment International
8 Queen Street
London W1X 7PH
Tel: 071 493 3362
Fax: 071 409 0503

Network Screen Production
Pinewood Film Studios
Iver Heath
Bucks SL0 0NH
Tel: 0753 651700
Fax: 0753 656844
Kevin Moran, ACTT director/producer
Film and TV production company

New Era Productions
23 West Smithfield
London EC1A 9HY
Tel: 071 236 5532
Fax: 071 236 5504
Marc Samuelson
Peter Samuelson
Caroline Hodgson

New Media
12 Oval Road
London NW1 7DH
Tel: 071 482 5258
Fax: 071 482 4957
Alison Turner
Multimedia design and production company providing a comprehensive service for the production of LaserVision, CD ROM, CD ROM XA, DVI, CD-I and CDTV

North South Productions
Woburn Buildings
1 Woburn Walk
London WC1H 0JJ
Tel: 071 388 0351
Fax: 071 388 2398
Film and video production company that specialises in programmes on environmental issues, world development and other international themes. Productions include BBC series *Only One Earth*, Channel 4 series *Stolen Childhood* and many other documentaries and current affairs programmes for Channel 4

Nub Television
(formerly Seventh Art Productions UK)
1st Floor
116 Grafton Road
London NW5 4BA
Tel: 071 485 7132
Fax: 071 284 0260
Michael Whiteley
Recent productions include series on modern Spain *Spain – In the Shadow of the Sun* for Channel 4, *Talkin' Turkey* Channel 4's alternative Christmas lunch and for Channel 4's *Dispatches* a programme shot on location in Nigeria

OG Films
Pinewood Studios
Pinewood Road
Iver Heath
Bucks SLO 0NH
Tel: 0753 651700
Fax: 0753 656844
Oliver Gamgee
Production, packaging, and distribution company for feature films and TV

Opix Films
Pinewood Studios
Pinewood Road
Iver Heath
Bucks SL0 0NH
Tel: 0753 651700
Fax: 0753 656904
Terry Ryan
Productions include *Owain Prince of Wales*, a TV feature with S4C, a four-part series *Boyce Goes West*, co-produced with Brent Walker for the BBC, *American Carrott*, made for Channel 4 and HBO, and two films for TV, *Going Home* and *Heaven on Earth*, co-produced with Primedia (Canada), BBC and CBC. In production *The Fourth Dimension*, a 13 half-hour fantasy series, feature films *Puckoon* from the novel by Spike Milligan and *The Brylcream Boys*

Orbit Films
14 Campden Hill Gardens
London W8 7AY
Tel: 071 221 5548
Fax: 071 409 0503
Currently producing independent shorts; comedy, music programmes for television broadcast

Orchid Productions
Garden Studios
11-15 Betterton Street
Covent Garden
London WC2H 9BP
Tel: 071 379 0344
Fax: 071 379 0801
Jo Kemp
Sovereign House
Sovereign Street
Pendleton
Manchester M6 3LY
Neil Molyneux
Tel: 061 737 2816
Fax: 061 745 7248
Network animation series *The Raggy Dolls* for Yorkshire TV. Also live action co-productions

Orion Pictures Corporation
5-8 Warwick Street
London W1R 5RA
Tel: 071 753 8753
Stuart Salter
Productions include *Alice, Silence of the*

Lambs, Mermaids and *State of Grace*

Orlando TV Productions
20 Lealand Road
London N15 6JS
Tel: 081 802 5067
Fax: 081 809 6800
Mike Tomlinson
Producer of television documentaries for Channel 4, BBC and WGBH Boston, specialising in science and technology subjects

Oxford Film Company
2 Mountfort Terrace
London N1 1JJ
Tel: 071 607 8200
Fax: 071 607 4037
Mark Bentley
Producers of feature films and television including most recently *Sisters* (MGM) and *Promised Land* (Vestron). Produced the six-hour documentary series *Naked Hollywood* for the BBC. Films in development include Greenpeace Chairman David MacTaggart's *Journey into the Bomb* and *Touching the Void* based on Joe Simpson's book. TV projects include *Under Fire* – the Simon Hayward story

Oxford Scientific Films
Long Hanborough
Oxford OX7 2LD
Tel: 0993 881881
Fax: 0993 882808
OSF specialises in natural history and environmental documentaries, commercials, corporate and medical videos, sports programmes. See also under Facilities and Distributors (Non-Theatrical)

PAC Video Productions
Rosehill
Erbistock
Bangor on Dee
Wrexham
North Wales
Tel: 0978 780181
Corporate, promotional, training and educational programmes

Pacesetter Enterprises
11 Wythburn Place
London W1H 5WL
Tel: 071 437 5725
Fax: 071 706 1704
Production and co-production of international broadcast programming. A subsidiary of Colstar Communications and Entertainment. Credits include *The Wandering Company, In Search of Wildlife* (series), *Defending Wildlife, Antarctic Challenge.* In production *In Search of Wildlife* (second and third series), *Smith Island Antarctica* (working title), a series of adventure/environmental programmes. Currently looking at co-production properties in drama, documentary and the arts, sciences and nature

Pacesetter Productions
New Barn House
Leith Hill Lane
Ockley
Surrey RH5 5PH
Tel: 0306 70433
Fax: 0306 881021
Adele Spencer
On-going feature, documentary, TV drama and sponsored production

Palace Productions, Pictures, Video
16-17 Wardour Mews
London W1V 3FF
Tel: 071 734 7060
Fax: 071 437 3248
Nik Powell
Stephen Woolley
Daniel Battsek
Robert Jones
Made *Absolute Beginners, Company of Wolves, Shag, High Spirits, Scandal, The Big Man, Hardware, Dust, A Rage in Harlem, The Miracle* and *The Pope Must Die*

Palace TV Productions
56 Whitfield Street
London W1P 5RN
Tel: 071 580 9592
Fax: 071 631 3523
Leigh Blake
Martyn Auty
Valerie Ryan
Noel Bennett

Red, Hot & Blue, A Woman at War, Lenny Henry Live & Unleashed, Beyond the Groove

Panoptic Productions
296a Latimer Road
London W10 6QW
Tel: 081 960 5588
Fax: 081 964 0616
Nicholas Fraser
Michael Jones
Jean Newington
Producer of *Dispatches (Hungary), Sex on TV, Trial of Lady C (Sexual Intercourse Began in 1963),* 3 programmes in Channel 4's *Banned* season, *Lost Lawrence* and *Sex and the Censors*

Paramount Pictures
European Production
Paramount House
162-170 Wardour Street
London W1V 4AB
Tel: 071 287 6767
Fax: 071 734 0387
Ileen Maisel

Paramount Revcom
Balfour House
46-54 Great Titchfield Street
London W1P 7AE
Tel: 071 636 5066
Fax: 071 436 3252
Michael Deakin
Drama, mini-series and TV movies. Co-produced Jeffrey Archer's *Not a Penny More, Not a Penny Less* with BBC for USA Network. Co-producing *The Doomsday Gun* with TVS and HBO

Paravision (UK)
114 The Chambers
Chelsea Harbour
London SW10 0XF
Tel: 071 351 7070
Fax: 071 352 3645
Linda Agran
Nick Barton
Roy Stevens
Tony Kenber
Paravision (UK) is the international production arm of Paravision International – the major French media group. The company is currently developing feature films, telemovies, drama series and documentaries

Partridge Films
38 Mill Lane
London NW6 1NR
Tel: 071 435 8211
Fax: 071 431 1715
Michael Rosenberg
Makers of natural history films for television distribution worldwide. Producer of *Okavango: Jewel of the Kalahari* and *Seasons of the Sea,* winners of the Wildscreen Golden Panda in 1988 and 1990

Partridge TV & Video
Ellerncroft
Wotton-under-Edge
Glos GL12 7AY
Tel: 0453 521111
Fax: 0453 844556
Derek Anderson
Carol O'Callaghan (Library)
Makers of wildlife documentaries and videos for television and educational distribution. Extensive natural history stock shot library

Pelicula Films
7 Queen Margaret Road
Glasgow G20 6DP
Tel: 041 945 3333
Fax: 041 946 8345
Mike Alexander
Producer of programmes for TV, including Channel 4 and BBC TV

Pennies from Heaven
83 Eastbourne Mews
London W2
Tel: 071 402 0051/ 081 576 1197
Kenith Trodd
Kenith Trodd is a prolific producer of films for the BBC and others. Recent work includes *After Pilkington, The Singing Detective, She's Been Away, Old Flames, They Never Slept, For the Greater Good* and *Common Pursuit* all for the BBC. He also produced for PFH the features *Dreamchild* and *A Month in the Country.* Much of this work has been from screenplays by Dennis Potter, the company's other principal director. Currently Kenith Trodd is developing *Circle of Friends* (feature), *Maria's Child* (BBC) and several other projects for large and small screen

Penumbra Productions
21a Brondesbury Villas
London NW6 6AH
Tel: 071 328 4550
Fax: 071 328 3844
Producers of cinema and TV documentary and drama programmes specialising in current affairs and culture of developing countries, and their people living in the West

Persistent Vision Productions
133 Ravenslea Road
London SW12 8RT
Tel: 071 639 5596/081 673 7924
John Stewart
Carol Lemon
Short films completed include the award-winning *Crash* and *The Gaol.* In preparation is a short film *The Break-In* and a feature film *Straker*

Photoplay Productions
21 Princess Road
London NW1 8JR
Tel: 071 722 2500
Fax: 071 722 6662
Kevin Brownlow
David Gill
Patrick Stanbury
Originators of 'Thames Silents – Live Cinema' events. Producers of television versions of silent feature films. Specialist research and library services for silent cinema. Production credits: *Hollywood, Unknown Chaplin, Keaton – A Hard Act to Follow, Harold Lloyd – The Third Genius.* Currently working on *D W Griffiths – Father of Film,* a 3-part documentary for Channel 4

Picture Palace Productions
6-10 Lexington Street
London W1R 3HS
Tel: 071 439 9882
Fax: 071 734 8574
Malcolm Craddock
Recently completed *The Orchid House,* 4 x 1 hour drama series set in the Caribbean during 1918 and 1938 for Channel 4; 3 x *Eurocops* English episodes for Channel 4. In development Michael Stott's *The Fancy Man,* Po Chi Leong's *Passage to Heaven* and Sandra Goldbacher and Tony Grisoni's *Scarlet Women*

Picture Parade
3 Percy Street
London W1P 9FA
Tel: 071 580 1157
Fax: 071 436 4193
Recently completed *Gentleman Jim Reeves,* a co-production with TVS and SVT 1 Sweden for Channel 4. In pre-production *Hard on their Heels,* a thirteen-part drama series, *Chet Atkins,* 1 hour co-production with TVS and Channel 4, *Mycroft's Christmas* for the BBC and *Second Wind,* 10 part drama series with European co-producers in preparation

Picture Partnership Productions
see **Carnival (Films and Theatre)**

Pictures of Women
Top Floor
56 Carysfort Road
London N16 9AD
Tel: 071 249 9632

PolyGram International
30 Berkeley Square
London W1X 5HA
Tel: 071 493 8800
Fax: 071 499 2596
Co-produced *Chicago Joe and the Showgirl* and *Fools of Fortune* with Working Title

Portman Entertainment
Pinewood Studios
Iver Heath
Bucks SL0 0NH
Tel: 0753 630366
Fax: 0753 630332
Victor Glynn
Andrew Warren
Ian Warren
Chris Brown
Philip Hinchcliffe

Portobello Productions and Portobello Pictures
42 Tavistock Road
London W11 1AW
Tel: 071 379 5566
Fax: 071 379 5599/ 221 5991

Eric Abraham
Specialise in feature film and TV drama. Completed projects in 1990/1: John le Carre's *A Murder of Quality;* Roald Dahl's *Danny the Champion of the World* (feature); *Royal Ballet: Hobson's Choice; Murray Perahia's Mozart; Solti/Kiri – The Maestro and the Diva.* Projects in development 1991/2: Roald Dahl's *James and the Giant Peach; Darkness at Noon; Maiden; The Extraordinary Adventures of Private Ivan Chonkin*

Poseidon Productions
1st Floor
Hammer House
113 Wardour Street
London W1V 3TD
Tel: 071 734 4441/5140
Fax: 071 437 0638
Frixos Constantine
Productions include: *Autism – A World Apart* for Channel 4, *Lysistrata* a feature film co-production with the USSR, *Great Russian Writers,* a mini-series for Channel 4 and a documentary on *Dyslexia* for Channel 4

Praxis Films
14 Manor Drive
Binbrook
Lincoln LN3 6BX
Tel: 0472 83547
Fax: 0472 83683
John Goddard
Film and video production of documentaries and current affairs films world-wide. Recent credits include films for Yorkshire Television and for Channel 4's *Dispatches, Cutting Edge* and *World This Week* series. Extensive film/video archive of sea, rural, industrial and regional material

Primetime Television
Seymour Mews House
Seymour Mews
Wigmore Street
London W1H 9PE
Tel: 071 935 9000
Fax: 071 487 3975
Richard Price
Independent TV production/packaging company associated with distributors RPTA. Specialise in international co-productions. Recent projects include: *Jupiter Moon,* 150 half hours drama (Primetime/ Andromeda in association with Axel Springer/Multimedia), the RSC's *Othello* (Primetime for the BBC), *First Circle* 2 x two hours in association with Technisonor/ Communications Claude Heroux/Primedia

Productions Associates (UK)
The Stable Cottage
Pinewood Studios
Iver Heath
Bucks SL0 0NH
Tel: 071 486 9921
Fax: 0753 656844
Michael Baumohl

Prominent Features
68a Delancey Street
London NW1 7RY
Tel: 071 284 0242
Fax: 071 284 1004
Steve Abbott
Anne James
Company formed by Steve Abbott, John Cleese, Terry Gilliam, Eric Idle, Anne James, Terry Jones and Michael Palin to produce in-house features. Produced *The Adventures of Baron Munchausen, Erik The Viking, A Fish Called Wanda* and *American Friends*

Prominent Television
68a Delancey Street
London NW1 7RY
Tel: 071 284 0242
Fax: 071 284 1004
Steve Abbott
Anne James
Company formed by Steve Abbott, John Cleese, Terry Gilliam, Eric Idle, Anne James, Terry Jones and Michael Palin to produce in-house television programmes. In pre-production *Pole to Pole*

Quanta
Production Centre
40-44 Clipstone Street
London W1P 7EA
Tel: 071 323 3220
Fax: 071 637 2590
Old Forge House
Rodbourne Road
Corston
Malmesbury
Wiltshire SN16 0HA
Tel: 0666 825626
Fax: 0666 825626
Glyn Jones
Nicholas Jones
Developing international TV drama series, in addition to being specialists in TV science programming. Past commissions include *Equinox* (Channel 4) and *Horizon* (BBC2)

RM Arts
46 Great Marlborough Street
London W1V 1DB
Tel: 071 439 2637
Fax: 071 439 2316
RM Arts produces music and arts programming and co-produces on an international basis with major broadcasters including BBC, LWT, Channel 4, ARD and ZDF in Germany, NOS-TV in Holland, Danmarks Radio and TV2/Denmark, ORF in Austria, SVT in Sweden, RTVE in Spain and La Sept in France. Recent work includes live recordings of Beethoven's *Fidelio* and Strauss's *Die Fledermaus* from the Royal Opera House Covent Garden, ballet specials shot in studio with the Kirov Ballet and the Alvin Ailey American Dance Theatre, 35mm portraits of artists Max Ernst and Kazimir Malevich and a series of music documentaries exploring the all-pervasive presence and significance of 'Improvisation'

RSPB Film and Video Unit
The Lodge
Sandy
Bedfordshire SG19 2DL
Tel: 0767 680551
Fax: 0767 692365
Jeffery Boswall
Producers of *Osprey, Kingfisher, Where Eagles Fly* and most recently *The Year of the Stork.* The unit also acts as an independent producer of environmental films and videos

Ragdoll Productions
49 High Street
Henley in Arden
West Midlands B95 5AA
Tel: 0564 794076
Fax: 0564 794461
Anne Wood
Specialist children's TV producer of live action and animation. *Pob* for Channel 4, *Playbox* for Central, *Storytime* for BBC, *Magic Mirror* for ITV, *Boom!* for Channel 4, *Rosie & Jim* for Central and *Brum* for BBC

Recorded Development
8-12 Broadwick Street
London W1V 1FH
Tel: 071 439 0607
Fax: 071 434 1192
A subsidiary of Recorded Picture Co set up to bring projects to pre-production stage

Recorded Picture Co
8-12 Broadwick Street
London W1V 1FH
Tel: 071 439 0607
Fax: 071 434 1192
Jeremy Thomas
Thomas produced Nagisa Oshima's *Merry Christmas, Mr Lawrence,* Stephen Frears' *The Hit,* Nicolas Roeg's *Insignificance, The Last Emperor* and *The Sheltering Sky* directed by Bernardo Bertolucci. In production: *The Naked Lunch* directed by David Cronenberg

Red Rooster Films & Television Entertainment
11-13 Macklin Street
London WC2B 5NH
Tel: 071 405 8147
Fax: 071 831 0679
Linda James
Stephen Bayly
Non Morris
Carolyn Parry-Jones
Company formed in 1982 by Linda James and Stephen Bayly, producing quality television and feature films. Produced 24 hours of film including four TV movies and two features. In production in 1990 *The Diamond*

Brothers – South by Southeast. In development: *Keeping Clean, Cruikshank, Vanderpump and Styles, Safe House, The Scarer* and *Prat of the Argus*

Red Shadow Films
36 Ritherdon Road
London SW17 8QF
Tel: 081 672 0606
Fax: 081 672 6334
David Young
Jonathan Holloway
Red Shadow Films is a production company founded by Jonathan Holloway and David Young. First film *Eclipsed,* a half-hour anti-war drama, was broadcast by ITV on Remembrance Sundays 1988 and 1989

Rediffusion Films
c/o Buxton Films
5 The Square
Buxton
Derbyshire SK17 6AZ
Tel: 0298 77623
Jette Bonnevie
The production finance arm of a diversified communications company. In the past has provided finance for TV productions and feature films. Most recent involvements include a 13-part athletic coaching series financed in conjunction with the International Athletic Federation

Redwing Film Company
1 Wedgewood Mews
12/13 Greek Street
London W1V 5LW
Tel: 071 734 6642
Fax: 071 734 9850
Film, TV and commercial production

Regent Production
The Mews
6 Putney Common
Putney
London SW15 1HL
Tel: 081 789 5350
Fax: 081 789 5332
William Stewart
Productions for 1990/91 include two new series of the Channel 4 quiz series *Fifteen-to-One* (125 programmes). Two development deals in situation comedy and a four-part drama series

Revere Entertainment Company
24 D'Arblay Street
London W1V 3FH
Tel: 071 437 4551
John Goldstone
Goldstone produced *Monty Python's The Meaning of Life, The Life of Brian* and *Erik the Viking*

Rite Films
20 Bouverie Road West
Folkestone
Kent CT20 2SZ
Tel: 0303 52335
George Wright
Mainly engaged in corporate videos, documentary film productions, and TV news gathering

Riverfront Pictures
Dock Cottages
Peartree Lane
Glamis Road
Wapping
London E1 9SR
Tel: 071 481 2939
Fax: 071 480 5520
Jeff Perks
Carole Crouch
Specialise in music, arts and drama-documentaries. Independent productions for Channel 4 and the BBC. Latest production: *A Night at the Circus – Runaway to Archaosland* for Granada TV arts series *Celebration*

Roadshow Productions
c/o 6 Basil Mansions
Basil Street
London SW3 1AP
Tel: 071 584 0542
Fax: 071 584 1549
Kurt Unger
Daniel Unger
Recent productions include feature film *Return from the River Kwai*

SVP Communications
Jordans
Cakeham Road
West Wittering
Chichester
West Sussex PO20 8AA
Tel: 0243 511256/071 732 5413
Fax: 0243 511373
Jeremy Jacobs
Scriptwriting, production and direction of both drama and documentary productions in many different parts of the world

Sands Films
119 Rotherhithe Street
London SE16 4NF
Tel: 071 231 2209
Fax: 071 231 2119
Richard Goodwin
Goodwin produced *Stories From A Flying Trunk;* the puppet animation short *The Nightingale;* and features *Biddy* and the six-hour feature *Little Dorrit* both directed by Christine Edzard at the company's Rotherhithe Studios base. Latest production *The Fool* written and directed by Christine Edzard, and produced in the company's Rotherhithe studios

Stephen Saunders Films
32 Selwood Road
Addiscombe
Croydon
Surrey CR0 7JJR
Tel: 081 654 4495
TV, corporate, documentary productions

Scimitar Films
6-8 Sackville Street
London W1X 1DD
Tel: 071 734 8385
Fax: 071 602 9217
Michael Winner
Winner has produced and directed many films, including *Death Wish 3, Appointment with Death, A Chorus of Disapproval* and *Bullseye!*

Screen Ventures
49 Goodge Street
London W1P 1FB
Tel: 071 580 7448
Christopher Mould
Dominic Saville
Screen Ventures is a production company specialising in documentaries, current affairs and music production

Seventh Art Productions (UK)
see **Nub Television**

Shihallion Television
7 Queens Gardens
Aberdeen
Scotland AB1 6YD
Tel: 0224 642416
Fax: 0224 638383
Multi-camera light entertainment programme production

Siriol Productions
Phoenix Buildings
3 Mount Stuart Square
Butetown
Cardiff CF1 6RW
Tel: 0222 488400
Fax: 0222 485962
Robin Lyons
Formerly Siriol Animation. Producers of high quality animation for television and the cinema

Skan Productions International
21 The Quadrangle
Chelsea Harbour
London SW10 0GU
Tel: 071 354 5482
Fax: 071 352 4720
Malcolm Hossick
Shaie Selzer
Feature film production

Skreba Films
5a Noel Street
London W1V 3RB
Tel: 071 437 6492
Fax: 071 437 0644
Ann Skinner
Simon Relph
Produced *Return of the Soldier* and *Secret Places,* directed by Zelda Barron. Other projects include *Bad Hats, A Profile of Arthur J Mason, Honour, Profit and Pleasure* and *The Gourmet.* Relph produced the Bill Douglas-directed *Comrades* and Skinner was executive producer on *Heavenly Pursuits* and produced *The Kitchen Toto, A Very British Coup* and *One Man's War*

Skyline Film and TV Productions
4 Picardy Place
Edinburgh EH1 3JT
Tel: 031 557 4580
Fax: 031 556 4377
Trevor Davies
126 Rusthall Avenue
London W4 1BS
Tel: 081 747 8444
Fax: 081 995 2117
Steve Clark-Hall
Producers of *Scottish Eye, Walkie Talkie* and *The Big Day* for Channel 4

Speedy Films
8 Royalty Mews
Dean Street

London W1V 5AW
Tel: 071 437 9313/
494 4043
Fax: 071 434 0830
Keri Batten
Ren Pesci
Paul Vester
Barry Baker
Producers of commercials and shorts *Sunbeam* and *Picnic*

Spitting Image Productions

17-19 Plumbers Row
Aldgate
London E1 1EQ
Tel: 071 375 1561
Fax: 071 375 2492
Comedy-based production company specialising in international television and film, commercials and corporate video, using puppets, live action, cell and stop-frame animation. Productions include ten series of *Spitting Image* to April 1991, *The Winjin' Pom* and in co-production with the BBC *The Mary Whitehouse Experience*

Stagescreen Productions

12 Upper St Martin's Lane
London WC2H 9DL
Tel: 071 437 7525
Fax: 071 497 2208
Jeffrey Taylor
Derek Granger
Film, television and theatre company whose work includes *A Handful of Dust, Death of a Son* (for BBC TV) and *Where Angels Fear to Tread*

Stephens Kerr

113-117 Wardour Street
London W1V 3TD
Tel: 071 439 2001
Fax: 071 434 0617
Produced the 15 part series *Sex Talk* for Channel 4 in 1990 and are currently producing *Love Talk* for Channel 4 in 1991

Robert Stigwood Organisation

118-120 Wardour Street
London W1V 4BT
Tel: 071 437 2512
Fax: 071 437 3674
Robert Stigwood
David Land
David Herring
Theatre and film producer Stigwood is currently involved in the film of *Evita* and several other projects

Swanlind

The Wharf
Bridge Street
Birmingham
B1 2JR
Tel: 021 616 1701
Fax: 021 616 1520
Corporate communications, film and television producers

TKO Film and TV (formerly Kruger Leisure Organisation)

PO Box 130
Hove
East Sussex BN3 6QU
Tel: 0273 550088
Fax: 0273 540969
Jeffrey Kruger
A division of the Kruger Organisation, making music programmes for TV, satellite and video release worldwide as well as co-producing various series and full length feature films. Latest co-production with Central TV music division *21st Anniversary Tour of Glen Campbell*

TV Cartoons

39 Grafton Way
London W1P 5LA
Tel: 071 388 2222
Fax: 071 383 4192
John Coates
Norman Kauffman
Claire Braidley
TVC produced the Academy Award-nominated film *The Snowman*, and the feature *When The Wind Blows*, both adaptations from books by Raymond Briggs. Production was completed in May 1989 of *Granpa*, a half-hour television special for Channel 4 and TVS. Currently in pre-production with the feature-length film *The Adventures of Peter Rabbit* from the Beatrix Potter books and a half-hour TV special of Raymond Brigg's *Father Christmas*

TV Choice

80-81 St Martin's Lane
London WC2N 4AA
Tel: 071 379 0873

TVF
375 City Road
London EC1V 1NA
Tel: 071 837 3000
Fax: 071 833 2185
TVF is a large independent producer of factual programmes in the UK and supplies current affairs programmes to Channel 4. Produces entertainment and documentary programming for all four terrestrial channels as well as satellite broadcasters

D L Taffner UK
10 Bedford Square
London WC1B 3RA
Tel: 071 631 1184
Fax: 071 636 4571
Specialising in entertainment programming: *Talkabout*, ITV game show; *Winter with Flowers*, BBC sitcom; *The Saint*, LWT drama series. Also operate a joint venture with the Theatre of Comedy at the Shaftesbury Theatre. The parent company is a well known producer and distributor in New York, Los Angeles and Sydney

Talkback Productions
33 Percy Street
London W1P 9FG
Tel: 071 631 3940
Fax: 071 631 4273
Produced *Smith and Jones* for BBC1 and *A Life in Pieces* for BBC2. Current productions include *Blackheart the Pirate* (Central) and *Murder Most Horrid* (BBC2). Future series planned featuring Smith, Jones and Peter Cook

Tartan Television
35 Little Russell Street
London WC1A 2HH
Tel: 071 323 3022
Fax: 071 323 4857
Norrie Maclaren
Christopher Mitchell
Producing for both TV and film

Richard Taylor Cartoon Films
76 Dukes Avenue
London N10 2QA
Tel: 081 444 7547
Richard Taylor
Catherine Taylor

Team Video Productions
Canalot
222 Kensal Road
London W10 5BN
Tel: 081 960 5536

Television History Workshop
42 Queen Square
London WC1N 3AJ
Tel: 071 405 6627
Fax: 071 242 1426
Sharon Goulds
Marilyn Wheatcroft
Greg Lanning
Recent productions include a documentary for Channel 4 about morale in schools (Sep 1990) and a major series for BBC about youth culture since the war *Almost Grown* (Spring 1990). BMA Silver Award 1990 for *In the Club?* (Birth Control)

Teliesyn
3 Mount Stuart Square
Cardiff CF1 6EE
Tel: 0222 480911
Fax: 0222 481552
Colin Thomas
Richard Meyrick
Michele Ryan
Angela Graham
Producers of *Cracking Up* drama documentary series for Channel 4 and *The Enemy Within* for Channel 4. Drama co-productions include Richard Burton's *Christmas Story* for HTV Cymru/Wales and S4C

Tempest Films
33 Brookfield
Highgate West Hill
London N6 6AT
Tel: 081 340 0877
Fax: 081 340 9309
Jacky Stoller
Produced three two hour television movies filmed in Canada, Germany and Ireland based on the books of Dick Francis. Most recent credit *Shrinks* 7 1/2 hours for Euston Films. Four drama series in development (one with Canada); also Russian four part series, feature film and 26 half-hour films

Third Eye Productions
Unit 210 Canalot Studios
222 Kensal Road
London W10 5BN
Tel: 081 969 8211
Fax: 081 960 8780
Samantha Drummond-Hay
TV productions covering the worlds of arts, music, ethnography and developing world culture

Tiger Television
47 Dean Street
London W1V 5HL
Tel: 071 434 0672
Fax: 071 287 1448
Rowan Atkinson
Peter Bennet-Jones
Charles Brand
Made Golden Rose of Montreux-winning *Mr Bean* for Thames TV and ITV, *The Return of Mr Bean, The Curse of Mr Bean* and *Just for Laughs 1990* for Channel 4, *The Driven Man*, Central and ITV and *Omnibus: Life of Python* for the BBC

Time and Light Productions
5 Darling Road
London SE4 1YQ
Tel: 081 692 0145
Roger Elsgood
Works with European commissioning agencies to produce film and television programmes featuring the work of European artists and writers. Made *Time and Light* with writer John Berger. Current work includes *Between the Dog and the Fox* and *The Wrong Way*

Timeless Films
c/o Duncan Heath
Paramount House
162 Wardour Street
London W1V 3AT
Tel: 071 439 1471
Ian Emes has directed cinema shorts *French Windows, The Beard, The Oriental Nightfish, The Tent, The Magic Shop*, Paramount's Academy Award-winning *Goody Two Shoes*, his first feature for Enigma, *Knights and Emeralds, The Yob* for Channel 4, *How To Be Cool* for GTV, *Streetwise* for TVS, and, more recently, *The Wall* and *Kersplat* for Channel 4

Tiny Epic Video Co
138-140 Wardour Street
London W1V 3AU
Tel: 071 437 2854
Fax: 071 434 0211
Luke Jeans
Roger Thomas

Topaz Productions
Manchester House
46 Wormholt Street
London W12 0LS
Tel: 081 749 2619
Fax: 081 749 0358
Malcolm Taylor
David Jason
Produced *The Poetry Book* and *The Adventures of Dai Mouse* independently in 1990 with sales to Channel 4 and ABC (Australia). Currently developing several comedy/drama ideas for future production and continuing their current titles

Trans World International
TWI House
23 Eyot Gardens
London W6 9TN
Tel: 081 846 8070
Fax: 081 746 5334
Eric Drossart
Buzz Hornett
Chris Guinness
TV and video sports production and rights representation branch of Mark McCormack's International Management Group. TWI represents the television rights to many leading sports events including Wimbledon, British Open, US Open and Augusta Masters. Productions include the Men's ATP Tennis Tour, Volvo EDGA Golf Tour, the Australia v West Indies cricket series, the made-for-TV *Conquer the Arctic* and *The World's Strongest Man*

Transatlantic Films
100 Blythe Road
London W14 OHE
Tel: 071 727 0132
Revel Guest
Recent productions include a 10-part documentary series on the legacy of Ancient Greece in the modern world, *Greek Fire;* a 13-part series, *In Search of Paradise;* a four-part series directed by Peter Greenaway, *Four American Composers;*

Placido – A Year in the Life of Placido Domingo; and an eight-part series *The Horse in Sport* with Channel 4 and ABC Australia

Triple Vision
11 Great Russell Street
London WC1B 3NH
Tel: 071 323 2881
Fax: 071 323 0849
Terry Flaxton
Penny Dedman
Producers and off-line edit facility. Producing social documentaries, drama and arts programmes since 1982 for various sponsors including Channel 4 and the BBC and for non-broadcast purposes. Recent productions include: 1989: *Intensive Care* and *Soviet Cinema* for Channel 4. 1990: Programme on female circumcision and infibulation for Channel 4

Try Again
The Production Centre
5th Floor
Threeways House
40-44 Clipstone Street
London W1P 7EA
Tel: 071 323 3220
Fax: 071 637 2590
Michael Darlow
Rod Taylor
Produces documentary, drama, light entertainment, arts, music

Turner Lane Boyle Productions
9-12 St Anne's Court
London W1V 3AX
Tel: 071 439 0489
Fax: 071 434 0353
Ken Turner
David Lane
Robert Boyle
Producers of TV commercials and films

Twentieth Century Fox
31-32 Soho Square
London W1V 6AP
Tel: 071 437 7766
Fax: 071 437 1625

Twentieth Century Vixen
28 Southampton Street
Brighton
East Sussex BN2 2UT
Tel: 0273 692 336
Fax: 081 802 3911
Claire Hunt
Kim Longinotto
Film/video production and distribution, mainly social documentaries. Broadcast programmes include *Fireraiser* (1988), *Eat the Kimono* (1989 Channel 4) and *Hidden Faces* (1990 Channel 4). Also tapes about special needs issues and learning difficulties

Twenty Twenty Television
10 Stucley Place
London NW1 8NS
Tel: 071 284 2020
Fax: 071 284 1810
Claudia Milne
Mike Whittaker
The company continues to produce programmes exclusively for broadcast television, specialising in worldwide investigative journalism, current affairs, factually-based drama and science. Recent productions include a six-part series *An African Hospital* for Channel 4 plus three documentaries for *Cutting Edge,* current affairs for *Dispatches* and a network documentary for Granada

Ty Gwyn Films
Y Ty Gwyn
Llanllyfni
Caernarfon
Gwynedd LL54 6DG
Tel: 0286 881235
Gareth Wynn Jones

Tyburn Productions
Pinewood Studios
Iver Heath
Bucks SL0 0NH
Tel: 0753 651700
Fax: 0753 656844
Kevin Francis
Gillian Garrow
Long-established independent TV production company

UBA
Pinewood Studios
Iver Heath
Bucks SLO 0NH
Tel: 0753 651700
Fax: 0753 656844
Peter Shaw
Richard Gregson
Sarah Horne
Production company for cinema and TV projects. Past productions include: *Turtle Diary* for the Samuel Goldwyn Company, *Castaway* for Cannon, *The Lonely Passion of Judith Hearne* for HandMade Films, *Taffin* for MGM, and *Windprints* for MCEG Virgin Vision

Uden Associates
Chelsea Wharf
Lots Road
London SW10 0QJ
Tel: 071 351 1255
Fax: 071 376 3937
Adam de Wan
Patrick Uden
William Miller
Michael Proudfoot
Film and television production company for broadcast through Channel 4, BBC1 and BBC2. Corporate clients Ford Motor Company, British Nuclear Fuels, The Post Office

Umbrella Entertainment Productions
25 Denmark Street
London WC2H 8NJ
Tel: 071 379 6145
Sandy Lieberson
Formed in 1977. First production was *Performance,* and since then has produced a number of films, including *The Mighty Quinn* for MGM, *Stars and Bars* directed by Pat O'Connor for Columbia, and *Rita, Sue and Bob Too* for Channel 4. Sandy Lieberson is currently President of International Production at Pathe Entertainment

Umbrella Films
c/o Twickenham Film Studios
St Margaret's
Twickenham
Middlesex TW1 2AW
Simon Perry
Made Michael Radford's *Another Time, Another Place, 1984* and *White Mischief,* Richard Eyre's *Loose Connections,* Conny Templeman's *Nanou* and Jana Bokova's *Hotel du Paradis.* In development are *The Playboys,* to be directed by Gillies MacKinnon; *The Elixir,* to be directed by Michael Radford, and Agatha Christie's *Towards Zero*

Unicorn Organisation
Pottery Lane Studios
34a Pottery Lane
Holland Park
London W11 4LZ
Tel: 071 229 5131
Fax: 071 229 4999
Michael Seligman
Julian Roberts

VPL
1 Cowcross Street
London EC1M 6DR
Tel: 071 608 2131/2 & 490 8825
Fax: 071 490 1864
Sue Hayes
Sally French
Developing drama and documentary projects for Channel 4, Granada TV and the BBC

Verronmead
30 Swinton Street
London WC1X 9NX
Tel: 071 278 5523
Fax: 071 278 0643
Maureen Harter
David Wood
Produced *Back Home,* a TV film drama with TVS and the Disney Channel, corporate video for PACE on *Neuro Linguistic Programming*

Videotel Productions
Ramillies House
1/2 Ramillies Street
London W1V 1DF
Tel: 071 439 6301
Fax: 071 437 0731
Nick Freethy
Stephen Bond
Producers of educational and training packages for TV and video distribution including the series *Catering With Care, Working With Care, Chemical Plant Safety, Chemical Spills at Sea, Alcohol Beware, Coshh Dead Ahead*

Video Visuals
37 Harwood Road
London SW6 4QP
Tel: 071 731 0079
Fax: 071 384 2027
Currently produces *The Chart Show* for ITV

WTTV
1 Water Lane
Kentish Town Road
London NW1 8NZ
Tel: 071 911 6100
Fax: 071 911 6150
Antony Root

Simon Wright
Grainne Marmion
Tim Bevan
Sarah Radclyffe
Television programming including drama, comedy and children's/family. A sister company of Working Title Films

Wall To Wall Television
8-9 Spring Place
Kentish Town
London NW5 3ER
Tel: 071 485 7424
Fax: 071 267 5292
Alex Graham
Jane Root
Andy Lipman
Producers of *The Media Show, For Love or Money, Verdict* and *The Thing Is...* for Channel 4 and a range of other projects for BBC, Channel 4 and foreign broadcasters

The Walnut Partnership
Crown House
Armley Road
Leeds LS12 2EJ
Tel: 0532 456913
Fax: 0532 439614
Geoff Penn
Television, film and video production company

Warner Sisters
21 Russell Street
London WC2B 5HP
Tel: 071 836 0134
Fax: 071 836 6559
Lavinia Warner
Jane Wellesley
Producer of drama and documentary programmes, the company was founded following the success of *Tenko*. Recent productions include *Wish Me Luck* (3 x eight-part drama with LWT), *Tristan da Cunha* (documentary for Granada/WNET), *That's Entertaining* (Channel 4), *Madagascar* (Granada/WNET), *She-Play,* (6 short plays by new women writers for Channel 4), *In Search of the White Rajahs* (BBC/WNET/ABC), *Rides* (6-part drama series for BBC1), *Selling Hitler* (mini-series on the Hitler diaries scandal with Euston Films) and *£10 Poms* 8-part film drama (TVNZ/BBC)

Waterloo Films
Silver House
31-35 Beak Street
London W1R 3LD
Tel: 071 494 4060
Fax: 071 287 6366
Dennis Woolf
Ray Davies
Producer of *Return to Waterloo,* a fantasy film for Channel 4 written and directed by Ray Davies of The Kinks, which was co-financed by Channel 4 and RCA Video Productions. Other projects in development

Watershed Television
53 Queen Square
Bristol BS1 4LH
Tel: 0272 276864
Fax: 0272 252093
Video and film production. Broadcast as well as corporate and commercials

Westbourne Films
25 Westbourne Grove
London W2 4UA
Tel: 071 792 9801
Fax: 071 792 9646
John Purdie
Ron Johnston
Ingrid Darbyshire
Produced *The Lane* a six-part series for BBC, *Eton – Class of '91* and *Getting Better* for Channel 4 and *Storms* for BBC Enterprises

White City Films
79 Sutton Court Road
London W4 3EQ
Tel: 081 994 6795
Fax: 081 995 9379
Aubrey Singer
Current affairs and documentary productions

Michael White Productions
13 Duke Street
St James's
London SW1Y 6DB
Tel: 071 839 3971
Fax: 071 839 3836
Michael White
Trade product. Film and theatre producer. Recent films include *High Season, Eat the Rich, White Mischief,* and *Nuns on the Run*

David Wickes Productions
169 Queen's Gate
London SW7 5HE
Tel: 071 225 1382
Fax: 071 589 8847
David Wickes
Sue Davies
Currently producing two TV movies for US Networks; wrote *Jekyll & Hyde* for ABC starring Michael Caine, Cheryl Ladd. Produced, directed, co-wrote *Jack the Ripper* for CBS starring Michael Caine and Lewis Collins. Two series of *Marlowe Private Eye* for HBO

Richard Williams Animation
138 Royal College Street
London NW1 0TA
Tel: 071 437 4455
Richard Williams
1988 – *Who Framed Roger Rabbit?* (Touchstone/Amblin). In production 1990/1 *The Thief and the Cobbler,* an animated epic feature

Winkast Programming
Pinewood Studios
Iver Heath
Bucks SL0 0NH
Tel: 0753 651700
Fax: 0753 652525
Chantal Ribeiro
Elliott Kastner's company, independent producer of over 65 motion pictures in less than two decades, which include: *Where Eagles Dare, The Long Goodbye, Farewell My Lovely, Equus,* and *Angel Heart.* Currently developing *Jericho, Louie's Widow*

Witzend Productions
3 Derby Street
Mayfair
London W1Y 7HD
Tel: 071 355 2868
Fax: 071 495 3310
Television development and production

Woodfilm
61a Great Titchfield Street
London W1P 7FL
Tel: 071 631 5429
Elizabeth Wood
Producers of arts, features and TV drama; *The Pantomime Game* for The Arts Council, *The Future of Things Past, Stairs, Go For It, Sophie* and *Say Hello to the Real Dr Snide* for Channel 4

Dennis Woolf Productions
Silver House
31-35 Beak Street
London W1R 3LD
Tel: 071 494 4060
Fax: 071 287 6366
Specialising in current affairs *Dispatches,* documentaries *Cutting Edge,* music *Epitaph: Charles Mingus,* and studio reconstructions of contemporary trials *The Court Report* series for Channel 4, *The Trial of Klaus Barbie* for the BBC

Working Title Films
1 Water Lane
Kentish Town Lane
London NW1 8NZ
Tel: 071 911 6100
Fax: 071 911 6150
Sarah Radclyffe
Tim Bevan
Graham Bradstreet
Films include *My Beautiful Laundrette, Wish You Were Here, Sammy and Rosie Get Laid, A World Apart, The Tall Guy, Fools of Fortune, Dakota Road, Drop Dead Fred, Robin Hood* and *London Kills Me.* See also WTTV

Works On Screen
142 Albert Road
London N22 4AH
Tel: 081 889 6949
Alison Joseph

World Film Services
Pinewood Studios
Iver Heath
Bucks SL0 0NH
Tel: 0753 656501
Fax: 0753 656475
John Heyman
John Chambers

Worldmark Productions
The Old Studio
18 Middle Row
London W10 5AT
Tel: 081 960 3251
Fax: 081 960 6150
Recent productions include: *Greatest Goals II & III, Shoot Out, Every Day of your Life.* In production: *Man's Quest* and *Triple Crown,* 2 x three episode TV series, *Flyer,* the official film of the 1991 Rugby World Cup and *Olympic Experience II,* thirty years of Winter Olympics

World's End Productions

60 Berwick Street
London W1V 3PA
Tel: 071 439 7275
Fax: 071 494 1952
Adam Bullmore
Documentary and drama production. 1990 productions include: *Living with the Spill*, *Changing the Guard*, part two of *And the Walls Came Tumbling Down* (Channel 4) and *Dear Rosie* (Channel 4/British Screen). In production: *Ratlines* (Channel 4/ITEL) in association with Exposed Films

World Wide International Television

21-25 St Anne's Court
London W1V 3AW
Tel: 071 434 1121
Fax: 071 734 0619
The company produces a broad range of programmes including drama, children's programmes, light entertainment, documentary and current affairs. Recent productions include *The Fifteen Streets*, *The Black Velvet Gown* and *The Black Candle*, 3 TV films for ITV based on the books by Catherine Cookson. Children's programmes include *Kappatoo*, a science fiction comedy series for ITV, *Kids Court*, (26 part series for BSB), *Finders Keepers* (Quiz show for ITV). The company also produces Channel 4's religious magazine programme *Not on Sunday* (third series) as well as single documentaries for *Equinox* (Channel 4) and *Arena* (BBC)

Year 2000 Film and Television Productions

3 Benson Road
Blackpool FY3 7HP
Tel: 0253 395403/824057
Film and television producers

Yorkshire Film Co

Capital House
Sheepscar Court
Meanwood Road
Leeds LS7 2BB
Tel: 0532 441224
Fax: 0532 441220
Keith Hardy
Producers of satellite/broadcast sports documentaries, news coverage, corporate and commercials in film and video

ZED

29 Heddon Street
London W1R 7LL
Tel: 071 494 3181
Sophie Balhetchet
Glenn Wilhide
Ruth Walsh
Completed productions include two six-part drama series of *The Manageress*, directed by Christopher King, starring Cherie Lunghi for Channel 4 and the ECA. Also *The Missing Reel* a drama documentary special – co-produced with Channel 4, La Sept & Bravo; written and directed by Christopher Rawlence. ZED's new projects include a major new four-part series written by Stan Hey – *The Gun Club*, and an adaptation of Mary Wesley's *The Camomile Lawn* written by Ken Taylor and directed by Sir Peter Hall

Zenith North

11th floor
Cale Cross House
156 Pilgrim Street
Newcastle upon Tyne
NE1 6SU
Tel: 091 261 0077
Fax: 091 222 0271
Ian Squires
Subsidiary of Zenith Productions. Producers of *Byker Grove* for BBC1, *Big World* for Channel 4 and co-producers of *Gophers* for Channel 4

Zenith Productions

43-45 Dorset Street
London W1H 4AB
Tel: 071 224 2440
Fax: 071 224 3194
Charles Denton
Scott Meek
Film and TV production company, subsidiary of Carlton Communications and Paramount Pictures. Recent productions include feature film *Trust*, *Inspector Morse* for Central, *The Paradise Club* for BBC, *Shoot to Kill* for ITV and *Chimera* for Anglia. Zenith Productions, Zenith North and Action Time comprise The Zenith Group

Zero One

44 Newington Green
Mansions Green Lanes
London N16 9BT
10 Martello Street
London E8 3PE
Tel: 071 249 8269
Tel: 071 354 5965
Fax: 071 704 0135
Mark Nash
James Swinson
Producers of documentary and fiction. Most recent production *First Time Tragedy*... (documentary co-production with Australia). Currently producing *Memoirs of a Spacewoman* in association with the BFI

PRODUCTION STARTS

Below are listed British-made and/or financed features, USA productions based in Britain and some television films running over 73 minutes which began production during 1990 and the first quarter of 1991

▲

Afraid of the Dark

Telescope/Les Films Ariane
Studio: Twickenham
Location: London
Executive producer: Jean Nachbaur
Producer: Simon Bosanquet
Director: Mark Peploe
Screenwriter: Mark Peploe
Camera: Bruno de Keyzer
Editor: Scott Thomas
Cast: James Fox, Fanny Ardant, Paul McGann, Clare Holman, Robert Stephens

Alien III

20th Century Fox
Studio: Pinewood
Executive producer: Ezra Swerdlow
Producers: Gordon Carroll, David Giler, Walter Hill
Director: David Fincher
Screenwriters: Larry Ferguson, David Giler, Walter Hill, John Fasano
Camera: Jordan Cronenweth
Editor: Terry Rawlings
Cast: Sigourney Weaver, Charles Dutton, Charles Dance, Brian Glover, Paul McGann

L'Amant (The Lover)

Renn Production SA/Burrill Productions
Location: Vietnam/Italy/France
Producer: Claude Berri
Associate producers: Josee Benabent-Loiseau, Jacques Tronel
Director: Jean-Jacques Annaud
Co-producer: Timothy Burrill
Screenwriters: Gerard Brach, Jean-Jacques Annaud, from the novel by Marguerite Duras
Camera: Robert Fraisse
Editor: Noelle Boisson
Cast: Jane March, Tony Leung, Frederique Meininger, Arnaud Giovaninetti, Melvil Poupaud

American Friends

Prominent Features Ltd
Location: London/Oxford/Switzerland
Producers: Patrick Cassavetti, Steve Abbott
Director: Tristram Powell
Screenwriter: Michael Palin
Camera: Philip Bonham-Carter
Editor: George Akers
Cast: Michael Palin, Connie Booth, Trini Alvarado, Alfred Molina, David Calder

Assassin of the Tsar

Spectator Entertainment International/Mosfilm Production
Location: Moscow, Leningrad
Executive producers: Ben Brahms, Vladimir Dostal
Producers: Christopher Gawor, Erik Vaisberg, Anthony Sloman
Associate Producer: Alexander Moody
Director: Karen Shakhnazarov

▲ **American Friends**

Screenwriters: Alexander Boradyansky, Karen Shakhnazarov
Camera: Nicholai Nemolyaev
Editor: Lidia Milioli
Cast: Malcolm McDowell, Oleg Yankovsky, Armen Dzhigarkhanian, Yuri Sherstnyov, Angela Ptashuk

Backsliding
CaST Productions/Film Four International/ITEL
Location: Australia
Executive producers: Charles Target, Simon Target
Producer: Sue Wild
Director: Simon Target
Screenwriters: Simon Target, Ross Wilson
Camera: Tom Cowan
Editor: Nick Holmes
Cast: Tim Roth, Jim Holt, Odile le Clezio

Begin & Cease
Claro Films
Location: Leeds, Whitby
Producers: Peter M Kershaw, Jamie Nuttgens
Director/Screenwriter: Peter M Kershaw
Camera: Giles Nuttgens
Editor: Anna Zaluczkowska
Cast: Geoffrey Banks, Richard Colson, Sally Womersley

Bejewelled
TVS/Disney Channel
Location: Kent/London
Executive producers: Graham Benson, Wendy Dytman, Paula Weinstein
Producers: J Nigel Pickard, John Price
Director: Terry Marcel
Adapted for TV by Tom Astle
Camera: Ken Brinsley
Editor: Belinda Cottrell
Cast: Denis Lawson, Emma Samms, Dirk Benedict, Jerry Hall, Jean Marsh, Frances de la Tour

Best Intentions (Den Goda Viljan)
SVT 1 Drama/ZDF/Channel 4/RAI 2/La Sept/DR/YLE 2/NRK Norway/RUV
Location: Sweden
Executive producer: Ingrid Dahlberg
Producer: Lars Bjälkeskog
Director: Bille August
Screenwriter: Ingmar Bergman
Camera: Jörgen Persson
Editor: Janus Billeskov Jansen
Cast: Max von Sydow, Pernilla Östergren August, Samuel Fröler, Ghita Nørby

The Black Candle
Worldwide International TV/Tyne Tees TV
Location: Newcastle
Executive producer: Michael Chaplin
Producer: Ray Marshall
Director: Roy Battersby
Screenwriter: Gordon Hann, from the novel by Catherine Cookson
Camera: Witold Stok
Editor: Andrew Nelson
Cast: Samantha Bond, Nathaniel Parker, Sian Phillips, Robert Hines

▼

PRODUCTION STARTS

The Black Velvet Gown
Worldwide International TV/Tyne Tees TV
Location: North-east England
Producer: Ray Marshall
Director: Norman Stone
Screenwriter: Gordon Hann, from the novel by Catherine Cookson
Camera: Ken Westbury
Editor: John McDonal
Cast: Bob Peck, Janet McTeer, Jean Anderson, David Hunt, Geraldine Somerville

Blonde Fist
Blue Dolphin
Location: Liverpool, New York
Producers: Christopher Figg, Joe D'Morais
Director/Screenwriter: Frank Clarke
Camera: Bruce McGowan
Editor: Brian Peachey
Cast: Margi Clarke, Carroll Baker, Ken Hutchison

The Bridge
Moonlight (Bridge) Ltd
Location: Suffolk
Producer: Lyn Goleby
Director: Syd Macartney
Screenwriter: Adrian Hodges, from the novel by Maggie Hemingway
Camera: David Tattersall
Editor: Mike Ellis
Cast: Saskia Reeves, David O'Hara, Joss Ackland, Rosemary Harris, Anthony Higgins, Geraldine James

Can You Hear Me Thinking
BBC Screen One
Studio: BBC London
Executive producer: Richard Broke
Producer: Ruth Caleb
Director: Christopher Morahan
Screenwriters: Monty Haltrecht, Beverley Marcus
Camera: David Feig
Editor: Dave King
Cast: Dame Judi Dench, Michael Williams, Richard Henders

City of Joy
Lightmotive/Pricel
Location: India
Producer/Director: Roland Joffé
Producer: Jake Eberts
Co-producer: Iain Smith
Screenwriters: Mark Medoff, Gerard Brach
Camera: Peter Biziou
Cast: Patrick Swayze, Pauline Collins, Om Puri, Art Malik, Nabil Shaban

Close My Eyes
Beambright/Film Four International
Location: London/Surrey
Producer: Therese Pickard
Director/Screenwriter: Stephen Poliakoff
Camera: Witold Stok
Editor: Michael Parkinson
Cast: Alan Rickman, Clive Owen, Saskia Reeves, Karl Johnson, Lesley Sharp

The Commitments ▶
Beacon Communications
Location: Dublin
Producers: Lynda Myles, Roger Randall-Cutler
Associate producer: David Wimbury
Director: Alan Parker
Screenwriters: Dick Clement, Ian Le Frenais, from the novel by Roddy Doyle
Camera: Gale Tattersall
Editor: Gerry Hambling
Cast: Robert Arkins, Angeline Ball, Bronagh Gallagher, Maria Doyle, Andrew Strong

The Common Pursuit
BBC Screen Two/WNET/New York
Location: London/Cambridge/Oxford
Producer: Kenith Trodd
Director: Christopher Morahan
Screenwriter: Simon Gray
Camera: Ian Punter
Editor: Dave King
Cast: Stella Gonet, Kevin McNally, Tim Roth, Andrew McCarthy, James Fleet, Stephen Fry, Ian Bannen

The Count of Solar
BBC Screen Two
Studio: Ealing
Producer: Ruth Caleb
Associate producer: Carolyn Montague
Director: Tristram Powell
Screenwriter: David Nokes, based on an episode from 'When the Mind Hears' by Harlan Lane
Camera: Nigel Walters
Editor: Ardan Fisher
Cast: David Calder, John Standing, Tyron Woolfe, Georgina Hale, Susan Jameson

◀ Close My Eyes

PRODUCTION STARTS

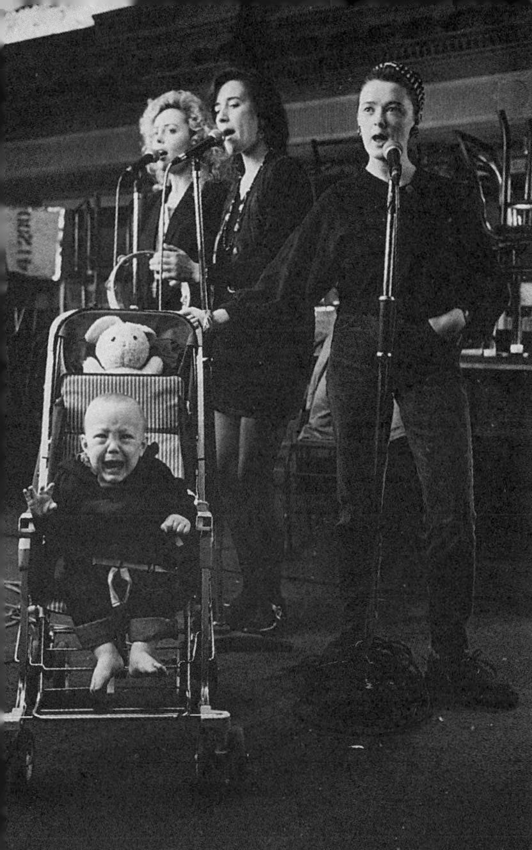

Dear Rosie

Worlds End/Film Four International/British Screen
Studio: Grip House
Location: London
Executive producer: Stewart Richards
Cast: Amelda Brown, Jason Carter, Charlotte Chatton, Alan Howard, Rachel Scott
Producer: Barnaby Thompson
Associate producer: Nicky Kentish Barnes
Director: Peter Cattaneo
Screenwriters: Peter Morgan, Mark Wadlow
Camera: Clive Tickner
Editor: Guy Bensley
Cast: Fiona Victory, Remy Beard, Terence Wilton, Roger Hammond, Su Elliot, Belinda Mayne

A Demon in My View

First City/Pro-ject Filmverlag Gmbh
Location: London/Germany
Executive producers: ▼ Theo Hinz, Herbert Rimbach
Producers: David Kelly, Martin Bruce-Clayton
Director: Petra Haffter
Screenwriter: Petra Haffter, from the novel by Ruth Rendell
Camera: Frank Bruehne
Editor: Moune Barius
Cast: Anthony Perkins, Uwe Bohm, Sophie Ward, Stratford Johns, Brian Bovell

Deptford Graffiti

Positive Partnership/ Channel 4
Location: Deptford
Producer: Judy Hunt
Director: Philip Davis
Screenwriter: Sheila Fox
Camera: Steve Bernstein
Editor: Alan Knight
Cast: Nabil Shaban, Sharon Maiden, Mark McGann, Nick Bartlett, Jag Plah

Do Not Disturb

BBC Screen Two/BBC Enterprises
Location: Norfolk
Producer: Simon Passmore

The Crucifer of Blood

Agamemnon/British Lion/Turner Pictures
Studio: Pinewood
Location: London
Executive producer: Peter Snell
Producer/Director: Fraser Heston
Associate producer: Ted Lloyd
Screenwriter: Fraser Heston, from the play by Paul Giovanni
Camera: Robin Vidgeon
Editor: Eric Boyd-Perkins
Cast: Charlton Heston, Richard Johnson, Susannah Harker, Simon Callow, Edward Fox

Dakota Road

Film Four International/British Screen/Working Title/British Film Partnership
Location: East Anglia, Fenlands
Executive producer: Sarah Radclyffe
Producer: Donna Grey
Director/Screenwriter: Nick Ward
Camera: Ian Wilson
Editor: Bill Diver

Associate producer: Chris Cherry
Director: Nick Renton
Screenwriter: Timberlake Wertenbaker
Camera: Dave Bennett
Editor: Frances Parker
Cast: Frances Barber, Eva Darlan, Peter Capaldi, Stefan Schwartz, Patrick Godfrey

Drop Dead Fred
Working Title
Location: Minneapolis
Executive producers: Tim Bevan, Sarah Radclyffe
Producer: Paul Webster
Director: Ate de Jong
Screenwriters: Carlos Davis, Anthony Fingleton
Camera: Sandi Sissel
Editor: Marshall Harvey
Cast: Phoebe Cates, Rik Mayall, Marsha Mason, Carrie Fisher, Tim Matheson, Bridget Fonda

A Duel of Love
Lord Grade/Turner Pictures/Gainsborough Pictures
Studio: Goldcrest
Location: Althorp House
Executive producer: Lord Grade
Producer/Director: John Hough
Associate producer/composer: Laurie Johnson
Screenwriter: Terence Feely, from the novel by Barbara Cartland
Camera: Terry Cole
Editor: Peter Weatherley
Cast: Alison Doody, Michael York, Geraldine Chaplin, Billie Whitelaw, Benedict Taylor

Edward II
BBC/British Screen/Working Title
Studio: Bray
Executive producer: Sarah Radclyffe
Producers: Steve Clark-Hall, Antony Root
Associate Director: Ken Butler
Director: Derek Jarman
Screenwriters: Derek Jarman, Ken Butler and Steven McBride, from the play by Christopher Marlowe
Camera: Ian Wilson
Editor: George Akers
Cast: Jody Grober, Steven Waddington, Kevin Collins, Andrew Tiernan, Tilda Swinton

◀ The Favour, the Watch and the Very Big Fish

Escape from Kampala
BBC Scotland
Studio: BBC Glasgow
Location: Prestwick
Producer: Aileen Forsyth
Director: Roy Battersby
Screenwriters: Margaret and Eric Ledere, from the novel by Wycliffe Kato
Camera: Alan Henderson
Editor: Peter Hayes
Cast: John Matshikiza, Rudolph Walker, John Adewole, Leo Wringer, Oke Wambu

The Favour, the Watch and the Very Big Fish
Films Ariane/Fildebroc/Umbrella Films
Location: Paris
Executive producer: Antoine de Clermont Tonnerre
Producer: Michelle de Broca
Associate producer: Simon Perry
Director/Screenwriter: Ben Lewin
Camera: Bernard Zitzermann
Editor: John Grover
Cast: Bob Hoskins, Jeff Goldblum, Natasha Richardson, Michel Blanc, Jean-Pierre Cassel

Filipina Dreamers
BBC Wales/BBC Screen One
Location: Philippines/Wales
Executive producer: Ruth Caleb
Producer: Jacinta Peel
Director: Les Blair
Screenwriter: Andrew Davies
Camera: Ashley Rowe
Editor: Tim Kruydenberg
Cast: Bill Maynard, Charlie Drake, Geoffrey Hutchings, David Thewlis, Lee Cornes

Finding Sarah
Jericho Productions/Channel 4
Location: Lancashire
Producer: Bernard Krichefski
Co-producer: Adrian Bate
Director: Carol Wiseman
Screenwriter: Julia Kearsley
Camera: Daf Hobson
Cast: Barbara Durkin, David Horovitch, Brenda Bruce, Frank Windsor

The Gift
Jam Pictures/Mark Forstater Productions/Canal Plus
Location: Natal, South Africa
Executive producer: Mark Forstater
Producers/Screenwriters: Lloyd Maroti, Cheryl Johnson
Director: Cheryl Johnson
Camera: Jeff Baustert
Editors: Mark Baard, Guy Spiller
Cast: Alfius Mabaso, Helen Mirren, Ian Roberts, Patrick Shai

The Grass Arena
BBC Screen Two
Location: London
Executive producer: Mark Shivas
Producer: Ruth Baumgarten
Director: Gillies MacKinnon
Screenwriter: Frank Deasy, from the autobiography by John Healy
Camera: Rex Maidment
Editor: Michael Parker
Cast: Mark Rylance, Andrew Bailey, Tim Barlow, David Bauckham, Lynsey Baxter

Hallelujah Anyhow
BBC Screen Two
Location: London
Executive producers: Mark Shivas, Colin MacCabe
Producer: David Stacey
Director: Matthew Jacobs
Screenwriters: Jean 'Binta' Breeze, Matthew Jacobs
Camera: Remi Adefarasin
Editor: Sue Wyatt
Cast: Dona Croll, Keith David, George Harris, Valerie Buchanan, Maynard Eziashi

Hamlet ▶
Marquis Productions
Studios: Lee International, Shepperton
Location: Kent/Scotland
Executive producer: Bruce Davey
Producer: Dyson Lovell
Director: Franco Zeffirelli
Screenwriters: Chris De Vore, Franco Zeffirelli, from the play by William Shakespeare
Camera: David Watkin

Editor: Richard Marden
Cast: Mel Gibson, Glenn Close, Alan Bates, Paul Scofield, Ian Holm

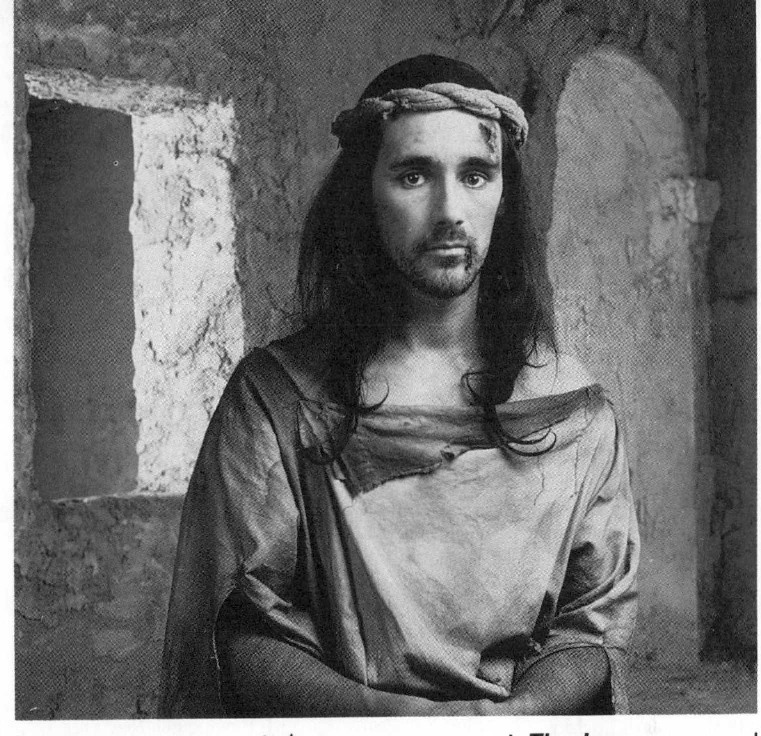

Hancock
BBC Screen One
Executive producer: Richard Broke
Producer: Paul Marcus
Director: Tony Smith
Screenwriter: William Humble
Camera: John McGlashan
Editor: Jerry Leon
Cast: Alfed Molina, Frances Barber, Mel Martin, Nick Burnell, Jim Carter

Heading Home
BBC Screen Two
Location: Bristol/South Wales/London
Executive Producer: Mark Shivas
Producer: Rick McCallum
Associate producer: Kathryn Farrar
Director/Screenwriter: David Hare
Camera: Oliver Stapleton
Editor: Frances Parker
Cast: Gary Oldman, Joely Richardson, Stephen Dillane, Stella Gonet, Michael Bryant

Hear My Song
Film Four International/British Screen/Windmill Lane/Limelight
Location: Ireland/UK
Executive producers: Simon Fields, John Paul Chapple, Russ Russell
Producer: Alison Owen
Associate producer: David Brown
Director: Peter Chelsom
Screenwriters: Peter Chelsom, Adrian Dunbar
Camera: Sue Gibson
Editor: Martin Walsh
Cast: Ned Beatty, Adrian Dunbar, Tara Fitzgerald, Shirley Anne Field, David McCallum

▲

Incident in Judaea
Brooke/Channel 4
Location: London
Producer: Anne Lapping
Director/Screenwriter: Paul Bryers
Co-Screenwriter: Mark Rogers
Camera: Simon Kossoff
Editor: Andrew Page
Cast: John Woodvine, Mark Rylance, Jim Carter, Jason Carter, Frank Baker

The Jazz Detectives
HTV West/HTV International
Location: Bristol
Executive producer: Derek Clark
Producer/Director: Alan Clayton
Screenwriter: Bob Baker
Camera: Bob Edwards
Editor: Viv Grant
Cast: Daniel Webb, Marella Oppenheim, George Irving, David Howey, Michael Povey

K2
Trans Pacific/Majestic Films International
Location: Pakistan/Canada/UK
Executive producers: Mel Estrin, Hal Weiner
Producers: Jonathan Taplin, Tim Van Rellim, Marilyn Weiner
Director: Franc Roddam
Screenwriter: Scott Roberts
Camera: Gabriel Beristain
Editor: Sean Barton
Cast: Michael Biehn, Matt Craven, Raymond Barry, Lucia Bercovici, Patricia Charbonneau

King Ralph
Ralph Productions Ltd
Studio: Pinewood
Executive producers: Mark Rosenberg, Sydney Pollack
Producer: Jack Brodsky
Associate producers: Julie Bergman, John Comfort
Director: David S Ward
Screenwriter: David S Ward, from the novel 'Headlong' by Emlyn Williams
Camera: Ken MacMillan
Editor: John Jympson
Cast: John Goodman, Peter O'Toole, John Hurt, Joely Richardson, Judy Parfitt

The Law Lord
BBC Screen Two/BBC Enterprises
Location: London/Oxford/Wales
Producer: Simon Passmore
Associate producer: Ralph Wilton
Director: Jim Goddard
Screenwriter: John Cooper
Camera: Alec Curtis
Editor: Ken Pearce
Cast: Anthony Andrews, Bernard Hill, John Rowe, Tom Baker, TP McKenna

Let Him Have It
Canal Plus/Film Trustees/British Screen/Vivid
Studio: Pinewood
Location: London/Liverpool
Executive producer: Jeremy Thomas
Producers: Luc Roeg, Robert Warr
Director: Peter Medak
Screenwriters: Neal Purvis, Robert Wade
Camera: Oliver Stapleton
Editor: Ray Lovejoy
Cast: Christopher Eccleston, Paul Reynolds, Tom Courtenay, Eileen Atkins, Mark McGann

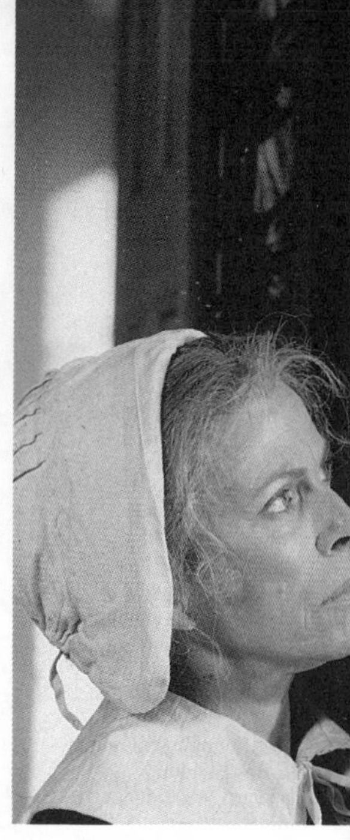

Liebestraum
Initial Film/Pathé Entertainment
Location: Binghamton/New York
Producer: Eric Fellner
Associate producer: Michael Flynn
Director/Screenwriter: Mike Figgis
Camera: Juan Ruiz-Anchia
Editor: Martin Hunter
Cast: Kim Novak, Kevin Anderson, Pamela Gidley, Bill Pullman

Life After Life
Lawson Productions/LWT
Studio: Bray
Executive producer: Nick Elliot
Producer: Sarah Lawson
Associate producer: Esta Charkham
Director: Herbert Wise
Screenwriter: Jonathan Lynn
Camera: Colin Munn
Cast: George Cole, Renee Asherson, Gudrun Ure, Leslie Phillips

Life is Sweet
Thin Man Films/Film Four International/British Screen
Location: London
Producer: Simon Channing-Williams
Director/Screenwriter: Mike Leigh
Camera: Dick Pope
Editor: Jon Gregory
Cast: Alison Steadman, Jim Broadbent, Jane Horrocks, Claire Skinner, Timothy Spall

London Kills Me
Working Title
Location: Notting Hill Gate
Executive producer: Tim Bevan
Producer: Judy Hunt
Associate producer: David Gothard
Director/Screenwriter: Hanif Kureishi
Camera: Ed Lachman
Editor: Jon Gregory
Cast: Justin Chadwick, Emer McCourt, Steven Macintosh, Naveen Andrews, Stevan Rimkus

▲ Lorna Doone
Thames TV/Working Title TV
Location: Scotland
Producers: Antony Root, Alan Horrox
Associate producer: Peter Richardson
Director: Andrew Grieve
Screenwriter: Matthew Jacobs, from the novel by R D Blackmore
Camera: Paul Wheeler
Editor: Scott Thomas
Cast: Clive Owen, Sean Bean, Polly Walker, Billie Whitelaw, Miles Anderson

Lost in Siberia
Spectator Entertainment International
Location: Moscow, Bukara
Executive producer: Benjamin Brahms
Producers: Gagik Gasparyan, Alexander Moody
Associate producers: James Brabazon, Christopher Gawor
Director: Alexander Mitta
Screenwriters: Alexander Mitta, Valery Fried, Yuri Korotkov, James Brabazon
Camera: Vladimir Shevtsik
Editors: Anthony Sloman, N Veselovskaya
Cast: Anthony Andrews, Yelena Mayorova, Vladimir Ilyin, Ira Mikhalyova, Yevgeni Mironov

Meeting Venus
Enigma
Location: Budapest, Paris
Producer: David Puttnam
Director: Istvan Szabo
Screenwriters: Istvan Szabo, Michael Hirst
Camera: Lajos Koltai
Editor: Jim Clark
Cast: Glenn Close, Neils Arestrup, Erland Josephson, Moscu Alcalay, Macha Meril

The Miracle
Palace/Film Four International/British Screen/Promenade
Location: Bray, County Wicklow
Executive producers: Nik Powell, Bob Weinstein, Harvey Weinstein
Producers: Stephen Woolley, Redmond Morris
Director/Screenwriter: Neil Jordan
Camera: Phillipe Rousselot
Editor: Joke van Wijk
Cast: Beverly D'Angelo, Donal McCann, Nial Byrne, Lorraine ◀ Pilkington, Mikkel Gaup

Mississippi Masala
Channel 4/Cinecom/Masala Films
Location: Mississippi and Uganda
Executive producer: Cheire Rodgers
Producers: Michael Nozik, Mira Nair
Director: Mira Nair
Screenwriter: Sooni Taraporerala
Camera: Ed Lachman
Cast: Denzel Washington, Sarita Choudhury, Roshan Seth, Sharmila Tagore, Ranjit Chowdhury

Misterioso
BBC Play on One
Location: York/Brighton/London/Glasgow
Producer: Norman McClandish
Associate producer: John Gibbons
Director: John Glenister
Screenwriter: Alan Plater from his own novel
Camera: Alex Scott
Editor: Bob Bathgate
Cast: Suzan Sylvester, Jack Shepherd, Hugh Ross, Eilidh Alexander, David Michaels

▲ Lost in Siberia

A Murder of Quality
Portobello/Thames TV
Location: Sherborne and London

Executive producer: Brian Walcroft
Producer: Eric Abraham
Director: Gavin Millar
Screenwriter: John le Carré
Camera: Denis Crossan
Editor: Angus Newton
Cast: Denholm Elliott, Glenda Jackson, Joss Ackland, Billie Whitelaw, David Threlfall

Naked Lunch
Naked Lunch Productions
Location: Toronto
Producer: Jeremy Thomas
Associate producer: Gabriella Martinelli
Director: David Cronenberg
Screenwriter: David Cronenberg, from the novel by William S Burroughs
Camera: Peter Suschitzky
Editor: Ron Sanders
Cast: Peter Weller, Judy Davis, Ian Holm, Julian Sands, Roy Scheider

▲ Needle
BBC TV Screenplay
Producer: George Faber
Associate producer: Ros Parker
Director: Gillies MacKinnon
Screenwriter: Jimmy McGovern
Camera: Barry McCann
Editor: Claire Douglas
Cast: Shaun McKee, Emma Bird, Peter Postlethwaite, Anna Keaveney, John Bennett, Paul Barber

O.M.
Film Cymru/BBC Wales/Ffilmiau Eryri
Location: North Wales/Oxford/Heidelberg
Executive producer: John Hefin
Producer: Norman Williams
Director: Emlyn Williams
Screenwriter: Eigra Lewis Roberts
Camera: Ashley Rowe
Editor: Tim Kruydenberg
Cast: Bryn Fon, Mari Rowland Hughes, Huw Garmon, Mirain Llwyd Owen, Olwen Rees

One Man's War
TVS Films/Skreba Films/HBO Showcase/Film Four International
Location: Mexico City/Vera Cruz
Executive producer: Graham Benson
Producer: Ann Skinner
Associate producer: David Ball
Director: Sergio Toledo
Screenwriters: Mike Carter, Sergio Toledo
Camera: Rodolfo Sanchez
Editor: Laurence Mery Clark
Cast: Anthony Hopkins, Norma Aleandro, Ruben Blades, Fernando Torres, Leonardo Garcia

102 Boulevard Haussmann
BBC Screen Two
Location: Scotland/London
Executive producer: Mark Shivas
Producer: Innes Lloyd
Director: Udayan Prasad
Screenwriter: Alan Bennett
Camera: John Hooper
Editor: Ken Pearce
Cast: Alan Bates, Janet McTeer, Jonathan Coy, Gillian Martell, Philip Rham ▼

Palmer
Palmer TV & Films/LWT
Location: Brighton/Reigate
Executive producer: Nick Elliot
Producer: Paul Knight
Director: Keith Washington
Screenwriter: Tony Hoare
Camera: Geoff Harrison
Editor: Paul Hudson
Cast: Ray Winstone, Gerard Horan, Dora Bryan, Lesley Duff, Louise Plowright

The Pleasure Principle
Psychology News
Location: London
Producer/Director/Script: David Cohen
Associate producers: Alistair Fraser, Joe McAllister, Jane Uder
Camera: Andrew Speller
Editors: JP McAllister, Bill Hopkins
Cast: Peter Firth, Hayden Gwynne, Lynsey Baxter, Lysette Anthony, Sarah Mair-Thomas

The Police
BBC Screen One
Executive producer: Richard Broke
Producer: Jacinta Peel
Director: Ian Knox
Screenwriter: Arthur Ellis
Camera: Jon Daly
Editor: Mark Day
Cast: Guy Faulkener, Oliver Ford Davies, Neville Watchurst, Arbel Jones, Caroline Ryder

The Pope Must Die
Palace/Michael White/Stephen Woolley
Location: Yugoslavia
Executive producers: Nik Powell, Michael White
Producer: Stephen Woolley
Associate producer: Paul Cowan
Director: Peter Richardson
Screenwriters: Peter Richardson, Pete Richens
Camera: Frank Gell
Editor: Katherine Wenning
Cast: Robbie Coltrane, Beverly D'Angelo, Herbert Lom, Ade Edmondson, Dawn French

Prince
BBC Screen One
Location: Bristol/South Wales
Executive producer: Richard Broke
Producer: Ruth Baumgarten
Associate producer: Ian Hopkins
Director: David Wheatley
Screenwriter: Julie Burchill
Camera: Andrew Godfrey
Editor: Roy Sharman
Cast: Sean Bean, Celia Montague, Janet McTeer, Jackie McGuire, William Armstrong

Prisoners of Honor
Warner Brothers Productions/HBO
Location: London
Producers: Judith James, Richard Dreyfuss
Director: Ken Russell
Screenwriter: Ron Hutchison
Camera: Mike Southon
Editor: Brian Tagg
Cast: Richard Dreyfuss, Oliver Reed, Peter Firth, Jeremy Kemp, Brian Blessed, Peter Vaughan

Prospero's Books
Allarts/Cinea/Camera One
Location: Amsterdam
Producer: Kees Kasander
Associate producers: Denis Wigman, Philippe Carcassonne, Jean-Louis Piel
Director: Peter Greenaway
Screenplay adapted from 'The Tempest' by William Shakespeare
Camera: Sacha Vierny

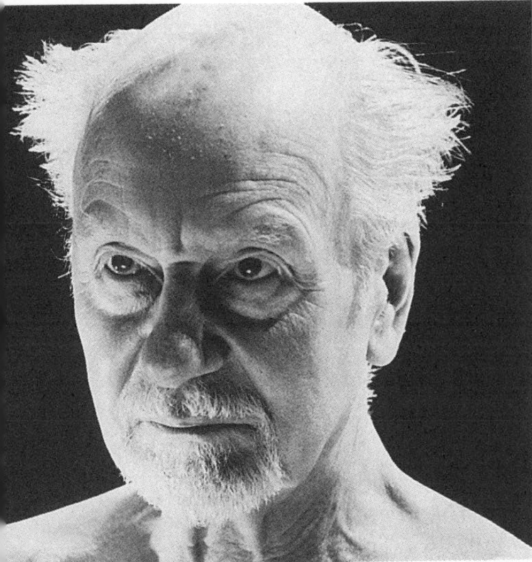

▲ Editor: John Wilson (England), Chris Wyatt, Marina Bodbijl (Holland)
Cast: Sir John Gielgud, Isabel Pascoe, Mark Rylance, Tom Bell, Kenneth Cranham

Revenge of Billy the Kid

Montage Films
Location: South Wales/Hertfordshire
Producer: Tim Dennison
Director: Jim Groom
Screenwriters: Tim Dennison, Jim Groom, Ross Smith
Camera: David Read
Editor: Harry Barnes
Cast: Michael Balfour, Samantha Perkins, Norman Mitchell, Jackie D Broad

Riff-Raff

Parallax/Channel 4
Location: London
Producer: Sally Hibbin
Director: Ken Loach
Screenwriter: Bill Jesse
Camera: Barry Ackroyd
Editor: Jonathan Morris
Cast: Robert Carlyle, Emer McCourt, Ricky Tomlinson, Jimmy Coleman, George Moss

Robin Hood

Working Title
Location: Cheshire
Executive producer: Francesca Barra
Producers: Sarah Radclyffe, Tim Bevan
Associate producer: Chris Thompson
Director: John Irvin
Screenwriter: Mark Allen Smith
Camera: Jason Lehel
Editor: Peter Tanner
Cast: Patrick Bergin, Uma Thurman, Jürgen Prochnow, Edward Fox, Jeroen Krabbé, Owen Teale

Robin Hood: Prince of Thieves

Morgan Creek
Studio: Shepperton
Executive producers: James G Robinson, David Nicksay, Gary Barber
Producers: John Watson, Pen Densham, Richard B Lewis
Co-producer: Michael Kagan
Director: Kevin Reynolds
Screenwriters: John Watson, Pen Densham, from a story by Pen Densham
Camera: Douglas Milsome

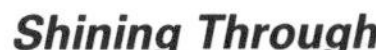

Editor: Peter Boyle
Cast: Kevin Costner, Morgan Freeman, Christian Slater, Mary Elizabeth Mastrantonio, Nick Brimble

Rubin & Ed

Working Title
Location: Utah
Executive producer: Tim Bevan
Producer: Paul Webster
Associate producer: David Stacey
Director/Screenwriter: Trent Harris
Camera: Bryan Dugga
Editor: Brent Schoenfeld
Cast: Howard Heffeman, Crispin Glover, Karen Black, Michael Green

The Runner

Living Spirit Pictures
Location: England/Wales
Producer: Genevieve Jolliffe
Director: Chris Jones
Screenwriter/Editor: Mark Talbot-Butler
Camera: Jon Walker
Cast: Terence Ford, Paris Jefferson, Andrew Mitchell, Raymond Johnson, Ivan Rogers

Separation

Mark Forstater Productions/BBC Scotland/American Playhouse
Studio: BBC Glasgow
Executive producers: Bill Bryden, Lyndsey Law
Producers: Mark Forstater, Paddy Higson
Director: Barry Davis
Screenwriter: Tom Kempinski
Camera: Nigel Walters
Editor: Martin Sharpe
Cast: David Suchet, Rosanna Arquette

Shining Through

Sandollar/20th Century Fox
Studio: Pinewood
Location: Berlin/Leipzig/Klagenfurt/Salzburg/London
Executive producer: Sandy Gallin
Producers: Carol Baum, Howard Rosenman, Nigel Wooll
Director: David Seltzer
Screenwriter: David Seltzer, from the novel by Susan Isaacs
Camera: Jan de Bont
Editor: Craig McKay
Cast: Michael Douglas, Melanie Griffith, Liam Neeson, Joely Richardson, Sir John Gielgud

▲ Riff-Raff

Shuttlecock

KM Films/Productions Belles Rives/Channel 4
Location: Portugal/London
Executive producer: Christian Arden
Producer: Graham Leader
Associate producer: Jean Ferber
Director: Andrew Piddington
Screenwriter: Tim Rose Price, from the novel by Graham Swift
Camera: Denis Lenoir
Editor: Jon Costelloe
Cast: Alan Bates, Lambert Wilson, Kenneth Haigh, Jill Meager, Beatrice Bucholz, Gregory Chisolm

The Revenge of Billy the Kid

PRODUCTION STARTS

A Small Dance
Thames TV
Location: Cambridge/Enfield
Executive Producers: Cathy Elliott, Emma Wakefield
Producer/Director: Alan Horrox
Screenwriter: Lucy Gannon
Camera: David Scott
Editor: Olivia Hetreed
Cast: Kate Hardie, James Hazeldine, Linda Bassett, Suzanne Burden, Mark Aiken

Sticky Wickets
BBC Wales/Screen One
Location: South Wales
Executive producer: Ruth Caleb
Producer: Jane Harris
Associate producer: Anji Dyer
Director: Dewi Humphreys
Screenwriter: Fletcher Watkins
Camera: Russ Walker
Editor: Rob Sylvester
Cast: Alun Armstrong, James Bolam, George Sewell, William Thomas

Sunday Pursuit
HTV International/Telecip
Executive producer: Patrick Dromgoole
Producer: Paul Sarony
Associate producer: Michael Guest
Director: Mai Zetterling
Screenwriter: N J Crisp
Camera: John Bulmer
Editor: Edward Roberts
Cast: Denholm Elliot, Rita Tushingham, Simon Shepperd, David Trevena, Dana Gillespie

Sweet Nothing
BBC Screen One
Location: London
Executive producer: Richard Broke
Producer: Louis Marks
Director: Tony Smith
Screenwriter: Vincent O'Connell
Camera: Pat O'Shea
Editor: Ken Pearce
Cast: Lee Ross, Charlotte Coleman, Joan Heal, Andrew Tiernan, Janet McTeer

Tell Me That You Love Me
BBC Screen One
Location: London
Executive producer: Richard Broke
Producer: Sarah Curtis
Director: Bruce MacDonald
Screenwriter: Adrian Hodges
Camera: John McGlashan
Editor: Mark Day
Cast: Judith Scott, Sean Bean, Rowena Cooper, David Lyon, Pippa Hinchley

The Thief and the Cobbler
Richard Williams/Allied Filmmakers
Executive producer: Jake Eberts
Producer/Director: Richard Williams
Producer: Imogen Sutton
Screenwriters: Richard Williams, Margaret French, John Patrick Shanley
Camera: John Leatherbarrow
Editor: Peter Bond
Voices: Vincent Price, Donald Pleasance, Sean Connery, Joan Sims, Anthony Quayle

Tickets for the Zoo
Cormorant Films
Location: Edinburgh
Producer/Screenwriter: Christeen Winford
Director: Brian Crumlish
Camera: Martin Singleton
Editor: Fiona MacDonald
Cast: Alice Broe, Tom Smith, Fiona Chalmers, Ashley Jenson, David McGowan

◀ Trust
Zenith/Last Moment
Location: Long Island, New York
Executive producer: Jerome Brownstein
Producer: Bruce Weiss
Director/Screenwriter: Hal Hartley
Camera: Mike Spiller
Editor: Nick Gomez
Cast: Adrienne Shelly, Martin Donovan, Rebecca Nelson, Edie Falco

Twenty-One
Anglo-International
Studio: Twickenham
Location: London/New York
Producers: Morgan Mason, John Hardy
Director: Don Boyd
Screenwriters: Zoe Heller, Don Boyd
Camera: Keith Goddard
Editor: David Spiers
Cast: Patsy Kensit, Jack Shepherd, Patrick Ryecart, Rufus Sewell, Sophie Thompson

Uncle Vanya
BBC TV/WNET New York
Producer: Simon Curtis
Associate producer: Glyn Edwards
Director: Gregory Mosher
Adapted by David Mamet from the play by Anton Chekhov translated by Vlada Chernomordik
Camera: Chris Miller
Cast: Ian Bannen, Roger Hammond, Ian Holm, Rachel Kempson, Mary Elizabeth Mastrantonio, Rebecca Pidgeon, Sandra Voe, David Warner

Under Suspicion
Columbia Pictures/Rank/LWT/Carnival Films
Studio: Shepperton
Location: Brighton/Wales/Miami
Producer: Brian Eastman
Associate producer: Vincent Winter
Director/Screenwriter: Simon Moore
Camera: Vernon Layton
Editor: Tariq Anwar
Cast: Liam Neeson, Laura San Giacomo, Kenneth Cranham, Alphonsia Emmanuel, Maggie O'Neill

Where Angels Fear to Tread
Stagescreen/LWT
Location: Tuscany/UK
Executive producers: Jeffrey Taylor, Kent Walwin
Producer: Derek Granger
Associate producer: Olivia Stewart
Director: Charles Sturridge
Screenwriters: Tim Sullivan, Derek Granger, from the novel by E M Forster

Camera: Mick Coulter
Editor: Peter Coulson
Cast: Helena Bonham-Carter, Judy Davis, Rupert Graves, Giovanni Guidelli, Helen Mirren

Who Needs a Heart
Black Audio Film Collective
Location: London
Producer: Lina Gopaul
Associate Producer: Avril Johnson
Director/Screenwriter: John Akomfrah
Camera: Nancy Schiesare
Editor: Brand Thumim

The Widowmaker
Central Films
Location: West Midlands
Executive producer: Ted Childs
Producer: Deirdre Keir
Director: John Madden
Screenwriter: Jeremy Brock
Camera: Michael Coulter
Editor: David Rees
Cast: Annabelle Apsion, David Morrissey, Aaron Dawson, Kenneth Welsh, Eileen Nicholas

Why Lockerbie? ▶

▲ Where Angels Fear to Tread

Young Catherine
Consolidated/Primedia/Lenfilm for Turner Network TV
Location: Leningrad
Executive producers: Michael Deeley, Stephen Smallwood
Producer: Neville Thompson
Associate producers: Pat Fearns, Chris Bryant
Director: Michael Anderson
Screenwriter: Chris Bryant
Camera: Ernest Day
Editor: Ron Wiseman
Cast: Vanessa Redgrave, Christopher Plummer, Maximilian Schell, Franco Nero, Julia Ormond

Young Soul Rebels
BFI/Channel 4/La SEPT/Kinowelt/Sankofa Film & Video
Location: London
Executive producers: Ben Gibson, Colin MacCabe, Angela Topping
Producer: Nadine Marsh-Edwards
Director: Isaac Julien
Screenwriters: Isaac Julien, Paul Hallam, Derek McClintock
Camera: Nina Kellgren
Editor: John Wilson
Cast: Valentine Nonyela, Mo Sesay, Dorian Healey, Frances Barber, Sophie Okenedo

▼

bfi – Produced and/or distributed by the British Film Institute

Why Lockerbie?
Granada TV/HBO Showcase
Location: Manchester/Germany/Malta/USA
Executive producers: Ray Fitzwalter, Colin Callender
Producer/Director: Leslie Woodhead
Screenwriter: Michael Eaton
Camera: Ken Westbury
Editor: Edward Mansell
Cast: Timothy West, Ned Beatty, Peter Boyle, Vincent Gardenia, Michael Wincott

The World of Eddie Weary
Fingertip/Yorkshire TV
Location: Leeds/Bradford
Executive producer: Keith Richardson
Producers: Terry Mellis, Steve Lanning
Associate producer: Loretta Ordewer
Director: Alan Grint
Screenwriter: Roy Clarke
Camera: Peter Greenhalgh
Editor: Mike Eustace
Cast: Ray Brooks, Celia Imrie, Connie Booth, Anita Dobson, Brian Glover

PUBLICATIONS

MAJOR REFERENCE BOOKS

The BFI Library (see p8) currently holds some 35,000 books in many languages. Below is a selection of its general cinema and TV reference books in English. The Library produces bibliographies on specific subjects and a list of these is obtainable from the Librarian

CINEMA

ACTT Directory of Members
London: PEAR Books, 1985-86. Ed Peter Avis
Contact information, credits

Academy Awards
New York: Frederick Ungar, 1982. Compiled by Richard Shale. 2nd ed
For 1927-1977, full lists of nominations organised by category and by year. With a supplement containing a chronological listing for 1978-1981. Cross-indexed by name and title

The American Film Institute Catalog of Motion Pictures Produced in the United States Feature Films 1911-1920
Berkeley, Ca: University of California Press, 1988. 2 vols

Feature Films 1921-1930
New York: R R Bowker, 1971. 2 vols

Feature Films 1961-1970
New York: R R Bowker, 1976. 2 vols
Alphabetical listing of US features released during these decades, with credits and plot synopses. Credit and subject indices

A Biographical Dictionary of the Cinema
London: Secker & Warburg, 1975 (revised 1980). By David Thomson
Over 800 entries on directors, actors, producers. Described by its author as 'personal, opinionated and obsessive'

British Film Actors' Credits, 1895-1987
Jefferson, NC: McFarland, 1988. By Scott Palmer
Short career sketches with lists of films

British Film Catalogue, 1895-1985
Newton Abbott: David & Charles, 1986. Ed Denis Gifford. 2nd ed
Basic reference work on British cinema, listing films by month and year of release. Includes footage or r/t, cast, basic technical credits and category

bfi British Films 1927-1939
London: BFI, 1986. Ed Linda Wood
Concise survey of the period followed by annual 'in production' charts, and comprehensive statistics for the British film industry 1927-1939

bfi British Films 1971-1981
London: BFI, 1983. Ed Linda Wood
Concise survey of the period followed by lists, with basic credits, of commercial features made and/or released in Britain between 1971 and 1981

Broadcast Production Guide 1991
London: International Thomson, 1991
Comprehensive directory of companies involved in film and broadcasting in Britain

Catalog of Copyright Entries: Motion Pictures, 1894-1981
(various vols)
Washington: Library of Congress
Entries give copyright date and owner, production company, sound, colour, r/t, director, writer, editor and where appropriate, author and title of original story and composer. Indices of series, authors and organisations

Cinema. A Critical Dictionary
London: Secker & Warburg, 1980. Ed Richard Roud. 2 vols
Biographical and critical entries on over 200 major filmmakers in world cinema

Directors Guild of Great Britain Directory of Members 1991
London: Directors Guild of Great Britain, 1991
Type of work, credits, contact addresses

bfi Directory of International Film and Video Festivals 1991-92
London: British Council/BFI, 1991
Film, television and video festivals, contact addresses, coverage and requirements for awards

Encore Directory 1991
Darlinghurst, NSW: Trade News Corporation, 1991
Australian directory of film, video and television companies, technicians and services

The Great Movie Stars: The Golden Years
London: Macdonald, 1989. By David Shipman. Revised ed
Entries for 200 stars, tracing their lives and careers during the peak years of Hollywood and

mentioning all their films

The Great Movie Stars: The International Years
London: Macdonald, 1989. By David Shipman. Revised ed
Life and career entries for over 230 stars who have become known in the post-war years

The Great Movie Stars: The Independent Years
London: Macdonald, 1991. By David Shipman
Entries for over 90 current major international film stars

The Guinness Book of Movie Facts and Feats
Enfield, Middx: Guinness Books, 1988. By Patrick Robertson. 3rd ed
Illustrated compendium of facts and figures on cinema

Halliwell's Film Guide
London: Grafton, 1989. By Leslie Halliwell. 7th ed
Alphabetical listing of over 10,000 film titles with main credits, brief summary of plot and evaluation

Halliwell's Filmgoer's and Video Viewer's Companion
London: Grafton, 1988. By Leslie Halliwell. 9th ed
Biographical dictionary with entries also on subjects and fictional characters

The Illustrated Guide to Film Directors
London: Batsford, 1983. By David Quinlan
Career studies and full filmographies for 550 directors

The Illustrated Who's Who in British Films
London: B T Batsford, 1978. By Denis Gifford
Outline biographical entries with lists of credits for 1,000 British actors and directors

The International Dictionary of Films and Filmmakers
London: St James Press, 1984-87. 5 vols
Dictionary of world cinema

The International Encyclopedia of Film
London: Michael Joseph, 1972. Ed Roger Manvell and others
Articles on national cinema, technical developments, genre and other topics as well as entries for individuals

The International Film Encyclopedia
London: Macmillan, 1980. By Ephraim Katz
More than 7,000 entries mainly biographical but including industry and technical processes

International Film Guide 1991
London: Andre Deutsch, 1991. Ed Peter Cowie
Regular features include worldwide production surveys, film books and magazines, film schools, and festivals. Also special features and studies of directors

International Motion Picture Almanac 1991
New York: Quigley, 1991.
Yearbook of the US industry, including who's who section, running index of releases from 1955, market analyses from some 50 countries, awards and top US box-office films

Kay's Database: video, film, television 1990-91
London: B L Kay Publishing Co, 1990
Annual UK directory of film, video and television companies and services

Kay's International Production Manual 1987
London: B L Kay Publishing Co
International directory of film, video and television companies and technicians organised by country (and state for USA, Canada and Australia), then by activity

Kemp's International Film and Television Yearbook 1990/91
London: Kemp's Printing and Publishing Co
Information on a wide range of companies and technical services in the UK plus directory entries for the industry abroad

The Knowledge 1991
London: PA Publishing Co, 1991
Annual directory of British film and TV companies and services

The Motion Picture Guide 1927-1990
Evanston, Ill: Cinebooks, 1985 to date. 12 vols plus annual updates
A listing of 50,000 English and notable foreign film titles with credits and synopses

Movies on TV: 1991/92
New York: Bantam Books, 1991. Ed Stephen H Scheuer
Alphabetical listing, with brief notes on films available on TV in USA

New York Times Encyclopedia of Film
New York: Times Books, 1984. Ed Gene Brown. 13 vols
A collection of articles on film from the New York Times 1896-1979, arranged chronologically with an index

The Oxford Companion to Film
London: OUP, 1976. Ed Liz-Anne Bawden
3,000 entries on all aspects of world cinema

Quinlan's Illustrated Directory of Film Stars
London: B T Batsford, 1986. By David Quinlan. Revised ed
1,700 brief career studies of top players and full lists of credits

Reel Facts: The Movie Book of Records
London: Penguin Books, 1981. New York: Vintage Books, 1982 (revised ed). By Cobbett Steinberg
Lists of awards and prize winners, top box office films, most successful stars etc

Researcher's Guide to British Film and Television Collections
London: British Universities Film and Video Council, 1989. Ed Elizabeth Oliver. 3rd ed
Combines guidance for researchers with information about collections of film, video and relevant documentation and how to access them

Researcher's Guide to British Newsreels
London: British Universities Film and Video Council, 1983. Ed James Ballantyne
Full abstracts of writing published between 1901 and 1982 provide a history of British newsreels. Additional information includes lists of newsreel company staff and details of relevant film libraries and documentation centres, their holdings and policies. vol II, 1988

Screen International Film and TV Yearbook 1991/92
London: International Thomson. Ed Peter Noble
A who's who of British film and TV with directory information on cinemas, studios, companies etc, with a foreign section

Screen World 1990
London: Frederick Muller, 1990. Ed John Willis
Pictorial and statistical record of the movie season

60 Years of the Oscar
New York: Abbeville Press, 1989. By Robert Osborne
The official history of the Academy Awards, with full lists of nominations and awards. Index by name and title

The Studio Blu-Book: 1991 Directory
Hollywood: Hollywood Reporter, 1991
Directory of California film and TV specialist services

Variety Film Reviews 1907-1986
New York, London: R R Bowker, 1983-86. 19 vols
Chronologically arranged collection of 'Variety' film reviews, with a title index

Variety International Show Business Reference
New York, London: Garland Publications, 1983. Ed Mike Kaplan
Includes career biographies, credits for films and TV programmes released 1976-1980, major awards

Who Played Who on the Screen
London: B T Batsford, 1988. By Roy Pickard
An A-Z guide to film portrayals of famous figures of fact and fiction

Who Was Who on the Screen
New York: R R Bowker, 1984. By Evelyn Mack Truitt. 3rd ed condensed
Biographical dictionary of over 9,000 screen personalities who died between 1905 and 1975

Who Wrote the Movie, and What Else Did He Write?
Los Angeles: Academy of Motion Picture Arts and Sciences, 1970
An index of American screenwriters and their works, 1936-1969, compiled from Academy publications

Who's Who in the Motion Picture Industry 1989
Hollywood, California: Packard Publishing, 1989. Ed Rodman Gregg
A-Z of directors, producers, writers and executives with credits, addresses, agents

The World Encyclopedia of the Film
London: Studio Vista, 1972. Ed John M Smith and Tim Cawkwell
Biographical entries with filmographies and a film index of 22,000 titles

TV/VIDEO

Actors' Television Credits 1950-1972
Metuchen, NJ: Scarecrow Press, 1973. Supplement 1 (1973-1976), 1978. Supplement 2 (1977-1981), 1982. Supplement 3 (1982-1985), 1986. By James Robert Parish
Each name is followed by a list of titles with transmission date and US TV company

The American Vein; Directors and Directions in Television
London: Talisman Books, 1979. By Christopher Wicking and Tise Vahimagi
Critical evaluation and credits for American TV directors

BBC Annual Report and Accounts 1989/90
London: BBC, 1990.
The Corporation's annual report and accounts

BBC Annual Report and Handbook 1987
London: BBC, 1987.
The Corporation's annual report and accounts with details of organisation, programmes, etc

Broadcast Yearbook and Diary 1991
London: International Thomson, 1991. Ed Nick Radlo
Diary containing information on British television industry and services

The Complete Directory to Prime Time Network TV Shows
New York: Ballantine Books/Random House, 1988. By Tim Brooks and Earle Marsh. 4th ed
The detailed information, from 1946 to the present, includes broadcasting history, front of camera credits and descriptive and evaluative comment

Halliwell's Television Companion
London: Grafton, 1986. By Leslie Halliwell with Philip Purser. 3rd ed
Revision of Halliwell's Teleguide. An A-Z of programmes and personalities in UK television with critical comment

International TV and Video Guide 1987
London: Tantivy Press, 1986. Ed Richard Paterson
The TV and video companion volume to the International Film Guide

International Television and Video Almanac 1991
New York: Quigley, 1991.
Record of US television industry and its personalities. UK and World Market sections

Leonard Maltin's TV Movies and Video Guide, 1991
New York: New American Library, 1991. Ed Leonard Maltin
Brief credits and plot synopses for 15,000 films appearing on US television

Les Brown's Encyclopedia of Television
New York: Zoetrope, 1982. By Les Brown
A-Z guide to programmes, people, history, and business of American television

Professional Video International Yearbook 1987-88
Croydon: Link House, 1985
Directory of technical information for the TV and video industries

TV Facts
New York: Facts on File, 1985. By Cobbett S Steinberg. Revised ed
'50,000 facts about American TV.' Ratings, awards, revenues, prime-time schedules, etc

TV Guide Almanac
New York: Ballantine Books, 1980. Ed Craig T and Peter G Norback
Encyclopedia of information on television in the US

Television and Radio 1988
London: IBA, 1987
Annual IBA guide to independent broadcasting

Television Drama Series Programming: Comprehensive Chronicle 1959-1975
Metuchen, NJ: Scarecrow Press, 1978. Supplements (1975-1980), 1981. (1980-1982), 1983. (1982-1984), 1987. By Larry James Gianakos
Provides a season by season breakdown of American TV drama series. Gives title of each episode, date of first transmission, series stars and guest stars

Television Programming Source Books
Philadelphia: North American Publishing Co, 1990
Annual listing with supplements including all feature films and TV series currently available

to American TV companies or which have already been televised. Includes brief technical and credit information with a plot synopsis and names of export and domestic sales agents

Who's Who on Television
London: Independent Television Publications, 1990/91
Alphabetical listing of information on over 1,000 personalities in British television

PUBLICATIONS AVAILABLE FROM THE INTERNATIONAL FEDERATION OF FILM ARCHIVES

The International Federation of Film Archives (FIAF) was founded in 1938 to encourage the establishment of film archives throughout the world. Its specialist publications are often the only detailed research works available in this field. The titles below can be ordered from: FIAF, Room 113, Canalot Studios, 222 Kensal Road, London W10 5BN. (Prices include p & p)

International Index to Film Periodicals
Published since 1972, this indexes literature on film in over 100 of the world's most important film magazines under general subjects, film and personalities
Available as: microfiches cumulating 15 years, 1972-86, including directors index at £280. 1987-89 cumulation at £35. 1990 cumulating microfiche service (6 despatches per year) £465
Annual published volumes from 1974-88 (£56.00), 1989 (£60.00)

International Index to Television Periodicals
Published since 1979, this indexes literature on television in over 40 media journals under general subjects, television programmes and personalities.
Available as: microfiches cumulating 1979-86, including directors index at £75, 1987-89 cumulation at £15. 1990 cumulating microfiche service (6 despatches per year) at £215
Published volumes cumulated as 1979-80, 1981-82 (£25.00 each), 1983-86 (£56.00), 1987-88 (£35.00)

FIAF Classification Scheme for Literature on Film and Television
By Karen Jones and Michael Moulds, 1990. 52nd ed
120pp, £30

The following FIAF publications are available from the FIAF Secretariat, rue Franz Merjay 190, 1180 Brussels, Belgium. (Prices, in Belgian francs, include p & p)

FIAF Bulletin
Published twice a year by FIAF Brussels. Annual subscription BF400 + bank costs

Annual Bibliography of FIAF Members' Publications
Prepared by the National Film & TV Archives, Ottawa from 1979.
BF300 + bank costs

Bibliography of National Filmographies
Compiled by Dorothea Gebauer. Edited by Harriet W Harrison, 1985
Annotated list of filmographies, journals and other publications
80pp, BF800

Cinema 1900-1906: An Analytical Study

Proceedings of the FIAF Symposium at Brighton 1978. Vol I contains transcriptions of the papers, Vol II contains an analytical filmography of 550 films of the period. Prepared by the National Film Archive, London, 1982
372pp and 391pp, BF1500

Evaluating Computer Cataloguing Systems – A Guide for Film Archivists

By Roger Smithson for the Cataloguing Commission, 1989
35pp BF900
(Available with 'Study on the Usage of Computers for Film Cataloguing' for BF1500)

50 Years of Film Archives 1938-1988

FIAF yearbook published for the 50th anniversary, containing descriptions of its 78 members and observers and a historical account of its development. 1988
203pp, BF950

Glossary of Filmographic Terms

Compiled by Jon Gartenberg, 1985. Lists and defines English, French, German, Spanish and Russian terms
141pp, BF1000

Glossary of Filmographic Terms, Version II

Compiled by Jon Gartenberg, 1989. Includes terms and indexes in English, French, German, Spanish, Russian, Swedish, Portuguese, Dutch, Italian, Czech, Hungarian, Bulgarian
149pp, BF1300

Manuel des Archives du Film

Edited by Eileen Bowser and John Kuiper, 1980. Basic manual on the functioning of a film archive. French version
151pp, BF1000

Preservation and Restoration of Moving Images and Sound

A report by the FIAF Preservation Commission, covering the physical properties of film and sound tape, their handling and storage, and the equipment used by film archives to ensure permanent restoration, 1986
268pp, BF1300

The Slapstick Symposium

Edited by Eileen Bowser, 1988. Dealings and proceedings of the Early American Slapstick Symposium held at the Museum of Modern Art, New York, May 1985
121pp, BF800

Study on the Usage of Computers for Film Cataloguing

Edited by Roger Smithson, 1985. A survey and analysis on the usage of computers for the cataloguing of material in film and television archives
275pp, BF900
(Available with 'Evaluating Computer Cataloguing Systems – A Guide for Film Archivists' for BF1500)

Technical Manual of the FIAF Preservation Committee

A user's manual on practical film and video preservation procedures. Ongoing loose leaf publication in A4 + folder. 1987-
150pp (by end 1989), BF1500

ENGLISH LANGUAGE FILM, TV, VIDEO AND CABLE PERIODICALS

A select list of film, television, video and cable journals, most of which can be studied in the BFI Library (see p8)

£ Afterimage

(irregular)
20 Landrock Road
London N9 7HL
Each issue deals with a specific area of film and/or critical theory

American Cinematographer

(monthly)
1782 N Orange Drive
Hollywood CA 90028
USA
International journal of film and video production techniques. Published by the American Society of Cinematographers

American Film

(10 pa)
BPI Communications Inc
1515 Broadway
39th Floor
New York NY 10036
USA
Journal of the AFI. A magazine of the Film and Television Arts

Animator

(quarterly)
13 Ringway Road
Park Street
St Albans
Herts AL2 2RE
Intended for all levels of animators and animation fans

Ariel (weekly)

BBC
Room G1
12 Cavendish Place
London W1A 1AA
The BBC staff magazine. Contains articles of general interest about the BBC

Audio Visual

(monthly)
PO Box 109
Maclaren House
Scarbrook Road
Croydon
Surrey CR9 1QH
Tel: 081 760 9690
Aimed at management and businesses which use audiovisual materials

Audiovisual Librarian (quarterly)

Library Association Publishing
7 Ridgmount Street
London WC1E 7AE
Tel: 071 636 7543
The official organ of the audiovisual groups Aslib and the LA. Includes articles, book reviews and a bibliographic update

bfi British National Film and Video Catalogue

(quarterly)
British Film Institute
21 Stephen Street
London W1P 1PL
Tel: 071 255 1444
Details of films and videocassettes made available for non-theatrical use in the UK, classified by subject. Cumulates annually

Broadcast (weekly)

International Thomson Publishing
2nd Floor
7 Swallow Place
London W1R 7AA
Tel: 071 491 9484
Television industry news magazine. Regular sections devoted to video, cable and industry news. Now incorporates Television Weekly

Broadcasting

(weekly)
Broadcasting Publications Inc
1705 De Sales Street
NW Washington DC 20036
USA
America's main broadcasting trade weekly

Bulgarian Films

(8 pa)
Bulgarian Cinematography State Corporation
135-a Rakovski Street
Sofia
Bulgaria
News of the Bulgarian cinema in English

The Business of Film (monthly)

24 Charlotte Street
London W1P 1HJ
Tel: 071 580 0141
Aimed at film industry professionals – producers, distributors, exhibitors, investors, financiers

Cable and Satellite Europe (monthly)

531-533 Kings Road

London SW10 0TZ
Journal covering the European cable and satellite industry

Cineaste
(quarterly)
200 Park Avenue South
New York NY 10003
USA
Reviews, interviews, articles on the art and politics of cinema. International in scope

Cinema Papers
(6 pa)
MTV Publishing
43 Charles Street
Abbotsford
Victoria
Australia 3067
Australia's leading film journal

Combroad
(quarterly)
Commonwealth Broadcasting Association
Broadcasting House
London W1A 1AA
Tel: 071 580 4468
Articles on Commonwealth television, radio and broadcasting in general

Commercials
(monthly)
EMAP Commercials
12-13 Kingly Street
London W1V 5LP
Tel: 071 494 2035
Articles and news from the commercials industry

Communication Research Trends
(quarterly)
Centre for the Study of Communication and Culture
221 Goldhurst Terrace
London NW6 3EP
Tel: 071 328 2868
Information on international communications research

Czechoslovak Film
(quarterly)
Czechoslovak Filmexport
Press Department
Praha 1
Vaclavske Namesti '28
Czechoslovakia
News from the Czech cinema in English

Direct (8 pa)
Directors' Guild of Great Britain
125 Tottenham Court Road
London W1P 9HN
Tel: 071 387 7131
Journal of Directors' Guild of Great Britain

EMMY (6 pa)
Academy of Television Arts and Sciences
3500 West Olive Avenue
Suite 700
Burbank CA 91505
USA
Published by the Academy of Television Arts and Sciences

Empire (monthly)
42 Great Portland Street
London W1N 5AH
Tel: 071 436 5430
Articles, news and reviews of films, videos and books

Encore
(fortnightly)
PO Box 1377
Darlinghurst
NSW 2010
Australia
Entertainments magazine now incorporating The Australian Film Review

European Journal of Communication
(quarterly)
Sage Publications
6 Bonhill Street
London EC2A 4PU
Tel: 071 374 0645
Publication covering diverse aspects of communication theory and research in Europe

FTT and BETA News (10 pa)
111 Wardour Street
London W1V 4AY
Tel: 071 437 8506
The official journal of BECTU (Broadcasting Entertainment and Cinematograph Technicians Union)

Fact (monthly)
Producers Alliance for Cinema and Television
Paramount House
162-170 Wardour Street
London W1V 4LA
Tel: 071 437 7700
PACT members monthly

bfi **Film**
(monthly)
British Federation of Film Societies
Film Society Unit
BFI
21 Stephen Street
London W1P 1PL
Tel: 071 255 1444
Non-commercial aspects of film. See also p166

Film Comment
(bi-monthly)
140 West 65th Street
New York NY 10023
USA
Published by the Film Society of Lincoln Center. Aimed at intelligent American filmgoers

£ **Film Dope**
(irregular)
88 Port Arthur Road
Nottingham NG2 4GE
Mainly an A-Z of international film personalities but also includes some long interviews

Film Monthly
Argus House
Boundary Way
Hemel Hempstead
H12 7ST
Film-fan magazine incorporating 'Photoplay'

Film Quarterly
University of California
Berkeley CA 94720
USA
International critical journal with particular emphasis on film literature and book reviews

Film Review
(monthly)
Orpheus Publications
4th Floor
Centro House
Mandela Street
London NW1 0DU
Tel: 071 387 3848
All English-speaking films on release and in production covered in reviews, interviews, articles and pictures, book and record reviews. Now incorporating 'Films and Filming'

Films in Review
(10 pa)
PO Box 589
Lennox Hill Station
New York NY 10021
USA
Popular magazine aimed at 'film buffs'. Notable for career articles and historical information

£ **Framework**
(irregular)
Sankofa Film and Video
Unit K
32-34 Gordon House Road
London NW5 1LP

Historical Journal of Film, Radio and Television (bi-annual)
Carfax Publishing
PO Box 25
Abingdon
Oxfordshire OX14 3UE
Academic journal founded by IAMHIST in 1981. Articles, book reviews, archival reports and reviews of film, television and radio programmes of historical or educational importance

The Hollywood Reporter (daily)
6715 Sunset Boulevard
Hollywood CA 90028
USA
International showbusiness trade paper

Impact (bi-monthly)
Producers Alliance for Cinema and Television
Paramount House
162-170 Wardour Street
London W1V 4LA
Tel: 071 437 7700

In Camera (quarterly)
Kodak
Motion Pictures & TV Products
PO Box 66
Station Road
Hemel Hempstead
Herts HP1 1JU
Magazine published as a service to the Film and Television industry

Independent Media
(monthly)
7 Campbell Court
Bramley
Basingstoke
Hants RG26 5EG
Tel: 0256 882032
A broadsheet designed for makers and consumers of independent film and video productions. Covers television and radio media, with items on international, education and art topics, news, interviews and reviews. Sponsored by the Arts Council of Great Britain and Channel 4

Intermedia (bi-monthly)
International Institute of Communications
Tavistock House South
Tavistock Square
London WC1H 9LF
Tel: 071 388 0671
Articles on international communications and broadcasting

International Broadcasting (monthly)
7 Swallow Place
London WC1R 7AA
Tel: 071 491 9484
Tracks key developments worldwide in broadcast quality video and audio technology and systems. Independent comment and analysis on issues influencing European production and broadcasting strategies

International Media Law (monthly)
21-27 Lamb's Conduit Street
London WC1N 3NJ
A monthly bulletin on rights clearances and legal practice. Includes a regular update section

Journal of Broadcasting and Electronic Media (quarterly)
Broadcast Education Association
1771 N Street
NW Washington DC 20036
USA
Articles on current research mainly in the US; book reviews

Journal of Communication (quarterly)
Oxford University Press
200 Madison Avenue
New York NY 10016
USA
Theoretical and research articles and book reviews

Journal of Film and Video (quarterly)
Division of Mass Communication
Emerson College
100 Beacon Street
Boston MA 02116
USA
Articles on current academic research in film and television, as well as film and video practices, book reviews, video and film reviews

The Journal of Media Law and Practice (3 pa)
Frank Cass
11 Gainsborough Road
London E11 1RS
Tel: 071 530 4226
Covers media law relating to copyright and video recording. Includes articles, news and book reviews

The Journal of Popular Film and Television (quarterly)
Heldref Publications
4000 Albemarle Street
NW
Washington DC 20016
USA
Dedicated to popular film and television in the broadest sense. Concentration on commercial cinema and TV

Jump Cut (quarterly)
PO Box 865
Berkeley CA 94701
USA
Radical critical journal with a special interest in politics of cinema

Kino (irregular)
Dina Lom
Century House
4th Floor
100 Oxford Street
London W1N 9FB
Tel: 071 580 4422
Official publication in English on German cinema published by the German Film Board and the German Film Export Union

£ **Media, Culture and Society** (quarterly)
Sage Publications
6 Bonhill Street
London EC2A 4PU
Tel: 071 374 0645
Articles on the mass media in their political, cultural and historical contexts

Media Report to Women (bi-monthly)
3306 Ross Place
NW Washington DC 20008
USA
Published by the Women's Institute for Freedom of the Press, this journal deals with what women are thinking and doing to change the communications media

£ **Movie** (irregular)
PO Box 1
Moffat
Dumfriesshire DG10 9SU
Tel: 0683 20808
Journal of theory and criticism with special emphasis on American cinema

Moving Pictures International (weekly)
26 Soho Square
London W1V 5FJ
Tel: 071 494 0011
Worldwide coverage of television, film, video and cable

Onfilm (bi-monthly)
PO Box 6374
Wellington
New Zealand
The magazine of the NZ picture industry

£ **Picture House** (irregular)
5 Coopers Close
Burgess Hill
West Sussex RH15 8AN
The magazine of the Cinema Theatre Association, presenting historical articles on cinema buildings, circuits, architects, etc

Postscript (3 pa)
Jacksonville University
Jacksonville FL 32211
USA
Journal of essays in film and the humanities

Premiere (monthly)
Murdoch Magazines
2 Park Avenue
New York NY 10016
USA
News, reviews and interviews

£ **Primetime** (irregular)
Wider TV Access
c/o Flashbacks
6 Silver Place
London W1R 3LJ
Primetime is published by WTVA, a society devoted to the wider circulation of, and discussion about, old TV programmes, with reviews of TV material available on video

Quarterly Review of Film and Video
University of Southern California
School of Cinema-Television
University Park
Los Angeles
CA 90089-2211
USA
Academic journal dealing with cinema in context of larger aesthetic or sociopolitical issues

Radio Times (weekly)
BBC
35 Marylebone High Street
London W1M 4AA
Tel: 071 580 5577
Guide to all programmes on UK television and BBC radio

£ **Screen** (quarterly)
(incorporating Screen Education)
Department of Theatre, Film and Television Studies
University of Glasgow
Glasgow G12 8QF
Aimed at teachers/ lecturers in film theory

Screen Digest (monthly)
37 Gower Street
London WC1E 6HH
Tel: 071 580 2842
An industry news digest covering film, TV, cable, satellite, video and other multimedia presentations. Has a centre page reference section every month on subjects like law, statistics or sales

Screen Finance (fortnightly)
Financial Times Business Information
30-31 Great Sutton Street
London EC1V 0DX
Tel: 071 490 8994
International financial news for the film and television industry

Screen International (weekly)
7 Swallow Place
249-259 Regent Street
London W1R 7AA

Tel: 071 734 9452
Cinema industry magazine mainly focused on the cinema, with a regular section which has industry news and information about upcoming productions for TV and video

Sight and Sound (monthly)
British Film Institute
21 Stephen Street
London W1P 1PL
Tel: 071 255 1444
International critical journal of film and television relaunched in May 1991 incorporating 'Monthly Film Bulletin', and including synopses and reviews of all films theatrically released. See also p12

Soviet Film (monthly)
9b Gnezdnikovsky Pereulok
Moscow 103009
USSR
News in English of Soviet films and filmmakers

The Stage and Television Today (weekly)
47 Bermondsey Street
London SE1 3XT
Tel: 071 403 1818
'Television Today' constitutes the middle section of 'The Stage' and is a weekly trade paper

TV Times (weekly)
Independent Television Publications
247 Tottenham Court Road
London W1P 0AU
Tel: 071 636 3666
Guide to all UK television programmes

Television (monthly)
The Royal Television Society
Tavistock House East
Tavistock Square
London WC1H 9HR
Tel: 071 387 1970
Articles on the television industry, technical and general

Television Week
67 Clerkenwell Road
London EC1R 5BH
Tel: 071 251 6222
News magazine for the television industry

Televisual (monthly)
Centaur Publications
St Giles House
50 Poland Street
London W1V 4AX
Tel: 071 437 4377
Glossy publication aimed at the industrial and business user of video. Features, details of shows and exhibitions, a hardware catalogue and new programmes of interest to the industrial user

Trade Guide (weekly)
Manek Chambers
Lamington Road
Bombay 400 004
India
Trade journal

Variety (weekly)
475 Park Avenue South
New York NY 10016
USA
The American showbiz journal including worldwide coverage of cinema and other media

The Velvet Light Trap (irregular)
PO Box 9240
Madison
Wisconsin 53715
USA
Critical journal in which each issue addresses a particular aspect of film theory or culture

Video Today (monthly)
Argus Specialist Publications
Argus House
Boundary Way
Hemel Hempstead
Herts
Consumer-orientated magazine with short reviews of new releases. It also includes readers' problems, hardware tests, articles, with information on London and regional dealers

Video Trade Weekly
20 Bowling Green Lane
London EC1R 0BD
Weekly newspaper aimed at the retail trade, with news about the distribution industry, new products, festivals, awards and so on

Viewfinder (3 pa)
British Universities Film and Video Council
55 Greek Street
London W1V 5LR
Tel: 071 734 3687
News and reviews of new productions available to workers in higher education, articles on, for example, storing and handling videotape. Includes some book reviews

Wide Angle (quarterly)
Johns Hopkins University Press
701 W 40th Street
Baltimore MD 21211
USA
Academic journal with each issue concentrating on a single aspect of film culture

FOREIGN LANGUAGE FILM PERIODICALS

L'Avant-Scène Cinéma (monthly)
16 rue des Quatre Vents
75006 Paris
France
Articles, reviews, interviews, often complete scripts

Cahiers de la Cinémathèque (irregular)
Palais des Congrès
66000 Perpignan
France
Published with the Cinémathèque de Toulouse. Each issue treats one subject

Cahiers du Cinéma (monthly)
9 Passage de la Boule Blanche
75012 Paris
France
Leading critical journal with a special interest in US cinema

Chaplin (bi-monthly)
Box 27 126
102 52 Stockholm
Sweden
Journal of the Swedish Film Institute

Cine Cubano (irregular)
Calle 23 no 1155
Havana
Cuba
Critical journal mainly concerned with Latin-American cinema

Cineinforme (bi-monthly)
Gran Via 64
28013 Madrid
Spain
Trade magazine on Spanish and Latin-American cinema

Cinema & Cinema (quarterly)
Editrice Clueb Bologna
Via Marsala 24
40126 Bologna
Italy
Critical journal with a special interest in Italian cinema

Cinema Nuovo (bi-monthly)
Casello Postale 362
70100 Bari
Italy
Serious critical journal – features many book reviews

Cinéma (monthly)
49 rue Faubourg-Poissonnière
75009 Paris
France
Reviews of current releases in France, articles, interviews, book reviews, plus a section on films on television

Film (monthly)
Westerbachstrasse 33-35
6000 Frankfurt 90
Germany
Authoritative film journal featuring articles and criticism

Film a Doba (monthly)
Halkova 1, 120 72
Praha 2
Czechoslovakia
International film journal with emphasis on eastern European cinema

Film Echange (quarterly)
16 rue des Quatre-Vents
75006 Paris
France
Substantial journal of information on international law, economics and sociology of the audiovisual media

Film Echo/Film Woche
(72 pa)
Wilhelmstrasse 42
6200 Wiesbaden
Germany
German trade magazine

Film Français
(weekly)
90 rue de Flandre
75943 Paris
France
Trade paper for French cinema professionals. Includes video information

Filmowy Serwis Prasowy (2 per month)
ul Mazawiecka 6/8
00-950 Warszawa
Poland
Official journal of Polish film contains information on films and filmmakers

Frauen und Film
(irregular)
Verlag Stoemfeld/Roter Stern
Postfach 79
CH-4007 Basel
Switzerland
Concentrates on issues concerning women and film

Griffithiana
(quarterly)
La Cineteca del Friuli
Via Osoppo 26
3304 Gemona (UD)
Italy
Italian/English journal devoted to silent cinema and animation

Iskusstvo Kino
(monthly)
A-319
ul. Usievicha 9
125319 Moscow
USSR
Leading Soviet journal concentrating on national cinema with credits

Kosmorama
(quarterly)
Det Danske Filmmuseum
Store Søndervoldstraede
1419 København K
Denmark
Leading Danish periodical containing essays, credits and film and book reviews

Positif (monthly)
Nouvelles Editions Opta
1 Quai Conti
75006 Paris
France
International critical journal with wide festival coverage

Revue du Cinéma/ Image et Son
(monthly)
86-88 avenue du Docteur-Arnold-Netter
75012 Paris
France
Reviews of films, television and video. Aimed at cine-club audience

Skoop
(10 pa)
Postbus 871
2300 AW Leiden
Netherlands

INDEXES TO FILM AND TV PERIODICALS

For many years BFI Library Services (see p8) has been indexing periodicals from around the world for information and articles about film and TV programme titles, personalities, organisations, festivals, awards and other subjects. All of this information is keyed into the department's database SIFT (Summary of Information on Film and TV). As the number of periodicals published has grown, so the proportion which the department can index has diminished. Happily there has been a corresponding increase in the number of published indexes which complement the service provided by the department. A selection of such publications is listed below

The Critical Index: A Bibliography of Articles on Film in English, 1946-1973
By John C Gerlach and Lana Gerlach. New York; London: Teachers College Press, 1974

The Film Index: A Bibliography
Vol 1 The Film as Art: compiled by Workers of the Writers' Program of the Work Projects Administration in the City of New York. New York: Museum of Modern Art Film Library; HW Wilson, 1941. Vol 2 The Film as Industry. White Plains, NY: Kraus, 1985. Vol 3 The Film in Society. White Plains, NY: Kraus, 1985

The Film Literature Index
Quarterly Author-Subject Periodical Index to the International Literature of Film 1973 to date. Albany, NY; Film & Television Documentation Center, 1975 to date. Quarterly issues with annual cumulations

Index to Critical Film Reviews in British and American Film Periodicals
Compiled by Stephen E Bowles. New York: Burt Franklin, 1974

Index to Motion Pictures Reviewed by Variety, 1907-1980
By Max Joseph Alvarez. Metuchen, NJ; London: Scarecrow Press, 1982

International Index to Film Periodicals 1972 to date International Index to Television Periodicals 1979 to date
These annotated guides are published as monthly cumulative microfiche and annual volumes. Over 100 journals from over 20 countries are indexed to include general subjects, reviews and personalities together with author and director indexes. London: International Federation of Film Archives

Motion Picture Directors: A Bibliography of Magazine and Periodical Articles, 1900-1972
Compiled by Mel Schuster. Metuchen, NJ: Scarecrow Press, 1973

Motion Picture Performers: A Bibliography of Magazine and Periodical Articles, 1900-1969
Compiled by Mel Schuster. Metuchen, NJ: Scarecrow Press, 1973. Supplement 1 (1970-74), 1976

The New Film Index: A Bibliography of Magazine Articles in English, 1930-1970
By Richard Dyer MacCann and Edward S Perry. New York: EP Dutton, 1975

Performing Arts Biography Master Index
Ed Barbara McNeil and Miranda C Herbert. 2nd ed Detroit: Gale Research Co, 1981

Retrospective Index to Film Periodicals 1930-1971
By Linda Batty. New York; London: R R Bowker, 1975

 – BFI publication

 – BFI-supported

RELEASES

Listed here are films of 40 minutes and over, both British and foreign, which had a theatrical release in the UK during 1990 and the first quarter of 1991. (For early 1990 releases, see the 1991 edition of the Handbook). Entries quote the title, country of origin, director/s, leading players, distributor, release date (NB the production date may vary substantially from this), duration, gauge if other than 35mm, and the Monthly Film Bulletin reference. A list of distributors' addresses and telephone numbers can be found on p140. Back issues of MFB are available for reference from BFI Library Services

A.W.O.L.
(18) USA Dir Sheldon Lettich with Jean-Claude Van Damme, Harrison Page, Deborah Rennard. Guild, 21 Sep 1990. 108 mins. MFB Oct 1990 p286

Acque di primavera (Torrents of Spring)
(PG) Italy/France Dir Jerzy Skolimowski with Timothy Hutton, Nastassja Kinski, Valeria Golino. Curzon, 18 May 1990. 101 mins. English version. MFB May 1990 p144

The Adventures of Ford Fairlane
(18) USA Dir Renny Harlin with Andrew Dice Clay, Wayne Newton, Priscilla Presley. 20th Century Fox, 15 Feb 1991. 104 mins. MFB Mar 1991 p70

Air America
(15) USA Dir Roger Spottiswoode with Mel Gibson, Robert Downey Jnr., Nancy Travis. Guild, 11 Jan 1991. 118 mins. MFB Jan 1991 p8

▼ Akira

Akira
(12) Japan Dir Katsuhiro Otomo with the voices of Mitsuo Iwata, Nozumo Sasaki, Mami Koyama. ICA Projects, 25 Jan 1991. 124 mins. Subtitles. MFB Mar 1991 p65

All Dogs Go to Heaven
(U) Eire Dir Don Bluth with the voices of Burt Reynolds, Judith Barsi, Dom De Luise. Rank, 6 Apr 1990. 84 mins. MFB Apr 1990 p93

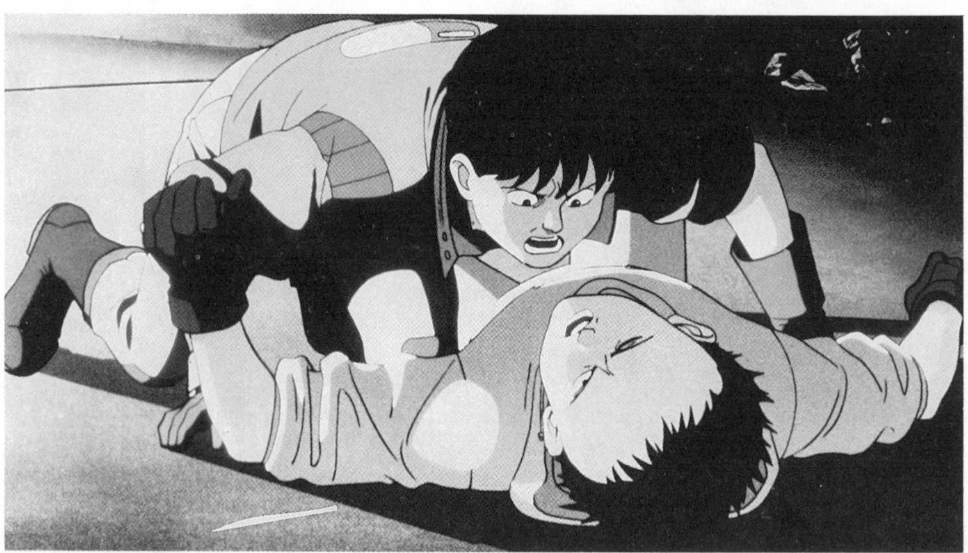

Almost an Angel
(PG) USA Dir John Cornell with Paul Hogan, Elias Koteas, Linda Kozlowski. UIP, 26 Dec 1990. 95 mins. MFB Feb 1991 p38

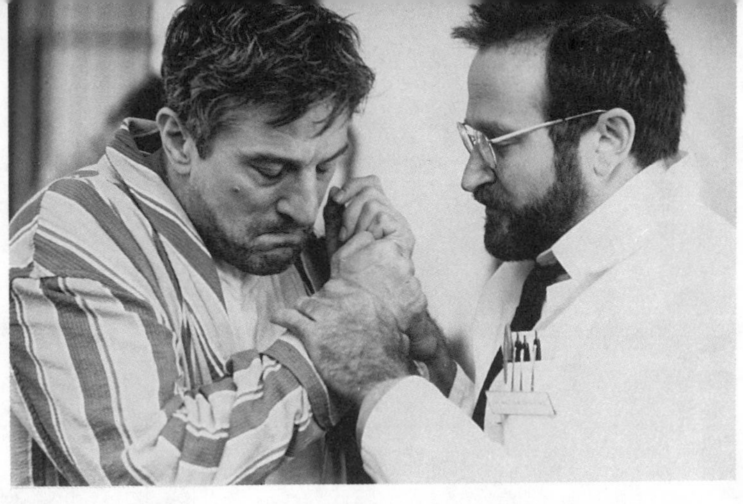

American Friends
(PG) UK Dir Tristram Powell with Michael Palin, Trini Alvarado, Connie Booth. MCEG Virgin Vision, 22 Mar 1991. 96 mins. MFB Apr 1991 p98

L'Ami Retrouvé (Reunion)
(12) France/West Germany/UK Dir Jerry Schatzberg with Jason Robards, Christien Anholt, Samuel West. Rank, 6 July 1990. 101 mins. English version. MFB July 1990 p189

An Angel at My Table
(15) New Zealand Dir Jane Campion with Kerry Fox, Karen Fergusson, Alexia Keogh. Artificial Eye, 28 Sep 1990. 160 mins. MFB Nov 1990 p314

▼

Anita: Dances of Vice
see **Anita: Tänze des Lasters**

Anita: Tänze des Lasters (Anita: Dances of Vice)
Germany Dir Rosa von Praunheim with Lotti Huber, Ina Blum, Mikael Honesseau. ICA Projects, 13 July 1990. 85 mins. Subtitles. MFB Aug 1990 p215

Another 48 HRS
(18) USA Dir Walter Hill with Eddie Murphy, Nick Nolte, Brion James. UIP, 21 Sep 1990. 96 mins. MFB Sep 1990 p252

Arachnophobia
(PG) USA Dir Frank Marshall with Jeff Daniels, Julian Sands, John Goodman. Warner Bros, 4 Jan 1991. 110 mins. MFB Jan 1991 p9

L'Atalante
(PG) France Dir Jean Vigo with Michel Simon, Jean Dasté, Dita Parlo. Artificial Eye, 20 July 1990. 88 mins. Subtitles. Newly restored 35mm print

¡Atame! (Tie Me Up! Tie Me Down!)
(18) Spain Dir Pedro Almodóvar with Victoria Abril, Antonio Banderas, Loles Leon. Enterprise Pictures, 6 July 1990. 102 mins. Subtitles. MFB July 1990 p189

Aufzeichnungen zu Kleidern und Städten (Notebook on Cities and Clothes)
(U) Germany Dir Wim Wenders. Documentary with Yohji Yamamoto. Artificial Eye, 8 June 1990. 80 mins. English version; some English subtitles. MFB July 1990 p190

Avalon
(U) USA Dir Barry Levinson with Armin Mueller-Stahl, Elizabeth Perkins, Joan Plowright. Columbia Tri-Star, 1 Mar 1991. 128 mins. MFB Mar 1991 p71

▲ Awakenings
(12) USA Dir Penny Marshall with Robin Williams, Robert De Niro, Julie Kavner. Columbia Tri-Star, 15 Mar 1991. 121 mins. MFB Mar 1991 p72

Babar: The Movie
(U) Canada/France Dir Alan Bunce with the voices of Gordon Pinsent, Elizabeth Hannah, Lisa Yamanaka. Winstone Films, 27 July 1990. 76 mins. MFB Sep 1990 p253

La Baule-les pins (C'est la vie)
(12) France Dir Diane Kurys with Nathalie Baye, Richard Berry, Julie Bataille. Electric Pictures/Contemporary, 1 Mar 1991. 96mins. Subtitles. MFB Mar 1991 p68

Beautiful Dreamers
(15) Canada Dir John Harrison with Colm Feore, Rip Torn, Wendel Meldrum. Blue Dolphin, 18 Jan 1991. 108 mins. MFB Jan 1991 p10

▲ **Anita: Tänze des Lasters (Anita: Dances of Vice)**

Back to the Future Part III
(PG) USA Dir Robert Zemeckis with Michael J Fox, Christopher Lloyd, Mary Steenburgen. UIP, 13 July 1990. 124 mins. MFB July 1990 p192

Bad Influence
(18) USA Dir Curtis Hanson with Rob Lowe, James Spader, Lisa Zane. Entertainment, 5 Oct 1990. 100 mins. MFB Oct 1990 p286

Berlin Jerusalem
France Dir Amos Gitai with Lisa Kreuzer, Rivka Neuman, Marcus Stockhausen. ICA Projects, 8 Mar 1991. 89 mins. MFB Apr 1991 p96

Betsy's Wedding
(15) USA Dir Alan Alda with Joey Bishop, Madeline Kahn, Alan Alda. Warner Bros, 26 Oct 1990. 94 mins. MFB Nov 1990 p315

▲ *The Big Man*
(18) UK Dir David Leland with Liam Neeson, Joanne Whalley-Kilmer, Billy Connolly. Palace Pictures, 31 Aug 1990. 116 mins. MFB Oct 1990 p287

The Big Picture
(15) USA Dir Christopher Guest with Kevin Bacon, Emily Longstreth, J T Walsh. Hobo, 30 Nov 1990. 100 mins. MFB Dec 1990 p348

The Big Steal
(15) Australia Dir Nadia Tass with Ben Mendelsohn, Claudia Karvan, Steve Bisley. Hobo, 29 Mar 1991. 100 mins. MFB Apr 1991 p100

Bill and Ted's Excellent Adventure
(PG) USA Dir Stephen Herek with Keanu Reeves, Alex Winter, Robert V Barron. Castle Premier, 13 Apr 1990. 89 mins. MFB Apr 1990 p96

Bird on a Wire
(12) USA Dir John Badham with Mel Gibson, Goldie Hawn, David Carradine. UIP, 10 Oct 1990. 111 mins. MFB Nov 1990 p316

Black Rain
see ***Kuroi Ame***

Black Rainbow
(15) UK Dir Mike Hodges with Rosanna Arquette, Jason Robards, Tom Hulce. Palace Pictures, 20 July 1990. 103 mins. MFB June 1990 p160

Blind Fury
(15) USA Dir Phillip Noyce with Rutger Hauer, Terrance O'Quinn, Lisa Blount. Columbia Tri-Star, 13 July 1990. 85 mins. MFB Aug 1990 p218

Blood Oath
(15) Australia Dir Stephen Wallace with Bryan Brown, George Takei, Terry O'Quinn. Rank, 15 Mar 1991. 108 mins. MFB Apr 1991 p100

▼ **Blue Steel**

Blue Heat (The Last of the Finest)
(15) USA Dir John MacKenzie with Brian Dennehy, Joe Pantoliano, Jeff Fahey. Rank, 21 Sep 1990. 106 mins. MFB Sep 1990 p254

Blue Steel
(18) USA Dir Kathryn Bigelow with Jamie Lee Curtis, Ron Silver, Clancy Brown. Vestron, 23 Nov 1990. 102 mins. MFB Nov 1990 p311

Boda secreta (Secret Wedding)
Argentina/ Netherlands/Canada Dir Alejandro Agresti with Tito Haas, Mirtha Busnelli, Sergio Poves Campos. Metro Pictures, 4 Jan 1991. 95 mins. MFB Jan 1991 p11

The Boost
(18) USA Dir Harold Becker with James Woods, Sean Young, John Kapelos. Hemdale, 27 July 1990. 95 mins. MFB Aug 1990 p219

The Brave Little Toaster
(U) USA Dir Jerry Rees with the voices of Jon Levitz, Deanna Oliver, Tim Stack. Castle Premier, 3 Aug 1990. 90 mins. MFB Oct 1990 p288

Breaking In
(15) USA Dir Bill Forsyth with Burt Reynolds, Casey Siemaszko, Sheila Kelly. Castle Premier, 31 Aug 1990. 94 mins. MFB Sep 1990 p255

Buddy's Song
(12) UK Dir Claude Whatham with Roger Daltrey, Chesney Hawkes, Sharon Duce. Castle Premier, 1 Mar 1991. 106 mins. MFB Mar 1991 p74

Bullseye!
(15) USA Dir Michael Winner with Michael Caine, Roger Moore, Sally Kirkland. Castle Premier, 2 Nov 1990. 92 mins. MFB Nov 1990 p317

Bye Bye Blues
(PG) Canada Dir Anne Wheeler with Michael Ontkean, Rebecca Jenkins, Luke Reilly. Artificial Eye, 21 Sep 1990. 117 mins. MFB Oct 1990 p289

▲ **The Brave Little Toaster**

Cadillac Man
(15) USA Dir Roger Donaldson with Robin Williams, Tim Robbins, Pamela Reed. Rank, 5 Oct 1990. 98 mins. MFB Oct 1990 p291

bfi ***Captain Johnno*** ▶
(U) Australia Dir Mario Andreacchio with John Waters, Damien Walters, Rebecca Sykes. 16mm. Subtitles for the deaf. BFI, 7 Apr 1990. 100 mins. MFB May 1990 p127

Carnival of Souls
(15) USA Dir Herk Harvey with Candace Hilligoss, Frances Feist, Sidney Berger. Palace Pictures, 24 Aug 1990. 95 mins. MFB Sep 1990 p274

Catchfire
(15) USA Dir Alan Smithee with Dennis Hopper, Jodie Foster, Dean Stockwell. First Independent, 25 Jan 1991. 99mins. MFB Feb 1991 p39

C'est la vie
see ***La Baule-les pins***

Chicago Joe and the Showgirl
(18) UK Dir Bernard Rose with Kiefer Sutherland, Emily Lloyd, Patsy Kensit. Palace Pictures, 6 Apr 1990. 103 mins. MFB Apr 1990 p99

Child's Play 2
(15) USA Dir John Lafia with Alex Vincent, Jenny Agutter, Gerrit Graham. UIP, 11 Jan 1991. 84 mins. MFB Jan 1991 p13

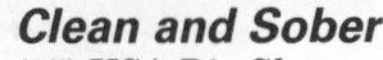

▲ **Cold Dog Soup**

Clean and Sober
(15) USA Dir Glenn Gordon Caron with Michael Keaton, Kathy Baker, Morgan Freeman. Warner Bros, 8 June 1990. 124 mins. MFB June 1990 p161

Cold Dog Soup
(15) USA Dir Alan Metter with Randy Quaid, Frank Whaley, Christine Harnos. Palace Pictures, 15 Feb 1991. 88 mins. MFB Mar 1991 p75

Cold Feet
(15) USA Dir Robert Dornhelm with Keith Carradine, Sally Kirkland, Tom Waits. MCEG Virgin Vision, 27 Apr 1990. 94 mins. MFB May 1990 p123

Come See the Paradise
(15) USA Dir Alan Parker with Dennis Quaid, Tamlyn Tomita, Sab Shimono. 20th Century Fox, 30 Nov 1990. 131 mins. MFB Dec 1990 p349

The Comfort of Strangers
see ***Cortesie per gli ospiti***

Coming Out
(15) Germany (formerly East) Dir Heiner Carow with Matthias Freihof, Dagmar Manzel, Dirk Kummer. Metro Pictures, 15 Mar 1991. 113 mins. Subtitles. MFB Apr 1991 p101

RELEASES

Common Threads: Stories from the Quilt ▶
USA Dirs Robert Epstein, Jeffrey Friedman. Documentary narrated by Dustin Hoffman with Gregg Baker, Robert Bazell. ICA Projects, 31 Aug 1990. 75 mins. 16mm. MFB Feb 1991 p40

Communion
(15) USA Dir Philippe Mora with Christopher Walken, Lindsay Crouse, Joel Carlson. Vestron, 12 Oct 1990. 101 mins. MFB Oct 1990 p291

Conte de printemps (A Tale of Springtime)
(U) France Dir Eric Rohmer with Anne Teyssèdre, Hugues Quester, Florence Darel. Artificial Eye, 15 June 1990. 112 mins. Subtitles. MFB June 1990 p151

Cortesie per gli ospiti (The Comfort of Strangers)
(18) Italy/UK Dir Paul Schrader with Christopher Walken, Rupert Everett, Natasha Richardson. Rank, 30 Nov 1990. 105 mins. MFB Jan 1991 p5 ▼

Courage Mountain
(U) USA Dir Christopher Leitch with Juliette Caton, Charlie Sheen, Leslie Caron. Entertainment, 6 Apr 1990. 98 mins. MFB Apr 1990 p100

Crazy People
(15) USA Dir Tony Bill with Dudley Moore, Daryl Hannah, Paul Reiser. UIP, 14 Sep 1990. 92 mins. MFB June 1990 p256

Creator
(15) USA Dir Ivan Passer with Peter O'Toole, Mariel Hemingway, Vincent Spano. Entertainment, 8 June 1990. 107 mins. MFB July 1990 p193

Crimes and Misdemeanors
(15) USA Dir Woody Allen with Alan Alda, Martin Landau, Woody Allen. Rank, 27 July 1990. 104 mins. MFB Aug 1990 p220

Criminal Law
(18) USA Dir Martin Campbell with Gary Oldman, Kevin Bacon, Karen Young. Hemdale, 16 Nov 1990. 117 mins. MFB Nov 1990 p318

The Crossing
(15) Australia Dir George Ogilvie with Russell Crowe, Robert Mammone, Danielle Spencer. Enterprise Pictures, 11 Jan 1991. 94 mins

Cry Baby
(12) USA Dir John Waters with Johnny Depp, Amy Locane, Susan Tyrell. UIP, 20 July 1990. 85 mins. MFB Aug 1990 p222

Cyrano de Bergerac
(U) France Dir Jean-Paul Rappeneau with Gérard Depardieu, Jacques Weber, Anne Brochet. Artificial Eye, 11 Jan 1991. 138 mins. Subtitles. MFB Jan 1991 p14

Daddy's Dyin', Who's Got the Will?
(12) USA Dir Jack Fisk with Beau Bridges, Beverly D'Angelo, Tess Harper. Palace Pictures, 25 Jan 1991. 96 mins. MFB Feb 1991 p41

Dances with Wolves
(12) USA Dir Kevin Costner with Kevin Costner, Mary McDonnell, Graham Greene. Guild, 8 Feb 1991. 179 mins. MFB Feb 1991 p42

Darkman
(15) USA Dir Sam Raimi with Liam Neeson, Frances McDormand, Colin Friels. UIP, 16 Nov 1990. 91 mins. MFB Nov 1990 p319

▲ Cyrano de Bergerac

Dark Angel
(18) USA Dir Craig R Baxley with Dolph Lundgren, Brian Benben, Betsy Brantley. Entertainment, 13 July 1990. 91 mins. MFB July 1990 p193

Dark Habits
see ***Entre Tinieblas***

Days of Thunder
(12) USA Dir Tony Scott with Tom Cruise, Robert Duvall, Nicole Kidman. UIP, 10 Aug 1990. 107 mins. MFB Sep 1990 p257

Death Warrant
(18) USA Dir Deran Sarafian with Jean-Claude Van Damme, Robert Guillaume, Cynthia Gibb. UIP, 7 Dec 1990. 88 mins

December Bride ▶
(PG) UK Dir Thaddeus O'Sullivan with Donal McCann, Saskia Reeves, Ciaran Hinds. BFI, 8 Feb 1991. 87 mins. MFB Feb 1991 p43

Delta Force 2
(18) USA Dir Aaron Norris with Chuck Norris, John R Ryan, Billy Drago. UIP, 4 Jan 1991. 105 mins

Desperate Hours
(15) USA Dir Michael Cimino with Mickey Rourke, Anthony Hopkins, Mimi Rogers. 20th Century Fox, 29 Mar 1991. 105 mins. MFB Mar 1991 p76

Diamond Skulls
(18) UK Dir Nick Broomfield with Gabriel Byrne, Amanda Donohoe, Michael Hordern. MCEG Virgin Vision, 8 June 1990. 87 mins. MFB July 1990 p194

Dick Tracy
(PG) USA Dir Warren Beatty with Warren Beatty, Madonna, Al Pacino. Warner Bros, 6 July 1990. 105 mins. MFB Aug 1990 p215

Die Hard 2
(15) USA Dir Renny Harlin with Bruce Willis, Bonnie Bedelia, William Atherton. 20th Century Fox, 17 Aug 1990. 120 mins. MFB Sep 1990 p258

Diexue Shuang Xiong (The Killer)
(18) Hong Kong Dir John Woo with Chow Yun-Fat, Danny Lee, Sally Yeh. Palace Pictures, 10 Aug 1990. 111 mins. Subtitles; also available in dubbed version. MFB Sep 1990 p260

Dom za Vesanje (Time of the Gypsies)
(15) Yugoslavia Dir Emir Kusturica with Davor Dujmovic, Bora Todorovic, Ljubica Adzovic. Enterprise Pictures, 7 Dec 1990. 142 mins. Subtitles. MFB Apr 1990 p102

Dr. M
(18) Germany/Italy/France Dir Claude Chabrol with Alan Bates, Jennifer Beals, Jan Niklas. Hobo, 30 Nov 1990, 115 mins. English version. MFB Dec 1990 p351

▲ ***Dreams***
(PG) USA Dir Akira Kurosawa with Akira Terao, Mitsunori Isaki, Martin Scorsese. Warner Bros, 25 May 1990. 120 mins. Japanese dialogue, English subtitles; some English dialogue. MFB June 1990 p159

The Emperor's Naked Army Marches On
see ***Yuki Yukite Shingun***

The Enchantment
see ***Yuwakusha***

Enemies, A Love Story
(15) USA Dir Paul Mazursky with Anjelica Huston, Ron Silver, Lena Olin. 20th Century Fox, 6 Apr 1990. 120 mins. MFB Apr 1990 p103

Entre Tinieblas (Dark Habits)
(15) Spain Dir Pedro Almodóvar with Cristina S Pascual, Marisa Paredes, Carmen Maura. Metro Pictures, 24 Aug 1990. 100 mins. Subtitles. MFB Oct 1990 p292

The Exorcist III
(18) USA Dir William Peter Blatty with George C Scott, Ed Flanders, Brad Dourif. 20th Century Fox, 23 Nov 1990. 109 mins. MFB Dec 1990 p352

Fear
(18) USA Dir Rockne S O'Bannon with Ally Sheedy, Pruitt Taylor, Lauren Hutton. First Independent, 8 Mar 1991. 95mins. MFB Mar 1991 p77

Fire Birds

see ***Wings of the Apache***

The First Power
(18) USA Dir Robert Resnikoff with Lou Diamond Phillips, Tracy Griffith, Jeff Kober. Castle Premier, 21 Sep 1990. 98 mins. MFB Oct 1990 p294

Flatliners
(15) USA Dir Joel Schumacher with Kiefer Sutherland, Julia Roberts, Kevin Bacon. Columbia Tri-Star, 9 Nov 1990. 114 mins. MFB Nov 1990 p320

The Fool
(U) UK Dir Christine Edzard with Derek Jacobi, Cyril Cusack, Ruth Mitchell. Hobo, 18 Jan 1991. 140 mins. MFB Dec 1990 p353 ▼

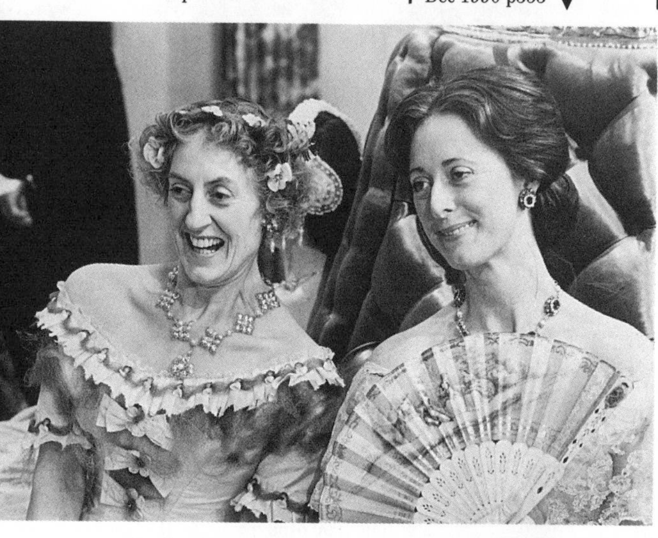

Felix the Cat: The Movie
(U) USA Dir Tibor Hernádi with the voices of Chris Phillips, Maureen O'Connell, Peter Neuman. Transatlantic, 3 Aug 1990. 82 mins. MFB Oct 1990 p293

The Field
(12) UK Dir Jim Sheridan with Richard Harris, John Hurt, Tom Berenger. Granada, 22 Feb 1991. 110 mins. MFB Mar 1991 p78

Fools of Fortune
(15) UK Dir Pat O'Connor with Mary Elizabeth Mastrantonio, Iain Glen, Julie Christie. Palace Pictures, 22 June 1990. 104 mins. MFB July 1990 p195

The Fourth War
(15) USA Dir John Frankenheimer with Roy Scheider, Jürgen Prochnow, Tim Reid. Guild, 22 June 1990. 91 mins. MFB July 1990 p196

Frankenstein Unbound ▲
(18) USA Dir Roger Corman with John Hurt, Bridget Fonda, Raul Julia. Blue Dolphin, 11 Jan 1991. 85 mins. MFB Jan 1991 p3

Fresh Horses
(15) USA Dir David Anspaugh with Molly Ringwald, Andrew McCarthy, Patti D'Arbanville. Columbia Tri-Star, 29 June 1990. 103 mins. MFB July 1990 p197

The Freshman
(PG) USA Dir Andrew Bergman with Marlon Brando, Matthew Broderick, Bruno Kirby. Columbia Tri-Star, 2 Nov 1990. 103 mins. MFB Dec 1990 p354

The Garden
(15) UK Dir Derek Jarman with Tilda Swinton, Johnny Mills, Kevin Collins. Artificial Eye, 4 Jan 1991. 92 mins. MFB Jan 1991 p15

Georgette Meunier
Germany Dirs Tania Stöcklin, Cyrille Rey-Coquais with Tiziana Jelmini, Diana Stöcklin, Dina Leipzig. Electric Pictures, 1 Apr 1990. 82 mins. Subtitles. MFB May 1990 p128

Ghost
(12) USA Dir Jerry Zucker with Patrick Swayze, Demi Moore, Whoopi Goldberg. UIP, 5 Oct 1990. 127 mins. MFB Oct 1990 p295

The Godfather Part III
(15) USA Dir Francis Ford Coppola with Al Pacino, Andy Garcia, Talia Shire. UIP, 8 Mar 1991. 162 mins. 70mm. MFB Apr 1991 p91

The Gods Must Be Crazy II
(PG) South Africa Dir Jamie Uys with N!xau, Lena Farugia, Hans Strydom. 20th Century Fox, 18 May 1990. 98 mins. MFB July 1990 p198

Golden Braid
(15) Australia Dir Paul Cox with Chris Haywood, Gosia Dobrowolska, Paul Chubb. Artificial Eye, 29 Mar 1991. 91 mins. MFB Apr 1991 p103

GoodFellas
(18) USA Dir Martin Scorsese with Robert De Niro, Ray Liotta, Joe Pesci. Warner Bros, 26 Oct 1990. 146 mins. MFB Dec 1990 p355

Green Card
(12) USA Dir Peter Weir with Gérard Depardieu, Andie MacDowell, Bebe Neuwirth. Warner Bros, 1 Mar 1991. 107 mins. MFB Mar 1991 p79

Gremlins 2: The New Batch
(12) USA Dir Joe Dante with Zach Galligan, Phoebe Cates, John Glover. Warner Bros, 27 July 1990. 106 mins. MFB Aug 1990 p224

La Grieta (The Rift)
(15) Spain Dir J P Simon with Jack Scalia, R Lee Ermey, Ray Wise. Warner Bros, 22 June 1990. 83 mins. English version. MFB Aug 1990 p225

The Grifters
(18) USA Dir Stephen Frears with Anjelica Huston, John Cusack, Annette Bening. Palace Pictures, 1 Feb 1991. 119 mins. MFB Feb 1991 p31

The Guardian
(18) USA Dir William Friedkin with Jenny Seagrove, Dwier Brown, Carey Lowell. UIP, 31 Aug 1990. 93 mins. MFB Sep 1990 p262

The Handmaid's Tale
(18) USA/Germany Dir Volker Schlöndorff with Natasha Richardson, Faye Dunaway, Aidan Quinn. MCEG Virgin Vision, 2 Nov 1990. 108 mins. MFB Nov 1990 p321

Hard to Kill
(18) USA Dir Bruce Malmuth with Steven Seagal, Kelly Le Brock, Bill Sadler. Warner Bros, 1 June 1990. 96 mins. MFB July 1990 p198

▲ Heart Condition

▼ Heavy Petting

Harlem Nights
(15) USA Dir Eddie Murphy with Richard Pryor, Redd Foxx, Eddie Murphy. UIP, 25 May 1990. 116 mins. MFB July 1990 p200

Hardware
(18) UK Dir Richard Stanley with Dylan McDermott, Stacey Travis, John Lynch. Palace Pictures, 5 Oct 1990. 90 mins. MFB Oct 1990 p296

Havana
(15) USA Dir Sydney Pollack with Robert Redford, Lena Olin, Raul Julia. UIP, 25 Jan 1991. 145 mins. MFB Feb 1991 p45

Heart Condition
(15) USA Dir James D Parriot with Bob Hoskins, Denzel Washington, Chloe Webb. Enterprise Pictures, 12 Oct 1990. 95 mins. MFB Nov 1990 p322

Heavy Petting
USA Dir Obie Benz. Documentary with David Byrne, Paula Longendyke, Sandra Bernhard. ICA Projects, 14 Dec 1990. 80mins. MFB Jan 1991 p16

Henry & June
(18) USA Dir Philip Kaufman with Fred Ward, Uma Thurman, Maria De Medeiros. UIP, 23 Nov 1990. 136 mins. MFB Jan 1991 p17

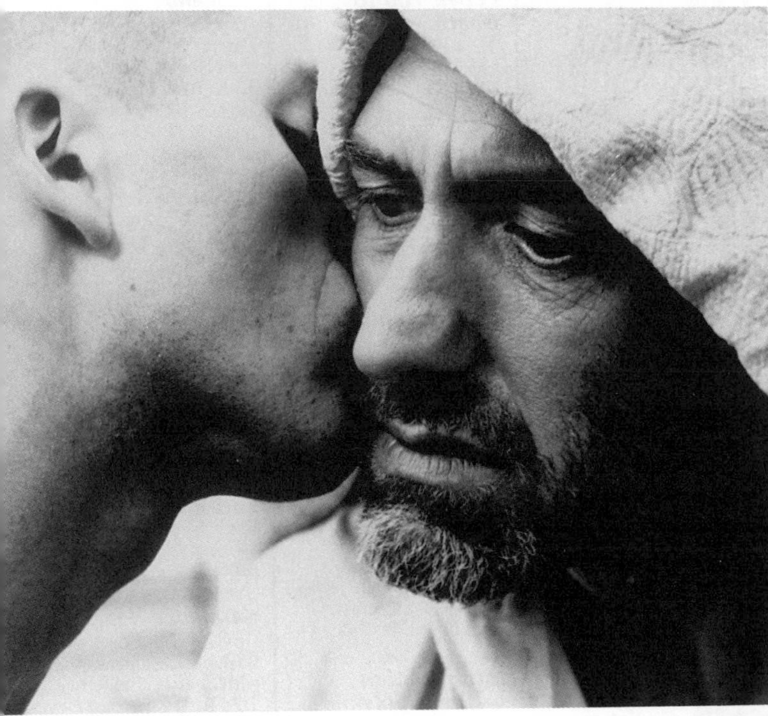

◀ The Garden

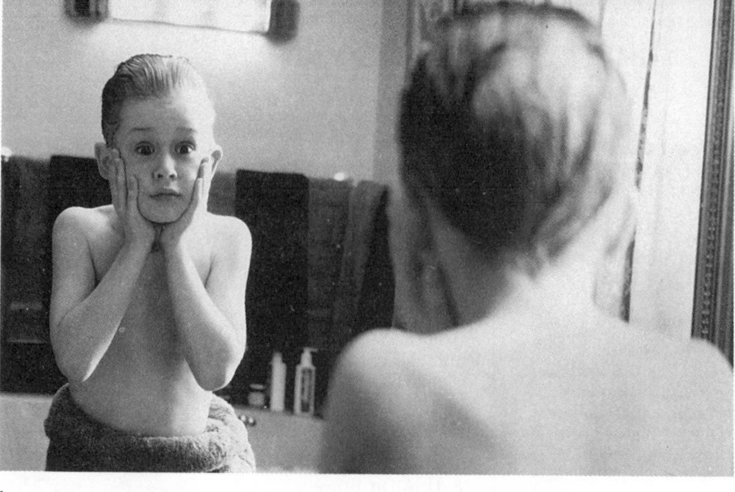

Hidden Agenda
(15) UK Dir Ken Loach with Brad Dourif, Brian Cox, Frances McDormand. Enterprise Pictures, 11 Jan 1991. 108 mins. MFB Jan 1991 p19

Home Alone ▶
(PG) USA Dir Chris Columbus with Macaulay Culkin, Joe Pesci, Daniel Stern. 20th Century Fox, 7 Dec 1990. 103 mins. MFB Jan 1991 p19

The Hot Spot
(18) USA Dir Dennis Hopper with Don Johnson, Virginia Madsen, Jennifer Connelly. Rank, 7 Dec 1990. 130 mins. MFB Dec 1990 p343

◀ House Party

House Party
(15) USA Dir Reginald Hudlin with Christopher Reid, Robin Harris, Christopher Martin. Enterprise Pictures, 31 Aug 1990. 104 mins. MFB Sep 1990 p262

The Hunt for Red October
(PG) USA Dir John McTiernan with Sean Connery, Alec Baldwin, Sam Neill. UIP, 18 Apr 1990. 135 mins. 70mm Panavision. MFB Apr 1990 p108

Hush-a-Bye-Baby
N Ireland Dir Margo Harkin with Emer McCourt, Michael Liebman, Sinéad O'Connor. ICA Projects, 27 July 1990. 72 mins

I Bought a Vampire Motorcycle
(18) UK Dir Dirk Campbell with Neil Morrissey, Amanda Noar, Michael Elphick. Hobo, 6 July 1990. 105 mins. MFB July 1990 p200

I Hired a Contract Killer
(15) Finland/Sweden Dir Aki Kaurismäki with Jean-Pierre Léaud, Margi Clarke, Kenneth Colley. Electric Pictures/Contemporary, 15 Feb 1991. 80 mins. Filmed in English. MFB Feb 1991 p46

I Love You to Death
(15) USA Dir Lawrence Kasdan with Kevin Kline, Tracey Ullman, Joan Plowright. Columbia Tri-Star, 21 Sep 1990. 97 mins. MFB Sep 1990 p263

The Icicle Thief
see ***Ladri di saponette***

An Innocent Man
(18) USA Dir Peter Yates with Tom Selleck, F Murray Abraham, Laila Robins. Warner Bros, 28 Sep 1990. 114 mins. MFB June 1990 p163

Internal Affairs
(18) USA Dir Mike Figgis with Richard Gere, Andy Garcia, Nancy Travis. UIP, 4 May 1990. 115 mins. MFB May 1990 p130

Interrogation
see ***Przesluchanie***

bfi ***James Baldwin: The Price of the Ticket*** ▶
(PG) USA Dir Karen Thorsen. Documentary with James Baldwin, Maya Angelou, Amiri Baraka. BFI, 20 Apr 1990. 87 mins. 16mm. MFB June 1990 p164

Jetsons: The Movie
(U) USA Dirs William Hanna, Joseph Barbera with the voices of George O'Hanlon, Mel Blanc, Penny Singleton. UIP, 22 Mar 1991. 83 mins. MFB Mar 1991 p80

Joe Versus the Volcano
(PG) USA Dir John Patrick Shanley with Tom Hanks, Meg Ryan, Lloyd Bridges. Warner Bros, 6 July 1990. 102 mins. MFB July 1990 p201

Johnny Handsome
(15) USA Dir Walter Hill with Mickey Rourke, Ellen Barkin, Elizabeth McGovern. Guild, 11 May 1990. 94 mins. MFB May 1990 p130

Ju Dou
(15) China/Japan Dirs Zhang Yimou, Yang Fengliang with Gong Li, Li Baotian, Li Wei. ICA Projects, 22 Mar 1991. Mandarin dialogue; English subtitles. 94 mins. MFB Apr 1991 p105

Kamikaze Hearts
(18) USA Dir Juliet Bashore. Documentary with Sharon Mitchell, Tigr Mennett, Jon

Martin. Metro Pictures, 20 July 1990. 77 mins. 16mm. MFB Aug 1990 p226

Kickboxer 2
(18) USA Dir Albert Pyun with Sasha Mitchell, Peter Boyle, Dennis Chan. Entertainment, 1 Feb 1991. 90 mins

The Killer
see ***Diexue Shuang Xiong***

Kill Me Again
(18) USA Dir John R Dahl with Val Kilmer, Joanne Whalley-Kilmer, Michael Madsen. Palace Pictures, 3 Aug 1990. 95 mins. MFB Oct 1990 p297

▲ I Love You to Death

Kid
(18) USA Dir John Mark Robinson with C Thomas Howell, Sarah Trigger, Brian Austin Green. Entertainment, 2 Nov 1990. 91 mins. MFB Nov 1990 p323

Kindergarten Cop
(12) USA Dir Ivan Reitman with Arnold Schwarzenegger, Penelope Anne Miller, Pamela Reed. UIP, 1 Feb 1991. 110 mins. MFB Feb 1991 p47

King of the Wind
(U) USA Dir Peter Duffell with Frank Finlay, Jenny Agutter, Nigel Hawthorne. HTV International, 25 May 1990. 102 mins. MFB June 1990 p165

King Ralph
(PG) USA Dir David S Ward with John Goodman, Peter O'Toole, Camille Coduri. UIP, 29 Mar 1991. 97 mins

Komitas
Germany Dir Don Askarian with Samuel Ovasapian, Onig Saadetian, Margarita Woskanjan. In Armenian with subtitles. ICA Projects, 20 Apr 1990. 96 mins

Korczak
(PG) Poland/ Germany/France/UK Dir Andrzej Wajda with Wojtek Pszoniak, Ewa Dałkowska, Piotr Kozlowski. Artificial Eye, 26 Oct 1990. 113 mins. Subtitles. MFB Nov 1990 p324

The Krays
(18) UK Dir Peter Medak with Billie Whitelaw, Gary Kemp, Martin Kemp. Rank, 27 Apr 1990. 119 mins. MFB Apr 1990 p110

◀ *Kuroi Ame (Black Rain)*
(PG) Japan Dir Shohei Imamura with Yoshiko Tanaka, Kazuo Kitamura, Etsuko Ichihara. Artificial Eye, 29 June 1990. 123 mins. Subtitles. MFB Aug 1990 p227

Kvinnorna på taket (The Women on the Roof)
(15) Sweden Dir Carl-Gustaf Nykvist with Amanda Ooms, Helena Bergström, Stellan Skarsgård. Curzon, 14 Sep 1990. 90 mins. Subtitles. MFB Sep 1990 p264

Ladri di saponette (The Icicle Thief)
(PG) Italy Dir Maurizio Nichetti with Maurizio Nichetti, Caterina Sylos Labini, Federico Rizzo. Metro Pictures, 16 Nov 1990. 90 mins. Subtitles. MFB Nov 1990 p325
▼

Last Images of the Shipwreck
see ***Ultimas imagenes del naufragio***

The Last of the Finest
see ***Blue Heat***

Leviathan
(18) USA/Italy Dir George P Cosmatos with Peter Weller, Richard Crenna, Amanda Pays. 20th Century Fox, 11 May 1990. 96 mins. MFB May 1990 p132

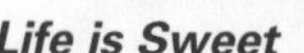

Life is Sweet ▲
(15) UK Dir Mike Leigh with Alison Steadman, Jim Broadbent, Claire Skinner. Palace Pictures, 22 Mar 1991. 103 mins. MFB Mar 1991 p81

Limit Up
(12) USA Dir Richard Martini with Nancy Allen, Dean Stockwell, Brad Hall. Medusa, 22 June 1990. 88 mins. MFB June 1990 p165

Auberjonois, Christopher Daniel Barnes, Jodi Benson. Warner Bros, 19 Oct 1990. 82 mins. MFB Oct 1990 p298

Longtime Companion
(15) USA Dir Norman René with Stephen Caffrey, Patrick Cassidy, Brian Cousins. Palace Pictures, 21 Sep 1990. 99 mins. MFB Nov 1990 p326
▼

Listen to Me
(15) USA Dir Douglas Day Stewart with Kirk Cameron, Jami Gertz, Roy Scheider. Columbia Tri-Star, 6 July 1990. 110 mins. MFB Aug 1990 p228

The Little Mermaid
(U) USA Dirs John Musker, Ron Clements with the voices of René

Look Who's Talking
(12) USA Dir Amy Heckerling with John Travolta, Kirstie Alley, Olympia Dukakis. Columbia Tri-Star, 6 Apr 1990. 96 mins. MFB Apr 1990 p113

Look Who's Talking Too
(12) Dir Amy Heckerling

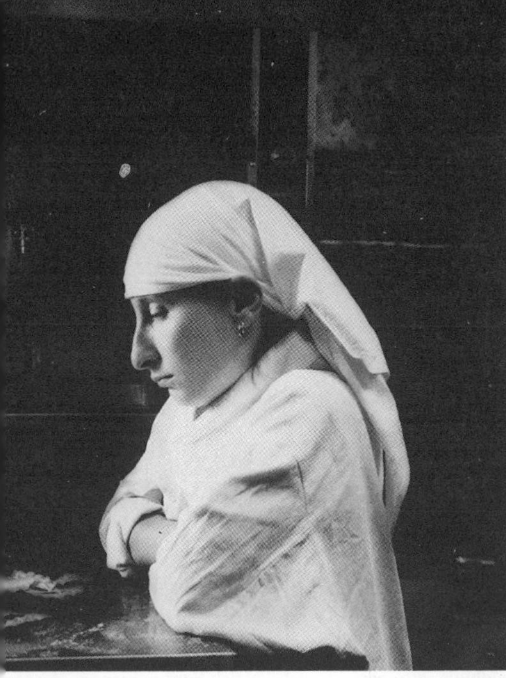

with John Travolta, Kirstie Alley, Olympia Dukakis. Columbia Tri-Star, 22 Mar 1991. 80 mins. MFB Mar 1991 p82

Lord of the Flies
(15) USA Dir Harry Hook with Balthazar Getty, Chris Furrh, Danuel Pipoly. Palace Pictures, 29 June 1990. 90 mins. MFB July 1990 p203

Lost Angels
see ***The Road Home***

Love at Large
(15) USA Dir Alan Rudolph with Tom Berenger, Elizabeth Perkins, Anne Archer. Rank, 2 Nov 1990. 97 mins. MFB Nov 1990 p327

Love Hurts
(15) USA Dir Bud Yorkin with Jeff Daniels, Cynthia Sikes, Judith Ivey. Vestron, 30 Nov 1990. 101 mins. MFB Dec 1990 p357

Loverboy
(15) USA Dir Joan Micklin Silver with Patrick Dempsey, Kate Jackson, Kirstie Alley. Columbia Tri-Star, 25 May 1990. 98 mins. MFB June 1990 p166

Madhouse
(15) USA Dir Tom Ropelewski with John Larroquette, Kirstie Alley, Alison LaPlaca. Rank, 16 Nov 1990. 90 mins. MFB Nov 1990 p329

The Mad Monkey
see ***El Mono Loco***

Le Mahabharata (The Mahabharata)
(U) France Dir with Peter Brook with Urs Bihler, Ryszard Cieslak, Georges Corraface. MCEG Virgin Vision, 26 Dec 1990. 171 mins. English version. MFB Jan 1991 p20

The Mahabharata
see ***Le Mahabharata***

Le Maître de musique (The Music Teacher)
(U) Belgium Dir Gérard Corbiau with José Van Dam, Anne Roussel, Philippe Volter. Mainline, 12 Oct 1990. 98 mins. Subtitles. MFB Oct 1990 p281

Maniac Cop 2
(U) USA Dir William Lustig with Robert Davi, Claudia Christian, Michael Lerner. Medusa, 25 Jan 1991. 87 mins. MFB Jan 1991 p22

▲ Memphis Belle

The Match Factory Girl
see ***Tulitikkutehtaan Tyttö***

Max mon amour
(18) France/USA Dir Nagisa Oshima with Charlotte Rampling, Anthony Higgins, Bernard-Pierre Donnadieu. Electric Pictures/Contemporary, 18 May 1990. 92 mins. Partly subtitled. MFB May 1990 p132

Meet the Applegates
(15) USA Dir Michael Lehmann with Ed Begley Jnr, Stockard Channing, Dabney Coleman. Castle Premier, 22 Feb 1991. 89 mins. MFB Feb 1991 p48

Memphis Belle
(12) UK Dir Michael Caton-Jones with Matthew Modine, Eric Stoltz, Tate Donovan. Warner Bros, 7 Sep 1990. 102 mins. MFB Sep 1990 p265

Men at Work
(12) USA Dir Emilio Estevez with Charlie Sheen, Emilio Estevez, Leslie Hope. Entertainment, 15 Feb 1991. 90 mins. MFB Feb 1991 p49

Men Don't Leave
(15) USA Dir Paul Brickman with Jessica Lange, Arlis Howard, Joan Cusack. Warner Bros, 3 Aug 1990. 114 mins. MFB Aug 1990 p230

Metropolitan
(15) USA Dir Whit Stillman with Carolyn Farina, Edward Clements, Christopher Eigeman. Mainline, 23 Oct 1990. 98 mins. MFB Dec 1990 p358

Miami Blues
(18) USA Dir George Armitage with Fred Ward, Jennifer Jason Leigh, Alec Baldwin. Rank, 14 Dec 1990. 97 mins. MFB Dec 1990 p359

Mignon è partita (Mignon Has Left)
Italy/France Dir Francesca Archibugi with Stefania Sandrelli, Jean-Pierre Duriez, Leonardo Ruta. Metro Pictures, 17 Aug 1990. 90 mins. Subtitles. MFB Aug 1990 p231

▲ Milou en mai (Milou in May)

Mignon Has Left
see **Mignon è partita**

Miller's Crossing
(18) USA Dir Joel Coen with Gabriel Byrne, Marcia Gay Harden, Albert Finney. 20th Century Fox, 15 Feb 1991. 115 mins. MFB Feb 1991 p50

Milou en mai (Milou in May)
(15) France/Italy Dir Louis Malle with Michel Piccoli, Miou-Miou, Michel Duchaussoy. Curzon, 31 Aug 1990. 106 mins. Subtitles. MFB June 1990 p167

Milou in May
see **Milou en mai**

Miracle Mile
(15) USA Dir Steve DeJarnatt with Anthony Edwards, Mare Winningham, John Agar. Hemdale, 18 Jan 1991. 87 mins. MFB Feb 1991 p51

Miss Firecracker
(PG) USA Dir Thomas Schlamme with Holly Hunter, Mary Steenburgen, Tim Robbins. Rank, 15 June 1990. 103 mins. MFB June 1990 p168

Mister Frost
(15) France/UK Dir Philippe Setbon with Jeff Goldblum, Alan Bates, Kathy Baker. Blue Dolphin, 7 Dec 1990. 103 mins. Filmed in English. MFB Dec 1990 p361

Mister Johnson
(12) USA Dir Bruce Beresford with Maynard Eziashi, Pierce Brosnan, Edward Woodward. 20th Century Fox, 29 Mar 1991. 102 mins

Mo' Better Blues
(15) USA Dir Spike Lee with Denzel Washington, Spike Lee, Wesley Snipes. UIP, 28 Sep 1990. 130 mins. MFB Oct 1990 p299

Un Monde sans pitié (A World Without Pity)
(15) France Dir Eric Rochant with Hippolyte Girardot, Mireille Perrier, Yvan Attal. Artificial Eye, 7 Dec 1990. 88 mins. Subtitles. MFB Dec 1990 p361

El Mono Loco (The Mad Monkey)
(18) Spain Dir Fernando Trueba with Jeff Goldblum, Miranda Richardson, Anémone. Hobo, 9 Nov 1990. 108 mins. English version. MFB Nov 1990 p329

Monsieur Hire
(15) France Dir Patrice Leconte with Michel Blanc, Sandrine Bonnaire, Luc Thuillier. Palace Pictures, 27 Apr 1990. 80 mins. Panavision. Subtitles. MFB Apr 1990 p114

Moon 44
(15) Germany Dir Roland Emmerich with Michael Paré, Lisa Eichhorn, Malcolm McDowell. Medusa, 6 July 1990. 99 mins. Filmed in English. MFB Sep 1990 p266

Mountains of the Moon
(15) USA Dir Bob Rafelson with Iain Glen, Patrick Bergin, Fiona Shaw. Guild, 20 Apr 1990. 136 mins. MFB Apr 1990 p115

Mr. and Mrs. Bridge
(PG) USA Dir James Ivory with Paul Newman, Joanne Woodward, Margaret Welsh. Palace Pictures, 22 Feb 1991. 124 mins. MFB Jan 1991 p23

Music Box
(15) USA Dir Costa-Gavras with Jessica Lange, Armin Mueller-Stahl, Frederic Forrest. Guild, 15 June 1990. 126 mins. MFB May 1990 p135

▼ Mo' Better Blues

The Music Teacher
see ***Le Maître de musique***

My Blue Heaven
(PG) USA Dir Herbert Ross with Steve Martin, Rick Moranis, Joan Cusack. Warner Bros, 9 Nov 1990. 96 mins. MFB Nov 1990 p330

Narrow Margin
(15) USA Dir Peter Hyams with Gene Hackman, Anne Archer, James B Sikking. Guild, 18 Jan 1991. 97 mins. MFB Jan 1991 p23

The Nasty Girl
see ***Das schreckliche Mädchen***

The Neverending Story II: The Next Chapter
(U) Germany Dir George Miller with Jonathan Brandis, Kenny Morrison, Clarissa Burt. Warner Bros, 14 Dec 1990. 90 mins. Filmed in English. MFB Dec 1990 p362

Next of Kin
(15) USA Dir John Irvin with Patrick Swayze, Liam Neeson, Adam Baldwin. Warner Bros, 27 Apr 1990. 109 mins. MFB June 1990 p169

Nightbreed
(18) USA Dir Clive Barker with Craig Sheffer, Anne Bobby, David Cronenberg. 20th Century Fox, 28 Sep 1990. 101 mins. MFB Oct 1990 p279

A Nightmare on Elm Street: The Dream Child
(18) USA Dir Stephen Hopkins with Robert Englund, Lisa Wilcox, Kelly Jo Minter. Enterprise Pictures, 11 May 1990. 90 mins. MFB June 1990 p169

Nikita ▶
(18) France/Italy Dir Luc Besson with Anne Parillaud, Jean-Hugues Anglade, Tcheky Karyo. Palace Pictures, 12 Oct 1990. 116 mins. Subtitles. MFB Nov 1990 p331

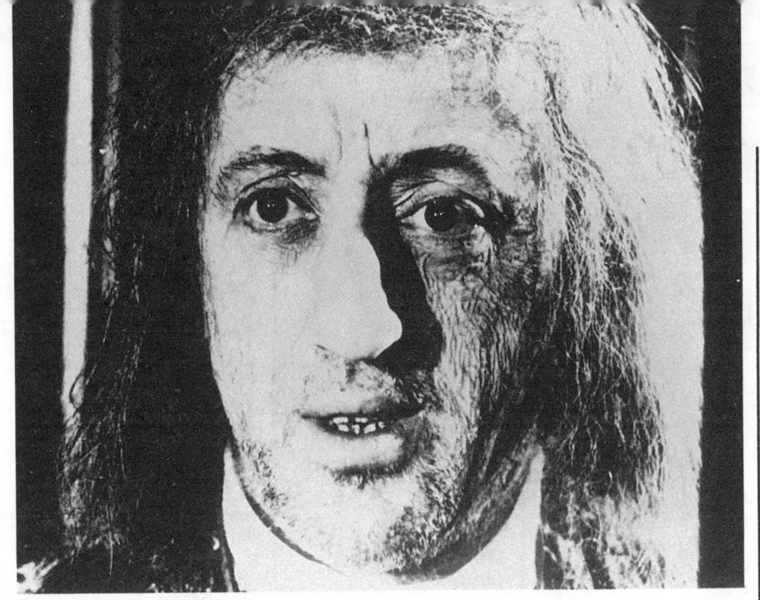

bfi ***Noi Tre (The Three of Us)*** ▲
(PG) Italy Dir Pupi Avati with Christopher Davidson, Lino Capolicchio, Gianni Cavina. BFI, 11 Jan 1991. 93 mins. Subtitles

Notebook on Cities and Clothes
see ***Aufzeichnungen zu Kleidern und Städten***

Nuns on the Run
(12) UK Dir Jonathan Lynn with Eric Idle, Robbie Coltrane, Camille Coduri. Palace Pictures, 4 May 1990. 95 mins. MFB June 1990 p171

Out Cold
(15) USA Dir Malcolm Mowbray with John Lithgow, Teri Garr, Randy Quaid. Hemdale, 17 Aug 1990. 89 mins. MFB Sep 1990 p267

Pacific Heights
(15) USA Dir John Schlesinger with Melanie Griffith, Matthew Modine, Michael Keaton. 20th Century Fox, 22 Feb 1991. 104 mins. MFB Feb 1991 p52

The Package
(15) USA Dir Andrew Davis with Gene Hackman, Joanna Cassidy, Tommy Lee Jones. Rank, 8 June 1990. 108 mins. MFB June 1990 p172

Paper Mask
(15) UK Dir Christopher Morahan with Paul McGann, Amanda Donohoe, Frederick Treves. Enterprise Pictures, 14 Sep 1990. 105 mins. MFB Sep 1990 p268

Paura e amore (Three Sisters)
(12) Italy/France/ Germany Dir Margarethe von Trotta with Fanny Ardant, Greta Scacchi, Valeria Golino. Curzon, 14 Dec 1990. 112 mins. English version. MFB Feb 1991 p53

Phantom of the Opera
(18) USA Dir Dwight H Little with Robert Englund, Jill Schoelen, Alex Hyde-White. Castle Premier, 15 June 1990. 93 mins. MFB June 1990 p172

Der Philosoph (3 Women in Love)
(18) Germany Dir Rudolf Thome with Johannes Herrschmann, Adriana Altaras, Friederike Tiefenbacher. Mainline, 8 June 1990. 83 mins. Subtitles. MFB Feb 1990 p46

The Plot Against Harry
(PG) USA Dir Michael Roemer with Martin Priest, Ben Lang, Maxine Woods. Electric Pictures/Contemporary, 5 Oct 1990. 81 mins. MFB Oct 1990 p301

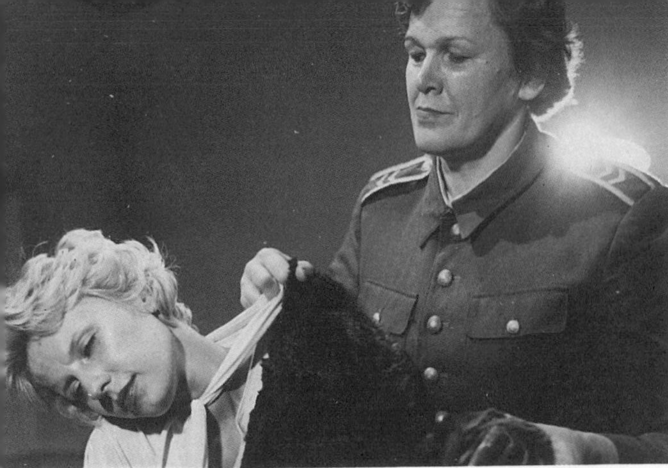

▲ Przesluchanie (Interrogation)

Postcards from the Edge
(15) USA Dir Mike Nichols with Meryl Streep, Shirley MacLaine, Dennis Quaid. Columbia Tri-Star, 25 Jan 1991. 104 mins. MFB Feb 1991 p54

Powwow Highway
(15) UK Dir Jonathan Wacks with A Martinez, Gary Farmer, Joanelle Nadine Romero. HandMade, 11 May 1990. 91 mins. MFB May 1990 p136

Presumed Innocent
(15) USA Dir Alan J Pakula with Harrison Ford, Brian Dennehy, Bonnie Bedelia. Warner Bros, 28 Sep 1990. 126 mins. MFB Nov 1990 p332

Pretty Woman
(15) USA Dir Garry Marshall with Richard Gere, Julia Roberts, Ralph Bellamy. Warner Bros, 11 May 1990. 120 mins. MFB May 1990 p136

Przesluchanie (Interrogation)
(18) Poland Dir Ryszard Bugajski with Krystyna Janda, Adama Ferencego, Agnieszka Holland. Gala, 20 July 1990. 114 mins. Subtitles. MFB Aug 1990 p231

The Punisher
(18) Australia Dir Mark Goldblatt with Dolph Lundgren, Louis Gossett Jnr., Jeroen Krabbé. Castle Premier, 1 June 1990. 88 mins. MFB June 1990 p174

Quigley Down Under
(12) Australia Dir Simon Wincer with Tom Selleck, Laura San Giacomo, Alan Rickman. UIP, 29 Mar 1991. 120 mins. MFB Apr 1991 p109

The Reflecting Skin
(15) UK Dir Philip Ridley with Viggo Mortensen, Lindsay Duncan, Jeremy Cooper. MCEG Virgin Vision, 16 Nov 1990. 95 mins. MFB Nov 1990 p334

Repossessed
(15) USA Dir Bob Logan with Linda Blair, Ned Beatty, Leslie Nielsen. Guild, 30 Nov 1990. 85 mins. MFB Dec 1990 p364

Requiem for Dominic
see ***Requiem für Dominic***

bfi ***Requiem für Dominic (Requiem for Dominic)***
(15) Austria Dir Robert Dornhelm with Felix Mitterer, Viktoria Schubert, August Schmölzer. BFI, 16 Dec 1990. 89 mins. Subtitles

Reunion
see ***L'Ami Retrouvé***

Revenge
(18) USA Dir Tony Scott with Kevin Costner, Anthony Quinn, Madeleine Stowe. Columbia Tri-Star, 22 June 1990. 124 mins. MFB July 1990 p204

Reversal of Fortune
(15) USA Dir Barbet Schroeder with Glenn Close, Jeremy Irons, Ron Silver. Rank, 11 Jan 1991. 111 mins. MFB Feb 1991 p55

The Rift
see ***La Grieta***

The Road Home (Lost Angels)
(15) USA Dir Hugh Hudson with Donald Sutherland, Adam Horovitz, Amy Locane. Rank, 15 Mar 1991. 116 mins. MFB Mar 1991 p83

RoboCop 2
(18) USA Dir Irvin Kershner with Peter Weller, Belinda Bauer, Nancy Allen. Rank, 12 Oct 1990. 116 mins. MFB Oct 1990 p301

Rocky V
(PG) USA Dir John G Avildsen with Sylvester Stallone, Talia Shire, Burt Young. UIP, 25 Jan 1991. 104 mins. MFB Feb 1991 p56

Roger and Me
(15) USA Dir Michael Moore. Documentary. Warner Bros, 20 Apr 1990. 91 mins. MFB Apr 1990 p116

Romuald & Juliette
see ***Romuald et Juliette***

Romuald et Juliette (Romuald & Juliette)
(12) France Dir Coline Serreau with Firmine Richard, Pierre Vernier, Daniel Auteuil. Gala, 10 Aug 1990. 112 mins. Subtitles. MFB Aug 1990 p234

The Rookie
(15) USA Dir Clint Eastwood with Clint Eastwood, Charlie Sheen, Raul Julia. Warner Bros, 18 Jan 1991. 120mins. MFB Feb 1991 p58

The Russia House
(15) USA Dir Fred Schepisi with Sean Connery, Michelle Pfeiffer, Roy Scheider. UIP, 22 Feb 1991. 123 mins. MFB Mar 1991 p84

The Salute of the Jugger
(18) Australia Dir David Peoples with Rutger Hauer, Vincent Phillip D'Onofrio, Joan Chen. MCEG Virgin Vision, 19 Oct 1990. 92 mins. MFB Nov 1990 p334

Santa Sangre
(18) Italy Dir Alejandro Jodorowsky with Axel Jodorowsky, Blanca Guerra, Guy Stockwell. Mainline, 13 Apr 1990. 123 mins. English version, partly subtitled. MFB Apr 1990 p117

Das schreckliche Mädchen (The Nasty Girl)
(PG) Germany Dir Michael Verhoeven with Monika Baumgartner, Lena Stolze, Michael Garr. Mainline, 4 Jan 1991. 94 mins. Subtitles. MFB Jan 1991 p24

Secret Wedding
see ***Boda secreta***

See You in the Morning
(12) USA Dir Alan J Pakula with Jeff Bridges, Alice Krige, Farrah Fawcett. Warner Bros, 4 May 1990. 119 mins. MFB May 1990 p138

Santa Sangre ▶

She-Devil
(15) USA Dir Susan Seidelman with Meryl Streep, Roseanne Barr, Ed Begley Jnr. Rank, 11 May 1990. 99 mins. MFB May 1990 p140

The Sheltering Sky
(18) UK/Italy Dir Bernardo Bertolucci with Debra Winger, John Malkovich, Campbell Scott. Palace Pictures, 30 Nov 1990. 138 mins. MFB Jan 1991 p25

She's Out of Control
(12) USA Dir Stan Dragoti with Catherine Hicks, Wallace Shawn, Tony Danza. Columbia Tri-Star, 13 July 1990. 94 mins. MFB Aug 1990 p236

Shocker
(18) USA Dir Wes Craven with Michael Murphy, Peter Berg, Cami Cooper. Guild, 20 Apr 1990. 110 mins. MFB May 1990 p141

A Shock to the System
(15) USA Dir Jan Egleson with Michael Caine, Elizabeth McGovern, Peter Riegert. Medusa, 26 Oct 1990. 87 mins. MFB Dec 1990 p365

Short Time
(12) USA Dir Gregg Champion with Dabney Coleman, Teri Garr, Matt Frewer. Rank, 8 Feb 1991. 97 mins. MFB Mar 1991 p85

Silent Scream
(15) UK Dir David Hayman with Iain Glen, Paul Samson, Andrew Barr. BFI, 19 Oct 1990. 85 mins. MFB Oct 1990 ◀ p303

Ski Patrol
(PG) USA Dir Richard Correll with Roger Rose, Yvette Nipar, T K Carter. Entertainment, 15 June 1990. 91 mins. MFB July 1990 p205

Society
(18) USA Dir Brian Yuzna with Bill Warlock, Devin DeVasquez, Evan Richards. Medusa, 6 Apr 1990. 99 mins. MFB Apr 1990 p91

Spaced Invaders
(PG) USA Dir Patrick Read Johnson with Douglas Barr, Royal Dano, Ariana Richards. Medusa, 3 Aug 1990. 100 mins. MFB Aug 1990 p237

Spoorloos (The Vanishing)
(12) Netherlands/France Dir George Sluizer with Bernard-Pierre Donnadieu, Gene Bervoets, Johanna Ter Steege. Metro Pictures, 1 June 1990. 105 mins. MFB June 1990 p175

Stanley and Iris
(15) USA Dir Martin Ritt with Jane Fonda, Robert De Niro, Swoozie Kurtz. UIP, 22 June 1990. 104 mins. MFB June 1990 p177

Staying Together
(15) USA Dir Lee Grant with Stockard Channing, Melinda Dillon, Sean Aston. Hemdale, 8 Feb 1991. 91 mins. MFB Dec 1990 p366

Stella
(15) USA Dir John Erman with Bette Midler, John Goodman, Trini Alvarado. Rank, 7 Sep 1990. 109 mins. MFB Sep 1990 p269

Stockade
(12) USA Dir Martin Sheen with Charlie Sheen, Martin Sheen, F Murray Abraham. Entertainment, 23 Nov 1990. 98 mins. MFB Dec 1990 p367

Sweetie
(15) Australia Dir Jane Campion with Genevieve Lemon, Karen Colston, Tom Lycos. Electric Pictures/Contemporary, 4 May 1990. 90 mins. MFB May 1990 p142

A Tale of Springtime
see **Conte de printemps**

Teenage Mutant Ninja Turtles
(PG) USA Dir Steve Barron with Judith Hogg, Elias Koteas, Josh Pais. MCEG Virgin Vision, 23 Nov 1990. 93 mins. MFB Dec 1990 p344

Texasville
(15) USA Dir Peter Bogdanovich with Jeff Bridges, Cybill Shepherd, Annie Potts. Guild, 7 Dec 1990. 126 mins. MFB Jan 1991 p27

Three Men and a Little Lady
(PG) USA Dir Emile Ardolino with Tom Selleck, Ted Danson, Steve Guttenberg. Warner Bros, 8 Feb 1991. 104 mins. MFB Apr 1991 p111

The Three of Us
see **Noi Tre**

Three Sisters
see **Paura e amore**

3 Women in Love
see **Der Philosoph**

Tie Me Up! Tie Me Down!
see **¡Atame!**

Tilaï ▶
(PG) Burkina Faso/Switzerland/France Dir Idrissa Ouedraogo with Rasmane Ouedroago, Ina Cissé, Roukietou Barry. Artificial Eye, 22 Feb 1991. 81 mins. Subtitles. MFB Mar 1991 p63

Time of the Gypsies
see **Dom za Vesanje**

Torrents of Spring
see **Acque di primavera**

To Sleep with Anger
(12) USA Dir Charles Burnett with Danny Glover, Paul Butler, Mary Alice. Metro Pictures, 15 Feb 1991. 102 mins. MFB Mar 1991 p86

Total Recall
(18) USA Dir Paul Verhoeven with Arnold Schwarzenegger, Rachel Ticotin, Sharon Stone. Guild, 27 July 1990. 113mins. MFB Aug 1990 p238

Treasure Island
(PG) USA Dir Fraser C Heston with Charlton Heston, Christian Bale, Richard Johnson. Warner Bros, 15 June 1990. 132 mins. MFB July 1990 p206

Tremors
(15) USA Dir Ron Underwood with Kevin Bacon, Fred Ward, Finn Varter. UIP, 29 June 1990. 96 mins. MFB Aug 1990 p239

Triumph of the Spirit
(15) USA Dir Robert M Young with Willem Dafoe, Edward James Olmos, Robert Loggia. Guild, 22 June 1990. 120 mins. MFB June 1990 p177

Tulitikkutehtaan Tyttö (The Match Factory Girl)
(15) Finland/Sweden Dir Aki Kaurismäki with Kati Outinen, Esko

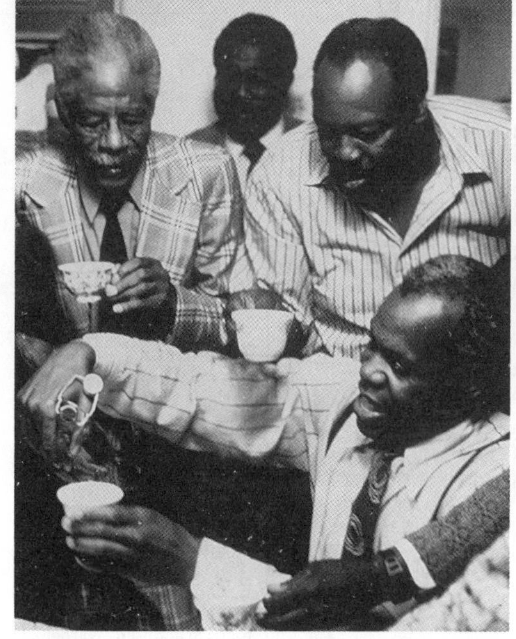

Nikkari, Vesa Vierikko. Electric Pictures/ Contemporary, 19 Oct 1990. 70 mins. Subtitles. MFB Nov 1990 p335

Ultimas imagenes del naufragio (Last Images of the Shipwreck)
(15) Argentina/Spain Dir Eliseo Subielo with Lorenzo Quinteros, Noemi Frenkel, Hugo Soto. Palace Pictures, 23 Nov 1990. 127 mins. Subtitles. MFB Dec 1990 p368

The Unbelievable Truth
(15) USA Dir Hal Hartley with Adrienne Shelly, Robert Burke, Christopher Cooke. Electric Pictures/ Contemporary, 18 Jan 1991. 98 mins. MFB Feb 1991 p59

▲ **To Sleep with Anger**

Uncle Buck
(12) USA Dir John Hughes with John Candy, Jean Louisa Kelly, Gaby Hoffman. UIP, 13 Apr 1990. 100 mins. MFB Feb 1990 p52

Vampire's Kiss
(18) USA Dir Robert Bierman with Nicolas Cage, Maria Conchita, Jennifer Beals. Hemdale, 30 Nov 1990. 103 mins. MFB Dec 1990 p369

The Vanishing
see ***Spoorloos***

Vincent and Theo
see ***Vincent et Théo***

▼ **Where the Heart Is**

Vincent et Théo (Vincent and Theo)
(15) France/UK Dir Robert Altman with Tim Roth, Paul Rhys, Johanna Ter Steege. Blue Dolphin, 22 June 1990. 140 mins. English version. MFB July 1990 p183

Waiting for the Light
(PG) USA Dir Christopher Monger with Teri Garr, Hilary Wolf, Shirley MacLaine. Entertainment, 7 Sep 1990. 94 mins. MFB Sep 1990 p270

We're No Angels
(15) USA Dir Neil Jordan with Robert De Niro, Sean Penn, Demi Moore. UIP, 1 June 1990. 106 mins. MFB June 1990 p178

Where the Heart Is
(15) USA Dir John Boorman with Dabney Coleman, Uma Thurman, Joanna Cassidy. Guild, 10 Aug 1990. 107 mins. MFB Sep 1990 p247

White Hunter, Black Heart
(PG) USA Dir Clint Eastwood with Jeff Fahey, Charlotte Cornwell, Clint Eastwood. Warner Bros, 31 Aug 1990. 112 mins. MFB Oct 1990 p304

Why Me?
(15) USA Dir Gene Quintano with Christopher Lambert, Christopher Lloyd, Kim Greist. Entertainment, 7 Sep 1990. 87 mins. MFB Nov 1990 p336

Wild at Heart
(18) USA Dir David Lynch with Nicolas Cage, Laura Dern, Diane Ladd. Palace Pictures, 24 Aug 1990. 124 mins. MFB Sep 1990 p271

Wild Orchid
(18) USA Dir Zalman King with Mickey Rourke, Jacqueline Bisset, Carré Otis. Entertainment, 3 Aug 1990. 112 mins. MFB Oct 1990 p306

Windprints
(15) UK Dir David Wicht with John Hurt, Sean Bean, Marius Weyers. MCEG Virgin Vision, 29 June 1990. 99 mins. MFB Sep 1990 p273

Wings of the Apache (Fire Birds)
(15) USA Dir David Green with Nicolas Cage, Sean Young, Tommy Lee Jones. Medusa, 19 Oct 1990. 86 mins. MFB Nov 1990 p337

The Witches
(PG) USA Dir Nicolas Roeg with Anjelica Huston, Mai Zetterling, Jasen Fisher. Warner Bros, 25 May 1990. 92 mins. MFB May 1990 p146

The Women on the Roof
see ***Kvinnorna på taket***

A World Without Pity
see ***Un Monde sans pitié***

Young Guns II
(12) USA Dir Geoff Murphy with Emilio Estevez, Kiefer Sutherland, Lou Diamond Phillips. 20th Century Fox, 2 Nov 1990. 104 mins. MFB Nov 1990 p338

Yuki Yukite Shingun (The Emperor's Naked Army Marches On)
Japan Dir Kazuo Hara. Documentary with Kenzo Okuzaki, Shizumi Okuzaki, Kichitaro Yamada. ICA Projects, 14 Sep 1990. 123 mins. Subtitles. MFB Apr 1991 p114

Yuwakusha (The Enchantment)
Japan Dir Shunichi Nagasaki with Kumiko Akiyoshi, Kiwako Harada, Takeshi Naito. ICA Projects, 19 Oct 1990. 109 mins. Subtitles. MFB Apr 1991 p115

bfi – Produced and/or distributed by the British Film Institute

WARNER BROS. DISTRIBUTORS LTD.
A TIME WARNER COMPANY

SPECIALISED GOODS AND SERVICES

Agfa-Gevaert
Motion Picture Division
27 Great West Road
Brentford
Middx TW8 9AX
Tel: 081 560 2131
Fax: 081 569 7868
Film stock

Agricius
c/o Robin Browne
Tel: 081 903 9922
Special effects cinematography. Specialist camera equipment. In the process of relocating

Any Effects
64 Weir Road
London SW19 8UG
Tel: 081 944 0099
Fax: 081 944 6989
Mechanical (front of camera) special effects
Pyrotechnics: simulated explosions, bullet hits
Fine models for close up camera work
Weather: rain, snow, fog, wind
Breakaways: Shatterglass, windows, bottles, glasses, collapsing furniture, walls, floors
Specialised engineering rigs and propmaking service

Barclays Bank
27 Soho Square
London W1A 4WA
Tel: 071 439 6851
Fax: 071 434 9035
Nicki Davies
Large business centre providing a comprehensive range of banking services to all aspects of the film and television industry

Boulton-Hawker Films
Hadleigh
Ipswich
Suffolk IP7 5BG
Tel: 0473 822235
Fax: 0473 824519
Time-lapse, cinemicrography and other specialised scientific filming techniques

Cabervans
Caberfeidh
Cloch Road
Gourock
Renfrewshire PA19 1BA
Mobile wardrobe, make-up, transport etc

Clifford and Smith Productions
2 Eton Hall
Eton College Road
London NW3
Tel: 071 586 8215
Sukie Smith
Workshop for scriptwriters and production companies; professional actors read the script and a script advisor aids discussion concerning development. Workshops also held for non-professional writers.

Cool Million
Unit 16A
149 Roman Way
Islington
London N7 8XH
Tel: 071 609 9191
Caroline Harris
Merchandising products

Crews Employment Agency
111 Wardour Street
London W1V 4AY
Tel: 071 437 0721/0810/0350
Fax: 071 494 4644
A licensed employment agency set up by the ACTT-section of BECTU (see under Organisations) in 1989. Operating a computerised database, they are able to scan for freelance union members by grade, geographical location, foreign languages, specialist skills and experience, etc. This is a free service to the film and television industry

De Wolfe
80-88 Wardour Street
London W1V 3LF
Tel: 071 439 8481
Fax: 071 437 2744
Major production music library of tapes and CDs, controlling 26,000 titles as publisher. Offices in New York, Tokyo, Paris, Holland, Italy and Brussels. Specially composed film and TV scores; 24-track studio; film cutting rooms; sound effects CDs

Diverse Design
Gorleston Street
London W14 8XS
Tel: 071 603 4567
Fax: 071 603 2148
Steve Billinger
Full service design company from Storyboard to Series. Designers of innovative programmes which include: *Dispatches, Small Objects of Desire, Obsessions, Europe Express, Check Out, And the Walls Came Tumbling Down, West of Moscow, QED Panic Attack*

EOS Electronics AV
EOS House
Weston Square
Barry CF6 7YF
Tel: 0446 741212
Fax: 0446 746120
Specialist manufacturers of Video Animation, Video Time Lapsing and Video Archiving Equipment. Products: Supertoon Low Cost School Animation System, AC580 Lo-Band Controller, BAC900 Broadcast Animation Controller and IRIS (Instant Recording Image System)

ETH Screen Music
York Lane
22 Broughton Street
Edinburgh EH1 3RH
Tel: 031 557 2721
Harald Tobermann
Original music production for film, TV and video; composers, arrangers, musicians. Past productions in Europe and UK include drama, comedy, documentary. Specialists for live music accompaniment with restored silent films

Eureka Location Management
16 Broadwick Street
London W1V 1FH
Tel: 071 734 4100
Fax: 071 734 0150
Finds and manages locations for film and television in Britain and abroad. Offices in London and Toronto

FTS Filmbond
Aerodrome Way
Cranford Lane
Hounslow
Middx TW5 9QB
Tel: 081 897 7973
Fax: 081 897 7979
Total care for all moving media

Film Finances
1-11 Hay Hill
Berkeley Square
London W1X 7LF
Tel: 071 629 6557
Fax: 071 491 7530
Graham Easton
David Wilder
Provide completion guarantees for the film and television industry

The Film Stock Centre
68-70 Wardour Street
London W1V 3HP
Tel: 071 734 0038
Fax: 071 494 2645
Approved distributor of film, video tape, magnetic recording stock and spacing – all major brands

Harkness Screens
The Gate Studio
Station Road
Borehamwood
Herts WD6 1DQ
Tel: 081 953 3611
Fax: 081 207 3657
Projection screens and complete screen systems

Jim Henson's Creature Shop
1b Downshire Hill
Hampstead
London NW3 1NR
Tel: 071 431 2818
Fax: 071 431 3737
Animatronics, puppets and prosthetics

Hirearchy Classic and Contemporary Costume
45 Palmerston Road
Boscombe
Bournemouth
Dorset BH1 4HW
Tel: 0202 394465
Fax: 0202 309660
Specialise in twentieth century costume hire

Image Diggers Picture and Tape Library
618b Finchley Road
London NW11 7RR
Tel: 081 455 4564
35mm slides, stills, postcards, sheet music, magazine and book material for hire (NB no film footage). Audio/visual tape resources in performing arts and other areas, plus theme research

Kodak
Motion Picture and Television Products
PO Box 66
Hemel Hempstead
Herts HP1 1LU
Tel: 0442 61122
Fax: 0442 232505
Film stock

Lip Service Casting
Unit 131 Canalot Studios
222 Kensal Road
London W10 5BN
Tel: 081 969 8535
Fax: 081 968 6911
Voiceover agency for actors, and voiceover casting agency. Publishers of 'The Voice Analysis' – a breakdown of actors' vocal profiles

Location Works
8 Greek Street
London W1V 5LE
Tel: 071 434 4211
Fax: 071 437 3097
Locations library, location finding and management (London, UK and world)

Media Education Agency
5A Queens Parade
Brownlow Road
London N11 2DN
Tel: 081 888 4620
David Lusted
A search facility for consultants, lecturers and teacher in-service education (INSET) in aspects of film, television and media studies. A membership of over 100 includes broadcasters and actors for occasional lectures

Ocean Film and Research
Studio 12
39 Tadema Road
London SW10 0PY
Tel: 071 352 7913
Fax: 071 376 4510
Marine productions. Floating production facility, location support and exploration charter, based on the m/s O-LUCIA. On board equipment: Betacam SP cameras. Audio: Hi-band SP edit suite with digital FX and 8-track. Sub Aqua. Flying Boat. Radio/telephone comms linked to computer and fax. 240/110v power to shore

Oxford Scientific Films (OSF)
Long Hanborough
Oxford OX7 2LD
Tel: 0993 881881
Fax: 0993 882808
10 Poland Street
London W1V 3DE
Tel: 071 494 0720
Fax: 071 287 9125
Specialists in macro, micro, time-lapse, high-speed and snorkel optic photography for natural history programmes, commercials, corporate videos and videodiscs

Persona Films
33 Castle Arcade
Cardiff CF1 2BW
Tel: 0222 231680
Fax: 0222 342235
Richard J Staniforth
International film development house for the commercial development of feature film projects from concept to fully scripted production package. Development finance available to producer/writer teams

Radcliffes Transport Services
5-9 Willow Lane
Willow Lane Industrial Estate
Mitcham
Surrey CR4 4NA
Tel: 081 688 7258
Fax: 081 681 0409
Alba Way
Barton Dock Road
Manchester M32 0XL
Tel: 061 865 0071
Fax: 061 864 2345
The supply of transport, from small box vans through to 40' articulated vehicles

The Screen Company
182 High Street
Cottenham
Cambridge CB4 4RX
Tel: 0954 50139
Fax: 0954 52005
Pat Turner
Manufacture, supply and installation of all types of front and rear projection screens for video, slide, film and OHP

Security Archives
Saref House
135 Shepherdess Walk
London W1 7PZ
Tel: 071 253 0027
Fax: 071 608 0640
Film and video storage and retrieval services

Simon Olswang & Co
1 Great Cumberland Place
London W1H 7AL
Tel: 071 723 9393
Fax: 071 723 6992
Established in 1981, one of the country's leading firms of entertainment and media solicitors. The firm specialises in all aspects of film, television and video production, distribution and finance, cable, satellite and other communications media, recording and other music industry contracts and sponsorship

Stanley Productions
147 Wardour Street
London W1V 3TB
Tel: 071 439 0311
Fax: 071 437 2126
Ronnie Arlen, Sales Director
Distributors worldwide of videotape, video equipment, audiotape, film stock, and accessories

Ten Tenths
106 Gifford Street
London N1 0DF
Tel: 071 607 4887
Fax: 071 609 8124
Props service specialising in vehicles (cars, bikes, boats and planes) ranging from 1901 to present day – veteran, vintage, classic, modern – with additional wardrobe facilities

Touche Ross & Co
Hill House
1 Little New Street
London EC4A 3TR
Tel: 071 936 3000
Fax: 071 583 8517/1198
Gavin Hamilton Deeley
Mark Attan
Robert Reed
Advisors to film, television and broadcasting organisations. Business plans and financial models for companies, tax planning and business advice for individuals, and information on legal and regulatory developments affecting the sector

STUDIOS

Bray Studios
Down Place
Water Oakley
Windsor Road
Windsor
Berks SL4 5UG
Tel: 0628 22111
Fax: 0628 770381

STAGES

1 (sound)	955 sq metres
2 (sound)	948 sq metres
3 (sound)	235 sq metres
4 (sound)	173 sq metres
5 accoustic rehearsal 30 x 20ft	

FILMS/PROGRAMMES
Hope and Glory for John Boorman
The Manageress for Zed
Saracen for Central TV
Tecx for Central TV
The Witches for Henson Organisation
Forever Green for Picture Partnership
Jeeves & Wooster for Picture Partnership
Inspector Morse for Zenith
For Queen and Country for Working Title
Edward II for Working Title
Gone to the Dogs for Central Films

Elstree Studios
Borehamwood
Herts WD6 1JG
Tel: 081 953 1600
Fax: 081 207 0860

STAGES

7	480 sq metres
8	720 sq metres
9	720 sq metres

Other stages are under construction during re-development of the studios

FILMS/PROGRAMMES
Duel of Love for Gainsborough (Film & TV) Pictures
Capital City II for Euston Films
Shrinks for Euston Films
Birds of a Feather II for Alomo Productions

Halliford Studios
Manygate Lane
Shepperton
Middx TW17 9EG
Tel: 0932 226341
Fax: 0932 246336

A	334 sq metres
B	223 sq metres

Isleworth Studios
Studio Parade
484 London Road
Isleworth
Middx TW7 4DE
Tel: 081 568 3511
Fax: 081 568 4863

STAGES

A	292 sq metres
B	152 sq metres
C	152 sq metres
D	152 sq metres
Packshot stage	141 sq metres

Jacob Street Studios
9-19 Mill Street
London SE1 2DA
Tel: 071 232 1066
Fax: 071 252 0118

STAGES

A	1250 sq metres
B	600 sq metres
C	170 sq metres
D	235 sq metres
E	185 sq metres
F	185 sq metres
G	170 sq metres

FILMS/PROGRAMMES
London's Burning
Spitting Image

Lee International Studios Shepperton
Studios Road
Shepperton
Middx TW17 0QD
Tel: 0932 562611
Fax: 0932 568989

STAGES

A	1674 sq metres
B	1116 sq metres
C	1674 sq metres
D	1116 sq metres
E	294 sq metres
F	294 sq metres
G	629 sq metres
H	2790 sq metres
I	657 sq metres
J	284 sq metres
K	120 sq metres
L	604 sq metres
M	260 sq metres
T	261 sq metres

FILMS/PROGRAMMES
Hamlet starring Mel Gibson, Glenn Close; director Franco Zeffirelli; producer Dyson Lovell
A Kiss Before Dying starring Matt Dillon, Sean Young; director James Dearden; producer Eric Fellner
Prince of Thieves starring Kevin Costner, Morgan Freeman; director Kevin Reynolds; producers John Watson, Michael Kagan
Henry V starring Kenneth Branagh, Paul Scofield, Derek Jacobi; director Kenneth Branagh; producer Bruce Sharman
To Be the Best starring Christopher Cazenove, Lindsay Wagner, Stephanie Beacham, Anthony Hopkins; director Tony Wharmby; producers Aida Young, Robert Bradford

Limehouse Television
128 Wembley Park Drive
Wembley
Middlesex HA9 8HQ
Tel: 081 900 1188
Fax: 081 900 2860

STAGES

A	605 sq metres
B	605 sq metres

(May be combined to form one stage of 1227 sq metres)

Pinewood Studios
Pinewood Road
Iver
Bucks SL0 0NH
Tel: 0753 651700
Fax: 0753 656844

STAGES

A	1685 sq metres
B	827 sq metres
C	827 sq metres
D	1685 sq metres
E	1685 sq metres
F	700 sq metres
G	247 sq metres
H	300 sq metres
J	825 sq metres
K	825 sq metres
L	880 sq metres
M	880 sq metres
007 (silent)	4350 sq metres
South Dock (silent)	1548 sq metres
North Dock (silent)	628 sq metres
Large Process	439 sq metres
Small Process	226 sq metres

FILMS
Alien III
Buddy's Song
Crucifer of Blood
King Ralph
Let Him Have It
Prisoners of Honour
Shining Through

Rotherhithe Studios
169 Rotherhithe Street
London SE16 1QU
Tel: 071 231 2209
Fax: 071 231 2119
STAGES

A	800 sq metres
B	177 sq metres
C	158 sq metres

Theed Street Studios

12a Theed Street
London SE1 8ST
Tel: 071 928 1953
Fax: 071 928 1952
STAGES

A	151 sq metres

FILMS/PROGRAMMES
The Museum of Madness for BBC
Snub TV

Twickenham Film Studios

St Margaret's
Twickenham
Middx TW1 2AW
Tel: 081 892 4477
Fax: 081 891 0168
STAGES

1	701 sq metres
2	186 sq metres
3	516 sq metres

Westway Studios

8 Olaf Street
London W11 4BE
Tel: 071 221 9041
Fax: 071 221 9399
STAGES

1	602 sq metres
2	520 sq metres
3	169 sq metres
4	242 sq metres

Below are listed all British television companies, with a selection of their key personnel and programmes. The titles listed are a cross-section of productions initiated (but not necessarily broadcast) during 1990 and the first quarter of 1991. 'F' and 'V' indicate whether productions were shot on film or video. For details of feature films made for television, see Production Starts (p252)

INDEPENDENT TELEVISION

ANGLIA
Television Limited

Anglia Television

Anglia House
Norwich NR1 3JG
Tel: 0603 615151
Chairman: Sir Peter Gibbings
Chief Executive: David McCall
Managing Director, Broadcasting Division: Philip Garner

A Brief History of Time
Production companies: Anglia Television/Gordon Freedman Productions/Amblin Entertainment
Producers: Gordon Freedman, David Hickman
Director: Errol Morris
1 x 90 mins V
A documentary special, based on the life and work of brilliant Cambridge physicist Professor Stephen Hawking, taking a stunning visual journey into his conception of the fundamental mysteries of the universe

The Chief
Production company: Anglia Films
Producer: Ruth Boswell
Director: Brian Farnham
Writer: Jeffrey Caine
Cast: Tim Piggott-Smith, Karen Archer, Judy Loe
6 x 1 hour V
The outspoken Chief Constable John Stafford returns in a new series. The crusading Chief is back at the helm of Eastland Police after clashes with the Home Office led to his suspension. But his brand of policing causes conflict and threatens to rock the boat again as he tackles contentious issues

Chimera
Production company: Zenith Productions
Producer: Nick Gillott
Director: Lawrence Gordon Clark
Writer: Stephen Gallagher
Cast: John Lynch, Christine Kavanagh, Kenneth Cranham
4 x 1 hour V
A prophetic drama set in the chilling world of genetic engineering where science fact has overtaken science fiction. A journalist's investigations into a mass murder lead to the discovery of a secret so terrible the highest authorities want him silenced

Growing Rich
Production company: Anglia Films
Producer: Roger Gregory
Director: Brian Farnham
6 x 1 hour V
The financial fortunes of three teenage girls eager to improve their lot in life unfolds in a new six part drama written for Anglia by Fay Weldon

Knightmare
Production company: Broadsword Productions
Producer: Tim Child
Director: Jimmy McKinney
Writer: Tim Child
Cast: Hugo Myatt, John Woodnutt
16 x 25 mins V
Children's fantasy adventure game using computer graphics and animations

Other productions include:
Anything Goes
Castle's Abroad
Farming Diary
Folio
Food Guide
Go Fishing
Heirloom
Jumble
Lucky Ladders
A Place in the Sun
Relationships
Survival

Border Television

The Television Centre
Carlisle CA1 3NT
Tel: 0228 25101
Chairman: Melvyn Bragg
Managing Director: James Graham
Head of Production & Assistant Controller of Programmes: Neil Robinson

Enterprize Challenge
Producer: Tony Nicholson
7 x 30 mins
A yearly competition for small businesses in the Border Television region

Union and the League
Producer: Jack Johnstone
10 x 30 mins
A monthly series which proves that rugby union

and rugby league can be covered in one programme

C.U.4
Producer/Director: Harry King
6 x 30 mins
Saturday morning summer children's magazine for youngsters in the Border Television region

7th Heaven
Producer: Christian Dymond
Director: Tony Nicholson
10 x 30 mins
Broad based arts programme covering venues, performances etc in the Border region

Wide Angle
Producer: Paul Baird
Director: Ron Smith
8 x 30 mins
Local current affairs and community issues programme

Central Independent Television

Central House
Broad Street
Birmingham B1 2JP
Tel: 021 643 9898
East Midlands Television Centre
Lenton Lane
Nottingham NG7 2NA
Tel: 0602 863322
35-38 and 43-45 Portman Square
London W1H 9AH
Tel: 071 468 6688
45 Charlotte Street
London W1P 1LX
Tel: 071 637 4602
Unit 9 Windrush Court
Abingdon Business Park
Abingdon
Oxon OX14 1SA
Tel: 0235 554123
Chairman and Chief Executive: Leslie Hill
Managing Director, Central Broadcasting: Andy Allan
Deputy Managing Director, Central Broadcasting: Bob Southgate
Controller, Regional Programmes: Steve Clark
Controller, News: Laurie Upshon
Controller, Sport: Gary Newbon
Managing Director, Central Productions: Mike Watts
Controller, Entertainment & Daytime: Tony Wolfe
Controller, Young People & MD FilmFair: Lewis Rudd
Controller, Features & Documentaries: Roger James
Controller, Drama & MD Central Films: Ted Childs

Soldier, Soldier
Production company: Central Productions for Central Television
Producer: Chris Kelly
Directors: Laurence Moody, Zelda Barron
Writer: Lucy Gannon
Camera: Ray Goode, Peter Greenhalgh
Editors: Kevin Lester, Alan Jones
Cast: David Haig, Cathryn Harrison, Annabelle Apsion, Holly Aird, Robson Green, Miles Anderson
7 x 1 hour F
Officers, squaddies, wives and girlfriends learn to live with the highs and lows of mixing military and domestic life in this realistic look at life in the modern British army. With a six-month tour of duty behind them, the officers and men of the King's Fusiliers infantry regiment look forward to an emotional return to their Midlands' headquarters but their homecoming is tinged with some sadness

Inspector Morse
Production company: Zenith Productions for Central
Producer: David Lascelles
Directors: Adrian Shergold, John Madden, Roy Battersby, Colin Gregg
Writers: Julian Mitchell, Alma Cullen, Peter Nichols, Geoffrey Case, Daniel Boyle
Camera: Paul Wheeler
Editor: Andrew Nelson
Cast: John Thaw, Kevin Whately
5 x 2 hours F
Crosswords, real ale and classical music are the trademarks of Britain's top detective, the enigmatic Chief Inspector Morse. The cerebral sleuth returns to the dreaming spires of Oxford to solve more perplexing murder mysteries

Gone to the Dogs
Production company: Central Films for Central Television
Producer: Michele Buck
Directors: Sandy Johnson, Tony Dow
Writer: Tony Grounds
Camera: Richard Greatrex
Editors: Brian Freemantle, Peter Krook
Cast: Alison Steadman, Jim Broadbent, Harry Enfield, Warren Clarke
6 x 1 hour F
When a charismatic multi-millionaire greyhound owner and a romantic loser fall in love with the same woman it should be a one dog race. But when the winning post keeps moving – the lady's heart is up for grabs

The Upper Hand
Production company: Central Television
Producer: Christopher Walker
Directors: Martin Dennis, Mike Holgate
Camera: Peter Sanderson
Editor: Nigel Miller
Cast: Joe McGann, Diana Weston, Honor Blackman, Kellie Bright, William Puttock
13 x 30 mins V
Hunky ex-footballer Charlie Burrows hangs up his boots and picks up a duster when he takes a job as housekeeper to successful business-woman Caroline Wheatley. The couple are aided and abetted by Caroline's young son, her mother-next-door and Charlie's teenage daughter

Hello, Do You Hear Us?
Production company: Central Television
Executive Producer: Richard Creasey
Producer, Soviet Union: Veronyka Bodnark
Director: Yuris Podnieks
Camera: Yuris Podnieks, Guido Zvaigzne
Editors: Steve Barclay, Antra Tsilinska, Mark Davies
5 episodes F
Three years of great change in the Soviet Union are the backdrop to a major documentary series, directed by a renowned Soviet film maker, giving a unique and remarkably frank insight into the changing social and political mood of Russia today

Press Gang
Production company: Richmond Film and Television for Central
Producer: Sandra C Hastie
Directors: Bob Spiers, Lorne Magory
Writer: Steven Moffat
Camera: Trevor Coop
Editors: Geoff Hogg, Michael Bateman
Cast: Julia Sawalha, Dexter Fletcher, Lee Ross, Kelda Holmes
12 x 30 mins F
Focusing on the lives of the newshounds at the Junior Gazette. School's out for good and the cub reporters are out on their own facing serious deadlines and a serious budget

Other productions include:
About Face
Bob's Your Uncle
Boon
Chancer
Cook Report
Cool Head
Family Pride
Find-a-Family
Legacy – Origins of Civilisation
Spitting Image
The Widowmaker
Woof

Channel Television

Television Centre
La Pouquelaye
St Helier
Jersey JE2 3ZD
Tel: 0534 68999

Fax: 0534 59446
Television Centre
St George's Place
St Peter Port
Guernsey
Tel: 0481 723451
Fax: 0481 710739
Chairman: Major J R Riley
Managing Director: John Henwood

Channel Report
Director: Paul Brown
News Editor: Martyn Farley
Presenters: Cathy Le Feuvre, Peter Rouse
News magazine broadcast Monday to Friday jointly presented from Channel's Jersey and Guernsey news studios – also featuring live or taped inserts from the smaller islands Sark and Alderney

Link Up
Producer: Marcel Le Masson
Presenter: The Rev Colin Hough
Religious Adviser: Canon David Mahy
A once monthly religious magazine programme covering all aspects of religious affairs throughout the Channel Island region

Gerald Durrell and the Quest of the Magic Finger
Producer: Bob Evans
Director: Frank Cvitanovich
Camera: Tim Ringsdore
Editor: John Le Signe
With Gerald Durrell, Lee Durrell
1 x 1 hour V
Gerald and Lee Durrell travel to Madagascar in search of the aye-aye, one of the world's most mysterious animals

Mauritius – Island of the Dodo
Producer/Director: Bob Evans
Camera: Tim Ringsdore
Editor: John Le Signe
1 x 30 mins V
The story of how Jersey Zoo is helping to prevent more Mauritian animals following the Dodo into extinction

Morning Worship
Producer: Bob Evans
Director: Paul Brown
1 x 1 hour V
Sunday service from Wesley Grove Methodist Church in Jersey

Highway
Producer/director: Bob Evans
2 x 30 mins V
With Sir Harry Secombe. Guernsey – Faith; Jersey – Christian Love

Other titles include:
Antiques – Fakes and Forgeries
Azitiz
Beat the Hammer
Great British Isles (second series)
Greenstuff
Midnight Clear
Mind's Eye
The Pianist and the Painter
Religion – Accident of Birth?
Rhino Sanctuary
Sporting Scenes
The Success Factor

CHANNEL FOUR TELEVISION

Channel Four Television
60 Charlotte Street
London W1P 2AX
Tel: 071 631 4444
Chairman: Sir Richard Attenborough
Chief Executive: Michael Grade
Director of Programmes: Liz Forgan
Deputy Director of Programmes & Controller of Factual Programmes: John Willis
Director of Programme Acquisitions & Sales: Colin Leventhal
Director of Advertising Sales and Marketing: Stewart Butterfield
Head of Drama: David Aukin
Deputy Director of Programmes & Controller, Arts & Entertainment: Andrea Wonfor
Commissioning Editors: David Lloyd (Senior Commissioning Editor, News & Current Affairs); Gwynn Pritchard (Senior Commissioning Editor, Education); Alan Fountain (Senior Commissioning Editor, Independent Film and Video); Peter Ansorge (Deputy Head of Drama: Series and Serials); Seamus Cassidy (Entertainment); Farrukh Dhondy (Multicultural Programmes); Stephen Garrett (Youth); Waldemar Januszczak (Arts); Bob Towler (Education and Religion); Avril MacRory (Music); Mike Miller (Sport); Peter Moore (Documentaries); Michael Attwell (Talks & Features)
Chief Film Buyer: Mairi Macdonald

Film on Four
Continues through the 90s with further runs of highly acclaimed feature films funded wholly or in part by Channel 4. TV premiers include such critical cinema successes as *A World Apart, Hope and Glory, Drowning by Numbers, We Think the World of You, Smack and Thistle, The Dressmaker* and *Riff-Raff*

Fragile Earth
The award-winning environmental series continues – covering issues where a threat to the living environment is at the heart of the matter. A harder investigative approach balances visually compelling material

Friday at the Dome
The music series for the 90s, presenting live music in a new context together with filmed features and fronted by comedian Craig Ferguson of *The Rocky Horror Show* fame

GBH
Robert Lindsay, Michael Palin, Lindsay Duncan and Julie Walters star in Alan Bleasdale's first original drama series since *Boys from the Blackstuff* and his first for Channel 4

GRAMPIAN TELEVISION

Grampian Television
Queen's Cross
Aberdeen AB9 2XJ
Tel: 0224 646464
Fax: 0224 635127
Chairman: Sir Douglas Hardie CBE JP
Chief Executive: Donald H Waters CA
Director of Television: Robert L Christie
Director of Finance: Graham Good CA
Director of Programmes: George W Mitchell

The Energy Alternative
Grampian producer: Ted Brocklebank
Grampian director: Michael Steele
InCA producer: William Woollard
InCA director: John Shepherd
3 x 60 mins V
This series asks what steps can be taken to reduce western energy consumption by over 50% during the next 40 years to allow the third world to reach current western standards without creating the worst effects of the first industrial revolution

Grundig UK Mountain Bike Championship
Production company: TSL
Commissioning editor: George Mitchell
1 x 60 mins V
The world's top mountain bikers compete for the honours, from the spectacular setting of the Scottish highlands, in this British round of the World Cup series

Hot Property
Executive producer: George Mitchell
Director: John Pluck
6 x 30 mins V
A magazine series, presented by Judith Chalmers, on all aspects of running and owning a home, with each programme having a housing-related story.

The programme also visits the stars at home for a peep into the private world of public faces

Portrait of the Wild
Production company: Shearwater Productions
Commissioning editor: Ted Brocklebank
4 x 30 mins V
The magic of the wild is captured on canvas by top Scottish wildlife artists as the programmes follow the flora and fauna of the country through the seasons

Scotland's Larder
Production company: Cinécosse
Commissioning editor: Ted Brocklebank
6 x 30 mins V
The doyen of British food writers, Derek Cooper, takes a unique look at Scottish food, asking why we eat as we do and what the reasons are behind the production of certain foods. Each programme takes a particular foodstuff as its theme and each week, top chefs prepare some of their favourite dishes

Scotland the Grave
Producer: Ted Brocklebank
Director: Bernd Schulz
1 x 60 mins V
Scotland has the worst record for heart disease in the world and this documentary asks what are the underlying reasons and what can be done to reduce the level of fatalities

Other programmes include:
Abair!
The Art Sutter Show
Country Matters
Crann Tara
Crossfire
Fionnan-Feoir
Grampian Sheepdog Trials
North Tonight
Pick a Number
Scotland the What?
Top Club
You'd Better Believe It

Granada Television

Granada Television Centre
Quay Street
Manchester M60 9EA
Tel: 061 832 7211
Fax: 061 832 7211 x3405
Granada News Centre
Albert Dock
Liverpool L3 4BA
Tel: 051 709 9393
Fax: 051 709 3389
Granada Television
White Cross
South Road
Lancaster LA1 4XH
Tel: 0524 60688
Fax: 0524 67607
Granada News Centre
Bridgegate House
5 Bridge Place
Lower Bridge Street
Chester CH1 15A
Tel: 0244 313966
Fax: 0244 320599
Granada News Centre
Daisyfield Business Centre
Appleby Street
Blackburn BB1 3BL
Tel: 0254 690099
Chairman: David Plowright
Managing Director: Andrew Quinn
Director of Programmes: Steve Morrison
Programme Board: Rod Caird, Paul Doherty, Ray Fitzwalter, Stuart Prebble, David Liddiment, Sally Head

The Case-Book of Sherlock Holmes
Producer: Michael Cox
Directors: Patrick Lau, John Madden, Michael Simpson, June Howson, Tim Sullivan
Dramatised by: T R Bowen, Jeremy Paul, Gary Hopkins, John Hawkesworth, Robin Chapman
Camera: Ken Morgan, Mike Popley, Doug Hallows, Lawrence Jones
Cast: Jeremy Brett, Edward Hardwicke
6 x 1 hour F
Jeremy Brett and Edward Hardwicke return in their definitive roles as Holmes and Watson. The great man is in superb form – and now entering a new century as Victorian London gives way to the Edwardian era

You've Been Framed
Producer: Kieran Roberts
Director: Wendy J Dyer
VTR Editor: Chris Barham
7 x 30 mins V
Jeremy Beadle hosts an hilarious collection of home videos. In their rush to record historical moments, people have accidentally captured hysterical moments ... and the only thing that gets hurt is their pride

Watching
Executive producer: David Liddiment
Producer/Director: Les Chatfield
Scriptwriter: Jim Hitchmough
Cast: Emma Wray, Paul Bown, Liza Tarbuck, John Bowler, Patsy Byrne
10 x 30 mins V
Centring around the unlikely romance between sharp talking Brenda and her bird-watching boyfriend Malcolm. A new face appears in the fifth series – Lucinda, as a rival for Malcolm's affections, sharing his love of wildlife and presenting Malcolm with a broken 2CV to mend

Compass
Executive producer: Rod Caird
Producers: Sue Hayes, Ken Grieve, Jane Wellesley
Directors: Roger Mills, Ken Grieve, Patrick Lau
Camera: Jorge Vignati, Mike Thomson, Chris O'Dell
3 x 1 hour F
Three new films from the Compass series. Each film will be a unique journey, a record of a dream fulfilled or the solving of a personal mystery

The Shape of the World
Executive producer: Rod Caird
Producers: Simon Berthon, Mark Anderson
Directors: Peter Swain, Simon Berthon, Patrick Lau, Mark Anderson
Camera: Nick Plowright, Mike Thomson
6 x 1 hour V
From the earliest times people have sought to chart and understand their environment, to express through drawings, diagrams, ritual and legend the world around them and to use maps to navigate, to communicate and to dominate. The series traverses the globe to tell that story and to reveal the political, social and cultural impact map-making has made throughout history

Other programmes include:
Busman's Holiday
Cluedo
Coasting
Families
Made in Heaven
Medics
My Left Foot
Stars in their Eyes
This Morning

HTV Cymru/Wales

Television Centre
Culverhouse Cross
Cardiff CF5 6XJ
Tel: 0222 590590
HTV Ltd
126 Baker Street
London W1M 2AJ
Tel: 071 224 4048
Fax: 071 224 3750
HTV Group
Chairman: Louis Sherwood
Chief Executive: Charles Romaine
Director Television Group: H H Davies
Director Finance and Administration: Alan Burton
HTV Cymru/Wales Ltd
Chairman: I E Symonds
Chief Executive: H H Davies
Director of Programmes and Deputy Chief Executive: Emyr Daniel

Chestnut Soldier
Producer/Director: Pennant Roberts
Scriptwriter: Julia Jones from a story by Jenny Nimmo

Cast: Siân Phillips, Cal Macaninch, Osian Roberts, Sharon Morgan, Robert Blythe, Gareth Thomas
4 x 25 mins
Set in the present, the third part of Jenny Nimmo's trilogy that began with the award-winning *The Snow Spider* and continued with *Emlyn's Moon*

Old Scores
Producer: Richard Meyrick
Director: Alan Clayton
Scriptwriters: Dean Parker, Greg McGee
Locations: Cardiff Arms Park and Eden Park, New Zealand
Cast: Windsor Davies, Glyn Houston, Robert Pugh
1 x 2 hours
Comedy drama based on rugby union with appearances by former All Blacks and Welsh International rugby stars. A co-production with South Pacific Pictures of New Zealand

Other programmes include:
Farming Wales
Stopwatch
Wales and Westminster
Wales at Six
Wales on Sunday
Wales this Week

HTV West

Television Centre
Bath Road
Bristol BS4 3HG
Tel: 0272 778366
Fax: 0272 722400
Chairman: Ron Evans
Managing Director: Ted George
Director of Programmes: Derek Clark
Head of News: Steve Matthews

Ask Oddie
Chain Reaction
Flowering Passions
Garden Club
Good Neighbour Show
History on Canvas
Looking Back
Press Your Luck
Problems
Rolf's Cartoon Club
Scene
Simply the Best
Sportsmasters

ITN

Independent Television News

200 Gray's Inn Road
London WC1X 8XZ
Tel: 071 833 3000
Chairman: David Nicholas
Chief Executive: Robert Phillis
Editor-in-chief: Stewart Purvis

Independent Television News provides programmes of national and international news for the independent television network. It also produces the award-winning Channel Four News each weekday evening and since March 1989 has produced the World News for the Channel Four Daily. ITN also operates the first international English language news programme. ITN World News is a daily programme specifically designed for a worldwide audience and is now seen on four continents.

Other programmes for the other ITV companies include *The World This Week* and *The Parliament Programme* for Channel Four; elections at home and abroad, the budget, royal tours, state visits, overseas events and special celebrations. ITN also provides general, sport and business news for Oracle

Channel Four News
Eurodiario
5am Morning News
ITN Radio News
ITN Telephone News
ITN World News
Morning Bulletins
News at One
News at 5.40
News at Ten
Night Time Bulletins
Oracle
The Parliament Programme
Special Programmes
The World This Week
World News on Channel Four Daily

LWT

LWT (Holdings) plc

South Bank Television Centre
London SE1 9LT
Tel: 071 620 1620
Chairman: Christopher Bland
Deputy Chairman: Brian Tesler
Managing Director: Greg Dyke
Director of Programmes: Marcus Plantin
Director of Corporate Affairs: Barry Cox
Controller of Arts: Melvyn Bragg
Controller of Drama: Nick Elliott
Controller of Entertainment: John Kaye Cooper
Controller of Features and Current Affairs: Robin Paxton
Controller of Sport: Stuart McConachie

A Perfect Hero
Production company: Havahall Pictures
Executive producers: Nick Elliott and Michael Whitehall
Producer/Director: James Cellan Jones
6 x 60 mins V
Nigel Havers stars as a World War II fighter pilot who has to completely reassess his life after being badly burnt in a Battle of Britain dog-fight

London's Burning
Executive producer: Nick Elliott
Producer: Paul Knight
10 x 60 mins F
The fourth series of the ratings hit which chronicles the life and times of Blue Watch at Blackwall Fire Station in London's East End

The South Bank Show
Editor: Melvyn Bragg
Executive Producers: Nigel Wattis, David Thomas
1 x 120 mins, 1 x 90 mins, 1 x 75 mins, 21 x 60 mins F/V
ITV's flagship arts strand covering subjects as diverse as Rudolf Nureyev and George Michael, Kiri Te Kanawa and Steve Martin, August Wilson and Spitting Image, 30 Years of Private Eye and Vera Lynn

Breadline Britain 1990s
Production company: Domino Films
Executive producer: Robin Paxton
Series editor: Joanna Mack
Producer/Director: Stewart Lansley
6 x 30 mins F
A follow-up to the mould-breaking documentary series of 10 years ago which gave a new definition to the meaning of the word 'poverty'

Aspel & Company
Executive producer: Nick Barrett
Producer: Lorna Dickinson
Director: Alasdair MacMillan
13 x 45 mins plus 2 specials V
Television's top talk show host meets the showbusiness names who make the headlines

You Bet!
Executive producer: John Kaye Cooper
Producer: Linda Beadle
10 x 60 mins V
Matthew Kelly hosts the people show with unusual challengers benefiting celebrities' favourite charities

Other programmes include:
Agatha Christie's Poirot
Blind Date
Come Home Charlie and Face Them
Faith in the Future
Forever Green
Hale & Pace
The London Programme
The Piglet Files
Second Thoughts
Sex Now
Surprise Surprise
Walden

S4C

S4C
Parc Tŷ Glas
Llanishen
Cardiff CF4 5DU
Tel: 0222 747444
Chairman: John Howard Davies CBE DL
Chief Executive: Geraint Stanley Jones
Programme Controller: Deryk Williams
Director of Marketing: Christopher Grace

Noson yr Heliwr
Production company: Lluniau Lliw (for S4C and YTV)
Executive producers: Dafydd Huw Williams, Brian Harries
Producer/Director: Peter Edwards
Scriptwriters: Siôn Eirian, Lyn Ebenezer
Cast: Hywel Bennett, Phillip Madoc, Sue Jones-Davies, Nicola Beddoe
1 x 90 mins
Thriller concerning the conflict between a detective and an academic as a serial killer stalks the streets of a small university town

Traed Mewn Cyffion
Production company: Ffilmiau Eryri
Producer: Norman Williams
Director: David Lyn
Scriptwriter: John Ogwen, from a novel by Kate Roberts
Cast: Bethan Dwyfor, Maureen Rhys, Bryn Fôn, Mair Tomos Ifans
3 x 60 mins
The stoic struggle for survival of a slate quarrying community in North Wales during the early years of this century, seen through the eyes of one woman

Shakespeare – The Animated Tales
Production company: Shakespeare Production Ltd in association with Dave Edwards' Siriol Animation
Executive producer: Christopher Grace
Series director: Dave Edwards
Scriptwriter: Leon Garfield
Cast: Susan Fleetwood, Tilda Swinton, Nicholas Farrell
6 x 25 mins
Six of Shakespeare's immortal plays uniquely brought to life by animation. The series will include *Hamlet, The Tempest* and *A Midsummer Night's Dream*

Scottish Television
Cowcaddens
Glasgow G2 3PR
Tel: 041 332 9999
Fax: 041 332 6982
114 St Martin's Lane
London WC2N 4AZ
Tel: 071 836 1500
Fax: 071 528 9390
The Gateway
Edinburgh EH7 4AH
Tel: 031 557 4554
Fax: 031 557 4554 x239
Chairman: William Brown CBE
Managing Director: Gus Macdonald
Director of Programmes: Alistair Moffat
Head of Programmes – Scotland: David Scott
Controller of Drama: Robert Love
Controller of Entertainment: Sandy Ross

Taggart
Executive Producer: Robert Love
Glasgow detective series

The Advocates
Executive producer: Robert Love
Legal drama set in Edinburgh

Take the High Road
Producer: Frank Cox
Drama serial set on Loch Lomond

Wheel of Fortune
Executive producer: Sandy Ross
Popular network game show

The Disney Club
Executive Producer: Sandy Ross
Sunday morning children's network entertainment

Other programmes include:
In Verse
The Munro Show
NB
Scotland's War
Scotland Today
Scotsport
Scottish Books
Scottish Frontiers on Medicine
Scottish Women
Sick Kids
Win, Lose or Draw

TSW – Television South West
Derry's Cross
Plymouth
Devon PL1 2SP
Tel: 0752 663322
Chairman: Sir Brian Bailey OBE
Managing Director: Harry Turner
Deputy Managing Director: Ivor Stolliday
Director of Programmes: Paul Stewart Laing
Head of News and Current Affairs: Jon Williams
Head of Sport: Pete Barraclough
Head of Community Unit: Thomas Goodison
Head of Features: Frank Wintle
Head of Presentation and Programme Planning: Tony Smith

The TSW Documentary 'A Grin of Bitterness'
A documentary unlocking the secret behind Thomas Hardy's marital relationships

The Man Who Went Mad On Paper
This programme counterpoints the hilarity of the work that won cartoonist H M Bateman fame with the sombre obsessions which destroyed his marriage and turned him into a dour recluse

Mitchin'
An episode for the Dramarama series on Children's ITV about two boys from opposite ends of the social ladder who cause chaos when they take a forbidden day off school because of family problems

Sonia's Report
Producer: Frank Wintle
Director: Chris Watson
Scriptwriter: Frank Wintle
Camera: Mike Ford
Editor: Jim de Wan
1 hour
Ruth Werner, the spy who successfully passed Klaus Fuchs' nuclear secrets to Moscow from 1940s Britain, revealed her amazing story to the West for the first time in this remarkable documentary

Sounds Like Music
Bobby Crush returns to the small screen to compere a musical quiz testing knowledge of film and musicals

Stranger in a Strange Land
Production company: Cheriton Enterprises
Producer: John Pett
Executive Producer: Frank Wintle
Director: John Pett
Scriptwriter: Vicky Pett
Camera: Mike Ford
Editor: David Taylor
1 hour
This programme is about Karen Gershon, a Jewish daughter robbed of her parents by Riga concentration camp ... a mother who lost the confidence to fully love even her own children ... a grandmother whose scattered grandchildren lack even a common language

TV-am

Breakfast Television Centre
Hawley Crescent
London NW1 8EF
Tel: 071 267 4300
Fax: 071 267 4332
Chairman and Managing Director: Bruce Gyngell
Director of Programmes: Bill Ludford
Director of Regions and Training: Dave Davidovitz
Director of Sales: Tony Vickers
Director of Finance: Stratis Zographos
Controller, News and Current Affairs: Jeff Berliner

Good Morning Britain/After Nine
Presenters: Maya Even, Mike Morris, Lorraine Kelly, Kathy Tayler, Lisa Aziz, Lizzie Webb, Geoff Clark, Ulrika Jonsson, David Frost
News, current affairs, weather, sport and features on a wide range of topics

TVS

Television Centre
Vinters Park
Maidstone
Kent ME14 5NZ
Tel: 0622 691111
Television Centre
Southampton SO9 5HZ
Tel: 0703 634211
84 Buckingham Gate
London SW1E 6PD
Tel: 071 976 7199
Chairman: Rudolph Agnew
Managing Director: Tony Brook
Director of Programmes: Alan Boyd
Director of Regional Programming: Clive Jones
Controller of Factual Programmes: Peter Williams
Controller of Drama: Graham Benson
Controller of Children's Programmes: J Nigel Pickard
Controller of Entertainment: Gill Stribling-Wright
Head of News: David Morris Jones
Head of Sport: Gary Lovejoy

The Ruth Rendell Mysteries: A New Lease of Death
Executive producer/Controller: Graham Benson
Producer: Neil Zeiger
Director: Herbert Wise
Writer: Peter Berry
Cast: George Baker, Christopher Ravenscroft, Louie Ramsay, Diane Keen, Dorothy Tutin, Peter Egan, Sharon Maughan
3 x 1 hour F
A persistent vicar arrives in Kingsmarkham with a mission: to prove that his prospective daughter-in-law's father was not guilty of the murder he was hanged for 30 years ago

The Tale of Little Pig Robinson
Executive producer: J Nigel Pickard
Producer: Timothy Woolford
Director: Alan Bridges
Screenplay: John Michael Phillips
Editor: Mike Hunt
Cast: Timothy Spall, Jennifer Saunders, Dawn French, Edward Fox, Gorden Kaye, Toyah Wilcox, Bill Maynard, Prunella Scales, Thora Hird
Beatrix Potter's classic tale about a gullible young pig called Robinson is brought to life with an all-star cast. Robinson is sent to market by his two aunts but on his way is 'pig-napped' by ruthless sailors who want to eat him

Perfect Scoundrels
Executive producer: Graham Benson
Producer: Terence Williams
Directors: Jan Sargent, John Gorrie
Scriptwriters: Willis Hall, Kieran Prendiville (2 episodes), Barry Delvin, Tim Aspinall, Anthony Couch
Camera: Michael D Smith
Editors: Nick McPhee, Michael Hunt
Cast: Peter Bowles, Bryan Murray, Thora Hird, Richard Griffiths, Sian Phillips, Frances Tomelty, Beryl Reid, Leslie Ash, Derek Fowlds
6 x 1 hour F
Peter Bowles and Bryan Murray continue as the stylish duo Guy Buchanan and Harry Cassidy, who always have an eye on other people's money, in this second series of the popular drama. Buchanan is even thinking of robbing his own grandmother . . . with Cassidy's help. And Cassidy dresses up as a nun to con a nun!

Motormouth III
Executive producer/Controller: J Nigel Pickard
Producer: Vanessa Hill
Director: David Crozier
Presenters: Andy Crane, Neil Buchanan, Gaby Roslin, Steve Johnson, Francis Wright
Live on Saturday mornings with top pop artists, video stars, special guests from around the country, and the fast-moving game show 'Mousetrap' with celebrity contestants

Human Factor
Controller: Peter Williams
Editor: Andrew Barr
Presenters: Ted Harrison, Rosemary Hartill, Peter Williams, Mike Field
An eighth series of documentaries in which the human spirit is revealed in all its unpredictability and strength

That's Love
Production company: Lawson Productions
Executive producer: Gill Stribling-Wright, Sarah Lawson
Producer: Humphrey Barclay
Director: John Stroud
Scriptwriter: Terence Frisby
Cast: Jimmy Mulville, Diana Hardcastle
7 x 30 mins V
The continuing story of a young married couple's attempt to resolve their marital differences

Other programmes include:
Art Attack
Country Ways
Facing South
Finders Keepers
It's a Dog's Life
Moneywise
Nature and Wildlife
Skyrunners
South by South East
TV Weekly
Taste of the South
This Way Out

Thames Television

306 Euston Road
London NW1 3BB
Tel: 071 387 9494
149 Tottenham Court Road
London W1P 9LL
Tel: 071 387 9494
Teddington Lock
Teddington
Middlesex TW11 9NT
Tel: 081 977 3252
Fairview House
71-73 Woodbridge Road
Guildford
Surrey GU1 4YZ
Tel: 0483 302708
2-4 The Priory Centre
Dartford
Kent
Tel: 0322 277200
Mobile Division
Twickenham Road
Hanworth
Middlesex TW13 6JH
Tel: 081 898 0011
Regional Sales
Norfolk House
Smallbrook Queensway
Birmingham B5 4LJ
Tel: 021 643 9151
Clarence House
4 Clarence Street
Manchester M2 4DW
Tel: 061 835 2876
Chairman: Lord Brabourne

Chief Executive: Richard Dunn
Director of Finance: Derek Hunt
Company Secretary & Director of Personnel: Ben Marr
Director of Sales & Marketing: Jonathan Shier
Director of Production: Ewart Needham
Director of Programmes: David Elstein
Director of Corporate Communications: Sue Farr
Controller of Network Factual Programmes: Roger Bolton
Controller of Sport & Outside Broadcasts: Bob Burrows
Controller of Programme Administration: James Corsan
Controller of Light Entertainment: John Howard Davies
Co-ordinator of Independent Productions: Roy English
Head of Variety: John Fisher
Executive Producer: James Gilbert
Controller, Children's & Education: Allan Horrox
Head of Purchased Programmes: Pat Mahoney
Controller, Sales & Marketing: David Mansfield
Head of Music & Arts: Ian Martin
Head of Features: Mary McAnally
Controller, News & Current Affairs & Documentaries: Barrie Sales

Sea Dragon
Producer: Alan Horrox
Director: August Gudmundsson
Writer: David Joss Buckley
Camera: Geoff Harrison
Editor: Olivia Hetreed
Cast: Graham McGrath, Janek Lesniak, Holly Aird, Anna Massey, Pat Roach
1 x 95 mins F
A Viking chieftain dies in this stirring tale of friendship and betrayal, set in the far off tenth century. Thormod the Viking and his slave Jestyn the Briton join forces in an epic search to find the murderers

A Small Dance
Producer/Director: Alan Horrox
Writer: Lucy Gannon
Camera: David Scott
Editor: Olivia Hetreed
Cast: Kate Hardie, James Hazeldine, Linda Bassett
1 x 94 mins F
Filmed in the Cambridge Fenlands, this powerful film tells the story of 16 year old Donna, trapped between her domineering father and her soulless job in a local food processing plant. She grasps at a moment of warmth with a passing stranger, and when she ends up pregnant, hides her condition and abandons the baby. But her decision returns to haunt her

Hope It Rains
Producer/Director: John Howard Davies
Writers: John Esmonde, Bob Larbey
Cast: Tom Bell, Holly Aird, Eamon Boland
7 x 30 mins V
Harry Nash's self-contained little world is disturbed when his eighteen year old god-daughter comes into his life. The fact that he hasn't set eyes on her for those eighteen years and that it's mutual dislike on second sight does not make for a happy reunion

Men Behaving Badly
Production company: Hartswood Films for Thames Television
Producer: Beryl Vertue
Director: Martin Dennis
Writer: Simon Nye
Cast: Harry Enfield, Martin Clunes, Leslie Ash, Caroline Quentin
6 x 30 mins V
Dermot and Gary are two young men in their mid-twenties. Although they share a flat, their approach to life is very different. Dermot has devoted his life to the pursuit of women and Gary has a steady job and regular girlfriend. They don't mean to, but somehow they always end up behaving badly

Murder Squad
Production company: Argo Productions
Producer/Director: Robert Fleming
Camera: Paul Williams
Editor: Roger Shufflebottom
1 x 60 mins, 6 x 30 mins F
A 'fly-on-the-wall' look at the work of the Metropolitan Police's murder squad. Made by the production company which made Thames' successful documentary *Flying Squad*

Selling Hitler
Production company: Euston Films
Producer: Andrew Brown
Director: Alastair Reid
Writer: Howard Schuman
Camera: Clive Tickner
Editor: Don Fairservice
Cast: Alexei Sayle, Jonathan Pryce, Alison Doody, Alison Steadman, Alan Bennett, Barry Humphries
5 x 1 hour F
Satirical drama portraying the Hitler Diaries publishing scandal of 1983

Titmuss Regained
Production company: New Penny Productions
Producer: Jacqueline David
Director: Martyn Friend
Writer: John Mortimer
Camera: Colin Munn
Editor: Chris Wimble
Cast: David Threlfall, Kristin Scott Thomas, Bill Oddie
3 x 1 hour F
Continuing the rise of thrusting young Tory MP, the Hon Leslie Titmuss; a love story set against the battle over a new town

Victor & Hugo
Production company: Cosgrove Hall
Producers: Brian Cosgrove, Mark Hall
Writers: Jimmy Hibbert, Brian Trueman
Voices: David Jason, Jimmy Hibbert, Brian Trueman
39 x 22 mins F
Victor and Hugo are a pair of incompetent French crooks who are the sole proprietors of Naughtiness International, an organisation run from their mobile headquarters – a ramshackle van. Together with their parrot Interpoll who doubles up as a telephone answering machine, no job is too big for Victor and Hugo

Truckers
Production company: Cosgrove Hall
Producers: Brian Cosgrove, Mark Hall
Adapted by: Brian Trueman
Voices: Joe McGann, Debra Gillett, Rosalie Williams, Sir Michael Hordern
13 x 10 mins F
Based on the novel by Terry Pratchett, and focusing on the adventures of a population of nomes – characters who are only four inches tall, who live in the world of humans, but who move at ten times their speed

French Fields
Producer: James Gilbert
Director: Mark Stuart
Scriptwriter: John Chapman, Ian Davidson
Cast: Anton Rodgers, Julia McKenzie
6 x 25 mins V
A second series continuing Hester and William's adaptation to their new way of life in France

Tyne Tees Television
Television Centre
City Road
Newcastle upon Tyne
NE1 2AL
Tel: 091 261 0181
Fax: 091 261 2302
Chairman: Sir Ralph Carr-Ellison TD
Deputy Chairman: R H Dickinson
Chief Executive: David Reay
Managing Director: Ian Ritchie
Director of Programmes: Adrian Metcalfe
Controller of Regional

Programmes: Steve Ireland
Controller of Public Affairs: Peter Moth
Head of Programme Organisation: Paul Black
Head of Education: Sheila Browne
Director of Resources: James Lancaster

Crosswits
Production company: Tyne Tees Television
Producer: Christine Williams
Director: Andy Martin
Presenter: Tom O'Connor
40 x 30 mins
Tom O'Connor hosts the compulsive word game for crossword fanatics. A host of celebrity guests are lining up to help crossword contestants solve the crossword clues and 80 contestants from all over the country test their crossword skills. The object of each round is to guess a keyword by solving the crossword clues

Ghost Train
Series Producer: Billy MacQueen
Producer: Angelo Abela
Presenters: Frances Dodge, Angelo Abela, Sabra Williams, Nobby the Sheep
20 x 60 mins
ITV's live soap opera. Evil funfair boss Barry Mafia has a new ally in Mervyn Mafia – a failed magician – and the duo have the Ghost Train in their clutches. But Frances is determined to get it back and together with Gerard, Sabra and Nobby the Sheep she sets off on a rollercoaster chase around Britain in pursuit of the Mafia mob and the Ghost Train

Don't Try This at Home
Producer: Lesley Oakden
Director: Malcolm Dickinson
Presenters: Frank Bruno, Eddie Kidd
1 x 60 mins
Frank Bruno and Eddie Kidd head an all-star cast of British stunt doubles from the World Cinema Stunt Festival in Toulouse, an hilarious event which gives stunt artists a rare opportunity to play themselves

The Black Candle
Production company: World Wide International Television
Producer: Ray Marshall
Director: Roy Battersby
Scriptwriter: Gordon Hann
Camera: Alistair McKenzie
Editor: Andrew Nelson
Cast: Samantha Bond, Nathaniel Parker, Denholm Elliott, Sian Phillips
1 x 102 mins
The latest in a long line of Catherine Cookson best-sellers about a modern-minded young woman who inherits her father's mill and turns it into a successful business. But her comfortable life begins to fall apart when her works manager is accused of murder and her sister marries the wayward son of an impoverished aristocrat

The Black Velvet Gown
Production company: World Wide International Television
Producer: Ray Marshall
Director: Norman Stone
Scriptwriter: Gordon Hann
Camera: Alistair McKenzie
Editor: John McDonal
Cast: Janet McTeer, Bob Peck, Jean Anderson, David Hunt, Geraldine Somerville, Brendan Healy, Christopher Benjamin
1 x 120 mins
Based on one of Catherine Cookson's most popular novels and set against a rural backdrop of Northumberland in the 1830's, the story centres on a strong-minded widow and her wilful daughter whose strong personalities clash as they challenge the prejudices around them. And when the mother accepts a job as housekeeper to a scholarly, embittered recluse, storm clouds gather and the family is torn apart

Other programmes include:
The Back Page
Echoes of the Past
Elements
Flashback
Listening Eye
Mystery of the Derbyshire
Northern Eye
Northern Life
Northern Life Review
North Tonight
Thank You and Good Night
the Useful Guide

Ulster Television
Havelock House
Ormeau Road
Belfast BT7 1EB
Tel: 0232 328122
Fax: 0232 246695
6 York Street
London W1H 1FA
Tel: 071 486 5211
Chairman: J B McGuckian
Managing Director: J D Smyth
Assistant Managing Director: J A Creagh
General Manager: J McCann
Controller of Programming: A Bremner
Commissioning Editor (Documentaries, Music): A Crockart
Commissioning Editor (News and Current Affairs): M Beattie

December Bride
Ulster Television, as one of the co-producers, hosted the Northern Ireland premiere of the film, based on Sam Hanna Bell's famed novel

William's War
A colourful hour-long drama featuring three kings and a host of actors. A costume production, it was filmed on locations in Holland and Ireland. One of several programmes to mark the Tercentenary of the Battle of the Boyne

Once Upon a Place
An out-and-about series of programmes exploring the history of many Ulster places, including Portavogie, Upper Lough Erne and the Waterside in Londonderry

High Days and Holidays
A series of cookery programmes presented by popular cookery expert Jenny Bristow. She also featured in another big viewer-response series, *Kitchen Garden*

Fleadh Fever
A rich musical programme looking at the traditional Irish music festival scene and the musicians who make them such colourful events. It went on to win its section in the Celtic Film Festival

Kelly
Into its second successful season, this 90-minute weekly programme hosted by Gerry Kelly provides a varied mixture of music and chat with well-known faces from today and yesterday

Yorkshire Television
The Television Centre
Leeds LS3 1JS
Tel: 0532 438283
Fax: 0532 445107
Television House
32 Bedford Row
London WC1R 4HE
Tel: 071 242 1666
Fax: 071 405 8062
Chairman: Sir Derek Palmar
Managing Director: Clive Leach
Director of Programmes: John Fairley
Controller of Drama: Keith Richardson
Controller of Entertainment: Vernon Lawrence
Head of Documentaries and Current Affairs: Grant McKee
Head of Science and Features: Duncan Dallas
Head of Education, Children's Programmes and

per4mance

Religion: Chris Jelley
Head of Local Programmes: Graham Ironside
Head of Sport: Robert Charles
Controller Corporate Affairs: Geoff Brownlee

Rich Tea & Sympathy
Executive producer: Vernon Lawrence
Producer: David Reynolds
Directors: David Reynolds, Michael Simpson
Writer: David Nobbs
Editors: John Allen, Lance Tattersall
Cast: Patricia Hodge, Dennis Quilley, Lionel Jeffries, Jean Alexander
6 x 1 hour
All about the relationships – whether they are bumpy, smooth, funny or serious – which develop between two contemporary families, the Rudges and the Merrygroves

Stay Lucky
Executive producer: David Reynolds
Producer: Andrew Benson
Directors: David Reynolds, John Glenister, Graeme Harper
Camera: Peter Jackson, Allan Pyrah
Writers: Geoff McQueen, Michael Aitkens, Steven Moffatt
Editors: Clive Trist, David Aspinall, David Stocks
Cast: Dennis Waterman, Jan Francis, Niall Toibin, Emma Wray
7 x 1 hour
Thomas Gynn (Dennis Waterman), the refugee Cockney up North, and Sally Hardcastle (Jan Francis), the tough young businesswoman with a soft centre, get together again for further hair-raising hilarious adventures

Emmerdale
Executive producer: Keith Richardson
Producer: Stuart Doughty
Directors: various
Writers: various
Story Editor: Morag Bain
Script Editor: Ann Tobin
Cast: Sheila Mercier, Arthur Pentelow, Ronnie Magill, Frazer Hines, Jean Rogers, Clive Hornby, Richard Thorp, Stan Richards, Malandra Burrows, Christopher Chittell, Cy Chadwick, Glenda McKay, Craig McKay, Norman Bowler, Claire King, Madeleine Howard, Leah Bracknell, Peter Amory, Matthew Vaughan, Kate Dove, Naomi Lewis, Diana Davies, Tony Pitts
Twice weekly serial which was first transmitted in 1972

The Darling Buds of May
Executive producers: Vernon Lawrence, Richard Bates, Philip Burley
Producers: Robert Banks Stewart, Richard Bates
Adapted by: Bob Larbey, Robert Banks Stewart
Directors: Rodney Bennett, Robert Tronson, David Giles
Camera: Peter Jackson
Editor: Robin McDonnell
Cast: David Jason, Pam Ferris, Philip Franks, Catherine Zeta Jones
6 x 1 hour
The Larkins, created by H E Bates, are one big happy loving family. Ma and Pop and their six children radiate happiness and have hardly a care in the world. The world is 'perfick', even with the arrival of the Inland Revenue!

First Tuesday
Executive Producer: Grant McKee
Deputy Editor: Chris Bryer
Producers: various, including Jill Turton, Mark Halliley, Jill Nichols
Directors: various, including Ian McFarlane, Kevin Sim
Camera: Mike Shrimpton, Alan Wilson
Editors: Terry Warwick, Clive Trist, Barry Spink, David Aspinall
12 x 1 hour (monthly)
Yorkshire's award winning documentary showcase which brings home and international issues to the screen. Recipient recently of an international Emmy, a BAFTA award and the Grand Award at the International Film and TV Festival of New York for its film 'Four Hours in My Lai'

Jimmy's
Executive Producer: Grant McKee
Producer/Director: Irene Cockcroft
Camera: Russell Glavin
Editors: Steve Fairholme, Tim Dawson, Don MacMillan
14 x 30 mins
Set in Britain's largest general hospital, tells the everyday stories of joy and anguish, pain and sorrow of the staff and patients, and behind the scenes workers at St James's University Hospital in Leeds

Other programmes include:
All Change
Countdown
Fiddlers Three
Haggard
How We Used to Live
The James Whale Radio Show
The New Statesman
Runaway Bay
Scrumdown
Singles
Through the Keyhole
Yorkshire Glory

BBC TELEVISION

British Broadcasting Corporation

Television Centre
Wood Lane
London W12 7RJ
Tel: 081 743 8000
Broadcasting House
Portland Place
London W1A 1AA
Tel: 071 580 4468
Chairman: Marmaduke Hussey
Director-General: Michael Checkland
Deputy Director-General: John Birt
Managing Director, Network Television and Chairman BBC Enterprises: Will Wyatt
Managing Director, Regional Broadcasting: Ronald Neil
Assistant Managing Director, Network Television: Jane Drabble
Controller of BBC1: Jonathan Powell
Controller of BBC2: Alan Yentob

BBC TV Children's Programmes

Television Centre
Wood Lane
London W12 7RJ
Head: Anna Home
Tel: 081 743 8000

Blue Peter
Programme editor: Lewis Bronze
Presenters: Yvette Fielding, John Leslie, Diane-Louise Jordan
Continuing x 25 mins F and live V
Blue Peter began on October 1958. The programme is named after the blue and white flag which is raised within 24 hours of a ship leaving harbour: the idea is that the programme is like a ship setting out on a voyage, having new adventures and discovering new things

Going Live!
Programme editor: Chris Bellinger
Cast: Sarah Greene, Phillip Schofield
Continuing x 3 hours F and live V
A mixture of cartoons, live music, videos, competitions and the chance to speak to famous guests on the telephone

Grange Hill
Producer: Albert Barber
Script Editor: Leigh Jackson
Writers: Barry Purchese, Kevin Hood, Margaret Simpson, Chris Ellis, Alison Fisher
20 x 25 mins V
Fictional characters face true-to-life situations at a large comprehensive school

Others programmes include:
Hart Beat
The Really Wild Show
Take Two

BBC Community Programme Unit

39 Wales Farm Road
North Acton
London W3 6XP
Tel: 081 743 8000
Editor: Jeremy Gibson
This Unit is responsible for programmes made by and with the general public, usually as a direct response to public request. A voice is given to those who feel that the media distorts or ignores their point of view, and so offers viewers new perspectives on issues of social concern they would not expect to find aired elswhere on television. Currently the Unit's output is presented under three main titles, *Open Space, Video Diaries* and *Inside Out*

Inside Out
A series of occasional documentaries consisting of a pair of films exploring two sides of an institution. Covered so far: Swansea jail and an infantry battalion

Open Space
Contributors make their own programme on their chosen subjects with production help from the Unit but keeping full editorial control, or in 'partnership' with the Unit if they prefer. Alternatively members of the public can simply suggest programme ideas

Video Diaries
A unique series of programmes giving people self-operated video cameras to record the unfolding events of their lives

BBC Continuing Education & Training Television

White City
201 Wood Lane
London W12 7TF
Tel: 081 752 5252
Head: Alan Rogers

Help Your Child with Reading
Producer: Robert Albury
Presenter: Maggie Philbin
8 x 15 mins
Advice and information for parents, grandparents and childminders to help them help their children read well. Children can enjoy books and words from babyhood; practical examples show how to encourage children taking their first steps towards reading. Plus, listening to children read, choosing books and what do they learn at school?

Making Their Mark
Producer: Dick Foster
6 x 30 mins
Six artists demonstrate their drawing skills, discuss their sources of inspiration and give an insight into the creative process. Mike Wilks explores his obsessive and surreal approach to art in an award winning programme. Also featuring Sir Hugh Casson, Maggi Hambling, David Gentleman, Charlotte Fawley and Roy Marsden

Where On Earth Are We Going?
Executive producer: Paul Kriwaczek
Presenter: Jonathon Porritt
6 x 50 mins
Reporting from around the globe on the major environmental problems facing the planet – and the radical and lasting changes needed to save them. Porritt's proposals on energy, agriculture, inner cities, the developing world and 'green' politics are discussed by expert panels. In an award winning programme on 'Industrial Futures' Porritt visits the US to look at ways of limiting the destructive powers of manufacturing industry

A Way With Numbers
Series producer: George Auckland
Presenter: Carol Vorderman
20 x 25 mins
Maths in everyday situations, such as dressmaking and gardening for the one in ten adults who have problems with simple number skills. Comedy sketches help introduce fractions, measuring, percentages and simple statistics to interest general viewers as well as those who want to improve their maths through study

A Certain Age
Producer: Tony Matthews
6 x 50 mins
The changes and choices of life over 50. Beating age discrimination at work, caring for older relatives, the menopause, bereavement and what happens when you 'chuck up everything and just clear off'. Featuring newsreader Richard Whitmore who took early retirement to begin a new stage career as a variety artist

Mosaic
Series producer: John Twitchen
6 x 30 mins
Racism in the British state and strategies for change explored in classic documentary style, looking at health services, the magistrates system, bi-lingual teaching, pre-school education, fair recruitment and the different ways that ethnic minority communities use the English language. Part of a major 5 year anti-racism initiative

Other programmes include:
Bazaar
Business Matters
Clean Slate
Into Print
Last Exodus
Mexico Vivo
OK2 Talk Feelings
See Hear and Sign Extra
Sum Chance
When in France
Women Talk Safety
You and '92

BBC TV Documentary Features

Kensington House
Richmond Way
London W14 0AX
Tel: 081 895 6611
Head: Colin Cameron

40 Minutes
Series Editor: Caroline Pick
26 x 40 mins F
A series of documentary films about the way we live now

Holiday 9z
Series Producer: Jane Lush

Inside Story
Executive producer: Paul Hamann

Saturday Night Clive
Producer: Beatrice Ballard
Executive producer: Richard Drewett
Presenter: Clive James
Clive James attempts to make some sense of the new and de-regulated universe of ever expanding media

Taking Liberties
Series producer: Elizabeth Clough
Presenter: David Jessel

Rough Justice
Series producer: Steve Haywood
Presenter: David Jessel

Film 91
Producer: Bruce Thompson
Presenter: Barry Norman

BBC TV Drama Films

Television Centre
Wood Lane
London W12 7RJ
Tel: 081 743 8000
Head of Drama Group, BBC Television: Mark Shivas

Screen One
Executive Producer, BBC1 Films: Richard Broke
An annual series of popular feature-length films for television on BBC1. Highlights from the 1990 season include *Newshounds, Can You Hear Me Thinking, The Police* and *Frankenstein's Baby*

Screen Two
Executive Producer, BBC2 Films: Mark Shivas
BBC Television's original feature-length film

strand. Highlights of the 1991 season include *102 Boulevard Haussman, Heading Home, They Never Slept, Morphine & Dolly Mixtures, Hallelujah Anyhow* and *Fellow Traveller*

BBC TV Light Entertainment Comedy Programmes

Television Centre
Wood Lane
London W12 7RJ
Tel: 081 743 8000
Head: Robin Nash

'Allo 'Allo
Producer/Director: Michael Stephens
Scriptwriters: Jeremy Lloyd, Paul Adam
Cast: Gorden Kaye, Carmen Silvera

Bread
Producer/Director: John B Hobbs
Scriptwriter: Carla Lane
Cast: Graham Bickley, Jean Boht, Nick Conway, Hilary Crowson, Ronald Forfar, Melanie Hill, Victor McGuire, Jonathan Morris, Bryan Murray, Eileen Pollock, Pamela Power, Kenneth Waller, Giles Watling

Last of the Summer Wine
Producer/Director: Alan Bell
Scriptwriter: Roy Clarke
Cast: Bill Owen, Peter Sallis, Brian Wilde

Only Fools and Horses
Producer: Gareth Gwenlan
Director: Tony Dow
Scriptwriter: John Sullivan
Cast: David Jason, Nicholas Lyndhurst, Buster Merryfield

Brush Strokes
Producer/Director: John B Hobbs
Scriptwriters: John Esmonde, Bob Larbey
Cast: Karl Howman, Elizabeth Counsell

One Foot in the Grave
Producer/Director: Susan Belbin
Scriptwriter: David Renwick
Cast: Richard Wilson, Annette Crosbie

Keeping Up Appearances
Producer/Director: Harold Snoad
Scriptwriter: Roy Clarke
Cast: Patricia Routledge

On the Up
Producer/Director: Gareth Gwenlan
Scriptwriter: Bob Larbey
Cast: Dennis Waterman

Waiting for God
Producer/Director: Gareth Gwenlan
Scriptwriter: Michael Aitkens
Cast: Graham Crowden, Stephanie Cole

Brittas Empire
Producer/Director: Mike Stephens
Scriptwriters: Richard Fegen, Andrew Norris
Cast: Chris Barrie

You Rang M'Lord
Producer/Director: David Croft
Scriptwriters: Jimmy Perry, David Croft
Cast: Paul Shane, Su Pollard, Jeffrey Holland

KYTV
Producer: Jamie Rix
Director: John Kilby
Scriptwriters: Angus Deayton, Geoffrey Perkins
Cast: Angus Deayton, Geoffrey Perkins, Helen Atkinson Wood, Michael Fenton Stevens, Philip Pope

Lazarus & Dingwall
Producer: Kim Fuller
Director: Bob Spiers
Scriptwriters: Kim Fuller, Vicky Pile
Cast: Stephen Frost, Mark Arden

Birds of a Feather
Producer: Nic Phillips for Alomo Productions
Directors: Nic Phillips, Charlie Hanson, Sue Bysh
Scriptwriters: Laurence Marks, Maurice Gran
Cast: Pauline Quirke, Linda Robson, Lesley Joseph

May to December
Producer: Sharon Bloom for Cinema Verity
Director: Paul Harrison
Scriptwriter: Paul A Mendelson
Cast: Anton Rodgers, Lesley Dunlop

Smith & Jones
Executive producer: Peter Fincham for TalkBack
Producer: Jon Plowman
Director: Graham C Williams
Cast: Mel Smith, Griff Rhys Jones

BBC TV Light Entertainment Variety Programmes

Television Centre
Wood Lane
London W12 7RJ
Tel: 081 743 8000
Head: Jim Moir

French and Saunders
Producer: Jon Plowman
Scriptwriters: Dawn French, Jennifer Saunders
Cast: Jennifer Saunders, Dawn French, with Raw Sex
7 x 30 mins

The Paul Daniels Magic Show
Producer/director: Geoff Miles
Host: Paul Daniels
9 x 45 mins
Magician Paul Daniels and speciality act guests

The Rory Bremner Show
Script Editor: John Langdon
Cast: Rory Bremner, John Fortune, John Bird
6 x 30 mins

The Russ Abbot Show
Producer/Director: John Bishop
Script Associates: Barry Cryer, Peter Vincent
Cast: Russ Abbot, Les Dennis, Bella Emberg, Sherrie Hewson, Tom Bright, Lisa Maxwell
12 x 30 mins
Zany comedy and music show

Takeover Bid
Producer/director: David Taylor
Programme Associates: Colin Edmonds, Wally Malston
Cryptic Questions: Norman Beedle
Host: Bruce Forsyth with Claire Sutton
14 x 30 mins
A unique game show in which the contestants begin with all the prizes and try to keep them

Wogan
Executive Producer: Peter Estall
Producers: Jane O'Brien, Graham Owens
Assistant Producers: Natalie Elsey, Cari Rosen
3 x 30/45 mins per week
Talk show hosted by Terry Wogan

The Generation Game
Producer: David Taylor
Director: Sylvie Boden
Programme Associates: Wally Malston, Garry Chambers
Hosts: Bruce Forsyth, Rosemarie Ford
13 x 60 mins plus Christmas Special

Noel Edmonds Saturday Roadshow
Producer/Director: Michael Leggo
Script Associate: Charlie Adams
Assistant Producer: Jon Beazley
Host: Noel Edmonds
16 x 45 mins

BBC TV Music and Arts

Kensington House
Richmond Way
London W14 0AX
Tel: 081 743 1272
Head: Michael Jackson
Arts Features Editor: Keith Alexander

Arena
Editors: Anthony Wall, Nigel Finch

The Late Show
Editor: Roly Keating

Music on Two
Executive Producer: Dennis Marks

Omnibus
Editor: Andrew Snell

Bookmark
Editor: Nigel Williams

Young Musician of the Year
Executive producer: Roy Tipping

BBC TV News and Current Affairs
Television Centre
Wood Lane
London W12 7RJ
Tel: 081 743 8000
Fax: 081 749 6972
Director, News and Current Affairs: Tony Hall
Editor of daily news programmes: Peter Bell
Editor of weekly and special programmes: Samir Shah

Main news programmes: BBC1 1.00pm, 6.00pm, 9.00pm; hourly summaries
Breakfast News 6.30am – 9.00am
BBC2 10.30pm
Newsnight

Other programmes include:
Assignment
The Money Programme
On The Record
Panorama
Public Eye
Question Time

BBC TV Programme Acquisition
Centre House
56 Wood Lane
London W12 7RJ
Tel: 081 743 8000
General Manager: Alan Howden
Purchased Programmes Head: June Morrow
Selects and presents BBC TV's output of feature films and series on both channels

Business Unit
Business Manager: Felicity Irlam
Contact for commissioned material and acquisition of completed programmes, film material and sequences for all other programme departments

BBC TV Religious Programmes
Television Centre
Wood Lane
London W12 7RJ
Tel: 081 743 8000
Head: Stephen Whittle

Everyman
Editor: Jane Drabble
26 x 40 mins F
Reflective religious documentary series

Heart of the Matter
Producer: Olga Edridge
18 x 35 mins F
Immediate and topical reports on moral and religious issues

Songs of Praise
Editor: Roger Hutchings
39 x 35 mins V
Community hymn-singing

This is the Day
Editor: Helen Alexander
34 x 30 mins live and V
Morning worship from a viewer's home, with the viewing audience itself making up the congregation

When I Get to Heaven
Editor: Helen Alexander
6 x 30 mins V
Interviews on ultimate belief

Global Reports
Producer: Peter Firstbrook
6 x 40 mins
Reports on development issues

Other programmes include:
Articles of Faith
The Cry
Five to Eleven
Home on Sunday
Praise Be!

BBC School Television
White City
201 Wood Lane
London W12 7TF
Tel: 081 752 5252
Head: Terry Marsh

Global Environment
Executive producer: Len Brown
10 x 20 mins
An International Broadcasting Trust Production for BBC-tv for 11-13 year olds exploring world environmental problems and solutions. Combines comedy-mime sequences with film from around the globe including the pavement dwellings of rapidly urbanising India and Canada's ancestral (but now polluted) Mohawk fishing grounds. Demonstrates the interdependence of people and their environments and between the industrialised and underdeveloped countries of the world

Thinkabout Science
Executive producer: Judy Whitfield
20 x 12 minutes
The first 'science soap' using a drama format to introduce children to the early stages of science, technology and maths. The day to day activities of two neighbouring families show how science is found in everyday situations such as riding a bike, cooking a meal and the birth of a pet

English File
Series producer: Paul Ashton
20 x 30 mins
Fresh approaches to poetry and the classics for GCSE students. Modern poets Liz Lochhead and Seamus Heaney talk about their writing and there are drama reconstructions of Christina Rossetti at work (A Double Exposure Production for BBC-tv). Plus making the classic texts relevant to modern teenagers – teaching 'Wuthering Heights' and 'Great Expectations' in the classroom today

Search Out Science
Producers: Lambros Atteshlis, Neil Ryder
10 x 25 mins
Science for 9-11 year olds encouraging them to discuss and build on what they've learnt in and out of the classroom. 'Planet Earth' looks at waste, recycling, the weather and dinosaurs. Plus, Dr Who makes a special visit to 'Search Out Space'. 'Moving About' explores how animals and machines move in, on and through earth, air and water

LernExpress
Producer: Susan Paton
10 x 15 mins
German language, people and culture for GCSE language students. Young presenter Sonja Zimmer introduces German language in real life situations including fast food eating, TV advertisements and interviews with young German people. This informative and up-to-date picture of modern Germany forms the second part of a two-stage course

Health Education
Producer: Ed Hayward
3 x 30 mins
A programme for teachers in primary and secondary schools made with the support of the Health Authorities in England, Wales, Scotland and Northern Ireland. Advice and information on good practice in 'the healthy school', dealing with exercise, diet, safety hygiene, sex education and good personal relationships

Other programmes include:
Diez Temas
The Geography Programme
Landmarks
Lifeschool
Mathscope
Music Time
Scene
Science Challenge
Techno
Who-me?
Words & Pictures
Zig Zag

BBC TV Science and Features
Kensington House
Richmond Way
London W14 0AX
Tel: 081 895 6611
Head: Graham Massey
Manager: Maggie Bebbington

Antenna
BBC2
Editor: Caroline Van den Brul
50 mins
Monthly science series exploring the unexpected in science, medicine and technology

Horizon
BBC2
Editor: Jana Bennett

24 x 50 mins
Single subject documentaries presenting science to the general public and analysing the implications of new discoveries

QED
Executive producer: David Filkin
14 x 30 mins F
Documentary films, each on a single subject. Topics vary enormously, using a very broad interpretation of science

Tomorrow's World
BBC1
Executive producer: Dana Purvis
Presenters: Judith Hann, Peter Macann, Howard Stableford, Kate Bellingham
Continuing x 30 mins live
Studio-based programme which includes filmed items investigating and demonstrating the latest in science and technology

Your Life In Their Hands
BBC2
Executive producer: David Paterson
5 x 40 mins
Series about medicine

BBC TV Serials

Television Centre
Wood Lane
London W12 7RJ
Tel: 081 743 8000
Head of Drama Group, BBC Television: Mark Shivas
Head of Serials: Michael Wearing

Clarissa
BBC2
Producer: Kevin Loader
Director: Robert Bierman
Scriptwriters: Janet Barron, David Nokes
Camera: John McGlashan
3 x 50 mins F
An adaptation of Samuel Richardson's innovative 18th century novel about a young woman ruined by her refusal to submit to an arranged marriage

The Men's Room
BBC2
Producer: David Snodin
Director: Antonia Bird
Scriptwriter: Laura Lamson
Editor: Sue Spivey
Cast: Harriet Walter, Bill Nighy, Mel Martin, Charlotte Cornwell, Amanda Redman
5 x 50 mins F
A spikey love story spanning the Thatcher years adapted from the novel by Ann Oakley. Charity Walton, sociologist, mother of four and embryonic feminist, falls passionately in love with her professor, Mark Carleton, an inveterate womaniser. She is persistently in his thrall, but after heartache and a tough fight, she discovers true liberation

Downtown Lagos
BBC2
Producer: Fiona Finlay
Scriptwriter: Leigh Jackson
3 x 52 mins F
A London solicitor's life changes irrevocably when he takes on a Nigerian client, but this seemingly open and shut case has hidden complications

A Fatal Inversion
BBC1
Producer: Phillipa Giles
Director: Tim Fywell
Scriptwriter: Sandy Welch
Camera: Barry McAnn
Editor: Paul Garrick
3 x 60 mins F
A three-part film serialisation of the psychological thriller by Ruth Rendell writing as Barbara Vine. A compelling story about the tragedy that befell five students during the long hot summer of 1976 as revealed through the eyes of the present

Jute City
BBC1
Producer: John Chapman
Director: Stuart Orme
Scriptwriter: David Kane
Camera: David Jackson
Editor: Arden Fisher
Cast: David O'Hara, John Sessions, Alan Howard, Annette Crosbie, Ion Caramitru, Fish, Vittorio Amandola
3 x 50 mins F
A Buchanesque thriller – a picaresque story set in the city of Dundee and the depopulated wastes of the Scottish highlands

Goodbye Cruel World
BBC2
Producer: David Snodin
Director: Adrian Shergold
Scriptwriter: Tony Marchant
Camera: Remi Adefarasin
Editor: Philip Kloss
Cast: Alun Armstrong, Sue Johnston
3 x 50 mins F
A moving tale of love and grief and an uncompromising examination of the hard-nosed world of charitable fund-raising

Screenplay
BBC2
Executive Producer: George Faber
A mixture of plays on tape or film between 60′ and 90′, presenting a season of challenging and contemporary drama, risking innovation in form or content. Titles from the 1991 season include *Redemption, The Fallout Guy, The Union Jack Connection, Murder in Oakland, The Hour of the Lynx, Events at Drimaghleen, Journey to Knock, Arise and Go Now, City Shorts*

BBC TV Series

Television Centre
Wood Lane
London W12 7RJ
Tel: 081 743 8000
Head of Drama Series: Peter Cregeen

Casualty
Producer: Geraint Morris
Directors: Steve Goldie, Jim Hill, Margy Kinmonth, Charles McDougal
Scriptwriters: Brian Elsley, David Fox, Bill Gallagher, Jacqueline Holborough, Ginnie Hole, Barbara Machin, Robin Mukherjee, Stephen Wyatt
Principal cast: Derek Thompson, Cathy Shipton, Mamta Kaash, Nigel Le Vaillant, Robson Green, Patrick Robinson, Maria Friedman, Adrienne Allen
15 x 50 mins V
Derek Thompson leads the cast of the top-rated hospital drama series, now in its sixth season

The House of Eliott
Executive producer: Ken Riddington
Producer: Jeremy Gwilt
Directors: Rodney Bennett, Jeremy Silberston, Richard Standeven
Scriptwriters: Peter Buckman, Deborah Cook, Jill Hyem, Michael Robson, Alan Seymour
Principal cast: Aden Gillett, Stella Gonet, Barbara Jefford, Louise Lombard
12 x 50 mins V
England in the Twenties: two sisters battle to make a living after their father dies, leaving them virtually penniless. They use their talent for designing clothes to create a new fashion house as they come to terms with their past

Lovejoy
Producer: Emma Hayter
Directors: John Crome, Barber Flemming, Sarah Hellings, Francis Megahy, Ian McShane, Baz Taylor
Scriptwriters: T R Bowen, Steve Coombes & Dave Robinson, Terry Hodgkinson, Roger Marshall, Geoff McQueen, Francis Megahy, Jeremy Paul, Andrew Payne, Douglas Watkinson
Principal cast: Ian McShane, Phyllis Logan, Chris Jury, Dudley Sutton
11 x 50 mins + 100 mins special F
The further adventures – and misadventures – of the East Anglian antiques dealer, starring Ian McShane, in a third series

Making Out
Producer: Carol Wilks
Directors: Tom Cotter, John Woods

Scriptwriter: Debbie Horsfield
Principal cast: Tracie Bennett, Margi Clarke, Alan David, Rachel Davies, John Forgeham, Melanie Kilburn, Shirley Stelfox, Heather Tobias, Gary Beadle, Moya Brady
8 x 50 mins V
The raucous and raunchy gang of women at a Manchester electronics factory return for a third series of the hit comedy by Debbie Horsfield

Spender
Producer: Martin McKeand
Scriptwriters: Ian La Frenais, Jimmy Nail
Principal cast: Jimmy Nail
6 x 50 mins F
Jimmy Nail's smash-hit series about an undercover cop in Newcastle returns for a second season

Trainer
Producer: Gerard Glaister
Directors: Tristan De Vere Cole, Frank Smith, Jeremy Summers
Scriptwriters: Colin Blumenau, Brian Finch, Gawn Grainger, Chris Green, John Pennington
Principal cast: Mark Greenstreet, David McCallum, Susannah York, Nigel Davenport
13 x 50 mins F
A new series set in the international world of horse-racing, centred round the attempts of one trainer to find a winner

Other programmes include:
Absolute Hell
Bergerac
The Boys from the Bush
EastEnders
Growing Pains
Love Hurts (Ind: Alomo)
Miss Marple: They Do It With Mirrors
Moon and Son
Nona
Old Times
Rides (Ind. Warner Sisters)
Top Girls
Uncle Vanya

BBC TV Sport and Events

Kensington House
Richmond Way
London W14 0AX
Tel: 081 895 6611
Fax: 081 749 7886
Head: Jonathan Martin
Deputy Head: John Rowlinson
Head of Events Programmes: Philip Gilbert

Football
Editor: Brian Barwick
Producer: John Shrewsbury
Director: Vivien Kent
Presenters: Desmond Lynam, Jimmy Hill

Grandstand
Editor: John Philips
Producer/Director: Martin Hopkins
Presenter: Desmond Lynam

One Man and His Dog
Producer: Ian Smith
Presenter: Phil Drabble

Royal Tournament
Producer/Director: Peter Hylton Cleaver

Sportsnight
Editor: Brian Barwick
Producer: Vivien Kent
Presenter: Steve Rider

BBC TV Topical Features

Lime Grove Studios
Lime Grove
London W12 7RJ
Tel: 081 743 8000
Head: John Morrell
Manager: Judith Parker

That's Life!
BBC1
Editor: John Getgood
Weekly consumer programme presented by Esther Rantzen which mixes serious investigations with light and musical items

Watchdog
BBC1
Editor: Sarah Caplin
Weekly consumer programme presented by Lynn Faulds Wood and John Stapleton

Primetime
BBC1
Editor: Bryher Scudamore
Weekly magazine programme aimed at the older viewer, presented by David Jacobs

Behind the Headlines
BBC2
Editor: Charles Miller
Daily discussion programme hosted by a regular team of presenters which provides intelligent conversation and debate on topical issues

Family Matters
BBC1
Editor: Anne Tyerman
Weekly programme on dilemmas facing families in the 1990s, presented by John Humphrys

Fifth Column
BBC2
Editor: Anne Tyerman
Weekly comment programme in which individuals provide personal perspectives on a subject of current interest, often presenting underrepresented or alternative points of view (see also BBC Community Programme Unit, part of Topical Features)

BBC TV Youth Programmes

Centre House
56 Wood Lane
London W12 7RJ
Tel: 081 743 8000
Head: Janet Street-Porter

Def II
The twice weekly Youth Programmes strand combines innovative original programming (**Reportage, Rough Guide to the World**) with cult series such as American hit **Fresh Prince of Bel Air** and the European pop show **Rapido**

Rough Guide to the World
Series producer: Rachel Purnell
Presenters: Magenta de Vine, Sankha Guha
Electronic scrapbook of cities and countries giving inside information on how to survive there

Reportage
Series editor: Sebastian Scott
Presenter: Aminatta Forna
Fast moving current affairs series, focusing on youth issues in the UK and around the world

283 Useful Ideas from Japan
Executive producer: Janet Street-Porter
Producer/Director: George Heggarty
Series of short films on contemporary life in Japan

The Full Wax
Producer: Janet Street-Porter
Associate producer: Olivia Hill
Off-beat talk show featuring American comedienne Ruby Wax

Extra
Executive producer: Janet Street-Porter
Series producer: Sharon Ali
Five European partners co-produced the thematic magazine show

Smash Hits Pollwinners Party
Producer: Sharon Ali
Director: Terry Jervis
Live broacast from the hippest awards presentation party

Other programmes include:
Dance Energy
First Bite
Rapido
Rough Guide to Careers
Snub
Forthcoming programmes include:
P's & Q's
A Soap Opera – The Vampire

VIDEO LABELS

These companies acquire the UK rights to all forms of audiovisual product and arrange for its distribution on videodisc or cassette at a retail level (see also under Distributors). Listed is a selection of titles released on each label

A & M Sound Pictures
136-144 New King's Road
London SW6 4LZ
Tel: 071 736 3311
Fax: 071 731 4606
Joan Armatrading: The Very Best Of Joan Armatrading
Carpenters: Yesterday Once More
Janet Jackson: Rhythm Nation 1814
Suzanne Vega: The Video

Albany Video Distribution
Battersea Studios
Television Centre
Thackeray Road
London SW8 3TW
Tel: 071 498 6811
Fax: 071 498 1494
Coffee Coloured Children
Framed Youth
Jean Genet is Dead
Looking for Langston
Ostia
The Passion of Remembrance
Perfect Image
Territories
Two in Twenty

Artificial Eye
211 Camden High Street
London NW1 7BT
Tel: 071 267 6036/482 3981
Fax: 071 267 6499
An Angel at my Table
Cyrano de Bergerac
Trop Belle Pour Toi

BBC Video
Woodlands
80 Wood Lane
London W12 0TT
Tel: 081 576 2236
Fax: 081 743 0393
Distributed by Pickwick International
Black Adder: Four Series
Blake's 7
Rosemary Conley: Whole Body Programme
Dr Who
Fireman Sam
Great Rugby Moments
The Lion, The Witch and The Wardrobe
Match of the Day series
Up Pompeii
Yes Prime Minister
The Young Ones

Braveworld
Symal House
Edgware Road
London NW9 0HU
Tel: 081 905 9191
Fax: 081 205 8619
Amadeus
Babette's Feast
One Flew Over the Cuckoo's Nest
Pelle the Conqueror
The Running Man

Buena Vista Home Video
3 Centaurs Business Park
Grant Way
Off Syon Lane
Isleworth
Middx TW7 5QD
Tel: 081 569 8080
Distribute and market Walt Disney, Touchstone and Hollywood Pictures product on video

Capital Home Video
Crown House
2 Church Street
Walton-on-Thames
Surrey KT12 2QS
Tel: 0932 223550
Fax: 081 546 4568
Blood Moon
Breaking In
Halloween 5
Opportunity Knocks
Pale Blood
Streethunter

CIC Video
4th Floor
Glenthorne House
5-17 Hammersmith Grove
London W6 0ND
Tel: 081 846 9433
Fax: 081 741 9773
Another 48 HRS
Bird on a Wire
Cry Baby
Darkman
Days of Thunder
Ghost
The Godfather part III
Henry and June
Internal Affairs
Mo' Better Blues

Channel 5 Video Distribution
see **PolyGram Video**

Chrysalis Records
Chrysalis Building
Bramley Road
London W10 6SP
Tel: 071 221 2213
Fax: 071 221 6455
Distributed by Pickwick Video
Adeva: Live In Concert
Deborah Harry: The Complete Picture
Sinéad O'Connor: Year Of The Horse
World Party Video EP

bfi Connoisseur Video
Glenbuck House
Glenbuck Road
Surbiton
Surrey KT6 6BT
Tel: 081 399 0022
Fax: 081 399 6651
A joint venture between the BFI and Argos Films, France, with films covering five decades of world cinema. Titles include:
The Aardman Animation Collection
The Gospel According to St Matthew
Jour de Fête
King and Country
Mon Oncle
Orphée
Playtime
The Seven Samurai
The Vanishing
Weekend
Wings of Desire

Walt Disney Co
see **Buena Vista Home Video**

Elephant Video
Tivoli Cinema
Station Street
Birmingham B5 4DY
Tel: 021 616 1021
Fax: 021 616 1019

Video distribution of feature films

Entertainment in Video
27 Soho Square
London W1V 5FL
Tel: 071 439 1979
Fax: 071 734 2483
The Ambulance
Bad Influence
Best of the Best
Courage Mountain
Dark Angel
Flesh Gordon II
Kickboxer 2
Martial Law
Why Me?
Wild Orchid

First Independent (formerly Vestron UK)
69 New Oxford Street
London WC1A 1DG
Tel: 071 379 0221
Fax: 071 528 7771
Backtrack
Blue Steel
Cannonball Fever
Communion
Far North
Fear
Little Monsters
Sundown
Upworld
Winter People

Fox Video
Unit 1
Perivale Industrial Park
Greenford
Middx UB6 7RU
Tel: 081 997 2552
Fax: 081 991 0251
Die Hard 2
The Exorcist III
Home Alone
Miller's Crossing
Nuns on the Run
Pacific Heights
Predator 2
Sleeping with the Enemy
The War of the Roses
Young Guns II

Guild Home Video
Crown House
2 Church Street
Walton-on-Thames
Surrey KT12 2QS
Tel: 081 546 3377
Fax: 081 546 4568
A.W.O.L.
Air America
Cover Up
Lock Up
Narrow Margin
Next of Kin
Repossessed
Total Recall

Hendring
8 Northfields Prospect
Putney Bridge Road
London SW18 1PE
Tel: 081 877 3313
Fax: 081 877 0416
Chapayev
Hamlet
In the Shadow of the Wind
I've Heard the Mermaids Singing
Mother Goose
Night Zoo
Que viva Mexico
Slade in Flame
We are from Kronstadt
War and Peace

Hollywood Pictures
see **Buena Vista Home Video**

ITC Home Video
24 Nutford Place
London W1H 5YN
Tel: 071 262 3262
Fax: 071 724 0160
Broken Dream
David
Fearstalk
Kill Me Again
Killer Instinct
Night of the Fox
Settle the Score
True Betrayal
UFO Cafe
Zandalee

Ingram Entertainment
(formerly Parkfield)
103 Bashley Road
London NW10 6SD
Tel: 081 965 5555
Fax: 081 961 8040
Blue Heat
Flatliners
Flesh Gordon 2
GoodFellas
Havana
Promise to Keep
Rookie
The Sheltering Sky

Island Visual Arts
22 St Peter's Square
London W6 9NW
Tel: 081 741 1511
Fax: 081 748 0841
Distributed by PolyGram Video

Jubilee Film and Video
Egret Mill
162 Old Street
Ashton-under-Lyne
Manchester
Lancashire OL6 7ST
Tel: 061 330 9555

London Weekend Television
South Bank Television Centre
London SE1 9LT
Tel: 071 620 1620
Another Bouquet
Bouquet of Barbed Wire
Come Home Charlie and Face Them
Frederick Forsyth Presents...Just Another Secret and *A Little Piece of Sunshine*
A Little Princess
The Mysterious Affair at Styles
No Honestly
The Seven Dials Mystery
Upstairs, Downstairs
Distributed by WH Smith for VCI

MCEG Virgin Vision
Atlantic House
1 Rockley Road
London W14 0DL
Tel: 081 740 5500
Fax: 081 967 1360
Belinda Carlisle: Runaway Videos
Diamond Skulls
Everybody Wins
Harlem Roots
Q & A
Reflecting Skin
Robocop

MGM/UA Home Video
Pathé House
76 Hammersmith Road
London W14 8YR
Tel: 071 603 4555
Fax: 071 603 4277
American Ninja IV
Death Warrant
Rocky V
The Russia House
Stanley and Iris

Media Releasing Distributors
27 Soho Square
London W1V 5FL
Tel: 071 437 2341
Fax: 071 734 2483
Day of the Dead
Eddie and the Cruisers
Kentucky Fried Movie
Return of Captain Invincible
Distributed through Entertainment in Video (qv)

Medusa Communications
Medusa Pictures Video Division
Regal Chambers
51 Bancroft
Hitchin
Herts SG5 1LL
Tel: 0462 421818
Fax: 0462 420393
Back Stab
Dark Side of the Moon
House IV
Maniac Cop 2
976-EVIL II
A Shock to the System
Spaced Invaders
Wings of the Apache

Mogul
35-37 Wardour Street
London W1A 4BT
Tel: 071 734 7195
Land Of The Giants
Wacky Weekend

Odyssey Video
15 Dufours Place
London W1V 1FE
Tel: 071 437 8251
Fax: 071 734 6941
Cul-de-Sac
The First of the Few
Flying Deuces
A Killing in a Small Town
Repulsion
Scum
She Said No
A Woman of Substance

Palace Video
16-17 Wardour Mews
London W1V 3FF
Tel: 071 734 7060
Fax: 071 437 3248
Asterix and the Big Fight
The Cook, the Thief, His Wife and Her Lover
Jean de Florette
Killing Dad
King of New York
Manon des Sources
My Left Foot
Roselyne and the Lions
Shag
When Harry Met Sally

Parkfield
see **Ingram Entertainment**

Pathé Video
see **MGM/UA Home Video**

Pickwick Video
Hyde Industrial Estate
The Hyde
London NW9 6JU
Tel: 081 200 7000
Fax: 081 200 8995
Carole Caplin's Holistix
Jungle Book
Lennon: A Tribute
Nursery Rhymes
Peter Pan
Reach for the Sky

Thomas, Percy and Harold
Wind in the Willows

Picture Music International
20 Manchester Square
London W1A 1ES
Tel: 081 486 4488
Fax: 081 465 0748
Blue Note
Marc Bolan: Born to Boogie
Kate Bush: The Whole Story
Nat King Cole: The Unforgettable Nat King Cole
Duran Duran: Decade
EMI Classics
MC Hammer: Hammertime and *Please Hammer Don't Hurt 'Em*
Iron Maiden: 1st Ten Years
Now That's What I Call Music
Pink Floyd: Delicate Sound of Thunder
Queen: Live at Wembley
Cliff Richard: From a Distance – The Event
Tina Turner: Foreign Affair

PolyGram Video International
6 Castle Row
Horticultural Place
Chiswick
London W4 4JQ
Tel: 081 994 9199
Fax: 081 994 6840
A subsidiary of PolyGram International making programmes for video release with such bands as Bananarama, Bon Jovi, Def Leppard, Dire Straits, Tears for Fears

PolyGram Video
PO Box 1425
Chancellors House
72 Chancellors Road
Hammersmith
London W6 9QB
Tel: 081 846 8515
Fax: 081 741 9781
Video catalogue includes music videos, feature films, sport, special interests and children's videos. New titles available through retail/sell-through outlets include:
Field of Dreams
INXS: Greatest Video Hits
Elton John: Greatest Hits
Thunderbirds

Quadrant Video
37a High Street
Carshalton
Surrey SM5 3BB
Tel: 081 669 1114
Fax: 081 669 8831
Sports video cassettes

RCA/Columbia Pictures Video UK
Horatio House
77-85 Fulham Palace Road
London W6 8JA
Tel: 081 748 6000
Fax: 081 748 4546
Blind Fury
The Boost
Casualties of War
Criminal Law
Glory
House Party
I Love You to Death
The Krays
Postcards from the Edge
The Punisher

Revision Jettisoundz
28-30 The Square
St Annes-on-Sea
Lancashire FY8 1RF
Tel: 0253 712453
Fax: 0253 712362
Kenneth Anger's *Magick Lantern Cycle*
William Burroughs' *Thee Films*
Cud
Derek Jarman's *Time Zones*
Killdozer
The Man from Delmonte
Klaus Maeck's *Decoder*
Psychic TV
Ska Explosion
Throbbing Gristle

Shiva Video
Unit 3 Pop In Building
South Way
Wembley
Middx HA9 0AJ
Tel: 081 903 6957
Fax: 081 903 3309
Indian videos

Telstar Video Entertainment
Suite 8
The Old Power Station
121 Mortlake High Street
London SW14 8SN
Tel: 081 392 2966
Fax: 081 392 2995
Carrott's Commercial Breakdown
Country's Greatest Hits
A Lesson with Leadbetter
The Official Liverpool Season 1990/91
The Official Review of the Rugby League Division I & II 1990/91 season
Thoughts of Home – Daniel O'Donnell

Thames Video
149 Tottenham Court Road
London W1P 9LL
Tel: 071 387 9494
Fax: 071 388 9604/6073
The BFG
Button Moon
Learn with Sooty
Rainbow
Rod, Jane & Freddy
Rumpole of the Bailey
Tommy Cooper

Touchstone
see **Buena Vista Home Video**

20.20 Vision Video UK
Horatio House
77-85 Fulham Palace Road
London W6 8JA
Tel: 081 748 4034
Fax: 081 748 4546
The Big Picture
Comfort of Strangers
Hamlet
Madhouse
Reversal of Fortune
Staying Together

Vestron (UK)
see **First Independent**

The Video Collection
Strand VCI House
Caxton Way
Watford
Herts WD1 8UF
Tel: 0923 55558
Fax: 0923 816744
Carry On England
Chancer Parts I and II
Fire and Ice
Healthy Skin
Lizzie's Slimming Program
Spitting Image

Video Gems
1st Floor
Acorn House
Victoria Road
London W3 6UL
Tel: 081 993 7705
Fax: 081 993 0209
Ashes: 1991 Australia Series
Mud and Monsters
Return To Treasure Island
Robin Of Sherwood
Yoga in Pregnancy

Video Programme Distributors (VPD)
Building No 1
GEC Estate
East Lane
Wembley
Middx HA9 7FF
Tel: 081 904 0921
Fax: 081 908 6785
Distributors for VPD, American Imperial and Rogue
Angel Down
Black Eagle
Chinawide
Dragons Forever
No Holds Barred
Police Story 2

Virgin Vision
see **MCEG Virgin Vision**

Warner Home Video
135 Wardour Street
London W1
Tel: 071 494 3441
Fax: 071 494 3297
Warner Home Video markets and distributes all Warner Bros product, films from Warner subsidiaries, together with MGM/UA releases for UK rental and retail markets
All Dogs go to Heaven
Graffiti Bridge
Gremlins 2
Joe vs The Volcano
Memphis Belle
My Blue Heaven
Presumed Innocent
Roadhouse
Tango & Cash
The Witches

WORKSHOPS

The film and video workshops listed below are non-profit-distributing and subsidised organisations. Some workshops are also active in making audiovisual product for UK and international media markets. Those workshops with an asterisk (*) after their name were ACTT-franchised in the period up till 31 March 1991

A19 Film and Video
21 Foyle Street
Sunderland SR1 1LE
Tel: 091 565 5709
Mick Catmull
Nick Oldham
Video production, distribution and exhibition. A19 makes films and videotapes which reflect the needs, concerns and aspirations of people on Wearside. Also offers production facilities, training and advice to schools, community groups and institutions

AVA (Audio Visual Arts)
7b Broad Street
The Lacemarket
Nottingham NG1 3AJ
Tel: 0602 483684
Two woman independent video production company specialising in arts and education. Wide range of commissioned work for artists, museums, galleries and educational organisations, including *Video Showcase* series on contemporary craftspeople. Grant aided production of *Great Expectations/Wedding Album,* a video installation funded by East Midlands Arts. Co-productions, residencies, placements with schools, colleges, PH day centres and community groups. Co-ordinators/producers of *'91 Degrees Fine Art*

Aberystwyth Media Group
see **Ceredigion Media Association**

Activision Irish Project
Roger Casement Centre
131 St John's Way
London N19 3QR
Tel: 071 281 5087
Fax: 071 281 4973
79 Wardour Street
London W1V 3TH
Tel: 071 287 0243
(Thursday, Friday only)
AIP collects and makes available for individual viewing, Irish films and videos. The archive is accessible on U-Matic and VHS, and booking must be made in advance. Also supplies a catalogue of titles held, as well as providing information relating to Irish film and video

Alva Films
Island House
16 Brook Street
Alva
Clackmannanshire
FK12 5JP
Tel: 0259 60936
Fax: 0259 69436
Russell Fenton
Bill Borrows
Film/video production, distribution and exhibition. Offers production, post-production and exhibition facilities to others

Amber Side Workshop*
5 Side
Newcastle upon Tyne
NE1 3JE
Tel: 091 232 2000
Fax: 091 230 3217
Murray Martin
Film/video production, distribution and exhibition. Most recent production *In Fading Light*

Avid Productions
Keswick House
30 Peacock Lane
Leicester LE1 5NY
Tel: 0533 539733
Laura McGregor
Video production mainly for local authorities and the voluntary sector. Training, promo, education, public information, with back-up publications where required. Training in video/photography within the community, particularly gay groups, women's and special needs groups

Azadi Asian Women's Film Project
3 Brown Street
Sheffield S1 2BS
Tel: 0742 727170/755676
Maya Chowdhry
Davinder Kaur
Suki Shergill
Community video project for Asian women. Productions, screenings and training workshops organised on an ad hoc basis run voluntarily by Asian women

Barnet Arts Workshop
1 Thomas More Way
East Finchley
London N2 0UL
Tel: 081 346 7120
Ann Latimer
Alan Everatt
Regular training in video at beginners and intermediate levels. Video production with local community organisations. Hire of production and post-production equipment (2-machine VHS edit)

Bath Community Television
7 Barton Buildings
Bath
Avon BA1 2JR
Tel: 0225 314480
Ray Brooking
Andrew Graham
Community video resource. VHS and lo-band U-Matic equipment for hire at reasonable prices. Reduced rates for community projects. Training courses for all levels, free advice, productions including a regular video programme for local elderly people. Flexible opening hours to suit clients. Recent productions for British Gas, Bath City Council

Belfast Film Workshop
37 Queen Street
Belfast BT1 6EA
Tel: 0232 326661
Fax: 0232 246657
Alastair Herron
Kate McManus
Only film co-operative in Northern Ireland offering film/video/animation production and exhibition. Offers both these facilities to others. Made *Acceptable Levels* (with Frontroom), *Thunder Without Rain* and various youth animation pieces

Birmingham Film and Video Workshop
The Bond
180/182 Fazeley Street
Birmingham B5 5SE
Tel: 021 766 7635
Alan Lovell
Film/video distribution and script development. Catalogue of films and videos in distribution plus accompanying education packs available on request

Black Audio Film Collective*
89 Ridley Road
London E8 2NH
Tel: 071 254 9527/9536
Lina Gopaul
Avril Johnson
Film/video production, distribution, exhibition and consultancy in the field of black filmmaking. Produced *Handsworth Songs, Testament, Twilight City, Mysteries of July* and *Who needs a Heart*

Black Witch (Women's Independent Cinema House)
Trading Places
Holmes Building
46 Wood Street
Liverpool L1 4AH
Tel: 051 707 0539
Ann Carney
Barbara Phillips
Video production, distribution and exhibition. Workshops in video and photography. Also screenings

Cambridge Video Unit
The Enterprise Centre
Haggis Gap
Fulbourn
Cambridge CB1 5HD
Tel: 0223 881688
Fax: 0223 881678
Anna Kronschnabl
Andy Lomas
Sangita Basudev
Video production co-operative. Production of experimental, community and commercial videos with specialisation within health/hi-tech fields. Workshops in video production with S-VHS/VHS editing suite available for hire

Cambridge Women's Resource Centre
Hooper Street
Cambridge CB1 2NZ
Tel: 0223 321148
Ila Chandavarkar
Mary Knox
Video classes for women include scriptwriting, basic camera techniques, lighting, production and editing using U-Matic equipment

Caravel Media Centre
The Great Barn Studios
Cippenham Lane
Slough SL1 5AU
Tel: 0753 34828
Fax: 0753 70383
Nick Gee
Training, video production, distribution, exhibition and media education. Offers all these facilities to others. Runs national video courses for independent videomakers and general training in arts administration

Ceddo Film and Video
Entrance B
South Tottenham Education and Training Centre
Braemar Road
London N15 5EU
Tel: 081 802 9034
Fax: 081 800 6949
Film/video production and training. Offers equipment resource base in 16mm, lo-band U-Matic, VHS (production and post production). Currently establishing an archive. Productions include: *Street Warriors, We are the Elephant, The People's Account, Time and Judgement, Omega Rising, Flame of the Soul* and *Racism – A Response*

CREU COF (of the Ceredigion Media Association)
Blwch Post 86
Aberystwyth
Dyfed
Wales SY23 1LN
Tel: 0970 624001
Catrin M S Davies
Media education for all ages and interests with specific reference to Welsh speakers and to rural themes and issues. Comprises training, teaching and development of photography, audio work, basic S8 film and VHS video. Runs longer term practical projects

Chapter Film and Animation Workshop
see **Make It Media**

The Children's Film Unit
Unit 4
Berrytime Studios
192 Queenstown Road
London SW8 3NR
Tel: 071 622 7793
Fax: 071 498 0593
A registered educational charity, the CFU makes low-budget films for television and PR on subjects of concern to children and young people. Crews and actors are trained at regular weekly workshops in Battersea. Work is in 16mm and video and membership is open to children from 8-16. Latest films for Channel 4 *Hard Road, Doombeach, Survivors.* For the Samaritans *Time to Talk*

Cinema Action
27 Winchester Road
London NW3
Tel: 071 586 2762
Fax: 071 722 5781
Gustav Lamche
Film/video production, distribution and exhibition. Offers all these facilities to others. Productions include *Rocking the Boat, So That You Can Live, The Miners' Film, People of Ireland, Film from the Clyde* and *Rocinante*

Cinestra Pictures
The Co-op Centre
11 Mowll Street
London SW9 6BG
Tel: 071 793 0157
Women's video production and training company. Aim to promote an alternative women's cinema and TV culture through production and training. U-Matic video courses from beginners to specialist advanced

City Eye Southampton
1st Floor
Northam Centre
Kent Street
Northam
Southampton SO1 1SP
Tel: 0703 634177
Film and video equipment hire. Educational projects. Production and post-production services. Screenings. Community arts media development. Training courses all year in varied aspects of video production/post-production. Committed to providing opportunities for disadvantaged/under-represented groups. 50% discount on all non-profit/educational work

Clapham-Battersea Film Workshop
Wandsworth Adult College

Latchmere Road
London SW11 2DS
Tel: 071 223 5876
Offers a range of 16mm filmmaking courses including a one year part-time course in film, video and photography. 16mm production facilities are available to those completing courses. Weekly screenings of experimental and avant-garde films. Equipment: Eclair ACL and Bolex cameras; Steenbecks and Pic-syncs, sound recorders, lighting kits, Xenon double band projector

Clio & Co

91c Mildmay Road
London N1 4PU
Tel: 071 249 2551
Rosalind Pearson
Produce documentaries about women's history. Latest documentary for Channel 4 is a sequel to *Women Like Us* (49 minutes), where older lesbians discuss their lives and the issues which affect them. Shown on Channel 4 in July 1991

Colchester Film and Video Workshop

see ***Signals, Essex Media Centre***

Community Productions Merseyside

see ***First Take Video***

Connections

Palingswick House
241 King Street
London W6 9LP
Tel: 081 741 1766/7
Video project providing short and long term training in production and post-production. Undertakes commissioned productions and training programmes. Editing facilities in S-VHS and VHS. Editing facilities are wheelchair accessible

Cornwall Video Resource

First Floor
Royal Circus Buildings
Back Lane West
Redruth
Cornwall TR15 2BT
Tel: 0209 218288
Lee Berry
An access and training based video resource working mainly on broadcast standard U-Matic primarily for independent video makers, workshops, disadvantaged groups and non-commercial sector. Commercial use possible subject to availability. Upgrading to three machine hi-band SP

Counter Image

3rd Floor
Fraser House
36 Charlotte Street
Manchester M1 4FD
Tel: 061 228 3551
Ivor Frankell
Janet Shaw
Paul Grivell
Independent media charity. Film/video production, distribution and exhibition. Offers production and exhibition facilities to independent film and video makers and photographers. Productions include *Fever House, Land of Colagne* and *Concrete Chariots*

Cultural Partnerships

90 De Beauvoir Road
London N1 4EN
Tel: 071 254 8217
Fax: 071 254 7541
Carys Pearce
Arts, media, communications group. 3 month access to media production course covering video/sound/computer graphics. Studio facilities for hire – fully air conditioned and purpose built. BVU-SP 3 Machine edit suite with dynamic tracking. BVE 900 Edit Controller, DV5 Vision Mixer with Apple Mac graphics. 8-track recording studio midi and mac, which can be used with video edit suite for sound dubs. 800 square ft production studio. Also make training, promotional videos, an area which they are developing

Despite TV

178 Whitechapel Road
London E1 1BJ
Tel: 071 377 0737
Fax: 071 377 0737
Video co-operative providing training through production for people living or working in Tower Hamlets, Hackney, Newham. The co-op produces both local topic and single-issue magazine tapes which are available for hire, as well as documentary for Channel 4 *Battle of Trafalgar*

Doncaster Independent Film Group

Basement Flat
6 Regent Square
Doncaster
South Yorks DN1 2DS
Tel: 0302 342982
Rodney Challis
Community media organisation. Video programmes for local authorities, schools and community groups. Some commercial clients. Training courses to order

*Edinburgh Film Workshop Trust**

29 Albany Street
Edinburgh EH1 3QN
Tel: 031 557 5242
David Halliday
Cassandra McGrogan
Robin MacPherson
Edward O'Donnelly
Scotland's only franchised Workshop. Broadcast, non-broadcast and community integrated production. Facilities include lo-band U-Matic production; VHS and lo-band edit suites; Neilson Hordell 16mm Rostrum camera; 8mm and 16mm cameras; film cutting room. Women's unit. Projects 1990-91 include *World Music, Focal Point* and *Gaelic Animation* for BBC Scotland

Edinburgh Film Workshop Trust Animation Workshop

address as above
Edward O'Donnelly

Electronic Arts Video

30 Estate Buildings
Railway Street
Huddersfield HD1 1JY
Tel: 0484 518174
Fax: 0484 450239
Stan Sagan
Community-based video production, training and facilities/equipment hire. Facilities include industrial standard S-VHS and VHS shooting kits, S-VHS and VHS edit suite, Amiga graphics system, 4-track sound recording, lights, mics etc. Training in S-VHS and VHS production techniques at Basic and Intermediate levels

Exeter Film and Video Workshop

c/o Exeter and Devon Arts Centre
Gandy Street
Exeter EX4 3LS
Tel: 0392 218928
Mark Jeffs
Film/video production, distribution, exhibition, facilities hire. Membership based, we offer these facilities to others together with training for individuals, groups and schools. Programme of broadcast standard training supported by ACTT, TSW and others

Faction Films

28-29 Great Sutton Street
London EC1V 0DU
Tel: 071 608 0654/3
Fax: 071 608 2157
Dave Fox
Sylvia Stevens
Group of independent filmmakers. Production facilities for hire include 6-plate 16mm Steenbeck edit suite; sound transfer; VHS edit suite with 6 channel mixer; U-Matic and VHS viewing and transfer; production office space; Nagra 4.2; redhead lighting kit. Spanish/English translation services. Titles include *Irish News: British Stories, Year of the Beaver, Picturing Derry, Trouble the Calm* and *Provocation or Murder*

Falmouth Film and Video

c/o 22 High Terrace
Ponsanooth
Cornwall TR3 7EW
Tel: 0872 864572

Lee Berry
Dave Evans
Mainly for independent film and video makers, artists and arts based groups. Training is available to meet clients/users needs from formal courses to one-to-one skills sharing etc. Equipment is mainly VHS Video/Super 8 and 16mm film making. Access can be arranged for U-Matic and other equipment. Assistance with fundraising/grant applications etc. Organising exhibition/ screenings/festivals. Independent productions also

Film Work Group
Top Floor
79-89 Lots Road
London SW10 0RN
Tel: 071 352 0538
Fax: 071 351 6479
Michael Tomkins
Charlotte Moss
Video post-production facilities. Offers three-machine hi-band SP suite, lo-band offline, telecine, transfer facilities and DTP to others with special rates for grant-aided and non-profit groups

Filmshed
9 Mill Lane
Harbledown
Canterbury
Kent CT2 8NE
Tel: 0227 769415
Tim Reed
Open-access collective for the promotion and production of independent film. Film production and exhibition. Offers exhibition facilities to others; filmmakers on tour and regular screenings of political/workshop films

First Take Video
(formerly Community Productions Merseyside)
Merseyside Innovation Centre
131 Mount Pleasant
Liverpool L3 5TF
Tel: 051 708 5767
Offers training and production services to the voluntary, arts, community and education sectors across the North West. Joint projects with other arts groups and special needs groups. Training courses, both basic and intermediate, for the public in video production and editing. Commissioned productions for local authorities

Forum Television
11 Regent Street
Bristol BS8 4HW
Tel: 0272 741490
David Parker
Co-operative with emphasis on South West film and video production, distribution and exhibition. Offers film/video editing suites and Beta SP Camera kit. Recent work has involved social and political issues around work, unemployment, the police and judiciary, racism and community education. Titles for Channel 4 include: *Lands at the Margin, A Question of Cornwall, A Gilded Cage?, Like Mothers, Like Daughters*. For the BBC: *The School Belongs to All of Us, Dying for a Job, Liberating Literacy*. For HTV: *Hurried Orders, Songs of the Forest, Time Goes on Quick, Harry Brown, Trotting* and *Women Farmers*

Fosse Community Studios
Fosse Neighbourhood Centre
Leicester City Council
Mantle Road
Leicester LE3 5HG
Tel: 0533 515577
Alan Wilson
Kiran Ravel
Sue Wallin
Nick Thornton
Sean Wainwright
An audio-visual resource providing training in all aspects of video production, computer graphics, sound recording, photography. Specialist and individual training on request, and City and Guilds 770 certificate course. Have a wide range of equipment for hire at low cost including VHS shooting kits, 8 track recording studio, video/photography studio with full lighting rig, darkroom, 3 machine lo-band and two 2 machine VHS edit suites; range of musical equipment

bfi Four Corners Film Workshop
113 Roman Road
London E2 0HU
Tel: 081 981 4243/6111
James Van der Pool
Provides access to film production courses, technical theory classes and film theory courses. A full programme runs all year round. Provides subsidised film equipment for the low budget independent film maker and has a 40 seat cinema. 16mm and Super 8 production and post-production facilities available

Fradharc Ur
11 Scotland Street
Stornoway
Isle of Lewis PA87
Tel: 0851 705766
The first Gaelic film and video workshop, offering VHS and hi-band editing and shooting facilities. Production and training in Gaelic for community groups. Productions include *Under the Surface, Na Deilbh Bheo, The Weaver, A Wedding to Remember* and *As an Fhearran*

Free Focus
The Old Co-op
38-42 Chelsea Road
Easton
Bristol BS5 6AF
Tel: 0272 558973
Free Focus promotes community development in Avon through the use of video. We help community groups make their own videos and to develop their video making skills through training, consultancy, information and cheap equipment hire

Glasgow Film and Video Workshop
Dolphin Arts Centre
7 James Street
Glasgow G40 1BZ
Tel: 041 554 6502
GFVW is a training/ access resource for film/ video makers in Scotland. Runs basic video familiarisation courses and provides advanced specialist courses in lo- and hi-band video, 16mm and Super 8. Occasionally offers bursaries to filmmakers and continues to programme showings of independent film and video work in the city

Gog Theatre Co
Ostia
Overleigh
Street
Somerset BA16 0TJ
Tel: 0458 47353
Stephen Clarke

Grapevine TV
Hebron House
Sion Road
Bedminster
Bristol BS3 3BD
Tel: 0272 637973/637634
Fax: 0272 631770
Jayne Cotton
Lynne Harwood
Adrian Mack
Video production, distribution and exhibition. Programmes made for voluntary and statutory organisations, including: *A Working Alternative* for Community Service Volunteers, *The Star Centre* for Hounslow and Spelthorne Health Authority and *Thinking Skills* for Somerset Education Authority

Guildford Video Workshop
c/o The Guildford Institute
Ward Street
Guildford
Surrey GU1 4LH
Michael Aslin
Video production and training facilities

Gweithdy Fidio Cydweithredol Scrin Cyf (Community Screen Film and Video Workshop)
Safle ATS
Ffordd Bangor
Caernarfon
Gwynedd LL55 1AR
Tel: 0286 4545
Mair Jones

HAFAD 1st Chance Project
(formerly 'I Can' 1st Chance Project)

The Masbro Centre
87 Masbro Road
London W14 0LR
Tel: 071 603 7481/602 5739
Basic training in video mainly aimed at people with disabilities. VHS camera and edit suite for hire. Remote control for camera/recorder. Other adaptations for disabled people are available soon. Also run video club for people with and without disabilities

Hall Place Studios
4 Hall Place
Leeds LS9 8JD
Tel: 0532 405553
Alf Bower
Jacqui Maurice
Ali Hussein
Anna Zaluczkowska
Facility and training centre offering film/video/sound production facilities on site and for hire on sliding scale. Also offers programme of training and events, some for women or black peoples only, membership scheme, community video development programme, and in-service training for youth/community workers

Hibiscus Productions
Delaunay House
Scoresby Street
Bradford BD1 5BJ
Tel: 0274 390404
Fax: 0274 393296
Pearline Hingston
Workshops and training in all aspects of film and video production. Organise regular training sessions. Work on commissions for training, information and promotional videos and films. Produce work in languages other than English, eg Punjabi

Hull Community Artworks
(formerly Outreach Community Arts)
Northumberland Avenue
Hull HU2 0LN
Tel: 0482 226420
Tony Hales
Film/video production, distribution and exhibition. Offers production and exhibition facilities to others. Holds regular training workshops

Hull Time Based Arts
8 Posterngate
Hull HU1 2JN
Tel: 0482 216446
Fax: 0482 218103
Mike Stubbs
Film/video production, exhibition and education. Also promotes, produces and commissions experimental film, video, performance and music. Provides annual summer school and *Junk Music/Found film* workshop. Equipment for hire includes video projector and U-Matic production facilities

'I Can' 1st Chance Project
see **HAFAD 1st Chance Project**

Intermedia Film and Video (Nottingham)
110 Mansfield Road
Nottingham NG1 3HL
Tel: 0602 505434
Malcolm Leick
Leaza McCloud
Offers training, facilities, production, information and advice. Training based on established short course programme in 16mm film, video and related areas together with industry retraining

Ipswich Media Project
202 Brunswick Road
Ipswich
Suffolk
Tel: 0473 716609
Mike O'Sullivan
Super 8 film and VHS video production equipment. Familiarisation training and media work

Island Art Centre
The Tiller Center
Tiller Road
Millwall
London E14 8PX
Tel: 071 987 7925
Peter Ellis
Facilities for local groups and individuals; video workshops and productions

Jackdaw Media
96a Duke Street
Liverpool L1 5AG
Tel: 051 709 5858
Fax: 051 709 0759
Laura Knight
Animated film making for school children and adults with or without the use of film. Daytime and evening sessions. Specialising in educational consultancy. Production commissions accepted. 16mm rostrums, Amiga computer, video animation facilities and 6-plate Steenbeck available for hire

Jubilee Arts
84 High Street
West Bromwich
West Midlands
Tel: 021 553 6862
Fax: 021 525 0640
Multi-media arts development based in the West Midlands, using video, film, photography, music, performance and visual art. Working in partnership with community groups and local authorities

Lambeth Video
Unit F7
245a Coldharbour Lane
London SW9 8RR
Tel: 071 737 5903
Lambeth Video is a part-funded video workshop. Runs production-based training and hire equipment (hi-band production kit, 3-machine edit suite and VHS edit). A one year training course is run with Brixton College, open only to women and black applicants, who must be unemployed. Also runs South London Documentary Project, open to women and black people, on-going training and production. Applicants at any time

Latin American Independent Film/Video Association
Latin American House
Kingsgate Place
London NW6 4TA
Tel: 071 372 6442
Offers 16mm film and VHS equipment (production and post-production) for hire. Film and video courses, workshops and exhibitions

bfi Leeds Animation Workshop*
45 Bayswater Row
Leeds LS8 5LF
Tel: 0532 484997
Jane Bradshaw
A women's collective producing and distributing animated films on social issues. Offers production, distribution and training. Productions include: *Risky Business, Give Us a Smile, Crops and Robbers, Out to Lunch, A Matter of Interest* and *Alice in Wasteland.* Free catalogue available on request

Light House Media Centre
Art Gallery
Lichfield Street
Wolverhampton
WV1 1DU
Tel: 0902 312033
Fax: 0902 26644
Frank Challenger
Krysia Rozanska
Raj Chahal
Isaiah Ferguson
Video production with 3-machine edit, computer graphics/animation; cinema and galleries. Training includes 16 week video courses specialising in editing. Films, conferences, events, courses and exhibitions. Joint Wolverhampton Borough Council/Wolverhampton Polytechnic development with Arts Council and West Midlands Arts support

Lighthouse Film and Video
19 Regent Street
Brighton
BN1 1UL
Tel: 0273 686479
Jane Finnis
A training and resource centre providing courses, facilities, exhibition and production services to the south-east. S-VHS, U-Matic and 16mm production and post-production facilities. Productions include *Bhashahara (Lost Voice)*

Line Out
138 Charles Street
Leicester LE1 1VA
Tel: 0533 621265
Nick Hunt
Ash Sharma
Kim Chenoweth
Professional and small format video facilities specialising in Super 8 film, all available for hire. Also running short courses, workshops and media education programmes. A membership organisation providing advice, information and lobbying

London Deaf Video Project
Room 303
South Bank House
Black Prince Road
London SE1 7SJ
Tel: 071 735 8171 ext 115 (voice) & 071 587 0817 (minicom)
Fax: 071 820 1312
Translates information from English into British Sign Language for London's deaf community. Recent productions include videos about solicitors, electricity, women's health and the work and aims of LDVP (all available for sale to others). Offers occasional courses, use of lo-band/VHS equipment and S-VHS edit suite to deaf people. Exhibitions to deaf community. Interested to liaise with any other video projects who feel they should use Sign Language to make their own material accessible to deaf people

London Fields Film and Video
10 Martello Street
London E8 3PE
Tel: 071 241 2997
Sophie Outram
James Swinson
Prue Waller
Computer generated images for film and video including pre-online visualising, titles and animation. Lo-band video and 16mm production and editing facilities. Current productions include: Arts Council/11th Hour *Five Steps Backwards, Four Steps Forwards*

London Film Makers' Co-op
42 Gloucester Avenue
London NW1
Tel: 071 722 1728
Administration & Distribution 071 586 4806
Cinema 071 586 8516
Film workshop, distribution library and cinema enables filmmakers to control the production, distribution and exhibition of their films. Workshop runs regular practical and theoretical film courses. Distribution has 2,000 experimental films for hire, from 20s to current work. Cinema screenings twice weekly. Work with cultural aesthetic/ political aims which differ from the industry

London Media Workshops
101 King's Drive
Gravesend
Kent DA12 5BQ
Tel: 0474 564676
Training agency specialising in short intensive courses in writing for radio, television, video and press, and in directing and producing television and video programmes. Regular one and two day courses in London, specially tailored in-house courses by commission.
Mail order booklist.
Top working tutors.
Small numbers allow individual attention

London Screenwriters Workshop
1 Greek Street
London W1V 6NQ
Tel: 081 551 5570
Ray Frensham
Screenwriting workshops range from discussion of short TV scripts and film treatments to the development of full-length screenplays and analysis of deep structure. A range of seminars bring screenwriters together with producers, agents, development executives and other film and television professionals

London Video Access (LVA)
23 Frith Street
London W1A 4XD
Tel: 071 734 7410
Fax: 071 734 2003
LVA is Britain's national centre for video and new media art. Offers a complete range of services including production based training, facility hire (production and post-production), distribution and exhibition of video and new media art and film

London Women's Centre
Wesley House
4 Wild Court
London WC2B 5AU
Tel: 071 831 6946
A women's resource providing facilities for women and women's organisations to hire with a sliding scale of charges. Facilities include lo-band U-Matic video filming and editing equipment and 16mm, lo-band and VHS playback facilities including screening space. All equipment for use on the premises only. Rooms available for hire range from the 'Theatre Space' with a PA and lighting rig (capacity 150), to a variety of seminar/ meeting rooms. The centre houses a cafe and sports facilities

Lothian Video Users Group
29 Albany Street
Edinburgh EH1 3QN
Tel: 031 557 8211
Pete Gregson
A membership-based association which provides resources and training for individuals and community groups to work with video. Courses are short and at basic or specialist level. Has VHS production facilities, runs monthly newsletter and information service. In 1990 'enabled' 95 videos and helped 10 members into film schools or jobs in the industry

Make It Media
(formerly Chapter Film and Animation Workshop)
c/o Chapter Arts Centre
Market Road
Canton
Cardiff CF5 1QE
Tel: 0222 396061
Christine Wilks
Solveig Jorgensen
Dane Gould
Film, animation, video, photography, print and exhibition production. Offers film, animation, video production and post-production facilities to others. Training courses in film, video, animation, sound, scriptwriting, photography, print and exhibition design. Projects include: *What Next?* a video for deaf and hearing impaired audiences

Media Arts
Town Hall Studios
Regents Circus
Swindon SN1 1QF
Tel: 0793 493451
Fax: 0793 490420
Carol Comley
Steve Chapman
Production, distribution, exhibition, education and training. Well-equipped studios in film, video, photography and sound. Small media library, viewing facilities, multimedia events, archive. Productions include *Plant the Town Green, Today is a Good Day, When I Was a Girl* and *The Weaver's Wife*

Media Education Centre
Leigh College
Railway Road
Leigh WN7 4AH
Tel: 0942 675830
Steve Brennan
Julie Cox
Carol Dahl
Paul Grimshaw
Provides video production and exhibition facilities for schools, colleges and local community groups. Facilities include community cinema/small TV studio, teachers resource material and advisor team with technical support

The Media Workshop

Peterborough Arts Centre
Media Department
Orton Goldhay
Peterborough PE2 OJQ
Tel: 0733 237073
Clifton Stewart
Roger Knott-Fayle
Video and photography productions, workshops and exhibitions. Offers U-Matic and VHS production/edit facilities, dark room, gallery and studio space suitable for film performances. Committed to equal access for all sections of the community

Migrant Media Collective

90 De Beauvoir Road
London N1 4EN
Tel: 071 254 9701
Nasser Bakhti
Ken Fero
Dipak Mistry
Hidie Hormoz
Production, training, advice and support for migrant and refugee media workers. Work centres mainly around Middle East communities. Currently working on a four part series on 'Black Resistance' in Europe – Germany, France, Britain, Italy. Networks with similar organisations in Europe and in Arab countries

Moonshine Community Arts Workshop

1090 Harrow Road
London NW10 5XQ
Tel: 081 960 0055
Jeff Lee
Offers video production facilities to others. Provides training in production and post-production with U-Matic and VHS edit suites and special effects. Also has 16 track recording studio with effects, and silk screen and offset litho printing facilities. Works with Brent-based groups and individuals with emphasis on young people and black community groups producing work including documentaries, music videos and video art

Moviola

40a Bluecoat Chambers
School Lane
Liverpool L1 3BX
Tel: 051 709 2663
Fax: 051 709 2575
Moviola presents, promotes and commissions work by artists using video, film and electronic media through exhibitions, projects, training and education

Northern Visions*

4-8 Donegal Street Place
Belfast BT1 2FN
Tel: 0232 245495
Fax: 0232 326608
Co-operative providing video production, distribution and exhibition. Offers hi-/lo-band recording, editing and 16 track sound recording. Commercial work undertaken. Training sessions. Special rates for community and campaign groups. Productions include 1988 *Our Words Jump to Life*, 1989 *Moving Myths*, 1990 *Schizophrenic City* and *The Write Off*

The Old Dairy Studios

(formerly York Film Workshop)
156b Haxby Road
York YO3 7JN
Tel: 0904 641394
Video production, distribution and exhibition, 8-track sound recording studio and a darkroom equipped for full disabled access. Courses are held in production, sound recording and photography

Outline Arts Trust

69 Rothbury Terrace
Heaton
Newcastle upon Tyne
NE6 5XJ
Tel: 091 276 3207
Heather Holmes
A community arts trust using video mostly for very specific and local use

Oxford Film and Video Makers

The Stables
North Place
Headington
Oxford OX3 9HY
Tel: 0865 60074
We offer specialised courses to meet the particular needs of various groups, open access courses covering the entire production process in film and video, equipment hire, distribution and exhibition, and productions which give voice to people normally denied one, such as *Futures on the Line*, *Journeys*, *Stopping the Press* and *Women in Rock*

Oxford Independent Video

Pegasus Theatre
Magdalen Road
Oxford OX4 1RE
Tel: 0865 250150
Maddie Shepherd
Arts and issue-based video project working with under-represented groups in Oxfordshire to produce tapes for national distribution. Work includes tapes about women in film noir, Eisenstein, integrated dance residencies with people of differing abilities, arts in schools projects, etc

Paxvision

The Albany
Douglas Way
London SE8 4AG
Tel: 081 692 6322
Fax: 081 692 6322
Video project providing services, video facilities and training (beginners to advanced) mainly targeted at the local community, independent video and film makers and disadvantaged groups or individuals. Also collaborate with local community groups and artists in video production; undertake commissions on production and music scoring. Facilities include S-VHS production equipment, VHS edit suite and S-VHS edit suite with Amiga 2000 computer, graphics and titling. All services available at community and commercial rates

Picture This

(formerly Watershed Media Centre)
Unit G
Arnos Castle Trading Estate
Junction Road
Brislington
Bristol BS4 3JP
Tel: 0272 721002
Shafeeq Vellani
Lulu Quinn
Film/video production, distribution, exhibition, training and media education. Offers all these facilities to others, primarily grant-aided and independent producers, community groups and educational institutions. Recent productions include *Walking Away with the Music* and *Celebration*

Pimlico Arts and Media Scheme

St James the Less School
Moreton Street
London SW1 2PT
Tel: 071 976 6133
Fax: 071 630 9517
Carolyn Shrives
Carol Swords
One of the biggest media training centres in London, running courses in video, photography and graphic design exclusively for unemployed people to give them a grounding in these three areas and prepare them for employment.
Offers graphics studio, VHS, U-Matic equipment, hi-band SP, fully-equipped darkroom and exhibition space, and can accommodate 165 trainees. Also weekend and evening courses for private individuals

Platform Films

13 Tankerton House
Tankerton Street
London WC1H 8HP
Tel: 071 278 8394
Chris Reeves
Film/video production and distribution. Also Panasonic VHS Hi-Fi sound VHS edit suite available for dry hire. Special rates for non-commercial and student productions

Plymouth Arts Centre

38 Looe Street
Plymouth PL4 0EB
Tel: 0752 660060

Projects UK
1 Black Swan Court
Westgate Road
Newcastle upon Tyne
NE1 1SG
Tel: 091 232 2410
Fax: 091 221 0492
Sandra Lathbury
Organises festivals and events concentrating on contemporary arts and media. Offers courses, training, product work, production facilities and distribution in their main areas of activity which are: photography, visual arts, performance, electro-acoustic music and public events

Real Time Video
Newtown Community House
117 Cumberland Road
Reading RG1 3JY
Tel: 0734 351023
Clive Robertson
Process-based community access video workshop. Video production, training and exhibition. Runs courses and workshops, organises screenings and projects and offers consultancy on community video

Red Flannel Films*
Maritime Offices
Woodland Terrace
Maesycoed
Pontypridd
Mid Glamorgan
Tel: 0443 401743/480564
Fax: 0443 485667
Red Flannel is a women's collective working on film and video production, distribution, exhibition, education, training, archive and video library. Productions for hire and purchase are *Mam* (16mm and video), *If We Were Asked* (video) and *Special Delivery* (16mm and video). Facilities for hire include S-VHS, VHS and 16mm editing, VHS production equipment

Retake Film and Video Collective
19 Liddell Road
London NW6 2EW
Tel: 071 328 4676
Fax: 071 372 1231
Mahmood Jamal
Seema Gill
Sebastian Shah
Ahmed Jamal
Film/video production, distribution and training. Facilities hire: 2 machine U-Matic suite, 16mm cutting room. Productions include two feature dramas, *Majdhar* and *Hotel London* and documentaries *Living in Danger, Environment of Dignity, Who Will Cast the First Stone?, Sanctuary Challenge* and *Hidden Worlds*. Hire of 16mm/lo-band U-Matic editing

Sankofa Film and Video
Unit K
32-34 Gordon House Road
London NW5 1LP
Tel: 071 485 0848
Fax: 071 485 2869
Maureen Blackwood
Robert Crusz
Isaac Julien
Nadine Marsh-Edwards
Film/video production and distribution. Offers production facilities to others, runs training workshops in film and video. Organises screenings and discussions. Productions include *The Passion of Remembrance, Perfect Image, Dreaming Rivers, Looking for Langston* and *Young Soul Rebels*

Screenworks – Portsmouth Media Trust
The Hornpipe
143 Kingston Road
Portsmouth PO2 7EB
Tel: 0705 861851
Steve Jackman
Claire Shearman
Dy Noszlopy
Film/video production, training workshops and projects. Regular exhibition of independent film and video in Rendezvous cinema

Second Sight
Zair Works
111 Bishop Street
Birmingham B5 6JL
Tel: 021 622 4223 (productions), 021 622 5750 (training)
Fax: 021 622 1554 (fao Second Sight)
Dylis Pugh
Glynis Powell
Pauline Bailey
Anne Cullis
Video production company specialising in arts, social issues and training programmes. Showreel and tapelist available on request. Runs practical training courses for women from beginners to hi-band production. Provides an information resource on all aspects of AV media. Gives consultancies on training programme construction and production within socially sensitive arenas

Sheffield Film Co-op*
Brown Street
Sheffield S1 2BS
Tel: 0742 727170
Chrissie Stansfield
Women's film and video production workshop reflecting women's views on a wide range of issues. Distribute work on film/tape including *Changing Our Lives, Women of Steel, Let Our Children Grow Tall!, Bringing It All Back Home, Diamonds in Brown Paper, Thank You, That's All I Knew* and *Running Gay*

Sheffield Independent Film
Avec
Brown Street
Sheffield S1 2BS
Tel: 0742 720304
Alan Robinson
Lucy Rumney
Gloria Ward
Jo Cammack
Carol Sidney
A resource base for independent film and videomakers in the Sheffield region. Regular training workshops; access to a range of film and video equipment; technical and administrative backup; and regular screenings of independent film and video

Signals, Essex Media Centre
(formerly Colchester Film and Video Workshop)
21 St Peters Street
Colchester CO1 1EW
Tel: 0206 560255
Film/video resource for community. U-Matic, S-VHS and VHS production and post-production, Super 8 and 16mm film. Services in training, media education, equipment hire and production

Siren Film and Video Co-op
6 Harris Street
Middlesbrough
Cleveland TS1 5EF
Tel: 0642 221298
Dave Eadington
Wendy Critchley
Sarah Shaw
Wendy McEvoy
Film/video production, distribution and exhibition. Offers production facilities to others. Workers' co-operative producing for community groups and television. Recent works include *My Little Sister* and a Women's Video project

Star Productions/ Studios
1 Cornthwaite Road
London E5 0RS
Tel: 081 986 4470/5766
Fax: 081 533 6597
Raj Patel
Film/video production company working from an Asian perspective. Multi-lingual productions. Offers studio for hire, video editing suite, 16mm cutting room. Production and exhibition facilities. Output includes community documentaries, video films of stage plays and feature films

Steel Bank Film Co-op*
Brown Street
Sheffield S1 2BS
Tel: 0742 721235
Jessica York
Simon Reynell
Dinah Ward
Noemie Mendelle
Film/video production and distribution. Work includes documentaries, art programmes, campaign tapes and fiction films. Productions include *Winnie, Security, Clocks of the Midnight Hours, Great Noises that Fill the Air, For Your Own Good, Spinster, Crimestrike* and *Custom-Eyes*

Studio 9, The Video Producers
Monyhull Hall Road
Kings Norton
Birmingham B30 3QB
Tel: 021 444 4750/0831 307728
Fax: 021 444 5674
Alison Richards
Gary Liszewski
An independent Birmingham based video production house. Documentary/ promotional/ entertainment/training films undertaken – broadcast and non-broadcast – from script to screen. Offers freelancer crew and rig service, computer graphics and edit suite hire

Swingbridge Video
Norden House
41 Stowell Street
Newcastle upon Tyne
NE1 4YB
Tel: 091 232 3762
Hugh Kelly
Sarah McCarthy
A community video project making productions for broadcast and non-broadcast distribution, with and on behalf of community and campaign groups in the North East. Film and video production and distribution

TURC Video
7 Frederick Street
Birmingham B1 3HE
Tel: 021 233 4061
Marian Hall
Video production, distribution and exhibition. U-Matic and VHS facilities, 3 machine editing. Offers all these facilities to others. Works mainly on trade union and campaign issues, locally and nationally. Productions include *Rights Wot Rights, P & O... Profit before People* and *The Journalist's Tale*

33 Video Co-operative
Luton Community Arts Trust
33-35 Guildford Street
Luton
Beds LU1 2NQ
Tel: 0582 419584
Dermot Byrne
3 machine lo-band, 2 machine VHS, lo-band and VHS shooting kits

bfi Trade Films*
36 Bottle Bank
Gateshead
Tyne and Wear NE8 2AR
Tel: 091 477 5532
Fax: 091 478 3681
Derek Stubbs
Film/video production, distribution and exhibition. Offers production and post-production (hi-/lo-band, 16mm) facilities to others. Workshop comprises Trade Films (fiction/documentary) and Northern Newsreel (current affairs), together with the Northern Film and Television Archive

Trilith Video
Corner Cottage
Brickyard Lane
Bourton
Gillingham
Dorset SP8 5PJ
Tel: 0747 840750/840727
Trevor Bailey
John Holman
Sue Holman
Specialises in rural video on community action, rural issues and the outlook and experience of country-born people. Produces own series of tapes, undertakes broadcast and tape commissions and gathers archive film in order to make it publicly available on video. Distributes own work nationally. Current work includes TSW feature

Valley and Vale Community Arts
Blaengarw Workmen's Hall
Blaengarw
Mid Glamorgan
Tel: 0656 871911
Justine Ennion
The Holm View Centre
Skomer Road
Gibbonsdown
Barry
South Glamorgan
Tel: 0446 742289
Video production, distribution and exhibition. Open-access workshop offering training to community groups in VHS, lo-band U-Matic and hi-8 formats

Vera Productions
30-38 Dock Street
Leeds LS10 1JF
Tel: 0532 428646
Fax: 0532 426937
Alison Garthwaite
Catherine Mitchell
Film/video production (broadcast/non-broadcast), training, exhibition and distribution. Teach women and mixed groups. Speak on representation of women in film and TV. Information resource and networking newsletter

Video in Pilton
30 Ferry Road Avenue
West Pilton
Edinburgh EH4 4BA
Tel: 031 343 1151
Joel Venet
Hugh Farrell
Community-based training facilities; broadcast productions; production work for national campaigning groups, trade unions and local authority; exhibition at the Edinburgh Film Festival

The Video Workshop/ Y Gweithdy Fideo*
Chapter Arts Centre
Market Road
Canton
Cardiff CF5 1QE
Tel: 0222 342755
George Auchterlonie
Video production, distribution and exhibition in English and Welsh. Offers production facilities to others. Working with community and arts organisations and trades unions on social, political and cultural issues

Vokani
Unit 40
Devonshire House
High Street
Digbeth
Birmingham B12 0LP
Tel: 021 773 4260
Tony Small
Black and Third World film and video exhibition circuit based in the West Midlands, offering media education packages developed around film by or about Black and Third World peoples. Membership available to provide access to video library and film information resource. Some distribution of new titles by new black film makers

Watershed Media Centre
see **Picture This**

WAVES (Women's Audio Visual Education Scheme)
London Women's Centre
Wesley House
4 Wild Court
London WC2B 5AU
Tel: 071 430 1076
A new initiative, launched March 1991, designed to offer training for women in the area of audio and visual media culture. The overall aim is to promote the ability of women to both enter the industry and make their own work. It is planned to offer training through inter-related modular courses and to create links with existing educational providers. The educational and training programme will also attempt to redress the inequalities of opportunity faced by specific groups of women, as well as ensuring that all courses are as accessible as possible, culturally and physically

Welfare State International
The Ellers
Ulverston
Cumbria LA12 0AA
Tel: 0229 581127/57146
Fax: 0229 581232
A consortium of artists, musicians, technicians and performers. Film/video production, distribution and exhibition. Output includes community feature films and work for television

West Glamorgan Video and Film Workshop
F6-7-10, Burrows Chambers
East Burrows Road
Swansea SA1 1RQ
Tel: 0792 476441
Lynfa Protheroe
Community co-operative dedicated to increasing the use and understanding of video, film and photography amongst all sections of

the local community in England and Wales. VHS, lo-band, hi 8mm, darkroom and sound facilities. Regular training courses, production groups and screenings (brochure and rate card available). Supported by Welsh Arts Council

West London Media Workshop

118 Talbot Road
London W11 1JR
Tel: 071 221 1859
Fax: 071 792 8085
Tricia King
John Goff
R K Saroff
Video production, distribution and exhibition. Offers production facilities to others. WLMW runs a bursary scheme aimed to encourage new makers to debate various cultural/social issues. Multimedia publishing and interactive technology

Wide Angle Video, Film, Photography

Birmingham Community Association
Jenkins Street
Small Heath
Birmingham B10 0HQ
Tel & Fax: 021 772 2889
Tracy Symonds
Wide Angle is a centre for production, exhibition and training in video, film and photography. Offers regular programme of short courses on a variety of levels. Membership scheme provides access resource, support and advice to independent film and video makers

Women's Media Resource Project (WMRP)

85 Kingsland High Street
London E8 2PB
Tel: 071 254 6536
Offers sound engineering courses, video exhibition equipment, hire of equipment and studio, women only screenings and discussion

Workers' Film Association

Media and Cultural Centre
9 Lucy Street
Manchester M15 4BX
Tel: 061 848 9785
Wowo Wauters
Rosemary Orr
Main areas of work include media access and training with a full range of production, post-production and exhibition equipment and facilities for community, semi-professional and professional standards. Video production unit (ACTT). Distribution and sale of 16mm films and videos, booking and advice service, video access library. Cultural work, mixed media events.
Bookshop/outreach work

Wrexham Community Video

The Place in the Park
Bellevue Road
Wrexham
Clwyd LL13 7NH
Tel: 0978 358522
Serena Rule
Video production, distribution and exhibition. Offers production and exhibition facilities to others. Runs short training courses in video production and studio sound recording

bfi – Workshops in receipt of BFI revenue funding for the year up to 31 March 1991

LIST OF ABBREVIATIONS

ABSA Association of Business Sponsorship of the Arts
ABW Association of Black Film and Video Workshops
ACGB Arts Council of Great Britain
ACTT Association of Cinematograph, Television and Allied Technicians
AFI American Film Institute/Australian Film Institute
AFRS Advertising Film Rights Society
AFVPA Advertising Film and Videotape Producers' Association
AGICOA Association for the International Collective Management of Audiovisual Works
AIC Association of Independent Cinemas
AID International Association of Cable Distribution Organisations
AMPAS Academy of Motion Picture Arts and Sciences (USA)
APC Association of Professional Composers
BABA British Advertising Broadcast Awards
BABEL Broadcasting Across the Barriers of European Language
BAFTA British Academy of Film and Television Arts
BARB Broadcasters' Audience Research Board
BASCA British Academy of Songwriters, Composers and Authors
BATC British Amateur Television Club
BBC British Broadcasting Corporation
BBFC British Board of Film Classification
BCC Broadcasting Complaints Commission
BCS British Cable Services
BECTU Broadcasting Entertainment and Cinematograph Technicians Union
BETA Broadcasting and Entertainment Trades Alliance
BFFS British Federation of Film Societies
BFI British Film Institute
BIEM Bureau Internationale des Sociétés Gérant les Droits d'Enregistrement
BKSTS British Kinematograph Sound and Television Society
BNFVC British National Film and Video Catalogue
BPI British Phonographic Industry
BSAC British Screen Advisory Council
BSC Broadcasting Standards Council
BSkyB British Sky Broadcasting
BUFVC British Universities Film and Video Council
BVA British Videogram Association
CAVIAR Cinema and Video Industry Audience Research
CD Compact Disc
CDI Compact Disc Interactive
CD-Rom Compact Disc – Read Only Memory
CEA Cinematograph Exhibitors' Association of Great Britain and Ireland
CEPI Co-ordination Européenne des Producteurs Indépendantes
CFC Cinematograph Films Council
CFTF Children's Film and Television Foundation
CFU Children's Film Unit
C4 Channel Four
CICCE Comité des Industries Cinématographiques et Audiovisuelles des Communautés Européennes et de l'Europe Extracommunautaire
CILECT Centre Internationale de Liaison des Ecoles de Cinéma et de Télévision
CNN Cable News Network
COI Central Office of Information
COMEX Consortium of Media Exhibitors
CORAA Council of Regional Arts Associations
CPBF Campaign for Press and Broadcasting Freedom
CTA Cinema Theatre Association
CTBF Cinema and Television Benevolent Fund
DADA Designers and Art Directors' Association
DBC Deaf Broadcasting Campaign
DBS Direct Broadcasting by Satellite
DELTA Development of European Learning through Technological Advance
DES Department of Education and Science
DGGB Directors' Guild of Great Britain
DTI Department of Trade and Industry
DVI Digital Video Interactive
EATC European Alliance for Television and Culture
EAVE European Audio-Visual Entrepreneurs
EBU European Broadcasting Union
ECF European Co-production Fund
EEC European Economic Community
EETPU Electrical, Electronic, Telecommunications and Plumbing Union
EFDO European Film Distribution Office
EGAKU European Committee of Trade Unions in Arts, Mass Media and Entertainment
EIFF Edinburgh International Film Festival
EIM European Institute for the Media
EITF Edinburgh International Television Festival
ESPRIT European Strategic Programme for Information Technology
EURO-AIM European Organisation for Audiovisual Production
EUTELSAT European Telecommunications Satellite Organisation
EVE Espace Vidéo Européen
FAA Film Artistes' Association
FACT Federation Against Copyright Theft
FBU Federation of Broadcasting Unions
FEMIS Fondation Européenne des Métiers de l'Image et du Son
FEPACI Fédération Pan-Africain des Cinéastes

LIST OF ABBREVIATIONS

FESPACO Festivale Pan-Africain des Cinémas de Ouagadougou
FFU Federation of Film Unions
FIA International Federation of Actors
FIAD Fédération Internationale de Distributeurs
FIAF Fédération Internationale des Archives du Film
FIAPF International Federation of Film Producers Associations
FIAT Fédération Internationale des Archives de Télévision
FICC Fédération Internationale des Ciné-Clubs
FIPFI Fédération Internationale des Producteurs de Films Indépendants
FOCAL Federation of Commercial Audio-Visual Libraries
FSU Film Society Unit
FTT Film and Television Technician
FTVLCA Film and Television Lighting Contractors Association
FVL Film and Video Library
FX Effects/special effects
GLA Greater London Arts (now LAB, London Arts Board)
HBO Home Box Office
HDTV High Definition Television
HTV Harlech Television
HVC Home Video Channel
IABM International Association of Broadcasting Manufacturers
IAC Interim Action Committee
IAMHIST International Association for Audio-Visual Media in Historical Research and Education
IBA Independent Broadcasting Authority
IBT International Broadcasting Trust
ICA Institute of Contemporary Arts
IFDA Independent Film Distributors' Association
IFFS International Federation of Film Societies (aka FICC)
IFPA Independent Film Production Associates
IFPI International Federation of Producers of Phonograms and Videograms
IFTA International Federation of Television Archives (aka FIAT)
IIC International Institute of Communications
ILR Independent Local Radio
INR Independent National Radio
IPA Institute of Practitioners in Advertising
IPPA Independent Programme Producers' Association
ISA International Songwriters Association
ISBA Incorporated Society of British Advertising
ITC Independent Television Commission
ITN Independent Television News
ITSC International Television Studies Conference
ITV Independent Television
ITVA Independent Television Association
IVCA International Visual Communications Association
IVLA International Visual Literacy Association
LAB London Arts Board (formerly GLA, Greater London Arts)
LAIFA Latin American Independent Film/Video Association
LFF London Film Festival
LFMC London Film Makers' Co-op
LSW London Screenwriters' Workshop
LVA London Video Access
LWT London Weekend Television
MAP-TV Memories - Archives - Programmes
MCPS Mechanical Copyright Protection Society
MEDIA Measures to Encourage the Development of the Industry of Audiovisual Production
MFB Monthly Film Bulletin
MFVPA Music, Film and Video Producers Association
MGM Metro Goldwyn Mayer
MHMC Mental Health Media Council
MIDEM Marché International du Disque et de l'Edition Musicale
MIFED Mercato Internazionale del TV, Film e del Documentario
MIPCOM Marché International des Films et des Programmes pour la TV, la Vidéo, le Câble et le Satellite
MIP-TV Marché International de Programmes de Television
MoMA Museum of Modern Art (New York)
MOMI Museum of the Moving Image
MPA Motion Picture Association of America
MPEA Motion Picture Export Association of America
MU Musicians' Union
NATPE National Association of Television Programme Executives (now formally NATPE International)
NAVAL National Audio Visual Aids Library
NCET National Council for Educational Technology
NCVQ National Council for Vocational Qualifications
NFA National Film Archive
NFDF National Film Development Fund
NFT National Film Theatre
NFTC National Film Trustee Company
NFTS National Film and Television School
NHMF National Heritage Memorial Fund
NTSC National Television Standards Committee
NUJ National Union of Journalists
NUT National Union of Teachers
NVALA National Viewers' and Listeners' Association
OAL Office of Arts and Libraries
PACT Producers Alliance for Film and Television
PAL Programmable Array Logic and Phase Alternation Line
PRS Performing Right Society
RAA Regional Arts Association
RAB Regional Arts Board
RACE Research and Development in Advanced Communication Technologies in Europe
RETRA Radio, Electrical and Television Retailers' Association
RFT Regional Film Theatre
RTS Royal Television Society
S&S Sight and Sound
SCET Scottish Council for Educational Technology
SCFVL Scottish Central Film and Video Library
SCTE Society of Cable Television Engineers
SECAM Sequential Couleur à Mémoire
SFC Scottish Film Council
SFD Society of Film Distributors
SFX Special Effects
S4C Sianel Pedwar Cymru
SIFT Summary of Information on Film and Television
SMATV Satellite Master Antenna Television
TSW Television South West
TVRO Television receive-only
TVS Television South
UA United Artists
UIP United International Pictures
UNESCO United Nations Educational, Scientific and Cultural Organisation
URTI Université Radiophonique et Télévisuelle Internationale
VCPS Video Copyright Protection Society
VCR Video Cassette Recorder
VHS Video Home System
WGGB Writers' Guild of Great Britain
WTN Worldwide Television News
WTVA Wider Television Access
YTV Yorkshire Television

ADVERTISERS

A

B

C

D

E

INDEX

F

G

H

I

INDEX

Q

R

S

T

U

V

W

Y

Z